ECODESIGN

Published in Great Britain in 2006 by Wiley-Academy, a division of John Wiley & Sons, Ltd

Copyright © 2006   Ken Yeang
                    Llewelyn Davies Yeang
                    Brook House, Torrington Place
                    London WC1E 7HN UK
                    T +44 (0) 20 7637 0181
                    F +44 (0) 20 7637 8740
                    D +44 (0) 20 7612 9465
                    Email : kynnet@pc.jaring.my & k.yeang@ldavies.com
                    www.ldavies.com

Email (for orders and customer service enquiries): cs-books@wiley.co.uk
Visit our Home Page on www.wileyeurope.com or www.wiley.com

This publication is designed to provide accurate and authoritative information in regard to the subject matter covered. It is sold on the understanding that the Publisher is not engaged in rendering professional services. If professional advice or other expert assistance is required, the services of a competent professional should be sought.

Other Wiley Editorial Offices
John Wiley & Sons,Inc, 111 River Street, Hoboken, NJ 07030, USA
Jossey-Bass, 989 Market Street, San Francisco, CA 94103-1741, USA
Wiley-VCH Verlag GmbH, Boschstr. 12, D-69469 Weinheim, Germany
John Wiley & Sons, Australia, Ltd, 42 McDougall Street, Milton, Queensland 4064, Australia
John Wiley & Sons, (Asia) Lte, Ltd, 2 Clementi Loop #02-01, Jin Xing Distripark, Singapore 129809
John Wiley & Sons, Canada, Ltd, 5353 Dundas Street West, Suite 400, Etobicoke, Ontario, Canada M9W ILI

983-2726-40-9

Book design by Imaan Yenniu Lim and Ridzwa Fathan for ADF Management Sdn. Bhd.

Printed and bound in Malaysia by Printelligence Sdn. Bhd.

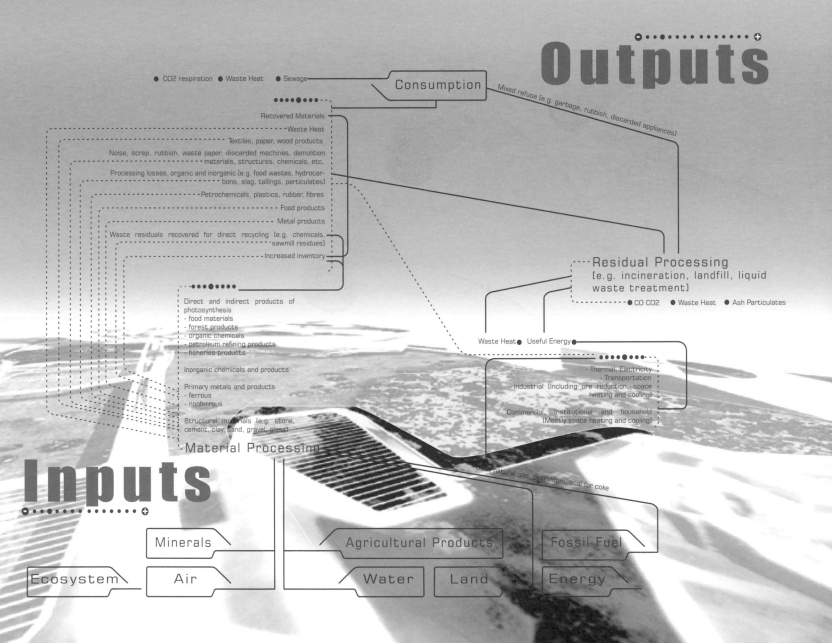

Outputs

● CO2 respiration ● Waste Heat ● Sewage

Consumption

Mixed refuse [e.g. garbage, rubbish, discarded appliances]

Recovered Materials
Waste Heat
Textiles, paper, wood products
Noise, scrap, rubbish, waste paper, discarded machines, demolition materials, structures, chemicals, etc.
Processing losses, organic and inorganic [e.g. food wastes, hydrocarbons, slag, tailings, particulates]
Petrochemicals, plastics, rubber, fibres
Food products
Metal products
Waste residuals recovered for direct recycling [e.g. chemicals, sawmill residues]
Increased inventory

Residual Processing
[e.g. incineration, landfill, liquid waste treatment]

● CO CO2 ● Waste Heat ● Ash Particulates

Direct and indirect products of photosynthesis
- food materials
- forest products
- organic chemicals
- petroleum refining products
- fisheries products

Inorganic chemicals and products

Primary metals and products
- ferrous
- nonferrous

Structural materials [e.g. stone, cement, clay, sand, gravel, glass]

Material Processing

Waste Heat ● Useful Energy ●

- Thermal, Electricity
- Transportation
Industrial [including ore reduction, space heating and cooling]

Commercial, institutional and household [Mostly space heating and cooling]

Inputs

Gas, natural gas, petroleum, coal for coke

Minerals

Agricultural Products

Fossil Fuel

Ecosystem

Air

Water

Land

Energy

A Manual for Ecological Design

Ken Yeang

WILEY-ACADEMY

This book is dedicated to my mother Louise and my father C.H.

I would like to acknowledge and thank the following whose help has been absolutely invaluable: my commissioning editor Helen Castle for her patience and encouragement, Mariangela Palazzi-Williams for her efficient and firm managing of the production of the book, Lucy Isenberg for editing my rough texts, Lord Norman Foster for his support and encouragement, Professor Bryan Lawson (Sheffield University, UK) for his advice on the topic, Professor Jeremy Till (Sheffield University, UK) for his review of the manuscript and suggestions on writing a design manual, Professor Ivor Richards (Newcastle University, UK) for his critical conversations and comments, Max Fordham for his comments and advice, Professor John Frazer for his advice and thoughts on biological design, Dr Kisho Kurokawa for his encouragement on writing and advice on biological design (metabolism), Charles Jencks for his ideas on biomorphic design. Professor Richard Frewer (Hong Kong University) for his advice and encouragement, Professor Peter Cook for his critical advice, Professor Alan Balfour for his incisive criticism of the work, Professor Mohsen Mostafavi (Cornell University, USA) for his comments and encouragement, Masayuki Fuchigami for his advice on green design, Professor Ingo Hagemann (Aachen University, Germany) for his comments on photovoltaics, Professor Colin Meurk (University of Auckland, New Zealand) for his advice on ecological migration, Simon Fisher for his research on ecological connectivity, Professor Klaus Daniels (Eidgenössische Technische Hochschule) for his advice on environmental systems, Professor Lam Khee Poh (Carnegie Mellon University, USA) for his advice on building performance, Paul Hyett for his conversations on green design, Guy Battle and Chris McCarthy (Battle McCarthy Engineers) for their advice on environmental systems and their encouragement, Steve Featherstone (Llewellyn Davies Yeang) for his support, Sym van der Ryn for his comments, Professor Dieter Schempp (Tübingen University, Germany) for his advice on building-vegetation integration, David Balcombe (Head of Built Environment Branch (Essex County Council, UK) for the Essex Design Initiative Sustainability Workshop, the late Professor Ian McHarg (University of Pennsylvania, USA) for his memorable lessons on ecological planning, Professor Kazuo Iwamura (Musashi Institute of Technology, Japan) for his ideas and comments, Ridzwa Fathan for giving alluring forms to my ideas, Lucy Chew for patiently typing the many versions of the manuscript, Yenniu Lim for the book design, Teh Sook Ay and Ives Kok for drawing the illustrations, my business partner Tengku Robert Hamzah for providing the environment to enable the work on this manual to be realised, and, finally, my family for tolerating my incessant racket and nuisance from early evenings through to the early hours of the morning during my writing and researching of this monograph.

While acknowledging the help of these and others, I am nevertheless solely responsible for the defects in this publication.

Designing for ecological nexus

Guide to using the manual: The designer should not regard what follows as a formal and rigid prescription for design, although the chapters are ordered to reflect the sequence of the crucial steps and considerations (ie from design brief to site analysis to schematic design, etc) that a designer would generally follow in any design assignment. The designer is free to modify the sequence.

1. For the beginner in ecodesign, it is recommended that the entire contents page is read for an immediate overview of everything that needs to be taken into account in the design process.

The quick way to grasp the ecodesign approach is to read each of the chapter headings in the instructions section (B1 to B31) together with the introductory paragraph to each chapter and the respective summaries at the end of each chapter. Between the introductions and the summaries the design considerations and descriptions of prescriptive action are elaborated.

2. For the expert or advanced designer, each chapter can be read on its own as providing information on that particular topic; or the entire Contents list can be used as a framework and checklist of items to be addressed in design. The designer may, however, prefer to follow the procedure as outlined by this guide.

3. A balance is sought between describing technical details and systems and providing sufficient practical information to enable the designer to proceed with design. To include all the available technical information and systems in this manual would simply make it too voluminous and unwieldy. The approach here is to provide at the start of each chapter a brief overview of the particular aspect to be considered by the designer, and its rationale. At the end of each chapter is a summary of instructions for the designer.

4. The manual is organised in three sections. Section A (A1 to A5) is the general introduction to ecodesign and sets out the fundamental premises.

5. A1 to A5 should be read first to enable the designer to understand the considerations in ecology and so acquire the basic level of ecoliteracy necessary for ecodesign; they set out the premises for ecodesign and planning. A2 sets out the principle of ecodesign as biointegration. A3 discusses the ecosystem concept, which is the fundamental basis for ecodesign based on the design of our built environment as emulation of the systems, structures and processes of ecosystems. A5 provides the theoretical basis for ecological design and constitutes a matrix that can also serve as a conceptual and structural checklist/tool for assessing any ecological design assignment.

6. With any common design assignment, the designer will usually first prepare a design brief of the set of requirements to be addressed and

fulfilled by the design. Chapters B1, B2 and B3 detail the considerations to be taken into account in the initial approach to any design assignment, whether for a built structure, infrastructure or product, and are intended to assist the designer in writing the brief.

7. In the case of built structures or infrastructures, their production takes place in a locality or on a site where they are to be erected. Chapters B4 through B11 discuss those aspects of the site and the natural environmental context that must be evaluated. These are the L22 considerations given in the Interactions Matrix in A5.

In the case of a product as a design assignment, its production and manufacture, distribution, retailing and consumption or utilisation all take place at different sites and localities and each of the processes and activities at each of these localities (including storage and transportation) has consequences for the respective site or locality. The ecological consequences of all these must be considered in totality (in B4 to B11).

8. B4 provides the designer with a taxonomy for assessing the ecological history of the site for the intended built system and gives a broad basis for initial site selection. It also helps establish the extent of ecological site analysis that the designer will need prior to embarking on the design and enables subsequent future monitoring of the consequences of L11 and L12 considerations (from the Interactions Matrix) over the life cycle of the designed system.

9. Following the general assessment of the ecological history of the site (in B4), B5 describes the process and approach to site analysis and eventual site layout, planning and physical/systemic integration. The method discussed here is the ecological land-use planning method as commonly employed by landscape architects.

For a more thorough ecological site analysis, the designer will need to have an ecological analysis carried out (by an ecologist, for instance), to examine the spatial, systemic and other properties of the locality's ecosystem (eg its biotic diversity; state of succession; energetics and materials, flow through the ecosystem; the level of contamination of biotic and abiotic components).

The outcome of the inventory and the mapping analysis of the site's ecology and the examination of its properties and performance will give the carrying capacity of the ecosystem for the designer as the initial basis for design, such as how to lay out the built configuration of the designed system, its output assimilation, etc.

10. B6 is useful for the designer in carrying out site planning to delineate in as much detail as possible the site's ecosystem boundaries. The designer may refer to B8 as the basis for improving existing ecological linkages of the locality or creating new linkages to enhance the ecological connectivities of the site and habitat biodiversity.

Book indicator

Chapter indicator

11. B7 is crucial to any ecodesign endeavour as most of all our existing built environments are essentially inorganic and wholly abiotic. A3 and A4 remind the designer of the need to balance any ecodesign assignment or site with both organic and inorganic components and to emulate the structures, processes and functions of natural ecosystems where practical or where possible.

In doing this, the designer may begin to develop ecologically driven aesthetic values for the designed system (see C1) – for instance, the designed system may move to acquire a more organic appearance when its biotic component increases both externally and internally (see B18 and B21).

12. B8 is particularly crucial in instances where the site for the designed system is sizeable (eg over 1 hectare) and needs to relate to the greater environmental context of the ecosystem in which it is located, and B8 thus seeks to identify its preferred ecological connectivities.

13. B9 serves to remind the designer to increase the biotic context of the designed system (in B7). Where the designed programme is sizeable, the designer may need to adopt either more intensively clustered or more spread-out patterns of built forms and to consider the provision of a related infrastructure, access routes (ie roads) and paved areas in relation to the vegetated areas.

The areal disposition of inorganic structures, roads and paved surfaces on a locality creates (and contributes to the increase in) the locality's heat-island effect. Hence the designer is reminded to increase the organic context of the designed system, including the way it is laid out or configured (eg using the patterns discussed in B7), to ensure that the heat-island effect build-up is eliminated.

14. B10 requires the designer to consider the energy requirements of the designed system, including the consequences of transportation to and from the designed system which, in most urban locations, is generally high in consumption of non-renewable energy sources. The layout of the regional and local transportation routes will also affect the site's ecology (in B5) and may reduce the extent of uninterrupted ecological corridors within the site (see B8).

15. B11 reminds the designer to integrate the patterns, functions and processes of the designed system with the greater planning and urban context within which the project site is located for greater synergy.

16. B12 to B29 are considerations that need to be taken into account as the designer proceeds to articulate the design of the environmental or comfort-related systems of the built system or the designed product.

This step follows on from the completion of the assessment of the premises for the creation, production and construction of the built system (in B1 to B3) and the assessment of the site context upon which the built system is to be located (B4 to B11), which becomes the context for the shaping of the built forms of that design assignment and its systems. These are the L11, L21 and L12 considerations given in the Interactions Matrix in A5.

17. B12 establishes the basic strategy for approaching the shaping and orientation of the built system. This requires analysis and study of the climatic conditions of the locality over the entire year in order to use these as the basis for influencing the design's built disposition and configuration (by passive modes driven by design) together with analysis of the site's features and ecology in B5.

B12 to B17 detail the considerations to be taken into account in formulating the built form's comfort conditions and the internal environment systems of the designed system to be employed to create these conditions. These constitute L11 of the Interactions Matrix.

18. Strategically, in the design approach the designer must optimise all the design options in B13 (passive mode), particularly in response to that locality's climatic conditions before progressing to consider the set of B14 design options (mixed mode) and, thereafter, to B15 (full mode) design options. When all the previous design options and strategies have been exhaustively assessed for inclusion, the designer can then progress to B16 (productive mode) and to B17 (composite mode), although B16 may be a prerequisite in certain design assignments.

19. In most instances the method adopted for designing the built form's internal environmental systems and for creating its internal comfort conditions will be composite mode (B17). This applies particularly to those designed systems located in climatic zones that experience significant fluctuation in conditions over the year (ie a hot summer, cold winter and two mid-seasons).

20. B18 and B29 are considerations relating to the inputs (L21 in the Interaction Matrix) of the designed system and its outputs (L12 in the Interaction Matrix). They include all those items that make up the designed system's built structural system, enclosural system (eg, its facade system), its materials and its furniture, fittings and equipment (FF&E), all of which eventually, of course, become potential wastes or outputs from that built system (ie L12 from the Interaction Matrix). Their use, reuse, recycling and their eventual destination in the biosphere need to be adequately considered and integrated.

21. B19 examines water as one of the inputs to the designed system (L21 from the Interaction Matrix), the need for its conservation and prudent use and the need for its return back into the ground as against its discharge into drains.

Chapter Demarcator

22. B20 discusses the sewage waste and emissions from the built environment and its recycling.

23. B21 discusses the need for local food production and independence.

24. B22 examines the issues of reuse, recycling and eventual reintegration of all the materials used in the built environment in ways analogous to those involved in the recycling of materials within natural ecosystems (see A3 and A4).

25. B23 requires the designer to seek means to integrate the designed system's inorganic mass with organic mass not only horizontally (see A2, B3, B7 and B8) but also vertically, to ensure more comprehensive biointegration.

26. B24 outlines an approach to evaluating the designed system as a series of energy flows, materials, people, machines, etc, through the built system as inputs and outputs (ie L21 and L12 from the Interaction Matrix) and their consequences.

27. B28 to B29 discuss the approach to the assembly and fixing of materials and components within the designed system as designing for disassembly (DFD) to facilitate their reuse, recycling and eventual reintegration.

28. In B30, the designer completes the circle and reassesses the designed system in its totality, with particular regard to its benefits and consequences for the natural environment in addition to its aesthetic outcome.

29. C1 to C3 cover other relevant issues that may preoccupy the designer in the implementation of this instruction manual.

C3 draws an analogy between the ecodesign of our built environment and prosthesis design; both design endeavours involve the integration of a human-made artificially designed system with a host organic system to which it is connected and the criterion of success is simply measured in the extent of the effectiveness of their biointegration. In the case of the human-built environment, the organic host system to which it is connected and with which it must effectively integrate is the ecosystems, the biosphere and global biospheric processes.

Contents

Contents

Chapter C • Chapter B • Chapter A

015

Ecodesign calls for a revisioning of both architecture and our built environment.

Preface

Today, the single most compelling question for designers concerned with the ecological consequences of human activities on the natural environment is how to design (and in some instances, also redesign) our built environment, which includes all the artefacts that are part of our everyday lives, so that it will be environmentally benign and neither be destructive nor cause environmental problems to the natural world on whose continued well-being our own survival as one of nature's species depends.

This instruction manual offers answers to this question in an informed and orderly basis for action. Despite the current plethora of literature on ecodesign, none exists that provides a comprehensive set of fundamental considerations and criteria in an organised approach to design. This then is the objective and usefulness of this manual.

Ecodesign is not just about proscribing one material or system in favour of another from a technical standpoint, but rather about the overall perception of how our human communities and built environment can become an integral and benign part of life on the planet. Ecodesign must be applied to all aspects of our built environment (such as land use, building design, product design, energy systems, transportation, materials, waste, agriculture, forestry, urban planning, etc. Ecodesign calls for a revisioning of both architecture and our built environment as we understand them. The text defines what such an architecture must be and how it is to function not only in order for it to be sustainable or green, but also for it to play a long-term permanent role integrable with the natural environment. The existing built environment is dissected to show how its roles, functions and processes have to be reinvented for us to be fully able to address the global issues of biointegration for the future benefit of humankind. This manual's relevance lies not just in providing a proactive basis for design but also in its role as a comprehensive body of instructions that inform the reader of what constitutes ecodesign.

This assessment calls for a total change, not just in how we currently perceive architecture and the built environment but also in the environmental context of our design and how we must respond to these by configuration and by process. It is evident that a radically different model of those human activities that can be permitted in the natural environment and of the way that we design our built environment is needed.

The manual is also intended to enable businesses to understand their environmental consequences and help them envision what their companies would look like if they were sustainable, and then realise this vision with new processes, materials and attitudes.

In addressing these points, we must first acknowledge that this manual does not contain all the answers to ecological design. Inevitably, there remain a significant number of theoretical and technical issues that are still unresolved because ecological design is, relatively speaking, still in its infancy. While recognising such shortcomings, this manual nevertheless serves to provide the designer with a methodical basis for design that seeks to be as comprehensive as possible. It is to be hoped that this groundwork will be augmented in the future and revised as the field advances and develops.

A strategic set of guiding design principles is also provided here so that, where solutions to any theoretical or technical problem are not prevalent, the manual remains useful in providing the designer with a fundamental framework for approaching these issues as a set of desirable ecological goals in design.

We need to acknowledge that compliance with the instructions and principles in this manual alone will not automatically generate a design. If the reader is expecting this, then he or she will be disappointed. Generally, data collection, analysis and compliance with green criteria will not result in a design, although in the process of carrying these processes out and in the resolution of the various problematic aspects of ecodesign, potential clues may be derived as to what might be the best shape, form and systems for the emergent design and these may lead to the indication of an eventual design form.

We must be clear that the design process will in all cases require a creative act of form-making by the designer, where, in the process of assembling a series of aphorisms together as a whole, the design is realised. Ultimately, this process and the envisioning of the aesthetics of the designed system depend entirely upon the design skills of the designer, and obviously these will vary with the individual.

The term 'designer' is used here to refer not only to architects, product and industrial designers, engineers, urban planners and those in the design profession, but also to include all those other professionals whose activities impinge in one way or another on the natural environment.

Although the set of instructions for ecodesign provided here is set out in what it is hoped is an orderly manner, we need to caution that ecodesign is not sequential in application and that the order in which these instructions are followed may vary, depending on the design assignment at hand.

Much of ecodesign has to start from empirical thinking, hence much of the initial thinking and knowledge is obviously abstract. The challenge is to take these abstractions and make them work in practice; this falls short of formulating a design, making production drawings or producing construction specifications, all of which are beyond the scope of this book. Ecodesign is multidisciplinary and the imperative here is to give a global view of what constitutes ecological design and its fundamental principles.

Included in the manual is a description of the theoretical basis for ecological design. We might contend that in academia, in politics and in professional practice, in terms of priorities, the sustainability debate currently occupies the middle ground in its advance from the marginal to the mainstream, for which reason a confident theory–practice framework such as is provided here (in A5) is critical to legitimise and affirm ecodesign's position in the mainstream.

Notwithstanding the above, this manual provides a unified conceptual basis and theoretical framework of the ecological determinants influencing built form whether it is for a built structure or infrastructure, as a designed system tied to the land upon which it is located, or for a product whose use and subsequent life-after-use, together with its eventual environmental assimilation, need to be pre-designed.

At its simplest level of utility, this text sets out those aspects of human activity and of our built environment, and similarly those aspects of the natural environment, that must be considered in their totality and their biointegration accommodated without planetary impairment if our long-term survival as a species is to be assured.

Theoretically, we can contend that just like a beehive or a foxes' den, our human-built environment (although existent on a scale much larger than the communities of bees and foxes) need not be destructive but can be benign to the ecosystems and global biospheric processes, as long as the natural environment's ecological integrity is preserved.

While the human animal is the most polluting one in nature, it is also the only species that has the capability to plan and manage its own future. It is this capability, based on the principles and directives set out in this manual, that must be effectively exercised now.

Ken Yeang

kynnet@pc.jaring.my

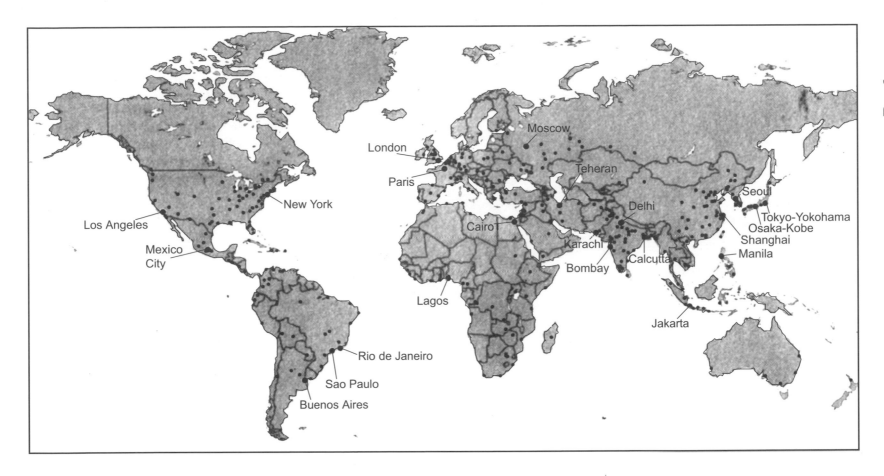

Preface-1   World's largest cities in 2000 (projected)
- ● Cities of greater than 10 million population
- • Cities with 1 million to 10 million population

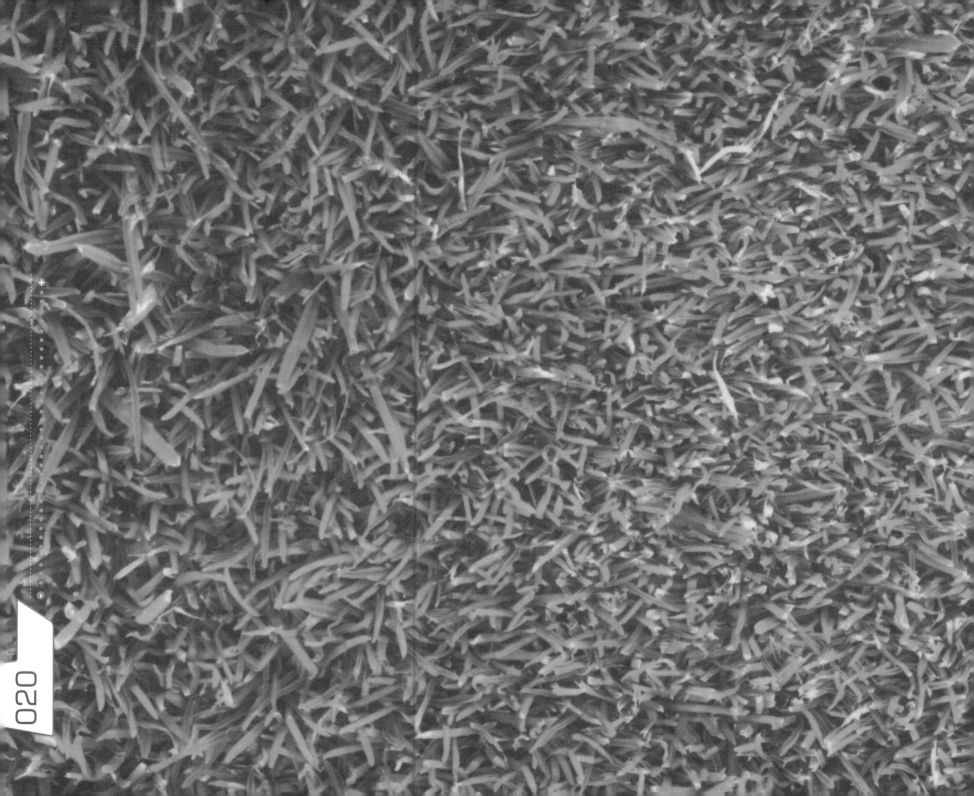

General Premises and Strategies

Chapter C • Chapter B • Chapter A •

A1

What is ecodesign? Designing the biointegration of artificial-systems-to-natural-systems

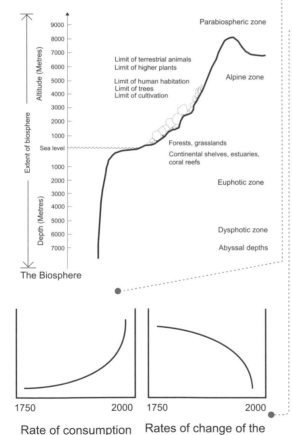

The Biosphere

Rate of consumption
of resources

Rates of change of the
quality of our environment

A1 What is ecodesign? Designing the biointegration of artificial-systems-to-natural-systems

Simply stated, ecological design or ecodesign is the use of ecological design principles and strategies to design our built environment and our ways of life so that they integrate benignly and seamlessly with the natural environment that includes the biosphere, which contains all the forms of life that exist on earth. This goal must be the fundamental basis for the design of all our human-made environments.

This definition, as a clear description of ecodesign, leads us directly to the key issues that are vital to design as they are formulated in the chapters below.

The basic premise for ecodesign is that our health, both as human beings and as one of the millions of species in nature, depends upon the air that we breathe and the water that we drink, as well as on the uncontaminated quality of the soil from which our food is produced. In the coming decades the survival of humanity will depend on the quality of the natural environment and, crucially, on our ability to continue to carry out all our human activities – including the sustaining of our built environment – without further impairment and pollution of the natural environment. Ecodesign is based on these fundamental conditions. Simply stated our health as human beings depends on the continued health of our natural environment.

Humans are a polluting species in nature. In fact, of all the species in nature, humans are the *most* polluting. This was not always the case as, until about two hundred years ago, the human race was, on the whole, a good neighbour in the community of species in the biosphere. However, humans have now begun to behave like 'dogs as careless defecators'. They have strewn their faeces and other rubbish and debris carelessly about the landscape. For the past two hundred years, humanity has been gradually polluting and modifying the natural environment at an increasing rate. Although humans account for only one quarter of the 1 per cent of the earth's entire biomass, they are responsible for 99 per cent of all the earth's pollution and cover 8 per cent of the biosphere's land surface with their built environment.

Added to the pollution of the natural environment is the quantum of depletion of non-renewable energy in fossil fuels. If we removed fossil fuels from the human equation our present modern industrial civilisation would cease to exist. Virtually every aspect of our modern human existence is made from, powered by or effected by fossil fuels. Current projections indicate that the timeline to global peak production of crude oil may be between eight and 18 years and that humanity is fast approaching one of its great historical crossroads. What will happen when there is no electricity? Without electricity, air conditioners, computers, credit-card machines, petrol pumps and cash registers will all cease to function. A few hours after the power runs out, most long-distance automotive traffic will run out of fuel and come to a halt. If these two cornerstones of our society, petroleum and electricity, are knocked out, human society might well stumble back into the Stone Age.

The imperative, then, is for a deep and prescriptive ecological basis for designing the nexus of our built environment with ecology to reflect the intimate symbiotic relationship between our human-made environment and the natural environment. Inevitably, ecological considerations have to become an integral part of the practice of the design of all of our artefacts, structures and infrastructures, indeed, of all our built environment. The question of how this is to be achieved now becomes a matter of critical debate among ecological designers.

There is currently much misunderstanding as to what constitutes ecodesign. The subject of the green built environment is not just one of another set of problems that can be resolved through advanced technology. Many designers wrongly believe that if they stuff a building with enough ecogadgets such as solar collectors, wind generators, photovoltaics and biodigestors then they will instantly have an ecological design. Of course, nothing could be further from the truth. While we should not deny the experimental usefulness of these technological systems and devices, which may eventually lead us to the ideal ecological product or structure or infrastructure or plan, they are certainly not the be-all and end-all in ecodesign. Many of these are just empty attempts at an ecological architecture. There is a sanctimonious mythology around what is basically a collection of admirable engineering innovations. Unfortunately, the architectural journals perpetuate this popular view and contribute to much of the misperception of what is ecodesign. This has given rise to the view that if you put an architect together with a mechanical and electrical (M&E) engineer familiar with the engineering design of such systems, then they will produce eco-architecture as an outcome – unfortunately, all they will in fact produce is just an ecogadget architecture, an illusory vision of technological salvation. There is nothing particularly compelling about a built form with photovoltaic cells, solar panels and thermal glass as a low-energy structure and, furthermore, green design is not just about low-energy design. What must be made clear is that ecodesign is not the facile assembly in a single structure of ecological-technological systems and gadgets. Such technology may be part of the ecological designer's tool kit, but the ultimate objective is environmental integration by design. Often such technological obsessions can distract the designer from understanding the bigger picture of ecology and ecosystems in the biosphere.

There are fundamental differences between an engineering approach to green or ecodesign and the ecological approach. In the engineering approach, the designer begins with the end, a picture of the desired outcome governed by the process of efficiency, and ends with the

- Ecodesign is not an assembly of ecogadgets

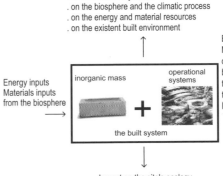

. on the local ecosystems
. on the biosphere and the climatic process
. on the energy and material resources
. on the existent built environment

Energy inputs
Materials inputs
from the biosphere

inorganic mass

operational systems

+

the built system

Energy outputs
Materials outputs
discharged to the biosphere (including the built system at the end of its useful life)

Impact on the site's ecology

- Integrating the built environment's impacts with the natural environment

A1

Chapter C ● Chapter B ● Chapter A ●

What is ecodesign? Designing the biointegration of artificial-systems-to-natural-systems

A1

Chapter C ● Chapter B ● Chapter A ●

What is ecodesign? Designing the biointegration of artificial-systems-to-natural-systems

goal of production. In contrast, the ecological design approach begins with environmental discernment (ie seeing what there is) and is governed by the process of achieving environmental harmony.

The shape, content and functioning of our designed systems must at the outset be directed towards this simple goal of benign environmental integration, starting from the production of our built environment and leading to its eventual environmental assimilation. However, this task is easy to define but complex and difficult to achieve comprehensively.

This manual sets out to address this imperative, to provide a clear and useful definition of ecodesign, and to present a sound, comprehensive and unifying theoretical framework for a definitive approach and basis for ecodesign to facilitate our production of built forms and the designing of their related systemic properties and functions.

Summary

Ecodesign is designing for the benign and seamless biointegration of our built environment with the natural environment. More specifically, the manual sets out to discuss what needs to be done to achieve this benign biointegration, why this is necessary, what the factors and aspects to be considered by design are, how these affect and influence the shaping of built forms (including their content and processes) and how such built forms might look (see C1).

It must be clear that ecodesign is still in its infancy. Humans are tampering with the biosphere, and from the devastation already inflicted and from studies by ecologists it is evident that ecosystems and their reaction to human activities are not fully understood. It is not likely that humans will understand them in the time period that they have to make decisions.

A2 The objective of ecodesign: design for benign and seamless environmental integration

The objective of ecodesign is benign biointegration with the environment. In essence, ecodesign is the process by which our human purposes are carefully and harmoniously meshed with the larger patterns, flows and processes, and physical disposition of the natural world. Simply stated, ecodesign is the seamless benign environmental integration of all our human-made environment and all our human activities with the natural environment, from source to production to operation to demolition and eventual assimilation into the ecosystems and biospheric processes. The vital premise and the predominant issue in ecological design or ecodesign is essentially one of effective integration of all of our human-made systems with the natural systems and processes in the biosphere.

This description is useful because it enables us to focus all our design activities on fulfilling the single objective of environmental biointegration.

The human-made environment that is referred to here consists inclusively of all the items, parts and components of our human-made world. These include our buildings and structures, urban infrastructure (eg roads, drains, sewerage, bridges, ports, etc), all the things that we extract, manufacture and produce, which includes all our artefacts (eg refrigerators, toys, furniture, etc), in effect, everything that is made by humans. Set against this is the natural environment, which consists of the ecosystems in the biosphere including all the biotic and abiotic constituents of the earth and the biospheric processes. The ecology of the earth is the ultimate context, the environmental matrix with which all our human activities and our built environment have to integrate.

The term biosphere is used here to describe the atmosphere, the earth's surface, the oceans and ocean floors or the region within which organisms live. It forms a thin layer around the earth, including the surface of the lithosphere, the hydrosphere and the lower atmosphere. It is the source from which our built environment is derived, and its ultimate sink.

The key word in ecodesign is integrate. It is this aspect and this emphasis on environmental integration and its systemic articulation that is absent from most other works on ecodesign. In effect, seamless ecological integration is regarded here as the foremost single fundamental issue that we as humans must resolve, not just in ecodesign but in all our activities. If humans are able successfully to integrate their entire human-made environment, its functions and all its processes in their totality in a benign, seamless and symbiotic relationship with the natural environment, we would have eliminated virtually all the significant problems arising from the negative consequences of human activity on the natural environment.

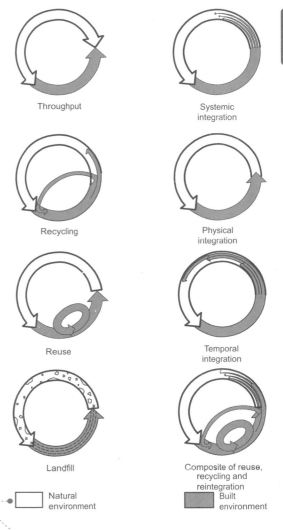

Throughput

Systemic integration

Recycling

Physical integration

Reuse

Temporal integration

Landfill

Composite of reuse, recycling and reintegration

☐ Natural environment

■ Built environment

● Integration of the built environment with the natural environment

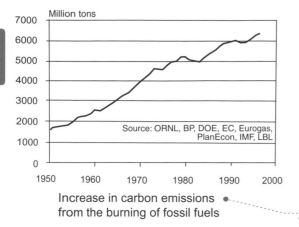

Million tons

Source: ORNL, BP, DOE, EC, Eurogas, PlanEcon, IMF, LBL

Increase in carbon emissions from the burning of fossil fuels

By gas	(%)
Carbon dioxide (CO_2)	49
Methane (CH_4)	18
Nitrous oxide (N_2O)	6
CFC-11 and CFC-12	14
Tropospheric ozone (O_3)	8
Other	5

By sector	(%)
Energy	57
CFCs	17
Agriculture	14
Forestry	9
Other industrial	3

Contributions to global warming by gas and by sector

Some designers regard green design as designing with minimal negative consequences for the natural environment; or as producing a built environment that takes less from the earth and gives more to people; or as designing the built environment analogous to a tree (ie that produces oxygen, uses solar energy, purifies water, etc). All these approaches are indeed inclusive but if the resultant design systems fail to integrate with the natural environment in terms of their production, operation (in-use) and eventual reuse, recycling or reintegration, then they will only ameliorate the present rate of environmental impairment but will not lead to an end-solution. The eventual criteria by which to judge success have to be how seamlessly, benignly and inclusively the built environment integrates with the natural environment. The ultimate test remains integration.

For instance, if we are able to integrate systemically and assimilate all the emissions and waste materials (solids, gases, liquids) from our industrial built environment harmlessly within the natural cycles and processes in the ecosystems without their disruption or impairment, then there will in effect be no such things as waste or environmental pollution.

If we were able to integrate temporally (ration and conserve) our rate of energy use (whether from renewable or non-renewable energy resources) with the availability and the natural rates of resource renewal in the biosphere, then there would be absolutely no problem of depletion of non-renewable energy resources or global warming due to the environmental effects of greenhouse gases, nor any need for concern over their sustainability for future generations. By using natural and energy resources too quickly, humans throw away that part of solar energy that will still be reaching the earth for a long time after humankind has departed. Humans' consumption of energy resources over the last 200 years has been profligate, such resources should not be used for non-vital needs. The natural resources (eg fossil fuels, metals and other materials) should not be temporally extracted at a faster pace than their slow degradation and reintegration back into the earth's crust or their absorption by nature. Similarly, substances produced in the built environment must not systemically increase or be produced at a faster pace than they can be broken down.

If we are able to integrate physically all of our built structures and infrastructures with the ecosystems in the biosphere we will not encounter any disruption of habitats or loss of biodiversity or the problems they cause.

Of course, while we may insist that this is the most vital issue and design problem confronting ecological design today, we must also recognise that achieving this comprehensively and successfully (see A5) in an environmentally benign and seamless way is a difficult endeavour, but herein lies the great challenge for ecological design.

To articulate this basis for ecodesign further, we need to approach the objective of [biointegration] from three separate levels: physical, systemic and temporal. Physical integration is the dispositional, geographical and locational integration of our built environment with the physical features and processes of the ecosystems. [Systemic-integration] is the integration of the flows, functions, operations and processes of our built environment with the processes and functions of the ecosystems and the biosphere. Temporal integration is the integration at a sustainable rate of the use and consumption of the natural resources, ecosystems and biospheric processes by humans and by our built environment with the natural rates of renewal and regeneration occurring in the ecosystems and in the biosphere. Each of these levels of integration must obviously be achieved benignly and seamlessly (ie with zero or minimal negative consequences) and, ideally, with positive consequences for the natural environment. Such are the fundamental principles of ecodesign and planning.

In resolving this issue of ecointegration, we can refer to our ecological design 'interactions model' (in A5) to inform us of all those aspects of the built environment that must be taken into account. For instance, the range of ecological integration can be broken down as follows. The designer must address the ecological integration of the primary production of the materials, products and urban infrastructure supporting our built systems (including their installation and construction, their operations in-use and their impacts on their immediate environment including the climatic processes in the biosphere). The next component of ecointegration is the flow and transportation of people and things to and from the built system during its period of use. Then there are the spatial impacts of the built system itself (and its subsequent alteration and renovation) all impinging upon the site's ecosystem. The final component consists of the consequences of the built system's emissions and outputs and of their reuse or recycling within the existing human-made environment including their eventual assimilation or reintegration into the natural environment. These processes encompass the built system's own content of materials and equipment since these too have to go somewhere at the end of their useful life.

Ecodesign is therefore a complex undertaking. As with all matters dealing with the natural environment, there are multiple linkages and multiple levels of effect that are interdependent. The effective resolution of all these aspects into built form becomes a complex design and technical endeavour. Each of the acts in the design and creation of our built environment can impose significant negative impacts on the natural environment as can each step of their flow from production, through operation, transportation, recycling and reuse to their eventual environmental reintegration. Therefore, ecological design should set out to achieve a total physical, systemic and temporal integration of our human-made systems with those in nature but in a benign and positive way. In practice, it may be difficult to achieve biointegration in

Hierarchy	Level of integration		Linkages
Biosphere	↑	↓	Macroscale environment
Biomes	↑	↓	Mesoscale environment
Ecosystems	Increasing complexity of organisation	↓	Defined envelope of environment and biota conditions
Functional groups	↑	Decreasing number of individual organisms	Sets of environmental pressures within tolerance range of species making up functional group
Communities	↑	↓	Sets of environmental pressures within tolerance range of species making up community
Population	↑	↓	Other population and microscale environments
Organisms	↑	↓	Other individuals, of the same and other species, and microscale environments

● Levels of integration and linkages in ecodesign

Biodisintegratable
Outputs benignly biodisintegrate and turn into mulch. Generally, biodisintegrating takes place in the presence of moisture. Biodisintegration may be inhibited or may not be possible, in landfills. Biodisintegration may perform slightly better when outputs are compressed. Degradation must be 100% less than 2 months after outputs are exposed to the outside environment.

Biodegradable
Outputs benignly biodegrade 100% rather than biodisintegrate (eg, manufactured by micro-organisms.)

Bioregenerative
Outputs benignly biodegrade completely within 3 months, leaving no residues (eg paper products laminated with layers of corn-based cellulose materials) and can resist water for 6 to 8 hours (eg containers for drinks and fast foods.)

Bioenhancing
Outputs benignly bioenhance (eg use artificial burrs designed to prevent erosion in arid climates). Carry additives to stimulate plant growth (eg plant seeds and seedlings embedded in growth stimulants)

Note: All outputs must be benign to the natural environment

● Systemic integration

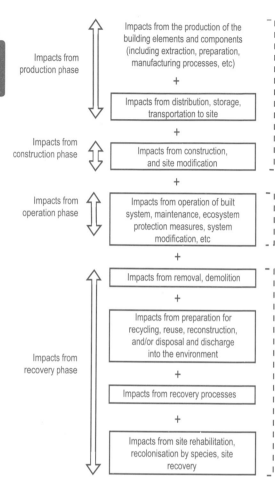

Impacts from production phase

Impacts from the production of the building elements and components (including extraction, preparation, manufacturing processes, etc)

+

Impacts from distribution, storage, transportation to site

+

Impacts from construction phase

Impacts from construction, and site modification

+

Impacts from operation phase

Impacts from operation of built system, maintenance, ecosystem protection measures, system modification, etc

+

Impacts from removal, demolition

+

Impacts from preparation for recycling, reuse, reconstruction, and/or disposal and discharge into the environment

+

Impacts from recovery phase

Impacts from recovery processes

+

Impacts from site rehabilitation, recolonisation by species, site recovery

Impacts in the life cycle of a designed system

absolute terms (in B3). Thus ecodesign becomes a process of prioritising those aspects of biointegration crucial to the design programme and to the particular ecological conditions pertaining to a given site (see B3).

Some of the techniques currently used in ecological design, such as the ecological land-use planning method as developed by landscape architects in the 1960s (see B5), are particularly relevant to achieving these objectives. Although they are not entirely satisfactory, these techniques give us a greater likelihood of achieving the physical and mechanical integration of our built forms and infrastructures with the ecosystem features and processes of the site. However, in most instances, the level of integration reached has essentially been one of the mechanical and physical integration of our built forms and infrastructures with the site's ecosystem features, as opposed to the sought-after systemic integration with the ecosystem processes. For example, the systemic integration of our built form's operations systems and the flows of the infrastructural systems with the ecosystems remain, in many instances, inadequately integrated.

What is sustainable design? Broadly speaking, sustainable design is synonymous with ecological design. It can be defined as designing to ensure a society that is able to satisfy its needs without diminishing the chances of future generations. It includes any form of design that minimises environmentally destructive impacts by integrating itself physically, systemically and temporally with the natural environment's living processes (see Appendix 2).

Arising from this definition with regard to 'future generations' is the question of precisely how far into the future we are referring. The answer is most probably a mere hundred years from today. The world as it exists today, even if there are no significant changes to humankind's impact on the environment, can probably continue for another hundred years, probably to 2100; but the prospects beyond that date do not appear optimistic if we do not change our way of life and our built environment. Already it has been indicated that, at humankind's present rate of consumption, oil as a non-renewable energy resource will not last for more than 50 years.

In the case of built structures (architecture, structures of any sort and infrastructure), ecodesign considerations include not just the design of the entire built systems but also what happens during their manufacture, transportation and construction through to their eventual reuse, recycling and reintegration. This covers all related issues from the preparation of the design brief to site selection, conceptualisation and development of the design, construction techniques, landscaping, management of construction waste, consumption during use, ecosystem protection and occupant health. To these ecodesign considerations might be added the conservation of the site upon which these structures are placed; the site's ecosystem and its biotic and abiotic components with which the processes in the structures must integrate; and the conservation of water, energy, material and other biological resources as well as the issues of biointegration (see B4 to B8). This consideration must also extend to all the internal items, fittings, products and equipment in the built system itself.

Summary

Ecological design, or ecodesign as used here for short, is the design of our artificial human-made environment to integrate with nature. This involves the territorial shaping of that human-made environment's form and (in the case of the ecodesign of a product) the determining of its content, functions and processes and the monitoring of its passage during its life cycle, where the environmental consequences of its creation as well as the environmental consequences of its total set of environmental interactions, its inputs and outputs and the other related aspects and activities, such as transportation, etc, are carried out so as to integrate benignly, seamlessly and symbiotically with the natural environment.

This definition of ecodesign is useful as a set of references for the designer to ensure that all those crucial aspects of our design endeavours will be taken into account in biointegration and also be realised in the process of determining its built form by design.

Our first task in any ecodesign endeavour is to avoid any further deterioration in the environment and design to sustain it, Ultimately ecodesign should aim to restore the previous environmental conditions that existed before the age of industralised mass corruption.

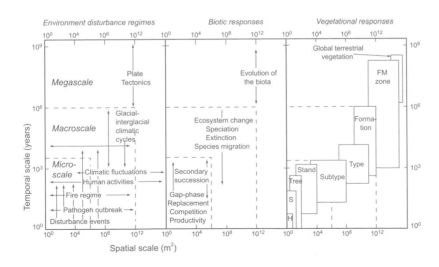

Environmental disturbance regimes, biotic responses and vegetational patterns •·····

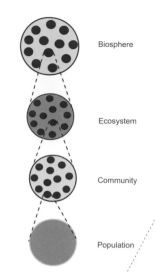

Biosphere

Ecosystem

Community

Population

System of biological organisation ●

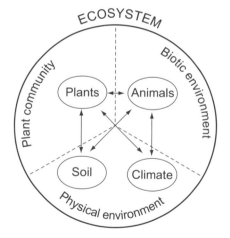

ECOSYSTEM

Plant community

Biotic environment

Plants ↔ Animals

Soil — Climate

Physical environment

Plants, animals and their biotic and physical ●
environment as components of the ecosystem

The plant community is viewed as a collection of individuals patterned
by their unique interaction with the environment, a highly integrated
whole that was set in a particular physical environment

A3 The basis for ecodesign: the ecosystem concept

Ecodesign must always be based on the ecosystem concept. First articulated by the British botanist Arthur George Tansley (1871-1955) in 1935 and developed into a general system by Eugene P. Odum (1913-2002), the ecosystem is defined as a discrete unit in nature that consists of living and non-living parts, together with its total environment, interacting to form a stable system. The whole earth can be considered as an ecological unit and within it is a system of biological organisation. This concept is vitally important for us here as it forms the cornerstone of ecodesign.

The ecosystem concept is derived from the term ecology, coined by the German biologist Ernst Heinrich Haeckel (1834-1919) in 1866. It denotes the scientific study of ecosystems and the interrelationships among organisms and between them and all aspects of their environment, both living and non-living, and is concerned with the effects that organisms have on the inanimate environment.

An important characteristic of an ecosystem is that it can be of any size. No ecosystem stands alone. All ranks of ecosystems are open systems, not closed ones. This means that all ecosystems are connected by flows of energy and materials. Each system draws in energy and materials from the systems around it and in turn exports energy and material to them. In drawing the boundaries of an ecosystem, we need to consider the flows that link it to its neighbour. Ignoring these connections, these imports of energy and materials, leads to ecosystem impairment.

It is necessary for the designer to study ecology and be ecoliterate as an understanding of ecology enables us to see and comprehend the interconnections and processes that make up the environment, and gives us the reason and basis to protect it by design. We need comprehensively to apply our knowledge of ecology and ecosystems to the redesign of our technologies, our social, economic and political institutions, to our existing industrial complexes, and to our built environment so as to bridge the current gap between the present ecologically damaging design of our built environment and technologies and the systems of nature.

Ecology is the study of plants and animals in their natural habitat (from the Greek word oikos, a house). The science of ecology examines all the interactions among living things in relation to their environment and involves the study of the interactions of organisms and their environment (which includes other organisms). It is the study of patterns, networks, balances and cycles rather than of the straightforward causes and effects that distinguish the disciplines of physics and chemistry. It is the study of the function and structure of the natural world. Ecological principles can be applied at all scales.

Generally stated, an ecosystem operates sustainably if its inputs and outputs (of both energy and materials) are balanced over time without substantial loss of nutrients, a situation that can be described as a state of dynamic equilibrium or a 'steady state', although there may be fluctuations. Achieving this equilibrium or steady state by analogy (see A5) must also be the design objective of our human-made built environment. A robust human-made ecosystem is an extension of the natural ecosystems in the biosphere.

A basic level of ecoliteracy is therefore fundamentally crucial and vital for the designer who must be critically aware of the ecological consequences of all the actions effected on the natural environment and be able to understand ecology and the ecosystem concept. This is essential for at least two reasons: first, ecological knowledge will enable the designer to understand clearly the causes behind environmental degradation due to humankind's development and progress. Second, a comprehensive grasp of ecological concepts gives the designer a tool to assess, measure and reasonably predict any environmental damage that may ensue as a consequence of his or her design. Most importantly, it will enable the designer to prescribe design solutions based on ecological principles and to design on the basis of the strategy of ecomimesis (see A4).

The biosphere is the thin skin around the earth, an envelope that extends 30 to 40 miles from the depth of the oceans to the upper stratosphere, and it contains all the forms of life that exist on earth. Within this narrow vertical band, living creatures and the earth's geochemical processes interact to sustain life. In the greater global context, the biosphere can be regarded as divided into a number of bioregions within which live characteristic plants, animals, birds, insects, fish and other inhabitants adapted to the region's climate, landforms and soils. Each bioregion contains ecological units or ecosystems. Tropical rainforest and tropical seasonal forest represent roughly 20 per cent of the total vegetated land surface of the earth (of which temperate forests, including evergreen, deciduous, and boreal forest, account for another 19 per cent). Open woodlands, shrublands and savannas represent 19 per cent, temperate grasslands 7 per cent, tundra and alpine areas slightly more than 6 per cent, and desert and near desert 14 per cent. All wet habitats, such as lakes, rivers and marshes, combined make up 3 per cent. Cultivated land accounts for the balance of slightly more than 45 per cent.

Within each ecosystem, then, are the organisms making up the living community in balance with their environment. For instance, the overall climate and topography within an area are major factors determining the type of ecosystems that develop, but within any ecosystem there are complex interactions, and minor variations give rise to smaller communities within which plants and animals occupy their own particular niches. It is to this concept of the ecosystem that our text will make constant reference.

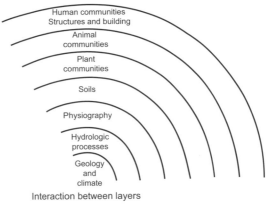

- Factors determining the type of ecosystems that develop

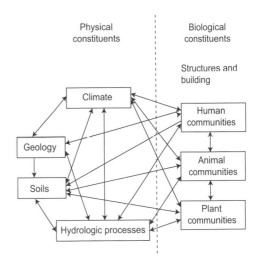

- Interactions between the layers within the ecosystem (ie the physical constituents and biological constituents) from the 'layer-cake' model

Ecosystem

Community of plants and animals
- Plant community (plant community = vegetation)
- Animal community
- Community of plant and animal microbes
} Biological constituents (biotic)

Physical environment
- Site characterised by given climate features
- Site characterised by given edaphic features
} Physical constituents (abiotic)

Ecosystem constituents ●

There are many definitions of ecosystems. Tansley describes the ecosystem as 'the basic unit of nature on the face of the earth'. Other interpretations include regarding the ecosystem as an energy-processing system the components of which have evolved together for a long period of time as communities of plants and animals, fungi and other organisms, with different degrees and kinds of interdependence among the component species, or simply as a dynamic complex of plant, animal and micro-organism communities and their non-living environment interacting as a functional unit.

The following are the key aspects of ecology and ecosystems that are crucial for the ecological designer to comprehend:

• The components of an ecosystem which are:

Layers

– Green belt or autotrophic layer, in which the organisms, plants fix light energy and utilise simple inorganic substances. The build up of complex substances from simpler material predominates.
– Brown belt or heterotrophic layer, in which the organisms utilise, rearrange and decompose complex materials. The breakdown of complex substances predominates.

Structural components

– Inorganic substances, carbon (C), nitrogen (N), carbon dioxide (CO_2), water (H_2O), etc involved in the materials cycles.
– Organic substances and compounds, proteins, carbohydrates, lipids, humic substances and the like that link the biotic and abiotic.
– Climatic system, including temperature, rainfall, etc.
– Producer organisms – autotrophic; primarily green plants that are able to synthesise foodstuffs from simple substances and light energy. ('Producers')
– Consumer organisms – phagotrophic; animals-that ingest particulate organic matter or other organisms. ('Consumers')
– Decomposer organisms–saprotrophic; primarily bacteria, protozoa, fungi and the like-that break down complex substances with the release of both organic and inorganic products which are then recycled by plants or provide energy sources and have a regulatory effect on other biotic components. ('Decomposers')

Processes

– Energy flow.
– The food chains or trophic relationships.
– Diversity patterns, spatial and temporal.

- Mineral, cycling of nutrients aside from food.
- Development and evolution.
- Control or cybernetic aspects.

• Within the ecosystems are habitats. A habitat is the place or type of site where an organism or population naturally occurs. The organisms produce food for other organisms (for instance, plants photosynthesise and grow, to be eaten by herbivores, etc). There are also other organisms present such as the decomposers that break down matter into the basic elements again. In an ecosystem there is a complete cycling of nutrients (from living organisms to organic wastes back to living organisms) and a net balance of energy flows (energy input from sunlight balances energy output during the production of matter, and heat). The designer must be aware that these complex processes and functions within the project site can easily be disrupted by the imposition of built systems, structures and human activity upon it; it is therefore crucial for the designer to study these processes systemically and areally in the designated ecosystem prior to any projected human activity taking place there (see B4 to B5).

• The key factors in an ecosystem are not just its size but the flow of energy and the physical circulation of matter.

• The earth is made up of many ecosystems of all kinds and sizes, and these in turn are linked. Designers must regard all their actions as being ecologically and environmentally interconnected, with consequences that are not just local and regional but also global.

• Natural ecosystems change by the process of succession. Ecological succession begins with the arrival of species, the growth and acquisition of resources, competition and facilitation as processes that lead to full ecosystem development. Limitations to succession are set by resource availability in that locality. The subsequent success of an ecosystem's development depends on the development of internal processes of recycling of materials. This involves decay of organic matter, release and reuse of nutrients, and the activities of soil organisms. Since ecosystems change over time, the designer must monitor the state of the ecosystems within which the designed system is located in a continual assessment of the system's impact on that locality over time. Ecodesign is not a one-off act.

• Within any ecosystem each organism, however large or small, plays a vital role in maintaining the stability of that community. Its habitat is where that organism – animal, bacterium, protist, plant or fungus lives. Every organism has its territory where conditions are conducive – its survival. The most important factor for any organism is its source of energy or food. From an ecological perspective, all species (including humans) have

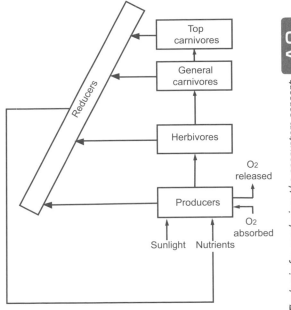

• The cycling of materials within an ecosystem

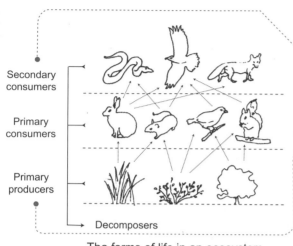

Secondary
consumers

Primary
consumers

Primary
producers

Decomposers

The forms of life in an ecosystem

evolved together on the planet and each species, however seemingly insignificant, has a claim to continue its life. Within any ecosystem, there are complex patterns of feeding relationships or food chains that are built up. The number of links within a food chain in ecosystems is normally three or four, with five, six and seven occurring less frequently. The main reason for the limited length of food chains is that a major part of the energy stored within the plant or animal is lost at each stage in the chain. Designers must be aware of the fragility of these patterns and be sensitive to disruptions brought about as a consequence of human activity interfering with food chains.

• Plants are the primary source of food and energy in any ecosystem. They derive energy through photosynthesis, a process that utilises environmental factors such as light, water, carbon dioxide and minerals. Herbivores then obtain their food by eating plants. In their turn, herbivores are preyed upon by carnivores, who may also be the source of food for other carnivores. Animal and plant waste is decomposed by micro-organisms within the habitat, and this returns the raw materials to the environment. The designer should note that this process within the ecosystem is cyclic whereas the process in our current human-made built environment is a one-way throughput in which the discharges at the end of the flow disrupt nature's cyclic processes causing environmental impairment.

• The forms of life in an ecosystem depend entirely upon the sensitive balance within its environment, and any change by humans that sets in train local, regional and worldwide effects could lead to further devastating consequences that will impact on humans and life in general. The body of knowledge and insights unique to ecology are not only significant in their own right, but are also important in the development of environmentalism.

• All species evolve to interact with one another physically and behaviourally. For example, pollinating insects and birds have evolved probosces and beaks suitable to the task, and the flowers that they pollinate have adapted to facilitate and encourage this cooperation so that during the process of feeding, insects and birds act as efficient pollinators. All creatures respond to and change their habitats in relation to climatic and atmospheric processes and to the locality's soil chemistry. If humankind wants to live sustainably then we too need to adapt our habitats (our built environment) to the processes of the natural environment, for instance by building and living in response to the climate and ecology of the given locality (see B5, B6 and B13). (It is estimated that an annual average of 50,000 species – including mammals, birds, insects and plants – could be lost over the next several decades. If this rate continues, more than two-thirds of all living species could disappear over the course of the 21st century.)

• In studying ecology, the designer is not studying the individual organism per se but the organism within its community of other living things. Ecodesign is about designing our built environment within its community of other living things, and concerns its relationship to other structures in nature, to the life of the whole natural community and to the ecosystems in the biosphere.

- Perhaps least obvious to many is the effect of the animals and plants in nature that are organised into highly complex communities. These communities not only ensure an orderly cycle of material and energy transformation as mentioned above but also regulate the moisture economy, cushion the earth's surface against violent physiographic change, and make possible the formation of soil. In short, humans are dependent upon these organisms both for their own immediate means of survival and for maintaining the habitat conditions under which their survival is possible. The changes to these organisms induced by humans, whether precipitated by wanton destruction or indirectly by accelerating natural processes, are probably more serious for humans than the 'natural changes' for which they are not responsible. The designer must be aware of such communities in each of the project sites and ensure that the ecological integrity of such communities is sustained.

- Generally stated, a fundamental aspect of natural systems is that the ecosystems and the entire biosphere are relatively stable and resilient. Their resilience to withstand disturbances and to recover from regular 'shocks' (eg from human action) are essential to keep the biosphere's life-support systems operating. Maintaining the integrity of the web of species, functions and processes within an ecosystem and the webs that connect different systems is critical for ensuring stability and resilience. If ecosystems become simplified and their webs become disconnected, they become more fragile and vulnerable to catastrophic and irreversible decline. Human-induced changes such as global climate change (notably warming) and the breakdown of the ozone layer, the biodiversity deficit, the collapse of fisheries, the increasingly severe floods and droughts, etc, provide ample evidence that the biosphere is becoming less resilient. Our current and future design endeavours must not further impair that resilience and should be designed to be within the ecosystems carrying capacities. It is for these reasons that an ecological design approach is vital for all of our built environments and activities.

- It is the ecosystem's components (organisms, populations, species, habitats, etc), processes (nutrient cycling, carbon cycles, ecological succession, etc) and properties (resilience, health, integrity, etc) that provide us with a life-supporting environment. But owing to the gradual loss of natural resilience over time, the ecosystems in the biosphere are growing more constrained, with the result that with their reduction and elimination the ecological impacts of our designed systems and activities grow correspondingly more

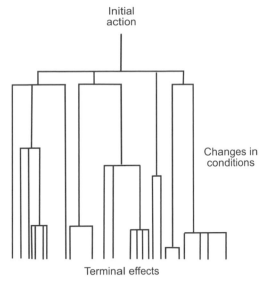

Initial action

Changes in conditions

Terminal effects

Escalating and multiple changes to the existing conditions in an ecosystem as a result of a single action

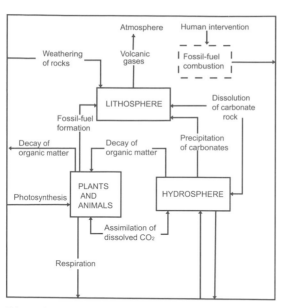

Disruption to the carbon cycle in the biosphere by human intervention through fossil-fuel combustion

important. Therefore, greater environmental design care and monitoring will be required with regard to our impacts on the ecosystems.

- All our endeavours at the design stage in relation to the earth's ecological systems are geared to the future; they therefore should be prognostic and anticipatory. In order to avoid designing further built environments that are one-way throughput systems, our built environment should be designed with prior regard to the potential recovery, reuse and recyclability of its constituents (eg its materials and components); this, then, is the need and the basis for ecodesign (see B29).

- The uniqueness and specificity of the ecological features of each site are mirrored by the specificity of our designed systems. A designed system that works for one particular site may not be transferable to another, even if they share superficial similarities. Because of this specificity, each site must be evaluated in terms of its individual ecological components even if it appears devoid of any ecological features. Even the site's ground-water conditions, topsoil, existing trees and other such elements are site specific and may respond differently to disruptions due to human action (see B4 to B6).

- Our earth is essentially a closed materials system with a finite mass, and all the ecosystems within it, along with all of the earth's material and fossil energy resources, form the final contextual limit to all our human activities. Acknowledging this limitation is crucial to understanding sustainability in ecodesign. All design inevitably takes place within the confines of this limit. For example, one of the planet's first ecosystem functions was the production of oxygen over billions of years of photosynthetic activity, which allowed oxygen-breathing organisms such as humans to exist. Our future depends upon the ecosystems that are responsible for maintaining the proper balance of these atmospheric gases such as oxygen and carbon dioxide. We must acknowledge that there are no human-made technological systems that can ever substitute for these vital services that nature provides and it is crucial that all our current and future design endeavours do not deplete or eliminate the resilience of these services (see A4).

- Ecodesign is the rational and managed use of an ecosystem's processes and non-renewable resources. (NB The term 'resources' is used here to refer to these components in nature although its context normally implies exploitation.) Such was not the case when designers used to build, manufacture and produce as if the natural environment was essentially infinite – in its capacity to supply resources for the human-built environment and in its ability to act as a final sink or dump for the discharge of waste material. It must be clear to all humans that such a view can no longer be maintained. The ecologically responsive designer must design within the very real limitations of the biosphere and the finite capacity of an ecosystem to recover, from the loss of resources on the one hand and the influx of waste products on the other.

- The designer who is aware of the ecosystem concept will appreciate that ecodesign is a conservation-driven approach (see B19, B26). The issue of the prudent and sustainable use of non-renewable resources is critical to ecodesign. The production, operation and eventual disposal of the designed system over its useful life will consume a large quantity of energy and material resources, something of which the designer must be aware and quantify. The designer must also be informed about the degree to which non-renewable resources are utilised or reused, ie of the efficiency of resource consumption by the built system. In the case of the built environment, one factor is the spatial accommodation (eg built-up area) that the designer has designed into the system, which may be excessive in terms of meeting the building users' requirements. Should there be a significant increased difference in this provision of spatial and physical accommodation, it will result and be reflected in the low efficiency of energy and resource use by the built structure in question. Such differences can also be quantified as a measure of the built system's impact on the biosphere and its consumption of the earth's resources. Ecological design in effect involves designing for temporal integration: essentially the prudent utilisation of non-renewable and renewable resources at rates less than the natural rate at which they regenerate; and designing to optimise the efficiency with which non-renewable resources are used (see B26).

- Ecosystems are also dynamic systems and are always changing and in a state of flux. Their organisms, numbers and relationships change in a process of succession. The species present and their physical environment control the patterns, rates and limits of this succession. Even the most stable ecological systems change when affected by cyclic or catastrophic disturbances. Cumulative changes in many smaller ecological systems can add up to significant impacts on larger ecological systems. Because of this ongoing state of change in the natural environment, designers must constantly monitor the natural environment for its changes and for the consequences of the similarly changing human-built environment.

- Ecological processes function on many time scales, and change through time. Some processes take place almost instantaneously, such as metabolic functions, whereas some take longer than a human lifetime, such as decomposition, forest growth and soil formation and the formation of fossil fuels. Ecosystems also change from season to season, and year

Ecosystem attributes	Developmental stages	Mature stages
Community energetic		
- Gross production/community respiration (P/R ratio)	Greater or less than 1	Approaches 1
- Gross production/standing crop biomass (P/B ratio)	High	Low
- Biomass supported/unit energy flow (B/E ratio)	Low	High
- Net community production (yield)	High	Low
- Food chains	Linear, predominantly grazing	Weblike, predominantly detritus
Community structure		
- Total organic matter	Small	Large
- Inorganic nutrients	Extrabiotic	Intrabiotic
- Species diversity ~ variety component	Low	High
- Species diversity ~ equitability component	Low	High
- Biochemical diversity	Low	High
- Stratification and spatial heterogeneity (pattern diversity)	Poorly organised	Well organised
Life history		
- Niche specification	Broad	Narrow
- Size of organism	Small	Large
- Life cycle	Short, simple	Long, complex
Nutrient cycling		
- Mineral cycles		
- Nutrient exchange rate, between organisms and environment	Open	Closed
- Role of detritus in nutrient regeneration	Rapid	Slow
Selection pressure		
Growth form	For rapid growth (R -selection)	For feedback control (R -selection)
Production	Quantity	Quality
Overall homeostasis		
Internal symbiosis	Undeveloped	Developed
Nutrient conservation	Poor	Good
Stability (resistance to external perturbation)	Poor	Good
Entropy	High	Low
Information	Low	High

A model of ecological succession: Trends to be expected in the development of an ecosystem

1. Initiation
The starting point of any succession is a bare surface. It may be 'new', eg an emergent shoreline, or more commonly a surface stripped of any previous vegetation cover by natural or human agencies.

2. Colonisation
The first plant growth is based on a small number of specialised, highly stress-tolerant plant species. Total biomass is low, and soil is rudimentary, generally lacking organic matter and balanced available nutrients. Typical colonisers are bryophytes, and vascular plants with tolerance of extreme water and nutrient status conditions (either high, low or alternating).

3. Development
As soil conditions improve, highly stress-tolerant species are replaced by more productive and competitive ones which include grasses and weeds. Both of these are quite tolerant of disturbance, which is often a feature of the development of sere, in which substrate conditions may remain unstable and alternation between different environmental conditions may occur.

4. Maturity
By this point the ecosystem has developed to the extent that vegetation cover is dominated by competitive species, though not necessarily those with a very long life cycle. Soil conditions are stable, and nutrient and water conditions are not major problems in the ecosystem. Typical species are competitive grasses, bushes and smaller trees. Non-vascular plants are minor components, and the range of higher trophic and decomposer species is considerable.

5. Climax
The final stage sees the development of a vegetation cover that is relatively stable and persistent. It is often dominated by large trees, with a long life cycle. There is little or no evidence of the initial abiotic or biotic environmental conditions of the area which existed at the beginning of the successional sequence. The issue of whether or not there is such a condition as a stable climax is controversial.

Stages in a typical plant succession ●

to year, as well as in response to climatic changes and disturbances. They are also in continual flux as they go through successional changes. Through their disruptive activities, humans cause widespread ecosystem impairment and alter the biological, chemical and physiographic flows through the ecosystems. Some of the effects of human disturbances on the ecosystem require a long time scale before they become evident.

- Ecosystems are characterised by the nesting of systems: their interdependence, change and cycling. Enhancing ecological connectivity by design can be a beneficial effect of ecodesign (see B8).

- In ecosystems, particular species or the links between certain species may have large impacts on their functions. Two key concepts in ecological studies are the use of indicator species and keystone species. One way of assessing the health of a specific ecosystem is to use indicator species. When carefully selected, an indicator species can provide information to the designer about particular habitats, and in particular provide the information necessary to help solve conservation problems. An indicator species can be defined as an 'organism (often a micro-organism or a plant) that serves as a measure of the environmental conditions (or ecosystem health) that exist in a given locale'. For example, the designer may note that the presence of mosses indicates acid soil or that of tubifex worms indicates oxygen-poor soil and be alerted by stagnant water that is unfit to drink; the presence of certain plant species suggests whether other species would thrive, and so on.

- An understanding of the way that an ecosystem is structured, including which species are intricately linked to other species, as well as a knowledge of their physiographic and edaphic factors, can be useful to designers in their assessment of an ecosystem's health. The designer can employ particular species as indicators of the ecosystem's habitat integrity. For example, in marine ecology, butterfly fishes are used to monitor the health of coral reefs as an indicator of overall reef health or biodiversity. Should the population and species diversity of butterfly fish decline in a particular reef, it can be taken as a sign that reef health has been compromised. In intertidal ecosystems, the sampling and chemical analysis of filter feeders such as molluscs (as well as their species diversity and dynamics) can indicate to what extent their habitat has been polluted.

- Keystone species, on the other hand, have greater effects on ecological processes than would be predicted from their abundance or biomass alone. Keystone species affect ecosystems through such processes as competition, mutualism, dispersal, pollination, and by modifying habitats and abiotic factors. Keystone species usually govern biological diversity in their given habitat. For example, the starfish *Pisaster ochraceus* holds the intertidal community in a fine balance. If this predator species is removed, dramatic changes result in the varieties and population densities of all the other species in the community. No such changes result from the removal of other species. Insect pollinators are another example of keystone species because more than two-thirds of flowering plants depend on them for their reproduction needs. A reduction of pollinator species, such as that caused by the conversion of land to monoculture agriculture or urban spread, can lead to reduced reproductive success, subsequently affecting other species that feed on seeds and fruit. The keystone species' place in an ecosystem is so important that it has been proposed as a foundation for management efforts to protect the biodiversity of the world's ecosystem. The designer must be aware that the ecological impact of single species matters. In order to manage, understand and restore ecological assemblages, the roles of individual species have to be understood and considered.

- The impacts of land-use changes on keystone species can spread well beyond the boundaries of the land-use unit upon which human activities are imposed, and are difficult to predict. Unfortunately for humans, keystone species are usually noticed only when they are removed or disappear from an ecosystem, resulting in drastic changes to the rest of the ecological community.

- In the same way that the reduction of a keystone species can affect an ecological community, the introduction of alien species can have the same sort of drastic effects on ecosystem processes via their roles as predators, competitors, pathogens or vectors of disease. For instance, the introduction of salt cedars into the western USA as windbreaks to prevent soil erosion resulted in reduced plant and animal diversity, increased evapotranspiration, a lower water table, and increased soil salinity as the salt cedar invaded riparian and wetland ecosystems. Its negative effects on nutrient cycling in the ecosystem were not difficult to observe.

- Species interaction also includes those which occur within trophic levels, ie to the flows and stages of food chains, such as producers (or autotrophs, primary producers), herbivores, decomposers and other heterotrophs. Changes in the abundance of a certain species or groups of organisms on a trophic level will affect other trophic levels and can result in dramatic changes in biodiversity, community or even total productivity. For instance, the designer must be aware that in designing and planning the land use for a particular locality, the proposed layout patterns of the built structure or infrastructure can effect this change in the natural species balance and can have long-term implications for the productivity of the ecological systems.

- Just like the professional ecologist, the designer can use indicator species to measure the environmental conditions and changes within our built ecosystem. Ecodesign is deemed

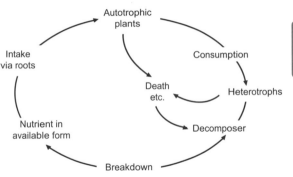

Flows within the ecosystem

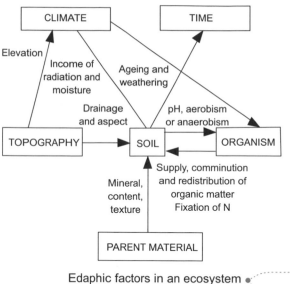

CLIMATE

TIME

Elevation

Income of
radiation and
moisture

Ageing and
weathering

Drainage
and aspect

pH, aerobism
or anaerobism

TOPOGRAPHY → SOIL ⇄ ORGANISM

Supply, comminution
and redistribution of
organic matter
Fixation of N

Mineral,
content,
texture

PARENT MATERIAL

Edaphic factors in an ecosystem

successful if we find the species of the same ecoregion returning to our designed built environment (eg as a result of our increasing the biomass of the designed system and providing more habitats; see B7). For instance, the designer would need to know the naturally occurring species of the locale (therefore the ecology) before the area is disturbed by any building activities, and then design so that these species' habitats are maintained and are contiguous with the larger ecosystem through ecological corridors, etc, which can be designed on to the site (see B8). Ecological monitoring would be essential throughout to assess the changes that occur. Nor does the use of indicator species begin and end with undisturbed habitats. Ecological studies show that there are some appropriate indicators for fragmented habitats (eg the presence/loss of the red-spotted newt, ring-necked snake and grey tree frog). The area sensitivity of reptiles and amphibians can make them indicator species for habitat fragmentation.

- Apart from the biotic factors discussed above, the designer must be aware that ecological processes are also dependent upon local climate, hydrology, and edaphic and other geomorphologic factors (see B5). The rates of key ecosystem processes (primary production and decomposition) are governed by edaphic factors (soil nutrients, temperature, moisture level) and the temporal pattern of these factors is controlled by the climate of the locality. In particular, edaphic factors are key in balancing ecological nutrient cycles. Within the soil are a multitude of decomposers, in the form of bacteria, fungi and mycorrhizal fungi, which ultimately affect productivity and the respiratory ratios on which ecosystem energy flows are based. They should be considered keystone groups of organisms as well. This point emphasises the role that soil plays in ecosystem stability. In designing changes to a specific site, the designer must take into consideration the role of the edaphic factors of that ecosystem and must ensure the retention of the topsoil of the locality.

- Natural patterns of ecosystem structure and function provide models that can guide sustainable land-use planning and design. Species assemblages are adapted to the constraints of a locale. Imposing land uses that go beyond the ecological constraints of a place will entail long-term costs and have broad-scale implications. Therefore the designer must ensure that the types of land-use, development, building or landscape design that are adopted are compatible with local conditions. This highlights the importance of knowledge of local ecological processes and the need for an inventory of the site's ecosystem prior to disruption (in B5).

- Human-made disturbance can significantly shape and change ecosystem processes and functions by its type, intensity, duration, frequency and timing. Human-made disturbance has the capacity fundamentally to change the character of an ecosystem as it affects both above- and below-ground processes, species composition, nutrient cycle and habitat structure. For instance, our act of building construction is akin to large-scale disturbances of ecosystems, with the capacity to change the course of ecological processes.

- Ecosystem processes are affected by the character of the landscape, its size, shape and patterns. Species composition and abundance will suffer as the size of habitat patches decreases, or if the distance between two habitat patches increases (eg as a result of human intervention). Larger patches, with their higher local variability tend to contain more species than smaller patches. The edges and interiors of patches also harbour different species. The designer should design to link patches and thus enhance ecological connectivity (see B8).

- The amount of connectivity needed between patches varies from species to species and depends on the abundance of the focal species, its spatial arrangement and movement capabilities. These new connectivities, or ecological corridors (see B8), have myriad functions: as habitat, conduit, filter, barrier, source and sink. In the provision of new ecological corridors within a locality by the designer, it is necessary to define the goal or implied functions to be achieved. There has previously been much confusion resulting in conflicting definitions of the term 'corridor', and the designer should address all the possible functions of the corridors when these are designed. Proper design and management of an ecological corridor will depend critically on a clear assessment of its intended ecological functions at the outset.

- The ecological importance of a habitat patch can be greater than it might seem from its size and distribution, for example riparian vegetation, which may occur as relatively narrow bands along a stream or as small patches of wetlands. Although the patches may be small and discontinuous, they have ecological functions that exceed their spatial extent. This scrappy corridor can play an important role in storing excess nutrients that would otherwise end up in water bodies and cause eutrophication or acidification. There is a constant danger that the designer may over-engineer and so overlook these seemingly unimportant skimpy habitats. Other habitats that may be more ecologically important than they at first seem are brownfield sites and neglected patches of land within the urban and city landscape (B4).

- The physical substance and form of the built environment is constructed from renewable and non-renewable energy and material resources all of which are derived from the earth's mantle and its ambient resources. In other words, our built systems are dependent upon the earth as a supplier of energy and material resources for their continued healthy existence and conservation. As a consequence, ecological design is a form of prudent management of the use of these resources. Our human-built environment should no longer be designed as one-way throughput systems but as closed or cyclic systems (B27).

• The designer must be aware of the 'services' provided by ecosystems to our built environment. These are the flows of materials, energy and information from the biosphere that support all human existence. Such natural services provided by ecosystems are vital; without them humankind as a species will not be able to survive. They can be summarised as follows:

* Primary productivity – photosynthesis, oxygen production, the removal of CO_2 from the air and its fixation into plant materials, which form the basis of the food chain
* Pollination
* Biological control of pests and diseases
* Habitat and refuge protection (maintaining genetic resources for food, disease resistance and medicines)
* Water supply, regulation (ie flood control – vegetated slopes dramatically reduce runoff relative to denuded hillsides) and purification
* Waste recycling and pollution control (by a vast array of decomposers)
* Nutrient cycling
* Raw materials production (lumber, fodder, biomass fuel)
* Soil formation and protection
* Ecosystem disturbance regulation
* Climate and atmospheric regulation

It is not feasible for humans to replace these free services of nature by any sustained and affordable technological systems or substitutes without using non-renewable sources of energy. It is for this simple reason that ecodesign should utilise as many passive and non-technological means as possible because such design modes will not make demands on the use of non-renewable energy resources. To ensure the continued existence of these ecosystem services from nature, it is vital for humankind to restore and maintain the environmental health of the ecosystems in the biosphere, which in return will sustain our human life (B13 to B17).

Networks

At all levels of the natural world, we find living systems nesting within other living systems – networks within networks. Their boundaries are not boundaries of separation but boundaries of identity. All living systems communicate with one another and share resources across their boundaries.

Cycles

All living organisms must feed on continual flows of matter and energy from their environment to stay alive, and all living organisms continually produce waste. However, an ecosystem generates no net waste, the waste of one species being the food of another. Thus, matter is cycled continually through the web of life.

Solar energy

Solar energy, transformed into chemical energy by the photosynthesis of green plants, drives the ecological cycles.

Partnership

The exchanges of energy and resources in an ecosystem are sustained by pervasive cooperation. Life did not take over the planet by combat but by cooperation, partnership and networking.

Diversity

Ecosystems achieve stability and resilience through the richness and complexity of their ecological webs. The greater their biodiversity, the more resilient they will be.

Dynamic balance

An ecosystem is a flexible, ever-fluctuating network. Its flexibility is a consequence of multiple feedback loops that keep the system in a state of dynamic balance. No single variable is maximised; all variables fluctuate around their optimal values.

Understanding ecology affects the way that the designer approaches the form of the designed system. The designer is not just shaping the form but is also determining the content of the designed system, as well as its systems and processes (and their consequences) and also the reuse, recycling and eventual biointegration of the afterlife of the designed system.

Summary

The above are the key aspects of ecology and ecosystems (their properties and functions) that need to be understood by the designer as the fundamental premises for ecodesign or designing for ecological integration. Appreciating these may seem onerous, but it is crucial for the designer to be aware of them as they establish a fundamental level of ecological literacy and understanding necessary for approaching ecodesign, compared to an entirely technological engineering approach.

Circulation of energy in the biosphere

Design	Ecosystems	Engineering
Emphasis on	Ecology and environmental biology	Technology and engineering
Starts with	Environmental discernment	Predetermined specifications
Uses process of	Systemic integration	System efficiency
Goal	Environmental symbiosis	Production
Characteristics	Organic Holistic Natural	Mechanistic Incremental Artificial

Comparison between the ecological approach and the engineering approach

Ultimately, ecodesign is based on three main ethical principles:

1. The responsibility of the current generation for the welfare of future generations

2. The limitations and fruitfulness of the earth's resources and carrying capacity

3. The right to life of all species including humans

We need to define a model for a new type of life style and an environmental model upon which social consensus worldwide can be reached.

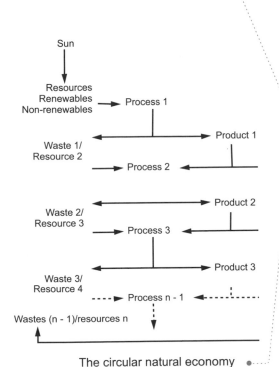

Resource ⟶ Process ⟶ Products ⟶ Wastes / Wastes

The linear human economy ●

Sun

Resources
Renewables
Non-renewables ⟶ Process 1

Waste 1/
Resource 2 ⟷ Product 1

Process 2

Waste 2/
Resource 3 ⟷ Product 2

Process 3

Waste 3/
Resource 4 ⟷ Product 3

Process n - 1

Wastes (n - 1)/resources n

The circular natural economy ●

A4 Ecomimicry: designing based on the ecosystem analogy

Ecodesign can be regarded as design based on ecomimicry, which is defined as designing architectural ecosystems to emulate the properties, structure, functions and processes of ecosystems in nature. This is necessary because designing for biointegration would be greatly facilitated if our designed system had properties and characteristics similar to those of the ecosystems in nature. The principles of designing by ecomimicry are similar to those in bionics or biomimicry – to design based on the general principle that nature's 'designs' and 'technologies' are by far superior to any of our human designs and technologies.

Key to an understanding of ecological design and sustainability is the realisation that we do not need to invent our human communities and built environment from scratch but that we can model these by imitating nature's ecosystems, which are naturally occurring sustainable communities of plants, animals and micro-organisms. Essentially, our design must have an ecomimetic culture. Evident to the ecologist is the outstanding characteristic of the earth's biosphere's inherent ability to sustain life. It follows that to design a sustainable human community it must be designed so that its ways of life, businesses, economy, physical structures and technologies do not interfere with nature's inherent ability to sustain life. The sustainable communities in nature are those that evolve their patterns of living over time in continued interactions with other living systems, both human and non-human. Ecological sustainability does not mean that things do not change. It is a dynamic process of co-evolution rather than a static state.

The design approach is ecomimicry (as in biomimicry), which uses ecosystems as design models, hence design is based on lessons learnt from ecology. The design approach requires the study of ecological models and processes and their reproduction as potential design solutions for the built environment. To illustrate this, some of the principles of ecology that are critical to sustaining life are: networks, cycles, solar energy, partnership, diversity and dynamic balance. These principles can be emulated in our design of the built environment.

The rationale for ecomimicry is self-evident. Stable ecosystems in the biosphere exist without any interference by humankind. They are self-sustaining, albeit that each ecosystem may be at various stages of its ecological succession and maturity. The rationale behind ecomimicry is that the inherent operations and organisation of ecosystems (ie being 3.8 million years in the making) are vastly superior to those artificial ecological systems produced by man. As shown in the description of the design of prosthetic (artificial) limbs and organs (in C3), we now have the ability to imitate nature, albeit only partially successfully in our human-made built environment and, in the case of biotechnology, for the benefit of humankind. Ecomimesis not only provides us with new models of nature as the source of new generative strategies for the design of our built environment but it is also the source of new forms and new ways of constructing and operating the built environment. The objective of ecomimicry is to design and build our human-built environment so that it functions as a collection of human-made ecosystems that will coexist in stability with the ecosystems in nature.

In designing our built environment to imitate the properties of ecosystems, our human-made ecosystems must function in a way analogous to their natural counterparts (eg the consumption of energy and material must be optimised, waste generation minimised, and the effluents of one process serve as raw materials for another). At the same time, we must not lose sight of the prime ecological design objective – to have our built environment exist in a seamless relationship with the natural environment and be more than a passive artificial device in nature. Its processes must emulate ecosystems in virtually all their functions in ways beneficial both to humankind and to the natural environment while interacting systemically in a benign way with nature's ecosystems. We must model in its entirety our built environment's systemic design on the systemic design of the biological ecosystems. In doing so, our designed systems will further enhance the extent of their functional integrity with those ecosystems. Ecomimicry is the analogical basis for ecological design. To accomplish this may entail designing our built environment as a hybrid or composite containing both artificial and natural components, so that it resembles as closely as possible the composition, structure and functions of ecosystems.

The ecosystem concept was first used as a largely arbitrary system defined by the specific considerations for a particular application. This definition is the most relevant to our purposes because it is formulated relative to the objectives of the given study. In ecomimicry, designers consciously look to ecosystems for inspiration to create design as a nature-based innovation. The designer can assess a design for ecological appropriateness, measuring the extent to which it preserves the integrity and stability of the existent biotic community. It is inappropriate or wrong when it tends otherwise.

Some of the characteristics of ecosystems which our built environment and built systems could mimic by ecodesign are given below.

Elimination of the concept of waste in ecosystems

Virtually all of life, down to the basic cell, is interconnected, responds to its environment, communicates, thrives within diversity and generates no net waste. The exception is present-day human life and its built environment. In natural systems there is no such thing as 'waste' as everything is reassimilated and reintegrated into the ecosystems. In the natural world,

Layers
- Green belt or autotrophic layer, in which the organisms and plants fix light energy and utilise simple inorganic substances. The buildup of complex substances from simpler material predominates.
- Brown belt or heterotrophic layer, in which the organisms utilise, rearrange and decompose complex substances.

Structural components
- Inorganic substances, carbon (C), nitrogen (N), carbon dioxide (CO_2), water (H_2O), etc, involved in the materials cycles.
- Organic substances and compounds, proteins, carbohydrates, lipids, humic substances and the like that link the biotic and abiotic.
- Climatic system, including temperature, rainfall, etc.
- Producer organisms autotrophic; primarily green plants that are able to synthesise foodstuffs from simple substances and light energy.
- Consumer organisms phagotrophic; animals that ingest particulate organic matter or other organisms.
- Decomposer organisms saprotrophic; primarily bacteria, protozoa, fungi and the like that break down complex substances with the release of both organic and inorganic products which are then recycled by plants or provide energy sources and have a regulatory effect on other biotic components.

Processes
- Energy flow.
- The food chains or trophic relationships.
- Diversity patterns, spatial and temporal.
- Mineral, cycling of nutrients aside from food.
- Development and evolution.
- Control or cybernetic aspects.

● Ecosystem properties as the basis for ecomimicry

waste is food. Analogous to the mode of operation of ecosystems, ecodesign should ensure that there is nothing from our human-made built environment that cannot be absorbed benignly somewhere else in the system. In nature, a mature ecosystem optimises by keeping the bulk of its matter and nutrients 'on the stump', as in the case of perennials, rather than passing it through to decay every year as annuals do. In some ecosystems, perennial plant species take over the roles of annual plant species, and eventually the growth rate slows down and the productivity per unit of biomass slows down. The system no longer maximises on throughput, but shifts to optimising, such as by closing nutrient and mineral flows. One of the key lessons to be learnt from ecology is that as the system's biomass increases, more recycling loops and complex interactions are needed to prevent it from collapsing. In emulating ecosystems, we must design our human-built environment to contain more recycling loops and interactions. In nature, the more mature the ecosystem, the more self-contained it becomes. It circulates what it needs within the system without losing any matter to the outside environment. This it does with its diverse assembly of producers, consumers and decomposers. There is complex organisation with a rich array of interconnections. All waste becomes food to one thing or another within the system. The only thing it imports is energy from sunlight, and the only energy it exports is the by-product of energy use: heat. All these are relevant properties that our human-built environment can integrate.

For example, the ecosystem retains within itself the cycling of materials through rigorous internal reuse and recycling. In a similar way, by ecomimesis, we must design our built environment so that the materials are continuously reused and recycled; where these can no longer be retained within the built environment, they must be seamlessly and benignly reintegrated into the natural environment's cycles and processes, and not callously dumped as waste into a landfill site.

In the human-built environment, our construction and development process of sheltering and accommodating our needs and activities is the single most wasteful process that we conduct. Waste is created when something appears to have no further value. Therefore what is needed is a design/build/recycle process in our economics and building industry that is more connected to the evolutionary process of life, rather than the making of isolated, disconnected, inanimate objects of consumed natural materials.

This principle of recycling is clearly evident in ecosystems; everything in natural systems is absorbed constructively back into the system somewhere else. In the same vein, nutrients for one species are derived from the death and decay of another. In this regard what is waste for one organism is nutrient for another. The process of organic-matter decomposition is the main process that recycles nutrients back into the soil. Decomposition of organic matter begins with large soil organisms like earthworms, arthropods (ants, beetles and termites), and gastropods (slugs and snails). These organisms break down the organic matter into smaller pieces, which can then be decomposed by smaller organisms like fungi and heterotrophic bacteria. Bacteria play a central role in some of the earth's most important nutrient cycles. Their adaptability means that they use substrates other than oxygen for respiration to assimilate and metabolise a diverse range of organic and inorganic substrates. Materials and energy in the ecosystems are continually circulated and transformed in various ways.

In principle, there are no such things as pollutants in natural systems because the toxins that are not stored or transported in bulk at the systems level are synthesised and used as needed only by individual species. Toxins are dealt with mostly by organisms in soils within the ecosystems where they are broken down.

In contrast, 85 per cent of the human-made items in our built environment quickly become waste through the manufacturing process. It is this high percentage that we must reduce and eventually eliminate. The ecomimicry lesson to apply here is to slow down the throughput of materials in our built environment. One approach is to design to emphasise quality and for longevity, rather than for quantity of new products and artefacts (B29) that then require rigorous reuse and recycling. To achieve this, we could close nutrient and mineral flows by designing for recycling, reuse and remanufacture at the outset as well as by using waste as a resource. Although there are now examples of functioning 'industrial ecology' in our human-built communities where industrial manufacturers are able to share some of their resources (ie one manufacturer using another's waste as a resource), our built environment still lacks an adequate diversity of functions and relevant organisation in its economic framework to make full use of recycling processes.

In a mature ecosystem, organisms live on 'harvestable interest' instead of 'principal', to use a financial metaphor. Species in nature will not utilise their prey species, or food plants, until there is nothing left. In a stable ecosystem, prey species are never completely eliminated and food plants are allowed to grow back. In hard times when food sources start to run out and become more difficult to find, when it will take more energy to hunt than the eventual meal will supply, it is usually easier for the wild animal to move to an alternate food source, leaving the old stock to renew itself. The lesson here for our human ecomimics is to use renewable sources only at the rate at which they can renew themselves, and not to use non-renewables faster than renewable substitutes can be developed (eg making plastics from plants, and fuel from corn). In practice, it is not possible for humans to wait for fossil fuels (as a non-renewable) to be produced as the time scales for their production exceed human life spans. In the past humans have been consistently failing on both counts. Humankind has been living on a legacy of resource-depleting and badly managed timber removal, environment-impairing agriculture, excessive fish farming and ranching, which have resulted in marked decreases in the productive capacity of our land and oceans. The ecomimetic designer will take only what will grow back (essentially living on 'interest'), the 'sustainable yield' concept that is applied in sustainable forestry and fishery sectors (see B29 for a discussion of recycling, reuse, remanufacture, etc).

In the case of the built environment, ecodesign must ensure that as far as possible its discharges and emissions are recycled or reused within the built environment itself or within its larger overall urban system (eg by continuous recycling and reuse of wastewater, waste heat, rainwater, wastepaper, etc) as well as facilitating their eventual benign reintegration. If humans are unable to recycle these wastes within the built system, then these should be recycled within the entire urban-wide system within which the designed system is located (for example, within the city's infrastructure; see B12). Essentially, what this means is that at the outset in our design process, the larger-scale human-made systems of urban recycling, reuse and repair must be in place and be effective. This applies not just to volumetric waste but also to molecular waste (eg the CO_2 discharges from the building's stand-by generators, heating systems, etc) as well as to emissions of waste heat (eg thermal discharges).

The efficient use of energy in ecosystems

Ecosystems run entirely on ambient solar energy, which is essentially free energy and is abundant as a renewable source of energy. Over time nature stores this energy in the form of fossil fuels. Humans use fossil fuels which, being a non-renewable energy source, have a high entropic rate in the system. Energy, unlike nutrients and minerals, cannot be circulated through the weblike connections of an ecosystem. In nearly all ecosystems, energy is harnessed from the sun by photosynthesisers, and transformed into sugars and carbohydrates. Only 2 per cent of the sunlight that reaches the earth is used, and these green plants, blue-green algae and certain bacteria can achieve up to 95 per cent efficiency of use.

The carrying capacity of the land has everything to do with how much energy there is to go around in the ecosystem. As efficient as photosynthesisers are in trapping and transforming sunlight into energy, only 10 per cent is available to herbivores, and only 10 per cent of that is available to the next level in the food chain, the carnivores, and so on. Thus ever decreasing amounts of energy become available to the upper trophic levels, and hence animals tend to be highly energy efficient. Plants and animals have evolved behaviours and mechanisms that are akin to energy-saving tactics.

In a mature ecosystem, energy is harnessed from the sun as a renewable source and is used efficiently. By analogy, humans should be using a similar renewable source of energy and reducing their dependence on non-renewable energy. Solar, wind, tidal and biodiesel forms of energy are 'current' solar energy, termed here renewable sources of energy, as opposed to 'ancient' sunlight energy, which is fossil fuels, termed here non-renewable sources of energy (B16). Fossil fuels are formed from the anaerobic breakdown of ancient plants and animals, the decay process of which was not completed, and their regeneration rate is much longer than the human rate of their consumption.

High-efficiency energy use is evident in ecosystems as they reach a state of succession whereas burning fossil fuels completes the decaying process and in turn releases the stored carbon into our atmosphere in vast quantities. Such large fluxes are unheard of in stable and mature ecosystems in nature. Ultimately, ecodesign should direct the built environment to shift to an economy run on current solar energy as in ecosystems. Until this is achievable, ecodesign should be directed towards energy conservation and efficiency where it optimises every unit of energy efficiently out of these non-renewable fuels in all our designed systems. The opportunities for tightening energy leaks and curbing inefficient use are plentiful (eg from using compact fluorescent lights to providing better insulation for the built environment). However, these strategies are by no means the be-all and end-all of energy efficiency. Ecodesign needs to ensure that humans and their built systems use energy in the same way that natural systems use their energy – to maximise diversity so that they can be more efficient in terms of mineral and nutrient cycling. Humans need to re-evaluate what they are maximising (throughput) and optimise instead (see discussion on non-renewable energy in B26).

An application of ecomimicry is the imitation of the photosynthesis process in plants by the use of nano-structures. Photosynthesis is one of the most basic processes of life and is key to the ecological relationship between plants and animals. This is the process by which plants and bacteria transform light energy into chemical energy through molecule synthesis and proton gradients.

A dynamic and information-driven system in ecosystems

The identity of components in the ecosystem is defined in terms of processes. Mature ecosystems have numerous interaction channels that carry feedback to all communities, ensuring high environmental control and overall system stability. They can be regarded as running on 'information'. Resource availability is controlled within the biotic system by mechanisms that have evolved to reward efficient behaviour. A mature community runs on a rich feedback system that permits changes in one component of the community to

Standard economics

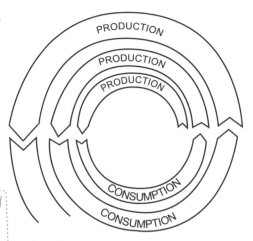

Standard economics considers ever growing cycles of production and consumption but does not consider the role of the supporting ecosystems. Such a view encourages an economy that ultimately strains the surrounding natural environment

Steady-state economics

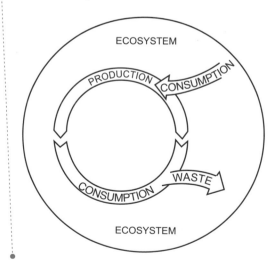

Steady-state economics considers cycles of production and consumption that take the surrounding ecosystems into account and try to achieve a state of equilibrium

influence the whole system, while allowing for adaptability (which is what drives evolution) in a changing environment. Mature ecosystems survive, adapt and evolve in situ. This should be the goal in ecomimicry too. Ecodesign must be able to withstand environmental perturbation by implementing innovative adaptations and a rich feedback mechanism that self-corrects to reach and maintain system stability. Ecodesign should ensure that energy and material resources are not squandered but conserved, so that our human-made system is essentially buffered should there be significant disturbances, and so that it possesses the ability to cope with change. For example, it is well known that tropical rainforests are a vast storehouse of chemicals that could be potential medicines, a resource that we have barely begun to tap. Having this resource will help humans to cope with and fight constantly evolving diseases and plagues that thrive, proliferate and mutate in our human-made systems. As human-made systems are, in most instances, large-scale 'disturbances' in the natural ecosystem, they reduce the diverse gamut of functional services in nature to a much simpler system, and so it becomes even more crucial that the natural ecosystems in our biosphere are conserved to absorb any future shocks to the system.

Interlinked cooperation and competition within the ecosystem

In ecosystems, species' cooperation and competition are interlinked and held in balance so that the system permits independent activity on the part of each individual of a species, yet cooperatively meshes the activity patterns of all species. All living systems are interconnected and dependent upon each other for sustained life. At the same time we must recognise the dependency of our own built environment upon ecosystems. This sense of the interdependency of our constructed (the artificial) and the given (the natural) could be regarded as a 'connectedness'. It requires a departure from the limitations of current science, and the social, political and economic contexts that implicitly valorise human enterprise as dominant over, and essentially independent of any need to connect and integrate with nature. Ecodesign must seek to integrate as fully as possible the literally thousands of ways in which a built system and its users connect to the natural world. This in itself makes ecodesign a difficult and complex endeavour to achieve well in totality and over time, but nonetheless ultimately vital.

More specifically, when we design for biointegration (see A2), our designed systems must handle and creatively adapt the connections and linkages and the interdependencies with the ecosystems as opposed to regarding ecological design as compartmentalised casuality (ie without linkages). Ecodesign requires a holistic integration by design, entailing the prudent management of energy and materials in the built system alongside the ecosystems in the biosphere. In doing so, the design reduces its detrimental impacts on the ecosystems.

One of the outcomes of the interaction of the array of diverse species and niches in an ecosystem is a 'cooperative' strategy where organisms spread out to utilise all possible niches so that every material left over by one species is 'cleaned up'. This is exemplified by the roles of the producer, consumer and decomposer species in their functional niches that together create a dynamic system stability. Through highly organised species communities and the interconnections between them, the ecosystem allows each individual of a species to act independently yet integrates the activity patterns of all species into a cooperative whole. Cooperation and competition in the ecosystems are interlinked and held in balance.

By analogy, in the case of our human-made ecosystems the provision of the equivalent of community and functional diversity will be the presence of a balance of equivalent producers, manufacturers, services (including nutrients, sewage and waste) and consumers (recycling and reuse), each occupying different niches in the built environment, producing different system services and using different resources (often each other's waste products) all of which must be highly organised with myriad networks linking each one to the others.

High structural diversity and spatial efficiency in ecosystems

Ecosystems have a high structural diversity with compact spatial efficiency. Our designed systems, whether large or small, whether their built forms are laid out laterally or vertically, can come in a variety of forms and functions and should emulate the high structural diversity and spatial efficiency in ecosystems.

Within ecosystems, ecological diversity is comprised of three main types of diversity. The first is the compositional element, which refers to the most basic and well-known type: species diversity. Also included are genetic diversity and diversity of communities and ecosystems.

Functional diversity includes the many ecological interactions among species such as competition, predation, mutualism, as well as ecological functions such as nutrient cycling. It also includes the episodic natural disturbances that many species and communities count on, such as annual fires. It is by functional diversity that many ecological services are provided.

Apart from diversity of species and niches, diversity in an ecosystem is also taken to mean structural diversity. Plants and animals generally occupy space very efficiently. This spatial efficiency is reflected in the variety of structural diversity, which refers to the size, shape and distribution of species, habitats and communities across the landscape.

Ecosystem 'services' and natural controls

Ecosystems provide 'services' to support the human-made built environment through their processes and flows of materials, energy and information from the biosphere that create a healthy environment for humans, from production of oxygen to soil genesis and water detoxification. In designing our built environment ecomimically, our designed systems must mimic all the natural 'services' provided so efficiently by ecosystems (see A3).

Ecosystems in nature have built-in natural controls, such as the nurturing of innumerable species that are not harvested directly but which provide important 'free' services to the ecosystems. In this way, species pollinate crops, keep potentially harmful organisms in check, build and maintain soils, and decompose dead matter so that it can be used to build new life. These ecosystem 'service providers', which include, for instance, birds, bees, insects, worms and microbes, show how such small and seemingly insignificant functions and organisms can be of disproportionate value to the ecosystem.

Unfortunately, with the current impairment of the natural environment, such ecosystem services are increasingly becoming deficient. Rather than integrating the built environment with these ecosystem services, humans have fragmented and destroyed habitats and have drastically reduced their extent and ability to function. In the present state of the built environment, humankind has created a situation where they must now ecomimically return to natural ecological controls, or develop new ones or design some new combination of integration. Ecodesign's fundamental basis is benign and seamless biointegration, which, as mentioned earlier, is the integration of our human-made systems with those of the natural environment symbiotically, so as to make use of existing natural controls (eg passive systems), and/or combining both human-made and ecosystem (or biological) control structures.

Complexity in ecosystems

Ecological systems are complex. Within the ecosystem is an integrated balance of living and non-living components, which are interconnected and interdependent; a dynamic continuum interacting as a whole. There is also tremendous complexity in many of the cause and effect interrelationships in ecosystems. Our human-made systems need to ecomimic the integrated balance of abiotic constituents (eg the built components, which currently are mainly inorganic) in ecosystems with the biotic constituents (see B7 and B18).

There are obviously challenges at every step in mimicking the ecosystem approach for our urban built environment. For example, we can consider the structure of an ecosystem such as a forest ecosystem. The forest's structure is a function of the growth form of the mix of tree species that make up the forest and this is constrained by topography, climate, edaphic factors, etc, whereas our human-made built environment (eg the city) is built and designed often without any constraints prompted by the locality's topography, climate, edaphic factors, etc. Besides topographical and other ecological factors of the locality, there are in our human-made urban environments artificial human-designed landscapes. Along with the additional structure of social institutions and social groups, it can become a very complex endeavour to measure our urban environment using standard ecosystem techniques. Biomimicry and ecomimicry must become much more than just novel ways of examining the natural world as the bases for design. In light of the current rate of species and habitat loss, it becomes a race and 'rescue' mission for our future and for that of our human-built environment.

Besides ecomimicry, biomimicry can, for instance, be applied to buildings to make materials stronger, self-assembling and self-healing; natural processes and forces should be used for basic building functions, as well as to allow the buildings to produce resources by integrating natural systems. Biomimicry in building engineering systems is still a new research area, in which solutions are being sought to the usual constructional problems such as scaling in pipes, toxic adhesives and finding an alternative to concrete production. However, our approach to biomimicry goes beyond its application to just the one individual building and the materials of which it is made. Just as a forest is comprised of more than an individual tree, is in fact a community of trees and other organisms whose life cycles are interlinked, so a built environment (such as a city) is much more than just individual buildings; it has to be a linked and integrated community of biotic constituents with both human-made and natural features where, ultimately, nature's laws are still applicable.

Ecomimicry could be used as an approach to redesign existing human-made systems in our built environment by deriving solutions and models from those found in natural systems, for example inventing a non-toxic adhesive by mimicking the adhesiveness of lizard feet; by learning how to build self-assembling walls without concrete by mimicking the physical and chemical structure of an abalone shell; and how to prevent pipe-scaling by producing a protein for coating the inside of pipes which mimics that produced by abalone to stop the accretion of calcium carbonate on their shells. These solutions are still very much at the primary research stage. Here, when we seek to employ ecomimicry as a more specialised form of biomimicry of ecosystem properties, the study of ecology and ecosystems can already furnish us with much more knowledge of these properties, although this is far from complete. Nevertheless, this incompleteness should not inhibit designers from implementing ecomimicry now.

Furthermore, addressing and resolving ecological design objectives is not a one-off goal. The designer has to manage and monitor the designed system's consequences over its entire life cycle. This complexity is dynamic, extends over time and is mirrored in the workings of natural systems, where ecosystem processes function in many time scales.

We must not regard ecological design as a rearguard action in which we are just designing to reduce our design's negative impacts on the environment. Ecological design must also be about designing for planned positive and restorative outcomes that will contribute beneficially to the ecosystems. These positive outcomes can include, for instance, improving biodiversity, the creation of pure water, the conservation of local landscapes and ecology, the reduction of consumption of energy resources and greenhouse gas emissions, the reduction of waste and pollution (eg greenhouse gases) and the reduction of the design's ecological footprint. Our ecodesign can and must effect positive acts of repair, restoration and renewal of the natural systems of the environment. Ecomimicry has the potential to provide the designer with existent models in nature upon which the design can draw, as analogies and as inspiration.

Aspects of ecological succession (from developing to mature stages)

We should take the properties of ecosystems at the mature stage of the ecosystem as a template for ecomimicry. The ecodesign of our human-made built environment can follow analogously those ecosystem attributes in ecological succession at the mature stages of the development of an ecosystem. A set of ecosystem attributes and their characteristics during the developing stages and at their mature stages as the basis for ecomimesis is given below.

Ecosystem attributes	Developing stages	Mature stages
• Food chain	Linear	Weblike
• Species diversity	Small	Large
• Life cycles	Short, simple	Long, complex
• Growth strategy	Emphasis on rapid growth	Emphasis on feedback control
• Production (body mass and offspring)	Quantity	Quality
• Internal symbiosis (cooperative relationships)	Undeveloped	Developed
• Nutrient conservation (closed-loop cycling)	Simple	Good
• Pattern diversity (vertical canopy layers and horizontal patchiness)	Simple	Complex

• Biochemical diversity (such as plant/herbivore competition)	Low	High
• Niche specialisations (functions in the ecosystem)	Broad	Narrow
• Mineral cycles	Open	Closed
• Nutrient exchange rate between organisms and environment	Fast	Slow
• Role of detritus (dead organic matter) in nutrient regeneration	Unimportant	Important
• Inorganic nutrients (minerals such as iron)	Extrabiotic	Intrabiotic
• Total organic matter (nutrients tied up in biomass)	Small	Large
• Stability (resistance to external perturbation)	Poor	Good
• Entropy (energy lost)	High	Low
• Information (feedback loops)	Low	High

All the aspects detailed above can become the basis for design ecomimicry. In practice, at our present level of ecotechnology, it seems unlikely that we can construct artificial systems in our built environment that can achieve a satisfactory steady state of total biointegration without the use of non-renewable energy resources, such as happens in ecosystems. Accomplishing these by design becomes humankind's single most important ecodesign and technological objective for research and invention.

Advancing from the above, the key properties of ecosystems at the stage of maturity, and how we can base our built environment's design on them to achieve effective biointegration, is given overleaf.

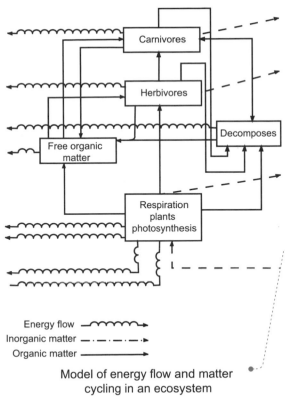

Energy flow 〰〰〰→
Inorganic matter —·—·—·—▸
Organic matter ————→

Model of energy flow and matter
cycling in an ecosystem

Ecosystem properties
(at the stage of maturity)

Human-made ecomimetic objectives

Energy

- Reduced gross photosynthetic activity

- Uses renewable source of energy (solar)

- High-efficiency energy flow
- Uses the energy that is needed

- Reduce dependency on non-renewable
  energy (in system's life cycle from
  production to recovery)

- Change from use of non-renewable sources
  of energy to renewable sources of energy

- Increase efficiency in energy use
- Reduce wasteful use of non-renewable
  energy resources

Materials

- Recycling of nutrients

- Recycle materials and outputs

Diversity

- A balance of producers, consumers,
  decomposers and integrative species

- Many functional niches and engenders
  diversity

- Balance producers, manufacturers,
  services (include nutrients, sewerage,
  waste, etc) and consumers (recycling)

- Increase high functional diversity

Spatial efficiency

- Compact spatial efficiency

- High structural diversity (small and large,
  lateral and vertical, large variety)

- Increase compact spatial efficiency

- Provide high structural diversity
  (small and large, lateral and vertical,
  large variety)

Information and organisation

- High species and community
  interconnections

- High community organisation (many
  interconnections)

- Attain high community diversity

- Have high community organisation
  (many networks)

Systemic control

- High environmental control and effective monitoring response system of the natural environment

- Provide global protection from environmental perturbations

- Resources availability controlled within biotic system

- Conserve resources, sustainable use and increase ability to buffer and cope with changes

- Symbiotic system stability and rewards systemic cooperation

- Adopt self-correcting systems for environmental stability

Form

- Fits form to function

- Imitate nature by analogy and ecomimesis

These factors and characteristics will obviously influence the shape and processes of our designed systems. Our resultant built environment should be more responsive to these while respecting ergonomic and other human functional requirements.

Summary

In designing for biointegration, the key properties and features of ecosystems can provide the designer with the principles, inspiration and basis for design and invention through ecomimicry. These can be applied and reinterpreted as characteristics and design objectives for the design of our built forms, facilities, infrastructures and the products in our built environment. The resultant built form may well be a hybrid or a composite of human-made and organic features. The ideal ecodesign is a hybrid of human-made technology integrated with nature. The resultant form is likely to be a hybrid biotechnology that is part inorganic and part organic, where the designed form is a technology that is alive, that is a living technology or a living structure and serves as a surrogate habitat for wildlife and plants.

A5 The general law and theoretical basis for ecodesign: the system-to-environment Interactions Matrix

Presented here is the theoretical reference and basis for ecodesign in the form of an Interactions Matrix. The form is that of a Partitioned Matrix and interactions framework that informs the designer of all those aspects that a design must take into consideration in order to be comprehensive in its approach to ecodesign. In summary, these considerations are: the environment of the designed system; the designed system itself and all its activities and processes; the inputs of energy and materials (including people) to the designed system; the outputs of energy and materials (and people) from the designed system; and, in aggregate, all of these interacting with each other as a whole over the entire life cycle of the designed system.

Establishing the theoretical basis for ecodesign here is crucial because a commonly agreed and useful definition of what constitutes ecological design still remains to be satisfactorily formulated. Furthermore, a satisfactory theory for 'green' design that embodies a total set of generally recognised principles is still undertheorised and not found elsewhere. In the absence of a satisfactory and commonly accepted definition and theoretical framework for ecological design, there is the problem that ecodesign remains partial, inconsistent and misunderstood. Should this situation continue, further criticisms might be levelled at the very legitimacy of ecodesign and could even lead to its eventual negation and demise once ecological design is no longer the topic of the day or able to provide satisfactory solutions in critical or urgent situations due to this discrepancy or misperception.

To avert this worst-case scenario, it is essential that a fundamental 'law' of ecological design can be formulated. The Interactions Matrix described below constitutes the 'law' and theory for ecological design. In establishing academic fields, theory is the integral component of the understanding and development of the field, hence affirming a theoretical basis for ecological design is vital. The theory provides a framework through which knowledge in this field can be both progressively structured and tested.

Our 'law' here requires the designer to look at the designed system in terms of its component parts. (The inputs, outputs and internal and external relations), and then to see how these interact with each other (both statically and dynamically) over time, each representing the four components of the Partitioned Matrix. In effect it informs the designer which of the designed system's ecological impacts need to be given priority and which need to be taken into account or adjusted in its design.

To begin with, we should acknowledge that ecological design is complex, certainly considerably more complex than is currently recognised by many ecological designers. The Interactions Matrix more specifically informs the designer that ecodesign involves the incorporation of a set of 'interdependent interactions' or connections with the environment (both global and local), which must be regarded dynamically (ie over time). It provides a holistic structure of the anticipatory properties of ecological design. In comparison, what is generally found to be inadequate in other theoretical constructs in this field is their incompleteness or failure to include an environmentally holistic property (eg 'connectedness') crucial to the ecological approach, which is an inherent property of the Partitioned Matrix.

It must be clear that the fundamental premise for ecological design is this interconnectedness between all aspects of the human-made environment and the natural environment. Therefore, any approach to design that does not take into account this aspect of connectedness or the full range of interactions that are thus connected as indicated in this framework cannot then be considered holistic, and hence must either not be ecological or at best be an incomplete approach to ecological design.

At the same time environmentally sustainable objectives require ecodesign to minimise (and be responsive to) the negative impacts that the interactions have on the earth's ecosystems and resources, in which case each of these interactions (in the framework) can be the ecological cause of uses that may need to be taken into account. We should, of course, be aware that ecological design is not a rearguard action, and a designed system can contribute productively to the environment (eg through production of energy using photovoltaics) as well as restore and repair damaged ecosystems through such mechanisms as ecosystem rehabilitation and biodiversity enhancements.

What we need is a simple and general framework that structures, integrates and unifies the entire set of the ecological interactions of a designed system with the earth's ecosystems and resources. This framework must identify those impacts so that the designer can then assess which are undesirable and which need to be minimised or altered through design synthesis. The theoretical basis for ecological design must provide the designer with an easy-to-apply set of structuring and organising principles. This can be in the form of an open structure with which the selected and relevant design constraints (eg ecological considerations) can be holistically and simultaneously organised and identified. Furthermore, the open structure must facilitate the selection, consideration, and eventual incorporation of the design objectives in our subsequent design synthesis.

This open structure can be simply a conceptual or theoretical framework. It should enable the designer to decide which ecological considerations to incorporate in his design synthesis

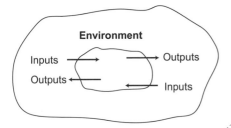

Environment

Inputs

Outputs

Outputs

Inputs

A simple model of a system and its environment and the exchanges between the two

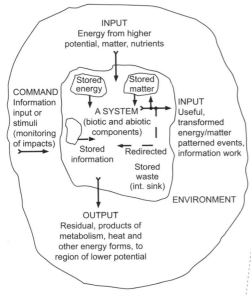

INPUT
Energy from higher potential, matter, nutrients

Stored energy

Stored matter

COMMAND
Information input or stimuli (monitoring of impacts)

A SYSTEM
(biotic and abiotic components)

INPUT
Useful, transformed energy/matter patterned events, information work

Stored information

Redirected

Stored waste
(int. sink)

ENVIRONMENT

OUTPUT
Residual, products of metabolism, heat and other energy forms, to region of lower potential

Where:

⟶ = Fluxes across system boundaries

— ⟶ = Internal relationships

An input-output structural model of the built environment

while ensuring a basis for a comprehensive check of other interdependent factors influencing design and, crucially, demonstrating their interrelationships, the last being an essential property of the connectedness of all ecological systems in the biosphere.

For the purpose of developing a theory for ecological design, we can start by using the General Systems Theory approach, which considers the outcome of our design as a system (ie a designed system or a built system) that exists in an environment (ie including both the human-made and natural environments). The general systems concept is fundamental in the same way that the ecosystem concept is fundamental in ecology. Generally, in the analysis of the relationship of any system with its environment, there is no limit to the number of variables that we can include in the analysis or in a description of the design problem. In fact, this applies to all design endeavours. For no matter how fortunate may be our choice of the extent of inputs and outputs to enter into the description of that system and its environment, they cannot be expected to constitute a complete description. The crucial task in design and, similarly, in the conceptualising of any theory is therefore to pick the right variables for inclusion in the design resolution process (see also B3).

By using this open structure as a design map, in seeking a design solution the designer can also include any other related and pertinent disciplines that are similarly concerned with the problems of environmental protection and conservation (eg waste disposal, resource conservation, pollution control, applied ecology). These interactions are then the essential properties of this theory for ecological design: it has to be inclusive, comprehensive and open.

As ecological design is both prognostic and anticipatory (as mentioned earlier), the design process becomes essentially a 'statement' of its anticipated environmental impacts and benefits (see B3) and the level of 'greenness' that it can realistically achieve. From the earlier examination of ecology and ecological concepts, we have determined that the extent of the environmental consequences of any built system can be gauged in relation to the extent of its dependencies (ie demands and contributions) on the earth's ecosystems and processes and on the earth's energy and material resources (eg for a specific product or a specific service). These dependencies are at both the global level (eg use of non-renewable resources) and the local level (eg local ecology). Thus, if the designer is aware of the ecological consequences (ie both detrimental and beneficial) of the design, then this awareness in effect represents a summation of the extent of its impacts on the environment as accepted and anticipated by the designer.

Defining the design task in this way should in no way entail an exploitative role for humankind in the biosphere. On the contrary, this approach further emphasises the extent of humankind's dependency and that of their built structures on the biosphere and on the earth's resources. Working from such a viewpoint should help direct our attention to those aspects of the designed system that have ecological implications, and should indicate critical areas where the undesirable impacts might be eliminated, reduced or remedied.

These various functions and aspects of the environment and humankind's use of them are interrelated and overlapping; they meet each other at a 'transfer point', where the designed system interacts with the surrounding ecosystem and where benign and seamless biointegration is crucial. These transfer points are vitally important to green design precisely because bad design at the points where exchange occurs frequently results in damage to the ecosystem. The realisation of any designed system is therefore dependent directly or indirectly upon the biosphere for specific elements and processes, which can be identified as including the following:

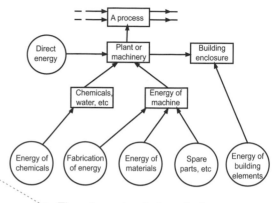

● The primary inputs to a single process in the built environment

- use of renewable and non-renewable resources including minerals, fossil fuels, air, water and food;

- use of biological, physical and chemical processes, eg decomposition, photosynthesis and mineral cycling;

- as an end point for processing of waste and discharges resulting from human activities, including life processes as well as the functioning of human-made systems (eg landfill waste disposal); and

- as a physical space in which to live, work and build.

It is in these areas that effective environmentally unimpairing integration has to be achieved by design.

It should be remembered, however, that it is physically impossible to design anything in which none of these transfer points will result in impacts on the ecosystem. The mere physical existence of the building or a product by design, as we have seen, causes some spatial displacement (ie it takes up space) of the ecosystem and use of land that represents a loss to the biosphere volumetrically. We must be clear that an absolute ecological compatibility is physically impossible to achieve because of this most basic impact on the environment. However, we can produce built systems and products that have less (not greater) destructive effects on the environment, and they can even have some results that are beneficial. The objective of green design is to minimise negative impacts and maximise beneficial interactions between built systems and natural ecosystems.

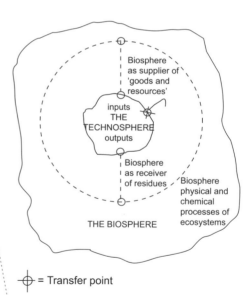

⊕ = Transfer point

● The linkages between the built environment and its external environment

From the ecologist's point of view, architecture as the consequence of design results in a built form (with attendant operational systems) that represents a net statement of its physical and potential demands and influences on the ecosystems and on the earth's resources. To determine these demands and influences, we must trace the uses of energy and materials in the designed systems in the form of the routes that they take from their environmental sources to the designed system's dependencies and to the end of their useful life. If we accept this principle, then it means that all the attributes of a designed system (whether functional, spatial, economic, cultural, etc) would have to be seen in the context of their relationship to the earth's ecological environment throughout its life cycle. Hence the life cycle concept is crucial to ecological design. However, life cycle in ecodesign extends from extraction and production all the way through to reuse, recycling and benign reintegration. The rationale is that only by identifying the dependencies associated with each design decision can the undesirable impacts on the ecosystems be assessed and minimised, and preventive action taken. In practice, this is impossible to identify or quantify in totality. Nevertheless, indices can be used and a broad theoretical framework can be applied to show the interdependencies.

The theoretical framework of green design must be developed in line with a number of concepts, which will be briefly summarised here.

The theoretical framework of green design

A building or a designed system or a product exists both in terms of its physical being (form, siting and structure) and its functional aspects, ie the systems and operations that sustain it during its useful life. Both aspects involve the built structure in relationships with the natural environment, which take place over time. The designed system acts like a living organism; in place of food, it uses energy and materials, and also produces outputs into its environment. Our theoretical structure should therefore model all these exchanges.

Three components are essential for an ecological model of the designed system. Our theoretical framework must include a description of the built system itself, a description of its environment including the ambient ecosystem and natural resources, and a mapping of the interactions between these two components (ie between the building and its environment).

The first step is systematically to take account of the internal processes of the designed system (eg in B12 to B17). The second step is to measure, based on a thorough knowledge of the building's physical and functional requirements, its interactions with the earth's ecosystems in the form of the energy and resources removed from the environment by the construction and ongoing operation of the structure. Also to be measured are the amounts of matter and energy that are sent back into the natural environment as a result of the functioning of the building's internal systems (the 'metabolism' that makes it function as a built environment; see B4 to B11, and B18 to B29). In the case of a built structure this includes the transportation consequences of moving people and goods to and from the built structure.

A supplementary issue is the relationship of the built structure as an element in the spatial configuration of the environment. Its existence as a built environment within the natural one implies further interactions and effects on the biosphere. Analysis of any such impacts will also have to be factored into the theoretical framework.

An open general systems framework can be used to visualise 'sets of interactions' taking place between the designed system and its environment.

The concept of an open system in contact with its environment as formulated in the General Systems Theory is useful here. Based on the above analysis of the fundamental interactions of the built and natural environments, the interactions can be grouped into the following four sets:

Set 1. external interdependencies, consisting of the designed system's relations to the external environment;

Set 2. internal interdependencies, being the designed system's internal relations;

Set 3. external-to-internal exchanges of energy and matter – ie system inputs; and

Set 4. internal-to-external exchanges of energy and matter – ie system outputs.

The four sets also usefully describe the 'transfer points' between the built and natural environments discussed above. Green design must take account of all four sets as well as the interactions between them. In this way, our framework allows us to determine how our designed system impinges on terrestrial ecosystems and natural resources whenever we address any design task.

Elsewhere ecodesigners have developed a 'Partitioned Matrix' (LP), which unifies these sets of interactions in a single symbolic form. We can demonstrate this conceptualisation of the relationship of the designed system to its environment ('1' stands for the system, '2' the environment) in the figure overleaf. If the letter L stands for interdependencies within the

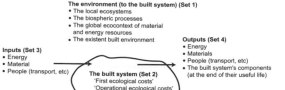

The General Systems Theory model for ecological design

Interactions	Symbol	Description
The external inter-dependencies of the designed system (its external relations)	L22	This refers to the totality of the ecological processes of the surrounding ecosystems, which intersect with others which interact with other ecosystems elsewhere within the biosphere, and the totality of the earth's resources. It also includes the slow biospheric processes involved in the formation of fossil fuels and other non-renewable resources. These may influence the built environment's functioning and are in turn also influenced by the built environment. It is these elements that are either altered, depleted or added to by the built environment.
The internal inter-dependencies of the designed system (its internal relations)	L11	This refers to the sum of the activities and actions that take place in or are related to and associated with the built environment and its users. They include the operational functions of the built environment. These will directly affect the ecosystems of the location in which they take place spatially and the ecosystem elsewhere (systemically), as well as the earth's totality of resources. These can be considered in the pattern of a life cycle of the built environment.
The external/ internal exchanges of energy and matter (the system's inputs)	L21	This refers to the total inputs into the built environment. These consist of both the stock and the flow components of the built environment (or the energy and matter needed for the physical substance and form of the built environment and its attendant processes). The efforts taken to obtain these inputs from the earth's resources often result in considerable consequences to the ecosystems.
The internal/ external exchanges of energy and matter (the system's outputs)	L12	This refers to the total outputs of energy and matter that are discharged from the built environment into the ecosystems and into the earth. These outputs may include the built environment's own physical substance and form, which also may need to be disposed of at the end of its useful life. These outputs, if they are not assimilated by the ecosystems, result in environmental impairment.

Description of environmental interactions

framework, then four types of interaction can be identified. In the Partitioned Matrix, they are identified as L11, L12, L21 and L22.

$$(LP) = \begin{array}{c|c} L11 & L12 \\ \hline L21 & L22 \end{array}$$

This figure depicts the conceptualisation of the relationship of the designed system to its environment.

Remembering that '1' represents the built system and '2' the environment in which it is situated, we can map the four sets of interactions listed above on to the Partitioned Matrix. L11 represents processes that occur within the system (internal interdependencies), L22 represents activities in the environment (external interdependencies), and L12 and L21 refer to system/environment and environment/system exchanges, respectively. Thus, internal and external relations and transactional interdependencies are all accounted for. 'LP' in effect is ecological design, as a summary of the simultaneous consideration of all these four sets of interactions (ie L11, L12, L21 and L22) with each other over the life cycle of the designed system.

The Partitioned Matrix is itself a complete theoretical framework embodying all ecological design considerations. For instance, the designer can use this tool to examine interactions between the system or product to be built and its environment holistically and inclusively, taking account of all the environmental interdependencies described by the above four sets.

In this way, any designed system can be conceptually broken down and analysed, based on these four sets of interactions as follows:

L22

These interactions describe the designed system's external interdependencies or 'external relations'. By this is meant the totality of the ecological processes of the ambient ecosystem, which as we have seen interacts with other ecosystems; hence L22 takes in not only local but also global environments and terrestrial resources in their totality. It therefore also includes the processes by which earth's resources are created (eg the formation of fossil fuels, and non-renewable resources), which may be affected by, and themselves affect, the built structure's functioning. These external resources will be modified, depleted or added to by the creation and functioning of the built system.

L11

The internal interdependencies are the internal environmental relations of the built system. This means the sum of all the activities that go on inside the building, including all its operations and functions. The functioning of the built structure's internal metabolism will have larger effects, extending to the ecosystem where it is sited; these effects, by the principle of connectivity (see A4), will in turn affect other ecosystems and the biosphere's totality of resources. The L11 effects take place over and describe the whole life cycle of the building.

L21

This quadrant of the matrix describes the total inputs into the built system, including all of the exchanges of energy and matter (including people) that go into its construction. System inputs of a designed system include all of the resources that make up its component parts and the matter and energy upon which its operations and processes depend. Securing these resources that make the building 'run' (the extraction of infrastructural materials and energy from the earth) often causes damage to the biosphere and its ecosystems.

L12

The total outputs from the built environment into the natural one are the most obvious concern of the ecological designer, but they are only one quarter of the total interactions discussed here. These outputs, however, include not only discharges of waste and exhaust from the building's construction and operation, but also the physical matter of the structure itself, which must be disposed of at the end of the building's planned life span (as well as people). Obviously, if these outputs cannot be assimilated by the natural environment they result in ecological harm.

Any design approach that claims to be ecological and does not take into account these four components and their interactions over time cannot be considered a complete and holistic ecological design, as interconnectedness is a crucial characteristic of ecosystems. Failure to take this factor into consideration is non-ecological.

As stated earlier, holistic and ecological design must take into account both local and global environmental interactions: it must be anticipatory by design and is forward-looking. It is also dynamic in that it must consider effects over the entire lifetime of the designed system whether it is a built structure or a product. A further point is that green design is self-critical. It considers its own effects on the environment and tries to eliminate negative impacts on ecosystems and terrestrial resources.

The ecological designer has to work within the constraints imposed by the principles shown here, and seeks to maximise the utility and efficiency of the design while reducing the negative effects of the building's creation and functioning. Thus, the designer adopts as far as possible a 'balanced budget' approach, weighing environmental costs and using global resources in the least damaging, most advantageous manner possible.

The ecological design framework provides a structure for identifying linkages between environmental elements. Energy consumption, wastes generated, and resources used in the production of building materials, transportation of building occupants, operation of building services and systems, and other processes in the life cycle of a building can be linked to one or more changes in the quantity or quality of environmental components. The cascading effects of these changes can then be traced through to their effect on ecosystems and specific communities – as the end points of environmental concern where biointegration is essential. Assessing these effects enables us to evaluate the relative importance of various potential effects on the productivity of plant and animal communities.

Where the ecological designer looks at a specific environmental effect, the designer should look at the entire chain with which it is associated and avoid focusing only on intermediate impacts. The linkages between the effects are not simple linear chains but instead form complex webs; each emission or use of a natural resource can cause a number of changes in the quality or quantity of air, water, soil and resource stock. In turn, these changes in quantity and quality of air, water, soil and resource stock can affect different end points.

From the point of view of applied ecology, ecological design is essentially to do with energy and materials management concentrated on to a particular locality (ie the building site) or into a particular item or assembly (as in the case of a product design). By this we mean that the earth's energy and material resources (biotic and abiotic components) are in effect extracted, managed and assembled by the designer into a temporary human-made form whether as a built structure or product (as an item that has a period of intended use or 'useful life'). At the end of this period, this is then either reused or recycled within the built environment or assimilated elsewhere into the natural environment after optimising a useful life. But, however mechanistic this formula may seem, we must be clear that ecodesign is much more than simply the management of energy and materials. The designed system must create a balanced ecosystem of biotic and abiotic components or, what would be better, create a productive and even reparative (ie healing) relationship with the natural environment both locally and globally. Of course, in addition one has to consider the other conventional aspects of the design of a built system: design programme, costs, aesthetics, site, and so forth.

The theoretical framework here reminds the designer that the designed system is not just a spatial object, but that it has internal functions (L11) and external relations (L22) that are equally part of the designed system. Environmental interactions must always be taken into consideration in the design process, by which is meant not only the physical reality of the structure and its components but also the functional aspects of the building and its outputs over its useful life and the subsequent disposal of the structure itself, which are also parts of the Partitioned Matrix.

The Partitioned Matrix and the above breakdown of sets of interactions can be used by the designer to conceptualise, verify and check the environmental interactions and effects of the proposed designed system. The designer can also use the framework to analyse any design or 'deconstruct' it, separating out its component interactions into the quadripartite system of the matrix: resource inputs (L21) and outputs (L12); internal functions (L11); and external environmental relations (L22). It is worth emphasising that the designer's ethical responsibility extends over all the aspects of the matrix (ie it includes the totality of interrelations), which must be factored into the design. Beyond these design imperatives in the narrow sense is an overarching responsibility to keep 'green' principles always in mind, including the general aim of sustainable development (the ecosystems must remain viable after our intervention) and minimisation of the damaging side effects of human action on the environment in tandem with maximising beneficial and repairable effects on the environment.

A further aspect of the matrix is that, because it is systemic and comprehensive, it provides a check on environmental impact assessments. It reminds the designer of the scope of the anticipated impacts and interactions of his design. For example, it is possible that the designer could overlook one interaction, or emphasise the importance of a single factor at the expense of another, thereby producing lopsidedness in the design.

If a designer is particularly concerned with pollution (negative outputs) from the built system, the drive to reduce these outputs, even though it has a 'green' objective, could result in a design that required excessive energy inputs, thereby consuming more terrestrial resources and perhaps putting strain on other (possibly non-local) ecosystems. The use of the Partitioned Matrix prevents this 'seesaw' effect by requiring the designer to keep in mind that any design that does not deal with the totality of environmental interactions and ramifications over the building's entire functional life will be uncomprehensive and therefore environmentally unsatisfactory.

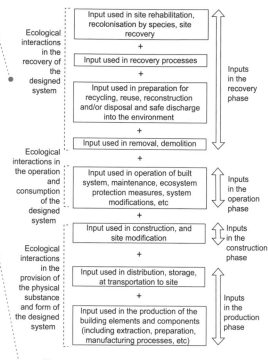

The total inputs in the life cycle of a designed system

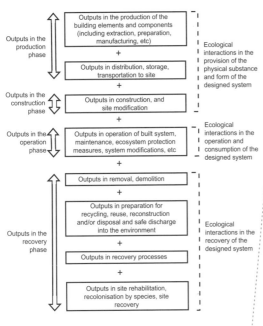

Outputs in the production phase

Outputs in the production of the building elements and components (including extraction, preparation, manufacturing, etc)

+

Outputs in distribution, storage, transportation to site

Ecological interactions in the provision of the physical substance and form of the designed system

Outputs in the construction phase

Outputs in construction, and site modification

+

Outputs in the operation phase

Outputs in operation of built system, maintenance, ecosystem protection measures, system modifications, etc

Ecological interactions in the operation and consumption of the designed system

+

Outputs in the recovery phase

Outputs in removal, demolition

+

Outputs in preparation for recycling, reuse, reconstruction and/or disposal and safe discharge into the environment

+

Outputs in recovery processes

Ecological interactions in the recovery of the designed system

+

Outputs in site rehabilitation, recolonisation by species, site recovery

The total outputs in the life cycle of a designed system

The matrix framework will also require the designer to integrate the designed system and its components into the ambient ecosystem in such a way as to be benignly assimilated or integrated, or even to achieve symbiosis. Once the designed system is physically in place, its outputs will have a greater or lesser environmental impact, which could reduce the ecosystem's ability to provide the inputs and natural resources specified in the design. A more comprehensive and complex model that encompasses the feedback loop must be further developed from the framework as it now stands.

The key feature of this theory is its comprehensiveness. Previous definitions of ecological design have been applied, without much precision, to any design method that expressed some environmental concern, but without providing any check on their validity or comprehensiveness. Thus, this theoretical framework can be used as an analytical tool to evaluate the ecological sensitivity of the design approaches of other designers and to test their comprehensiveness. Since the ecosystems approach as it is here set out is comprehensive and synoptic, those approaches that in one or more ways give a truncated version of the framework, leave out quadrants of the matrix or otherwise fail to take note of certain environmental interdependencies will not qualify as truly holistic, forward looking and 'green'. As we have shown above, an incomplete environmental approach is as capable of producing ecosystem damage as a pre-ecological one, and may actually add to the very problems that it aims to avoid. The validity of the matrix and the framework outlined here rests, therefore, on its comprehensiveness.

To summarise, the interactions framework described here has four prime functions:

- The designer is given a conceptual framework for organising and getting to grips with all the ecological ramifications of the proposed designed system. After identifying the totality of the interactions between structure and ecology, the designer is able to minimise negative environmental impacts through design decisions relating to various factors such as the materials to be used and their assembly into the built structure.

- The model can be shared, ie it can be used as a common frame of reference for the designer and other professionals in other disciplines who are evaluating the ecological impact of the designed system. This commonality promotes a 'multiple comprehensiveness' in that the examination of interrelated environmental issues is followed through in a continuous, harmonious manner.

- Over time, the establishment of a common frame of reference through this model creates the possibility of further theoretical elaboration. For environmental concerns to be resolved, various fields with similar concerns, heretofore separate, must be brought together. For example, efforts to conserve natural resources or provide alternatives can be contributory to the design process.

The real test of environmental commitment and principles is on the level of human action (ie, when ground is broken), and this model, by offering a comprehensive framework for understanding the interrelations of built systems and ecosystems, allows people in various fields to act in concert and contribute to ecological design philosophy.

• The theory of interactions presented here provides a single, unifying theory to bring together under one umbrella aspects of environmental science and protection efforts that have in the past been uncoordinated.

Just as it can unite disciplines, this design model can be extended to other disciplines. The designer can use the framework to describe and anticipate the environmental impact of the designed system, but other theorists and practitioners might employ it to model a broad range of human activities with ecological consequences, for example, tourism and the effects of recreational uses of natural sites.

Lastly, the theoretical structure developed here points out the discrepancies in other design practice and research on the subject. Ecodesign, when pursued comprehensively, demands certain kinds of data, which will have to be developed and quantified where not available. This comprehensive design framework offers a benchmark, which can be used by designers to evaluate on a consistent and quantitative basis any proposed design, or to compare one design with another (see B3).

The above premises provide the broad theoretical basis for ecological design, applicable to our designed system and other building types. From this starting point, a strategy for practical application in ecological design should begin by first addressing its design in terms of energy and materials conservation (ie L21 and L11), or more precisely in terms of the management of energy and materials in the designed system throughout its entire life cycle. This is the obvious beginning for the design process, since current statistics show that over 28 per cent of national energy use is in buildings, and that over 50 per cent of a nation's wastes as outputs that go to landfills come from buildings. Significant ecological benefits can be achieved by low-energy design and by concerted design efforts that seek to achieve cyclic use of materials within the built environment. Ecodesign needs to ask questions about the materials that are used in all components of our built system (eg its piling, structure, facade, infill walls, finishing materials, operational systems) (in B29).

We must be clear that the interactions framework is not a substitute for design invention. Invariably in any designed programme, the designer has still to synthesise by design the selected set of considerations into a physical form, though obviously based on informed decisions. In this process of design synthesis, the structural model described here is useful in determining ecological interactions and implications. In the case of a building, such design

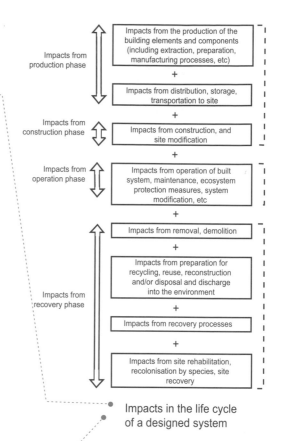

Impacts from production phase

Impacts from the production of the building elements and components (including extraction, preparation, manufacturing processes, etc)

+

Impacts from distribution, storage, transportation to site

+

Impacts from construction phase

Impacts from construction, and site modification

+

Impacts from operation phase

Impacts from operation of built system, maintenance, ecosystem protection measures, system modification, etc

+

Impacts from recovery phase

Impacts from removal, demolition

+

Impacts from preparation for recycling, reuse, reconstruction and/or disposal and discharge into the environment

+

Impacts from recovery processes

+

Impacts from site rehabilitation, recolonisation by species, site recovery

Impacts in the life cycle of a designed system

decisions are of course in addition to but should precede and govern the usual architectural and engineering decisions that need to be made.

The Partitioned Matrix also points out the fact that design decisions and materials selection can have impacts on ecosystems away from the project site. Every design problem represents a particular ecological balancing act between the relative importance of its principal elements and the demands arising from the form: in each case, the synthesis of a design that is related to that balance becomes the most effective way of designing an ecologically responsive built environment.

Different design methods might be viewed as alternatives, which are more or less advantageous depending on the design problem at hand (and on the particular designer). Our intention should not be to try to predetermine a set of standard solutions for design, for no single solution or set of solutions could be sketched out that would automatically correct all environmental problems. The aim here is not to provide a panacea (an impossible task, given the diversity of designs and situations), but rather to set out examples and options to provide the designer with insights into aspects of environmental impairment by built systems. In some instances, solutions may arise that do not require the synthesis of a physical system at all. The technical solutions discussed here are simply what is currently the state of the art.

The eventual impact of a designed system will reflect the degree to which the designer has been able to take in the whole spectrum of environmental effects during the design process. Yet, while the Partitioned Matrix is a comprehensive framework, it is not programmatic. That is to say, it includes all possible issues but not, for obvious reasons, particular situations and cases. It can act as the 'law for ecological design', but it is the individual designer who has to apply that law. All that can be predicted here is the type of design issue likely to be faced particularly in the area of ecosystem interactions and effects. The framework of green design has to be instituted from the outset because initial choices will largely determine the degree of environmental damage, the magnitude of the feedback effect into the designed system and the possibility of correction.

Even before any design begins to take shape, the designer should have analysed the strategic options under the Partitioned Matrix and the green design framework. The results of this analysis will have the effect of narrowing down the range of solutions and making clear the interrelationships that need to be understood in solving the design problem. The various factors and relationships might be represented graphically so as to highlight their most important features; this might also result in a schema that would be general enough to be used in a multiplicity of cases, ie in real design tasks and projects and not just idealisations. Thus, similarities or differences in design issues would be highlighted.

A5

The general law and theoretical basis for ecodesign: the system-to-environment Interactions Matrix   Chapter C • Chapter B • Chapter A

071

For now, the interactions model and the matrix present a general, overall picture of the design problems faced by ecological designers who follow green principles. In essence, it is a map that allows many paths to be taken on the way from problem recognition to resolution. How the designer goes about negotiating the obstacles and constraints depicted on this map of the design task is personal, both in terms of the designer's individuality and also the specific environmental and other factors of the site to be used. What is important is that in adapting the built system to the natural environment the designer does not neglect any of the interactions defined by the Partitioned Matrix; how they are addressed remains a matter of personal choice.

As with theory in general, the Interactions Matrix as a theoretical construct plays an important role in the ongoing development of research in this field. Within the scientific method, it is the primary focus for the generation of hypotheses that are tested in practice.

By considering the ecological design holistically in terms of the four factors in the Partitioned Matrix, it is clear that ecological design is interdisciplinary in encompassing not just architectural design, engineering design and the science of ecology but also other aspects of environmental control and protection such as resource conservation, recycling practices and technology, pollution control, energy embodiment research, ecological landscape planning, applied ecology and climatology. The Partitioned Matrix here demonstrates the interconnectivity of this multitude of disciplines, which must be integrated into a single approach to ecological design. The designed system's form is not finite but includes the hybrid with features, subsystems and functions that are a consequence of its interdisciplinary influences.

Having developed the theoretical foundation presented here, it is now possible to look at particular solutions to design problems on a technical level. These also mirror the Partitioned Matrix and the interactions depicted as:

- the management of inputs, or L21;

- the management of outputs, or L12;

- the management of the environmental context to the building, or L22;

- the design and management of the internal operational systems of our building in relation to the other three sets of factors, or L11; and

- the interactions of all the above sets acting symbiotically as a whole with the natural systems (and other human-made systems as well) in the biosphere.

To set out to fulfil the last (and broadest) goal, that is the global monitoring, synchronising and integrating of all the above aspects of our human-made built environment (ie its entire inputs, outputs, operational activities, environmental consequences) in its interface with the natural cycles in the biosphere and within the other human structures, communities and activities in the biosphere, may at first appear to be naively idealistic. Yet it is crucial to the realisation of ecodesign and sustainability at the global level of effectiveness. However, to accomplish this will require a consensus of global economic-political decision-making for the full exploitation of the opportunities afforded by the use of digital and satellite global information systems (GIS) technologies for the constant global monitoring of this interface of the biosphere's ecosystems and processes with the human-built environment. (For instance, this could involve using hyperefficient nanotech biosensors, fibre-optic devices as pollution-sensing systems that quickly and accurately sense and detect environmental impairment (air, water, land, etc), for example in sensing pathogenic organisms and microbial toxins in food, air and on surfaces in ecosystems and pinpointing loss of biodiversity, etc). The setting up of such a global ecosensing system is technologically possible and should be the prime objective of the major governments and international and national institutions.

Summary

Notwithstanding the existent limiting conditions for ecodesign, the Interactions Matrix given here provides the designer with the fundamental basis for theorising, examining and evaluating any proposed ecodesigned system. When confronted with any ecological design issue, we should refer back to the Interactions Matrix as a baseline reference to ensure that we have considered all the ecological aspects related to the design problem at hand. As mentioned earlier, the sustainability debate currently occupies the middle ground in the advance from the marginal to the mainstream, for which a confident theory-practice framework such as this is vital and urgently needed to legitimise and affirm sustainability's position in the mainstream.

Design Instructions

The human skin as the first layer

Clothing as the second layer and primary determinant of environment and comfort

Building envelope as the third layer and determinant of internal conditions of comfort

Layers of enclosure in the built environment

B1 Interrogate the premises for the design: deciding to build, to manufacture or not

At the outset of any design process, the designer must interrogate the initial premises and rationale behind the proposed design and decide whether to embark on that design project at all. We need to interrogate the basis for the design or the design brief itself, and to assess the proposed designed system for its anticipated consequences on both the built and natural environment and whether these can be mitigated right at the outset and, if so, at what environmental cost.

This process of interrogating the premises for the design is necessary because simply proceeding with a design assignment without questioning its rationale may eventually lead to further significant environmental disruption or pollution. In the ecological approach, the designer must start with the premise that the environmental impact of any designed system increases in relation to the increase in demand for conditions of our human way of life beyond those of a simple existence. The first question to ask prior to the commencement of design is: What is to be built or made and is it needed and crucial to humankind? The next step is to assess the designed system's validity and its projected consequences. For instance, in preparing the design brief for a building, the designer must find out the extent of shelter and comfort as layers of enclosure that must be designed for. All these depend on the performance standards expected by the users of the designed system and affect the extent of the built form. This can be illustrated by citing the case of planning a commercial building. Here, the designer usually asks at the outset whether the project is financially viable before he begins designing it. In the same way, at the very start the ecological designer must question the ecological viability of the project when assessing the set of design requirements. In effect we should start by not only asking how a proposed designed system should be made, but also what designed systems should be made to begin with, and whether these designed systems should be made at all.

Rather than taking the users' needs or the client's demands for granted, we need to look into ways in which the designer and others might inadvertently contribute to creating what may prove to be unsustainable expectations regarding the nature and form of our built environment. This is essentially an ethical issue for the designer. If the built system is a required commodity, then the first step is to assess the extent of manufacturing to be done, how to make this ecologically responsive and what might be its environmental consequences from its source to the end of its useful life. In the case of a building, the objective of ecological design includes ensuring that it can be designed in such a way that a minimum amount of non-renewable sources of energy is needed to service the structure in terms of heat, hot water, cooling, lighting, power, ventilation and other internal functions, as well as other impacts on the environment.

We might contend that a part of ecodesign involves the setting of society's standards. The further that people depart from a simple pattern of needs and use, the more complex is the support that must be derived from the natural environment and the more we have to plan for and expect environmental impairment. An overall reduction in the environmental impacts upon the earth can be effected if there is a similar reduction in the demand by humankind for certain needs (eg shelter, comfort level, mobility, food supply, etc). Ultimately, the extent of the impact of a design is a reflection of the society that commissioned it. In ecodesign it is necessary to avoid any over-design or over-provision and excess in general.

For instance, in the conservation of use of non-renewable resources an issue is the design temperature of the built environment. The average internal temperature of homes was about 13°C in the UK in 1970 whereas the average headed towards 19°C in 2004. Therefore if occupants are prepared to accept a lower comfort level, there will be significant energy savings. Generally, each extra 1°C requires 10 per cent more fuel. A lower indoor temperature simply means that occupants forgo wearing lighter clothing indoors and substitute warmer clothing. Energy savings effected by lifestyle changes include having fewer gadgets and electrical appliances. Households (in the UK) use 30 per cent of the country's total energy and are responsible for 28 per cent of the country's carbon dioxide emissions.

The four key overall strategies in the use of materials, non-renewable resources and ecosystems are: reduce, reuse, recycle and reintegrate. The first strategy is to reduce (see B22 for discussion on reuse and recycling). From the designer's point of view, it can be seen that a reduction in human environmental influence is possible, but only at the expense of a reduction in the provisions for shelter and comfort. As mentioned earlier, the less people demand from ecosystems, the less will be the human impact on them. If people had no need for shelter and comfort, then there would be no necessity for an ecological approach to the design of the built environment because human beings would be a completely integrated part of nature. For instance, with the use of digital technology, many of our current processes can be transacted electronically, in which case there will no longer be a need for many of the structures for direct human interaction. In an already industrialised world and in a society that already has high material expectations, the designer has a difficult task in balancing comfort levels and energy use with environmental impact. For example, the designer will note that the typical North American tall building uses 11.5 kilowatts of energy per day, and the designer would therefore need to evaluate whether the existing projected energy-consumption rates of the users for the built system in this locality might be reduced.

We need to ask: What is the size of the proposed system to be designed? The most significant determinant of building energy use is building size. Newer buildings tend to be larger than existing buildings, with more square footage per occupant and per function. To exacerbate energy use, additional space in a building increases energy use of the ambient systems (eg lighting and M&E systems) by as much as the square of the added floor space. For example, studies (in the year 2000) showed that in the UK although the number of households is expected to increase by 1 per cent a year, the residential energy demand will increase by 1.9 per cent, while an increase in commercial floor space of 1.3 per cent will produce a 2 per cent increase in electricity use. Energy reductions wrought by efficiency improvements are quickly subsumed and surpassed by the energy demands made to support the additional built-up space. The self-evident conclusion is that designers must reduce both the size of new constructions and built-form heights. Tall buildings, for instance, are particularly unecological and research has also shown that they take 30 per cent more embodied energy to build. The first aspect to interrogate in the case of a built structure is its extent of spatial provision (in square metres or square feet) and its height and built form.

Buildings as permanent shelters and workspaces are now considered prerequisites for human existence. Hence the problem for the designer, since such structures are going to be made and used anyway, is how they can be constructed so as to have as little effect as possible on terrestrial ecosystems and natural resources. The extent of the environmental impact of a structure reflects the values of the society that found a need for the building in the first place. For although it is a fundamental characteristic of all life to take in suitable materials (eg food and air) and convert them into products of value to its own or its species' survival (eg heat and metabolic energy), in contemporary human society the intake (ie inputs) includes materials such as fossil fuels to satisfy complex needs for energy, shelter and waste disposal, and the extent of this intake (and hence the related wastes) is tied to the standard of living or gross national product (GNP) of the people in the society where the project site exists. It is an inescapable fact that in order to provide people with the intakes required by their mode of existence, inevitable changes to the ecosystem will be incurred. Therefore, before finalising the design brief (which determines the built form's extent of construction in terms of spatial provision and enclosure), a questioning of the project programme and the users' need of that locality is beneficial. We might find, for instance, that these needs might be met by other means without the provision of any enclosure at all, or even by means of partial enclosures or simply by seeking a consensus among the users to reduce their level of resource intake and environmental requirements.

Therefore, prior to design, in establishing the pattern of needs and use the following questions would have to be asked and decisions made: What is the standard of living, in terms of spatial provision, conditions of comfort and consumption conditions, that is required? What are users willing to give up or tolerate to achieve this standard?

The ecological design approach has clearly to begin by questioning these needs and standards as a precursor to the preparation of the design brief and user requirements prior to commencing any design. Generally, the lower the requirements, the lower the impact. If the ecological designer is trying to reduce levels of society's consumption by setting lower values to comfort and energy levels than those prevailing in the locality, where the designer's structure or product is going to be more ecological and less spendthrift than these, then the end-users of the designed system will have to tolerate the designed changes in living comfort, expediency and consumption conditions. We need to acknowledge that the ecological designer has to deal with these issues in terms of professional liability, user education, etc, which are outside the scope of this book. This, then, is the societal consequence of ecodesign.

The conventional design brief would contain a definition of the function of the built system. In a process similar to value engineering, the ecodesigner needs to interrogate whether the intended objectives of the design (a built structure or a product) might be better served in other ways by what is already in existence, or whether its intended function can be replaced by another solution that will not require building (and/or manufacture) and which has less or no consequence on the use of materials and energy and the ecosystems. In other words, why build or make unless we really have to?

We further need to interrogate the premises for the design and to seek the answers to the following questions prior to design:

• What is the rationale for its existence? What is the purpose of the designed system? Has the designed system a justifiable purpose or value, without which it may, for instance, be just the creation of more trivial or novelty items that will eventually need to be disposed of into the environment after use and which will eventually create further problems of environmental disposal and reintegration? Is there a necessity for the design in the first instance? If there is no justifiable need for the built system or product other than as a novelty, then the outcome would simply be the production of more future waste material; when such material is no longer needed or serves no further useful purpose it will further clutter the biosphere, use up natural resources and may even cause further detrimental effects on the biosphere in its eventual assimilation.

Influencing the users' needs here can entail a simple management decision, such as requiring the male users to remove their ties. Alternatively, if occupants of a non-domestic building treated that building in the same way that they do their homes, energy management would be simplified. In winter, people are often willing to wear more clothes at home to reduce the impact of cold weather on heating bills. A reduction of 1.25°C in heating temperature can have a significant effect on lowering energy consumption, and can be achieved by encouraging a sensible attitude to seasonal and weather-related dressing. Similarly, in summer, light clothing and natural ventilation (ie opening windows) is preferable to mechanical ventilation or air conditioning, both on health grounds and in terms of energy impact. Some of these decisions are management and lifestyle decisions for the end-users of the building, but obviously if the building has been designed with windows that do not open certain options are foreclosed.

An energy efficiency strategy might be to limit the design temperature of the internal spaces to minimise winter and maximise summer temperatures (eg 19°C and 25°C, respectively).

Setting these standards is no easy task. At what point does it matter that a space is 'too hot' or 'too cold'? More significantly still, whose decision is this to be? When does 'discomfort' become a real problem? When is it a problem worth doing something about and what environmental costs are we prepared to pay to resolve it? People used to living in hot regions, especially in developing countries, may accept higher temperatures or humidity levels, not only because of natural acclimatisation but also due to lower expectations. Thus, such questions raise larger issues of lifestyles and culture.

What is the spatial requirement (gross floor area or GFA) and its efficiency?

The size and extent of spatial accommodation affect the quality of environmental comfort to be provided in the designed system, and this further affects not only the ambient conditions of the ecosystems of the project site but also the quantities of energy and materials (the earth's resources) that are consumed and depleted. As these obviously depend on the standard of needs and use by the people who will use the built environment, then it is clear that the higher the levels of needs and use, the more extensive will be the size of the designed system (see above) and the extent of its subsystems (operational systems), and consequently the greater will be its resource demands and ecological impact.

Essentially, in the case of a building, this means an evaluation of the design brief in terms of its level of enclosure (eg the extent of gross areas to be enclosed), and the level of environmental systems to be provided, as well as other factors, all of which are related to the building's consumption (ie L21 in the Partitioned Matrix) and emission levels (L12) and the efficiency of net to gross areas.

While there are commercial justifications in the case of building for achieving maximum plot to GFA ratios, the extent of enclosure may vary. The designer needs to assess the extent of total enclosure and reduce this by the provision of either partial enclosure or transitional spaces (eg sky courts and semi-covered areas) within the built form.

- What is the energy and material consumption vs benefits: will the designed system use up significant amounts of non-renewable energy and material resources without any justifiable social benefits to humankind? We need to assess at every stage the anticipated input and output impacts of the proposed built system (ie in its use of non-renewable sources of energy and materials and their impacts on the ecosystems) as a consequence of its production, its operation and its eventual reuse, recycling and/or its reintegration into the natural environment. One approach is the use of eco-footprinting, which is a form of energy audit that enables the estimation of the burden that the consumption of anything (from food to paper to building materials) puts on the environment.

Since users also affect the extent of waste and discharge from the building, the designer must be familiar with discharge figures and patterns for waste. Generally in urban conditions, as in cities, organic food waste is the highest, followed by paper/cardboard and plastic/rubber waste. Wastepaper production in commercial offices is about 0.110 kilograms per square metre per day (figures for the USA). This being the case, we can either ensure that appropriate provisions for recycling or reuse are in place, or we can seek to influence by design the behaviour of the users in that locality by ensuring that they reduce the extent of waste output. For example, economical urban waste production is regarded to be about 0.8 kilograms per person per day, whereas 'spendthrift' waste production is at about 1.5 kilograms per person per day. Savings can also be achieved by lowering cold water consumption from 150 litres per person per day to 80 litres.

The industry standard provides a set of industrial standards that are used as the description of a thermally comfortable environment that supports the productivity and well-being of a building's occupants, eg the ASHRAE Standard 55-1992. This includes humidity control within established ranges by climate zone. For naturally ventilated buildings, we may utilise the adaptive comfort temperature boundaries, applying acceptability limits (eg 90 per cent). The purpose of these standards is to establish temperature and humidity comfort ranges and design the building envelope and HVAC system to maintain these comfort ranges and to provide a thermally comfortable and supportive environment for the building's occupants.

Low-energy design requires us to install a permanent temperature- and humidity-monitoring system configured to allow operators to control thermal comfort performance and the humidification and/or dehumidification systems in the building, and requires us to establish temperature and humidity comfort ranges and design the building envelope and HVAC system to maintain them. We can, for instance, install and maintain a temperature- and humidity-monitoring system in the designed system to automatically adjust comfort conditions as appropriate.

Passive-mode design does not preclude using composite systems that also have mixed-mode and active-mode devices. For example, creating a climate-responsive building configuration requires the designer to respond inventively to the climate and ecology of the location (ie its latitude and ecosystems) through siting, orientation, layout and construction; but the designer must also selectively design the building's environment (M&E) systems for their contribution to energy consumption and conservation after first optimising the use of the natural ambient climatic energies. Of course, such an 'engineered' design solution should not in any way inhibit creative interpretation. The design needs to be evaluated quantitatively and to be based on a rationale. We need to be aware that the ecological approach is not a set of regimented design rules that result in a deterministic set of built forms. Variations are possible, and inventive means of compensation for deviations from the norms can be adopted.

It is important not only to re-evaluate user requirements but also to be aware that their patterns of use in the built structure are important as well. For example, if the pattern of use of paper in offices increased the rate of double-sided photocopying (eg through user education), it would save the equivalent of about 15 million trees. US businesses alone consume an estimated 21 million tons of office paper every year – the equivalent of more than 350 million trees. In fact, office paper is one of the top six contributors to waste outputs from offices and among the fastest growing by percentage.

It is useful to categorise the level of operational systems provided to our designed system types (ie the extent of its internal environmental servicing systems; see B12 to B17) into these five levels of provision:

• passive mode

• mixed mode

• full mode (or specialised mode)

• productive mode

• composite mode

The provision of the basic level of systems at the passive-mode level, if acceptable to all occupants, is ecologically ideal. It requires the optimisation of all possible passive-mode systems for the locality. The full conventional systems level of servicing is referred to here as the specialised level or the full mode. The in-between level or the mixed-mode level is the background level of servicing. Productive mode is the use of systems that generate energy (eg photovoltaics). The designer must decide at the outset which of these levels of operational systems is to be provided in the building (in B12 to B17).

- What are the anticipated consequences of production and delivery: will the realisation of the designed system cause environmental problems and can these be mitigated? For instance, the production facility or factory for its production may cause negative environmental impacts on the ecosystem in which it is located. Its production may result in emissions that cause environmental pollution. The transportation of raw materials for its production may use up a significant amount of energy resources. The extraction of the raw material(s) for its production may have significant environmental consequences.

- What are the site-specific consequences: will the creation and construction of the designed system (in the case of a built structure) or the facility or factory for the production of the designed system as a product have an impact on the site in which it is located?

- What are the consequences of use of the designed system: will the use or operation of the designed system (or use of the product) create environmental problems (eg emit waste heat and materials, require the transportation of people to and away from the designed system)?

- What are the consequences of reuse and recycling: what are the environmental consequences of reuse, recycling and reintegration of the designed system at the end of its useful life?

- What are the 'after useful life' consequences of the designed system: will the eventual disposal of the designed system create environmental problems of disposal and reintegration?

What are the users' needs and the functions of the designed system?

Right from the start, the designer must place greater priority on the evaluation of the proposed project's users (people) and their needs than on responding to the demands for provision of hardware (eg built enclosures, equipment, mechanical systems, etc). The tendency of most designers is to do the opposite. We need to ask first whether the users' needs can be met in a way that has low ecological impact, without the construction or manufacture of a new designed system or product, and whether the expected standards of living and standards for comfort may be too high.

What is the expected lifespan of the designed system?

At the outset we need to ascertain the product's expected lifespan as 'long life' or 'short life'. If it is designed for 'long life', this will mean minimal recycling of the item but it will still need to be designed with built-in redundancy and flexibility that will facilitate and enable continuous reuse after its useful life. If it is designed for 'short life', then it must be designed to enable maximum continuous reusability and to facilitate recycling (ie reconstitution) and eventual reintegration into the ecosystems.

What will be the footprint of the structure on the locality's ecosystem?

The determination of the floor-plate size and the built form further conditions the physical footprint of the designed system on the land and hence its impact on the site's physical features such as vegetation, hydrology/ground water (see B4 and B5). Further, the built structure's form will create shadows on surrounding land that will change over the course of the day and with the seasons, and will also influence the wind conditions at all levels of the surrounding landscape, streetscape and buildings. As a general strategy, we should build on a minimal site area using small footprint designs and leaving large portions of the site undisturbed and, where applicable, these should remain ecologically continuous.

What will be the configuration of the designed system?

The built configuration also needs to be questioned. For instance, do we need to have a tall built form or an extensively widespread built form? Could the design solution be low or medium-rise built form or a composite of these rather than a single tall built form?

Concurrent with determining the built form is the volume of enclosed space, which also needs to be questioned. Can some of the space requirements be externalised or be in semi-enclosed spaces? The reason being that the more space that is enclosed, the more energy and materials will be needed to produce and operate it.

What are the site conditions and ecological complexity of the territory on which the intended human activity or built structure facility or infrastructure is to be imposed?

The ecological quality of the site itself must be taken into consideration (B4 and B5). We must avoid placement of built structures and infrastructures on those areas within our site where the overall mass is likely to have a significant environmental consequence.

What is the extent of the internal environmental conditions of the built system?

As mentioned above, the initial impact of a design on the environment is proportionately related to the size and context of the users' design requirements. We can regard preparation of the design brief as the setting down of standards of comfort (both spatial and environmental) for the users of the designed system (eg acceptable internal designed temperature) and of consumption. Having established the extent of the designed system (ie its gross area) that is to be built or made, we next need to set down the extent to which we can lower internal environmental comfort standards for the structure (eg the internal designed temperature, air change per hour, indoor air quality and humidity, etc). These levels will depend on what is acceptable to the people who will use the built environment. Obviously, the higher the level of perceived needs, the more extensive will be the size of the built environment, and therefore the greater its ecological impact. For instance, if a lower working internal temperature is acceptable to the users of apartment buildings or office buildings, then the building's M&E systems can be designed operationally to consume less energy.

In evaluating the users' needs, consideration must be given not only to internal environmental standards, but also to the consistency of their provision. If passive-mode environmental systems are adopted (ie non-use of any electromechanical devices or operational systems), the consistency of internal conditions may vary since passive-mode systems are ambient-climate dependent. This becomes a subjective issue, dependent upon the individual preferences of the building's users. It might be argued that it is in the preliminary design stage that the designer is in a position to have the greatest influence on the extent of the impact of the built structure. In terms of energy inputs, half of all energy used by a nation is expended in the heating, lighting, cooling and ventilation of its buildings. In terms of outputs, the way buildings are designed, serviced and adapted over time all directly influence the volume of fossil fuels consumed, which relates directly to the volume of carbon dioxide released into the atmosphere, a factor in the raising of planetary temperatures (the greenhouse effect).

At the beginning of the production of the design brief, the designer should ascertain whether it is possible to meet the designed system's comfort requirements largely through a design incorporating passive-mode measures with a direct effect. In any event, the design strategy must begin by optimising all the passive-mode strategies before adopting others (B13). Then the designer must endeavour to use those mixed-mode systems that are viable and acceptable. The remaining energy needs in terms of heating, cooling, electricity and ventilation should be met by those active systems powered by ecologically sustainable forms of energy. The provision of the internal operational M&E environmental systems might be reduced if greater attention were given to the use of the location's ambient energies. This can be effected through application of bioclimatic design principles where users' needs can be met by climate-responsive building configuration, or by passive devices or by appropriate building orientation, rather than through the building's hardware as full-mode strategies. To achieve this goal, the designer has to be prepared to 'engineer' the architecture of the built structure and its configuration, orientation, external-wall design, M&E systems and other characteristics with careful consideration to the climatic features of the project site.

These features include the solar path, wind pattern and humidity (passive design is further discussed in B13).

Determining the internal environment and the operational consumption level of the built system is probably the most important decision affecting energy use. In a conventional building, these elements account for up to 65 per cent of the energy used in the building over its life cycle. These levels are often locality specific and related to the standard of living and welfare of the population of the project site. The extent of shelter and comfort required by the people who will use the designed system is often influenced by the socioeconomic and political structure of their society and its standard of living. It is these levels of needs and use that initially determine the size and extent of the pattern of built form and its servicing systems. It is therefore ridiculous to assume that specific internal environment conditions are universally applicable. As has already been mentioned, studies have shown that people living in hot regions, especially in developing countries, usually adapt to higher temperatures and/or humidity levels because of lower expectations and natural acclimatisation.

In low-energy social housing studies for temperate climatic zones (eg in Europe), the fuel energy consumption is about 125 kilowatt hours per square metre per annum in residential developments for two occupants per dwelling, and 166 kilowatt hours per square metre per annum for three- or four-occupant dwellings. The impact on and/or damage to the environment for which human beings are responsible is directly proportional to their living conditions and standard of living. Traditional, pre-industrial societies existing at subsistence level obviously make far fewer demands on their environment. Once human activities, modes of existence and expectations go beyond those of the traditional 'simple existence' (eg when they demand a greater or managed food supply, heated and cooled shelters, more developed locomotion, etc), environmental impact starts to be more noticeable. Indeed, as examples of rapid and unmanaged industrialisation show, it can become catastrophic. The more that people depart from a simple way of life, the more demanding and complex are their interactions with the environment, from which they draw (or drain) more and more support and resources. As a result, they will have to expect and anticipate more ecosystem impairment.

A simple quantifiable comparative rating or scoring system may be mapped out by the designer to evaluate and compare the consequences of one design solution or option against another. Another approach may be to use the Interactions Matrix (in A5). However, as with most evaluative systems, there are numerous subjective decisions and, in some cases, compromises to be made and many become value judgements by the assessor. For instance, even ecologists have difficulty in assessing some species as endangered – 'one man's weed is another's flower'. Nevertheless, while accepting the shortcomings of any such assessment methods, the designer will need to consider the above questions and use these to evaluate alternative design solutions.

Summary

When embarking on a design assignment a designer will usually start by preparing a design brief, and a financial brief establishing a preliminary broad estimate of production costs for the designed object (whether it is an artefact or a building, etc) as an accompanying budget and financial viability statement. In addition and similarly, prior to the object's design, construction or production the ecological designer needs to prepare the ecological equivalent of the design brief as an ecodesign brief that clarifies the projected design's ecological intentions and the extent of its ecological compliance, and to furnish a preliminary broad assessment of the designed system's anticipated environmental consequences, its benefits and what might be its likely after-life. A guide for the designer in preparing this may be found in the components in the Interactions Matrix (in A5), ie the designed system's estimated inputs, outputs, activities, etc on the ecosystems and the biosphere. Ecodesign therefore starts by preparing these three briefs: the design brief, the financial brief and the ecodesign brief. The design steps taken afterwards involve the cross-compliance of these three sets of requirements.

We should be aware that ecodesign is not a static design process but is 'design over time', which is designing the developing ecological future of our built environment, based on long-term environmental management that focuses on a continuously evolving and changing landscape.

Chapter C • Chapter B • Chapter A

B2

Differentiate whether the design is for a product (with no fixed abode or with a temporary abode) or for a structure or an infrastructure (both site specific)

White goods waste •------

B2 Differentiate whether the design is for a product (with no fixed abode or with a temporary abode) or for a structure or an infrastructure (both abode or site specific): determining the strategy towards the useful lifespan and the site specificity and fixation of the designed system

It is necessary at the outset of every design assignment for the designer to decide whether the designed system is a product or a built facility (structure) or infrastructure although all of them constitute our built environment. This differentiation is necessary as it determines the extent of the design attention that needs to be given to the content, form and process of the designed system in question, its flow through the built environment (ie its transportation energy and storage implications) and to the site (if any) upon which it is to be used, located or fixed.

In the case of most buildings, structures and infrastructures, these are site-bound in contrast to a product, which is potentially mobile. By being fixed to the land, most of the structures and infrastructures in our built environment are regarded commercially as financial investments and tend to increase in value as they age. A building can last from fifty to a hundred years. In the case of an office building, its commercially designed period of use is usually from eight to ten years to achieve the financial returns on investment. In which case, the broad design strategy is to design flexible built forms that can accommodate future changes in use, servicing and expansion.

In the case of products, equipment and fittings, these have a much shorter useful life. In fact they are often designed to be disposed of after use, and the ecological designer must now design into the product its life-after-use and after-life destination. We should design products so that when their useful lives are over, they do not become waste. We should ensure that they are biodegradable (eg they can be discarded to decompose and become food for plants and animals, and nutrients for soil) or alternatively that they can return into the built environment to industrial cycles to supply high-quality raw materials for new products, to be continuously reused or recycled. Such items should be designed to be energy efficient (conserve energy), water conserving, durable and easy to maintain, and manufactured to facilitate disassembly and recycling and environmental reintegration without further environmental impairment. One approach is to design at the outset the remanufacture of the product within the transition between its reuse and recycling. With conventional recycling, finished products that have outlived their useful lives are turned back into raw materials. In contrast, with remanufacturing the product and its components are reconditioned and reused again and again. A product in our built environment can be readily remanufactured if it is made of standardised interchangeable parts, if it costs less to take it apart and rebuild it than to make a new one, and if its technology is stable and not likely to change frequently. It must be recognised that a product's usage involves territorial changes in places other than its own site of manufacture on a magnitude of geographical range that is outside the control of the designer.

A product (or a piece of equipment), then, in most circumstances has no fixed abode and its impact on the ecosystem in which it is located is transient or may be of no great significance to the site's ecology, depending on where the product is used and where it is located, whether temporarily or permanently. Except for the locality in which it is used, produced or manufactured, the need to inventory a product's site ecology (B5) does not always apply. This is not the case with built facilities, structures and infrastructures whose impact on the site upon which they are located is crucial, and their site ecosystem characteristics must therefore be studied beforehand (see B4 and B5). Ideally, all our manufactured products, materials and wastes should become biological or technical nutrients that re-enter ecological cycles to be consumed by micro-organisms and other organisms in the soil, as effective components of biointegration. They should certainly not end up in landfills.

One approach to product design is to regard products as services where their after-life-use becomes the responsibility of the manufacturer. Here the products are regarded not as items to be owned and thrown away at the end of their useful lives, but as services that can be leased or rented. Ownership is in principle retained by the manufacturer. When the product is no longer needed or needs to be upgraded to a newer version, the manufacturer takes back the old product, breaks it down to its basic components (ie the technical nutrients) and reuses them in the assembly of new products or sells them to other businesses. This shifts the responsibility of a product's disposal away from consumers to manufacturers.

Similarly, this can also apply to packaging. Legislation can be introduced to enable consumers to leave all packaging materials at the point of sale. Retailers are then required to accept all packaging materials returned by the consumer. All products, including building products and equipment, pose this problem of dealing with their accompanying packaging. Packaging consumes energy and materials (eg paper, glass, aluminium, steel, plastic, wood and polystyrene) when it is made, generates harmful VOCs when it is printed and produces carbon dioxide when it is burned. Packaging is estimated to account for half of a nation's costs for waste disposal and should be designed for recycling.

Our food produces not only organic wastes; in addition there is the question of product packaging (which makes up half the volume of solid-waste material in landfills), which should be composed of biological nutrients. With current technology it is possible to make the

	(%)
Paper	56
Glass	16
Plastic	12
Wood	9
Metal	7

Packaging composition (by material)

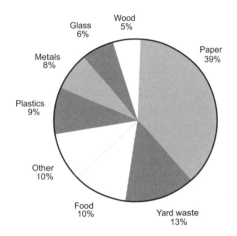

Waste material generated (by weight)

	2005%	2006%	2007%	2008%
Paper	66	68	69	70
Glass	55	68	69	70
Aluminium	28	30	33	35
Steel	55	58	60	61
Plastic	22	22	23	23
Wood	19	22	23	23
Overall recovery	65	67	69	70

Packaging recovery and recycling

Chapter C ● Chapter B ● Chapter A ●

B2

Differentiate whether the design is for a product (with no fixed abode or with a temporary abode) or for a structure or an infrastructure (both site specific)

090

- Design
- Choice of material
- Extraction of raw materials
- Material manufacture
- Use of recycled materials
- Transportation of materials and components
- Manufacture of components

- Packaging
- Transportation

- Operation
- Durability
- Reliability
- Use of energy
- Water use

- Collection, transportation
- Recycling
- Landfill, incineration

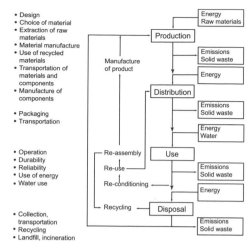

Life cycle of a typical product ●

packaging for all household products biodegradable (eg shampoo bottles, toothpaste tubes, yogurt cartons, juice containers).

The concept of regarding products as services can be extended to all the parts and components of our built structures and infrastructures. It makes no sense to own products merely to discard them at the end of their useful life or their after-useful-life. The resulting economy would no longer be based on the ownership of goods but on an economy of service and flow. Industrial raw materials and technical components would continually cycle between manufacturers and users, as they would between different industries.

In such a service-and-flow economy manufacturers must be able to take their products apart easily in order to redistribute the raw materials (eg design for disassembly in B28). This approach will have major design implications, applicable not only to product design but also to building design (ie built structures and infrastructures). The most successful products or buildings will then be those that contain a small palette of materials and components that can be easily disassembled or dismantled, separated, rearranged and reused.

In product design, greater attention needs to be paid to the ecological consequences of all the commercial aspects involved in the creation, use and eventual disposal of the product into the marketplace that are not applicable to built structures, facilities and infrastructures. For instance, we will need to consider the environmental consequences of the product's development, its after-useful-life, and its process and flow from source to its eventual sink or the point where it is no longer of use and needs to be reused, or recycled or reassimilated back into the environment (ie its design and prototyping, etc).

Besides the environmental consequences of a product's use of materials and natural resources and its industrial production, the ecodesign of products requires the designer to consider the environmental consequences of all the business-related aspects of that particular product such as its packaging, sales, marketing, advertising and promotion, transportation, distribution and delivery, bulk and retail storage and eventual disposal. The environmental consequences of these aspects of products are not covered here but can obviously have significant impacts on the environment.

Products may also be related to other products, as in the case of a building. One building product possesses a performance that can function relative to other products within the boundary of that particular project, and at another scale for that particular economy.

The manufacturer of a product should be responsible for the whole life cycle of his or her product. Products need to be designed and manufactured for continuous reuse, recycling and eventual reintegration into the environment. For most existing products in the built environment, their entire lines need to be redesigned to make them easier to disassemble for recycling. For example, some products may contain composite materials (eg bits of metal or rubber) that make recycling difficult, nearly impossible or uneconomical.

It is possible for the designer to design so that the manufacturer or producer is responsible for energy consumption and emissions during the use of the product. Ecodesign must take into account the product's repairability (eg designing to extend its useful life) and ability to be reused, recycled or disposed of (see B27 and B28).

The emissions from the production process should be designed to be another product or raw material that can be used, either directly or after processing, as an input into further production processes (see ecomimicry in A4). Production should be designed to minimise the use of non-renewable energy and material resources, and preferably to utilise reused or recycled (secondary use) materials or components (see design for disassembly in B28).

A product as referred to here need not be just an item or a piece of equipment, but can be anything made by humans (eg it can include food products).

This differentiation affects the form of the designed system (as in the case of the designed system as a built structure, facility or infrastructure), since its form needs to relate mechanically (eg in relation to the site's topography) as well as systemically to the ecological features and systems of the locality. Where the designed system is a product, which has (in most instances) no site or territorial specificity, its form should be geared to facilitate its continuous reuse, recycling and ease of eventual biointegration into the natural environment.

We need to design products (including appliances, furniture, fittings and equipment) that are:

• reduced in their consumption of materials and energy;

• already recycled or reused;

• better quality with a longer life that leads to users owning fewer but longer-lasting objects, which will be less energy intensive than having to acquire frequent replacements;

• repairable in order to extend their useful life for reuse;

• designed for reuse and not for disposal or to be thrown away after a short period of use or after a single use;

• designed for recycling and therefore not thrown away as waste;

B2

Chapter C • Chapter B • Chapter A

Differentiate whether the design is for a product (with no fixed abode or with a temporary abode) or for a structure or an infrastructure (both site specific)

Chapter C • Chapter B • Chapter A

B2

Differentiate whether the design is for a product (with no fixed abode or with a temporary abode) or for a structure or an infrastructure (both site specific)

- capable of reintegration into the environment and not thrown away as a landfill item; and

- devoid of use of hazardous materials either in the products themselves and/or in their manufacturing process.

Summary

At the outset, the designer should differentiate between the proposed designed system as a product or as a built structure or infrastructure. In the case of a product, the sequence of flow from its production to its use and eventual after-life role entails a series of consequences in multiple localities as well as significant transportation-related and storage consequences between these localities. Besides the need to assess the consequences of the use of the product itself at whatever locality this takes place, its life-after-use must be considered in advance and pre-designed, ie for reuse, recycling or reintegration. If its after-life is not pre-designed then the product will probably end up as landfill and/or as dissipated refuse, which is not reintegrated into the natural environment.

Where the designed assignment is for a built structure or infrastructure, the designer must take into account the entire set of interactions (as described in this manual) with the site upon which it is fixed.

Although a building or infrastructure may be fixed to a particular site, the fixation may be regarded as temporary in nature, as at the end of the useful life of the building or infrastructure, or at its demolition, a similar consideration of the after-life-use of all its components and items is needed.

B3 Determine the level of environmental integration that can be achieved in the design: establishing specific practical limitations

In practice, there is essentially no limitation to the extent to which our design can be ecologically responsive. The critical issue is, where do we stop and what is the extent of satisfactory biointegration that we can accomplish by design? Therefore, we need to ascertain at the outset what might be an acceptable level of designed ecological responsiveness and integration of the designed system or its level of greenness as a target that we can achieve by design. We need to prioritise those aspects of biointegration crucial to the design programme and to the particular site conditions. This, then, is a variable limitation in ecodesign and one that is difficult to define as there are no hard and fast limits to achieving finite biointegration.

- When a designer is attuned to the ecological consequences of the built environment, the designer is necessarily concerned with the life of the building after it has been handed over to the owner or user. If the designer takes the environmental approach seriously, then he or she will be able to inform the owner not only of the environmental consequences of the building as a built structure, the facility, or infrastructure or the product, but also of the consequences of its use and ultimate disposal once its useful life is over.

Ecodesign is certainly not just about meeting a checklist of predetermined standard 'green design' criteria as in, for example, achieving LEED (Leadership in Energy and Environmental Design) or BREEAM (Building Research Establishment Environmental Assessment Method) ratings, but rather about achieving the highest possible level of environmental integration, level of greenness and biointegration by a design appropriate to that particular system.

In ecodesign it is crucial for the designer to be aware that it is physically impossible to declare any design to be absolutely comprehensive in its response to all the design factors or to optimise all the conditions pertaining to ecodesign. This is just not possible to achieve in absolute terms. Key to each ecodesign assignment is establishing the level of green design that can be achieved. The difficulty may be compounded in part by the fact that many of the theoretical, technical and interpretive aspects have yet to be fully developed. Ecological design is, after all, still in its infancy. The best that the designer can accomplish is to take into account as many of the ecological considerations as possible, in particular the key aspects as defined by the Interactions Matrix (in A5) appropriate for the designed system and its locality's ecology. Further, the designer can ensure that the designed system has the least negative consequences for the natural environment over its life cycle and that it achieves the highest possible beneficial and reparative contributions to the natural environment. For instance, design should restore impaired habitats, rehabilitate brownfield land, conserve

- Human welfare
  is related to
- Material standard of living
  which depends on the
- Provision of manufactured goods
  which in turn requires
- Consumption of natural capital
  which means
- Extraction of natural resources
  which involves
- Discharges of waste
  which result in
- Human welfare

Ecological design essentially requires the establishing of standards and the determination of the extent of user requirements that is acceptable to society.

For instance, if we are to reduce the volume of our discharges of waste energy and materials to the natural environment, we need to reduce the extent and rate of our depletion of natural resources.

To do this means that we have to reduce the consumption of natural capital and the provision of manufactured goods. Reduction in the material standard of living enjoyed by the developed countries and a lowering of that standard of living will lead to a lowering of welfare for human communities. The question then becomes a subjective one: What are we prepared to give up for a sustainable future? The designer's role is to use innovation to help achieve this.

Standard of living versus environmental consequences

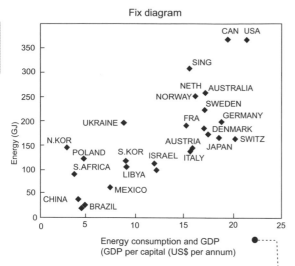

Fix diagram

Energy (GJ)

Energy consumption and GDP
(GDP per capital (US$ per annum)

the physical continuity of the existent ecosystems and enhance such ecological nexus (eg by land-bridges in B8). Nevertheless, at the outset the designer must first establish the extent or level of greenness that the ecodesign endeavour will achieve. While there may be general minimal performance operational standards (eg in energy consumption, waste recycling and harvesting, etc), ecodesign is also locality specific, and the maximum extent of biointegration that can be achieved in each ecodesign assignment varies depending on the project, local conditions, existent technological factors and physical practicalities besides other factors.

As with any design process, it is impossible to take comprehensive account of all the multitude of factors that affect design. As eventually became evident to researchers in design methods during the 1960s, these vary depending on the designer and it is not possible to research and take into consideration all the factors influencing a design prior to the actual design process. The designer has to be selective and must appreciate as far as possible what can be ascertained as the key design issues, and achieve a solution that can be tested and evaluated for its effectiveness. Nevertheless, the key components in the Interactions Matrix (in A5) must be taken into account as well as their interdependent interactions and their consequences.

If designers were to attempt to keep all the adverse environmental impacts of their designs to an absolute minimum, then society might have to return to a much simpler form of existence (ie to one lower than the current general standard of living; see B1), as well as having to accept living conditions that would make fewer demands for environmental comfort, shelter, energy and materials consumption than do the present ones. However, this would require a complex and extensive restructuring of the existing sociological, economic and political structures, which is obviously outside the remit of the designer here.

Without wishing to denigrate the various rating systems already in the marketplace, designing to meet rating targets will generally result in a design that is based on existing systems and therefore will not encourage innovations. While such systems provide useful indexes and checklists for comparing building and planning projects, the projects themselves need to be further evaluated in relation to the ecological and ecosystem criteria identified here. For instance, ecodesign's objectives must include design that can save natural ecosystems, repair those that are damaged and limit future environmental degradation, all of which could very easily be ignored if the focus of ecodesign was on compliance with the criteria on a predetermined checklist. Rather than start the design process by asking whether we can meet specific energy standards, we might start by asking how much energy we need, of what quality, at what scale and from what source to do the job in the most efficient low-energy way.

The ideal comprehensive framework for evaluation is the Interactions Matrix (in A5), applied over the entire life cycle of the product or the designed system and evaluated from source to source.

In implementing ecodesign, the designer needs to contend with the fact that, in practical terms, the level of ecological integration of a design is theoretically extensive and the full extent of ecological integration may not be achievable. Ultimately, the limitation may be the financial budget for the designed system and an awareness of the particular ecological constraints and those of the technological systems. Under such circumstances, the designer can only seek to ensure that the ecological consequences are kept to a minimum while the benefits are maximised. These then become the limiting factors beyond which the project for the designed system may not be viable. Therefore, in practice, the level of ecological integration may be restricted to what is practical and can be accomplished within a given construction or manufacturing budget and the available technical means, while ensuring that the outcome does not incur environmental impairment.

However, the designer must try to pre-empt a situation where such fiscal constraints may entail an unacceptable compromise of greenness for a particular ecodesign assignment. It will then depend on the designer to create the optimal conditions and level of environmental integration for that particular design within the given constraints; alternatively the designer should seek a liberalisation of the constraints, including the economic, or reject the assignment outright as ecologically unacceptable.

Ecology, unlike engineering, is based on discernment and there is much about ecological systems, their constituent species and their relation to their habitats, that still needs to be researched and understood. In this regard, the consequences of our built environment and its processes on the natural environment for certain ecosystems may be tentative. Nevertheless, the consequences of certain aspects of our built environment can be quantifiably defined, such as the loss of biodiversity, the loss of productivity in an ecosystem and the latter's loss of carrying capacity in its processes.

The energy used to construct a building is relatively small in comparison to that of the production of building materials. The direct energy is around 7-10 per cent of the total embodied energy (in the USA).

We should be aware that an embodied energy value for a designed system or a product is not a good indicator of its ecological impact because:

• The energy unit does not take into account the length of life of a product

• The energy unit does not take into account any subsequent reuse, remanufacture or recycling of the product.

- The energy unit is only a measure of environmental impact if the energy involved is produced from polluting sources (eg a high embodied energy value is not inherently a high ecological impact if much of the energy is produced photovoltaically).

- The energy unit is only an indicator of the 'first' initial consequences of the production of the designed system or product and does not take into account the environmental consequences of the product or material functioning over time.

There are a number of methods for assessing the embodied energy in a product or a built form: by input–output analysis, process analysis, statistical energy analysis and other hybrid analysis methods. Embodied energy tends to be high for single-storey built forms due mainly to poor surface area to volume ratio. As the number of storeys in the built form increases, the embodied energy initially decreases due to the savings from improving the surface area to volume ratio. Research studies have shown that the embodied energy of a built form starts to increase as the number of storeys approaches 10 storeys. High-rise built forms from 40 storeys upwards have approximately 60 per cent more embodied energy per unit GFA (gross floor area) than low-rise built forms due to having more materials to meet structural requirements and wind loads.

Summary

The set of factors highlighted in this manual provides the ecological design goals that the designer should seek to achieve in as close a fit as possible.

While the fundamental basis for ecodesign is environmental biointegration, in practice the designer may find this abstract and require more specific directives.

To elucidate, we can first establish three essential modes of integration: physical, systemic and temporal.

Physical integration means designing to integrate the physical presence and use (ie operations) of the designed system with the physical features and constituents of the project site's ecosystems. Optimally, this should entail minimal ecological consequences and, of course, maximum ecological benefits (eg rehabilitation of habitats, enhancement of biodiversity, restoration of devastated ecological systems, etc; in B4 to B8).

Systemic integration is the integration and assimilation of the designed system's processes and functions with those of the ecosystems and the biosphere (ie air, land, water) in terms of the system's inputs of energy and materials, its internal processes and its outputs of energy and materials (in B9 to B29).

Temporal integration is the use and conservation by the designed system of the natural environment and its resources at rates that ensure their continued enjoyment by future generations of humankind.

The achievement of all these three levels of biointegration will always be limited to the practical constraints of each design assignment. While specific targets can be established, eg in LEED, BREEAM etc, these are standards that need to be surpassed, to an extent that may vary in importance depending on the design assignment and site's conditions and ecology at hand.

The designer must be wary of the perception that just meeting these targets will result in a satisfactory environmental performance by the designed system. This is not the case. Meeting these prescribed targets simply means meeting an artificial generalised set of comparative customs. Ecodesign must set out to address all the issues that this manual outlines in as much detail as practically possible, as against simply meeting a set of checklist standards. Nevertheless, for each design assignment the designer can start by establishing the minimum performance standards that must be achieved, and the expected maximum biointegration that the design should aim to achieve within technological, practical and other limitations for that assignment.

Water-efficiency opportunities
- Reduction in use of water: reduce the flow in sanitary fixtures and HVAC equipment.
- Landscaping water efficiently: reduce the potable water requirements. Capture rainwater and recycle grey water.
- Wastewater innovative technologies: reduce sewerage quantity.

Site opportunities
- Redevelopment of urban sites: redevelop existing urban sites as opposed to developing rural sites, thereby reusing urban infrastructure.
- Redevelopment of brownfield sites: redevelop contaminated sites, thereby reducing development pressure on other sites.
- Site selection: do not develop inappropriate sites, ie those within flood zones, agricultural land or wetlands.
- Site disturbance reduction: restore damaged areas and conserve natural areas; use native vegetation.
- Transportation alternatives: promote alternative transportation methods, ie cycling, light rail and van pooling.
- Management of storm water: do not create a net increase in storm-water runoff or attempt to reduce the runoff; capture rainwater for use.
- Reduction of light pollution: keep outdoor lighting as low as possible.
- Reduce heat islands: use shading elements to reduce urban heat-island effects.

Resources and materials
- Reuse of resources: reuse of materials.
- Reuse of building: reuse of portions or all of a building.

  Recycle content: reuse of the recycle content.
- Management of construction and waste: recycle land clearing, demolition and construction waste; use life-cycle cost analysis in material selection.
- Use local and regional materials: the more local the materials the less money and fewer resources are spent bringing the material to the site.
- Wood certification: use wood from Forest Stewardship Council guidelines.
- Materials that rapidly renew themselves: use agricultural products that rapidly renew themselves, eg bamboo.
- Recycle content: use products high in recycled contents.
- IAO minimum performance: ASHRAE Standard 62-1999 for ventilation.

  Materials with low emissions of VOCs: carefully select adhesives and sealants, paints and coatings, carpets and wood products to reduce VOC of off gassing.

  Day-lighting: day-lighting a building can reduce energy consumption and increase comfort.

  Thermal comfort: the ASHRAE Standard 55-1992; permanent automated control systems are beneficial to human comfort.

  System control: operable window and individual controls can provide a higher degree of comfort.

  Monitoring of carbon dioxide (CO_2): monitoring of carbon dioxide levels is important for indoor air quality.

  Indoor air quallity management plan during construction phase: indoor air contamination reduced by implementing IAO plan during the construction phase.

  Environmental tobacco smoke (ETS): restrict smoking in the building to restricted rooms.

  Control of indoor pollutant sources and chemicals: mats can help maintain lower indoor pollution, isolate areas for working with hazardous chemicals.

● Examples of LEED criteria
(Leadership in Energy and Environmental Design)

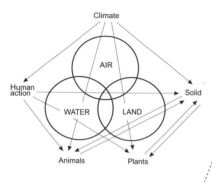

Land

Air

Water

Others

Some environmentalists wrongly conceive the environment in terms of discrete zones which do not interact with one another.

Environmental zones •------

The three layers of air, water and land, and their interaction with biotic factors

B4 Evaluate the ecological history of the site (for the designed system): site selection and establishing the overall site strategy

Where the designed system is a built structure, facility or infrastructure and is site specific, the designer must first evaluate the ecological history of that site's ecosystem to ascertain the level of ecological analyses required prior to design — and not as a series of discrete environmental zones. This is important because every locality in the biosphere is ecologically different, with a number of other factors affecting the environmental zones. This evaluation is therefore crucial in ecodesign as it enables the designer to determine how to lay out and physically integrate the built systems and structures, infrastructures and activities on to the site, ie where they are to be fixed or located and subsequently to systemically integrate their emissions. A simple method of categorisation for a project site is given here.

The project site's ecosystem: characteristics and features

Particularly in the case of a built facility design, we need to study the characteristics and features of the project site's ecosystem on which construction will take place. This must be done prior to any work on the site. In selecting the site, obviously the various optimal sites must be evaluated beforehand.

The earth's surface can be divided into large geographic regions characterised by distinctive patterns of vegetation. Such regions, called biomes, also have similar climates, soils and animals. The biomes are discontinuous but communities in separate biome parts generally resemble one another.

All sites within each of these communities, upon which building and infrastructure construction is intended to take place, have varying ecological histories of abiotic and biotic impairment and ecosystem simplification by humans. The ecological history of the site will indicate the history of past human intervention there and the current state of its succession. The level of ecological analysis needed for each site (B5) may vary depending on its ecological history and complexity.

In order to ascertain the extent of ecological analysis necessary for a particular site and the overall design strategy for its structure or infrastructure, at the outset the designer needs to assess its ecological complexity and history to decide in which of the following categories it lies:

- Ecologically mature ecosystems

These ecosystems are characterised by very high biodiversity. Ecologically mature ecosystems are those that have largely been undisturbed by people for a long time. They usually support a large variety of species. These species interact with one another on a relatively stable basis and use all available nutrients efficiently. Biodiversity varies depending on the locality of the ecosystem. For example, there are up to 400 tree species per acre present in a rainforest, around 40 in a New England (USA) hardwood forest and perhaps 10 in a forest in Maine. Ecologically mature ecosystems include forests, deserts, wetlands and rainforests and are essentially ecosystems that are not directly affected by any human-made interference. These are natural areas where succession is allowed to proceed into the mature and stable stages.

Adapting from the ecologist E.P. Odum's classification of land (productive areas, protective or natural areas, compromise areas, urban industrial or biologically non-vital areas), we can classify land areas for ecodesign purposes as follows:

- Ecologically immature ecosystems

There are ecosystems that, while still natural, are recovering from damage or are in the process of succession or regeneration (eg a site that is partially devastated by humans). This category can be regarded as ecologically protective or natural areas where ecological succession is allowed or encouraged to proceed to mature, and thus become stable if not at highly productive stages.

- Ecologically simplified ecosystems

These are sites that, though originally mature or immature, have now been savaged by grazing or controlled burning, by being mown or selectively logged, or by the removal of biotic components.

- Mixed artificial ecosystems

These are mixed ecosystems that are artificially maintained by man, eg through crop rotation, agroforestry, parks, gardens, etc. These are compromised areas with some combination of productive and protective areas and can be regarded as ecologically compromised areas where some combination of the first two ecological developmental stages exists.

- Monoculture ecosystems

These are again artificial, but monoculture, ecosystems (eg agricultural use, replanted forests for timber harvesting, plantations, crops, lawns). These are what ecologists call 'productive areas' where ecological succession is continually retarded by human controls to maintain high levels of productivity.

Ecosystem hierarchy of site
Ecologically mature
Ecologically immature
Ecologically simplified
Mixed artificial
Monoculture
Zeroculture
Contaminated

Taxonomy of site types as basis for ecodesign

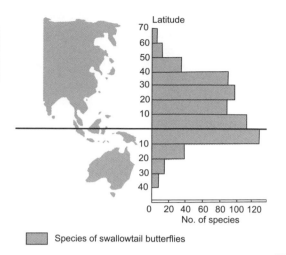

Latitude

No. of species

■ Species of swallowtail butterflies

Indicative biodiversity in relationship to latitude ●

- Zeroculture ecosystems

  These are totally artificial ecosystem sites with zero remaining ecological culture, eg urban sites (in a city-centre urban-site culture nothing of the original fauna and flora is left, its topsoil is probably all gone, and it is likely that only the bedrock and the affected subsoil hydrology remain), open-cut mines, etc. Similar to parts of our instant city, where there are no longer any historical reference points by which we can understand where we have come from, such zeroculture landscapes have lost remnant plant communities, traces of old landforms, and geological and cultural features that need to be retrieved as the basis for rehabilitation. This category can be regarded as urban industrial or biologically non-vital areas.

- Contaminated ecosystems

  These are brownfield sites or contaminated sites.

Going down the hierarchy from ecologically mature to contaminated ecosystems, we will note that the biodiversity of the project site decreases as we go down the list, as does the degree of natural (ecological) control of processes. At the same time, the demand for energy and maintenance input (eg addition of fertilisers, weeding, etc) increases as does the fragility of the ecosystems. At the start, the designer must ascertain to which of the above categories the project site belongs as this indicates the extent of ecosystem analysis and mapping to be carried out (see B5).

For the monoculture, ecologically mature and immature sites, it is essential to carry out an in-depth ecological analysis before starting to plan and design any structures or infrastructures on the site. Obviously, the extent of such analyses will depend on the complexity of the site's ecosystem. The site's ecological complexity obviously increases as we go up the list.

For zeroculture sites, the overriding strategy must be to bring as much biomass and landscaping back as possible. Urban land use has led to the construction of urban infrastructures (ie roads, drains, sewerage, water reticulation, electrical power supply, etc) that have changed the local hydrology and nutrient exchanges dramatically, altering ecosystem primary productions and the locus of secondary productions. We need to study the surrounding vegetation in the urban site (eg along roadside kerbs, nearby green areas, historical ecological information, etc) to identify what were the prevalent species on the site before it was cleared for building.

If the site is of an adequate size, one design approach is to provide it with a sizeable green area or an ecozone that will consist (where appropriate) of the site's original vegetation.

The design work involves researching the site's ecological heritage, and rehabilitating and regenerating its original ecological profile.

A strategic guide for implementation at the outset of the design process as the basis for approaching different sites and their biodiversities and for ascertaining the extent of site data needed is indicated below.

Guidelines for approaching different sites

Ecosystem hierarchy	Site data requirements	Design strategy
Ecologically mature	Complete ecosystem analysis mapping Highest level of detail in analysis	• Preserve • Conserve • Avoid any building to prevent any disturbances; build carefully only in no-impact areas (if any)
Ecologically immature	Complete ecosystem analysis mapping	• Preserve • Conserve • Build on impaired areas and areas of least impact and no ecological consequence
Ecologically simplified	Complete ecosystem analysis mapping	• Preserve • Conserve • Increase biodiversity • Build on low-impact areas
Mixed artificial	Partial ecosystem analysis and mapping	• Conserve • Increase biodiversity • Build on low-impact areas
Monoculture	Partial ecosystem analysis and mapping	• Increase biodiversity • Build on areas of non-productive potential (non-arable areas) and least ecological impact • Rehabilitate the ecosystem and habitats
Zeroculture	Analysis and mapping of remaining ecosystem components (eg hydrology, remaining trees, etc)	• Increase biodiversity and organic mass • Rehabilitate the ecosystem and habitats
Contaminated and brownfield sites	Mapping of those contaminated ecosystem components	• Assess cause of damage and source of contamination • Decontaminate and remediate • Rehabilitate the ecosystem and habitats

In the table above, the hierarchy of sites (in the first column) provides us with a guide to the extent of ecological inventory and studies that are needed for the site as the basis for design (in the second column). The options (in the third column) present the design strategy to be adopted for that particular site type.

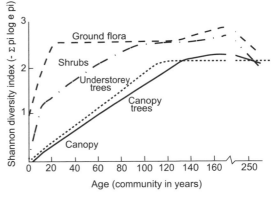

• Biodiversity index over time

	Mammals	Birds	Reptiles	Amphibians	Fish
Asia and Pacific	526	523	106	67	247
West Asia	0	24	30	8	9
Europe	82	54	31	10	83
North America	51	50	27	24	117
Latin America	275	361	77	28	132
Africa	297	217	47	17	148
Polar region	0	6	7	0	1

Threatened species by region ●--------

Site selection

If the designer is comparing a number of potential sites, then the information in the table above should form the basis for classifying the various sites with preference given first to contaminated ecosystems and last, in ascending order, to ecologically mature ecosystems as the most ecologically sensitive and therefore least suitable for disturbances by construction. Site selection is critical to ecodesign.

In selecting a site, the designer first ought to question whether it is appropriate to build or to interfere with the site at all. We need to avoid development on inappropriate sites (ie ecologically mature sites as defined above) and reduce the environmental impact from the location of a building on a site. The designer may need to look at the larger context of the site and examine the regional land-use patterns and impacts on the watersheds and wildlife habitats. Other factors for consideration include proximity to public transportation.

During the site selection process, preference should be given to those sites that do not include sensitive site elements and restrictive land types. Select a suitable building location and design the building with the minimal footprint to minimise site disruption. Strategies include stacking the building programme, tuck-under parking and sharing facilities with neighbours. We should not develop buildings, roads or parking areas on portions of sites that meet any one of the following criteria:

- prime arable land or farmland;
- flood-prone land, eg land whose elevation is lower than the elevation of the 100-year flood level (eg from 2 metres above the flood level);
- land which has already been specifically identified as a habitat of any species on the threatened or endangered lists;
- land close to water bodies, including wetlands and isolated wetlands or areas of special concern (eg within a proximity of 30 metres or more to water bodies), depending on the ecosystems;
- land which is parkland or conservation land.

In site selection, the preference is for sites from brownfield damaged and contaminated sites upwards (as in the categorisation given in the table above), rehabilitated contaminated land and reuse of previously developed or reclaimed land. Brownfield sites should be the first choice. To enable building to take place, the designer needs to implement a site remediation plan (eg using strategies such as pump-and-treat, bioreactors, land farming and in situ remediation). For these sites, we need to restore and repair the damage where building is complicated by real or perceived environmental contamination. The use of brownfield sites reduces the pressure on undeveloped land.

After brownfield sites, the next preference should be sites within urban areas with existing infrastructure and proximity to mass transport hubs. As far as possible, we need to protect greenfields and preserve habitats and their natural resources. In zeroculture and existent urban environments, the location of new, especially intensively built, developments should be at mass transport interchanges and hubs to reduce the energy cost of transportation.

Particularly in the case of the pristine and undisturbed ecosystems (eg ecologically mature and immature sites), if they have been undisturbed by humans for a long time they usually have a variety of species, which interact with each other on a relatively stable basis and use all nutrients efficiently. Diverse natural ecosystems tend to be more resilient to human activity.

Categorisation of the site provides indicators as to which general strategy should be adopted for that particular site. For instance, we need to restore and make habitable again, for both humans and other species, those sites that have been significantly devastated by man or are toxic-contaminated brownfield sites.

Even partially devastated land with a mixture of human-made and natural vegetation (ie mixed artificial sites), such as city parks, can be restored to a semblance of natural vegetation, so that they once more provide habitats for the small animals, birds and insects that were originally native there.

In the revegetation of devastated sites, such as abandoned building sites or brownfield sites, one approach to accelerating the revegetation process is selectively to introduce native plants and animals. This tactic helps increase the biodiversity of the region and allows the ecological 'corrections' to become quickly and firmly established.

An alternative approach might not entail trying to reconfigure the habitat to its state prior to disturbance. Instead, we might consider a restorative approach, introducing the native flora and fauna that can exploit and recognise the site as it stands. This type of restoration could occur side by side with that of the highest quality remnants of other habitat types.

The human-made built environment occupies space both on the ground and above it. A building and the related infrastructure needed to service it (such as roads, drainage, sewerage system, etc) are firmly embedded in the ground. They leave their footprint on the existing ecosystems. Designing for physical integration involves integrating the site's built system of infrastructure with the physical features of the ecosystem so that the physical displacement does not disrupt the site's ecosystem structure and functioning.

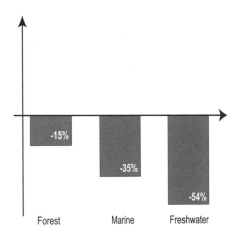

State of global decline in population by ecosystem

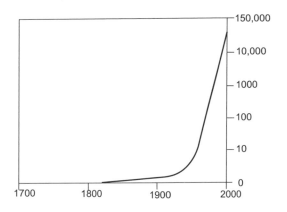

Number of species lost each year

This graph portrays the estimated loss of living species from 1700 to 1992. The normal or 'background' rate of extinction remained essentially unchanged for the last 65 million years from the disappearance of the dinosaurs along with countless other species at the end of the Cretaceous era until the last century

In site selection we also need to take into account the fact that our designed system will have effects on other human-made systems, such as other built environments and infrastructure either in the proximity or which are interconnected. This is especially true for urban buildings in the context of the densely built inner city. For example, in the case of tall buildings, their shadows may affect the ambient temperature and solar energy productivity potential of other buildings, a particularly crucial factor in the winter months in temperate and cold climate locations. One way of mitigating this effect is to apply the concept of 'solar envelope'. The solar envelope is defined as the largest hypothetical volume that can be constructed on a lot without overshadowing neighbouring properties during critical energy-receiving hours and seasons. It is, therefore, both a temporal and spatial calculation. Studies indicate that this concept applies to urban contexts with plot ratios up to 1:6.

The ecodesigner should aim to avert any human activity, including building, or other impacts on the natural environment, such as habitat destruction, introduction of invasive species, pollution, over-population and over-harvesting.

Our approach to site selection and site conservation must not focus solely on biodiversity, but must extend to protect larger ecological units, such as ecological systems. We need to use such descriptive/normative concepts as ecosystem health and ecosystem integrity, which apply at the ecosystems level and emphasise processes rather than elements.

As mentioned earlier, site selection should seek to avoid ecologically mature and immature sites. Ecologically mature sites mostly should be protected sites, ie geographically defined areas which are designated or regulated and managed to achieve specific conservation objectives. For those ecologically mature and immature sites where conservation is required, this should involve the conservation of their ecosystems and natural habitats, and the maintenance and recovery of viable populations of species in their natural surroundings.

In the case of mixed artificial sites, where there are mostly domesticated or cultivated species, the maintenance and recovery refers to those species that are within the surrounding area where they have developed their distinctive properties.

The sustainable use of components of biological diversity entails their use in a way and at a rate that does not lead to the long-term decline of biological diversity, thereby maintaining its potential to meet the needs and aspirations of present and future generations.

Generally, the next step after this broad analysis is to inventory and understand the particular ecosystem's properties and functioning. These processes, too, are vital prior to design and site planning. The impact of human activity on the site's biodiversity can have unexpected consequences. For instance, we may remove some old hedges on our site near an agricultural field, but this may make it impossible for birds to nest near the agricultural fields, so insect pests formerly eaten by the birds may suddenly multiply. If we understand the intricate and varied balances of biodiversity, we can avoid interfering with them.

Conservation strategies

For sites where conservation is needed, the ecosystem conservation strategies include:

- Identify protected areas or areas on the site where special measures need to be taken to conserve biological diversity. The objective is the protection of ecosystems, natural habitats and the maintenance of viable populations of species in natural surroundings.

- Determine the appropriate guidelines for the selection, establishment and management of protected areas or areas on that site where special measures need to be taken to conserve biological diversity.

- Regulate or manage those biological resources within the site that are important for the conservation of biological diversity whether within or outside the protected areas, with a view to ensuring their conservation and sustainable use.

- Review environmentally sound developments in areas adjacent to the protected areas of the site with a view to enhancing protection of these areas.

- Rehabilitate and restore those degraded ecosystems within the site and promote the recovery of threatened species, inter alia through the development and implementation of plans or other management strategies.

- Regulate, manage or control the risks associated with the use and release of any living modified organisms resulting from biotechnology that are likely to have adverse environmental impacts that could affect the conservation and sustainable use of biological diversity on that site, and also take into account the risks to human health.

- Prevent the introduction of, control or eradicate those alien species that threaten the site's ecosystems, habitats or species.

- Seek to provide the conditions needed for compatibility between present uses and the conservation of biological diversity and the sustainable use of its components.

- Where a significant adverse effect on biological diversity has been determined on the site, regulate or manage the relevant processes and categories of activities.

Designing for biointegration requires the designer to establish at the outset the ecological history and category of the project site for the designed system to inform his or her decision as to whether it should be selected or intervention be permitted on it. Appreciating the ecological history of the project site further provides the designer with a general strategy for addressing the relationship between the designed system and the site's ecology (see the table on Taxonomy of site types and design strategy).

Summary

In the design of any built structure or infrastructure, the designer must first ascertain the ecological history of the project site using the simple categorisation or taxonomy of sites given here (see table above). First, this will enable the designer to decide whether the project site is ecologically appropriate for the intended designed system or human activity or indeed, whether intervention in its ecosystem should be permitted at all. This taxonomy of sites provides the designer with the initial basis for site selection. Thereafter, the ecological history of the project site provides the designer with a general strategic approach for addressing the relationship between the proposed designed system and the site's ecology and, in particular, their physical and systemic integration.

The designer should take note that for any ecologically sensitive locality to accept our designed system without any impairment, we need first to inventory and study its ecological features and the characteristics of its ecosystem. These procedures will help achieve an understanding of the locality's resilience limitations and the ecosystem's resilience or its carrying capacity as the baseline for site integration in the planning and design of the proposed designed system (in B5). The extent of ecological site analysis and inventory to be carried out by the designer for that particular site will depend on its ecological history and sensitivity and the intended human activity, built structure, facility or infrastructure to be imposed upon it. The site's ecological history determines the design strategy to be adopted for that site, which in turn influences the extent of the permissible footprint and the intensity and the configuration of the designed system's built form, its access routes and other aspects of the performance of the designed system (eg assimilation of its outputs, etc).

B5 Inventory the designed system's ecosystem (site-specific design): establishing the ecological baseline and context for planning and design to protect the ecosystems and to restore disturbed or degraded ecosystems

Having established the ecological historical context and extent of previous human intervention on the project site's ecosystem, the designer next needs to study and inventory its ecosystem's characteristics, functions, structure, processes, etc, prior to determining how the proposed built structure, facilities and infrastructure, their extent, operations and use can (or cannot) be imposed and laid out upon it. The designer then needs to anticipate what the potential impacts and benefits might be. The simple objective is to work with nature. This site inventory and analysis are necessary because they will furnish the designer with information about the preferred form, intensity and patterns of the layout of the built structures and facilities, their related means of access and their configurations (eg roads, etc) and the extent of their infrastructure. Moreover, they will help determine the permissible level of the systemic operations that can integrate physically, systemically and temporally with the ecosystems of the locality, and provide an indication of how to achieve this with minimal negative consequences for the locality's ecosystems. At the same time, the designer can ascertain how the intervention can also positively contribute to the ecosystem's biodiversity and processes and, in this regard, ecodesign is designing the ecological future of the site.

It is necessary for all design to first examine critically the ecological and climatic characteristics and the natural boundaries of the project site as the prerequisite for design (ie the historical geology, climate, physiography, the water regimen, soils, plants, animals and land use). Biologists estimate that if the rate of species extinctions worldwide continues at the present rate, fully one-quarter of all life forms will be obliterated in 50 years.

When construction moves into a formerly wild area it reduces the habitats available for many species. The site's physical and biological profile, rather than technology or the patterns and mechanistic forms of the human-made environment and its artefacts, should determine the ultimate design. Any design that does not take into consideration the ecological and climatic characteristics of the project site and how they affect the designed system and its operation cannot be considered ecological. An evaluation of potential development impacts requires that a predevelopment ecological baseline or environmental model for the project site be produced. This model will describe the essential functions and interrelationships of the individual site factors and will establish acceptable limits of change during and after construction. Selected environmental monitoring and testing will need to continue during

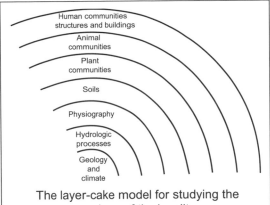

The layer-cake model for studying the ecology of the locality

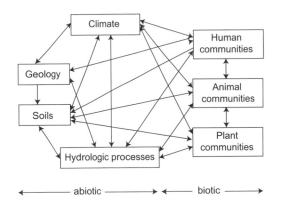

← abiotic → ← biotic →

The interactions between the layers

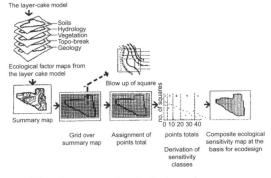

The sieve-mapping technique for ecological land-use planning.

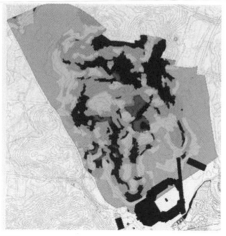

Slope 10 degrees and gentler
Slope 10 ~ 20 degrees
Slope 20 ~ 30 degrees
Slope 30 ~ 45 degrees
Slope 45 ~ 60 degrees
Slope 60 degrees and steeper

Most suitable for building
Moderately suitable for building
Building with caution to slope

Not suitable for building

Example of analysis of site topography

Masterplan
Example of site design developed from studying the ecology of the locality

construction. The entire building of the designed system can be planned to allow time between construction phases to monitor environmental impacts and to adjust the baseline model.

The basic objective is to limit destruction to existent habitats and any action that will reduce biodiversity and ecosystem processes and functions. Attention should also be given to the locality's hydrology and the design should follow natural drainage patterns (as natural storm-water treatment) using bioretention, bioswales, pervious paving and vegetated terraces and rooftops to reduce runoff and promote ground-water recharge.

Essentially, this applies to the design of structures and infrastructures that are site specific. In the case of products, this applies to the locality for the manufacturing facility for the product, its transportation and the various facilities where the product is used or stored or retailed.

The depth of analysis of ecosystem modelling and mapping of the site for our designed system depends on the level of complexity of the project site in the earlier hierarchy of sites (in B4). Obviously, the ecologically mature project site requires the most extensive analysis of its ecosystem and the greatest understanding of the effect of the intended human changes. This analysis decreases in complexity until we reach the zeroculture ecosystem site where most biotic components have already been removed. In practice, it is of course impossible to amass all the facts needed to describe completely even a very small landscape, but we have to work with what we can get.

This inventory further enables us to assess the carrying capacity of the locality's ecosystem. The rationale is that ecosystems have their own repair capabilities. They are able to maintain themselves against many natural disturbances, unlike machinery or buildings that require constant human maintenance. Pollution impacts upon ecosystems can be short term if the ecosystems possess enough capacity to absorb and transform pollutants. This, then, is the carrying capacity of a particular ecosystem. However, once this carrying capacity is exceeded, then the ecosystem becomes irreversibly impaired.

Designing for physical integration

This inventory is in effect a study of the biological phenomena of the locality's ecosystem and in order to produce it we need to understand this ecosystem's form, process and content. Generally, the necessary steps in designing for physical integration as part of the site masterplanning and built systems design are as follows:

- Model the ecosystem of the project site to establish an understanding of the latter's natural environment.

- Establish acceptable limits of change and protect those parts of the natural environment that must not be developed and should be buffered, either because they are rare, or ecologically fragile, or both.

- Based on the composite maps of those parts and patterns of the site that can withstand the intended intervention, design and lay out the built systems within social and environmental parameters and reintroduce natural and biodiversity enhancement features into already urbanised and built-up areas.

- Monitor site ecosystem factors throughout construction and operation.

- Re-evaluate design solutions between development phases.

- Repair and restore those natural systems and areas that have previously been damaged by human activities.

- Contribute productively to the site's ecology if it is in an urban context by increasing the biomass relative to the inorganic areas of the built systems.

In addition to the above, the designer should not neglect the usual social and economic considerations of the intended designed structure or infrastructure and their content.

We need to be aware that producing an ecological analysis or profile of the site of the proposed building can be a daunting task, requiring significant time and expertise. Because an ecosystem goes through natural seasonal changes, a complete analysis would have to include observation of the site at various times of the year – and the more diverse the site (ie the higher up on the scale of hierarchies), the more complex is the task. The flora and fauna of the locality provide the designer with clues to the condition of the site's ecology. The processes and organisms are distributed over the landscape in relation to climate and topography and their patterns have to be respected. As has been pointed out, a total ecological analysis including all interrelationships is a huge task, so the use of the condition of biotic communities as a benchmark is a helpful way to estimate the overall state of the local environment. An ecologist can use information about the status of the site's soil, micro-climate, hydrology and animal species. For example, a particular growth of vegetation and its state of succession tells us much about how recently there has been any ecological disturbance of the area, the biological productivity of the site, and the biodiversity and stability of the environment. Further inferences could be drawn about the interaction between the local ecosystem and other surrounding environments. By such careful observation of the site ecology, the designer can forecast both the degree to which the intended built system is suitable for the locality and the ecosystem's vulnerability to damage from such human intervention.

Ecological site mapping

An ecological analysis of a site is not something we can do over a week or a month but something that might need to be done over the seasons of the entire year. As designers, we do not have this luxury of time. One way of overcoming this is to use the 'sieve-mapping' technique for looking at the landscape. We can map the landscape as a series of layers as a simplified approach to studying the site's ecosystem. However, the prevailing tendency to adopt this approach as the be-all and end-all of ecological analysis should be resisted. The approach tends to regard the site's ecosystem statically and ignore both the constant dynamic forces that operate within an ecosystem and how ecosystem dynamics might change with time. Between each of these layers are complex interactions. This technique was advanced in the late 1960s and is still in use today, although subsequently enhanced by the use of satellite geographic information system (GIS) and other techniques. This 'layer-cake' method can be simplified into a series of steps, as follows:

- Identify biotic (faunal and floral) species present, including their diversity, distribution over the site and numbers.
- Create a hierarchy of species, ie determine which are most valuable and crucial to the functioning and viability of the ecosystem.
- Factor these conclusions into the design and building plan so as to minimise changes to biotic communities and permanent alterations in terrain, including other factors such as edaphic factors and land configurations.

This method involves the simplified mapping of the ecosystem in terms of its natural physical features (vegetation, soils, ground water, natural drainage patterns, typography, hydrology, geology, and so on) through the evaluative technique of 'sieve mapping', which produces a plan showing land areas suitable for different intensities of development and building types in relation to the carrying capacities of the natural systems. In the site planning or master – planning of built systems on large sites, the buildings and roads can then be located at appropriate points to ensure the least ecological impact and minimal interference with the ecosystem.

Site mapping and inventory

Physical evaluation: climate, soil and plants

Ecological analysis of a locality starts with historical geology. A place can only be understood through its physical evolution. The history of mountain building and ancient seas – uplifting, folding, sinking, erosion and glaciation – explains their present form. The effects of climate and later of plants and animals interacting upon geological processes lie in the record of the rocks. Both climate and geology can be invoked to interpret physiography, the current configuration of the place. Arctic differs from tropics, desert from delta, the Himalayas from the Gangetic plain. The historical geology, climate and physiography render the water regimen comprehensible – the pattern of rivers and aquifers, their physical properties and relative abundance, oscillation between flood and drought. Rivers are young or old, and vary by orders; their patterns and distribution, as for aquifers, are directly consequential upon geology, climate and physiography.

Knowing the foregoing and the prior history of the locality's plant evolution enables us to comprehend the nature and pattern of its soils. As plants are highly selective to environmental factors, by identifying physiographic conditions, climatic zones and soils we can perceive order and predictability in the distribution of constituent plant communities. The plant communities are more sensitive to environmental variables than we can be with available data, and we can thus infer environmental factors from the presence of plants. Animals are fundamentally plant-related so that given the preceding information, with the addition of the stage of succession of the plant communities and their age, it is possible both to understand and to predict the species, abundance or scarcity of wild animal populations. If there are no acorns there will be no squirrels; an old forest will have few deer; an early succession can support many. Resources also exist where they do for good and sufficient reasons – coal, iron, limestone, productive soils, water in relative abundance, transportation routes, fall lines and the termini of water transport. The land-use map becomes comprehensible when viewed through this perspective.

The information so acquired is a gross ecological inventory and contains the data bank for all further investigations. The next task is the interpretation of these data to analyse existing and propose future, land use and management. The first objective is the inventory of unique or scarce phenomena. In this category all sites of unique scenic, geological, ecological or historical importance are located. Enlarging this category we can interpret the geological data to locate economic minerals. Geology, climate and physiography will indicate dependable water resources. Physiography will reveal slope and exposure which, with soil and water, can

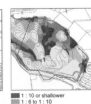

Topography

Slope analysis

■ 40
■ 50
■ 60
■ 70
■ 80

■ 1 : 10 or shallower
■ 1 : 6 to 1 : 10
■ 1 : 4 to 1 :6
□ 1 : 4 or steeper

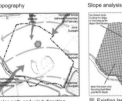

Solar path and wind direction
— Solar path
← Wind direction

Solar path and wind direction

■ Existing land clearing
░ Oil palm grid

Existing vegetation

● Ponds/lakes
∿∿ Existing boundary abutting and earthwork edge
➔ Major drainage/gulle channels
← Slope drainage runoff

Natural drainage

■ Land with relatively low gradient slope
□ Cleared land area
■ Unsuitable for development (steep contours)

Land suitability for development

✗ View extents
■ Vantage point above 60 m
■ Vantage point above 70 m

View analysis

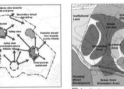

■ Academic zone
■ Residential zone
■ Recreational zone
■ Green zone

Composite Map

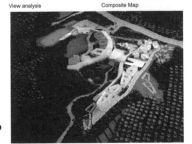

Example of the sieve-mapping technique for site planning (Nottingham University Masterplan, Kuala Lumpur)

be used to locate areas suitable for agriculture by types. The foregoing, with the addition of plant communities, will reveal intrinsic suitabilities for both forestry and re-creation. The entire body of data can be examined to reveal sites for urbanisation, industry, transportation routes and any human land-using activity. This interpretive sequence would produce a body of analytical material but the end product for a region would include a map of unique sites, the location of minerals and water resources, a slope and exposure map, a map of agricultural suitabilities by types, a similar map for forestry, and one each for re-creation and laying out the designed system.

- We need to conserve the site's topsoil. The topsoil abounds with life and is constantly changing, like all things ecological. Even a handful of soil contains innumerable termites, worms, millipedes, miniature arthropods related to crabs and spiders, bacteria and fungi. All these living systems are busy consuming nutrient materials from dead plants or animals and decomposing them into forms that can be taken up again by a new round of plants and animals and eventually returned into the soil. Water percolates through cracks, wormholes and root fissures down to the underlying permanently wet level that we call the water table.

Land use

These maps of intrinsic suitability would indicate highest and best uses for the entire study area. But this is not enough. These are single uses ascribed to discrete areas. In the forest there are likely to be dominant or codominant trees and other subordinate species. We must seek to prescribe all coexistent, compatible uses that may occupy each area. To this end it is necessary to develop a matrix in which all possible land uses are shown on each coordinate. Each is then examined against all the others to determine the degree of compatibility or incompatibility. As an example, a single area of forest may be managed for forestry, either hardwood or pulp; it may be utilised for water management objectives; it may fulfil an erosion control function; it can be managed for wildlife re-creation, and for built forms. Here we have not land use in the conventional sense but communities of land uses. The end product would be a map of present and prospective land uses, in communities of compatibilities, with dominants, codominants and subordinates derived from an understanding of nature as a process responsive to natural laws, having limiting factors, constituting a value system, and exhibiting opportunities and constraints to human use.

The above allows the designer to understand nature as a process insofar as the natural sciences permit. Second, it reveals causality. Third, it permits the designer to interpret natural processes as resources, to prescribe and even to predict for prospective land uses, not singly but in compatible communities. Finally, given information on demand and investment, the designer is enabled to produce a plan based upon natural processes.

Clearly, site inventory therefore requires more than just mapping. We need to understand the interlayer relationships as well. As we map the layers, we overlay them, assign points, evaluate the interactions in relation to our proposed land use and patterns of use of the site, and seek to produce the composite maps to help guide our site, road and drainage planning and the shaping of the built form(s).

It should be remembered that any description of these biotic and abiotic components of the site's ecosystem only serve to forecast the other functions and systems of the environment and do not constitute an exhaustive ecosystem map. A total analysis would have to look at the other subsystems as well and establish the links and interrelationships between them and the plant and animal populations.

Habitats

In understanding the ecology of the project site, we need to be aware that ecological elements can be broken down into several categories. Plant and animal species are one. Other factors are habitats and ecological processes. These elements can in turn be further specified. When the designer looks at the species present in the site, it is necessary to consider whether the following are present: rare, threatened or endangered plants or animals; game animals; migratory birds or colonies; and pestilential species (plant or animal) and/or parasites. A consideration of habitats will involve determining food chains, diversity of species and appropriate land use. The processes of the ecosystem include its productivity, hydrology and nutrient rates. There may be disagreement as to how, and even whether, one should prioritise these elements. Ultimately, this will be the designer's decision, for not even ecologists are agreed about how to protect an ecosystem from damage by humans. The approach may be total, or one might focus on preserving certain species in one's use of the site for development. The decision as to how much of the ecosystem will be conserved, and by what means, has to be taken in the context of the particular site and its unique qualities, as well as in the light of the designer's views and goals.

There are a number of other practical approaches currently adopted for studying ecosystems as the basis for planning (eg study of the trophic levels and energy flows through the ecosystem as in energetics), but we need to acknowledge that the study of ecosystems is complex and in most instances incomplete. For instance, although there have been numerous studies of the ecology of certain forests or lakes or streams, we still lack sufficient information to answer the full range of specific questions that might be asked about any given lake or forest.

In designing the pattern of the built structures, facilities and infrastructure on to the site, we need to note the following:

- As we learn more and more about a locality through obtaining ecological knowledge, we are brought face to face with the underlying paradox of our place on the earth today. We increase our understanding of the aesthetic of the intricacies, variety and complexity of life that can give endless delight, but together with this comes the desolation of seeing how grievously destructive to the web of life are our present industrial, agricultural and personal activities.

- The proposed design must respect and enhance the interconnectedness in nature (as opposed to the work of many designers who tend to think mechanistically about the natural environment). In ecology it becomes evident that all relationships are in some way reciprocal. For instance, without the carbon dioxide that we and other animals breathe out, plants, bacteria and algae could not get CO_2 from the air to build their cells and nourish themselves and other forms of life.

- The designed system must be based on an understanding of the living, natural world as an interlocking matrix of natural characteristics that the design should follow, rather than opposing the laws of life in the ecosystems. The design must ensure from the outset that our built systems are conceived, in this instance, physically, systemically and temporally to become an integrated part of the locality's ecosystem. For example, when trees are destroyed, a process called desertification begins. Trees are the main source of topsoil. Most shrubs and grasses do not have roots deep enough to work below the top metre of soil, but the deep roots of trees break up the rocks and combine minerals from the rocks with carbon from the air to feed the growth of leaves and branches. As this material falls to the ground and decomposes, it rebuilds and enriches the upper layers of soil which are vital to agriculture. It can take from 200 to 1000 years for nature to generate three centimetres of topsoil.

- In the design, achieving effective physical integration is a two-way endeavour. On the one hand, the designer needs to be fully aware of the characteristics and properties of his proposed design for built components, their systems (eg energy source, water supply, waste and sewage disposal, etc) and configuration, together with their related operational equipment (eg as in the case of an industrial facility the processes of which need to be integrated with the site's ecosystem). On the other hand, we need to ensure that the uniqueness of the ecosystem features of a specific site is mirrored by the specificity of the designed systems. A built system that works for one particular site may not be transferable to another, even if there are superficial similarities between them.

The designed system must respond to the site's ecosystems (eg its structure, processes, composition, carrying capacity, etc) before we can impose any built structures upon it. At the same time, the designer cannot view all project sites as being uniform, or as common economic commodities with uniform ecosystem features. In the same way that no two biological specimens are exactly the same, each site or location for building is ecologically heterogeneous even though some superficial similarities may appear. Every site's ecosystem has physical attributes, organisms, inorganic components and interactions that are unique. It is clear that only once the site's ecosystem, features and limitations are understood, can the designer then plan and design the built structures and systems appropriately to integrate these physically with the ecosystems.

- Prior to design, the extent and level of ecological analysis of a site depends on the complexity and state of the ecosystem (see B4). Where the design project extends beyond a single building and is to be located on highly ecologically sensitive land (ie ecologically mature land), then ecological design must be preceded by an even more thorough understanding of the ecology of the locality prior to, and as the basis for, preservation and conservation in the design and site planning process. In such ecologically sensitive localities, it may be best to avoid any interference with the ecosystem entirely.

- The ultimate but, of course, not the sole criterion of judgement of any ecological design would be the extent of its beneficial consequences and effects upon the health and further maturation of all the interdependent systems and species within the ecosystem and around the built system. For instance, this may range from earthworms aerating the soil on the building's roofs and its grounds, to the built-system users' engagement with and understanding of nature's cycles. Ecodesign can have positive consequences on a site, for instance by enhancing biodiversity (see B8).

- Starting with the surveying of the site's ecosystems and micro-climates, its geology and hydrology, and an understanding of their dynamic interdependencies, the designer integrates by design the proposed built structure and infrastructure using the data from the survey that are most beneficial for ecological health, beauty or rarity, and seeks to enhance these aspects rather than impinge upon them. Here architecture and engineering and landscape-architecture design converge as part of the design process in seeking a seamless integration of the human-made with the natural.

- Even if a site superficially appears devoid of any ecological features, it must still be evaluated in terms of its ecological components as those aspects that are not immediately visually apparent, such as the ground-water conditions, topsoil, existing vegetation and other such elements, may suffer ecological consequences arising from the intended imposition of a built system.

- The ecosystem in which the built system is located is itself made up of systems, cycles and functions that interact with each other. In a similar way, but on a larger scale, ecosystems interact with other ecosystems, generating further effects on the biosphere as a whole. Therefore the consequences of any action must be seen in the greater context of the biosphere as well.

- The design objective is to enable our designed system to achieve a symbiotic relationship with the ecosystem and to make the landscape surrounding the designed system into an intrinsic seamless part of its architecture, that is, to create 'building-as-landscape' and 'landscape-as-building'. By inventorying and studying the site's ecosystem, the designer can then take into account the external ecological interdependencies of the designed system and how they may be incorporated into the design process (see A5 for the interdependencies). This external ecological and physical context includes the ecology of the urban site as well as the ecological systems in the hinterland of the entire urban environment (see B11).

- The potential harm represented by the designed system and the tolerance level of the environment at the site (ie its carrying capacity) combine to determine the project's environmental impact. The degree of the impact will depend on a variety of factors, including the density and intensity of the activity, its duration, the strength or carrying capacity of the ecosystem involved, and the presence of other activities in the same area, which can either moderate or accentuate the effect. The ecosystem analysis of the project site provides the designer with the basis for determining the type of land use, preservation areas, conservation areas, the siting and built-form patterns and similar impacts during the life cycle of the designed system.

- The physical impact of the designed system on the site ecosystems can range from a minimal localised impact (such as the clearing of a small land area for the construction of a single house), to the total devastation of the entire land area (eg that can include the clearing of all trees and vegetation, removal and levelling of the topography, diversion of existing streams and waterways, etc). In the case of the latter, the site becomes what might be described as a totally artificial or manufactured site, one that is industrially modified into a totally human-made built environment and landscape. In such instances, the balancing of the imposed built system's biotic and abiotic components is crucial (see B7).

- The design must address the impacts on, for instance: the flora and fauna (eg biodiversity, endangered species); water (eg source, quantity, treatment and disposal); soil (eg contamination issues, removal, compaction, etc); air quality (eg the level of emissions, etc); the significance of energy used for plant operation and the transport of energy, etc (eg fuel).

- The designed system may result in what might be described as a 'manufactured site' (ie a mixed artificial–natural ecosystem or a habitat-restored ecosystem). This is not, of course, necessarily ecologically negative. It may make positive contributions and improvements to the locality's ecosystem, which may previously have been barren land of low biodiversity.

- The designed system has to be within the ecosystem's resilience or its limiting capacity if the ecosystem is to withstand the stresses that both construction and the built system impose on it. Every ecosystem has an ecological limit; if this is stressed beyond its capacity, the ecosystem becomes irreparably damaged. Every site also has its natural capital. Natural capital refers to 'a stock [of natural assets] that yields a flow of valuable goods and services into the future'. For example, a forest or a fish stock can provide a flow or harvest that is potentially sustainable year after year. The stock that produces this flow is 'natural capital' and the sustainable flow is 'natural income'. Natural capital also provides such services as waste assimilation, erosion and flood control, and protection from ultraviolet radiation (the ozone layer is a form of natural capital). These life-support services also count as natural income. Since the flow of services from ecosystems often requires that they function as intact systems, the structure and diversity of the system may be an important component of natural capital.

- In the process of design, assessing the carrying capacity is not a one-off activity but also includes assessing all inputs and outputs during the lifetime use of the designed system. We need to ascertain at the outset the relevant indicators to determine if the carrying capacity is within limits, and what might be the ecological footprint of the structure to be built, the indicators during its operation and its eventual demolition and the relocation of its content of materials and equipment.

- The site planning and design must go beyond combining and comparing site inventories, and attempt to determine the relationships between site factors and how those factors will adapt to change. Understanding these relationships further clarifies how the designed system's impacts from one area of the site may affect other areas. For example, we will frequently find that it is the location's hydrology that has been a major determinant of the shape of the land, the soils and, therefore, the plants and wildlife. By measuring water quality within the watershed, a good understanding of the functioning of the system can be derived as the basis for site planning.

- It is not only decisions about the scale and content of our urban built environment that are important; we should also examine their spatial distribution (ie their physical planning) in the ecosystems, which is crucial to creating a sustainable future. Spatial displacement through building physically destroys ecosystems. There are, furthermore, less obvious but related costs. For instance, our buildings are responsible for about 50 per cent of the total energy use in any given country, while the transport needed to get to these buildings and the provision of supplies to them from rural and outlying areas both account for another half of the remaining energy consumption. Thus, it is clear that the design of the transportation routes and patterns of vehicular and pedestrian access to any new proposed designed system and the consequences of people's vehicles and machines coming to and from the designed system, especially during its operational phase, must address the fact that these are highly energy-consuming activities. In aggregate, the urban built environment (with its complex matrix of buildings, activities, services and transportation) consumes 75 per cent of the world's energy resources and produces the vast bulk of its pollution and climate-changing gases.

- At the large-scale level, the external ecological interdependencies of the built environment (see A5) consist of the totality of all the earth's ecosystems and its resources (see B26). An awareness of the features of the ecosystems on which human activities are to be imposed provides baseline criteria for the management of the major spatial displacement brought about by building (ie including structures and infrastructures). Ecosystems provide diversity between and among the biotic communities. Natural systems, resources and reserves should be protected and managed for their long-term well-being (and ours). Some natural environments should not be developed because of their extreme fragility and designers can play a role in the safeguarding of natural places. Areas to protect include forests, storm-water storage areas, natural springs, rivers, streams, coastal waters and shorelines, recharge areas for aquifers, areas of high seasonal water table, mature vegetation, steep slopes, and wildlife and marine habitats.

- Considering some ecological features in detail, we will note, for instance, that the great value placed on watersheds comes from their ability to absorb and cleanse water, recycle excess nutrients, hold soil in place and prevent flooding. When plant cover is removed or disturbed, water and wind traversing across the land can take valuable topsoil with them, and it is a fact that soil, once exposed, is eroded at several thousand times the natural rate. Under normal conditions, each hectare of land loses somewhere between

0.004 and 0.05 tons of soil to erosion each year – far less than what is replaced by the natural soil-building process. On lands that have been logged or converted to crops and grazing, however, erosion rates are many thousands of times higher than that. The eroded soil carries nutrients, sediments and chemicals that are valuable to the system it leaves but often harmful to the ultimate destination. As a general strategy, where the impact of a designed system or an intended activity on the ecosystem could cause detrimental changes, the designer should weigh the implementation of the intended action against the prevention or corrective measures that could be incorporated into the design, as well as possible alternative design solutions. To do this adequately, a thorough understanding of the local ecosystem is crucial, as mentioned earlier.

- The impacts of all the interdependencies of the built environment on the earth's ecology and resources (L22 in the Partitioned Matrix) are vital considerations in the design process. The actions of the intended designed system on the site can have profound effects. For instance, deforestation (eg for timber harvesting and for urban development) contributes 15 per cent to global warming. The provision of inputs in the creation of a built system, the emission of outputs from a built system and the operational activities within a built system after it is constructed all have effects on the components and the airborne and waterborne processes of the ecosystems. Impacts must be considered over the life cycle of the designed system and should include local, regional and global effects. Clearly, an awareness of these effects at the onset of the design process would facilitate future computation of the ecological consequences of other intended built structures, as well as providing a basis for minimising undesirable future changes to the ecological environment of the locality of the project site. Observation of the site will reveal to the designer important physical features, such as the pattern of natural drainage, significant landforms, vegetation, and climatic conditions. In the case of urban centres, where most intensive buildings are located, we need also to mitigate the urban heat-island effect by increasing the volume of organic matter in the urban environment, eg through landscaping (see B9). Some of the ways to do this are by selective distribution of vegetation, revision of the layout of city blocks, choice of building configuration (size and clustering), the colour of roofs, surfaces and buildings, and the properties of surface materials (eg their reflectance, heat absorption and build-up consequences, etc) (see B9).

- We should acknowledge that these external interdependencies (L22) include global interdependencies of ecosystem processes and resources. The built environment is dependent on its external environment as a supplier of energy and material resources for its physical form and substance, as well as for maintenance of its operations. If the long-term supply of these resources is to be ensured, then a conservation approach to their use should be a design criterion. Immediate design objectives should be to provide potential for and flexibility in future resource use. The ecosystems of the project site can also serve as a limiting sink to assimilate the discharges from the designed system. As we have seen, the capacity for assimilation by the ecosystem is limited, and if the threshold is exceeded, the ecosystem will deteriorate.

- Biodiversity as a key method for comparing impacts is often held to be the broad foundation for assessing sustainability. It is necessary for the designer to understand the various types of biodiversity. Biological diversity means 'the variability among living organisms from all sources including inter alia, terrestrial, marine and other aquatic ecosystems and the ecological complexes of which they are part; this includes diversity within species, between species and the ecosystems' (in the (CBD) Convention on Biological Diversity). Simply stated, this term describes the diversity of living things including plants, animals and micro-organisms (species). It also refers to the diversity of their living places (habitats) and of the function performed in those places (riches). The concept also relates to the diversity of genetic material (genes) carried by the organisms. It is necessary for the ecological designer to be aware of each of these aspects of biodiversity so that his or her design is sensitive to biodiversity sustenance in securing a sustainable future for the natural environment and for human society.

An accurate, objective measure for biodiversity is assessing genetic diversity because this reflects the increasing phylogenetic divergence of the organisms present at any particular site. However, this method is deemed impractical and unrealistic. Counting species is by far the easier and the commonest approach among scientists. Counting species, however, does not often describe some of the subtleties of nature. For instance, all species, by their presence or absence, do not contribute equally to biological diversity. One approach is the concept of structural and interstitial species: structural species are those key species that determine the physical structure of ecosystems and influence the environment for the many other generally smaller, interstitial organisms (eg if an oak tree is present at a site, then a whole subset of fauna and flora will also be present). The implication is that not all species are of equal weight in their importance to biological diversity.

Biodiversity can be considered at four levels:

- species diversity;
- habitat diversity;
- niche diversity; and
- genetic diversity (within individual species).

The number of individual species in an area is sometimes called species richness. Ecosystems vary in richness. Examples of species-rich ecosystems are rainforests and coral reefs; species-poor ecosystems are alpine areas, deserts and most designed environments. There are also variations in how evenly/equitably the numbers of individuals within species are distributed. For example, there could be small numbers of many species as in a tropical forest, or large numbers of a few species as found in a eucalypt forest, an estuary or a designed landscape. Scientists have identified some 1.8 million species of living organisms. They estimate, however, that there are somewhere between 10 million and 100 million species, suggesting that our knowledge of the earth's biodiversity (particularly of insects and microscopic life forms) is still extremely limited.

There is no simple rule of thumb for the relationship of species diversity to stability. However, species loss can be catastrophic for both species-poor and species-rich ecosystems.

The term habitat diversity describes the number of different physical environments, or micro-climates, each with its own range of organisms, that occur within an ecosystem. Examples are snowfields and stream margins in an alpine area, or tree tops and forest floor in a eucalypt forest. The overall biodiversity of an area can be a result of great habitat diversity. Examples of low habitat diversity are grasslands, tidal flats, oceans and most designed landscapes. In evaluating the consequences of human intervention on ecosystems, the designer needs to be aware that habitat loss can have a more significant effect on biodiversity than species loss because new species can migrate into an area but habitats cannot repair themselves. Habitat preservation is more important than species conservation.

Niche diversity describes the variety of relationships that can occur between organisms and their habitat. Species specialise and adapt to specific conditions, which may involve exclusive relationships with other species, and the avoidance of competition for space and resources. For example, there are plants which can be pollinated by both bats and birds; bats and birds avoid competition by having different nesting sites, and visit the same plant species. Some habitats have high niche differentiation (eg eucalypt forests, semi-arid areas or coastal scrubs).

Niche diversity is related to both species and habitat diversity. In imposing a human intervention on to an ecosystem the designer needs to be aware that loss of habitat results

Group	Described species	Estimated species	Percentage of total already described
Micro-organisms			
Bacteria	30,000	2,500,000	0.1
Plants			
Algae	40,000	350,000	11
Bryophytes	17,000	25,000	68
Vascular plants	220,000	270,000	81
Fungi (including lichens)	69,000	1,500,000	5
Animals			
Nematodes	15,000	500,000	3
Arthropods	80,000	6,000,000	13
Fish	22,500	35,000	64
Birds	9040	9100	99
Mammals	4000	402	>99

The species diversity of a stated group at a particular place and time is termed alpha diversity. All species richness of a sample may be expressed by a diversity index, which is dependent on sample size.

One such index is Williams' alpha, derived from the equation:

$$\alpha = S/\log_e (1 + N/\alpha)$$

where N is the number of individuals and S the number of species in the sample, α is alpha

•• Estimates of global biodiversity and alpha diversity

in decreased niche diversity, which is evidenced by loss of species diversity. Grazing and mowing the undergrowth of forests reduce both niche and species diversity. Niches may then be occupied by less well-adapted species, such as feral animals and plants, which in turn may displace more indigenous species and destabilise the ecosystem.

Genetic diversity is the 'gene pool', and refers to the totality of all the genes in an ecosystem. It is a generally abstract term. However, it has the desirable quality of making us aware of the necessity to conserve and protect the information contained in the ecosystem and to realise that each species is precious, even spiders, fungi and bacteria, for the irreplaceable genetic resource that it contains.

It can be argued that it is important to maintain the diversity and abundance of plant life even if it is not required immediately for human needs. Only 12,000 of the 220,000 flowering plants that grow on the planet are utilised by humans, and of these only 150 are grown commercially. Of that 150, however, three species (wheat, rice and maize) provide 60 per cent of our global food requirements. The species diversity of a stated group at a particular place and time is termed 'alpha diversity'. When all the species cannot be accommodated for practical reasons, the species richness of a sample may be expressed by a diversity index, which is independent of sample size. One such index is Williams' alpha diversity index.

In designing for the conservation and sustainable use of biodiversity, the designer may choose to adopt an approach that conserves the site's ecosystem structure and functioning by its preservation. The rationale is that an ecosystem's functioning and resilience depend on a dynamic relationship within species, among species, and between species and their abiotic environment. The preservation of these interactions and processes is of greater significance for the long-term maintenance of biological diversity than the simple protection of species.

This approach has been reflected in recent global conservation practices where there has been a shift in emphasis from species conservation to ecosystem conservation. This shift was brought about by the simple observation that the cause of decline of species numbers is the loss of ecosystem integrity. Fluctuations in species numbers as well as the absence or presence of a species are normal within ecosystems; this is part of the dynamics of the larger system. At the core, and much more valuable to strive for in conservation management, is the constant functioning and resilience of whole ecosystems.

An awareness of the significance of the different aspects of biodiversity for key ecosystem attributes means that the designer should be able to focus on these. However, achieving this level of knowledge is a difficult task. The correlations between species and environmental attributes that scientists have found are too many and, often, found to be contradictory according to other ecologists.

Generally, species biodiversity increases towards the equator and declines with altitude because the majority of plant species are not cold-tolerant. Plant communities provide habitats for animal species. There are exceptions to this, of course – species of coastal sea birds increase away from the equator, for example.

The primary productivity of vegetation is positively correlated with plant species. This accounts for increased animal species as well. On the other hand, the artificial addition of nutrients, such as fertiliser, to some plant communities can decrease diversity, by allowing only those species either adapted to or able to tolerate high nutrient levels to thrive over other species.

The other obvious aspect of biodiversity is that it is changing all the time. It varies continuously on many different time scales linked to the generation times of the species under consideration, the seasonal aspects of lifecycle, longer-term successional processes and, finally, at evolutionary rates of change.

At the core of conserving biodiversity is the issue of land use by humans. Decisions about land use and the imposition of built development are inextricably linked to the issues of human tenure and resource valuation.

We can organise biodiversity on three levels. At the top are the ecosystems, such as rainforests, coral reefs and lakes. Next are species, composed of the organisms in the ecosystems, from algae and swallowtail butterflies to moray eels and people. At the bottom are the various genes making up the heredity of the individuals that compose each of the species. Each species is bound to its community in the unique manner by which it variously consumes, is consumed, competes and cooperates with other species. It also indirectly affects the community in the way it alters the soil, water and air. The ecologist sees the whole as a network of energy and material continuously flowing into the community from the surrounding physical environment, and back out, and then on round to create the perpetual ecosystem cycle on which our own existence is based.

Generally stated, the designer must ensure that the site's ecosystems are kept stable in part by the principle of maintaining biodiversity. If a species from the habitat disappears from a community, its niche will be more quickly and effectively filled by another species if there are many candidates for the role (in instances where there is high biodiversity) rather than few (ie on sites with low or reduced biodiversity).

It is difficult to predict the full future value of any kind of animal, plant or micro-organism. Its potential is spread across a spectrum of known and as yet unimagined human needs.

Our principal concern in ecodesign is the accelerating extinction of natural ecosystems and species as the consequence of our designed system. The damage already done cannot be repaired within any period of time that has meaning for the human mind. Fossil records show that new faunas and floras took millions of years to evolve to the richness of the pre-human world.

The threshold of tolerance of the ecosystem of the site is a key benchmark for the designer because it establishes the level of impacts that the ecosystem is able to adapt to and recover from. Design must recognise fundamental conservation theory, which supports the idea that there are irreplaceable elements in a mature, biologically diverse ecosystem whose importance must be seen in terms of their contribution to the stability of the biosphere over the long term.

The designer must ensure that action on any habitat does not result in a decrease in biodiversity and that all possible opportunities to restore and increase biodiversity are taken. Some of the actions to take to increase biodiversity in the design and planning of the built structures are as follows:

Activities that reduce biodiversity	Actions that increase biodiversity
Site works:	
• Clearing	Limit and restrict cleared areas and regard uncleared areas as a resource
• Grading	Accept greater limitations; retain/stockpile materials
• Tidying	Accept and design for greater diversity; resist interference
• Draining	Accept higher constraints; design for on-site water use
• Paving	Reduce hard surfaces to a minimum; use porous surfaces
• Excavating	Accept slope constraints; excavate only when essential
Building process:	
• Waste	Site sanitation: restrict waste to specific locations
• Pollution	Confine mixing eg lime and cement and washing of sites; regenerate on completion
• Compaction	Reduce and restrict heavy activities; regenerate sites

- Parking   Confine construction-personnel parking to off-site areas

- Contamination   Confine movements on site to designated areas; regenerate

- Indiscriminate damage   Supervise for minimum disturbance; fence off-limits areas

Design features of the built structure, facility or infrastructure

- Excessive site   Reduce footprint; consider going up; reduce internal circulation
  coverage   space; level space for wildlife movements

- Excessive bulk   Increase external circulation space; consider integrating indoor–
  outdoor spaces with habitats for wildlife

- Overshadowing   Orient and design to give solar access to surrounding areas as well
  as other built forms

- Wind effects   Design to avoid excessive wind speeds and turbulence in natural
  areas; avoid making wildlife corridors into wind tunnels

- Location of glass   Site glazed areas so as to avoid migration routes and flight paths
  surface   of birds; evaluate paths as part of site appraisal

- Obstruction of flora   Site and design to allow natural movement of animals, plants and
  and fauna   processes such as shifting fauna movements and water to pass
  under buildings where practically possible

- Excessive hard   Reduce hard surfaces to practical minimum; utilise porous
  surface   surfaces; use runoff water on site to re-create habitats

- Fauna-unfriendly   Use textured and natural materials where possible to provide
  surface   habitat for insects and thus food for birds and lizards

Materials and systems for the built system and landscape

- Polluting and space   Consider prefabrication of components off site
  intensive

- From industries   Consider alternative materials and suppliers
  which reduce
  biodiversity

- From locations   Consider alternative materials and suppliers
  where biodiversity
  is threatened

- Toxic outputs or
  – leachates   Use alternative materials

- Natural materials   Use more durable alternatives provided they are from sustainable
  with short life-   sources
  spans

- From unsustainable   Use alternative materials that preserve biodiversity
  sources

- Rare or threatened   Use only if available from sustainable sources, such as nurseries, or use
  sources   more common species

Landscape design

- Hard, formal   Consider using soft materials and designing for habitat
  schemes

- Excessive lawn and   Consider reducing monoculture and increasing diversity
  paving

- Water features   Consider creating water bodies with habitat; use water features
                       to detain storm runoff

- Low species diversity Consider schemes of higher species diversity and with a greater range
                       of plant forms, which can provide habitat diversity and enhance the
                       connectivity of habitats

Plant materials

- Rare or threatened   Preserve rare species so biodiversity can recover, provided they
  species   can be obtained sustainably

- From existing natural Use alternative materials or use materials from sustainable locations or
  landscapes   nurseries

- No habitat value   Consider using species with habitat value for indigenous wildlife

- Habitat for   Consider alternative indigenous species to provide refuge for native
  non-native species   wildlife

- Species with the   Use alternative species which are not invasive, and promote
  potential to become   their use
  pests

• Non-indigenous native species	Consider the use of alternative indigenous species so as to avoid the genetic pollution of surrounding areas by pollen

Landscape maintenance

• Mowing	Consider low-maintenance diverse landscapes instead
• Burning	Use appropriate-intensity, infrequent fires where possible and without endangering existent environments
• Herbicides/pesticides	Design for low maintenance and substitute labour
• Fertilisers	Use natural products and composts where necessary
• Animals	Recommend against feral pets or design effective containment away from wildlife habitat

The built form's presence also physically affects the environment around it. The other artefacts of our built environment, such as all those loose items that are part of our everyday lives, also use up space for their use and storage and eventual deposition at the end of their useful life (see B2). Their physical presence both on the ground plane and spatially has impacts on the ecosystems upon which they are located. The first step in ecological design is therefore to integrate the built environment's physical placement and built form on the ground with the ecosystems on which it is located. In the same way that a prosthetic device, such as an artificial arm or leg, must integrate physically with the human body to which it is attached, so the built environment must integrate physically with the host organism to which it is attached – in this case the ecosystems in the natural environment (see C3). The design objective, then, is to achieve as high a level of benign integration as appropriate for that ecosystem. This is the key challenge for ecological designers.

Unfortunately, the current state of site analysis by designers does not address these issues. At present, a designer generally looks only at the physical features of the site that the proposed designed system will occupy. This form of site analysis gives the designer a basis for determining the best location for the structures, creating the layout, making provision for vehicular access, and other aspects of the design such as shape and height. Ecological design, however, goes beyond these physical features of the site to include biological criteria and a knowledge of the surrounding ecosystem and its processes. The designer will have to understand and master these aspects of the proposed site to determine what type of built structure, facility or infrastructure could be allowed in that ecosystem by the criteria of sustainable development and 'green' design principles. To create a symbiosis between the designed and natural systems is the designer's task; on a physical level, the designed system's systemic features, processes and functioning have to be integrated with those of the ecosystem to avoid undesirable or destructive impacts as a result of human intervention in the natural environment.

As mentioned earlier, this is not just a once-only consideration but the physical consequences must encompass the designed system's entire life cycle. It starts from the time that any item used in the built environment is extracted, transported, manufactured, fabricated and used in the human-made environment until its eventual disposal and relocation or reintegration.

This is similarly the case for the design of products and artefacts (eg items for office, commercial, household and personal use, cars, etc) that are not site specific. Their integration should take account of their production, their use (which may physically displace an ecosystem) and what happens to them at the end of their useful life where they need to be either reused, remanufactured, recycled or benignly returned into the environment as part of the cyclic processes in the natural environment (see B2).

Spatially, a built system (ie a building or series of buildings or an engineering structure or infrastructure) will by its physical presence alone spatially displace the environment upon which it is located. The very construction and imposition of its physical presence on the site affects and changes the ecosystem processes and composition. Its configuration and structure, siting, layout, construction and eventual demolition are all aspects of its physical presence, which must be integrated in totality with the locality's ecosystem. All these aspects, therefore, have to be evaluated in terms of their effects on the corresponding natural systems embodied in the environment, including spatial pattern and functioning. It is the responsibility of the designer to make certain that the existing ecosystem survives the introduction of the foreign mass of the built system intact, and that no part of the ecosystem is irrevocably damaged or destroyed.

As discussed earlier, following an inventory of the project site's ecosystem, we can then carry out an interlayer analysis to prepare a composite map of the site, which the designer can then use for site planning and design. In the case of already existing, devastated, partially devastated and urban sites, we may next need to define the boundaries of the proposed urban ecosystem to be re-established and made whole (see B6). As a general strategy, we should build on a minimum footprint and leave large portions of the site area undisturbed or for vegetation.

Summary

Following on from the preliminary assessment of the project site's ecological history, for those sites within this taxonomy that are identified as ecologically sensitive or potentially ecologically sensitive, the designer must next inventory and model the locality's ecosystems to ascertain the site's resilience and carrying capacity in response to the imposition of new built forms, facilities, infrastructures and human activities upon the site's ecosystems. This procedure may consist of preparing a composite map of permissible interventions whereby the natural patterns for those ecosystems are delineated and so provide the basis for mapping the areas that may permit appropriate human activity or built forms. The mapping of areas that may permit such intervention then serves to influence and indicate the range of built configurations, their extent and the shaping of the built structures. These should be taken into account in layout planning together with the surface-water management and natural drainage for the territory (see also B19). The layout of the infrastructures and the systems to be used must be organised so that they integrate physically with the existent forms, patterns and processes of the physical and ecological characteristics of the locality's ecosystems. The inventory, modelling and mapping will also provide the basis for the design of the systemic operations of the designed system to biointegrate benignly with the ecosystems of the site without environmental impairment. However, once this inventory and ecological model have been completed, the designer will need to further continue to monitor the effects of the design on the ecosystems, and any changes occurring over the lifetime of the designed system as a consequence of its operation and its after-life (eg its eventual removal and disposal).

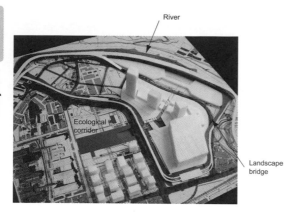

River

Ecological corridor

Landscape bridge

Aerial view of site

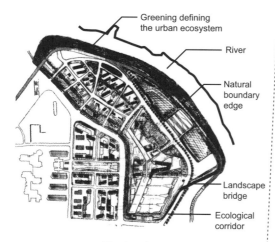

Greening defining the urban ecosystem

River

Natural boundary edge

Landscape bridge

Ecological corridor

Masterplan

Delineation of the boundaries of the urban ecosystem as the basic for ecodesign

B6 Delineate the designed system's boundary as a human-made or composite ecosystem in relation to the site's ecosystem: establishing the general extent for ecosystem and biodiversity enhancement

For site-related (ie non-product) design assignments, it may be useful for design purposes (depending on the geography of the site's ecological and natural features) to delineate the designed system's boundary as a human-made or composite ecosystem, emphasise the natural boundaries and define what might be the natural extent of the ecosystem or boundary conditions within which our designed system is to be located. These are not boundaries of separation but boundaries of identity. We need to recognise the importance of ecotones, or boundaries between discrete ecological communities, as zones for transfer of nutrients, sediments and energy, and ecological processes. A primary role of the management of urban biodiversity is to delineate boundaries or ecotones between discrete natural subsystems.

These are easier to delineate on sites that are bounded by natural features (eg coastal or riverine ecosystems). This delineation of the general boundary conditions can be useful because it provides the designer with an areal basis for subsequent ecological repair and restoration, particularly in locations where that ecosystem has been significantly disturbed by previous human intervention. It also provides the areal basis for biodiversity enhancement and integration by design. This may be difficult or arbitrary to delineate in urban sites surrounded by human-made structures. System theory defines a system boundary as a physical or conceptual boundary that contains all the system's (ie ecosystems) essential elements and effectively and completely isolates the system from its external environment except for inputs and outputs that are allowed to move across the system boundary. A key aspect to ecological site planning is the managing of storm-water and surface-water drainage. In undulating terrain, the natural drainage patterns and watershed can also be useful in delineating the designed system's boundary.

We must be clear that the inventory and mapping of ecosystem properties, etc (in B5), do not automatically result in a design by giving indications of patterns for the site design and planning. Viable ecodesign begins with study and analysis. This process does not immediately lead to active form-making that is central to landscape planning. Reams of ecosystem analysis and overlays will establish the parameters for ecological planning but they will hardly provide the design. The designer will first need to delineate the general natural boundary conditions of the ecosystem within which he is working (if the site is a large site) according to types of living species, watersheds, winds, drainage patterns, geographic and geological features and climates, and/or define the ecological zones that either are to be created or that need to have their habitat restored. In defining the natural limits and boundaries of the site, the designer is effectively defining the ecosystem and setting out the creation of specific habitats for its components and the human-made built facilities that might be integrated as human-made ecosystems (see A4 ecomimicry), and bearing in mind the location of potential green ways (landscaped bridges). At the same time, the designer can seek to restore degraded areas. In delineating such boundaries, the designer can follow the three basic modes of ecosystemic order, as found in natural landscapes, that combine to generate form, particularly where the natural landscape is the direct expression of its structural, functional and locational order as they exist at that particular moment.

Planning for biointegration

The designer can adopt, but not be limited by, the following key planning principles:

- Plan, manage and integrate the human-made vehicular and urban transportation system, network and infrastructure routes in a pattern that will minimise any divisive routes traversing across ecologically sensitive sites and avoid fragmentation of the existing ecosystems, which would create isolated island habitats, while at the same time shaping the routes and landscape to seek continuity of vegetation patterns from within the defined area to outside it.

- In defining the general boundaries, the designer must preserve the existent ecological continuity in the landscape or use opportunities in the landforms to create new ecological corridors with landscape bridges, etc.

- The design delineation may accentuate a memorable site feature, unusual rock formation and topographic configuration or a spectacular vista, etc, while still respecting the site's ecological functions. Here the ecological method is used to perceive natural form in the landscape.

- At the same time the designer must encourage and adopt those transportation systems and patterns that minimise the use of fossil fuels and the pollution from them as well as reducing greenhouse gas emissions.

- The design must identify and retain the existing natural ecosystems within intended and existent urban areas and protect the integrity of the locality's natural environment and ecological linkages.

- The design must also limit the amount of sewerage emissions and other outputs, such as waste generated for disposal off site.

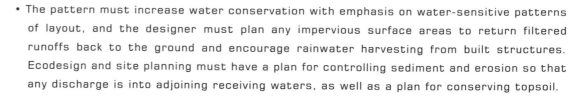

- The pattern must increase water conservation with emphasis on water-sensitive patterns of layout, and the designer must plan any impervious surface areas to return filtered runoffs back to the ground and encourage rainwater harvesting from built structures. Ecodesign and site planning must have a plan for controlling sediment and erosion so that any discharge is into adjoining receiving waters, as well as a plan for conserving topsoil.

- The landscape design must control noise emissions to achieve reasonable levels near human users and ecologically sensitive areas.

- The designer must assess the designed energy system to be adopted and its management.

- The designer must at the outset assess the entire human-made built ecosystem's input and output of materials for their environmental consequences.

- All the construction and demolition activities must be managed in order to minimise their effects on the ecological systems.

Summary

Our designed system cannot be designed in isolation, for instance as an autonomous system or organism, since no living system on earth can exist without connectivity to all the processes and functions of the biosphere. The designer must at the outset delineate as far as possible the general extent of the designed ecosystem's natural boundary in relation to the natural features and patterns of the locality, which then defines the geographical and areal form of the designed system. Having done so, the designer can next seek to design to enhance the designed system's ecological integration, connectivity, biodiversity, functions and processes in designing its ecological future.

B7 Design to balance the biotic and abiotic components of the designed system: integrating the designed system's inorganic mass vertically and horizontally with biomass and designing for the rehabilitation of degraded ecosystems

It is crucial that at the outset of the design process, the ecodesigner counterbalances the increasing artificiality and inorganicness of our human-made built environment. Essentially, in any ecodesign the designer must balance the designed system's inorganic content with its organic content. We should also endeavour to make the new designed system contribute positively to the ecosystem of the locality, as opposed to continuing to impose new inorganic and, in many instances, inert matter in the form of built structures and infrastructures on to the ecosystems and so cause further environmental impairment. This process is crucial for ecological designers to reverse the current trend of increasing the biosphere's artificiality as a consequence of humankind's continued extensive building and manufacturing activities. This counterbalancing also contributes to the creation of urban habitats and the rehabilitation of devastated habitats.

It is vital that we recognise that our existent built environment, which consists predominantly of our built structures, facilities and infrastructures, is essentially inorganic in content and by design with virtually zero biomass. In contrast, ecosystems have a balanced content of biomass consisting of the total mass of all living organisms (producers, consumers and decomposers) present. It should be obvious that if humankind continues to build extensively in this way and as our society is currently doing, and if in the continued process of doing this we do not balance the abiotic and inorganic components of our built structures with the biotic, then we are simply making the biosphere increasingly impervious, inert, inorganic and artificial. As humans spread out and appropriate more and more of the natural landscape for their needs, less and less land area becomes available for natural habitats. Trees and shrubby forests still cover about 40 per cent of the world's landmass, but that amount is rapidly shrinking, and the quality of that cover has declined. This endangers species large and small, pushing them to the brink of, and into, extinction. It is this trend that ecodesign must seek to reverse at every opportunity.

Biomass

In any ecodesign endeavour, the designer must set out by design systemically to balance the inorganic content of our designed system with equivalent (if economically permissible) organic and biotic components, or biomass, with the objective of creating a human-made built environment that functions as a built ecosystem. Biomass is the total mass of all

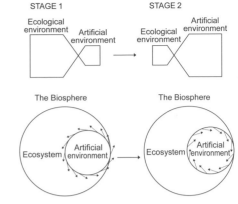

The present human-made environment has changed from being a contained system to the containing system where the biosphere becomes increasingly saturated with human-made elements.

Biosphere saturation with human-made artefacts: at least 15% of the biosphere land surfaces has been urbanised

Existing built environment mostly physical (abiotic) constituents

... where are the biological (biotic) constituents?

Design must balance the inorganic with the organic content

Sky courts detail (in Elephant and Castle Eco Tower, London)

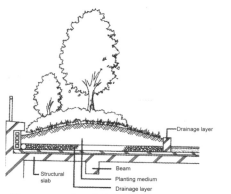

Sky courts detail (in Elephant and Case Eco Tower, London)

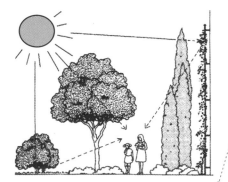

Use of vegetation for shading surfaces

living organisms (producers, consumers and decomposers) or of a particular set (eg species) present in an ecosystem or at a particular trophic level in a food chain, and it is this vital aspect that we must reintroduce into our built environment. Ecodesign must seek the integration of the built form and infrastructures with their context, using the elements of the earth and vegetation in such a way that the built environment appears to be part of the natural environment, as if it too grows from nature.

Plants as part of the biomass contribute to the environment in the following ways: produce oxygen and absorb carbon dioxide through photosynthesis; control water flow and filter water; cool and filter the air and form still air pockets; hold soil; produce food in the ecosystem; produce fibre; produce energy; provide food enclosure and cover for wildlife. It is these functions that we need to reintroduce into our built environment to produce human-made ecosystems. Plants are an important part of the cycle that maintains a healthy atmosphere. When animals breathe, they take oxygen out of the air to oxygenate their blood and digest their food. They exhale air with higher levels of carbon dioxide and release excess carbon produced by their metabolic processes. For plants the process operates in reverse. Plants absorb carbon dioxide and release purified oxygen into the air. Plants use the carbon from the air to combine with minerals gathered by their roots. The increase of vegetated areas and enhancement of biodiversity counteracts the effects of the degradation of land and therefore increases the land area available for photosynthesis, which creates the basic food supply for life. The biological importance of maintaining biodiversity and preserving habitats has been demonstrated by numerous ecological studies. Generally, the more species an ecosystem has, the more efficient it is. We might contend that the loss of biodiversity constitutes a planetary peril rather than just another episode in the evolutionary process or a chapter in the history of life.

Increasing the biomass through planting trees, for example, will not only moderate and reduce the heat-island effect in that urban locality (see B9), but the trees will also help ward off global warming by absorbing carbon dioxide from the air and at the same time giving off oxygen. Depending on the maturity and type of forest cover, 1 hectare of forest can absorb up to 16.3 tons of carbon dioxide per year. The thermal insulation provided by a green roof enhances internal energy efficiency (eg reducing the energy consumption in the heating and cooling systems). This not only reduces overall energy consumption but also lowers greenhouse gas emissions. The designer can compensate for the CO_2 emissions by the introduction of additional biomass into the designed system through the concurrent planting of compensating hectares of trees and the preservation of the appropriate extent hectares of trees. A single tree (10 metres high with a 6-metre crown) is estimated to be able to absorb 160 kilograms of CO_2 per annum.

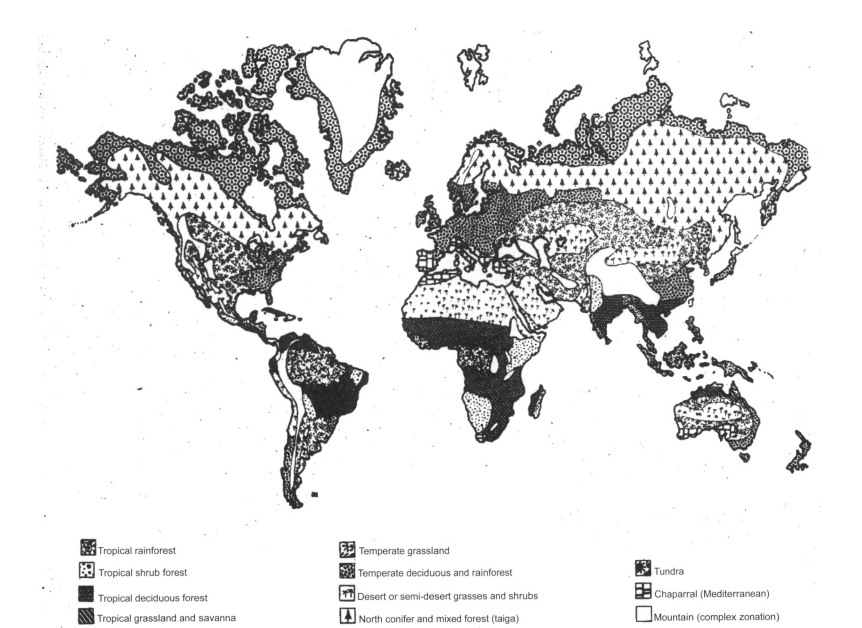

Tropical rainforest

Tropical shrub forest

Tropical deciduous forest

Tropical grassland and savanna

Temperate grassland

Temperate deciduous and rainforest

Desert or semi-desert grasses and shrubs

North conifer and mixed forest (taiga)

Tundra

Chaparral (Mediterranean)

Mountain (complex zonation)

Major biomes of the world

Roles of Plants Dominant trees, shrubs and groundcovers	Ecological control							Production			Wildlife	
	Oxygen/carbon dioxide	Filters air	Controls water flow	Filters water	Cools water	Forms still air pockets	Holds soil	Food	Fibre	Energy	Food	Cover
Pinus pinea	●	●	○	○	○		○			○	○	○
Sophora	○	○	○	○	●	●	○			○		○
Ginkgo biloba	●	●	●	○	○	○	○					○
Acacia			○	○	○							○
Avocado (Persea)	●	●	●	○	○		○	○	●		●	○
Citrus spp.	○	○	○	○	○		○	●			●	○
Arbutus unedo	○	○	○	○	○	○	○				○	○
Cassia artemisioides							○					
Cistus spp.			○	○			○					○
Carissa grandiflora			○	○	○		○	○			●	○
Heteromeles arbutifolia	○	○	○	○			○					
Rhus integrifolia	○	○	○	○			○				○	●
Yucca whipplei										○		○
Romneya coulteri				○								○
Baccharis pilularis				○			●					
Rosmarinus officinalis			○				○	●				
Gazania spp.				○								○
Strawberries			○				○	●			○	
Vegetables								●	●			
Herbs								●				

● Major

○ Significant

Example of roles of plants ●- - - - -

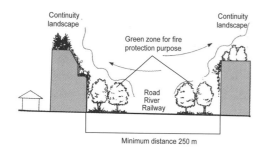

Continuity landscape

Green zone for fire protection purpose

Continuity landscape

Road River Railway

Minimum distance 250 m

Use of vegetation for fire protection

Putting plants into the built environment, including the planting of trees, is also crucial for global carbon sequestration, which is the permanent removal of carbon dioxide gas from the atmosphere so that it no longer contributes to the greenhouse effect. Trees and other plants and organisms absorb carbon dioxide from the atmosphere to increase their molecular structure. Such biological sequestration can also be achieved by reforestation to create 'carbon reservoirs'.

Vegetation can reduce the amount of direct sunlight that strikes and heats up a built form's surfaces. It can also prevent reflected light from carrying heat into a building from the ground or other surfaces. Landscape can be used to create different airflow patterns and can be used to direct or divert the wind advantageously by causing a pressure difference. Studies show that the ambient air temperature under a tree adjacent to a wall is about 2°C to 5°C lower than for an unshaded area.

Vegetation and forested land

The role of vegetation and forested land (eg, trees, shrubs and ground cover, etc) in the global carbon balance is as follows:

• Carbon reservoirs:

Global forests contain around four-fifths of the carbon stored in land vegetation. Of this total, about 60 per cent is held in tropical forests with the rest divided between temperate and boreal forests, mainly in the higher latitudes of the northern hemisphere.

• Carbon sinks:

Forests, soils and other vegetation currently absorb about 40 per cent of emissions from the built environment. There are two reasons for this. First, forests and soils are recovering naturally from past damage, and vegetation is regrowing and absorbing carbon dioxide. Second, there has been a global acceleration of photosynthesis (which governs the rate at which plants absorb carbon dioxide from the atmosphere) due to increasing levels of carbon dioxide in the atmosphere and, in some areas, nitrogen deposition. But as temperatures rise further, carbon uptake will be reduced, offsetting this trend.

• Sources of greenhouse gases:

Deforestation mainly in tropical regions and changes in land use cause approximately one-fifth of global warming.

Planting trees to offset carbon dioxide emissions requires long-term commitment. A tree plantation will absorb carbon dioxide as the trees grow, but eventually the growth rate and absorption of carbon dioxide slow until, in a fully mature plantation, the rate of tree growth and carbon sequestration are close to zero. Old trees die and release their carbon back into the atmosphere as carbon dioxide, while young trees grow and absorb carbon in roughly equal measure. If the sequestration benefit is to be maintained (for ever), there are three options. First, the mature plantation can be kept alive indefinitely and protected from fire and pest attack. Second, it can be harvested but the harvested material must be stored away from the atmosphere in perpetuity, for example by incorporating it in building construction. Third, the plantation can be harvested and the plant material burnt as an alternative to fossil fuels. These are stringent conditions.

We can define the 'biomass of the earth' as the total weight of the living things on it and above it in the atmosphere. Currently, studies estimate the earth's biomass to be about 75,000 million tons. This includes about 250 million tons of human biomass, about 100 million tons of other animal biomass, of which more than half is fish and about 10,000 tons of land plants.

These figures show that there is a predominance of plant biomass over animal biomass. Animals total around 2 to 3 per cent of the total plant biomass. As a single species, humans account for more than 10 per cent of the animal biomass, even though there are tens of thousands of animal species. Without the need to consider future disproportionate increases in human biomass (with birth rates increasing at an exponential rate), the above information provides the general basis for balancing the biomass in our designed systems. In so doing, the designer might be regarded as putting the wilderness back into the built environment.

Designing biomass to built systems

It is contended that there are essentially three basic strategies for designing plant and non-human biomass spatially into built systems: juxtapositioning; intermixing; and integrating. Juxtapositioning is the concentrated placement of greening material at one or a few locations in the built form. Intermixing is the distributed and patchy placement of greening material. Integrating consists of a woven blending of the greening material with the built form. The latter is preferred as the greening material is linked to the existent vegetation at the ground plane and enables species interaction and migration, thereby engendering a more diverse and stable ecosystem.

First, we can put all the greenery into one densely planted location in the built form. Second, we can have a scattered pattern of vegetated areas spotted over the built form, such as a series of greening troughs or sky courts. Third, we can have a more integrative relationship where a spiralling placement of vegetation is interwoven with the built form's inorganic mass as a single human-made vertical ecosystem, ie a linked nexus with the site's ecosystem horizontally at the ground plane.

Ecologically the preferred pattern is obviously the last, a spiralling continuous green biomass, as this provides greater opportunities for species interaction and migration, and in doing so

Juxtapositioning

Intermixing

Integrating

Designing plants and non-human biomass into built systems

Examples of continuous vertical landscaping

engenders a much more diversified ecosystem. A more diverse ecosystem is generally thought to function as a much more stable ecosystem and so require less external maintenance.

In parallel with the above architectural examples, the equivalent horizontal patterns for planning would, first, be the equivalent of the provision of a dense large central park in the city with all the greenery placed in one location (eg as in Central Park, New York). Second, we can disperse the greenery into a series of green 'squares' (eg such as those found in the squares of Georgian London). Finally, we can have a series of intertwining linked green 'corridors'. In the last pattern the green corridors, or ecological corridors, can extend to have secondary green fingers that can eventually link together to form a network of green corridors in the cityscape. Obviously, the linked pattern is to be preferred.

These two sets of patterns (those introduced vertically in the built form and horizontally in the planning patterns) can become the guiding patterns for the designer in integrating biomass with built form and built environment (eg for architectural design and master-planning work).

Biomass can be brought continuously upwards starting with a linked densely green zone at the ground plane, then climbing up diagonally along the facade of the built form using a series of stepped planters. Taking the example of a high-rise built form, at mid-level the biomass can traverse a mid-level transfer floor and then turn again diagonally up the high-rise form at its other side, ascending straight up to the rooftop. The connectivity (as against fragmentation) in the biomass ensures the maintenance of biodiversity (see above).

Starting from the ground plane, the series of linked stepped planting zones thus form a general nexus that links the greenery across the built form's facade right up to a potential rooftop garden. These planting zones or planter-box facilities can have a built-in gravity-fed water-sprinkler system that supplies water and nutrients to the planters.

What is evident in designing such systems is that the placement of greenery in built forms can depend on the sun's path for that locality as determined by its latitude. For instance, in designing for higher latitude zones, the designer must take into account that the sun's path traverses mostly from the southerly direction, which means that the placement of greenery should mostly be on the south, southeast and southwesterly facades. The floor-plate plan of the built form should conform with the location of vegetated terraces at these points, although in principle north-facing species that survive in these locations can also be introduced.

In temperate climates with two extreme seasons and two mid-seasons, it is important to select those species that can survive in winter and summer. Examples can be selected from those families of hardy species commonly found along the edges of railways and at roadsides.

For those sceptics concerned about the practicality of putting vegetation into buildings, there are already any number of proprietary systems in the marketplace for creating roof gardens.

This vertical landscaping is one variation on the creation of rooftop gardening. Another variation is the green-wall, which encapsulates the principle of a single element with multiple functions (eg the 'vertical wetland' incorporated in a Berlin apartment block). The exterior wall can be fitted with a cascade of terracotta basins, each filled with gravel and planted with reeds where grey-water trickles through the basins, removing pollutants through filtration, settlement and active uptake by roots and bacteria.

A more technically intensive approach to vertical greening is the 'breathing wall' or the totally vegetated facade. The focus becomes one of developing an ecologically complex and stable plant and microbial community, utilising hydroponic growing media that will further improve indoor air quality in an interface between natural processes and the built structure's environmental systems.

Research has shown that the more diverse an ecosystem, the better it can absorb carbon dioxide and nitrogen, which are on the rise due to human activities and industrial processes.

Balancing biotic and abiotic constituents

In balancing systemically the biotic and abiotic constituents in our designed system, we need to note the following:

- In any ecosystem, the climate of the locality is held to be the predominant ecological influence, even though other biotic factors such as flora, fauna and soils have an effect on the system. In most urban locations, all that remains of the site's ecosystem components is probably the topsoil with the upper geological stratum, and much simplified and reduced fauna. In any new built system, we should recognise the fundamental ecological value of greening in increasing the site's biological diversity. Vertical and horizontal landscaping of the built forms and surfaces in urban locations introduces vegetated organic mass into an otherwise high concentration of inorganic mass.

- Although soft-landscaping strategies for low- and medium-rise built forms are relatively well developed (common solutions include planter boxes and roof-planting), they are notably less advanced for tall and large buildings. Planting and organic material should be added to the facade, sky courts and balconies or inner sky courts of the built system to balance the biomass content.

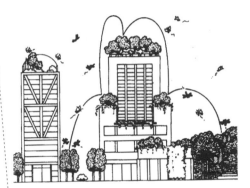

Roof gardens and sky courts create new urban habitats

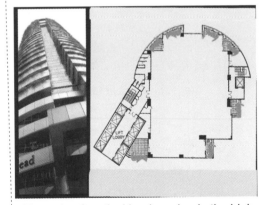

Example of vertical landscaping in the high-rise built form

Soil temperature

Indoor air temperature

Average outdoor air temperature

Winter   Spring   Summer   Autumn

The soil temperature around an earth-covered built form lags some 15 to 24 weeks behind that of the outside air. Midsummer heat reaches the underground roof by mid to late autumn and the floor by winter. The cold winter air then draws the heat slowly upwards to cool the built form in summer. This thermal flywheel effect keeps the indoor temperature comfortable.

Thermal flywheel effect ●

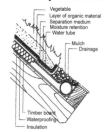

Vegetable
Layer of organic material
Separation medium
Moisture retention
Water tube
Mulch
Drainage

Timber board
Waterproofing
Insulation

planting medium
insulation
waterproofing
vapour barrier
protection board
L-shape plate
Rubble
Drainage
L-channel

Vegetated roof details ●

Planters with a gravity-fed system for watering and supply of nutrients

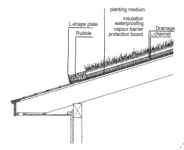

Plants can affect the indoor temperature and the cooling load of buildings in several ways:

Vegetation

- Trees with high canopies and pergolas near walls and windows provide shade and reduce the solar heat gain with relatively small blockage of the wind (shading effect).

- Vines climbing over walls and high shrubs next to the walls, while providing shade, also reduce the wind speed next to the walls appreciably (shading and insulation effects).

- Plants near a building can lower the air temperature next to the building's skin, thus reducing the conductive and infiltration heat gains. In winter, of course, they reduce the desired solar gain and may increase wall wetness after rains.

- Ground cover by plants around a building reduces the reflected solar radiation and the long-wave radiation emitted towards the walls from the surrounding area, thus lowering the solar and long-wave heat gain in summer.

- If the ambient temperature around the condenser of a building's air-conditioning unit can be lowered by surrounding plants, the coefficient of performance (COP) of the system can be improved, so that less electrical power is consumed for a given amount of cooling energy delivered to the building.

- The obvious areas in built forms that are immediately accessible and available for incorporation of vegetation are the roof surfaces, terraces, sky-courts and trellis structures on the built form's facades. These areas have higher evaporation rates than ground surfaces, because they are more exposed to sun and wind. Vegetation increases the area from which this evaporation can take place. Cumulatively, these effects are significant. From a light shower, there will be no runoff. From a moderate shower, only about half of the precipitation may be discharged from the roof or sky-courts. With a heavy shower, there may be a delay of an hour or more before there is any discharge from a previously dry roof. The total annual discharge may be halved. This further justifies the provision of roof gardens and sky-courts in the built environment. Vegetated roofs discharge less rainwater because:

  * roof water is retained by plants and used in their metabolic processes;

  * flat roofs and terraces have additional retention capacity;

  * roof water is returned to the atmosphere by evaporation.

- Vegetation on rooftops functions in the same way as at ground level in terms of its role in climate control. It would be a mistake to consider the roofs or the upper parts of tall buildings as too inhospitable an environment for climatically significant amounts of plant life. Hardy plants can adapt to such environments with minimum soil depth or humus content. Certain plants can grow on only 7 centimetres of soil consisting of pea gravel and silt sand. The depth of soil needed depends on the type of plant. For example, grasses need 150 to 300 millimetres; ground cover and vines need 300 millimetres; low and medium shrubs, 600 to 750 millimetres; large shrubs and trees, 600 to 1050 millimetres. New landscapes at the roof or sky-court level can contribute to improving the climatic conditions of the city by reducing urban mass heat absorption (see B9). Roof gardens can also be used for urban agriculture (eg most vegetables need no more than 200 milimetres of soil) (see B21).

- Plants can have aesthetic, ecological and energy-conservation benefits in addition to providing effective responses to wind and rain. Planting can shade the internal spaces and the external wall of the built form and can minimise external heat reflection and glare into the building. Plant evapotranspiration processes can be effective cooling devices on the built form's facade besides creating a healthier microclimate, affecting the facade's microclimate by generation of oxygen and the absorption of carbon dioxide. For example, studies have shown that 150 square metres of plant surface area can produce enough oxygen for one person for 24 hours.

- Vertical and horizontal landscaping can be used by the designer to reduce the ambient air temperature of those localities with heat-island problems (see B9). Facade planting can lower ambient temperatures (eg especially in summer in temperate climates) at street level by as much as 5°C. Heat loss in winter can be reduced by as much as 30 per cent. Vegetation on the facade of a building will obstruct, absorb and reflect a high percentage of solar radiation; the rest passes through the vegetation and reaches the built form's surfaces. Plant leaves can be 1°C lower than the ambient temperature, and damp surfaces like grass, soil or concrete can be 2°C or more below, and can contribute significantly to a cooler and healthier building as well as reducing energy costs by reducing the air-conditioning load.

- Biologically, the leaf is an efficient solar collector. In summer, leaves take advantage of solar radiation, permitting air to circulate between the plant and the building; cooling takes place by means of a 'chimney effect' and through transpiration. In winter, the overlapping leaves form an insulating layer of stationary air around the building. Even in regions too cold for evergreens to grow, summer cooling may still be an important factor, lending an energy saving and biological validity to incorporating planting in built forms.

- In the case of the tall built form, for example, its facade area can be up to four to five times the site area, perhaps even more. If the facade is covered with planting in its entirety,

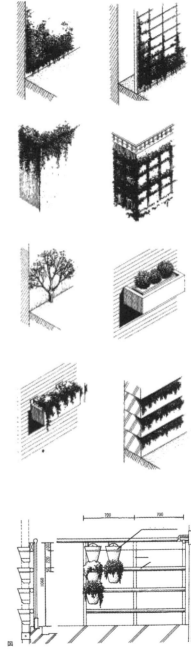

Examples of green wall systems

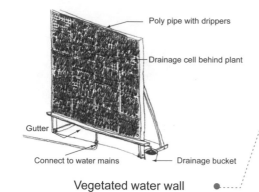

Poly pipe with drippers

Drainage cell behind plant

Gutter

Connect to water mains — Drainage bucket

Vegetated water wall

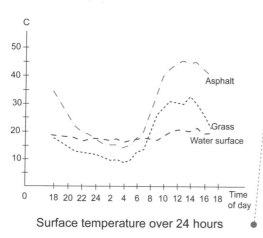

C

50

40

30

20

10

0   18 20 22 24 2 4 6 8 10 12 14 16 18   Time of day

Asphalt

Grass

Water surface

Surface temperature over 24 hours

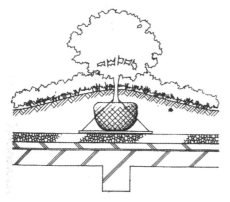

Mound for large plants for rooftop planting

the increase in vegetative cooling can be significant. The complete covering of the facade can greatly contribute to lowering the ambient temperature. Externally, vegetation can contribute to lowering urban temperatures in the boundary layer by 1°C, while vegetative canopies (ie trees) may lower external ambient temperatures by an additional 2°C in the area under the canopy.

• Studies have shown that not only do plants process carbon dioxide and release oxygen into the air; they also remove formaldehyde, benzene and airborne microbes, thereby contributing to a healthier internal environment (the required concentration is one plant per square metre of internal space). For example, the Boston fern removes 90 per cent of the chemicals that cause allergic reactions (see B18).

• The humidity of vegetated areas is related to the rate of evapotranspiration. The evaporation effect depends on the locality's albedo, and the morphology, rugosity and articular resistance of the leaf surface. The relative humidity of the air (in a humid subtropical climate) under vegetation is found to be between 3 and 10 per cent greater than in areas without vegetation, and the bigger differences are in the summer (eg in subtropical climates) because this effect is proportional to the density of the vegetation's leaf canopy. The smaller values are registered in the spring due to the action of winds and the existence of empty spaces in the crown during the flowering period. Through rooftop vegetation, the toxins in the rain can be absorbed or broken down by the soil, and the storm water can be retained for slow discharge. In arid climates, evapotranspiration can be enhanced in hot conditions by night-time spraying, which cools the built form and reduces the need for air conditioning. In temperate zones in winter, the snow cover and the ice-dried fibre-matrix can serve as insulation.

• Generally, a single large tree can transpire 450 litres of water a day (equivalent to 960,000 KJ of energy in evaporation), which is rendered unavailable to heat surfaces. The mechanical equivalent would be to have five average-size-room air conditioners, each operating at 10,500 KJ per hour, running for 19 hours a day. Air conditioners not only shift waste heat from indoors to outdoors, they also use electric power from non-renewable sources of energy. The heat is therefore still free to increase urban air temperatures and therefore the heat-island effect (demonstrating, incidentally, the need for designers to think in terms of the interconnectivity of environments; see B9). But with the tree, transpiration renders this same heat unavailable. To illustrate the importance of landscaping as a passive-mode strategy, studies of moisture sources in the urban air have concluded that advection and evapotranspiration are significant contributors to humidity and that a vegetated surface can be as effective as a high-albedo surface in reducing the sensible heat gain of the urban air. Studies have shown that near-surface air temperatures over vegetated areas appear to be 1–2.25°C lower than background air temperatures, and that vegetation may lower the urban temperatures in the boundary layer by 1–1.25°C.

- Ecologically, it is crucial for the designer to ensure physical continuity in the designed system by planting in the biomass to encourage species migration and contribute to greater diversity. To achieve viable continuity by 'vertical landscaping' of the urban building, the system should be linked (eg using stepped planter-boxes organised as 'continuous planting zones' up the face of the building). These should permit some extent of species interaction and migration, and provide a link to the ecosystem at the ground level. The alternative option would be to separate the planting into unconnected boxes. However, this can lead to species homogeneity, which necessitates greater external inputs (eg regular human maintenance) to remain ecologically stable. Examples have been found where the creation of these urban habitats has resulted in species returning to the urban environment where they were previously believed to have become extinct.

- As a general design strategy, we should reintroduce as far as possible the indigenous vegetation for that locality. We will probably find that the indigenous vegetation, reintroduced correctly within its own climatic range, typically requires less maintenance and makes fewer demands on other scarce resources such as water, fertiliser and energy.

- In considering the total carbon dioxide emissions from the built form, one strategy that has been suggested is to compensate for the embodied ecological impact of the production of the building arising from its CO and CO_2 emissions by adopting an area of forest equal to the extent of carbon dioxide emissions in the building. However, there is a flaw to this argument in that ecological design is then regarded as a battle to reduce the elimination of forests by the timber-producing countries. While this is a goal that must be achieved, the designer should also when designing, contribute to balancing the existent inorganic urban environment by adding organic matter and biomass seeking to achieve if possible the equivalent to the rate of 1 square metre of rainforest (capable of absorbing 1 kilogram of carbon dioxide per year). It has been estimated that 200 trees are required to absorb the carbon dioxide emissions per car. Therefore, to compensate for the car owners using the built system, an equivalent in mass of trees needs to be planted on the site or at that urban locality.

- As a general approach, the designer should free as much of the ground plane as possible and make available opportunities in the upper parts of the built system for its colonisation by flora and fauna.

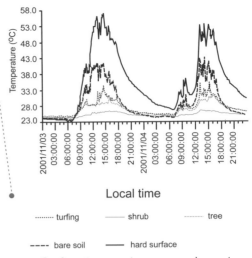

Local time

...... turfing   —— shrub   ---- tree

---- bare soil   —— hard surface

Surface temperature comparison at different times of the day

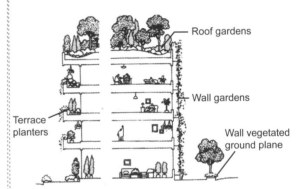

Roof gardens

Wall gardens

Terrace planters

Wall vegetated ground plane

Vertical planting design

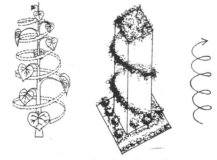

Continuous vertical landscaping

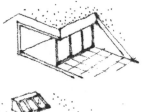

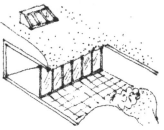

Earth integrated built forms •--------

Built forms can be earth integrated to varying
degrees. They can have a sheltered wall (top); a
floor at ground level with earth-cover to the whole
structure (centre); or be below ground level with a
sunken courtyard (below). The main glazed areas
face the sun for solar heat and to provide views.

External view of built form

Example of a continuously integrated planting
zone extending from the ground to roof

Ecological nexus •--------

Animal species and organisms

• We should be aware that any increase in biomass introduced into the urban ecosystem through ecological design will bring an attendant increase in accompanying organic life; as modern urban structures and human-made ecosystems are not biologically 'dead', this may affect human life. In fact, there are a number of species of creatures that make up urban biodiversity without any design help at all. It just happens that these species constitute those with which humans would rather not share their spaces. These are the cockroaches, rodents and rats, spiders, fruit flies, ants, dust mites, moulds and fungi that thrive in urban environments but are not obvious to the human occupants. They lurk in dark and damp places, cellars and basements, spaces between floors, walls, HVAC systems, and underneath furniture and appliances, for example.

Rats are usually found in basements. They carry fleas and other parasites into the building. Rats are usually nocturnal; as their population increases it might be possible to spot them during daylight. Their population, unfortunately, can expand rapidly – if unchecked, a pair can produce six to 12 young in just three weeks. Rats reach sexual maturity in just three months, so assuming there is adequate food, water and shelter, a single pair of rats may multiply into more than 640 in just one year. Rats are excellent swimmers, and often live in sewers and occasionally enter buildings through toilets.

Two species of rat are usually found in buildings. The brown or Norway rat and the black house rat arrived in North America from Europe with the early settlers, for instance. They nest under buildings and concrete slabs and in garbage dumps, or they might burrow under the foundations of buildings and develop an elaborate burrow system. Although they can climb, they prefer the lower floors of a multistorey building. Both these rat species are able to gnaw through wood, lead, aluminium, copper, cinder block and uncured concrete.

The house rat may also be found in trees, vine-covered fences or attics. They often enter buildings from the roof or utility lines. They are not as large as brown rats, and are agile. They are able to swing, jump and climb into upper parts of buildings, although they may nest outside in trees (especially palm), ivy and similar vegetation.

The house mouse weighs less than an ounce and prefers to live inside buildings. House mice spend much of their lives between walls, and behind cabinets and appliances. The only sign of mice occupancy is the evidence of gnawed food and droppings on floors, shelves and countertops. They will eat just about anything and survive with little or no water. Prodigious multipliers, a pair can have a litter of five to six young only 20 days after mating. These young are weaned in three weeks, and sexually mature at six to 10 weeks.

In a year, a single pair may multiply into several thousand.

Mice carry on their bodies a small mite, known as the house-mouse mite (*Allodermanyssus sanguineus*). These mites carry a bacterium, *Rickettsia akari*, which causes an infection called rickettsialpox.

Cockroaches find buildings ideal habitats in terms of protection, food, water and hiding places. They are nocturnal, and like warm damp places. For example in temperate climatic zones, during late autumn when central heating systems are activated, it is not uncommon to see a mass migration out of the walls (because the heat dries them up) and into water sources such as sinks. Cockroaches, such as the American cockroach, that live in contact with human faeces, can transmit bacteria such as *Salmonella* and *Shigella*, which cause food poisoning and dysentery. To control the population of cockroaches in buildings, sanitation is critical, as is limiting the availability of food and water; rubbish should be placed in roach-proof receptacles outdoors. Leaky taps and pipes should be repaired, and openings such as cracks in foundation walls, exterior walls around air conditioners, doors, windows, floor, ceilings, etc should be sealed. Rotting leaves and decaying matter should be cleared from doors and windows. Limiting moist areas in and around a structure helps to reduce areas that are attractive to cockroaches.

Spiders and insects are other species found in buildings. Apart from reactions from arachnophobes, spiders are good to have around buildings as they help curtail pest populations by eating insects. Fleas, on the other hand, are pests commonly found in homes where they are attracted to areas where dust and organic food matter accumulate. They thrive in wall-to-wall carpeting, and are the most common insect pests on cats and dogs. Cat fleas are suspected of transmitting murine typhus to humans and may also serve as intermediary hosts of dog tapeworms. In controlling flea populations, sanitation is again important. Vacuuming floors, carpets and upholstered furniture will remove flea eggs, larvae and adult fleas.

Bed bugs are another pest that thrives in a built environment. Three species attack people; of these, the most important is *Cimex lectularius*, which may also bite birds, bats and rodents. It is a pest that thrives where sanitary conditions are poor or where there are birds or mammals nesting on or near a house. Indirect measures, such as practising good sanitation and maintenance, can go a long way in controlling bed bugs, eg by keeping bats and birds away from houses.

It is crucial for the designer to be aware of these organic life forms and to design to help reduce their numbers and attract more undemanding faunal species, such as birds.

- Another unwanted form of organic life is indoor fungal growth. Fungal contamination has

External view of built form with vegetated edges (in Boustead Tower, Kuala Lumpur, 1985)

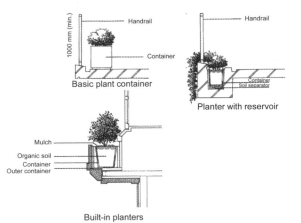
Examples of edge planting

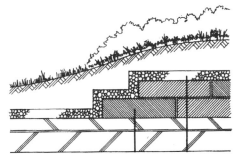
Lightweight method for changing grades on the vegetated roof

Design to balance the biotic and abiotic components of the designed system

Edge planting detail ●-----

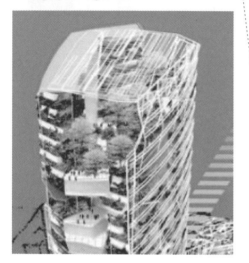

- Continuous planting to enable species interaction and integration

- Hardy plant species, such as those found on roadsides and in hedges, which will survive both cold and hot seasons

- Planter's soil-mix to relate to local climatic conditions

- Drainage floor-traps located at bottom of planters as well as the top (of soil mix) to allow for overflow

- Vegetation location in built form to relate to sun-path of the locality

- Ensure sunlight provision to back of vegetation

- Sliding 'wind breaker' shutters for high wind conditions with variable position for composite mode condition

- Gravity-fed irrigation system for plants and nutrients

- Design to be as complete as possible as an ecosystem

Aspects of green sky-court design ●

been shown to produce allergies in building occupants. Symptoms such as headaches, eye irritation and lethargy are cumulatively termed sick building syndrome (SBS) and often accompany contamination and allergies, though few studies have been able to verify this risk. SBS has been linked with elevated indoor levels of the fungi *Penicillium* and *Stachybotrys*, which are both implicated in causing respiratory diseases, asthma and pulmonary haemosiderosis. Asthmatics are notably more susceptible to environmental agents. Risks may be increased by a variety of things, including rat and cockroach infestations, unsanitary conditions and indoor and outdoor air pollution.

- These organisms and living things can be a nuisance to human life in buildings. Nevertheless, ecodesign must seek to provide a balanced biotic and abiotic built ecosystem on the one hand, and a habitable, healthy and safe environment through control of unwanted organic life on the other.

In seeking to balance the inorganic constituents of our designed system (which are site specific) with more organic constituents, the shape and appearance of our designed system may well become more organised and less formally geometrical and machine-made in appearance. The inclusion of vegetation, for instance, will probably produce a less finite built form with a more 'fuzzy' or 'hairy' aesthetic. The continuous pattern is preferred as this creates a geographically larger linked habitat.

Commensal/mutualist relationships

In enhancing the biomass of our built system, we need to distinguish whether the organisms involved will benefit from the interaction, be harmed by the interaction or derive neither benefit nor harm. The relationship that humans have with many of their associated species can be classified as either commensal or mutualist. Commensalism is an interaction in which one participant derives a large benefit while the other derives either no measurable benefit or harm. Examples of animal and plant species that are commensal with humans in most parts of the world include the black rat, the Norway rat, the house mouse, the pigeon, the starling, the cliff swallow, the house sparrow, the barn owl and the bed bug. Most of these are among the most cosmopolitan and abundant species within each of their respective genera. Plants commensal with humans include several hundred species of weeds, including members of the sunflower and mustard families.

The interaction between two organisms that results in a benefit for both participants is referred to as mutualism, where neither the human nor the companion species may kill and consume the other (if one participant is harmed to the benefit of the other, the relationship is termed predation).

Ecosystem rehabilitation

Besides altering the inorganic–organic balance of the existent built environment by vegetation and biomass, the introduction of biomass is also part of the rehabilitation of devastated or zeroculture sites (see B4). Rehabilitation of degraded ecosystems will become an increasingly important activity, particularly in the proximity of urban areas, where damaged lands are prevalent. Sometimes the first option for ecosystem management (ie the use of native and indigenous systems in ecologically correct associations and natural successions) is either not available or not sufficient to accomplish the deserved rehabilitation goals. For example, natural ecosystems may have low net productivity and, thus, limitations in situations where maximising net yield is necessary. When habitats are excessively damaged due to human activity, native systems and natural successions may not be effective for rehabilitation because native species may grow slowly and succession is therefore arrested. Under these conditions, the rehabilitation of degraded ecosystems may require the use of imported genetic materials from other geographic areas to accelerate the healing process of the ecosystems. The process of rehabilitation is often one of adaptive management where there is a loop between implementation of field actions, monitoring the affected ecosystem, comparing the results against expectations, and adjusting future actions, with each reiteration of activity being based on past experience.

It is possible for a simple grass-roof system to reach a K-value of 0.6 W/m²K without additional thermal insulation by simply using a layer of grass growing on a 15-centimetre layer of a special lightweight substrate.

On top of this good thermal insulation the thermal mass of the earth minimises the temperature amplitudes inside the built form. Particularly effective is the cooling effect, such as a grass roof has in summer. In moderate climates the temperature of the earth's surface will not exceed 25°C even if the atmospheric temperature is 35°C. In winter a grass roof reacts vice versa: the earth does not freeze even at atmospheric temperatures of –20°C, except a little just under the surface.

Beyond these positive effects on the indoor environment and the energy savings there are other ecological benefits. The total leaf surface of certain species of grass can be about 50 to 100 square metres per square metre of roof surface. This means that a grass roof of this type has about five to 10 times more green surface than a public park with trees, bushes, paths and a mown lawn (eg a cut lawn, 5 centimetres high, has only 9 square metres of leaf surface per square metre of ground area). This amount of green surface on a grass

1. Initiation
The starting point of any succession is a bare surface. It may be 'new', eg an emergent shoreline, or more commonly a surface stripped of any previous vegetation cover by natural or human agencies.

2. Colonisation
The first plant growth is based on a small number of specialised, highly stress-tolerant plant species. Total biomass is low, and soil is rudimentary, generally lacking organic matter and balanced available nutrients. Typical colonisers are bryophytes and vascular plants with tolerance of extreme water and nutrient status conditions (high, low or alternating).

3. Development
As soil conditions improve, highly stress-tolerant species are replaced by more productive and competitive species including grasses and weeds. This is often a feature of the development tolerance of sere in which substrate conditions may remain unstable and alternation between different environmental conditions may occur.

4. Maturity
By this point the ecosystem has developed to the extent that vegetation cover is dominated by competitive species, though not necessarily those with a very long life cycle. Soil conditions are stable and nutrient and water conditions are not major problems in the ecosystem. Typical species are competitive grasses, bushes and smaller trees. Non-vascular plants are minor components, and the range of higher trophic and decomposer species is considerable.

5. Climax
The final stage sees the development of a vegetation cover that is relatively stable and persistent. It is often dominated by large trees, with long lifecycles. There is little or no evidence of the initial abiotic or biotic environmental condition of the area that existed at the beginning of the successional sequence. The issue of whether or not there is such a condition as a stable climax is controversial.

● Stages in a typical plant succession

A typical proprietary vegetated roof system

roof is an inexpensive and effective device for purifying the air and reducing the formation of fog.

The importance of a grass roof will be demonstrated by the following example:
In intensive urban areas usually about 30 per cent of the ground is covered by built forms. If 10 to 20 per cent of the roofs (eg 3 to 6 per cent of the total area of the city) was covered by earth and wild grass they would create as much leaf surface as if 30 per cent of the entire built-up area was comprised of green areas. This is a simple and cost-effective way to reduce pollution in our densely built-up urban environments, and to provide an acceptable climate.

On the other hand, this leaf surface produces a large amount of condensing water. Before dawn, when the outdoor temperature is at its lowest in the grass layer, condensing water is formed. The heat developed in this process warms up the earth and therefore reduces the thermal loss of the built form (the condensation of 1 litre of water releases 530 kcal of energy). At the same time, irrigation is provided for the roofs. Moreover, the grass roof stores about 500 millimetres of water, which means that only 20 to 30 per cent of rainwater flows off the roof thus relieving the drainage runoffs.

In order to prevent the roots from growing through the roof a special reinforced plastic membrane can be used, which is waterproof and resistant to humic acid as well as ultraviolet radiation. There are a number of readily available proprietary systems for greening roof and terrace surfaces.

Summary
The ecological designer must assess the biotic content of the intended designed system. Most designed systems' contents are essentially totally inorganic (except for the human users and microbiotic life). It is therefore crucial for the designer to incorporate, systemically integrate and balance the necessary biotic components (eg in the form of greenery and related organic material) into the existent built environment of the locality, as well as to any proposed designed system, in order to create designed systems that are balanced human-made hybrid ecosystems and habitats in function and in content. This similarly applies to the rehabilitation of sites where all or virtually all of their biotic components and organic life have been removed. The designer can examine the structure and constituents of ecosystems and emulate their content and structure (see A3 and A4). In creating such a balanced environment the resultant built form may aesthetically become less mechanistic, inorganic and machine-like and acquire a more organic and amorphous configuration in response to the biointegrative demands of the organic matter.

Biophilia is defined as a partly genetic tendency by humans to respond positively to nature. It further justifies the increased addition of biomass into our built environment. Studies have shown that greenery can have restorative effects on humans, with measurable improvements in mental and physical health. In hospital environments, research studies have shown that patients heal more quickly in the presence of sunlight, trees and flowers than in biologically sterile, artificially lit, utilitarian internal environments.

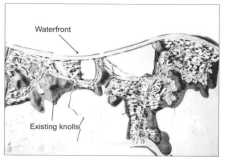

Example of an ecologically linked landscape using landscaped bridges (Huanan, China 2002)

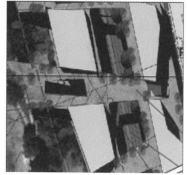

The landscaped bridge concept for reconnecting fragmented green areas

B8 Design to improve existing, and to create new, ecological linkages: enhancing the biodiversity of the designed system, conserving existent continuities of ecosystems and creating new ecological corridors and links (eg using ecological land-bridges, hedgerows, and enhancing horizontal integration)

It is crucial that our designed system conserve and enhance existent biodiversity and environmentally biological continuities present in the ecosystems and, where possible, create new ecological linkages. Ecodesign, especially in site planning, must involve the creation of new ecological corridors, linkages, networks and ecological land-bridges to enhance biodiversity. This is important because in the natural environment no living thing can survive without multiple connections with other organisms. This design goal is also vital because, by improving the existent ecological linkages and creating new ones, the locality's biodiversity has the opportunity to become enhanced.

Ecological corridors: land-bridges

Every ecodesign must seek to create ecological corridors as linear spatially continuous interconnected parks or open spaces in a green infrastructure, to link with a greater pattern for that locality and reduce habitat fragmentation. Impervious surfaces such as roads are barriers to faunal life. This green infrastructure or ecostructure is a continuous vehicular-free zone allowing for fauna and flora species movement. We need to recognise the requirement for connectivity between patches of natural habitat – isolated plots of ground are insufficient for many plants and animals to survive. Studies have shown that forest beetles and mice almost never cross two-lane roads, and even shy away from unpaved forest roads that are closed to public traffic. The designer can also use physical devices, such as a land-bridge that is vegetated or landscaped over, as 'landscaped bridges' between isolated or disparate habitats to increase habitat connectivity. The landscaped bridge is essentially a wide and well-vegetated platform that spans an otherwise inorganic area (such as an impervious road or a highway or some paved surfaces) that inhibits species migration and interaction. The landscaped bridge is organically planted over and by its bridging function ecologically links the habitats on either side of the bridge thereby increasing the size of those habitats and provides an active wildlife passage.

The theoretical proposition here is that the two previously disparate zones will now become joined together through this wide vegetated bridge. The new green bridge will provide an overhead ecological corridor that should enable flora and fauna species to interact, to share resources in a larger habitat and to migrate across thereby positively improving and increasing (by design) the biodiversity of the locality. In such circumstances, our design endeavours would no longer become a rearguard action to ensure minimal impacts on the ecosystems but would actually contribute positively to the ecosystems by enabling an increase and intensification in the locality's biodiversity or its probable enhancement and extending the ecological corridors to link other existing ecosystems. Existent urban built form has fragmented the landscape into islands and one of the key objectives of ecodesign is to reconnect the landscape and its organisms and create viable habitats. One of the major tasks in making our existent built environment sustainable and integrated with the surrounding natural areas is to maximise and enhance the viability of remnant ecosystems with increased linkages, through green corridors, with the supporting ecological functions from surrounding green areas. From the various patterns of integration of vegetation and non-human biomass with the built environment, the continuous ecological corridors with 'green fingers' and the network pattern are preferred.

Hedgerows

These are a linear form of ecological corridor. Although they are barriers to domestic animals, hedgerows are thoroughfares for many wild ones. English hedgerows embrace as many as 600 species of vascular plants and offer breeding sites to four out of five English woodland wildlife species.

Green corridors: ecological benefits

- These new connections enhance and increase the networks in the natural systems. In nature, we find living systems nesting within other living systems – networks within networks. Their boundaries are not boundaries of separation but boundaries of identity. All living systems communicate with one another and share resources across their boundaries.

- Ecological corridors support food chains and habitats. Elimination of existent corridors interrupts and changes the flows within ecosystems and migration routes and can lead to habitat pollution. Ecological corridors also provide support and pathways for migrating species.

- The creation of new ecological corridors will reconnect existent fragments of vegetation in the landscape to create larger linked tracts, so that the whole ecosystem with all its interacting inhabitants can be represented, and improve the movement of plants and animals from one area to another. Generally, organisms affect and modify the environment in which they live and the environment conditions the organisms that it contains. An ecosystem is characterised, therefore, by its organic components and by environmental factors and conditions and their interactions. In ecosystems the determining factors

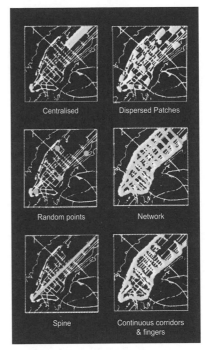

Centralised Dispersed Patches

Random points Network

Spine Continuous corridors & fingers

Horizontal patterns of integration of vegetation and biomass with the built environment © Ken Yeang

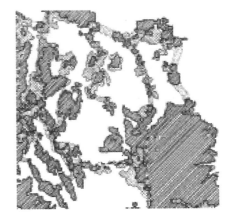

Creating linked vegetation zones in the landscape

Design to improve existing, and to create new ecological linkages

B8

151

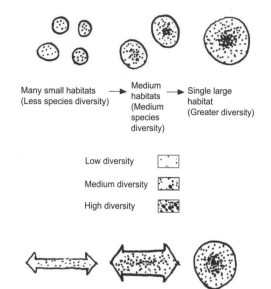

Many small habitats (Less species diversity) → Medium habitats (Medium species diversity) → Single large habitat (Greater diversity)

Low diversity

Medium diversity

High diversity

Ecological strip → Ecological corridor → Isodiametric

Less species diversity → Medium species diversity → Ecological zone

Design to increase biodiversity by linking vegetated areas

include population and territory, and the creation of new corridors and linkages enlarges the territory and provides opportunities for enhancing diversity and ecosystem stability.

• Ecologically, fauna and flora species do migrate across urban environments and between patches of greenery within the city despite built barriers, such as impervious surfaces and structures and built forms that separate the green areas. However, this inter-ecosystem migration is a gradual one and it may take 30 to 60 years or more for species to relocate (especially for the vegetation to become mature at another locality).

• The designer can enhance a locality's biodiversity by providing opportunities for fauna and flora species to interact with others, and by avoiding, at all costs, the making of habitat islands. These habitat islands are vulnerable to impairment by human activity and the invasion of alien organisms. The smaller the habitat reserve, the higher the rate of extinction. Reserves can be enlarged by encouraging the regrowth of natural habitat outwards from the periphery of the core reserve, while reclaiming and restoring developed land close by to create new reserves.

• The landscaped bridge and other linking devices such as ecological corridors increase ecological linkages and aggregation of habitats. This is important as all species rely on many other species in complex webs of interdependence. Strictly speaking there are no truly individual organisms. No living system exists in isolation from its ecological context; interdependence extends even to the genetic level. Symbiotic relationships, from the simple to the exotic, are a universal way in which life forms survive and coexist.

• Existent urban development and the construction of roads and impervious surfaces tend to fragment and separate the natural environment and ecosystems into disparate patches and green areas that become bounded by roads, highways, built structures, fences and impervious surfaces that obstruct and inhibit species interactions and migration. Habitat fragmentation affects the ecology of the locality, eg by altering biotic diversity and composition and changing existent ecological processes such as nutrient cycling and pollination. The designer must ensure that new road patterns reduce or eliminate such ecological divisiveness and maintain a continuous linked vegetation pattern within the ecosystem.

• The network in ecosystems is one of the very basic patterns of organisation of all living systems. At all levels of life, from the metabolic networks of cells to the food webs of ecosystems, the components and processes of living systems are interlinked in network fashion. It is this interlinking that we must seek to perpetuate in our designed systems and built environment.

- Increasing the linkages between green areas and ecosystems provides the opportunity for an increase in biodiversity. As an ecosystem gains greater diversity, it contains more species and this is further enhanced by increased opportunities for species to interact and to migrate. An ecosystem becomes impoverished when the number of species diminishes, as with any isolated island ecosystem where opportunities for increasing diversity are limited. Impoverishment happens when, for instance, a grassland with dozens of grasses and flowers, hundreds of insects and small mammals, and innumerable microbes is turned into a city or suburb, the paved and built-on land of which can support mainly rats, pigeons, English sparrows, Bermuda grass, certain species of tree, and cockroaches – all of which are hardy species that find ways to coexist with a large number of humans.

- Conservation biology should be used as a scientific approach to the protection of whole ecosystems in which ecological vigour can be maintained. Conservation studies show how large a protected reserve must be to safeguard an undisturbed, healthy core of biodiversity and how numerous and well distributed the members of rare or endangered species must be to survive over time. Conservation biology provides guidelines for the width of undisturbed ecological corridors between protected areas to allow safe passage of animals. The approach involves establishing priorities for new reserves and species needing immediate protection, proposing long-range preservation goals, and defining the conditions that restoration projects must meet if they are to establish truly sustainable ecosystems.

- When urban development encroaches on a formerly wild area it reduces the habitats available for many species. If its habitats are entirely obliterated a species is driven to extinction. When, as a result of development, we find that only small, isolated habitats remain we refer to these as fragmented or island habitats. The smaller the areas that are left the more destructive are the effects of fragmentation. For instance, if a North American forest ecosystem is broken up into housing tracts, then the forest-interior birds that need the safety of dense vegetation, such as wood thrushes and warblers, disappear leaving only the forest-edge species like blue jays, blackbirds and house wrens, which can survive in such conditions.

- At all scales of nature, we will find living systems nesting within other living systems as networks within networks. Their boundaries are not boundaries of separation but boundaries of identity. All living systems communicate with each other and share resources across their boundaries. Our layout design must facilitate rather than disrupt this linkage; it must not be divisive.

- The addition of new biomass and greenery into any built form also contributes to the biodiversity of the locality. For instance, the addition of roof gardens in cities, besides lowering the overall heat-island effect of the city, creates new urban habitats for wildlife.

- Studies have shown that original species, especially those particular to that locality prior to the advent of its urbanisation (eg birds, butterflies, etc), tend to return to these areas with the creation of new habitats such as rooftop gardens. Biodiversity breeds more diversity, and the overall abundance of plants, animals and micro-organisms increases to a corresponding degree. The more species that live together, the more stable and productive the ecosystems they comprise. The constituent species, by spreading out into multiple niches, seize and cycle more materials and energy than is possible in similar ecosystems.

  Ecosystems achieve stability and resilience through the richness and complexity of their ecological webs. The greater their biodiversity, the more resilient they will be.

- The cutting, excavating or altering of the earth has impact on the ecosystem and it is critical to pay attention when designing large spread-out buildings that require such extensive horizontal clearance of land area. This is not to say that all earthworks have negative ecosystem impacts, but all earthworks inevitably involve the removal of ground cover and topsoil and the alteration of the site's topography (whether to a greater or lesser extent) and its natural drainage routes. If these potential impacts are not considered and addressed in the design, such action on the site's terrain can radically affect the locality's natural drainage, clear and destroy all the existent vegetation (and related fauna), lower the hydrological regimen and ground-water table, and subsequently lead to siltation of the surrounding waterways and other secondary effects.

- In the case of a tall built form like a skyscraper, the planning of its access roads and related motorways (if applicable) and the impact of the layouts of these would generally not play an important role in its design except, perhaps, at the immediate ground plane to the built form and, in most instances, are of minimal importance unless the overall development is large and requires difficult road interchange patterns or related access roads. Clearly, ecological design must also consider the transportation consequences of the design, and acknowledge the relationship of the built form (see B10) with the traffic infrastructure of the locality. This is because any new intensification of land use would in all instances have significant energy consumption impacts arising from increased transportation occasioned by the increased number of users travelling to and from the new built form.

- For those built forms that are physically spread out in an urban sprawl, the layout of their access roads within and outside their built forms plays a more crucial role in their site planning design, particularly in the provision of all the horizontal access-ways, such as for pedestrians, service vehicles, visitors and parking and fire engine access (especially to gain service access to awkward parts of the built form). Their routing, built platform levels, access surface gradients, drainage, etc, must relate to the site's existent topography, as their patterns can inhibit or facilitate the provision of pedestrian vehicular-free routes, or inhibit the continuous organic relationships with the biomass and with other aspects of site planning. In particular, layout design should avoid any undesirable cross-overs of the key existent ecological corridors within the site, avoid the location of new impervious surfaces on those parts of the site that are prone to flooding and erosion, as well as taking into consideration natural vegetation diversity, natural drainage channels, soil factors, etc.

- There are complex and interconnected aspects of the site's ecosystem at the vegetation layer, soil layer and at the ground level that are particularly important when designing building layouts. At the outset, a slope analysis and drainage analysis of the site's existent topography and the projected integration of the site's existent topography and ecological features with the new built form and its access patterns are crucial to the ecological design and planning of the new built form.

- Similar attention must also be given to the pattern of the new pedestrian networks, the placement of new large areas of impervious surfaces (eg for car parking or plazas), to the routing of all the infrastructural engineering systems (roads, drains, sewerage, water reticulation system, surface water drainage channels, telecommunications, night-lighting, waste disposal routes, etc) and to the creation of new earthworks platform levels, drainage routes, etc.

- For essentially medium-rise and low-rise built forms, there are opportunities for linking groups of built forms together with, for example, overhead large umbrella-like canopies. These can provide protection from the climate for pedestrians, reduce solar heat-gain by shading the roof space from direct sunlight in the summer, make roofs available for recreational use and for open-air functions, and provide semi-covered transitional spaces below and between buildings. Nor need such a canopy always be solid. It can be permeable or trellis-like with planting over, or it can be a retractable structure that can be open or shut depending on the use below and the season of the year.

- An underground built form can also function as an urban regeneration device for urban locations where the site has complex issues involving multiple-ownerships of land titles

Landscaped bridges: new pedestrian linkages

Design to improve existing, and to create new ecological linkages

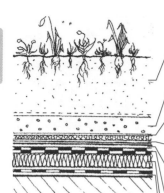

Soil and planting

Filter layer to prevent soil particles blocking the drainage

Drainage or water-retention system to prevent waterlogging/drying out

Protection layer to prevent damage to the layers below

Separation layer, to allow relative movement between the planted layer and the waterproofing below

Root barrier and second waterproof layer

Waterproofing and vapour equalisation layer

Insulation, which is able to withstand water and pressure of the soil

Vapour barrier bonded to roof deck

Roof garden detail

that make redevelopment problematic and require lengthy negotiations and land acquisition. An example is the case of the urban regeneration of important parts of existing cities with a streetscape where the facades need to be retained. Often, one of the major inhibitors of regeneration is the existence of multiple landownerships, which require large-scale and exorbitant acquisition of properties.

- The built form may be designed to be either totally or partially buried underground. However, we can compensate for the disturbed ground and soil by reintroducing it as a new roofscape that is totally revegetated. This will turn the excavated land surface into a natural habitat by creating an entirely new one where previously one did not exist.

- A linear underground built form can provide the prototype solution where the entire land area occupied by the street itself (which is usually publicly owned property) can become the zone for regeneration. First, the street has to be made into a traffic-free zone. In order to retain the present relationships between the existing buildings along the street, the concept is to sink the entire new development underground as a linear subscraping built form covering either the full or part extent of the length of the street itself between the abutting buildings. Inserted into this underground structure would be large air-wells to bring daylight and natural ventilation into the enclosed and semi-enclosed spaces below ground level.

Such linear built forms as new developments built within the land occupied by the street, become prototypes for urban regeneration for those sites with similar streetscape conditions, especially within the historic parts of existing cities. Here this becomes an alternative solution to the demolition of the existing buildings for redevelopment, especially along a historically important street.

To improve such connectivities, we might also incorporate high-level broad landscaped bridges between built forms, which can span the surrounding vehicular roads or streets. An alternative is to use a 'wedge-form' built form, where the landforms are mounded at the sides of the built structures to create vegetated mound forms that blend physically with the built form across the ground plane and with the landscape. The resultant built form is physically more integrated as a consequence of this landforming, and exhibits a high level of connectivity with the existent landscape and the ecosystems of the locality.

The maintenance or creation of corridors, either as continuous linkages or as stepping stones between disparate islands of remnant vegetation, has a relatively short history as a deliberate ecological management strategy in rural and urban areas, and has often come about as a by-product of land tenure and physical constraints (eg hedgerows, road easements and riparian vegetation along streams). In these environments, where the vegetation exists over relatively undisturbed ground, there is a small body of scientific and a greater amount of anecdotal evidence to suggest that physical linkages can enhance biodiversity by:

- assisting the movement of individuals through disturbed landscapes;

- increasing immigration rates to previously isolated habitats thus maintaining higher species richness and diversity, enhancing genetic variation, supplementing declining populations and allowing recolonisation;

- facilitating continuity of natural ecological processes in developed landscapes;

- providing habitats for animals moving through the landscape and plants and animals permanently living within the linkages; and

- providing ecosystem services such as water quality improvement and the reduction of erosion.

There are some reported disadvantages, in that corridors can:

- assist in the spread of disease and expose animals to predators;

- introduce new genes, which could disrupt local adaptations; and

- promote hybridisation through interbreeding of previously disjointed populations.

Some argue that the cost of creation and maintenance of corridors needs to be set against the preservation of other more homogeneous habitat areas by comparing the cost of not maintaining corridors and the effect on the ecological processes of the region.

There is an even greater paucity of scientific data that examine the effectiveness of corridors as part of an ecological design strategy, particularly where the corridor is established on impervious surfaces in an area that has experienced massive disturbance through large-scale development (eg on land that was once dockland).

While there is a need for more supporting data, some researchers have proposed the following:

- Habitat connectivity is a characteristic feature of natural environments and should be promoted as a means to counter isolation of natural environments.

- The 'precautionary principle' demands that where knowledge is limited, the alternative is to retain existing natural linkages in case they are beneficial.

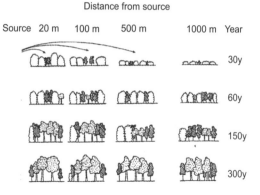

Distance from source

Source   20 m   100 m   500 m   1000 m   Year

30y

60y

150y

300y

Native plant colonisation of receptive habitats in the urban landscape

• The weight of evidence shows that isolation of populations and communities through loss of habitat has a detrimental effect.

Thus it is better to maintain or establish corridors as a matter of course, even if there is not enough scientific evidence fully to understand or predict the outcome of such work.

There are many variables that must be considered before the design and dimensions of the vegetated landscaped region can be determined. The species of fauna and flora that are or were indigenous to the area being developed have a significant bearing on the outcome of the project if they are to be catered for adequately. The habitat and food requirements of fauna will have a bearing on their 'robustness', or their ability to tolerate an environment disturbed by such things as excess noise, light and human interaction. Further considerations in respect of the fauna and flora of an area to be developed are:

• How much space do they need to forage, migrate and reproduce? Differences in home-range area are related to body size, food resources and foraging patterns.

• How do they move around? Do they move along the ground, through the tree tops, or fly?

• What is the pattern of movement? Some species will migrate or forage along the length of a corridor in one rapid journey, while some will move slowly, or move in an oscillating manner, making numerous small and seemingly random trips backwards and forwards over a short distance before reaching a destination.

• The interconnectivity must be adequate over a temporal scale so that individuals and populations can access suitable resources through time with variations in seasons, changes in the population dynamics of predator and prey, and changes in botanical composition as the habitat area matures and/or is affected by weather influences. This has a considerable bearing on how much management the corridors require.

It is well established by ecologists that diversity increases with the size of an ecosystem, but achieving a habitat size that permits great diversity or even approaches that of ecosystems in similar undisturbed ecosystems is unlikely to be compatible with the needs of the human residents and commercial pressures. In the resulting compromise, one must make hard choices about which species are most likely to survive and propagate in a human-altered environment. This obviously requires ecological research or some knowledge of at least some species' requirements and interrelationships, which of course may differ markedly between developments in different locations. Due to the previously mentioned paucity of scientific data, there will need to be an element of informed guesswork.

When the critical needs of the animal and plant species to be sustained or reintroduced are known, the botanical composition and the shape and size of the habitat can be determined.

The ratio of perimeter length to area is important as this governs the botanical composition possible (light penetration – abundance of pioneers and weeds) and hence the site's suitability as habitat or shelter (temperature, soil pH, moisture, disturbance, etc). In a vegetated corridor this will be a large ratio, and some species utilising it are likely to be subject to the edge effect, where they are exposed to higher levels of predation, human incursion and changes and fluctuation in micro-climate. However, while such a linkage may not be very suited to some species, others (usually with small ranges and/or tolerance to disturbance) will find that the linkage serves as a habitat, and that adequate genetic dispersal and population growth can occur.

Thus, there is no general solution for a linkage that will meet the requirements of all species. The type, quality and scale of the linkage must therefore match the needs and scale of the selected target species.

Connecting habitats over or, more commonly, under impervious surfaces has been successful for large animals such as elk in Canada. In these situations, the tolerance of the animals concerned means that there is no need to create a sophisticated habitat throughout the corridor. However, for most species this is not the case, and considerably more materials, energy and expertise will be required. To create a habitat style corridor over impervious surfaces, one must consider the energy required to transport soil and contain it over the impervious surfaces, and the energy required to maintain the soil and emerging vegetation until a nutrient cycle and functioning soil biota are sufficiently established to be self-sustaining and so minimise ongoing management of the ecosystem. Non-biological evidence that a restoration has succeeded could be an overall reduction in inputs such as the energy required to maintain a development, due to positive attributes of green spaces such as temperature regulation and water treatment.

Of course, there would need to be a commitment to periodic ecological assessment of these areas to quantify the benefits. If an area has been completely destroyed right down to the biotic and abiotic components of the soil, then perhaps the relevance of restoring the indigenous species is reduced and one could better serve the ecology of a region by using species that are native to the region but not indigenous to the site. Indeed, such an approach may still have a purpose in preserving species that may be endangered in other regions, much as a zoo does. This also may serve as an educational tool, to raise the environmental awareness of urban residents who may have lost touch with the concepts of human reliance on a healthy biosphere.

Design to improve existing, and to create new ecological linkages

A designed system need not have only negative impacts on the ecosystems. In designing with the ecosystems, the designed system may have positive relationships which:

• Preserve the ecosystem (eg nature-reserve management).

• Enhance the ecosystem by adding value to it as a resource (eg rehabilitation of derelict sites).

• Retard environmental deterioration by reducing the existing trend through change (eg the changing of an erosion-inducing drainage).

• Restore the ecosystem by replacing existing designed conditions (eg the revegetation of derelict land).

• Are net producers of energy.

Potential positive impacts of designed systems

In preserving and creating these ecological corridors and linkages, the resultant form and appearance make a continuous pattern across the landscape, urbanscape or the project site, thereby increasing the potential for biodiversity enhancement. They provide that background pattern as the basis for shaping the human-made built form; obviously, this must integrate physically in form and process with the existent natural corridors and new connections. Generally, large areal forms are preferred to linear forms.

Summary

In accommodating the wide planning, urban and ecological context of any design assignment, the designer must seek out opportunities during the planning and designing of the project site's layouts for improving and intensifying biodiversity, ecological connectivity within the ecosystems and biointegration with the habitats of that locality and region. A design can contribute positively to the environment, as against just having negative impacts. This is especially important where the project site is within an existent urban (ie totally built up) environment, which is overly inorganic in content, in context and in its built surfaces. Designing for habitat continuity may be particularly crucial in the case of those built forms that need especially wide ground coverages (ie where these have large inorganic built footprints laid on to the landscape). As part of the site-planning strategy in ecodesign, it is necessary for the designer to improve ecological linkages and, where possible, to create new ones while at the same time ensuring that the designed system does not inhibit such linkages. The overall site-planning strategy is to increase ecological norms by such linkages or ecological corridors, to enhance the locality's potential to increase biodiversity and to conserve existent continuities in its ecosystems, and to avoid any isolated land parcels that are segregated by impervious surfaces such as paved roads. The ideal ecological masterplan should be an interconnected single ecosystem where species can potentially traverse across the entire landscape and habitats uninterrupted by impervious surfaces or roadways.

B9 Design to reduce the heat-island effect of the built environment on the ecology of the locality: reducing and improving urban micro-climate impacts

The ecological designer must design to reduce the heat-island effects as the consequence of inserting new structures or infrastructures into a locality, particularly in existent urban built environments and where the environment has existent intensive concentrations of large quantities of inorganic mass on small land footprints and areas having extensive uncovered roof surfaces and impervious surfaces.

The heat-island effect

It is necessary to address this issue as there is now evidence for almost every city in the world that the temperature of its ambient environment is greater than that of its surrounding non-urban area. This difference in temperature is called the urban heat-island effect, which is essentially the warmer air temperature in the densely built-up areas of our built environment as compared to air temperatures in surrounding rural areas, and is defined as the thermal gradient differences between the built-up and non-built-up areas. Alternations in the land surface result in diverse micro-climates whose aggregate effect is reflected by the heat island. Globally this is increasing. The following factors are regarded as the main causes of the heat-island phenomenon in cities:

[1] Changes in ground cover

- Presence of high density of buildings on ground of varying levels, sunlight is repeatedly reflected off many surfaces. This means that buildings and ground surfaces absorb more solar radiation during the day, while the heat radiation towards the cold sky at night is disturbed by the dense built environment.

- Except in spots with strong winds, decreased wind velocity in densely built environments, compared with that in the sky above. Cities along the coast line provide a good example. In summer, although a cool sea breeze may blow high above the city during the day, the wind rapidly loses its velocity when it enters the built-up area and the potential for natural ventilation diminishes. Enclosed spaces such as high-rise 'canyons' are often unable to diffuse heat and pollutants when they receive only weak gusts of wind.

- Decrease in permeable ground surfaces, such as bare earth and greenery. This results in an increasing amount of heat radiation from the ground, as the capacity to retain water is reduced and thus the cooling effect of evaporation is lost.

- Ground plane in cities is covered with materials of high thermal capacity (eg asphalt pavement and concrete): solar heat absorbed during the day is emitted at night, producing uncomfortably hot temperatures even after dark.

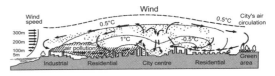

Heat-island effect in cities

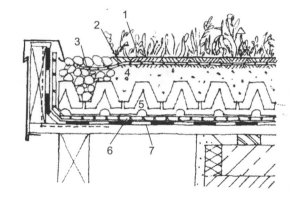

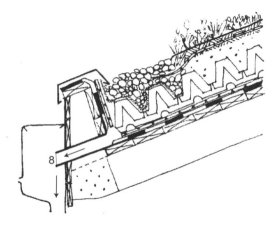

1. Vegetable
2. Layer of organic material
3. Anti-erosion sheet in open mesh jute, for roof slopes above 15 or very windy sites
4. Zincolit substrate
5. Profiled drainage element
6. Moisture retention/protection mat
7. Root-resistant waterproofing
8. Water outlet

Example of roof-edge greening details

[2] High energy consumption

In city centres for example, the heat generated by the consumption of energy by air conditioning equipment, lighting systems, automobiles and factories, is released into the atmosphere.

[3] Air pollution

Ambient pollution produces smog, which traps heat. This can raise temperatures by transforming an entire city into a 'glasshouse' enclosed in a layer of polluted air.

Recent studies using rainfall-measuring satellites confirm that urban heat islands create more summer rain downwind of major cities. The researchers found that mean monthly rainfall rates between 30 to 60 kilometres downwind of cities were on average about 28 per cent greater than for the upwind region. In some cities, the downwind area exhibited increases in rainfall as high as 51 per cent.

The temperature gradient between intensive urban conditions (such as the city) and surrounding rural areas creates air movement from the rural areas into the intensive urban zones, enhancing cloud formation and precipitation over cities. Then, as the dense urban zone such as the city holds the heat at night, it creates a low-pressure system. As hot air rises, cooler air from the surrounding areas rushes in to replace it. This cooler air condenses and forms thunderclouds. In other words, heat islands enhance convectional uplift, and the strong thermals generated in hot periods can result in violent thunderstorms over urban areas. It is also suspected that converging air due to the urban inorganic surfaces of varying heights also promotes the rising air needed to produce clouds and rainfall.

Climate change degrades ecosystems and is likely to encourage the spread of diseases among wildlife (ie affecting their distributions, population sizes, population density and behaviour), livestock, crops, forests, and coastal and marine ecosystems.

The ecodesign of our designed system must address this regional climate perturbation and the likelihood of new heat-island effects arising from any new intensive concentration of built forms. This should be approached not on the basis of individual built forms, but at the level of the overall planning of an existent or new urban area. Whereas, for example, in existing cities we can achieve a reduction of heat-island effects by increased tree planting and by creating extensive rooftop gardens, on greenfield sites we should avoid high and dense clusters of intensive buildings. This is important for several reasons. First, the increase in local temperature will affect the ecosystems of the locality and may cause biological impairment. Second, by reducing the heat-island effect, the need for the use of renewable energy in air conditioning and cooling is reduced.

Reducing the built environment's heat-island effect

The designer should take the following steps to reduce the heat-island effect of the built environment:

- Design to increase the extent of vegetated surfaces through selective distribution and layout of vegetation patterns and types on the urbanscape and maximise the area for planted or 'green' roof gardens (ie grass or other vegetative matter) and so help reduce the heat-island effects with vegetated surface areas greater than the inorganic surface areas.

- Reduce the extent of heat-absorbing surfaces such as paved, asphalt or concrete surfaces and increase their permeability.

- Revise existent and new urban city block layouts and configurations with layout patterns, materials and surfaces that absorb less solar energy.

- Ensure that the individual built form's configuration (eg size, clustering and form) does not encourage heat-island effects.

- Select roof, surface and building colours so as to reduce effects (eg avoid black or dark colours but use white and light colours).

- Use surface materials for the designed system the properties of which (eg their reflectance, heat absorption and built-up consequences) reduce heat-island effects.

- Add more urban landscaping such as trees or rooftop greenery and gardens to shade exposed surfaces (see B7). Trees also add oxygen to the atmosphere, break down some pollutants and reduce dust. It has been estimated that a total of 300 trees can counterbalance the amount of aerial pollution that a human being produces in a lifetime.

- Design the built form with the topography of the locality, to ensure that the heat-island effect does not affect the climate of the larger region surrounding the designed system and to reduce the wider impacts on people and on the surrounding natural and built environment.

- Shape and design the built forms' masses, densities and types with spacing and perforations to influence airflow, their views of the sun and sky, and their exposed surface areas.

- Design the roads and street canyons' width:height ratios and their orientations to control the warming up and cooling processes, the thermal and visual comfort conditions, and assist in air-pollution dispersal.

- Configure the built forms and design to influence building heat gains and losses, albedo and thermal capacity of external surfaces, including the use of transitional spaces.

Design to reduce the heat-island effect of the built environment on the ecology of the locality

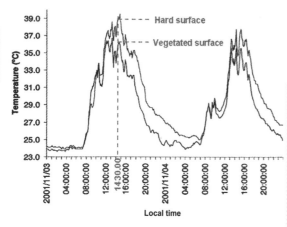

Vegetation lowers the ambient temperature of a locality and reduces the city's heat-island effect

- Adopt materials and surface finishes to control heat absorption, thermal mass storage and emissivity.

- Use the evapotranspiration and evaporative-cooling processes of vegetation on building surfaces and integrate open green spaces.

- Design traffic-systems reduction, diversion and rerouting to reduce the production of air and noise pollution, and heat discharges.

- Reduce heat islands (thermal gradient differences between developed and undeveloped areas) of other surfaces such as non-roof areas to minimise impact on micro-climate and human and wildlife habitats.

- Shade constructed surfaces of the designed system with landscape features and minimise the overall built footprint.

- Replace existent surfaces (ie roofs, roads, pavements, etc) with vegetated surfaces such as garden roofs and open-grid paving or specify high-albedo materials to reduce the heat absorption.

- Provide shade and use light-coloured high-albedo materials (eg reflectance of at least 0.3) and open-grid pavement for the site's non-roof impervious surfaces. These could be shaded (parking lots, walkways, plazas, etc) with trellises or a canopied roof.

- Place vehicular parking spaces underground or as covered structured parking. Use an open-grid pavement system (eg with impervious surfacing such as porous concrete) for the parking-lot areas.

- Reduce heat islands of roof areas and minimise impacts on micro-climate, human and wildlife habitats by installing high-albedo and vegetated roofs to reduce heat absorption.

- Use highly reflective and high emissivity roofing material (emissivity of at least 0.9 when tested) for the roof surface; or install a 'green' (vegetated) roof for the roof area. Combinations of high-albedo materials and a vegetated roof can be used provided that together they cover the roof area. Design must stipulate high-albedo and vegetated roof areas.

- Ensure zero use of CFC-based refrigerants in the built system's mechanical and electrical (M&E) systems. For reusing existing base-building M&E equipment, the design must adopt a comprehensive CFC phase-out conversion. When reusing existing M&E systems, the designer must conduct an inventory to identify equipment that uses CFC refrigerants and adopt a replacement schedule for these. For new buildings, design must specify new environmental systems and equipment (eg M&E equipment) that uses no CFC refrigerants.

In designing to ensure that the new designed system will not add to the heat-island effect of the existent built environment, the built form's roof surfaces, sloping surfaces and grade surfaces must all have entirely vegetated surfaces where possible (see B7) (ie natural as against artificial surfaces). Where this is achieved the resultant built form and built environment will become much greener and more vegetated, and in the process will create new habitats for wildlife with the likelihood of the return of species that were prevalent or were previously present prior to the urbanisation of the locality.

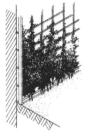

We might contend that trees are nature's equivalent to air conditioners. During photosynthesis trees suck up large amounts of water through their roots, which is released into the atmosphere through their leaves when they transpire. As this water evaporates, it cools the surrounding air – a similar effect to when humans sweat. In temperate climates during summer, an average-sized maple can release more than 190 litres of water in one hour. For instance, studies have shown that the maple tree has the cooling output of one large window airconditioner.

An average tree takes in up to 23 kilograms of carbon dioxide through its leaves annually during photosynthesis, storing up to 1 ton of carbon dioxide in its lifetime. During photosynthesis, the absorbed carbon dioxide and the energy from sunlight are broken down into carbon and oxygen, which are released into the atmosphere. The carbon is incorporated into the tree's growth. Because of transpiration and shading, the air surrounding a tree can be around 5°C cooler than its environment. Tree-shaded neighbourhoods can be up to 3.5°C cooler than those without trees.

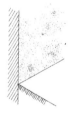

Where heat-absorbing greenery is incorporated into the site, the shape, form and appearance of the built form change from finite and hard-edged to a much more indeterminate, fuzzy vegetation-edged built form.

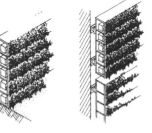

● Variations of green-wall design

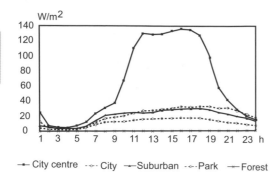

W/m²

```
140
120
100
 80
 60
 40
 20
  0
     1   3   5   7   9   11  13  15  17  19  21  23  h
```

-•- City centre   -◦- City   -▲- Suburban   -◦- Park   -×- Forest

Diurnal variation of anthropogenic heat from urban to vegetated zones

Summary

In design assignments where a designer will be imposing the significant volume and mass of new largely inorganic structures and infrastructures on to an ecosystem or on to an existent urban environment, he or she must seek by design to reduce the heat-island effects of the built environment's increased inorganic physical mass. Ecodesign involves reducing the negative thermal impacts of the imposition of the designed system on the surrounding ecosystems and habitats, and mediating its thermal consequences with the climate of the locality. To achieve this, the basic approach is to design with a more spread-out and horizontal pattern of built forms that are interlaced or intensified with an appropriate amount of vegetation or organic mass, with more organic or planted roof surfaces or roof gardens, and with water features and white or light-coloured roofs and wall surfaces. Implementing these strategies will also lead to a reduction in the use of non-renewable energy sources for air conditioning that would otherwise be increased as a result of the heat island's raised ambient urban temperature.

B10 Design to reduce the consequences of the various modes of transportation and of the provision of access and vehicular parking for the designed system

Ecodesign must take into account the ecological consequences of transportation at four levels: the provision of vehicular access to the designed system; the provision of vehicular parking to the designed system; the energy and material costs of transportation as a consequence of that system (eg of people and materials moving to and from the designed system and the building's vehicular infrastructure); and the ecological consequences of these three aspects. These considerations are important because transportation (vehicles and access infrastructures) uses large quantities of fossil fuels and non-renewable energy resources as well as material resources, besides having attendant consequences (eg design of more roads, car-park structures, etc). The basis of site selection for new buildings, facilities and infrastructure is not just the site's ecosystem history (see B4), but also its proximity to existent transportation hubs or stations.

	Car (km/litre)	Refrigerator (kWh/day)	Gas furnace (10^6 J/day)	Air conditioner (kWh/day)	Residence (10 J^3/m^2/hour)
Current average	6	4	210	10	190
New model average	10	3	180	7	110
Best model	18	2	140	5	68
Best prototype	27	1	110	3	11

Energy efficiency potential of various household devices

Reducing transportation and its infrastructure

Ecodesign must seek to reduce the use by transportation of non-renewable sources of energy (eg oil resources), which accounts for 35 per cent of the total energy consumption in a nation (UK) and 83 per cent of the distance travelled. Consumption of energy from non-renewable sources by transportation is nearly as large as that of the industrial sector. Increasing transport activity is a key feature of our built environment that must be reversed. The urban transportation aspect of our designed system must be considered in all ecodesign endeavours. In the case of built facilities, this includes the provision of car access (eg road and vehicular access), which has consequences for the landscape. For example, the USA has 132 million cars, 1.9 million trucks, 715,000 buses and 21,000 locomotives. The design strategy is to seek transport mode integration through the reduction of private-vehicle transportation in favour of public transportation (buses and trains) and pedestrianisation. This is the second most ecologically efficient way to conserve fossil fuels and improve effective air quality. The designer can have an effective impact on public transportation facilities by designing built structures and spaces to include easy access to these systems.

	Kilometres per litre		
Date	Passenger cars	Vans, pick-up trucks, SUVs	Trucks
1975	5.0	3.7	2.0
1980	5.7	4.3	1.9
1985	6.2	5.0	2.0
1990	7.2	5.7	2.1
1995	7.5	6.1	2.2
2000	7.8	6.2	2.0

Motor vehicle fuel consumption (USA, 1975–2000)

· Chapter C ● Chapter B ● Chapter A ·

B10

Design to reduce the consequences of the various modes of transportation and of the provision of access
and vehicular parking for the designed system

168

	Approximate passenger km/litre (direct energy consumption)	
	Potential (fully loaded)	Typical (average load)
Urban automobile	22.66	22.66
Compact automobile	42.5	14.9
Urban diesel bus (for 45 passengers)	76.11	20.9
Rail rapid transit	186	14.9

Energy efficiencies and capacities
of common transportation systems ●

Car and other vehicular parking provision uses up yet more material and energy resources in the provision of these structures in the designed system.

In addition, there are the environmental consequences of transporting materials and people to and from the designed system during construction and operation, plus the eventual transportation consequences entailed by the reuse and recycling of the system's materials. Compared to rail and buses, cars generate the highest carbon dioxide emissions per passenger for a given journey on land.

Where the designed system is a product, transportation considerations entail not only those leading to, and included in, its manufacture but also those entailed by its distribution and retail, and its subsequent collection for reuse and recycling.

Most design of built environments will involve the designing of roads as the means of access within the site and these have significant physical impacts on the ecosystems (eg the destination habitats for the physical structure, the division of existing habitats inhibiting species migration patterns, etc). Moreover, there are the energy and environmental costs of delivering and removing materials and wastes from the built environment and enabling people who use the built environment and its visitors to reach and leave it (eg in the evening to return home). In any event, transportation planning is a major design and planning determinant for cities and regional planning. The question, then, is how to address these aspects in ecodesign.

The motorcar is the least energy-efficient means of transportation. Strategically, in all aspects of its design, ecodesign must, therefore, first seek to discourage, reduce or eliminate the use of private motor vehicles. This tactic will reduce or eliminate the provision of access routes across the land.

Ecodesign as product design must also consider improving car design itself if its total elimination cannot be effected. The environmental consequences of its design should be reduced. 25 per cent of a car's lifetime environmental pollution and 20 per cent of its energy expenditure occur during its manufacture. Less steel used per car means less energy expenditure in the mining, refining, distributing, production and recycling of the steel in the car at the end of its useful life. During operation or use, in a typical car engine, only about 20 per cent of the high-quality energy in gasoline is converted into movements of pistons, gears and wheels. The other 80 per cent goes into the heat that is distributed, largely by the radiator, into the air and is lost in the engine heat and exhaust. In addition, half of the 20 per cent available for powering the car is used up in overcoming friction in the gears and tyres. In effect, only a tenth or less of the original fuel energy actually moves the car. The overall efficiency in terms of the proportions of fuel energy used to move the driver is 5 per cent of 20 per cent, being a mere 1 per cent.

Car design and its consequences

The designer must design cars that use less fuel. The cheaper the cost of fuel per mile, the further people are willing to drive. This may well be counterproductive as the better the gas mileage, the more the suburbs will sprawl out over greater landscapes, leading to increased demand for cars and freeways, and the need for ever more cars to service the expanding surburbia. Besides controlling sprawl, the designer must seek to produce an energy-efficient car – it will help create the energy-efficient city. The average fuel economy for a passenger vehicle is 20.8 miles per gallon (mpg). Hybrid electrical cars have been able to achieve 61 mpg in the city and 68 mpg on the highway.

Nor must the designer only reconsider car design (eg hybrid green cars); he must also assess the ecological impacts of motorcar production. This begins with the mining for metals, a process that releases large volumes of toxic emissions. Further enormous amounts of fossil fuel energy are expended in the mining, refining, smelting, casting and stamping of sheet metal for the car body and for engine parts. Eventually even the painting of cars creates air pollution, not to mention exhaust pollution during use and the eventual problem of disposal of used tyres and motorcar parts. The car production process generates about 29 tons of waste for every ton of car (eg Germany in the 1990s). Making a car emits as much air pollution as does driving a car for 10 years. Motor vehicle production (c 1990 in the USA) required about 10 to 30 per cent of the metals (mainly steel, iron and aluminium) used in the US economy. Half to two-thirds of the world's rubber goes into automobiles. In a 1999 advertisement, the Ford Motor Company boasted that it used enough steel to build 700 Eiffel Towers every year.

Car design: natural gas, electric, fuel cell

Ecodesign might consider the concept of natural gas cars which are 95 per cent cleaner than gasoline-powered cars, or the concept of hybrid cars. In addition to using cleaner fuels, natural gas or propane powered cars are designed not to be polluting or to emit carcinogenic particles, to have low fuel consumption and also to be less flammable.

We need to be aware that electric or fuel-cell cars are not the solution to replacing the internal combustion engine. They will not be available in large numbers nor will they single-handedly solve, or even make a significant impact on, the consumption of fossil fuels likely over the next decade or two. In a fuel cell, a chemical reaction converts hydrogen into

Class	MPG (city/highway)	
	High	Low
Two-seater car	61/68	8/12
Minicompact car	28/37	11/18
Subcompact car	42/49	10/15
Compact car	52/45	11/16
Midsize car	26/34	10/14
Large car	21/32	10/14
Small station wagon	42/50	17/21
Midsize station wagon	27/36	15/21
Sport utility vehicle	25/31	12/16
Minivan	21/27	15/20
Pick-up truck	24/29	12/16
Passenger van	16/20	13/17

*Vehicles over 8500 pounds gross weight rating are exempt from federal fuel economy requirements and are not included in the ratings.

Source: US Environmental Protection Agency

Highest and lowest fuel economy by vehicle class (2003)

B10

Chapter C ● Chapter B ● Chapter A ●

Design to reduce the consequences of the various modes of transportation and of the provision of access and vehicular parking for the designed system

Chapter C • Chapter B • Chapter A

B10

Design to reduce the consequences of the various modes of transportation and of the provision of access and vehicular parking for the designed system

170

Transportation means	Fuel efficiency
Helicopter	1.5
Supersonic plane	13.6
Boeing 707	21.0
Boeing 747	22.0
Automobile	32.0
Subway	75.0
Commuter train	100.0
Bus	125.0

Transportation fuel efficiency ●

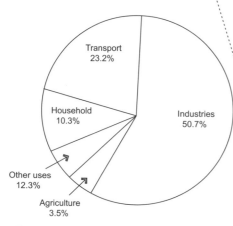

Transport uses over 20% of the energy consumption of a nation. Therefore the greater the intensification of development, the greater the saving in energy in transportation.

Energy consumption by sector (UK) ●

electricity, producing only water and heat. Fuel-cell technology is still in its early stages; the production of hydrogen is still mainly from fossil fuels. It is not yet a sustainable form of transport, not to mention the process of fuel-cell-car production itself, so fuel-cell cars – for all their comparatively green points – are still not good enough. Although fuel cells are two to three times more energy efficient than today's combustion engine, until the hydrogen in fuel cells can be derived from renewable sources such as water or even algae, it will not be emission-free because the main fuel currently used is methane, which needs to be burned to separate the hydrogen. In the case of electric cars, the problem is transferred to the electricity generating power plants. Electric cars bring emissions down to zero, but are not considered emission-free as fossil fuels are burned to produce the electricity at the power plant. Taking into account the fossil fuel origins, electric vehicles emit 67 per cent less carbon dioxide than gasoline powered cars. It is wrongly argued that conventional motorcars have greater environmental impacts than electric cars. A conventional motorcar creates 26 tons of hazardous waste for every ton the vehicle weighs, whereas a battery powered automobile produces twice as much, 52 tons, including lead and toxic acids.

There are, of course, those other problems that come with automobile transportation: violent accidents, dismemberment of the city and ecosystems, alienation, full cost of ownership, impervious paving surfaces, associated degradation of land, etc.

Then there is the consumption of energy in all the modes of transportation. About 32 per cent of the energy use in the developed world is in the operation of the various modes of transportation. In an industrialised nation, like the UK, private cars can account for 80 per cent of all the energy used for transport, and about 25 per cent of the nationwide output of carbon dioxide. By comparison, in the USA two-thirds of energy in the form of petroleum resources goes to fuelling the various modes of transportation.

Ecological design should seek to reduce air pollution simply by improving traffic regulation, as automobile traffic is one of the main causes of smog in cities and urban areas. Motorcars are responsible for 21 per cent of the world's global warming emissions (5443.2 kilograms of CO_2 per car per year). An average US passenger car gets around 23 miles per gallon while 1 gallon of petrol burned produces 23 pounds of carbon dioxide.

Addressing the implications of transportation

In considering the transportation implications, ecodesign must do the following:

• At the outset, eliminate the use of cars if possible. In 1995 there were over 530 million motorcars on earth. Their total ecological impact is significant. Their fuel requirements help propel the oil industry. Tractors and small trucks are used in agriculture.

- At the layout planning stage, seek to reduce the extent of road lengths and provision, to increase the provision of low-energy-consuming transportation systems and design to ensure interconnectivity with different modes of transportation meeting at the same point. This reduces the energy costs of connecting between different modes of transport and improves efficiencies. Plan and design to integrate the intensity of development (eg higher plot ratio permittance) with the surrounding community and with mass-transportation stations and nodes to save energy. For example, Hong Kong, which is a high-rise city, uses the least amount of petrol per capita in the world. Even the most energy-efficient use of energy in buildings achieves little if the building is distanced from accessible public transportation, cycle paths and pedestrian walkways.

- Discourage or totally desist from planning the urban environment around cars and automobile infrastructure (ie roads and highways, etc).

- Ecological design and planning should lay out the various land-uses and the access systems in the masterplan so as to encourage the use of public and mass transit as well as cycling and walking, and avoid the use of the motorcar. Once communities have been shaped by cars, they remain dependent on them.

- Design for higher density and diversity in order to be less dependent on motorised transport because the fewer resources that are required, the less impact there will be on nature. The quality of life largely depends, therefore, on how we build our cities in relation to the environmental consequences and impacts of transportation. High urban dwelling densities and development plot ratios generally allow for greater energy efficiency in mass transportation, as opposed to sprawl planning concepts. In specific areas, ecological planning might seek to intensify the urban density of population by design as studies show that the higher the density and diversity of a city the less dependent it is on motorised transport. In planning for urban growth in existent urban environments (eg cities), instead of expanding the city's boundaries or constructing satellite cities, it is better to optimise the land use within the existing/urban environments, for example by the reuse of brownfield sites to increase the intensity of the built environment and existent densities in specific areas that are already well served by public transport.

- Shift short-distance air transport to ground modes. For example, a 100-mile flight consumes 2~5 times as much fuel per passenger mile as a 1000-mile flight.

B10

Chapter C ● Chapter B ● Chapter A ●

Design to reduce the consequences of the various modes of transportation and of the provision of access and vehicular parking for the designed system

Sprawl patterns of urban built environment layouts

• Layout planning must avoid urban sprawl where people must drive to do virtually everything, using up non-renewable fossil fuels with their attendant ecological impacts. For instance, many American cities built after 1920 were shaped by mass ownership of automobiles (eg Los Angeles (LA), with its sprawl and freeways). In the 1940s, like several other American cities, LA dismantled its system of public trains to make way for cars. The city's automobile population quadrupled between 1950 and 1990 (to 11 million). The result is a city built for cars in a setting made for smog. By the 1960s the smog affected some 10 million people over hundreds of days a year and stunted the landscape's tree growth as much as 80 kilometres away. In 1976, the city's air was officially unhealthy three days out of four. Into the 1990s, the city's smog remained a regular health hazard.

Layout planning should cluster buildings, mix commercial and residential use, focus development around public transit routes, provide for bicycle and pedestrian commuting, and create cohesive neighbourhoods.

• Reshape the transportation mode and patterns in existing built environments. If we compare the energy consumed by the average person living in the suburbs to that consumed by the city dweller who does not own a car, a much greater level of energy (besides time and money) is expended by the suburbanite – equivalent to about 10 times the energy of the car-free city dweller in terms of the manufacture of cars and highways.

• Layout of vehicular access must not only ensure efficiency of land-use but also maintain the existent spatial ecological continuity within the site's ecosystems.

In designing for vehicles, their infrastructure and storage (eg surface car-parking), aim to reduce the land area to be provided for these uses (which serves to increase the land available for greening uses). Normally, in designing for these surface transportation land uses, the city's overall area is often forced to expand significantly to allow for public transportation vehicles and infrastructure. Access roads, which dominate the city and its transportation systems, become the single largest agent of resource depletion, habitat destruction, climate change and species extinction. For example, in providing land area for cars, the USA had laid 5.5 million kilometres of surfaced roads by 1990, exceeding the length of railways by a factor of 10 or 15. All these roads reorganised the nation's broad spaces into new patterns that attracted people, settlement and businesses, which in turn made car ownership almost essential for most adults. In North America, Europe and Japan land area for motorcars took up about 5 to 10 per cent of the land surface by 1990. Worldwide it took up about 1 to 2 per cent, matching the space taken by cities (and overlapping with it).

Pollution

- Educate people to reject driving cars and breathing smog and instead to accept limits on driving, and less smog. Historically, urban smog persisted for two main reasons: people had less choice since the public transit system was inadequate and the technology of automobile engines seemed the best option.

Lead emissions, mainly from automobile exhausts, increased from a yearly average of 22,000 tons between 1850 and 1900 to 430,000 tons between 1971 and 1980, before going down to 340,000 between 1981 and 1990, a reduction that reflected environmental awareness, new technologies and efficiencies.

It has been estimated that air pollution killed about 20 to 30 million people from 1950 to 1997. In addition, in the 20th century air pollution provoked or aggravated chronic illness among hundreds of millions more.

- Ensure that vehicular exhaust and air pollution do not affect or impair conservation of existing structures (eg monuments). For example, the car exhaust fumes (in Athens, Greece) did more damage to the ancient marble on the Acropolis in the space of 25 years than did all the weathering of the previous 2400 years. The statue of Michelangelo's David (in Florence) is so susceptible to the locality's air pollution that a replica stands in its place. In India, the refineries at Agra emitted sulphur dioxide that ate away at the Taj Mahal's structure. The Mayan limestone monuments in Tikal (Guatemala) showed the corrosive effects of oil combustion 100 kilometres away.

- Design to reduce car accidents. The human consequence of having cars is that car accidents kill a large number of people. In the USA it has been estimated that between two and three million people were killed in car accidents over the 20th century. Worldwide, 400,000 people were killed in such accidents every year by the end of the century. The number of accidents (including fatalities) per mile travelled in poor countries is 26 times higher than that in richer nations.

- Design to reduce the attendant costs of transport including shipping routes and pipelines.

The amount of petrol used per mode of transport is as follows:
Driving 32-kilometre round trip to a shopping mall: 4.546 litres
Shipping 1609-kilometre freight: 3 litres
Shipping 1609-kilometre via truck: 0.455 litres

Impact on pollution (output)	Impact on local ecosystem (output)	Impact on resource (output)
Emission of greenhouse gases CO_2, NO_2, and (indirectly) O_2	Health and fertility effects of CO_2	Increasing use of limited non-renewable energy resources (eg energy oil)
Contribution to acid rain SO_2, NO_2	Effects of lead on child mental development lead (PG)	Use of metals and other non-renewables in manufacturing
	Health effects of SO_2, black smoke, volatile organic compounds (VOCs) and low-level ozone (O_3)	Use of scarce land resources for roads and parking

● Environmental impacts of transport

Chapter C ● Chapter B ● Chapter A ●

B10

Design to reduce the consequences of the various modes of transportation and of the provision of access and vehicular parking for the designed system

Type of carrier	Speed (kilometres per day)	Volume carried (ton-kilometres per day)
Human porter	30	1.0
Pack animal	30	3.5 to 60
Two horses and wagon	30	60
Railway train	740	5,000,000
Motor truck	1125	20,000
Expressway motor truck	1600	60,000
Aeroplane (DC-3)	5800	15,800
Jet aeroplane (707 and DC-8)	18,500	360,000
Jumbo jet aeroplane (747)	19,300	1,750,000
Cargo ship	885	9,960,000
Container ship	970	25,400,400
Barge tow	200	7,000,000
Supertanker	640	175,000,000

Comparison of modes for transportation of goods

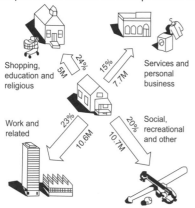

Shopping, education and religious — 24% 5M

Services and personal business — 15% 7.7M

Work and related — 23% 10.6M

Social, recreational and other — 20% 10.7M

Total household trips: each group of activities represents the average distance travelled

Existent domination of transportation routes over built form and landscape

• Design and plan for the proximity and disposition of other land uses in the context of the project site to reduce dependency on vehicles. An example is in the layout of shopping and retail facilities, as one of the major uses of motorcars is for shopping trips. Encourage on-line internet purchasing to reduce the number of such trips. Buying an item on-line and having it shipped via ground transport directly to the recipient saves more energy than any other type of on-line purchase. If domestic groceries are ordered on-line and delivered to the home each week, the household will save on the use of petroleum energy, plus hours of shopping and driving time.

• Optimise the modes of transportation that use the least energy. Including air conditioning in cars, which adds around 15 per cent to fuel use, we can compare road travel, aeroplane travel and rail travel in terms of energy consumption. In terms of fuel efficiency rail travel is the best. In comparing energy use by trains as against the aeroplane, trains are two to eight times as fuel efficient. Promoting well-operated high-speed regional rail systems would reduce costs and maximise energy efficiency, and in turn reduce the environmental and traffic pressures generated by highways and airports.

Aeroplane travel is responsible for roughly 8 per cent of the world's global warming emissions, although the number of people who travel by air is significantly smaller than those for car or rail use. For example, one round-trip flight New York–San Francisco will produce 2925.72 litres of carbon dioxide per passenger. The global warming effect of the carbon emissions from jet engines is tripled because of the fact that pollutants are injected high up into the earth's atmosphere where they can do the most damage.

Pollution measured by CO_2 emissions in grams per tonne per kilometre in a comparison of different transport modes is as follows:

Boat: 30

Rail: 41

Road: 207

Air: 1206

• Design and plan to take into account transportation within the project site itself, as well as transportation movement to the site. Transportation consumes about 23 per cent of the energy used in a nation and, directly or indirectly, buildings contribute towards energy use through the transport implications of the form, type and location of the development. For example, in 1996 Europe had one car per 2.5 persons making clear the importance of evaluating the transportation context and implications of large buildings that may have hundreds or even thousands of occupants.

Ensure that the imposition of a high-intensity building on a location is coordinated (where possible) with other buildings to manage the volume of traffic that will be generated and the impact on the roads and mass-transit systems, as well as the energy consequences. Clearly, the layout of the access routes and roads within the site is as much of design concern as are the energy implications of the distribution of goods from our built system and the bringing of materials to the site during construction. The energy used per mile per ton of freight (by road in the UK) averages 0.0056 GJ.

Promote cycling and walking

- Design the site planning to promote the proximity of food and other retail outlets to encourage walking and pedestrianisation of precincts. Shopping trips account for 13 per cent of all the personal mileage per year (in the UK). Shopping by car accounts for 86 per cent of the total mileage travelled (UK). In setting out the layout plan, ecodesign should encourage people to walk instead of using cars. Lazy walking distance standards are about 150 metres with a maximum walking distance of, say, 300 metres. If walking as a mode of transport is to be encouraged, then the layout must provide routes that are wide enough to cope with the population density. If covered verandas are preferred (in hot humid climates), then these should be provided. Buses, trams or trains are more energy efficient than cars. For instance, trains run on electricity and therefore help to reduce the pollution from petrol exhaust. It has been estimated that 200 trees are required to absorb the carbon dioxide from one car. Therefore, the designer must ensure that the energy impact of the design takes into account car ownership figures: 0.3 cars per person in the UK, 0.56 cars per person in the USA and 0.0012 cars per person in India.

- Design to encourage the switch to bicycles or walking for shorter journeys and the use of public transport (buses and trains) for longer journeys. In site planning we should maximise the use of public transport (and create bicycle and footpath systems), avoid further decentralised development (such as in new suburban and greenfield developments) and at the same time increase densities and intensities around existing suburban transport routes. The widely dispersed, single-land-use development has the effect of separating the demand for goods and services from the supply. To connect the two, people travel increasingly; but intensive developments such as skyscrapers help create more efficient, low-energy urban environments.

- Design to use alternative low-energy means of access such as walking or bicycling and other vehicles to reduce pollution and land development impacts from automobile use. Planning can provide transportation amenities such as alternative refuelling stations and carpool/vanpool programmes or the opportunity to share the costs and benefits of refuelling

Material	Distance (km)
Reclaimed tile	160
Reclaimed slate	480
Reclaimed bricks	112
Recycled aggregates	240
Reclaimed timber (eg floorboards)	1600
Reclaimed steel products	4000
Reclaimed aluminium products	12,000

Example of transport distances for reclaimed materials

Energy use	Kilograms coefficient
In the household for each kilowatt hour	
Electricity	x 0.45
Gas	x 0.19
Heating oil	x 2.975
In travel for each kilometre	
Petrol car: as driver	x 0.20
Diesel car: as driver	x 0.14
Rail: InterCity	x 0.11
Other services	x 0.16
Underground	x 0.07
Bus: London	x 0.09
Outside London	x 0.17
Express coach	x 0.08
Bicycle	x 0.00
Walking	x 0.00
Air travel:	
Within Europe	x 0.51
Outside Europe	x 0.32

Annual carbon dioxide emissions (kgCo$_2$)

B10

Chapter C ● Chapter B ● Chapter A ●

Design to reduce the consequences of the various modes of transportation and of the provision of access and vehicular parking for the designed system

stations with neighbours. On foot, humans can cover 24 miles in eight hours at the fairly fast pace of three miles per hour.

- Design the built systems to encourage the use of bicycles for shorter journeys and to provide related amenities such as bicycle racks and showering/changing facilities. For instance, commercial or institutional buildings can provide secure bicycle storage with convenient changing/shower facilities (within 200 yards of the building) for the regular building occupants. For residential buildings, covered storage facilities can be provided for securing bicycles for the occupants.

- Design and plan for the location of intensive land uses and new built environments to be in close proximity to existent public transportation (eg within half a mile of a commuter rail, light rail or underground station or quarter of a mile of two or more convenient bus routes). This will reduce pollution and land development impacts from automobile use.

- Design to reduce car use and the provision of car-parking and minimise the provision of parking lots, car park and garage size. This will reduce pollution and land development impacts from single occupancy vehicle use. Ecodesign should also allow for shared parking facilities with adjacent buildings and bumper-to-bumper parking. The designer can size parking capacity in line with local zoning requirements and provide preferential parking for carpools or vanpools capable of serving the building's occupants.

- In the case of a product, design the transportation implications to include the flow of materials leading to its manufacture and the subsequent transportation of the finished product to its storage, retail and distribution.

- Transportation design considerations must also include the encouragement of local food production (see B21). The carriage of food accounts for over 33 per cent of road freight (in the UK).

   The junctions (eg interchanges), provision of vehicular access, vehicular drop-off points and service points, vehicular parking, and the movement of people and materials to and from the designed system, all influence the shape, orientation and layout of the built form of the designed system.

- Transportation considerations must also include air travel. A reduction in international air travel is essential. Only 14 per cent of visits abroad by UK residents (in 2001) were for business.

- The consequences of transportation can be quantified in terms of the energy consumed in the movement of people, goods and wastes to and from our designed system. However, the impacts of transportation also include the provision of vehicular access (roads, etc) as well as vehicular parking and the consequences on other modes of transport (eg public transportation) as well as the emissions of all the above into the biosphere (see A5 as a checklist). Planning must at the outset avoid emphasising vehicular access.

Efficient energy use in transportation

Efficiency of energy use in the transport sector can relate to vehicles, passengers or journeys and each category needs to be measured differently. The three categories are:

- Vehicle efficiency: the efficiency of moving the vehicle around, measured as kilometres per litre (or miles per gallon).

- Passenger/freight efficiency: the efficiency of moving the passenger or goods around by that mode of transport, measured as energy per passenger kilometre or for freight per tonne kilometre.

- Journey efficiency: the fuel required to get from A to B by any method of transport.

Summary

The designer must consider the transportation implications of the designed system at every stage of the life cycle of the designed system. This includes assessing the energy consumption of moving people and goods to and from the built environment over every stage in its life cycle from its production, to operation, to reuse, recycling and reintegration. The location of the new built forms should be at or near existent public transportation nodes, interchanges or routes. Planning layouts and concepts should reduce the need for vehicular transportation (eg non-sprawl layout, intensified concentrated layouts that encourage pedestrian movement and discourage the use of vehicles, etc) and encourage the use of low-energy-movement systems. Ecodesign considerations must cover the transportation consequences of the inputs and outputs to the designed system including the moving of people, materials, energy, information and equipment to and from the designed system.

Generally, ecodesign must seek to reduce the environmental consequences of the use of non-renewable energy and seek the provision of low-energy-use access arising from and related to the transportation requirements of the designed system, whether it is a product or a built structure or infrastructure.

Country of origin	Energy costs of transportation to UK via container ship (GJ/tonne)
Papua New Guinea	2.4
Indonesia	2.2
British Columbia	1.0
Brazil	0.7
Ghana	0.6
Siberia	0.5
Finland	0.3
Sweden	0.1

Comparison of energy costs of transportation

B10

Chapter C ● Chapter B ● Chapter A ●

Design to reduce the consequences of the various modes of transportation and of the provision of access and vehicular parking for the designed system

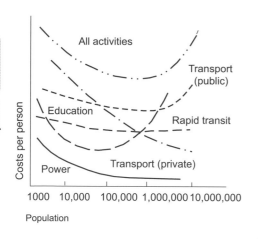

Costs per person

All activities

Transport (public)

Education

Rapid transit

Power

Transport (private)

1000 10,000 100,000 1,000,000 10,000,000

Population

Threshold to urban density: economies and diseconomies of scale in providing urban services

B11 Design to integrate with the wider planning context and urban infrastructure of the designed system

Ecodesign must not consider the designed system and its site in isolation, but in the larger context of the existent built and urban environment, as well as the natural environment (in B5) in which it is inserted and its connection and distance to the existent infrastructure systems of its utilities and vehicular routes. This is important to ensure a benign and seamless integration not only with the natural environment but with the existent human-made built urban environments and infrastructures. The objective is to create region-wide integrated green communities.

Very often a well-considered ecodesign scheme has the potential to change the urban context in which it is located ecologically. Furthermore, the individual site must not be seen in isolation but rather as an integrated part of the human-made greater urban context, especially in existent highly urbanised localities.

Conventional urban planning approaches have, in most instances, been more concerned with 'utopian' planning ideas than with natural processes as determinants of urban form. The planning approach has been to assert predetermined images of what urban places ought to be, rather than formulating what they actually are based on the locality's natural characteristics and features as determinants of urban form. Further, many landscape designers misguidedly transfer natural environments from their places of origin to places in existent built environments (ie the city) where they can be sustained only at high environmental cost at the expense of nature, and subsequently become a prescription for environmental catastrophe. The city of Tucson, Arizona (USA), in the 1950s employed intensive irrigation to support its green lawns and lush vegetation. However, legislation introduced in the 1960s required that ground-water withdrawal be balanced by natural replenishment. The result was that the energy-intensive high-maintenance greenery was replaced with indigenous desert plants. As a consequence, the city acquired a more regionalist sense of belonging to the landscape. What makes rational environmental sense is usually achieved only when change is perceived as absolutely necessary to survival.

We also need to look at urban and city planning in relation to the existent use of non-renewable energy. The fossil-fuel era brought with it new ways of planning and organising human society, including industrial enterprise, nation-state governance, dense urban settlement and the lifestyle of the developed world. The centralisation of power and economies of scale that so characterised the fossil-fuel era inevitably led to the concentration of human population in megacities that use up vast amounts of energy and are ultimately unsustainable. Many electricity power plants are located at great distances from the consumers of their output.

On average, electricity travels 220 miles (352 kilometres) or more from the power plant to the users.

Ecodesign in urban planning may be viewed in two ways. The first concerns the protection and restoration of the remaining biological phenomena and processes within the urban community itself in the greening of the city. Obviously, apart from its functional aspects, ecology is concerned with the aesthetic, educational, recreational and psychological benefits of natural areas within cities. The second concerns the impacts that urban built environments (eg cities) have upon the larger terrestrial, aquatic and atmospheric resources of the biosphere from which they draw sustenance and upon which they inflict harm. In this respect ecodesign must involve the resolution of urban problems such as those arising from transportation, energy conservation, air and water pollution abatement, material and nutrient cycling, etc, within existent built environments.

Site planning and conservation strategies

It is necessary for our design and planning ecological objectives to aim at the protection of most of the remaining ecosystems and species in the biosphere (see B4 and B5). The following broad planning strategies apply not just as conservation strategies but as planning strategies for regional as well as local sites:

- Salvage and conserve immediately those localities in the planning area that are ecologically critical.
- Keep intact the vegetated areas and remaining frontier forests.
- Cease all deforestation of sites with old growth and mature forests (see B4).
- Concentrate on the existent marine, lake and riverine ecosystems, especially those that are particularly threatened.
- Define precisely the critical places for ecological conservation in the locality.
- Carry out and complete the mapping of the biodiversity of the locality and region as a baseline to render the conservation efforts exact and effective.
- Use recent advances in mapping techniques to map the locality's terrestrial, freshwater and marine ecosystems, ensuring that their full range is included in the conservation strategy.
- Make ecological conservation integral with all the designed human systems and built environments.
- Use biodiversity more effectively to benefit all the human systems.
- Continuously initiate ecological restoration and rehabilitation of key areas in that locality.
- Increase the capacity of fauna and flora preservation zones and conservation areas and botanical zones in that locality.

- Design to include a re-examination of existent large concentrated built environments such as our cities, towns and suburbs, as urban ecosystems (albeit incomplete and currently throughput systems). Their multiscaled relationships to surrounding air, water, land, biota and human institutions are usually complex and poorly understood. Existent urban use has required urban infrastructures that have changed the local hydrology and nutrient exchanges dramatically, altering primary production (plant growth and tree cover), and the locus of secondary production (eg butterflies, birds) and decomposition within landfills and incinerators.

Although, currently, global urban areas occupy only 2 per cent of the world's land surface, they use 75 per cent of the world's resources and release a similar percentage of global wastes. For example, in 1996, London's footprint was 125 times its surface area, ie nearly 20 million hectares compared to 159,000, although it contains only 12 per cent of the population of the UK.

- Integrate planning considerations with existent built environments and their amelioration and revision.

- Design with patterns of site-planning layouts that facilitate ecosystem interactions and avoid those patterns that inhibit such interactions.

- Design with patterns of site planning, building configurations and linkages that encourage low-energy and pedestrian movements (in preference to the use of private transportation and cars) as well as enhancing ecological connectivities; introduce ecological corridors (see B7 and B8).

- Design to promote proximity of the built system to other existing community facilities such as shops, schools, workplaces, recreation areas, etc, to reduce transportation requirements and therefore their impact (see B10).

- Design and plan for proximity to an existing urban mass-transit station or mass-transportation collection point; the nearer the built system is to such a location, the less will be the dependency on the use of additional modes of transport.

- Design to avoid urban-sprawl patterns that lead to a high level of motorcar dependence with a minimal role for public transport, cycling or walking. The consequences of such patterns are high consumption of petrol and correspondingly high levels of smog, severe stress due to traffic congestion, and loss of street life, with compromised community and public safety (see B10). Urban sprawl is the widespread, generally low-rise, building over of natural landscapes around older, more compact settlements such as cities and urban centres. Components of sprawl include an extensive network of spread-out housing subdivisions and their supporting roads and highways. Sprawl is one outcome when long-established urban centres reach their boundaries, creating a creeping, extending pattern of development. This is suburbanisation, the development of areas that are neither urban, with complete amenities and facilities, nor rural, that is primarily suitable for agricultural use, nor forest, which encompasses an area's animals, plants, rivers and other natural life forms. Suburbs have been in existence for more than 50 years and, as two generations have been brought up within these sprawling areas, many have grown to assume that it is the best way to live – to fulfil human needs for contact, food, culture, recreation and work by driving. Few expect or demand that our planners and developers build more compactly, or plan so that such facilities are accessible by foot.

Sprawl is a threat to the environment. The ground may be levelled in hilly or undulating areas. The topsoil is removed and the ground cover, including all the plants and the animals living within them (many of which may be undiscovered and undescribed), is eliminated. Developers are also known to have covered up entire waterways or deflected their course to enable them to build more houses. If a swampy area or part of a wetlands system is filled in, whatever benefit the wetlands performed in the natural cycle of the surrounding habitat is lost for ever.

However, there is more to sprawl than its physical impact on our environment. People have to travel by car all the time. Humans are consuming land that could otherwise feed more people than the number of people housed in a single residence. In the Philippines, most new subdivisions are built over fertile agricultural land. Elsewhere, the biggest contaminant of some of the riverine systems is lawn fertiliser, and where the entire garden area is paved over to park cars all rainwater will add to the runoff from impervious surfaces. These areas are very rarely planted with food.

Like most environmental problems, sprawl can be stopped or slowed down. This can be done in several ways, for example by planning controls that allow judicious infilling or densification of already established urban areas or by allowing mixed developments that combine housing, commercial and other uses in a smaller area and so inhibit further construction of sprawling urban patterns.

- Design for intensification of built-up areas and increased population density in existing urban areas; studies have shown that energy consumption is thus reduced.

For example, in European cities compact dense developments have become more widespread. Major new growth areas are situated in locations within or adjacent to existing developed areas and are designed at relatively high densities. Such developments are designed to incorporate a mix of uses, balancing workplaces and housing with ecological features.

Large parts of these areas can be heated by means of district-wide heating supplied from power-plants that are situated close by and use waste energy. A double water system can provide both potable and recycled water for non-potable uses, together with storm-water management through a system of natural swales. Homes are low energy and must use sustainably harvested wood.

- Design and plan to optimise land uses in existent intensively built environments by the redevelopment and adaptive reuse of older deteriorated areas on recycled land within or near the city centre.

- Design all major new-growth built environments to have good public transport as a basic underlying design assumption in order to reduce the consumption of energy by private transport. Construction of these systems does not need to wait until the residential components have been built; rather the lines and investments should be concurrent with the built projects.

- Design and plan new built environments with a closed-loop or circular urban metabolism; where all waste represents input for other urban processes. For instance, ecodesign can ensure that governmental administration is reorganised so that the departments controlling waste, water and energy are grouped within an ecocycles division (eg to coordinate harvesting of biogas from sewage sludge to power public vehicles and as fuel for combined heat and power plants to provide district heating).

- Use clustered and compact urban-planning patterns to enable combined heat and power generation and district heating. For example, if the built system's buildings are connected to such a generation plant, it can result in substantially increased fuel efficiency and significant reductions in pollution emissions.

- Use street patterns to disperse rather than concentrate traffic.

- Design street patterns to conform to the site's natural topography to reduce the environmental impact and the alteration of the site's natural drainage patterns. This would also save costs by eliminating unnecessary over-engineering of road systems.

- Design and plan increased greenery with the streetscapes.

- Design and plan to reduce the areas of impervious surfaces. For instance, the designer can cluster built forms and extend them vertically, to enable shared driveways, and decrease side and rear garden setbacks to reduce impervious paving. Design can specify alternative paving surfaces (eg porous concrete). If impervious paving is necessary, recycled paving materials such as crushed glass, recycled tyres and aggregate should be used.

Generally, the form of our designed system must integrate not only with the natural environment and the characteristics of the ecosystem within which it is located, but it must also integrate with the existent planning context.

Summary

The designer should not limit the appraisal of the ecological implications of the proposed designed system to within the confines of the project site, but must include its consequences on, and integration with, the wider context of the human-made urban environment in the region within which the intended designed system is to be located. Having done so, the designer must then integrate the designed system's configuration, landscape pattern, ecological corridors and transportation requirements with this greater built context (which must, of course, also include its ecological context). Ecodesign is about designing the built system not as an isolated object or system but as a system integrated with other human-made built environments as well as the natural environment.

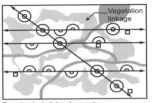

Transit-oriented developments

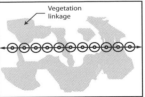

The linear city

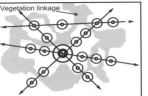

The polycentric net or regional city

- City forms, transportation linkages and linked ecological zones

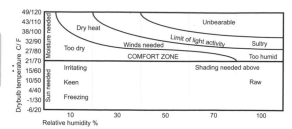

- Rooms should be as cool as is compatible with comfort.
- The velocity of air movements should be at least 10 m (33 ft) per minute in winter - less than 6 m (20 ft) per minute may cause stuffiness.
- Air movement should be variable.
- The relative humidity should not exceed an upper maximum of 70% and should preferably be substantially lower than that.
- The average temperature of internal surfaces should be above, or at least equal to, the air temperature.
- The air temperature should not be appreciably higher at head level than it is at floor level, and excessive radiant heat should not fall on the heads of occupants.

Comfort conditions ●┄┄┄┄┄

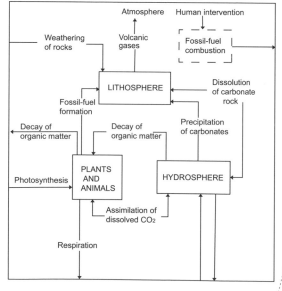

Disruption to the carbon cycle in the biosphere by ●┄┄┄ human intervention through fossil-fuel combustion

B12 Design for improved internal comfort conditions (of the designed system as an enclosure): designing the built system based on the progressive optimisation of modes (B13 to B17)

Where ecodesign involves the designing of an enclosure such as a building or built structure, then, in the designing and shaping of its built form, its enclosure and internal environmental systems, it is necessary for the designer to establish the level of internal conditions that will be acceptable to the users (see B1) and at the same time will be low in the consumption of non-renewable energy resources (eg fossil fuels, electricity, etc). One of the key ecodesign determinants is energy or how much non-renewable energy is consumed to create these comfort conditions. Obviously, the lower the comfort conditions, acceptable to the users, below standard design conditions (eg within ±1° of standards set by ASHRAE), the lower will be the overall consumption of energy. This type of energy conservation is vital because, for instance, if global oil production were to peak some time in the next decade or so, followed by a global peak in natural gas production, then a world economy without adequate electricity or fossil fuels could set off a cascade of events that could well unravel much of our current domestic and industrial way of life. Designing for the conservation of non-renewable energy resources is designing for temporal integration.

Comfort zones are usually between 18°C (65°F) and 24°C (75°F), but this varies depending on the relative humidity, which should remain between 30 and 65 per cent. Relative humidity is a measure of the amount of water vapour in the air, 100 per cent being saturated air. Within the above general limit the higher the relative humidity becomes the lower the air temperature needs to be in order for humans to feel comfortable. Thermal comfort is not just about air temperatures and temperature gradients, radiant temperature, air movement and ambient water vapour pressure, but also about the amount of clothing worn by the occupants and the occupants, level of activity.

At the same time that the designer is resolving the spatial requirements of the built form and selecting the materials and components to be used, consideration also needs to be given to the technology available for the operational systems. The latter is important to meet the objective of improving the building envelope and in developing passive mode (bioclimatic and solar driven) strategies to optimise internal comfort conditions while reducing energy demands on electricity and fossil fuels since people now spend roughly 90 per cent of their time inside buildings. Solutions should be chosen that meet the criteria of an overall energy balance and materials recovery and reflect the latest technical knowledge on the use of environmentally compatible forms of energy.

The existent built environment and globalisation are dependent on fossil fuels. Fossil fuels have allowed human commercial enterprises radically to compress time and shorten distances, making possible a single world market for the exploitation of raw resources and human labour and for the marketing of finished products and services. Ecologically, the cost of producing energy is our greatest energy cost. However, in the typical office building, the cost of energy saving is small compared to the office workers' salaries.

Internal comfort conditions: energy systems

We need to look at the use of non-renewable energy in relation to the five basic modes for creating internal conditions of comfort for users of built structures:

- Passive-mode systems. These systems use no non-renewable energy and are preferred over active systems (ie systems that use electromechanical devices); such passive systems should be maximised as the first basic step in ecodesign.

- Mixed-mode systems (ie partially electromechanically assisted systems that optimise other ambient energies of the locality).

- Full-mode systems. These are fully active systems and in ecodesign they should have low energy and low environmental impacts (eg low or even zero carbon dioxide emissions).

- Productive-mode systems. These are systems that generate on-site energy (eg photovoltaic systems, wind generators, etc).

- Composite-mode systems, being a composite of all the above.

In ecodesign it is crucial for the designer strategically, first progressively and then sequentially, to optimise all the passive-mode options for the designed system before proceeding to any of the other modes listed above as these systems use zero electromechanical systems to provide improved internal comfort conditions.

As a design strategy, this makes ecological sense because if we first optimise all the passive modes in our built form, then any subsequent strategies should serve to enhance its low-energy performance. If we do not adopt this strategy, we may end up with an inappropriate built form, which will then have to be supplemented or rectified thus making a total nonsense of low-energy design. Furthermore, if the built form is configured to be habitable without any external sources of energy, then in the event of power failure it is still comfortable to occupy. A wrongly configured passive-mode building, on the other hand, may be totally unusable in the event of a power failure. Then, having optimised the passive-mode strategies, if necessary the mixed-mode strategies can be implemented, followed by optimising the energy efficiency of full-mode systems.

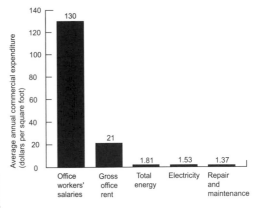

Comparison of energy costs with office workers' salaries

Mode	Internal systems	Example
Passive mode	No M&E systems	Traditional dwellings
Mixed mode	Partial M&E systems	Ceiling fans
Full mode	Full M&E systems	Conventional
Productive mode	Productive M&E systems	Photovoltaics
Composite mode	Composite of the above	Seasonal strategies

Modes for creating internal conditions of comfort

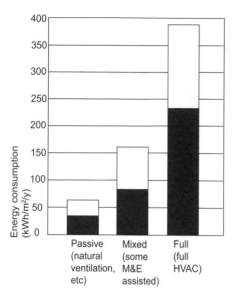

Energy consumption targets of various modes of operational systems in the built forms

This progressive selection of modes by design affects the configuring and planning of the built form and this step by step design can follow from or be designed concurrently with, the site's ecological analysis (in B5). In the process of shaping the built form, we need first to look at opportunities to optimise all the passive modes or bioclimatic design options in relation to controlling the external climatic conditions and ambient energies of that locality. Energy analysis may be used to refine the design. After construction is completed, the designer should utilise full systems building commissioning to ensure that systems perform as intended.

The basis for any built structure is its enclosed functions where its *raison d'être* is to provide an enclosure for some human or human-related activity (eg storage). The obvious function of an enclosure is to provide protection from the climate outside and to supply an improved level of internal conditions over the outside environment, and this can be achieved through the various modes indicated above.

In natural systems, the environmental conditions of the habitats of animals and other organisms are sustained by passive means (for example in ant-hills) or by some organic means. In the case of the human-built environment, the internal environmental conditions have now become sustained by mechanical means (eg using M&E equipment and technology) and the use of sources of energy that are not ambient to the project site (and thus are non-passive); instead, they are usually supported by non-renewable sources such as electricity generated from oil, coal, gas or other fuel. Ecodesign, in imitation of natural systems, should optimise the use of all passive systems of operation and of the climatic and diurnal conditions of the locality. The operational systems in our building are those systems that generate internal environmental conditions of comfort and facilitate materials recovery (ie L11 in A5).

A number of technical solutions presented here have aspects that require refinement and modification to meet ecological objectives fully. Nevertheless, as the technology for ecological design is still in its early developmental stages, such systems are not to be seen as panaceas. By applying our 'law of ecological design', all these operational systems need to be evaluated for their inputs, outputs, operational consequences and external consequences. Many of these analyses have still to be carried out. This section provides the broad strategy for the design of a large building's operational systems. Others elsewhere have covered the engineering aspects of various operational systems in great detail. The type of operational system to adopt – whether passive, mixed mode, full mode, etc – is dependent on the climate of the locality and its ecology (ie L22 in A5).

At the schematic design stage, the designer should have completed all the usual built-form design analyses for the project to enable the next set of decisions to be made, on the building's passive and active operational systems. These are the internal ecological interdependencies to consider (see A5). The building's total operational activity during its life cycle must be kept in mind, and design considerations should include all the ecological impacts and interactions that result from these activities (ie L11 in A5). The important factors include spatial displacement of the environment, energy and materials (both inputs and emissions), the activities of building users and the functional systems of the structure itself.

Our examination of the entirety of the resource flow and the use of materials and energy in the built environment's operational phases should make clear each building's individual pattern use. This pattern, in turn, is evaluated for its potential environmental impact and modified accordingly. For example, we can establish annual energy consumption targets per square metre as benchmarks for different building types. Similar sets of design criteria can be established for the primary embodied energy or the embodied carbon dioxide production for different building types. Similar discharge (output) indexes can be established for different building types (eg gross tonnage of wastepaper per annum per square metre, etc).

We have seen that the majority of energy use (L21 in A5) and a similar proportion of carbon dioxide emissions (outputs, L12 in A5) are associated with buildings, with 60 per cent attributed to the residential building type and 7 per cent to the commercial office building. Such statistics would seem to indicate that our design efforts should be directed first at minimising the energy use in the residential building type, followed by the commercial office building type; these figures emphasise the residential building type because of the greater volume of residential building. On a per-square-metre basis, however, commercial buildings consume greater energy than residential structures. In both types, about 60 per cent of the energy use during the operational phase (L11 in A5) is accounted for by space heating and air conditioning. For example, primary embodied energy for buildings (eg in Europe) does not vary much between different structural solutions (about 2.5 to 3.5 GJ/m²) and this represents only some 5 to 10 per cent of the total energy over a normal 60-year building life. In effect, the entirety of constructional components' requirements (including lifetime decisions) comprises only 35 per cent of total energy demand.

The measure of the success of the ecodesign of a built system's operational system lies in achieving a lower operational energy consumption level per annum (in kWh/m²) per year and the least pollutive emissions and impaired effects on the ecosystems. For instance, for built systems in the temperate zone, a general target for full-mode buildings should be less than 150 kWh/m² per year for typical conventional full-mode commercial buildings. Added to this would, of course, be the necessity to meet the ecological criteria of the other sets of interactions (L22, L12 and L21 in A5).

Design decisions to be made	Ecological criteria to be evaluated (interactions framework)	Examples of design strategies to be considered	Examples of technological applications and inventions needed
▪ Choice of servicing system	▪ Depletion of energy and material resources during production, construction, operation and disposal	▪ Use ambient sources of energy and materials	▪ Demountable structures and system to permit further reuse
	▪ Discharges of outputs over their life cycle	▪ Reduce overall standard of user needs and comfort, and reduce overall consumption levels	▪ Materials derived from renewable resources ▪ Recycled materials
	▪ Spatial impacts on the ecosystems of the project site	▪ Optimise use of energy and material inputs	▪ Biodegradable materials, that can be assimilated into the ecosystems
	▪ Ecosystems' impacts caused by the actions and activities over the life cycle	▪ Optimise use of energy and material inputs ▪ Others	▪ Development of low energy consumption and low-pollutive forms of materials
▪ Others		▪ Others	
Spatial planning of built form	▪ Impacts on the ecosystem of the project site	▪ Design on a site of least ecological impact	▪ Ecosystem analysis of the site prior to location and reaction

• Ecological criteria for selection of operational system

Regions and selected countries	1980	1990	2000
World	68	70	71
North America	300	293	301
Canada	416	418	446
Mexico	56	63	65
United States	362	355	367
Central and South America	41	43	53
Argentina	61	61	77
Bolivia	15	15	19
Brazil	35	43	57
Ecuador/El Salvador	24	26	28
Guatemala	11	12	19
Nicaragua	10	9	14
Panama	13	12	12
Venezuela	49	36	57
Western Europe	111	112	118
Austria	142	147	155
Denmark	149	158	182
France	175	164	173
Germany	165	163	185

• Energy consumption, per capita (million kJ, world)

Technology	Characteristics	Functionality	Reliability	Buildability	Maintenance requirement	Notes
Natural ventilation	Uses natural pressure differences to ventilate internal areas	For simple buildings, but pollution and daylight conflicts need to be designed	Vents, cowls and windows need maintenance	No use of non-renewable energy	Vents, windows and any automated actuators need maintenance	Dusty air in hot climates cannot be easily filtered
Full-mode ventilation	Uses fan energy to control airflow into the built form	Needs fan power, but heat can be recovered	Complex controls require good management	Maintenance dependent	Equipment needs maintaining and a supply of filters is needed	System can be used for active thermal storage and powered by renewable energy
Mixed-mode ventilation	Uses a combination of fans and windows, as needed, for ventilation	Offers flexibility between natural and mechanical ventilation	Needs careful attention to controls	Adjustment dependent	Equipment needs maintaining and a supply of filters is needed	System can be used for active thermal storage and powered by renewable energy
Harvesting rainwater	Harvesting of rainwater for drinking or flushing	Dependent on rates of rainfall	Climate dependent	Simple and component based	Low maintenance for flushing, high for drinking	Depends on rainfall
Grey-water recovery	Recovery and storage of washing water for toilet-flushing purposes	For areas with low rainfall or with unreliable supplies of drinking water	Health factors	Component based	High maintenance (for monitoring, filters and disinfectant)	Depends on the severity of context
Composting toilets	Alternative to the flush toilet where effluent is stored and composted	For areas without a sewerage system	Manual dependent	Few moving parts, self-assembly	Low and easy maintenance	Systems not reliant on an electrical supply to heat the compost
Passive thermal storage	Exposed built form structure that controls solar gains and stores heating and cooling energy	Climate dependent	Climate dependent	May be dependent on availability of materials	Low maintenance	Depends on climate
Active thermal storage	Full-mode mechanical or semi-mechanical system to control rates of energy storage and discharge	May need energy for fans and controls; climate dependent	Can fail to perform without good control	Requires fine tuning to deliver consistency	Depending on complexity	May be fragile without robust controls, needs facilities management ability
Ice stores	Maximises off-peak refrigeration energy to charge an ice store for release of cooling energy during daytime	Higher overall energy penalty	Complex systems need constant management	Component based, but takes up space	Chillers, pumps, pipework and ice vessels	Often fragile wthout skilled management, needs good controls and financial acumen
Ground-source heat pumps	Uses latent heat in the ground to power a heat pump for cooling or heating mode	Location dependent	System maintenance	Component based, but boreholes can be high cost	Heat pump and controls need maintaining; boreholes can silt up	Closed circuit boreholes most reliable, open circuit may provide flushing/ irrigation water

Use of various conservation technologies in built forms

If we look at energy consumption in the operations of a commercial building, by far the highest energy use in full mode are the M&E systems, followed by the artificial lighting systems. The other mechanical and electrical systems (such as elevators, plumbing and sewerage systems) contribute marginally to the operational energy costs of the built system. Therefore, the first area on which to focus our energy conservation and efficiency efforts is the M&E systems, followed by artificial lighting. Our ecodesign objective should be to adopt a built form and its respective operational systems that will make the most of available natural lighting and ventilation and minimise the built system's remaining energy demands.

It has been proposed that as operational energy efficiency improves, these components of energy used in the built system's life cycle will become less important than the embodied energy used in the construction of the built system in the first place, which would become proportionally more significant. However, unless the built system approaches virtually zero energy consumption in its operational phase, it is likely that the 'initial energy costs' will remain small compared to the 'operational energy costs'. For example, it has been said that the preferred standard for the annual primary energy consumption in Germany should be less than 1UU kWh/m² per year.

Generally, the management of the built system's operational systems (whether passive, active, mixed mode or a composite) affects the overal thermal and ecological performance and impact of the building. We should note that the full-mode (active) systems have the biggest effect on the total energy consumption in the built system's overall lifetime use of energy. But, in order to be effective in achieving real energy conservation, all three aspects should be taken into account – beginning at the design and planning stages.

The intention here is not to provide design guidelines for all climatic zones (which is better covered elsewhere), but simply to show how various modes of handling the building's operational systems are to be dealt with in ecodesign.

Simply stated, the total set of interactions caused by our design system (see A5) is not defined only by those inherent in the making and construction of the building and its components, but includes everything that arises from its operational use, its final disposal, recovery and reintegration into the ecosystem.

The extent of provision of comfort conditions acceptable to the users of the built structure, facility or infrastructure determines the provision of these designed systems and therefore influences the extent and size of their form and provision.

The rationale for optimising passive-mode design options in the design of the built form is twofold: first as low-energy design (ie low use of non-renewable energy resources), and

Year	Total consumption	Residential	Commercial	Industrial	Transportation	Electric power
1975	76.004	15.707	9.986	31.064	19.226	21.503
1980	82.730	16.815	11.197	33.959	20.779	28.887
1985	81.000	16.980	12.185	30.666	21.175	28.012
1990	89.375	17.812	13.892	33.488	23.780	32.180
1995	94.120	19.509	15.198	35.936	25.294	34.850
2000	104.208	20.880	17.336	37.635	28.375	38.166
2001	101.637	20.332	17.263	35.682	28.375	36.661

Consumption, total and by end-use sector, in quadrillion kJ*

Energy consumption for different sectors (USA)

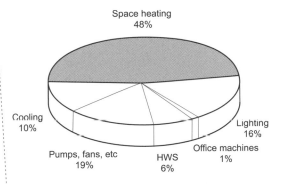

Delivered energy use in a typical air-conditioned office building

Air temperature (C)	Apparent temperature (C)		
35	34	42	58
30	29	32	38
25	23	25	27
RH (%)	20	50	80

What the body senses the temperature to be with various degrees of moisture in the air (RH = relative humidity). A combination of heat and humidity makes for heat exhaustion and discomfort – a different condition to that caused by dehydration in a hot dry climate, when it is necessary to drink sufficient water to replace salt lost through sweating.

Air temperature °(C)	Apparent temperature °(C)		
+10	+9	0	-3
+4	+3	-8	-12
-12	-14	-32	-38
Wind speed (m/sec)	2.0	9.0	18.0

Wind causes rapid evaporation of sweat and consequent cooling. When the air is cool, its movements sometimes cause wind chill, a combination that makes for considerable discomfort. The table shows the chilling effect of wind at various speeds, given as an apparent temperature, which is how people feel it to be, calculated from a formula based on the responses of a large number of people.

Comparison of air temperatures and apparent temperatures

second to relate the built configurations to the climate of the locality as a critical regionalist design.

If global oil and natural gas production peak, catching humankind unprepared, then the built environment (ie countries and energy companies) are likely to look to dirtier fossil fuels such as coal, heavy oil and tar sand as substitutes, leading to a serious increase in CO_2 emissions, an escalation in temperature rise and even more devastating effects on the earth's biosphere than have already been envisioned.

Excluding the ecological consequences of the physical presence of a built form, its outputs and transportation energy on the ecosystems of its locality, about 90 per cent of its environmental impact is from the creation of internal conditions of use and comfort (ie heating, cooling, lighting, etc) and only 10 per cent from its 'embodied energy' used to produce the fabric of the building itself (taken over a 60-year life cycle).

Summary

In those instances where the designer is designing a built structure, the usual approach will be to proceed with the planning of the layout and configuring of the built enclosures and their environmental systems while simultaneously considering the requirements of the project site (in B4 to B11). In designing the built enclosures and their environmental systems to provide improved comfort conditions over the external environment's conditions, the broad strategy is for the designer, progressively and sequentially, to first identify all passive-mode bioclimatic design options that are possible for that particular locality's climatic conditions and then to optimise these in the shaping, laying out (planning) and integrating of the built form with the locality's climate and ecology. This must be the crucial initial set of design steps adopted prior to moving on to any other design modes (in B13 to B17).

B13 Design to optimise all passive-mode (or bioclimatic design) options in the designed system: configuring the built form, its layout and plan, and designing for improved internal comfort conditions without the use of renewable sources of energy and as low-energy design in relation to the climate of the locality

Designing the enclosural system, the shape of the built form and the plan of our designed system is related first to the passive modes adopted for that design to create improved internal comfort conditions, which are significantly influenced by the climatic conditions and seasons for that locality. Ecodesign starts by optimising all the passive-mode design strategies to ensure an effective passive low-energy design at the outset (see B12). It is vital for ecodesign to adopt this approach in order to reduce the consumption of non-renewable energy resources and its associated negative consequences such as greenhouse emissions into the biosphere.

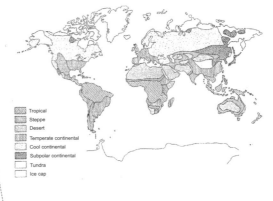

Tropical
Steppe
Desert
Temperate continental
Cool continental
Subpolar continental
Tundra
Ice cap

● Climatic zones around the world

In addition, the designer should undertake ecological analysis of the site's natural features (in B3 and B6) since these can significantly affect the layout of the built form and that of its roads and access routes. The other factors that can significantly affect the shaping of the built form are the passive-mode design options adopted, which are themselves influenced by the climatic conditions of the locality. These two aspects appear to be the primary determinants influencing built form.

As outlined in B12, there are five basic modes for designing suitable internal comfort conditions in the built environment: passive mode, mixed mode, full mode, productive mode and composite mode. Essentially, passive mode produces improved internal comfort conditions without the use of any non-renewable sources of energy. The rationale for strategically optimising and adopting as many as possible of the passive-mode design options prior to adopting any of the other modes is that such a strategy uses up relatively little or zero non-renewable energy and so has the least impact on the environment.

Passive-mode design is, in effect, bioclimatic design and requires an understanding of the climate of the locality to enable advantage to be taken of the ambient energies and climatic characteristics. Passive-mode systems provide thermal comfort by using natural energy sources and sinks, eg solar radiation, inside air, wet surfaces, vegetation, internal gains, etc. Energy flows in these systems are by natural means such as radiation, conduction and convection with no use of mechanical means. These vary from one climate to the other. In a cold climate, the ecodesign aim would be to design a built form in such a way that solar gains are maximised, but in a hot climate, the architect's primary aim would be to reduce solar gains and maximise natural ventilation.

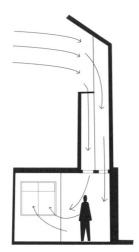

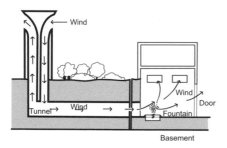

Basement

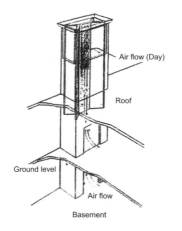

Examples of Windscoops

The type and order of the design responses adopted by the designer can have significant bearing on the built configuration, its spatial arrangements and layout; implementation of passive-mode design can be the greatest determinant in the shaping of the built form and its use of materials.

In design terms, passive-mode strategies and bioclimatic design exert significant influence over the shaping of the built form, its orientation, internal spatial disposition, colour, porosity, materials use, etc, which should all take maximum advantage of seasonal variations, the sun, wind and other climatic features. This includes optimising passive solar design and cooling when appropriate.

The built form itself might be regarded here as essentially an enclosure erected to offer protection to some human or human-related activity over the external environment with an improved level of internal comfort conditions. If the designer does not optimise all these passive-mode aspects to the built form (eg in its configuration and orientation), then the result may be an erroneously shaped or inappropriately oriented built form. In consequence, more energy resources may have to be used in its M&E systems to compensate for such errors, which makes nonsense of any attempt at a low-energy design.

Human activities alter many components of the earth's climate system. The climatic effect of a built-up area generally includes a higher temperature than in exposed countryside, weak winds, and variable sunlight exposure at ground level. Solar radiation, temperature and wind conditions vary greatly based on topography and surroundings and the effect of an urban area on local climate and weather can be great, sometimes devastating. Unfortunately, many urban areas and the layout of their built environment were planned before environmental issues were completely understood. Designers are now standing at an important threshold, and learning from past mistakes when energy use was profligate.

In nature, ecosystems use solar energy. Solar energy is transformed into chemical energy by the photosynthesis of green plants and drives the ecological cycles. For ecodesign to be ecomimetic, we should seek to do the same and use solar energy. However, at the moment the use of solar energy is limited to various solar collector devices and photovoltaic systems.

We need to return to our rationale for having buildings and enclosures. Humans improve the level of comfort conditions in their built environment. As standards of existence increase, the demands for comfort conditions also increase. The first level of enclosure is, of course, clothing. This is followed by the built environment as the second level of enclosure. Contemporary expectations of the internal comfort conditions of built environments are high; they cannot be achieved by passive means alone, with the result that external sources of energy are accessed; unfortunately, many of these are non-renewable. Humankind's recourse to external sources of energy predominantly means the use of fossil fuels. Buildings now account for about 40 to 50 per cent of delivered energy use and just under 50 per cent of all CO_2 emissions. Approximately 60 per cent of building-related CO_2 emissions are due to residential building sector activity and about 30 per cent are attributable to the service sector (public and commercial buildings). In the service sector, the total CO_2 emission is about 89 million tonnes and approximately 44 per cent of this is due to space heating (eg in the UK).

Today, we make use of electromechanical systems or mechanical and electrical (M&E) systems to modify the internal conditions of comfort in our built environment. As mechanical, electrical and plumbing systems developed and became prevalent, the natural techniques (passive modes) of heating, cooling and lighting homes became neglected by designers and disappeared. Ecodesign must seek the minimisation of the use of non-renewable sources of energy, and in this regard low-energy design is an important ecodesign objective. However, it must be clear that ecodesign is not just about low-energy design.

Humans have a remarkable ability to survive climatic extremes and adapt to hostile climatic conditions. The human species occupies climatic extremes more widely divergent than almost any other species (save the cockroach). Traditionally, this has been achieved by sustainable technologies that do not use fossil fuels. This would include the passive-design strategies in simple human shelters, for example.

Passive-mode design in the built environment implies a building that has no mechanical electrical systems, for instance the traditional dwellings and structures related to habitation that we see in any country in the world. Learning from traditional examples, it is important to adopt a design strategy that begins with design of the built form by optimising all the passive-mode strategies appropriate to the climate and ecology of that locality; the next step involves deciding whether other modes should be adopted to further enhance the energy performance of the designed system. Here, it is heartening to note that many designers are beginning to adopt passive-mode building strategies again, integrating passive cooling and natural ventilation in their plans. Implementation of passive-mode bioclimatic design strategies must be the first consideration when seeking to configure the built form.

Passive-mode design

Our first step in the ecodesign of our built forms must be to look at the range of options for passive design and systems based on the climatic conditions of their locality and to maximise these design opportunities. The approach is not to design architectural forms to

Design specification:		Detached 100–150 m²
Reference case Randomly oriented 'notional' building of compact form (complying with 1990 building regulations)	EI kWh/m² CO₂ kg/m²	100–115 25–29
Step 1 Most windows to south; no overshadowing	EI kWh/m² CO₂ kg/m²	85–100 25–30
Step 2 As above and all windows double glazed (0.75 ac/h)	EI kWh/m² CO₂ kg/m²	55–65 17–20
Step 3 All windows with insulated night shutters or low-emissivity-coated double glazing; window area within guidelines	EI kWh/m² CO₂ kg/m²	50–60 15–18
Step 4 As above envelope insulation to U-0.25	EI kWh/m² CO₂ kg/m²	35–40 11–12
Step 5 As above with mechanical ventilation and heat recovery (0.5 ac/h)	EI kWh/m² CO₂ kg/m²	< 30 < 9

Energy Index (EI) and carbon dioxide (CO_2) emission indices for residential built forms

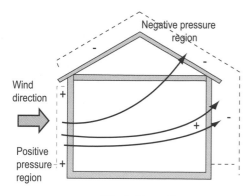

Wind-driven flow

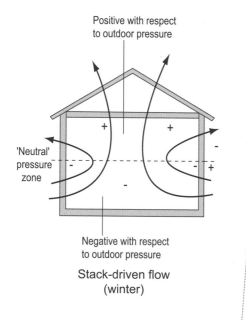

Stack-driven flow
(winter)

Natural driving mechanisms ●

follow the climate of the locality, but rather as a response to it. Climate does not determine built form but it does influence it. Priority must be given to passive-system over active-system options because this is the way to achieve the ideal level of servicing for ecological design since it represents the lowest level of consumption of energy from non-renewable sources. Passive design as low-energy design is not achieved by electromechanical means, but by the building's particular morphological organisation. Passive systems use various simple cooling and/or heating techniques to enable the indoor temperature of buildings to be modified through the use of the natural and ambient energy sources in the natural environment. Obviously, the range of opportunities depends on the latitude of the project site's location. Strictly speaking, passive systems should exclude any electromechanical devices that use non-renewable energy. Climate-responsive design (eg bioclimatic design) thus reduces consumption of non-renewable energy, minimising recourse to such mechanical systems. Although there are some who might argue that the use of a fan or pump may be permitted within this category, it is contended here that fully 'passive' systems mean operational systems without the use of any electromechanical devices or systems. 'Active' means energy dependent or partially assisted electromechanical systems.

For example, in temperate climates, bioclimatic principles seek to reduce heat gains by conduction, radiation and convection through walls and windows in the summer, and to reduce heat losses towards the exterior in winter. Passive cooling systems transfer incident energy to natural energetic deposits, or heat sinks, such as the air, the upper atmosphere, water and earth. Passive warming systems store and distribute solar energy without the need for complex controllers for its distribution. Applying passive systems in the summer, it is possible to reduce the average external temperature values and increase indoor temperatures in winter.

If the built form has passively improved comfort conditions over the external conditions, then, in the event of failure of energy supply from external sources, the built form remains habitable. The other scenario is that if the built form is entirely dependent on a full-mode or mixed-mode system, then it may be uncomfortable to occupy in the event of a failure of external sources of energy.

Passive-mode strategies include appropriate shaping of the building in relation to the locality's sun path, the use of natural ventilation, the use of vegetation, appropriate facade design, sun shading, etc. Generally, a locality's traditional buildings offer the best examples of appropriate passive-mode design or bioclimatic design because they were constructed when contemporary M&E systems using non-renewable sources of energy simply did not exist. Through trial, error and intuition, these buildings would have been designed to have improved internal over exterior comfort conditions and to provide protection from inclement weather, obviously without the use of any electromechanical systems.

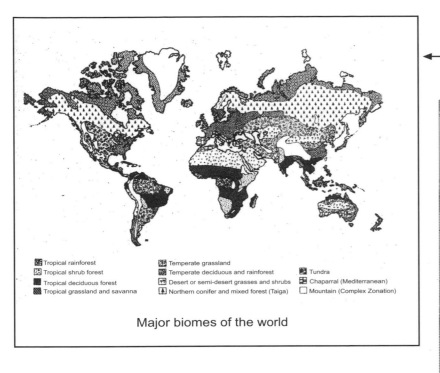

Tropical rainforest
Tropical shrub forest
Tropical deciduous forest
Tropical grassland and savanna
Temperate grassland
Temperate deciduous and rainforest
Desert or semi-desert grasses and shrubs
Northern conifer and mixed forest (Taiga)
Tundra
Chaparral (Mediterranean)
Mountain (Complex Zonation)

Major biomes of the world

Passive comfort measures	Active comfort measures	Ice caps	Tundra	Uplands	Continental	Temperate	Mediterranean	Subtropical	Tropical	Savanna	Steppe	Desert
Natural ventilation		O	O	1	4	6	6	7	7	7	7	7
	Mechanical ventilation	5	5	3	3	3	4	5	6	6	6	6
Night ventilation		O	1	2	3	5	6	7	7	7	7	7
	Artificial ventilation	O	O	O	1	1	3	5	5	5	5	6
Evaporative cooling		O	O	O	1	2	3	2	2	5	6	7
	Free cooling	O	O	O	4	3	5	6	6	7	7	7
Heavy construction		3	4	4	6	5	6	2	2	3	5	5
Lightweight construction		3	3	2	2	3	3	5	5	6	4	4
	Artificial heating	7	7	7	7	6	4	O	O	2	4	1
Solar heating		2	3	6	6	7	6	O	O	2	3	O
	Free heating	7	7	7	6	6	5	O	O	O	3	O
Incidental heat		6	6	6	6	6	6	O	O	6	6	O
Insulation/ permeability		7	7	7	7	6	5	O	O	1	3	4
Solar control/shading		O	1	3	4	5	6	6	6	6	7	7
	Artificial lighting during daytime	6	6	4	4	4	3	3	3	2	2	2
Daylight		6	6	6	6	6	6	5	5	5	4	4

Climatic zones

O 1 2 3 4 5 6 7
No importance — Very important

Energy-saving measures by global regions

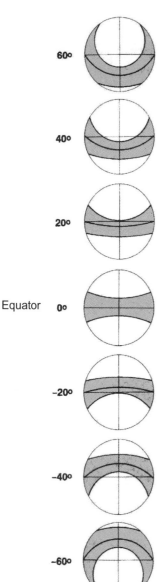

60°

40°

20°

Equator   0°

-20°

-40°

-60°

The pattern of changes of sun paths
from the Equator towards the poles

Passive-mode methods

The following are some of the passive methods to be applied to the built form to address any remaining needs for a higher level of internal comfort conditions; these may be met by active or mixed-mode systems powered by ecologically sustainable forms of energy:

- Built-form configuration and site-layout plannings
- Built-form orientation (of main facades and openings, etc)
- Enclosural (and facade) design (including window opening size, location and details)
- Solar-control devices (eg shading for facades and windows)
- Passive daylight concepts
- Wind and natural ventilation
- Roofscape
- Built-form envelope colour
- Landscaping (ie use of plants with the built form)
- Passive cooling systems
- Building mass

These methods are discussed below

Passive mode by building configuration

The built form, its spatial arrangements and layout are configured and planned in relation to the energies of the ambient environment and the meteorological data of the locality as a passive response. However, reducing the heating energy requirements (eg by optimising the incoming heat) is not simply a matter of building orientation; it is also influenced by the form of the building and the ratio of volume to surface. Making the built form in the configuration appropriate to the sun path for that latitude can reduce energy consumption by as much as 30 to 40 per cent at no extra cost.

The building form needs to be shaped and laid out on the site to function in a low-energy way in concert with other design intentions such as to capture an expansive view, to achieve privacy or security. This approach has been well developed by others for the low-rise and medium-rise building types, but less so for the high-rise building type. If a particular building has not been configured or oriented to maximise its passive benefits, then any electro-mechanical active systems and devices that are installed later may have to 'correct' for some of the earlier design 'errors' such as wrongly configured or oriented built forms.

It is generally held that the built form should have a 1:2 to 1:3 length ratio for climatic zones nearer to the equatorial zone, while at the higher latitudes the built form should be twice as long as it is wide. This configuration provides the added advantage of reducing shading impact on any buildings located to the south (if building is below the equator). We should ensure that the long axis of the built form is oriented east–west so that the long length of the building faces north–south. This enables the majority of the windows to be designed into the north wall for sites at the equator (and vice versa if above the equator) so that sun penetration into the building will be maximised.

The designer must consider the internal and external interfaces of the built form's fabric and comfort in relation to the site, climate and orientation together with the global ecological impact of the building. For instance, in the hot-humid tropical zones, one approach is to shape the building's floor plate so that the service core is placed appropriately in relation to the sun's path for the locality's latitude, to create a solar buffer to reduce solar penetration inside the building. Tall building types are more exposed than others to the full impacts of external temperatures, wind and sunlight and therefore their built form configuration, orientation, floor-plate shape and use of buffer components can have particularly important effects on energy-conservation design and natural lighting of the interior spaces.

The building's service core placement also determines which parts of the floor plate's periphery have openings (eg for ventilation and views); their location can benefit the building's thermal performance as well. The designer must consider the sun path and the winds of the locality in aggregate with other factors in making design trade-offs (eg direction of best views, site shape, neighbouring buildings). The service cores can be positioned on the 'hot' east or west sides of the building, or both, to serve as solar buffers in the tropical zone. Studies show that significant savings in air conditioning can be achieved from a double-core configuration with window openings running north–south and cores on the east and west, even in temperate and cold climate zones. However, this strategy is most applicable at the equator and at latitudes up to, say, 40° north of the equator. This placement prevents heat gain into the internal user spaces and provides spatial thermal insulation buffers to the hot sides, while at the same time maximising heat loss away from the user spaces. In cold and temperate climates, in the upper or southern regions of the biosphere, they could serve as wind buffers.

Peripheral service cores

Of the various possible service-core positions (ie central core, double core and single-sided core), the double-core position is to be preferred. The benefits of peripheral service-core position are:

• no fire-protection pressurisation duct, resulting in lower initial and operating costs;

• a view out with greater awareness of place for users;

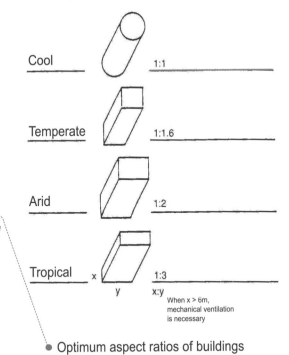

Cool   1:1

Temperate   1:1.6

Arid   1:2

Tropical   x   1:3
      y   x:y

When x > 6m, mechanical ventilation is necessary

● Optimum aspect ratios of buildings

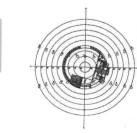

Elevator cores of hot sizes of built form

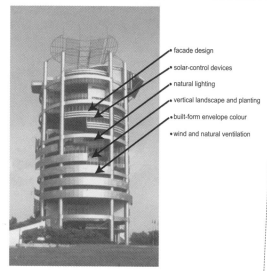

• facade design

• solar-control devices

• natural lighting

• vertical landscape and planting

• built-form envelope colour

• wind and natural ventilation

IBM (Mesiniaga), Subang Jaya

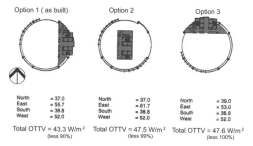

Option 1 (as built)	Option 2	Option 3
North = 37.0	North = 37.0	North = 39.0
East = 55.7	East = 61.7	East = 53.0
South = 38.8	South = 38.8	South = 38.8
West = 52.0	West = 52.0	West = 52.0
Total OTTV = 43.3 W/m² (less 90%)	Total OTTV = 47.5 W/m² (less 99%)	Total OTTV = 47.6 W/m² (less 100%)

Example of passive mode by built-form configuration and orientations

• provision of natural ventilation to the lift lobbies (ie increased energy savings);

• provision of natural sunlight to lift and stair lobbies;

• a safer building in event of total power failure; and

• solar buffer effects and/or wind buffer effects.

On sites located north of the equatorial belt, the service-core placements might be adjusted in accordance with the sun path, which would contribute to shaping the floor plate. By adopting the above strategy in the case of the high-rise built form the structure's configuration would be shifted away from the conventional central core one.

We might contend that there is a correlation of different core locations and orientation with the annual cooling load. The core type that provides the minimum air-conditioning load is clearly the double-core configuration, in which the opening is from north to south and the core runs from east to west. Conversely, the core type characterised by maximum air-conditioning load is the central core configuration, in which the main daylighting opening lies in the southeast and northwest directions.

Generally, in the tropics a high-rise building type, if arranged longitudinally from north to south, has to bear an air-conditoning load that in unoptimised conditions (ie without special facade treatment for the external walls) is 1.5 times that of a building arranged longitudinally from east to west.

In the temperate zone, careful consideration of a building's shape can also make considerable energy savings in terms of heating. Older office buildings were constructed to maximise the penetration of natural daylight. However, with a large surface area for their volume they lost heat quickly. Today, architects favour 'deep plan' designs that retain heat. A deep-plan building can cost 50 per cent less to heat than a shallow-plan building of the same floor area, but will receive less natural daylight in the deeper parts of the floor plate and therefore require more energy to supply artificial lighting. Elimination of heating and cooling is more cost effective than reducing heating and cooling.

Passive mode by built-form orientation

This strategy has to do with the shape of the building's floor plate, its position on the site and its orientation to the sun path and wind direction of the locality. For instance, in response to the sun path in the tropical zone, the building's shape should be rectangular along the east–west axis to reduce solar insolation on the wider sides of the building. This is because the greatest source of heat gain is by solar radiation entering through the windows. The gain, of course, varies markedly with the time of day and angle of incidence.

Built-form orientation is a significant design consideration, mainly with regard to solar radiation and wind. In predominantly cold regions, the built form should be oriented to maximise solar gain; the reverse is advisable for hot regions. In regions where seasonal changes are very pronounced, both the situations may arise periodically. For a cold climate, an orientation slightly east of south is favoured (c 15 degrees east of south), as this exposes the unit to more morning than afternoon sun and enables the built form to begin to heat during the day.

We must be careful to distinguish between true north (or solar north) and magnetic north, which are not the same. True north varies through time but is approximately 11° W of magnetic north. When designing, we must ensure that orientation is related to true north. Misunderstandings can seriously affect shadow diagrams.

If the site does not align with the sun's geometry on its east–west path, other building elements such as the building's service cores can follow the geometry of the site to optimise the effects on column grids, basement car-parking layouts and other features. However, other features may need to be introduced to correct the hot facades.

Some might assume that the square building floor plate will have a smaller peripheral area and therefore be less exposed to the effects of external air than the other built form shapes, resulting in lower air-conditioning loads. Studies show, however, that it is actually the circular floor plate that affords the least surface exposure. But despite this shape's advantage in terms of surface exposure, it is the rectanglar shape that is actually better for solar control.

Provided passive solar energy use is well considered, and will not result in overheating in temperate and cold climatic zones, we need to site the building to allow for use of solar gains to offset heating requirements. This is likely to be appropriate in buildings with low occupant density, because high internal heat gains from equipment will be less likely.

Above the equatorial zone, in temperate and cold climatic zones, there are two basic strategies to adopt in terms of shaping the built form to achieve minimum energy impact:

• Minimise surface area to volume ratio, design for high insulation levels and compact the building form to minimise heat losses in winter conditions. This strategy helps minimise both the building materials consumed and the direct energy requirement in fuel terms.

• Reduce plan depth to maximise opportunities for using natural ventilation and natural daylighting.

Current thinking in low-energy office-use building design favours the latter of these two options as the preferred passive solution whenever possible. It allows maximum use of natural

Basic floor surface (A)	Floor size only 100m² (B)	Wall surface only 2.5 m High (C)	Floor + wall + ceiling in m² (D)
1. Circle	P 35.44 m	WS 88.62 m²	F 100.00 m²; C 100.00; WS 88.62; Total 288.62 m²
2. Ellipse	P 37.59	WS 39.99	F 100.00; C 100.00; WS 93.99; Total 23.99 m²
3. Square	P 40.00	WS 100.00	F 100.00; C 100.00; WS 100.00; Total 300.00 m²
4. Square with patio	P 42.42	WS 106.06	F 100.00; C 100.00; WS 106.00; Total 306.00 m²
5. Gamuda	P 80.00	WS 200	F 100.00; C 100.00; WS 200.00; Total 400.00 m²
6. Rhombus	P 44.72	WS 111.80	F 100.00; C 100.00; WS 111.80; Total 311.80 m²
7. Trapezoid	P 48.28	WS 120.71	F 100.00; C 100.00; WS 120.71; Total 320.71 m²

Each floor = 100 m²
All floors are equal in size
All heights = 2.5 m

P = Perimeter
F = Floor
C = Ceiling
WS = Wall surface

Zoning for solar gain
Diagram indicating the location of space that can be used for solar heat gain. The location follows the sun path in each climate zone; in the tropical and arid zones, the spaces are on the east- and west-facing sides; in the temperate and cold zones, they are on the south-facing side.

● Surface exposure for different built forms

Design to optimise all passive-mode (or bioclimatic design) options in the designed system

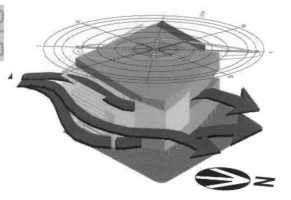

Configuring the built form to optimise
ambient wind and natural ventilation ●

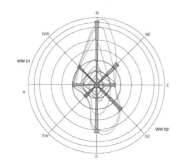

Wind rose for the locality diagram

Passive mode: by natural ventilation ●

ventilation and daylight to minimise energy consumption and is an approach that can be applied even if, at first glance, the scope for it appears limited. For example, when planning internal spaces, the designer must ensure that rooms without specific environmental requirements can benefit from natural light and ventilation. General offices can be located to make use of the external ambient energy resources available, while, conversely, areas with high heat gains (such as kitchenettes and computer rooms) should be sited to the north (if the site is south of the equator), or in the central core of a deep-plan building if they will require to be fully mechanically treated (eg clean rooms and some computer facilities). In other words, the design strategy is to make use of external ambient energy in spaces where the gain will be of benefit, and avoid solar gains and natural ventilation only if this will exacerbate an existing problem, or if it is completely inappropriate.

The first decision taken in relation to the orientation of the building on the site can affect every other later decision. Every building site is unique and therefore the design of the building is exclusively related to that site. This immediately places constraints on the ensuing design decisions. When deciding how to make an environmentally responsive intervention with a new building within the site, two major site factors must be addressed: the local climate and the environmental impact of the building on the site and vice versa. Local climate considerations can be positive and negative. The building's orientation can take advantage of free energy from the sun in terms of both heat and light. Wind effects can be mitigated by shelter-belt planting or permeable walling, or can be used (in combination with compatible devices) for natural ventilation. By building up a picture of basic micro-climatic information, it is possible to identify the most suitable siting and configuration for the building, eliminating unsuitable (polluted, overshadowed) areas of the site and harnessing the potential of the remaining land to the fullest through the building form, planting and shelter belts. Investigative studies include using overlay techniques for clarification. The final design should incorporate adequate fenestration to make use of free solar energy and natural daylight while minimising heat losses and avoiding glare. This will be achieved by glazing ratios (the ratio of glass to solid surfaces in the facade) of ideally above 20 per cent if single glazing (particularly in the temperate zone) but can be checked by manual calculation or computer modelling.

Recent advances in external wall systems include the use of special glass, double glazing, composite double glazing with blinds, double facades, etc, which permit higher glass-to-solid ratios.

Our intensive building should also be considered in relation to the other buildings within the site's proximity and, where relevant within the block. Aspects such as aesthetics, over-shadowing, self-shading, climate variations, vegetation and pollution should also be examined to avoid negative effects on existing and new buildings. An overall site strategy for energy use and an integrated energy policy should be developed at an early stage; this will include consideration of the use of waste heat, potential to generate electricity on site using a combined heat and power scheme (ie co-generations), and renewable energy sources (eg wind turbines, photovoltaics, etc). In other words, the site should be considered holistically and not in isolation. In shaping the floor plate and the facade design, the designer might also identify key 'view corridors' from the building to its surrounds that need to be maintained.

In temperate climates where the sun path is lower, adequate measures have to be taken to avoid excessive overheating in the summer while ensuring that the potential of useful winter solar gains is maximised. In temperate climates, the sun has to be designed 'out' as well as 'in'. A balance between heat losses from the north and heat gains to the south must be achieved. This can be assisted by careful material selection as well as space planning. For example, heat gains from the M&E plant rooms can reduce heating requirements in peripheral zones. Another strategy is to use the service cores and circulation spaces, stairwells and corridors as buffers between the accommodation areas and the outside, either by siting them on the north to help reduce heat losses, or on the south to reduce excess gain (if designed, for example, as walkways and galleries).

In temperate zones, solar gain will be of benefit in most built forms early in the morning when the structure is cold. This is particularly true in temperate and cold climate non-domestic built forms, where use of solar energy in east and southeast zones in winter can provide free early morning pre-heat to offset heating loads. The associated risk of summer overheating can be addressed by solar shading (see below).

In situations where internal heat gains are high, solar gains to rooms on southwest- and west-facing aspects may contribute to overheating, since during much of the year sunlight will fall on these facades later in the day when the interior is already warm. For instance, contrary to current recommendations for residential-use tall buildings such as apartment blocks and hotels, where north-facing glass should be minimised, in non-residential tall buildings north-facing glass should be maximised to make use of daylight while avoiding excessive heat losses. It is important to be aware that artificial lighting can account for up to 50 per cent of the overall electricity costs in a modern office building. Coupled with excess uncontrolled solar heat gain, the consequent raised internal temperatures can result in unnecesary energy expenditure on air conditioning – which could have been avoided by a clearer understanding of the cumulative impact of internal and external factors.

Beginning at the equator and moving north, the need for solar heating increases (white range), while the need for solar shading (black range) follows the opposite course.

● Annual % of required shading + solar heating

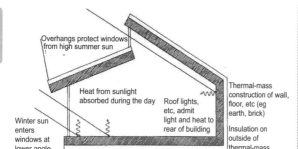

Overhangs protect windows from high summer sun

Heat from sunlight absorbed during the day

Roof lights, etc, admit light and heat to rear of building

Thermal-mass construction of wall, floor, etc (eg earth, brick)

Winter sun enters windows at lower angle

Insulation on outside of thermal-mass

Large glazed areas facing south

Little or no glazing to the north

Basic passive solar design principles ●········
(temperate zone)

Passive mode by enclosural (and facade) design

Our next task, facade design and the enclosural design should be given priority over the built form's contents (ie its operational systems) and should in effect be designed in combination with the optimisation of the passive systems, mixed mode and such active systems as are used. The permeability of the skin of the building to light, heat and air and its visual transparency must be controllable and capable of modification, so that the building can react to changing local climatic conditions. These variables include solar screening, glare protection, temporary thermal protection and adjustable natural ventilation options. A well-designed building envelope will yield significant energy savings. The building is like a third skin, after our physical skin and our clothes; all these layers of enclosure need to function naturally and in harmony with our bodies and the natural environment. By analogy, the building's facade, as our third skin, needs to breathe and function as a regulator, protector, insulator and integrator with the natural environment.

Thus, the ideal external wall should act as an environmentally responsive filter. The envelope should have adjustable openings that operate as sieve-like filters with variable parts to provide natural ventilation, control cross-ventilation, provide views to the outside, give solar protection, regulate wind-swept rain and discharge heavy rain, provide insulation during cold seasons (and in temperate zones, to meet the demands of a hot summer, a cold winter and two mid-seasons), and promote a more direct relationship with the external environment. In temperate zones and above, the designer should consider the angle for both summer sun penetration and winter sun penetration, as these differ. The green approach runs contrary to those facade designs that rely on hermetically sealed skins. The 'green' facade has to be multifunctional in its design. It can reduce solar heat gain to the space through external shading devices, provide fresh air ventilation, serve as an acoustic barrier, give maintenance access and make a contribution to the building's aesthetics.

Increased insulation

Insulation is of value when the built form requires mechanical heating or cooling. An effective passive way to reduce energy consumption in the building, particularly in temperate and cold climates, is to increase external-wall insulation to reduce leakages and thermal bridges, and to lower the ratio of solid to glass areas. Insulation reduces the rate at which heat can flow through the elements in which it is installed. In heated and cooled buildings, this will result in significant energy savings and thermal comfort.

External-wall surfaces having direct solar insolation should be insulated and the 'time lag' taken into consideration. External materials used might be those that are effective heat sinks (eg aluminium cladding) or that are designed to have a 'double-layered' (or even triple-layered) ventilating space. The thermal transfer properties of the window frame and glazing systems should be verified. For instance, aluminium framing fitted with thermal bridging can assist in reducing heat transfer. The current standard for external-wall insulation in temperate climates is around 0.45 kW/M²K. Design efforts should therefore be directed at achieving insulation levels lower than this. By reducing or using several times the insulation level, the carbon dioxide emissions can also be reduced (eg Vale and Vale, 1991); a figure for carbon dioxide emissions of only 28 kg/m²/y has been achieved in residential design by using three times the recommended levels of insulation. A single-glazed window has a heat loss rate over 10 times greater than the recommended UK building regulations (5.7 W/M²K for a wall element). Double glazing (depending on the width of the air gap) may reduce this to 2.8 W/M²K, and triple glazing may reduce this to 2.0 W/M²K. This might be lowered yet further by reducing the solid to glazing ratio of external walls.

It is often assumed that higher insulation levels in the facade and roof (although minimal in the case of the skyscraper) are the obvious solution to reducing energy use. However, more insulation is not necessarily the answer. The thermal performance of materials has to be considered in conjunction with other factors, among which are the following:

- In temperate and cold climatic zones, the loss of heat through air leakage can begin to dominate 'heat loss' if not addressed simultaneously with insulation levels.

- Similarly, the heating systems and components must be designed and selected with effective energy use in mind and must 'match' the building fabric and purpose. A well-insulated building with an inefficient or poorly controlled heating system will probably overheat – without saving energy. Domestic hot water production may also become a critical factor in the overall energy picture and so a holistic approach is needed.

Summer and winter

In temperate and cold climatic zones high insulation levels will reduce the rate of heat loss in both winter and summer. They also reduce the potential for heat gain. The thermal performance must be evaluated to optimise heat gains and losses to prevent trapping heat gain from internal sources in summer while avoiding excessive losses in winter. Simultaneously, potentially useful winter gains should not be eliminated by only considering avoidance of summer gains. The optimum solution will be achieved by maximising insulation levels, designing heating systems appropriately for high operating efficiency and providing solar protection in summer without compromising useful winter solar gains.

The above strategy does not, of course, exclude the benefits of high insulation standards but points out the fact that solutions should be carefully evaluated. It is possible to achieve

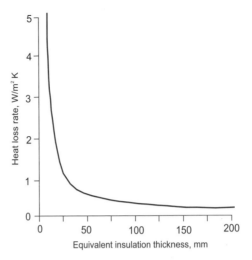

Relationship between thickness of insulation and heat loss through building elements

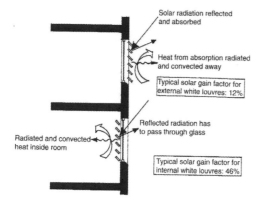

Solar radiation reflected and absorbed

Heat from absorption radiated and convected away

Typical solar gain factor for external white louvres: 12%

Reflected radiation has to pass through glass

Radiated and convected heat inside room

Typical solar gain factor for internal white louvres: 46%

Solar shading ●

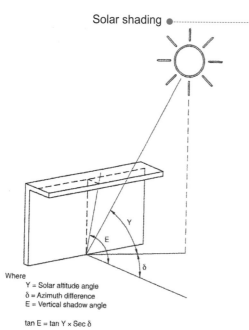

Where

Y = Solar altitude angle
δ = Azimuth difference
E = Vertical shadow angle

$\tan E = \tan Y \times \sec \delta$

Solar sunshade geometrical design ●

insulation values of well above the statutory requirements at little additional cost, using modern techniques and materials, and this approach should be adopted.

Passive mode through solar-control devices

Solar shading: louvres, tinted and reflective glass, etc

Generally, on the 'hot' sides of the built form (generally the east and west sides), regardless of the latitude, some form of solar shading is required, making due allowance for glare and the quality of light entering the spaces. A full-height glazed curtain wall may be used on the non-solar facades, provided it meets the other criteria (eg insulation values). The westward solar-facing wall has the highest intensity at the hottest time of the day. The correct form of angle control (through computer-aided design) is held to be the key to the optimisation of a facade, since direct radiation of internal areas should be avoided for lengthy periods during the year, while maintaining high daylight utilisations (radiation transmission). Depending upon the season and time of day, the angle control of the louvres achieves optimal natural daylight illumination in combination with minimal heat gain. 'Intelligent facades' operate with automated angle control, regulated by incident radiation and outside air temperature. During periods that could produce unwanted outside thermal gain, the louvres are positioned at a steeper angle than during periods when passive solar gain can be taken advantage of to reduce the energy costs for heating rooms. Angle control is thus an important factor with regard to total solar energy transmission. Another is the type of glazing used between the indoor space and the air cavity separating it from the outside.

In temperate climates, the designer should reduce the need for air conditioning in the summer and the need for heating in winter. The strategy is to extend the mid-seasons (spring and autumn) through enhanced cross-ventilation in the summer, late spring and early autumn. In the winter, we should capture as much solar benefit as possible and reduce the need for heating the internal spaces through enhanced external-wall insulation (eg movable shields).

The most efficient form of solar control is achieved by providing external shading devices over clear glass. Clear glass is often preferred, as it gives a more direct visual and natural relationship between the inside and the outside of the building. Recent advances in glass technologies have produced 'door' glass that gives good light transmission but has lower shading coefficients.

The most ecoefficient design can only come from an understanding of the solar geometry of the locality as the basis for determining the angles for the cross-section of the solar-shading devices at the facade.

Generally, solar heat gain through windows in the building can be reduced by sunshades, balconies or deep recesses (such as totally recessed windows) or sky courts. This sunshading cuts the huge solar heat gains that occur directly through window transmission and indirectly from hot surface conduction and radiation. Shading should be designed to reduce glare as well as to enable the passive transmission of light into the deeper reaches of the floor plate. This allows the designer to use clear glass and to provide better daylight penetration to internal spaces, which then reduces the lighting energy load as well as enabling a better aesthetic relationship between the inside and the outside of the building.

In temperate and cold zones, an adaptable facade is needed to let the sun in through the windows in the winter months to heat residential buildings, to reduce glare in offices and to provide sunshading in the summer to reduce heat gain. The building mass can be used to store thermal heat, but this is not possible in zones where the night-air temperatures do not fall below comfort temperature to discharge the heat.

It is useful to provide external or mid-pane solar shading in preference to internal shading in situations where heat gain and glare are to be controlled. As movable devices can provide additional protection against heat loss in winter, it is suggested that application of an external device, such as movable blinds or mid-pane protection, is preferable to providing fixed shading with internal blinds (particularly on the east and west facades). Integrating energy, amenity and biological considerations, a combination of fixed and movable, solid and planted shading devices can be cost effective.

In the past, fixed shading devices have been preferred to movable ones, in part because of simplicity, low cost and minimum maintenance, but also because limiting human intervention in some ways limits room for error or misuse. However, they are not as effective as movable shades for anything other than to shade buildings facing due south. If it is the intention to employ a fixed solution, this should be borne in mind. For example, in Britain a horizontal shelf-type screen of approximately 0.7 metres width will be required to shade each metre of height of exposed south-facing glass effectively in summer (from mid-May to early August) at a latitude of around 56°. Various configurations can be provided at the top of the glass, or a reduced depth of shelf can be installed lower down the pane. Alternatively, the shading device can be located partly inside and partly outside, providing a light shelf to throw light deeper into the space. Careful detailing is important to avoid excess glare or heat gain via an exposed upper pane. Louvred devices allow hot air to pass through, and are not subject to snow-or wind-loadings. Architecturally, louvres can be used to provide articulation, and less projection is necessary to achieve an equivalent degree of protection compared with a solid shelf arrangement.

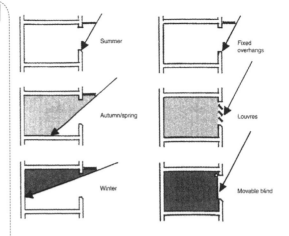

Types of shading devices that have different effects on view and ventilation

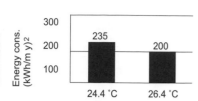

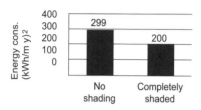

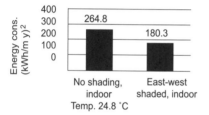

Energy reduced by shifting up indoor temperature and providing sun protection on east and west glass walls

The east facade of the building requires solar shading as it is subject to the morning sun. The vertical shadow angle determines the effectiveness of horizontal solar-shading devices. The horizontal component of the sun's angle of incidence '8' is the difference between the solar azimuth angle and the wall azimuth angle. The solar altitude angle 'y' is read from the concentric circles, all of which are obtained from the sun-path diagram for the latitude of the building's locality for a given time of day.

Fixed horizontal shading devices such as overhangs are very effective for south-facade windows in higher latitudes but have a disadvantage in that they operate on a 'worst case' basis, depending on sun altitude only and not external temperature. Thus, these shades may block out useful solar gain under certain conditions when heating is required. East- and west-facing facades will always require some degree of vertical shading.

Movable shading has two main advantages: it can be adjusted to suit outside conditions to allow maximum benefit from sun and to provide protection from glare and excessive heat gain; and in winter, in temperate zones, devices can be closed to reduce heat loss from the building through radiation to the night sky. In terms of protection from solar gain, external shading devices are more effective than internal devices; mid-pane shading is also preferable to internal solutions. External devices prevent sunlight from entering the space, while internal devices allow solar energy to penetrate, and then attempt to reflect the sunlight back out through the glass. The process is never 100 per cent efficient, but the most effective solution will be achieved by a light-coloured or reflective finish on blinds or curtains. The external shading elements for high-rise buildings also need to be integrated with the facade-cleaning strategy.

Tinted glass cannot be a substitute for sunshading. Tinting's best effect is to reduce thermal transmission to about 20 per cent, which is still ineffective in attenuating conditions in hot climates and summer conditions in temperate climates, with as much as 500–1000 W/m² solar radiation. Tinting absorbs heat and so the external wall gets hot, but the radiation heats the internal spaces and the air has to be made cooler to maintain comfort. Hot glass further conducts the heat, so the cooling load is still higher. Worse, tinting cuts out daylight, affecting the quality of internal spaces. Heat-absorbing glass absorbs short-wave solar radiation and thus reduces heat gain to the inside of a building. However, depending on coincident internal and external climatic conditions, this energy stored as heat may be 're-radiated' into the space as the temperature outside begins to fall in the late afternoon. At this time, the internal equipment and casual gains tend to be at a peak. Thus, summer overheating in buildings with tinted glass can be more severe than that which would have occurred with clear glass, and winter heat gain may occur too late in the day to achieve this heat absorption.

Studies have shown that the tints used can have two effects on building occupants:

- Long-wave (light) transmission is reduced, resulting in an increased need for artificial light, and/or larger window areas to achieve the same level of daylight illumination.

- The psychological effect of looking at the outside world through brown, grey or green glass can be disturbing to occupants and has been suggested as a contributory factor in building-related health problems.

Solar-reflective glass can be used to reduce solar penetration without affecting the view to the same extent as heat-absorbing glass. However, this solution reduces both short-wave (heat) and long-wave (light) transmission, which results in reduced useful winter heat gain and year-round use of artificial lighting at times when natural light could have been sufficient; in other words, heat gain is eliminated at the expense of good-quality natural lighting. Reflective glass can, however, be useful in situations where heat gain is not desired and where the use of external shading is not physically possible (particularly on west facades).

Low-emissivity glass reduces direct heat gain by transmitting a greater proportion of light than heat. It reduces heat loss by reflecting heat back into the space and has an appearance similar to that of clear glass. It is thus useful for situations where daylight is required but solar heat gain should be minimised. It also allows the use of slightly larger windows for admitting daylight, without necessarily incurring an energy penalty in winter.

New 'intelligent' glazing systems, which overcome the problems of differing summer and winter requirements, are currently being researched and some are available already but at a high cost. The use of photochromatics, phase-change materials, holographic or electrically responsive glass and other technologies may become more commonplace. In the meantime, the environmentally responsive approach tends to encourage the use of clear or low-emissivity glass, in high-quality double- or triple-glazed units, wherever possible with solar shading provided. Shading should preferably be by easily adjusted, external devices to allow occupant control. Failing that, fixed shading is effective on south facades and mid-pane shading is preferred to internal shading devices.

For an ecological approach, the built system's external wall system has to be evaluated not only in terms of its ecological costs in respect of inputs (eg embodied energy evaluation) but also by designing for future recovery.

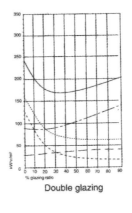

Double glazing

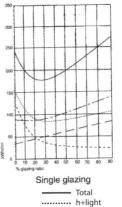

Single glazing

- Total
- h+light
- heat
- light
- cool

● Annual primary energy consumption

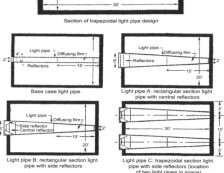

Section of trapezoidal light pipe design

Base case light pipe

Light pipe A: rectangular section light pipe with central reflectors

Light pipe B: rectangular section light pipe with side reflectors

Light pipe C: trapezoidal section light pipe with side reflectors (location of two light pipes in space)

Various light-pipe designs

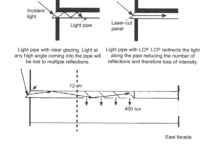

Light pipe with clear glazing. Light at any high angle coming into the pipe will be lost to multiple reflections.

Light pipe with LCP. LCP redirects the light along the pipe reducing the number of reflections and therefore loss of intensity.

12-m

400 lux

East facade

Light pipes section

Passive-mode daylight systems: light pipe

Light pipe building integration

Passive-daylight concepts

Passive mode includes the use of passive-daylight devices. The objective in ecological design is to maximise the use of daylighting and to decrease the need for energy-consuming artificial lighting.

Most passive-daylight techniques have worked to control incoming direct sunlight in order to minimise its potentially negative effect on visual comfort, ie glare, and reduce the building's cooling load by reducing heat gain. Direct sunlight, however, is an excellent interior illuminant when it is intercepted at the plane of the aperture and efficiently distributed throughout the building without glare. It is contended that windows and indoor spaces should be laid out in such a way that under overcast conditions (in temperate zones) with an external intensity of illumination of approximately 10,000 lux, a level of 200 lux can be achieved in the depth of rooms.

Transitional daylight designs can provide adequate daylight within about 4.6 metres of conventional height windows. The use of larger windows and higher transmittance glazings to provide sufficient levels of daylight at distances further from the window has proved to be ineffective. Daylight levels decrease asymptomatically with distance from the window, so that a disproportionate amount of daylight solar radiation must be introduced into the front of the room to achieve small gains in daylight levels at the back of the room.

There are a number of experimental perimeter daylighting systems that passively redirect beam sunlight further from the window using special optical films, an optimised geometry and a small glazing aperture and special glass (eg holographic optical elements or HOE). The objectives of these systems are:

• to increase daylight illuminance levels at 4–5 metres to 9 metres from the window aperture with minimum solar heat gains; and

• to improve the uniformity of the daylight luminance gradient across the room under variable solar conditions throughout the year.

Some of the advanced systems use 'articulated light shelves' and 'light pipes'. Studies have shown that passive light-shelf and light-pipe designs and HOE can introduce adequate ambient daylight for office tasks in a zone up to 12 metres from the external wall of a deep perimeter space under most sunny conditions with a relatively small inlet area; the light pipe has been shown to perform more efficiently throughout the year than the light shelf.

The design of light-collecting systems relies upon the transmission properties of the highly reflective surface materials used, as well as on their geometry, in order to redirect sunlight more efficiently.

The advanced optical daylighting systems are based on the following concepts:

- By reflecting sunlight to the ceiling plane, daylight can be delivered to the workplace at depths greater than those achieved with conventional windows or skylights, without significant increases in daylight levels near the window. This redirection improves visual comfort by increasing the uniformity of wall and ceiling illumination levels across the depth of the room.

- By using a relatively small inlet glazing area and transporting the daylight efficiently, lighting-energy savings can be attained without severe cooling load penalties from solar radiation.

- By carefully designing the system to block direct sun, direct source glare and thermal discomfort can be diminished. The challenge of the design stems from the large variation in solar position and daylight availability throughout both the day and the year.

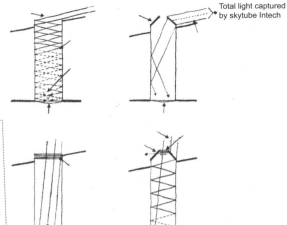

Total light captured by skytube Intech

Comparison between traditional and tubular skylights

A daylighted building, no matter how well designed, saves energy only if the daylighting can effectively and reliably displace electric lighting usage. Most daylighting designers agree that, in non-residential buildings, no amount of provision for convenient manual switching (even for 50 per cent reduction of fixtures in use) will result in useful savings.

Energy savings in artificial lighting can begin by using narrow-width floor plates to reduce artificial lighting and to optimise natural lighting (eg at around 14 metres to 16 metres external wall-to-wall plate size). Earlier high-rise built forms with central cores have about 8.2-metre depths from the external wall to the lift core wall.

The external shading devices used on the facade can have an effect on the amount of natural daylight that the building receives. Other devices include the use of overhangs from the floor above and external blinds. Provided the sun path of the locality justifies their use, light-shelf devices can be used to reflect light back into the inner reaches of the floor space. These devices do not enhance the quality of light but ensure a better distribution to the inside of the space. Detailed analysis would be required to ensure their effectiveness.

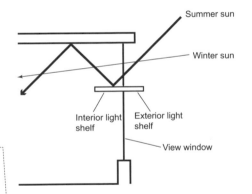

Summer sun

Winter sun

Interior light shelf

Exterior light shelf

View window

Light shelf preventing glare close to the window, and reflecting light deep into the room

There is, of course, an energy balance to be made between the savings in artificial lighting and the small increase in solar heat gain. We can also improve seating and work-surface layouts, reduce glare, and have natural light through better window and facade design. For more effective means, particularly in climatic zones with a low sun path, the use of holographic glass in the outer facade and the use of light shelves as scoops may extend natural light by 10 metres or more from the facade line. Studies have shown that access to sunlight and views provide a feeling of well-being. However, to guarantee a safe, comfortable working environment where visual tasks are performed, occupants should have control over the quantity and quality of light. A mixture of lowered levels of background light from low-energy, ceiling-mounted fittings and daylight from windows, together with task lighting for close work, is often found to provide the most acceptable visual environment.

Glare

In achieving an acceptable comfort level of daylight, one of the main 'discomforts' to be recognised and resolved is the problem associated with glare (both direct and indirect). Treatment of this problem reflects a lighting strategy and has implications for the energy performance of the building. Glare is a function of contrast and brightness and results from one of two causes. In the first, a bright light source (such as a sunlit window or a bright lamp) is viewed from a surrounding area that is in relative darkness. In this case, glare results from excessive contrast and can be relieved by increasing the brightness of the surroundings. This type of glare causes discomfort to occupants, resulting in poor visual performance and potential dissatisfaction with the visual environment. Often complaints manifest themselves as more general dissatisfaction with the environment as a whole due to the subjective nature of the problem, which is not always obvious.

If a space is 'over-lit' by a source that is so excessively bright that the eye mechanism becomes saturated, the result is 'disability glare'. Although less likely to occur, this can be debilitating or even dangerous. For example, a window in sunlight at the end of a dimly lit corridor can suddenly plunge a pedestrian into relative darkness and could prove hazardous.

Sky courts

Here, a useful device is the use of recessed terraces or 'sky courts' to serve as interstitial zones between the inside areas and the outside areas. These are parks-in-the-sky, the balancing of the inorganic mass of the building's hardware and components with the organic mass to effect a more balanced ecosystem.

The sky court is essentially a recessed balcony area with full-height glazed doors that open out from the internal areas to the terrace spaces. Besides providing shading to that portion of the building, these sky courts can also serve the following multiple functions: as emergency evacuation zones; as areas for planting and landscaping; as flexible interstitial zones for future expansion (eg in the event of future increase in permissible plot ratio); or as areas for the future spatial addition of executive washrooms, kitchenettes, etc. The skycourts also furnish the built form's users with a more humane environment as an optional open-to-the-sky zone for them to step out on to from the internally enclosed floor areas, to enable them to experience the external environment directly and to enjoy views.

These transitional spaces can also be located to protect the 'hot' sides of the urban building or to frame an important view. Positioned either centrally or peripherally, such multistorey transitional spaces essentially perform the same traditional transitional role (ie as in-between spaces) as the veranda in vernacular architecture. Such spaces are in effect 'open-to-the-sky' spaces under semi-enclosed conditions.

These spaces should also not be totally covered from above. They might be shielded by a louvred roof to encourage wind flow to the inner areas while letting the hot air out. These spaces may even extend over the entire face of the building to create a multistorey recessed atrium space, which might also serve as a wind scoop to vent the inner parts of the building. The hot air from the stack effect generates air movement through these atria and is often used in hot-arid and temperate zones (where the differences in the external and internal temperatures are sufficient to make this work).

Passive mode by natural ventilation

Natural ventilation may be used to increase comfort (air movement), for health (air change) or for building cooling (wind speed). Natural means of ventilation utilise the motive force of air pressure differentials from external wind effects on the building, and from temperature differentials. The designer must ascertain the basis for the use of the wind forces for the locality in question. The wind rate for that locality gives detailed information about wind direction and frequency for a month or a whole year.

Wind

One of the key ambient sources of energy of a location is wind. By optimising on the location's wind conditions during the time of the year and time of the day when good ventilation or when wind-assisted comfort ventilation is needed, we can shape the urban building's floor plate and external wall for natural ventilation and more effective cooling.

Natural ventilation includes a number of ways in which external air and wind can be used to benefit the occupants of buildings. At the simplest level, natural ventilation ensures a fresh air supply to the interiors (eg through vents in double-skin facades or as simple vents installed above windows). However, it must be taken into account that this could create dustier or noisier internal conditions, especially at the lower levels of the high rise (eg on the fifth to eighth storeys and below). Large projects may be dependent on the stack effect in mixed-mode systems, whereby fresh air is allowed to enter at low level, where it can be further cooled as it comes into contact with the thermal mass of the cold concrete floor slabs. As the air warms, it rises and is eventually expelled at roof level.

Construction and configuration of space

Ventilation and expected internal temperatures
- Stack effect
- Wind assistance
- Mechanical assistance
- Comfort and avoidance of overheating
- Room air movement

Supply air
- Normal path
- Possibility of heat recovery
- Bird screens

Extract air
- Source
- Tempering and heating generally
- Bird screens

Smoke ventilation and fire prevention

Avoidance of rain and wind-driven snow
- Prevention
- Draining if prevention fails

Lighting
- Daylighting and blackout facilities
- Interference with ventilation path
- Artificial

Acoustics
- Acceptable noise levels
- Room acoustics

Risk of condensation
- Interstitial
- On any part of exposed structure

Controls

Durability, access and maintenance

Appearance

Cost

Notes:
1. Naturally ventilated systems are not easily compatible with provision of incoming air filtration or the additional resistance that results.
2. Wind loads need to be assessed by a structural engineer.

● Checklist for natural-ventilation design

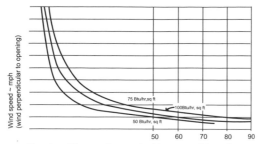

The size of the opening required to remove internally generated heat, as a percentage of floor area, assuming a difference of 3°F between inside and out, may be determined from the graph.

Cross-ventilation and required inlet area ●

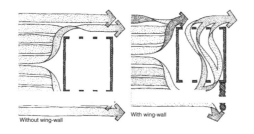

Without wing-wall

With wing-wall

Use of wing wall to increase internal cross-ventilation ●

Properly designed natural ventilation solutions can result in both capital cost and energy savings. In addition, it is also desirable to minimise the requirement for mechanical ventilation and air-conditioning systems in order to ensure a 'healthy' building. The use of natural ventilation is overwhelmingly supported by the fact that energy consumption is typically around half that of air-conditioned buildings in cases where natural methods are used. In addition, maintenance is reduced, there are fewer incidents of 'sick building syndrome' and there is a reduction in carbon dioxide emissions.

The ground floor could be entirely open to the outside space and used as a naturally ventilating space where possible in hot-humid and temperate zones (in the summer). It need not be enclosed or air-conditioned, if it is to be effective as a transitional space between the outside of the built form (the street environment) and its lift lobby area. However, care should be taken to keep out wind-driven rain and to avoid wind turbulence in these areas.

There are two ways in which ventilation can improve comfort. One is a direct physiological effect: by letting in more wind through opening the windows (for example, through the use of wing walls in combination with adjustable shutters and spoilers), the indoor air speed is increased which will make the occupants feel cooler. This approach is termed comfort ventilation. Introducing outdoor air with a given higher wind speed into a building may provide a direct physiological cooling effect even when the indoor air temperature is actually elevated; this is particularly the case when the humidity is high, as the higher air speed increases the rate of sweat evaporation from the skin, thus reducing the discomfort. Ceiling fans operate by the same principle. The other method is nocturnal cooling, ventilating the building only at night and thus cooling the building's interior mass during the day. The cooled mass reduces the heat build-up rate of the indoor temperature.

In temperate climates, the bioclimatic strategy is to extend the mid-seasons (and as mentioned earlier, reduce the need for heating in winter and air conditioning in summer through the use of a multiple-skin facade system that has different modes during the winter and summer). In winter, a part of the facade can become a Trombe wall and absorb the heat from the sun. Part of the wall also lets in the eastern and western sun. In the evening, the Trombe wall is used to heat up the interior and the internal blinds are pulled shut to insulate the insides to keep the heat in. The same wall is insulated on the outside in the summer to reduce the solar insolation, and natural ventilation is used. During the summer nights, the mass of the Trombe wall is ventilated to release the accumulated heat.

Enclosed central courtyards or atria can save energy by functioning as spaces that bring fresh air into the building and provide natural 'pre-heat'. In addition, a design incorporating such an atrium space should lend itself to natural ventilation by virtue of the fact that

Beaufort number	Wind speed (m/s)	Description	Land condition	Comfort
0	0–0.5	Calm	Smoke rises vertically	No noticeable wind
1	0.5–1.5	Light air	Smoke drifts	
2	1.6–3.3	Light breeze	Leaves rustle	Wind felt on face
3	3.4–5.4	Gentle breeze	Wind extends flags	Hair disturbed, clothing flaps
4	5.5–7.9	Moderate breeze	Small branches in motion, raises dust and loose paper	Hair disarranged
5	8.0–10.7	Fresh breeze	Small trees in leaf begin to sway	Force of wind felt on body
6	10.8–13.8	Strong breeze	Whistling in telegraph wires, large branches in motion	Umbrellas used with difficulty. Difficult to walk steadily. Noise in ears
7	13.9–17.1	Near gale	Whole trees in motion	Inconvenience in walking
8	17.2–20.7	Gale	Twigs broken from trees	Progress impeded. Balance difficult in gusts
9	20.8–24.4	Strong gale	Slight structural damage (chimneypots and slates)	People blown over in gusts
10	24.4–28.5	Storm	Seldom experienced inland. Trees uprooted, considerable structural damage	

Wind speeds: Beaufort scale

Example of wing walls (UMNO Tower, Penang, 1995)
Example of use of wing walls in a high-rise built form
to create internal conditions of comfort

Diagrams 3, 4 and 5 illustrate the
effect of a wing wall on the facade of a building

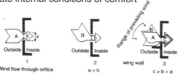

Guide to extent of window to be opened to
achieve required air-change
The wing wall device

the inclusion of the atrium will modify the building form to one that avoids deep-plan accommodation in favour of a layout with windows on inner and outer facades, allowing for good cross-ventilation.

Natural ventilation should be employed whenever possible without incurring heating (or cooling) energy penalties. Ventilation helps to control indoor air pollution by diluting stale indoor air with fresh outside air. Air movement will be encouraged by temperature and pressure differentials between inside and outside, particularly where temperature differences are enhanced by climate-sensitive considerations such as passive solar gains, atrium spaces and glazed courtyards.

However, not all buildings lend themselves to a completely natural approach; indeed in winter, care must be taken to avoid over-ventilation and consequent energy penalties due to excessive fresh-air cooling. As a result, in larger buildings, mixed-mode and displacement ventilation systems have begun to emerge as a means to conserve energy in winter.

The argument against natural ventilation is that there is an increase in air and noise pollution into the interior of the building. It is held that this defect also applies to many mechanical systems, in which a misplaced fresh-air inlet can recycle dirty air into the interior of a building.

Natural ventilation in buildings is encouraged by the provision of low-level inlets and high-level exhaust openings that allow fresh air to be drawn in and foul air to be expelled. This movement of air is the result of the simple mechanism of pressure differentials created by temperature differences (ie convections) and by the wind acting on the built form creating positive and negative pressures.

In any event, the service cores of buildings should be naturally ventilated spaces and should have natural sunlight. At the same time, there should be good views to the outside wherever possible. This again reaffirms the preference for the peripheral-core position. Further energy savings can be achieved through reduced requirements for mechanical ventilation, artificial lighting and the need for mechanical pressurisation ducts for fire protection. As mentioned earlier, the cores placed on the hot sides of the building can be used to absorb the heat build-up during the day and can then be flushed with cool air at night.

Internal open-plan layouts should ensure that occupants enjoy the advantages of daylight. By providing a view out from the lift lobby areas, the designed system's users can experience the outside environment immediately as soon as they exit from the lift. As they step out from the enclosed elevator into the lift lobby, they receive natural sunlight and access to ventilation, and in this way enjoy a greater awareness of place. In the central-core layout of the floor plate, the building's users exit the lift to enter into an artificially lit 'location-unspecific' lobby, often combined with a dark and dingy passageway, which is far less pleasant by comparison.

Wind-tunnel testing assists in the design of the built form's structural system; aids in the design of the outriggers (eg sky-bridges, steel balconies, etc); provides the basis for the exterior facade design (the varying wind speeds, surface pressures, suction effects and other factors); identifies opportunities for natural ventilation (at the lift lobbies, stairwells, lavatories and other areas); helps ascertain turbulences and conditions on the ground plane and in the sky courts (ie to identify locations with uncomfortable or unsafe wind speeds; the Beaufort scale level 9 is equivalent to gale-force winds); and identifies opportunities for using wind generators.

Natural ventilation may be optional, and not a constant provision, in the low-energy large building. When needed (as when air-conditioning systems break down), and for natural cross-ventilation to be effective, the best window opening arrangement is full wall openings on both the windward and leeward sides of the building in the summer (or all year round in the hot-humid zones), with adjustable or closing devices on the facade to assist in channelling the airflow in the required direction to match changes in wind direction.

Ideally, it should be possible to open windows very wide when required (about 4 square metres for most lift lobbies and around 2 square metres for staircases, achieving approximately six air changes per hour). However, high wind velocity at the upper reaches of tall urban buildings could make this impractical. Recessed windows with means of adjusting airflow and control of wind-swept rain could provide natural ventilation alternatives in the event of air-conditioning failure.

The provision of an adequate amount of fresh air is also essential for occupant health, for the removal of moisture and pollutants, and, depending on the climatic zone, as a source of heat dissipations and cooling when indoor temperatures are high. In temperate climates, the design objective is to ensure adequate air quality with no unnecessary increase in heat loss. A minimum fresh-air supply of 2–3 air changes per hour per person is recommended.

Air movement can generate cooling of occupants by air speeds of between 0.4 and 3.0 m/s. Air movement increases heat loss by both convection and evaporation; for instance, air movement of 1 m/s (walking pace) will reduce an air temperature of 30.25ºC to an effective temperature of 27.25ºC. Ceiling fans can be very energy efficient when compared to air conditioning, which uses at least six times as much energy.

In the case of the facade of the tall built form, wind performance grows exponentially as it moves upwards. Therefore, if natural ventilation is used in the building, then a series of

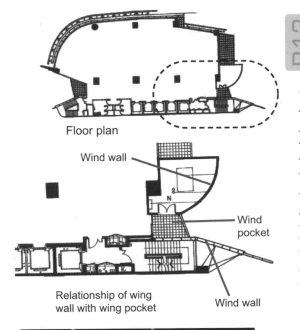

Floor plan

Wind wall

Wind pocket

Wind wall

Relationship of wing wall with wing pocket

Wind pocket viewed from inside the floor
Detail of wing wall device (see previous page)

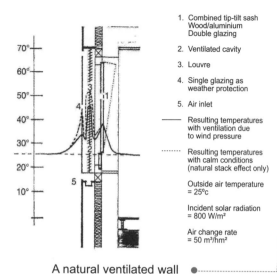

1. Combined tip-tilt sash
   Wood/aluminium
   Double glazing

2. Ventilated cavity

3. Louvre

4. Single glazing as
   weather protection

5. Air inlet

—— Resulting temperatures
     with ventilation due
     to wind pressure

······ Resulting temperatures
        with calm conditions
        (natural stack effect only)

Outside air temperature
= 25°c

Incident solar radiation
= 800 W/m²

Air change rate
= 50 m³/hm²

A natural ventilated wall ●┄┄┄┄┄┄┄┄┄┄┄┄┄┄┄

modified venting devices for different height zones is needed. The external facade can consist of a series of systems (eg double-skin, flue-wall, etc) depending on the desired thermal effect and venting system.

Stack ventilation

The taller the building, the greater should be its potential to ventilate itself by the stack effect. Passive stack ventilation is a system of natural (non-mechanical) ventilation that employs vertical 'stack' ducts that allow internal air to be expelled from the built system by the motive forces that create pressure differentials. Currently, this phenomenon is counteracted through the mechanical pressurisation of the corridor space and horizontal air barriers to dampen what would otherwise be an excessive stack effect, at the expense of using additional energy to ventilate the units.

Wing walls

Wing walls are also useful low-energy devices that can be designed into the built form to capture wind using a 'fin' at the facade to channel wind into the insides of the building to increase the internal airflow per hour and so create comfortable internal conditions similar to the effects of a ceiling fan.

Natural ventilation is valuable for sustainable design as it relies upon natural air movement and can save significant non-renewable fuel-based energy by lowering the need for mechanical ventilation and air conditioning. It addresses two basic needs in buildings: the removal of foul air and moisture, and the enhancement of personal thermal comfort.

Some European design codes dictate that in order to receive adequate natural light, the furthest desk from an outside wall should be in the range of 5–7.5 metres (eg depth at 2.5 times the external window height). It also becomes impractical to attempt natural ventilation with greater floor-plate depths, because natural ventilation becomes unsuitable – the air tends to become contaminated long before it is released to the outside.

As mentioned earlier, in those cities with high levels of outdoor air pollution, natural ventilation to the usable areas becomes problematic. Air needs to be introduced into the space via air-conditioning systems with efficient filters to optimise the quality of the internal environment. External traffic noise might also militate against natural ventilation through open windows, unless suitable acoustical barriers exist. Sky courts might need sliding screens as windbreaks to protect interiors on those occasions when high wind speeds occur.

Natural ventilation is generally suitable only for selective areas such as the lift lobbies, staircases and toilets, which can have openable windows or air gaps to the exterior, but these should also be ventilated by a calculated percentage of air loss that is permitted to seep in from the air-conditioned spaces. Large balconies can have full-height adjustable sliding doors to serve as operable vents in cases where such natural ventilation is needed.

In temperate and cold climates, the design challenge is to restrict incoming air to achieve the minimum necessary fresh-air change without causing cold draughts or excessive heat loss. Even under calm winter conditions, differences in temperature between the interior and exterior air will usually create a sufficient stack effect to draw in fresh air. The stack effect is brought about by warm air rising up to be emitted through high-level outlets and so allowing colder, heavier air to be drawn in from the outside. Natural ventilation is often absent from most user areas in tall buildings located in cold and temperate climates, partly because of excessive wind speeds at higher levels but also due to problems arising from the stack effect. A common strategy in temperate climates is to use tempered or cooled minimal mechanical ventilation with natural ventilation (or fan-assisted ventilation), which varies depending upon the seasons, while limiting winter design temperatures to 19°C and summer temperatures to around 25°C. Treating each season differently can enable the built form to achieve acceptable energy consumption targets (around 150 kw/h/m² over a normal year). Naturally ventilated buildings should be shaped and oriented to maximise exposure to the required summer wind direction, and designed with a relatively shallow plan (about 14-metre external wall-to-wall floor-plate depth) to facilitate the flow of air through the building as cross-ventilation. Solar-heated buildings require particular attention in order to optimise both the solar and ventilation requirements. Ideally, solar orientation and breeze paths need to coincide.

To be effective for personal comfort, the air path through the building must pass through the zone frequented by the building's occupants (that is, within about 2 metres from floor level). Airflow above the heads of occupants in offices is of little value in summer (except for night cooling purposes), but can be useful in winter for achieving minimum ventilation needs while avoiding draughts.

Natural ventilation can be further induced by creating different pressures across the building. The essential principle is that a building's walls obstruct airflow, and so it is necessary to create wind pressure differences between windward and leeward walls. The effective pressure difference tends to be c 1.4 times dynamic pressure at projected floor-overhang level or at the location of any wing walls in the facade. Where wall openings are about 15 to 20 per cent of wall area, the average wind speeds through wall openings can have the potential to be 18 per cent higher than the local wind speed.

During winter in temperate and cold climates, it is necessary to ensure an adequate exchange of indoor air to maintain indoor air quality. This natural ventilation can be achieved using wind pressure or the stack effect. During summer in warm humid climates, natural ventilation

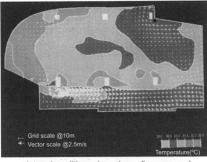

Internal conditions when wing walls are opened (Southwesterly wind at 2.5 m/s)

Grid scale @10m
Vector scale @2.5m/s
Temperature(°C)

Grid scale @10m
-5 -2.5 0 2.5 6 7.5
Pressure (Pa)

Wind flow around building (vertical section) in the form of air pressure contours.

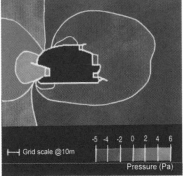

Grid scale @10m
-5 -4 -2 0 2 4 6
Pressure (Pa)

Wind flow around building (plan) in the form of air pressure contours

Use of Computational Fluid Dynamics (CFD) to analyse use of wind to create internal conditions of comforts

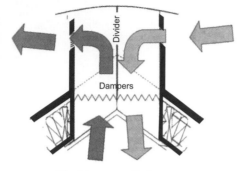

Wind tower ventilation

using wind pressure and/or the stack effect is useful for achieving airflow or indoor thermal comfort. The urban building in hot-arid desert climates can benefit from natural ventilation by the stack effect to draw airflow through evaporative cooling systems or by wind pressure at night to enhance night cooling of the building. Natural ventilation during the day can be achieved through an evaporative cooling system (to ensure that the temperature of the incoming air is lowered and its relative humidity raised).

The main aspects that affect indoor ventilation conditions are:

- geometrical configuration of the building's envelope – its shape and profile (projection, recesses, etc);

- location of openings with respect to wind direction;

- total area of openings in the pressure and suction regions of the built system's envelope;

- type of windows and details of their opening;

- vertical location of openings;

- interior obstructions to airflow from the inlet to the outlet openings, particularly when the air is flowing through more than a single room (this includes information such as the size and location of the openings connecting the adjacent rooms – the doors); and

- presence or absence of fly screens in the openings.

The full impact of these design details depends on the extent to which they enable or inhibit cross-ventilation in the built form both as a whole and in its individual rooms. Cross-ventilation is defined as the situation in which outdoor air can flow from openings on one side of the building (the inlet openings, or pressure zones around the building) through the building and out via openings on the suction sections of the building.

In evaluating the ventilation from the human comfort point of view, attention should be paid not only to the overall amount of airflow but also to the distribution of air velocities throughout the ventilated space. In any discussion of ventilation, quantitative criteria by which indoor ventilation conditions can be evaluated are needed. Examples of such criteria are:

- air speed at the inlet opening;

- maximum speed at any point in the space;

- average air speed in the space; and

- average speed at occupancy level (ie at about 1 metre above the floor).

In essence, bioclimatic design (ie passive mode) works with rather than against climate. To do this, we of course need to understand the climatic conditions of the locality and then to design in relation to these climatic conditions, not just to synchronise the built form's design with the local meteorological conditions but also to optimise the ambient energies of the locality into a low-energy building design. For by designing to improve the comfort conditions internally without the use of any electromechanical systems we minimise dependence on external energy sources and the use of non-renewable energy is reduced.

There is also a regionalist rationale to this approach. By designing with the climate of the place, we are producing a built form that is better linked to the locality and thus has a more regionalist benefit. This will be evident in the vernacular architecture of that locality which, without exception, will be highly resource efficient, will use local materials in construction, and will be well adapted to local climate and ecology. Many of today's green designers seek inspiration from such buildings.

The form of a building is crucial to its environmental performance as are its orientation and materials. At the more detailed level, the fixtures and fittings of environmental design are also crucial. These include: photovoltaic and solar panels (to include or exclude); (day)light shelves; (day)light tubes; architectural shading devices; buffer zones; planting; hybrid M&E systems – part mechanical, part passive – ventilation chimneys; etc.

Passive-mode design is demanding. It is not merely a question of a few simple, intuitive moves like shading a south-facing northern hemisphere facade in summer and protecting a north-facing northern hemisphere facade in winter. Environmental design began as building physics, and that's where it ends. Here, we find that the development of powerful environmental software is being driven by the need to test the complex physical behaviour of a passive or hybrid building before it is built to see whether the control of the internal environment is still satisfactory after the reduction or renunciation of conventional energy-expensive mechanical systems. The more ambitious the design, the more this modelling is necessary, since opening a building up to the outside again results in many more variables than a sealed building has to address – fluctuations in solar radiation, wind velocity, humidity, etc. At the same time, passive-mode designed buildings must meet much higher comfort and performance levels than the vernacular architecture, the model for a less energy-hungry architecture.

Once we have optimised the built-form configuring options passively, then any other systems that we add to the design further improve its low-energy performance.

Even if the sources of energy are ambient (eg solar collectors, photovoltaics, wind energy, etc), these systems generally require a higher or more sophisticated level of technological support systems, the result of which is to increase the inorganic content of the building, its embodied energy level and, indirectly, the material resources and hence attendant impacts on the environment.

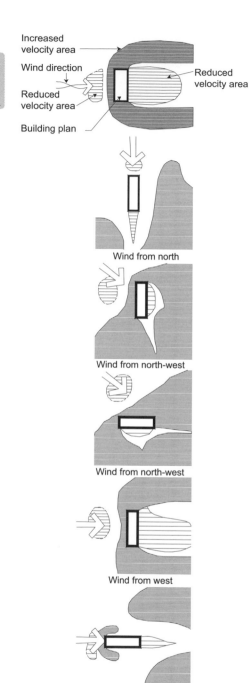

Increased velocity area

Wind direction

Reduced velocity area

Reduced velocity area

Building plan

Wind from north

Wind from north-west

Wind from north-west

Wind from west

Wind from west
Guide for landscape design considering wind on the built form

Vegetation

Studies have shown that visual comfort is afforded by vegetation in buildings. Another benefit is the physical improvement in air quality (see B18). Ecodesign should bring more nature into our built environment, and we should be designing characteristics similar to those that we have evolved in the natural world to provide a design that includes a rich and varied environment with a close relationship to nature.

Windows

The design of windows is one of the most important aspects of making a built system more energy efficient. Generally, glass is a poor insulator with a low R-value because heat passes through it very rapidly and at a very high percentage (about 95 per cent). The designer can use low-emissivity glass that reflects radiant heat to prevent it from entering a building where it would be absorbed by whatever surface it happened to shine on. It has an invisible, metallic coating that admits the full spectrum of sunlight but blocks the escape of radiant heat. Efforts are also being made to develop windows that can directly harness the sun's energy with embedded photovoltaic cells.

To reduce cooling costs, it is important to keep heat and sunlight out of a house during the day by closing all windows, doors, curtains and blinds, especially on windows that face east and west. However, if the temperature outside is cooler than 25.5°C, windows and doors should be opened to let in the breeze. In milder climates, ventilating the built form with cool night air can reduce the use of air conditioning during the day. Opening all curtains and blinds after dark will allow the heat in the house to escape through the windows.

Another way to cool a building is to stop the sun's heat from seeping in through the roof. One way to do this is to add a radiant barrier – an inexpensive type of aluminium foil – on the underside of the roof. This will stop at least 95 per cent of the heat from radiating into the attic or ceiling void.

Ecodesign seeks to provide as much natural daylight to the built form's internal spaces as possible. Use of clear glass (with proper shading) and natural daylight provides the building's occupants with a connection between indoor and outdoor spaces as well as allowing views into the regularly occupied areas of the building. Design needs to achieve a minimum daylight factor of 20 per cent (excluding all direct sunlight penetration) in as much of the space that is occupied for the performance of tasks requiring comprehensive lighting as possible.

Ecodesign should maximise interior daylighting. Design strategies to consider include building orientation, shallow floor plates, increased building perimeter, exterior and interior permanent shading devices, high-performance glazing and photo-integrated light sensors. Designers can predict daylighting through calculations or model daylighting strategies with a physical or computer model to assess use levels and daylight factors achieved.

Glare can be avoided by careful consideration of window design in relation to the room depth and height, surface attributes of the space and the relationship between the window, the exterior and the occupants. A room 3 metres high and 6 metres deep daylit on one side only should achieve a daylight factor of around 1.5–2 per cent at the back of the room, for around 15–20 per cent glazing/external wall ratios. In terms of the visual environment created by this scenario, these levels are described as 'cheerfully daylit'. A height-to-depth ratio of 1:2 allows good light penetration for the aforementioned glazing ratios, which can be applied to rooms with higher and lower ceilings or deeper and shallower plans pro rata. The effect of this ratio is to limit the depth of a non-residential building to about 12 metres, assuming it is lit on both sides.

Glare problems can be solved by improving or reducing contrasts – for example, by increasing internal surface reflectance. In schools, glare often occurs when light-coloured walls are concealed behind posters or friezes; this could be alleviated by concentrating such material on walls adjacent to the window, to allow the wall opposite the window to remain as free as possible of artwork and other coverings.

The built form's floor layout and shape, besides responding to commercial considerations, should take into account the local users, modalities and cultural patterns of working, privacy and community, all of which have developed in relation to the locality's climate. This should be reflected in the building's floor-plate configuration, its floor depth, the positioning of its entrances and exits, the provision for human movement through and between spaces, its orientation and its external views. The floor-plate configuration should provide a habitable environment, interest and scale, internally available sunlight, sufficient ventilation and so forth. For example, for offices, the workstations should not be located in the centre of each floor plate with the partitioned offices at the periphery but should be reversed, by planning the internal layout to enable the greatest number of users to receive natural sunlight.

Artificial lighting accounts for about 10 per cent of the energy used in the typical large building (whereas carbon dioxide emissions account for about 25 per cent of emissions). This is the next area for design efforts to minimise energy consumption in the built form's operational systems. Although artificial lighting loads can be reduced in part by making the building configuration maximise the accessibility of natural sunlight, they can also be reduced by using high-efficiency lamps, low-energy artificial lamps, electronic ballasts and high-quality fittings. For instance, replacing a 75-watt incandescent bulb with an 18-watt compact fluorescent bulb will, over the lifetime of the bulb, avoid emitting the equivalent of 4300 kilograms of carbon dioxide and about 10 kilograms of sulphur dioxide, which also

Example of vertical landscaping
(Palomas 2, Mexico City, 2003)

creates acid rain, from a typical generating plant (in the USA). Energy savings could be achieved by providing lighting switching systems coupled with the building's automation systems (BAS), or using local controls and ambient light sensors to adjust artificial lighting, depending on the amount of natural light entering the built form.

Artificial-lighting energy consumption can be improved in existing light fittings (either two or three tubes) by replacing these with single-output tubes with electronic ballasts and high-performance reflectors (eg '3M Silverlux') with a reflectivity of 0.8. This will increase the light output by about 60 per cent compared to the old fitting. By using electronic ballasts, the lamp flicker common with most standard magnetic ballasts is eliminated. An additional gain is the instant start-up of electronic ballasts as compared to the longer inconvenient start-up time of most magnetic ballasts.

The roofscape: the 'fifth facade' in the building shell

The designed system's green roofscape should be considered as the building's fifth facade. The roof of a high-rise built form is less important thermally compared to that of the lower-rise building type because of its small surface area compared to the extensive external wall area. Furthermore, extensive building height makes any roof overhangs irrelevant, except for the uppermost few floors.

Most traditional dark-coloured roof surfaces to built forms absorb about 70 per cent or more of the solar energy striking them, resulting in peak roof temperatures of 65–88°C. Cool roofs, on the other hand, which are roofs coated with light-coloured surface treatments, are 10–16°C cooler on hot days. The resulting reductions in the transfer of heat into the air-conditioned spaces below can decrease cooling costs by an average of 20 per cent.

However, the direct solar-heat absorption of the roof in the topmost floors needs to be considered. In any case, much of the roof is usually occupied by mechanical equipment, which offers some insulation. The alternative is to have a roof canopy or pergola, or to provide a roof garden or to design for permaculture (in B21).

For instance, in hot, humid climate zones, roofs should be constructed of low thermal capacity materials with reflective outside surfaces (where these are not shaded). The roof should preferably be of double construction and provided with a reflective upper surface.

The thermal forces acting on the outside of the built form are a combination of radiation and convection impacts, among others. The radiation component consists of incident solar radiation and of radiant heat exchanged with the surroundings. The convective heat impact is a function of exchange with the internal air and may be accelerated by air movement.

Roofs and terrace areas in our building might also be vegetated. If buildings are designed with vegetated roofs, rainwater is retained and evaporated, new wildlife habitats are created, internal insulation is improved and energy consumption is reduced. Roof vegetation can halve the rainwater collected (which must be discharged), reduce heat-island phenomena in dense urban centres by cooling the air by evaporation, add thermal and acoustical insulation, protect and increase the lifespan of the roof underlay, nourish habitable space for flora and fauna and increase the biodiversity of the locality.

The beneficial effects of vegetation are further treated under 'passive design by landscaping' (below).

Passive design by colour of the built form's envelope

Peak cooling can be reduced by as much as 40 per cent by using white or lighter-coloured materials, especially for the roof surfaces (which receive much more sun than other planes or facades, eg in temperate zones more in summer, when it is not wanted, than in winter when it is). Similar improvements can be achieved by placing vegetation, including large shade trees, around buildings. Both methods also contribute to reducing energy demand by minimising the urban heat island and by boosting urban temperatures when pavement and building surfaces absorb the sun's rays instead of reflecting them. Cooling needs can be cut by 30 per cent if enough trees are planted.

An effective protection against radiation impact for the external wall is the selective absorption and emission characteristics of certain materials, especially under hot conditions. Materials which reflect rather than absorb radiation, and which release the absorbed heat

Optical flat black paint	0.98
Flat black paint	0.95
Black lacquer	0.92
Dark grey paint	0.91
Black concrete	0.91
Dark blue lacquer	0.91
Black oil paint	0.90
Stafford blue bricks	0.89
Dark olive drab paint	0.89
Dark brown paint	0.88
Dark blue-grey paint	0.88
Azure blue or dark green lacquer	0.88
Brown concrete	0.85
Medium brown paint	0.84
Medium light brown paint	0.80
Brown or green lacquer	0.79
Medium rust paint	0.78
Light grey oil paint	0.75
Red oil paint	0.74
Red bricks	0.70
Uncoloured concrete	0.65
Moderately light buff bricks	0.60
Medium dull green paint	0.59
Medium orange paint	0.58
Medium yellow paint	0.57
Medium blue paint	0.51
Medium Kelly green paint	0.51
Light green paint	0.47
White semi-gloss paint	0.30
White gloss paint	0.25
Silver paint	0.25
White lacquer	0.21
Polished aluminium reflector sheet	0.12
Aluminised mylar film	0.10
Laboratory vapour deposited coatings	0.02

Solar absorptance of various materials

Item	Emittance (at 10–40°C)	Absorptance (for solar radiation)
Black non-metallic surfaces such as asphalt, carbon, slate, paint	0.90–0.98	0.85–0.98
Red brick and tile, concrete and stone, rusty steel and iron, dark paints (red, brown, green, etc)	0.85–0.95	0.65–0.80
Yellow and buff brick and stone, firebrick, fireclay	0.85–0.95	0.50–0.70
White or light-cream brick, tile, paint or paper, plaster, whitewash	0.85–0.95	0.30–0.50
Bright aluminium paint; gilt or bronze paint	0.40–0.60	0.30–0.50
Polished brass, copper, Monel metal	0.02–0.05	0.30–0.50

Solar emittances and absorptances of selected materials

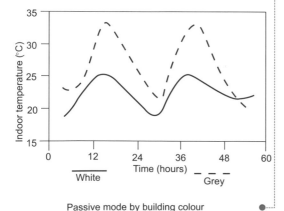

Passive mode by building colour

as thermal radiation more readily, bring about lower temperatures within the building. The external facade should be as light coloured as possible to reduce the heat-island effect and to lighten overall air-conditioning loads. Special coatings are available to improve thermal performance of the base materials, and these should be considered. Dark colours may be used on internal walls on those facades where high mass is used as part of the design strategy. Some pastel finishes reflect the radiated half of solar energy well whereas some visually 'white'-looking shingles absorb it.

Passive design by landscaping

A crucial factor in ecological design is the counterbalancing of the inorganic characteristic of buildings with the organic or the biotic components analogous to the ecosystem. This can be achieved in the building by the incorporation of vertical landscaping into the built form. Roofs can be clad in turf or other vegetation, walls can have climbing plants, car-parking bays can have reinforced grass, roads can be lightly vegetated so that they are porous to dust and water (see B7).

In addition to its organic counterbalancing role, vertical landscaping also serves as part of the passive means for lowering ambient temperatures around buildings, as well as reducing the overall urban heat-island effect (see B9). Plants evaporate water through the metabolic process of evapotranspiration. The water is carried from the soil through the plant and evaporated from the leaves during photosynthesis. The transpiration of water by plants helps to control and regulate humidity and temperature. Studies have shown that vertical plant cover on exposed wall surfaces improves the energy efficiency of the wall up to 8 per cent, partly by trapping pockets of air and partly by preventing rain from filling the air voids in the building facade with water (ie a wet wall is a weaker insulator than a dry one).

Another energy-efficient landscaping method is to grow vines on a trellis, which can reduce the surface temperature of the wall to which the trellis is attached by 4°C. The first step in energy-efficient landscaping should be to see where the sun hits a building throughout the day and then, depending on the climate, take steps to block the sun, let it shine through, or a mixture of both.

In hot-arid places, high-canopied trees create maximum shade on the roof, walls and windows. If air conditioners are used, breezes should be deflected from the building; conversely, if air conditioners are not used, breezes should be encouraged.

In temperate climates, deciduous trees provide excellent shade during summer, and allow maximum solar heat gain during winter. In hot-humid areas, breezes should be allowed to reach the building while as much shade as possible should be created in the summer with deciduous trees. In cool climates, a thin windbreak to deflect winter winds should be planted. South-facing windows are particularly helpful for solar heat gain in winter. Deciduous trees should be planted to prevent overheating in summer, if applicable.

Because of transpiration and shading, the air surrounding a tree is, on average, 5°C cooler than the ambient temperature. The United States Department of Energy has found that tree-shaded neighbourhoods are up to 3°C cooler than neighbourhoods without trees.

Passive-cooling systems

Passive cooling applies to various simple cooling techniques that enable the indoor temperature of buildings to be lowered through the use of natural energy sources.

Bioclimatic design techniques in hot-humid equatorial regions involve architectural designs and choices of materials that provide better comfort conditions (moderately better than the ambient internal conditions) while minimising the demand for energy used to cool a building. This involves minimising heat gain by the building, minimising the solar heating up of the building envelope and solar penetration through windows, providing comfort by natural ventilation and other techniques. The architectural means of achieving this have been discussed above (eg layout of building, orientation, the number, size, location and details of its windows, shading devices, the thermal resistance and heat capacity of its envelope). Appropriate applications of these design elements can bring the average indoor temperature to an improved comfort level better than the outdoor average. On the other hand, various passive-cooling systems are capable of transferring heat from a building to various natural heat sinks by providing 'active' cooling through the use of passive processes, which often use heat-flow paths that do not exist in non-green buildings that lack these systems. A passive mode in a hot-arid climate uses a thermal-siphon method to create a natural form of air conditioning.

The appropriate architectural bioclimatic design for the region of the project site with hot summers can be considered as a precondition to the application of passive-cooling systems, and the two approaches supplement and reinforce one another. Buildings can be cooled by passive systems through the utilisation of several natural heat sinks such as the ambient air, the upper atmosphere, water and the undersurface soil. Each of these cooling sources can be utilised in various ways, resulting in different systems. The various passive-cooling methods have been identified as follows:

- Comfort ventilation: providing direct human comfort, mainly during the daytime, through higher indoor air speeds which increase the rate of sweat evaporation from the skin, thus minimising the discomfort from the sensation of wet skin.

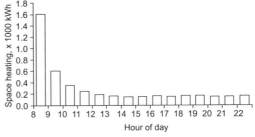

Simulated hourly amounts of useful energy supplied by conventional heating appliances summed up over the year

- Nocturnal ventilative cooling: cooling the structural mass of the building interior by ventilation during the night and closing building apertures during the daytime, thus lowering the indoor daytime temperature.

- Radiant cooling: transferring into the building cold energy generated during the night hours by radiant heat loss from the roof, or using a special radiator on the roof, with or without cold storage for the daytime.

- Direct evaporative cooling: mechanical or non-mechanical evaporative cooling of air. The humidified and cooled air is then introduced into the building.

- Indirect evaporative cooling: evaporative cooling of the roof, for example by roof ponds. The interior space is cooled without elevation of the humidity.

- Cooling of outdoor spaces: cooling techniques that are applicable to outdoor spaces, such as patios, that are adjacent to a building.

Passive mode using building mass

Thermal mass is comprised of building materials that absorb heat effectively, charging up like a thermal battery and then yielding this heat back into the built form's internal space through periods of time when the built form is not actively gaining heat from the sun or from some other source. Buildings are designed here as thermal systems, constructed with materials that have their own qualities of thermal inertia in combination with spaces that permit and generate the natural flow of air in, out, around and through the building, providing for the modification of temperature and speed, ventilation and cooling, without mechanical assistance. The form and elements of a built form can be made to respond to natural cycles both daily and seasonally and to exploit ambient energy sources and sinks. This can be achieved through the joint spatial and temporal interactions in natural and human-made environments, which combines the interactions of space dimensions, the size and shape of an open or enclosed space, to produce an effect.

Glazed thermal walls

The addition of glazing on the outer side of an external wall provides a means of trapping the solar radiation transmitted through the glazing by suppressing part of the convective and radiative heat losses from the face of the wall. Given a suitably dark colour, the surface of the wall behind the glazing will absorb the incoming radiation and release heat to the cavity between the wall and the glazing. The wall may also store heat in its mass. In consistently sunny climates (such as those around the Mediterranean belt) the magnitude of the radiation striking such a wall may be sufficient to produce temperatures in the air cavity that are high enough for the wall to operate as a natural heating appliance. It might then supply adjacent rooms with warm air by means of natural convection, as well as transfer indoors the heat stored in its mass. In more cloudy climates, however, temperatures in the cavity may not be high enough for this process and there may be little solar gain to store in the mass of the wall. In such circumstances, convection in the cavity and long-wave radiation from the surface of the wall should be discouraged in order to reduce heat loss. The key issue is whether the heat retained by the wall can match a dwelling's heat-demand pattern or compensate for the wall's heat losses.

The following are variants of the glazed thermal wall that differ in the way the heat absorption, storage and distribution functions are handled behind the glazing:

- A Trombe wall (after Felix Trombe) combines heat storage and transfer through the mass of an uninsulated solid wall with natural convection. It is a thermally effective system for storing and circulating sun-warmed air. At night the process can reverse, and warm air can be drawn back out of the internal space to escape through this cool glazing.

- A Trombe wall is a thermally massive wall with vents provided at the top and bottom. It may be made of concrete, of masonry or adobe and is usually located on the southern side (in the northern hemisphere) of a built form in order to maximise solar gains. The outer surface is usually painted black to maximise absorption and the wall is directly placed behind glazing with an air gap in between.

- The mass wall excludes heat distribution by convection, relying solely on heat transfer through the mass of the wall. Generally, thickness of the storage wall is between 200 millimetres and 450 millimetres, the air gap between the wall and the glazing is 50 to 150 millimetres and the total area of each row of vents is about 1 per cent of the storage wall area. The wall needs to be shaded in summer to reduce heat gains.

- Other types of solar walls are water-container walls.

- A thermosiphon air panel (TAP) includes a metallic absorber (separate from the wall) and relies mainly on natural convection, with heat distribution through channels in the floor and ceiling.

- A transparent insulation material (TIM) can be fitted behind glass on the external surface of a solid wall. TIM allows incoming radiation to be transmitted through its structure and absorbed by the surface of the wall while restricting heat losses back to the outside.

By optimising all the passive-mode options in the designed system prior to adopting any of the other design modes (eg mixed mode, full mode, productive mode, composite mode), the designed system operates as a low-energy design from the start. Being low energy and not initially dependent on the use of non-renewable sources of energy (eg fossil fuels) there will also be fewer attendant environmental consequences (eg CO_2 emission).

As mentioned earlier, if a built form is designed to optimise all the passive-mode options in the first instance, then even in the event of a power failure to its electromechanical systems, the built form remains acceptably comfortable to its occupants. If this design strategy is not adopted, the built form may become totally unoccupiable in the event of a power failure.

Having optimised all such passive-mode design options in the configuration and layout of the designed system, the designer can progress to the adoption of the next most ecologically sound modes of design.

Summary

As a broad ecodesign strategy, the designer must first optimise all the passive-mode options in the shaping, the enclosural design and the planning of the proposed designed system (in B12) as these will crucially influence its built form, orientation, enclosural design and the extent of openness in its site configuration, layout and massing. Only following this should the designer progress to the next set of design strategies (B14 to B17), which influence the designed and operational systems of the built form. Clearly, the proposed built form must first respond to the climate of the locality, which obviously varies depending on the latitude wherein the biosphere is situated. This design approach is commonly referred to as bioclimatic design and requires the designer to first analyse and understand the climatic conditions of that locality over the year, and then to design to improve the internal conditions of comfort of the intended built form in relation to these climatic conditions and seasonal variations (if any) without the use of any non-renewable sources of energy or mechanical and electrical (M&E) systems, and so create a low-energy built form.

Passive-mode design includes: built-form configuration and orientation, enclosural and facade design, solar-control devices, passive-daylight concepts, wind and natural ventilation, roofscape design, built-form colour, landscaping, passive-cooling systems, use of building mass, etc.

The designer is reminded here to review the intended designed system's level of environmental integration (in B3). The greater the demands placed on the designed system by its users and the higher the comfort level required (see B1), the further the design will depart from depending only on passive-mode systems (here in B13) and approach dependency on full-mode systems (in B15).

B14 Design to optimise all mixed-mode options in the designed system: designing for improved internal comfort conditions with partial use of renewable sources of energy and as low-energy design in relation to the climate of the locality

Having adopted and optimised as many passive-mode design options as possible in the built form (in B13), the designer can next proceed to adopt the appropriate mixed-mode options for the designed system as the next best ecologically beneficial mode. Mixed-mode design is essentially improved internal comfort conditions where there is partial use of mechanical and electrical (M&E) systems (eg fans, blowers, pumps, heat exchangers, etc) and partial use of renewable sources of energy.

As with passive-mode design, mixed-mode design can be considered as a form of bioclimatic design and requires an understanding of the climate of the locality so that it can take advantage of its characteristics. In mixed-mode systems, only the best performing, least consuming and most appropriate technologies should be utilised. Examples include ceiling fans, demister fans, double facades, flue atriums and Trombe walls.

The effectiveness of a mixed-mode design is dependent on the benign interaction between the interior of the built form and exterior ambient forces (as opposed to full-mode buildings where the interior of a building is fully isolated from the exterior ambient forces). Mixed-mode built forms usually have greater transparency and complexity because they admit and control ambient energy sources. The development of mixed mode in such a built form is dependent on the cost-effective exploitation of ambient energy sources without incurring any penalties in terms of discomfort. Design strategies usually associated with these buildings include use of solar gain for winter warmth, natural lighting and ventilation. Mixed-mode use aims to create as natural an environment as possible, and building occupants have control over their environment for their thermal comfort by opening windows and drawing blinds.

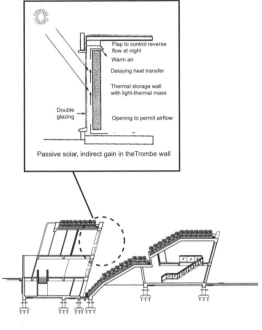

Passive solar, indirect gain in theTrombe wall

● Mixed mode using Trombe walls

Mixed mode
Considerations include:

Secondary glass skin
One approach is to wrap the built form in a secondary glass skin, outside the weather-excluding membrane. This lowers energy consumption by trapping a winter jacket of warm air, opens up to let breezes through on temperate days or on still days and creates stack-effect updraught breezes. Only on the hottest days is the inner skin sealed and the building ventilated mechanically. Other examples include double-skin glazed facades with siphoning systems. (It is important to ensure that this second skin is openable for natural ventilation purposes.)

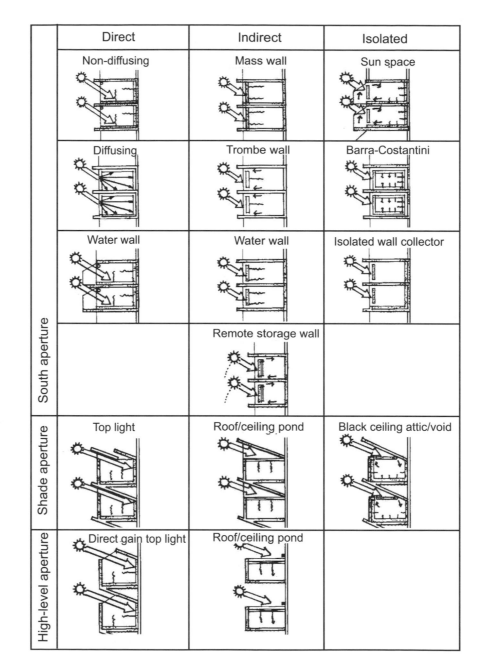

	Direct	Indirect	Isolated
South aperture	Non-diffusing	Mass wall	Sun space
	Diffusing	Trombe wall	Barra-Costantini
	Water wall	Water wall	Isolated wall collector
		Remote storage wall	
Shade aperture	Top light	Roof/ceiling pond	Black ceiling attic/void
High-level aperture	Direct gain top light	Roof/ceiling pond	

Mixed mode using various generic passive solar systems

The 'double-layered' facade system operates by means of a ventilated double 'skin' with an intermediate shading device. The intermediate shading device deflects most of the incoming solar radiation back through the external glass. The proportion of absorbed solar radiation is converted into 'sensible' heat and radiated back into the air space between the inner and outer glass units.

Wind pressure/stack effect

Ventilation of the heat gains in the air space is dependent on the effects of external wind pressures and/or the stack effect. The stack effect works on the principle that the heat absorbed and radiated out by the blind and glazing rises within the cavity. Cooler air is drawn into the air space to replace the buoyant warmer air, which is ventilated; thus an air-stream is used to ventilate solar heat gains. The system is most efficient when external wind pressure supplements the ventilation effect, but since the occurrence and intensity of wind are variable, optimum performance of the design also varies.

For the stack effect to work effectively, the depth of the air space between the layers must be greater than 250–300 millimetres and the external vent dimension must be at least 150 millimetres. This results in a very deep and heavy facade structure. While the system is effective in controlling solar heat gains, the introduction of cold external air into the cavity during winter means that the benefits of an air buffer are negated. Natural ventilation due to external wind pressures must also be carefully monitored as tests have shown that strong oscillations of the blinds were noted at external wind speeds of around 30 m/s. This is an important consideration in countries subject to high maximum wind gusts. However, the benefits of double facades include dampening of noise emissions, and reduction in high-wind pressures in built forms with natural ventilation. However, wind-pressure reduction within a facade also reduces the air exchange on calm days. The possibility of creating a greenhouse effect in front of each window can also moderate the outside air in winter, and creates a heat trap in summer. This prescribes the use of outside sunshading that is not subject to wind forces, so that tall buildings with clear glazing can be built without risking excessive solar gains.

Active and interactive walls

Active and interactive facades operate on the same principle as a naturally ventilated double-skin wall, but have a number of advantages. As with a naturally ventilated wall, the 'sensible' heat built up within the cavity is extracted by forced or controlled ventilation. The wall is more compact, requiring a much smaller overall section depth than a naturally ventilated wall.

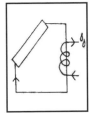

This configuration offers the advantages of both air and water systems. Solar-heated air from a collector can be passed through a heat exchanger to warm water which is then distributed for space heating or domestic water heating. There is no water to freeze in the exposed collector so no antifreeze is needed and there is no risk of collector leakage.
The hydronic system has the advantage of compactness. The disadvantages are the inherent inefficiency of air-to-water heat exchangers and cost.

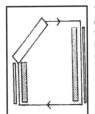

This system lends itself well to the retrofitting of older and poorly insulated buildings. Warm air from the collector is fan-forced through an air gap in the building envelope. Because the collector can operate at low temperatures it can achieve a high efficiency. By raising the surface temperature of the walls comfort is improved.
The large surface area of the walls, however, results in large losses of the low-temperature solar heat.

Warm air from a south sun space freely convects through floor and ceiling ducts to a sun space on the north side, effectively bracketing a model apartment within a tempered micro-climate. Another system is where the roof-collector-warmed air is fan-circulated behind a new facade, similarly creating a tempered climate for the apartment blocks in this retrofit project.

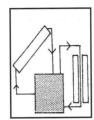

Here air circulates in a closed loop between the collector and storage, and in a separate closed loop between the storage and hypocausts or murocausts which radiate the heat into the rooms. Thereby, the discharge of the collector can be limited to the times when heat is needed and the storage can be fully charged without risk of overheating occupied spaces. Both advantages lead to a higher solar utilisation and improved comfort.

We can use a rock bin as a heat storage, charged by facade-and-roof-integrated collectors. Upon demand, hot air is circulated from the rock bin to channels behind the gypsum walls to heat the classrooms. This allows a fast response when heat is needed and no heating when internal gains are high. A facade collector can be used to provide latent heat storage, which is linked in a separate loop to the living space.

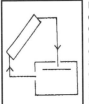

In this system, sometimes referred to as a daytime heater, sun-warmed collector air circulates directly into a room, ideally to a north room where demand is greater. In the summer the collector can act as a solar chimney, drawing cool air from the north side through the building. A criticism of this system is the absence of storage: solar gains can be useful only when the sun shines.
The facade can be constructed of black perforated sheet metal through which ventilation fresh air is drawn. Atria or sun spaces can also serve to pre-heat ventilation air.

Mixed mode using various solar collector systems (see Passive Solar systems)

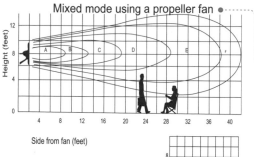

Mixed mode using a propeller fan •

Height (feet)

A	B	C	D	E	F

Side from fan (feet)

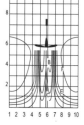

Distance from fan (feet)

A	B	C	D	E	F
1000 FPM	750 FPM	500 FPM	250 FPM	100 FPM	50 FPM

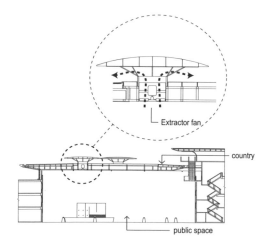

Extractor fan

country

public space

Example of mixed mode using extractor fans •

With an active wall, the heat gains are extracted using internal room air. In temperate and cold climatic zones during winter, the inner glass may be kept closer to room temperature (within 1–2°C), thus eliminating any cold radiation effects and allowing greater use of the perimeter area of the office building. The heat energy removed by an active facade can be used in conjunction with a heat-exchange system to provide further energy savings. An interactive wall is similar to a naturally ventilated facade, but the rate of ventilation is controlled by a small energy-efficient fan powered by solar energy or by conventional electrical means. This is a 'stand alone' system independent of the main building's mechanical systems.

A trombe wall is a self-standing heat storage wall placed on the inner side of the heat collection windows, and the heat flows through this wall and reaches the indoor space. This is how it provides a heating effect and is called 'Trombe' wall after the name of its inventor. The thicker the wall, the more heat storage capacity, resulting in a longer time lag of heat transfer. However, the heat attenuation increases as well. The thickness of the wall is in general 20 to 30 centimetres and the time lag about six to eight hours. In some cases, openings for air circulation are placed on the top and bottom of the thermal storage wall to enhance the heat transfer by air convection. In this case, some measures for avoiding overheating in summer are to be taken into consideration. The heat collection efficiency has been drastically improved by the recent development of the new construction method to fill the air layers between the glazing and the Trombe wall with transparent heat insulating material.

Propeller fans

Propeller fans are also mixed-mode devices and can be used in conjunction with air conditioners to help spread cooled air through the built form. In winter, ceiling fans set at a low speed will help distribute warm air that collects under the ceiling. In milder climates ceiling fans can actually replace air conditioners, while in hotter climates they can be used in conjunction with an air conditioner, which can be turned up to 33°C without discomfort. This can reduce cooling costs considerably, as running a ceiling fan for 24 hours on high speed costs considerably less than air conditioning. Ceiling or window fans are also good options for cooling individual rooms. A breeze makes us feel cooler than it really is, because wind makes it easier for water to evaporate and therefore easier for us to sweat and stay cool. The human comfort zone during the summer is 22–25.5°C but with the breeze of a ceiling fan, that comfort zone can be raised. Higher capacity extractor fans can be used for semi-enclosed areas.

Evaporative coolers

Evaporative coolers pull hot dry air from outside over wet pads inside the coolers. The drier outside air absorbs some of the water from these pads and becomes cooler as a result. A fan then blows the now cold air into the house. Because of their much simpler technology, swamp coolers use only a quarter as much energy as air conditioners. These devices can lower the temperature of outside air by up to 17°C, as well as being excellent ventilators. An evaporative cooler will replace an entire room of air every one to three minutes. But because they add humidity to the air they cool, they are not suitable for humid climates. However, there are two-stage models that produce cool, dry air for such climates.

Dehumidifiers

Dehumidifiers are also examples of mixed-mode systems (used, eg, in humid climates). These can cool a room using less energy than a room or central air conditioner. Reducing humidity will make a person feel cooler even though the actual temperature may still be high.

Passive solar systems

Passive solar systems are essentially mixed-mode systems as they are usually not full M&E or fully active systems. Like a living organism, the building using passive solar operational systems continuously seeks the path of the sun. The building becomes a skin that orients its occupants to a universal calendar. The time of day and season of the year synchronise the comfort (and aesthetics) in the natural world with those inside. It is projected that in approximately 20 to 30 years, between 20 and 30 per cent of the world's energy requirements will be supplied by solar energy. Clearly, the sooner measures are taken to convert existing systems to optimise solar energy, the better.

Solar energy can be harnessed in many ways for the purposes of heating, cooling and lighting. The sun delivers approximately 5000 times more energy per year than is consumed worldwide. Atmospheric solar radiation is approximately 1300 W/m2, of which approximately 1000 W/m2 reaches the earth's surface. The term 'passive solar' refers to systems that absorb, store and distribute the sun's energy without relying on mechanical devices like pumps and fans, which require additional energy. Passive solar design reduces the energy requirements of a building by meeting part or all of its daily heating, cooling and lighting needs with solar energy.

The three most common passive solar design systems are direct gain, indirect gain and isolated gain. A direct-gain system allows sunlight to pass through windows into an occupied space, where it is absorbed by the floors and walls. In an indirect-gain system, a medium for heat storage such as a wall located in one part of a building absorbs and stores solar

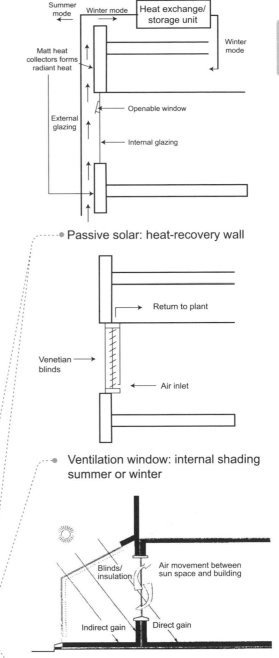

Passive solar: heat-recovery wall

Summer mode / Winter mode / Heat exchange/storage unit / Matt heat collectors forms radiant heat / Winter mode / External glazing / Openable window / Internal glazing

Return to plant / Venetian blinds / Air inlet

Ventilation window: internal shading summer or winter

Blinds/insulation / Air movement between sun space and building / Indirect gain / Direct gain

Passive solar-attached sun space

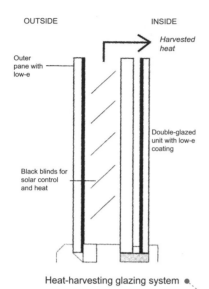

OUTSIDE   INSIDE

Harvested heat

Outer pane with low-e

Double-glazed unit with low-e coating

Black blinds for solar control and heat

Heat-harvesting glazing system ●

heat. The heat is then transferred to the rest of the building through conduction, convection or radiation. In an isolated-gain system, solar energy is absorbed and stored in a separate area, such as a greenhouse or solarium, and then distributed to the living space through ducts. In order to conserve more energy, insulation is incorporated into the most effective passive solar designs.

In climatic regions with wide seasonal fluctuations in temperature, passive solar heating systems typically require some kind of back-up heating. Nonetheless, passive systems contribute significantly to energy savings. Studies show that incorporating passive features typically adds 5 to 10 per cent to the cost of construction, yet the outlay is generally recouped in 5 to 15 years, depending on geographical location and regional energy costs.

In active systems, solar collectors are used to convert the sun's energy into available heat for producing hot water, space heating or industrial processes. Flat-plate collectors are typically used to gather the sun's energy. These are most often light-absorbing plates made of a dark-coloured material such as metal, rubber or plastic that is covered with glass. The plates transfer heat to a fluid – usually air or water – circulating above or below them, and the fluid is either used for immediate heating or stored for later use. These systems are referred to as active because external electromechanical-powered equipment, such as a fan or pump, is used to move the fluid. In domestic dwellings, active solar systems are generally designed to provide at least 40 per cent of the building's heating needs.

Open-loop solar hot-water systems are sometimes classified according to temperature and are used mainly for heating swimming pools, by means of low-temperature unit collectors that can warm water up to 7°C. Pool-heating systems typically use pumps to circulate the water; storage tanks are generally not needed because the water is in constant circulation. Where medium-temperature systems are installed, the temperature rises from 7°C to 28°C for water and space heating in residential and commercial buildings and for industrial-process heat. In high-temperature collectors, water warmed to 28°C or above is used for heat and hot water or for domestic and industrial processes such as cooking, washing, bleaching, anodising and refining.

Thermosiphon

One common type of solar water heater, the thermosiphon system, uses collectors and circulating water, yet it is actually a passive system since no pumps are involved. In this type of system, the storage tank is installed above the collector. As water in the collector is heated and becomes less dense, it rises into the tank by convection and cooler water in the tank sinks into the collector.

Radiant heat barriers

Passive solar technology can also be used for cooling purposes. These systems function by either shielding buildings from direct heat gain or by transferring excess heat outdoors. Carefully designed elements such as overhangs, awnings and eaves shade windows from the high-angle summer sun while allowing the light from the low-angle winter sun to enter the building. The transfer of heat from the inside to the outside of a building may be achieved either through ventilation or conduction, in which heat is lost through a wall or floor. A radiant heat barrier, such as aluminium foil installed under a roof, is able to block up to 95 per cent of the radiant heat transfer from the roof into the building. The Florida Solar Energy Center in Cape Canaveral has found that radiant heat barriers are the most cost-effective passive cooling option for hot southern climates.

Water evaporation

Water evaporation is another effective method used to cool buildings, since water absorbs a large amount of heat from its surroundings when it changes state from a liquid to a gas. Fountains, sprays and pools provide substantial cooling to the surrounding areas. The use of sprinkler systems to continually wet a building's roof during hot weather can reduce its cooling requirements by 25 per cent. Transpiration, the release of water vapour through pores (stomata) in the epidermis of higher plants, can reduce the air temperature in an immediate area.

Numerous approaches to active solar cooling have also been developed. Provided subsoil temperature permits, one method includes the use of earth cooling tubes – long, buried pipes with one end open to the outside air and the other opening into a building interior. Fans draw hot outside air into the underground pipes, and the air loses heat to the soil, which remains at a relatively constant, cool temperature year-round. The soil-cooled air is then blown into the building and circulated. In active evaporative cooling systems, fans draw air through a damp medium, such as a water spray or wetted pads. The evaporation of water from the medium cools the airstream.

Desiccant cooling

Desiccant cooling systems are designed to both dehumidify and cool air. These systems are particularly well suited to hot, humid climates where air conditioning accounts for the majority of a building's energy requirements. Desiccant materials such as silica gels and certain salt compounds naturally absorb moisture from humid air. Moisture-laden desiccant

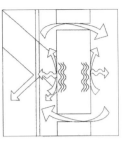

Glazed wall in heating mode transfering heat indoors through its mass and by natural convection

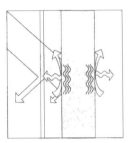

Glazed wall in heating mode excluding natural convection

Design criteria	Variable air volume	Fan-coil units	Displacement ventilation	Natural ventilation
Erase of installation	1	3	5	5
Commissioning requirements	3	3	5	5
Floor-to-floor height	2	3	3	2
Temperature control	4	5	2	1
Humidity control	2	3	4	1
Multi zone control	5	5	5	1
Air movement	4	3	4	2
Air cleanliness	4	3	4	2
Odour control	1	2	4	2
Noise control	2	3	4	1
Flexibility	1	2	3	3
Capital cost of plant	3	2	4	5
Maintenance costs	3	2	4	5
Total	36	38	52	35

A score between 1 and and 5 is given with 5 representing a positive feature.

Decision criteria for air-conditioning system (eg variable air volume (VAV) and fan-coil units (FCUs) vs natural ventilation systems)

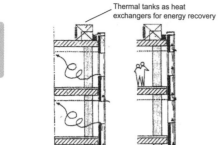

Thermal tanks as heat exchangers for energy recovery

Winter (cold days)   Summer (warm days)

Passive system

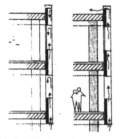

Winter (cold days)   Summer (warm days)

Mixed-mode system ●----------

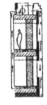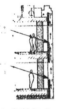

Winter (cold days)   Summer (warm days)

Full-mode system

False ceiling

Winter (cold days)   Summer (warm days)

Ventilation or pumping systems with heat exchangers and/or pumps

Various modes of using double-facade systems

materials will release the stored moisture when heated, a characteristic that allows them to be reused. In a solar desiccant system, the sun provides the heat needed to recharge the desiccants. Once the air has been dehumidified with desiccants, it can be chilled through evaporative cooling or other techniques to provide relatively cool, dry air.

Displacement ventilation

In displacement ventilation as a mixed-mode approach, the system employed introduces air at floor level, tempering only the occupied zone to around 1.8 metres above floor height. There are three main benefits to this technique:

- Energy is saved by allowing the space above 1.8 metres to 'float'. For this reason a higher than normal ceiling height is generally required to gain maximum benefit (a floor-to-ceiling height in the order of 3 metres is usual).
- Contaminants are encouraged to rise towards a high-level exhaust zone, and incoming clean air travels upwards from a low level.
- In summer, if the space temperature rises above the design set-point of say 27°C, air can be introduced at low level at the outside air temperature (which will be slightly cooler). The upward movement of this cooler air should produce a cooling sensation and will improve comfort for the occupants as a result.

In addition, the inert mass of concrete floors and ceiling voids may be used to provide some additional free cooling, as the slab temperature should be below the room air temperature. This can provide a further 1°C or so of free cooling. The cooling effect can be enhanced by running cold outside air through the system overnight for a few hours to remove residual slab heat. The effectiveness of this approach depends on the finished ceiling arrangement; for instance, suspended ceilings restrict the flow of air up and 'into' the slab.

Mixed-mode systems (as in passive-mode principles) can further influence the shaping and configuring of the design system and its orientation, material use, enclosural design and its operation. In many instances the mixed-mode design option depends on the climatic conditions of the locality.

In proceeding from passive-mode features in the designed system to mixed-mode features, the system begins to acquire some mechanical and electrical (M&E) equipment and systems. The designer has to be aware that the more 'equipment' intensive the designed system becomes, the higher will be its embodied energy content and the greater the number of components that will eventually need to be reused, recycled or reintegrated at the end of the system's useful life.

Summary

Once the designer has optimised all the passive-mode design options in configuring the designed system (in B13), the next step is to consider incorporating the appropriate mixed-mode operational systems and design options that, again, take advantage of the ambient energies of the climate of that locality. Mixed-mode design involves the use of some renewable sources of energy in combination with some mechanical and electrical (M&E) systems. It should now be evident to the designer that by designing in this way, the designed system heads progressively towards an increasingly efficient low-energy design. The designer also needs to be aware that the more 'equipment' (ie technology) intensive the designed system is or becomes, the higher will be its embodied energy content and the greater the number of items within its built system that will eventually need to be reused, recycled or reintegrated at the end of the designed system's useful life.

End use	Electricity for lights and appliances (%)
Cold (fridge, freezer, fridge-freezer)	24
Lighting	24
Cooking (hob, oven, kettle, plus other)	17
Wet (washing machine, tumble dryer, dishwasher)	16
Consumer electronics (TV, video, satellite, PC, etc)	14
Miscellaneous	4

Electricity use within an average residential unit in lights and appliances ●

B15 Design to optimise all full-mode options in the designed system: designing for improved internal comfort conditions with minimal full use of renewable sources of energy and as low-energy design in relation to the climate of the locality

Having adopted and optimised as many as possible of all the passive-mode and appropriate mixed-mode design system options (in B13 and B14) for our designed system, we can proceed to adopting the full-mode systems to create the required internal conditions of comfort while ensuring that these are as low energy consuming as possible. In this way the designing process becomes one of progressively improving the designed system's low-energy performance without having made any design decisions that go against this eventual goal.

In ecodesign it is crucial to ensure that any full-mode systems adopted work in tandem with the passive- and mixed-mode systems adopted, as an integrated total environmental system to provide improved internal comfort conditions over the external conditions. Full-mode systems enable the designed system to meet industry standards (eg ASHRAE standards) for comfort conditions.

Full mode, as the third option, refers to the conventional full environmental system where the mechanical and electrical (M&E) systems are used as for any conventional building. Basically, in full electromechanical systems, or full mode, special attention is paid to their energy-efficient performance, ecological impacts and use of building-automated systems for energy conservation. Full-mode provisions for heating, cooling, lighting and ventilation are all controlled artificially through energy-intensive mechanical plant and the internal environment may thus be protected from the fluctuations of the exterior environment. The system is also usually automated.

Full-mode systems design depends on:

• The equipment and service systems design that should be designed for optimal efficiency as a whole system adopting efficient equipment and control system that avoids unnecessary energy consumption

• M&E systems that are always properly operated and maintained to avoid wasting energy consumption

If the designer insists that consistent comfort conditions throughout the year are maintained for a building's users, then what is in effect a full-mode built form is created. Clearly, low energy consumption is essentially a user-driven condition. It is impossible that the low-energy condition of passive-mode and mixed-mode design can ever compete with the comfort level provided by the high-energy full-mode system.

In a full-mode building, built-form lighting can be responsible for as much as 15% of the building's electricity use in the case of a commercial building and 24% of the building's electricity use in residential buildings, and is estimated to be responsible for 20 to 25 per cent of the nation's overall electricity use. For instance, the use of daylight combined with occupancy and daylight sensors, dimmable ballasts and task lighting with reduced ambient light levels can achieve substantial savings, not only in energy required for lighting but also in that used for cooling as a result of the lighting. General office lighting should be less than 11.88 W/m² connected, and with lighting controls, it may be as low as 5.4 W/m².

Full-mode buildings consume more than half of the energy used worldwide, particularly in the case of tall buildings which add to their energy demand by their extensive cooling systems. These usually have huge air-conditioning systems that vent heat into the outside air. Not only does this energy usage create pollutants but it adds to the heat-island effects of the urban environment in cities. For instance, 35 per cent of energy supply and 60 per cent of annual electricity is used to operate buildings (in the USA).

Full-mode buildings can be designed for energy-use efficiencies by using automated systems combined with energy-simulation software to determine the most appropriate energy-efficient alternatives for M&E, lighting, exterior cladding materials and techniques. For example, such software can simulate the building's hourly energy performance and costs, taking into account local weather conditions. It allows users to compare potential energy savings and options.

One approach to reducing consumption of energy in the full-mode built form is to design the systems as a clustered group of built forms with local combined heat and power (CHP) units (eg as a system that consumes biomass that releases only the carbon dioxide it has withdrawn from the atmosphere).

Another strategic approach is broad corporate participation in which the government and the cooperating business community could collectively save on its use of energy for lighting and reduce air pollution from electric generation by a full 10 per cent (equivalent to taking 42 million cars off the road). Another example is to maximise opportunities for on-site power generation from high-efficiency conservation plants (plants able to capture waste heat from electricity generation, utilising it for the production of steam to provide chilled water or additional electricity).

Thus, following the previous design considerations (in B13 and B14), the designer should coordinate the passive-mode and mixed-mode (or background) systems with the full-mode (or active operational) systems provided. This will result in a composite-mode system (in B17). Once all the passive systems for the built system's design have been maximised, then design solutions can be sought for its other operational and active systems (eg lighting, heating, air-conditioning systems), depending on the level of servicing and comfort to be provided. As mentioned earlier, a significant proportion of the energy use in a building over its life cycle occurs during its operational phase as a result of its internal M&E engineering

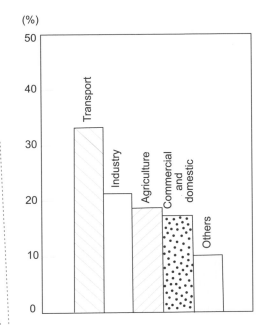

● Utilisation of hydrocarbon fuels (by sector)

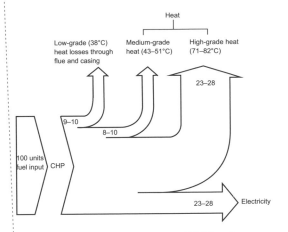

● Combined heat and power (CHP) units: typical energy balance

Device		Energy production	Energy source
Microturbines	Small combustion turbines that generate electricity	25–500kW	Natural gas, hydrogen, propane, diesel
Combustion turbines	Energy is extracted from the high-pressure, high-velocity gas flowing from the combustion chamber	500kW to 25MW	Natural gas, liquid fuel
Reciprocating engines	A reciprocating, or internal-combustion, engine converts the energy contained in a fuel into mechanical power	5kW to 7MW	Natural gas, diesel, landfill gas, digester gas
Fuel cells (phosphoric acid fuel cells)	A fuel cell is similar to a battery in that an electrochemical reaction is used to create current	100 to 200kW	Natural gas, landfill gas, biodigester gas, propane
Photovoltaic	Solar cells convert sunlight directly into electricity	Less than 1 to 100kW	Sunlight
Wind	A turbine with fan blades harnesses the wind to generate electricity	Up to 105 MW	Wind

Comparison of various energy production systems

systems. For example, in the 50-year life-cycle costs of a typical commercial skyscraper, the building's energy costs are at 34 per cent and more of the total costs. In the operation of a building in the temperate zone, its space heating accounts for at least 48 per cent of its total energy use.

The key economic benefit of the passive mode or bioclimatic approach is a building with lowered capital and operating costs, due to lower energy consumption during its operational mode (savings ranging from 20 to 40 per cent of energy costs can often be achieved over the building's entire life cycle). Operational cost savings mean lower use of electrical energy, particularly from non-renewable resources, which further reduces overall emissions of waste heat and particulates and the resultant urban heat-island effects. While this saving is small by comparison to total costs, the greater benefit is in enhanced productivity (eg as a result of reduction in eye irritation, etc).

In temperate and cold climates, where a composite-mode system is used, the building should operate differently in relation to the changing seasons of the year as they affect the locality. Of course, significant energy savings can also be achieved if users accept a lower designed room temperature in winter in temperate zones. In full-mode buildings in the summer in temperate and tropical zones the cooling load in the air-conditioning systems can be decreased by approximately 10 per cent by increasing the designed room temperature by 1°C. In the air conditioning of full-mode buildings, the designer can compare the three types of air conditioning: variable air volume (VAV) system, fan-coil units and displacement ventilation.

Significant energy savings can be achieved by using upgraded M&E systems (eg chillers, pumps, cooling towers, etc) with integrated building management systems (BMS), but over-design should be avoided. In temperate climatic zones, ecodesign should seek to achieve design targets of about 100 kW/h/m²/y or less, compared with 230 kW/h/m²/y for fully air-conditioned (and heated, if in a temperate zone) buildings and about 150–250 kW/h/m²/y for typical air-conditioned offices.

Full-mode design guidelines

For built forms where the use of full-mode air conditioning and heating is unavoidable, the following full-mode design guidelines should be applied:

- Avoid dual-duct systems or fixed volume terminal reheating, as both involve cooling air and reheating it as required at the point of use.

- Avoid high-velocity systems as they consume more energy, but use less material.

- Use variable air volume systems (and fan-coil units) to provide local control.

	Temperature		
	Maximum increase in temperature required	Neutral zone where internal temperature is satisfactory	Maximum reduction in temperature required
	Internal temperature needs to be raised towards ambient	Internal temperature needs lowering towards ambient	Internal temperature needs lowering below ambient
	Therefore heating required	Therefore mechanical ventilation to be considered	Therefore mechanical cooling required

	Ventilation		
	Fresh air required for respiration and control.	Fresh air required for respiration, odour control; and possibly a large amount to lower internal temperatures. (This is obviously variable since, during a hot day, one may want to restrict the amount of fresh air to avoid bringing in outside air that may be warmer than the air inside).	Fresh air required for respiration and odour control. (Fresh air alone or, more commonly, a mixture of fresh and recirculated air, can be cooled below the ambient temperature. The latter is normally more energy efficient.)

Composite-mode heating, cooling and ventilation design considerations

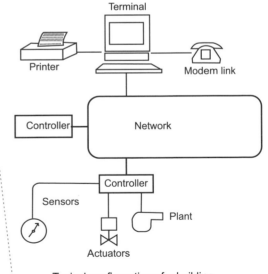

Typical configuration of a building automation management system

• Employ heat reclaimed from parts of the building with a heat surplus.

• Avoid any system incorporating CFCs and HCFCs.

• Select equipment that has maximum efficiency.

We need to be aware that mechanical cooling in air conditioning carries a range of potential environmental impacts. These include:

• greenhouse gas emissions from energy use;

• greenhouse gas emissions and ozone depletion from refrigerant leakage and disposal; and

• toxic-waste production from treated condenser waste.

There are methods of dealing with all of these, but most involve the compromising of other ecological parameters.

Refrigerants

The ecological designer needs to be aware that all refrigerants have some level of environmental impact, and all are therefore some form of compromise. There is no standard solution to refrigerant replacement in existing equipment, and even in new equipment different chiller manufacturers appear to champion different refrigerants. The direct environmental impacts of refrigerants can be summarised as follows:

• the ozone-depletion potential (ODP), a measure of the degree to which the chemicals deplete the ozone layer, measured relative to the CFC-based refrigerant R-11; and

• the global-warming potential (GWP), a measure of the degree to which the chemicals contribute to global warming, measured relative to carbon dioxide.

For any refrigerant choice, there is a technical trade-off between ODP, GWP, indirect GWP (ie effects on chiller efficiency) and impacts such as inflammability and toxicity.

It is therefore essential to minimise refrigerant emissions in operation. Estimates of annual leakage vary widely from as low as 1 to 2 per cent for best practice to as high as 30 per cent in poor-quality installations and servicing. While it is not possible at the design stage to prevent bad maintenance, care is required to ensure that good maintenance practice is possible through the configuration of plant and the provision of appropriate detection, isolation and drainage points. Design choices do, however, have an impact on what can be achieved through good maintenance. Open-drive chillers, for instance, are generally associated with an unavoidable 2 per cent leakage rate through seals. The loss of refrigerant not only causes a release of environmentally damaging – and expensive – refrigerants, it also causes the degradation of chiller performance.

Ecodesign requires the designer to take into account the embodied energy of the intensive equipment and fittings that accompany full-mode design options and their eventual reuse, recycling and reintegration at the end of their useful life or resulting from their replacement (in instances when their useful lifespan is shorter than that of the built form itself).

Summary

Having adopted and optimised all the passive- (from B13) and mixed-mode (from B14) design options appropriate to the project site's climatic conditions, the designer can progress to the adoption of full-mode options to achieve the desired conditions of comfort for the designed system. Again, the extent of full-mode systems (ie full mechanical and electrical building systems) depends on the comfort level expected by the users of the designated system (see B1). With full-mode systems, the designer is dependent upon full mechanical and electrical (M&E) systems achieving low energy consumption by the design and the use of energy-saving automated systems.

Whereas passive-mode design is about energy conservation which is reduced energy consumption through lower quality of energy service, full-mode design is about improving energy efficiency, which is simply increasing the ratio of energy services to energy output. It means getting the most out of every unit of energy.

The designer is reminded that ecodesign requires account to be taken of the embodied energy of all the intensive equipment (ie technological systems) and fittings that accompany full-mode design options, and consideration to be given to their eventual reuse, recycling and reintegration at the end of their useful life (as well as their replacement in instances when their useful life or after-lifespan is shorter than that of the built form itself).

Device	Net efficiency in %	Conversion type
Electric generator	~99	Mechanical to electrical
Hydroelectric	~92	Mechanical to electrical
Large electric motor	~92	Electrical to mechanical
Dry cell battery	90	Chemical to electrical
Large steam boiler	~88	Chemical to thermal
Home gas furnace	~85	Chemical to thermal
Fuel cell (potential)	~80	Chemical to electrical
Storage battery	~72	Chemical to electrical
Refuse to methane	~70	Chemical to chemical
Home oil furnace	~65	Chemical to thermal
Small electric motor	~63	Electrical to mechanical
Fuel	~60	
MHD	60	
Wind generator	~59	Mechanical to electrical
Liquid-fuel rocket	~47	Thermal to kinetic
Steam turbine	~46	Thermal to mechanical
Steam power plants*	~40	Thermal to mechanical
Gas laser	~38	Electrical to radial
Diesel engine	~38	Thermal to mechanical
Aircraft gas turbine	~36	Thermal to mechanical
Industrial gas turbine	~34	Thermal to mechanical
High-intensity lamp	~30	Electrical to radial
Solid-state laser	~28	Electrical to radial
Wave-powered buoy	~26	Mechanical to electrical
Automobile engine	~25	Thermal to mechanical
Turbojet	~24	Thermal to mechanical
Ramjet	~23	Thermal to mechanical
Fluorescent lamp	~20	Electrical to radial
New German solar cell	~18	Radiant to electrical
Wankel engine	~18	Thermal to mechanical
Silicon solar cell	~12	Radiant to electrical
Steam locomotive	~9	Thermal to mechanical
Thermocouple	~8	Thermal to electrical
Incandescent lamp	~5	Electrical to radial

* Natural gas, coal, oil, nuclear, geothermal

Comparison of energy-conversion efficiencies

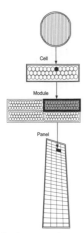

Relations between photovoltaic cell, module, panel and array

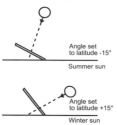

Angle set to latitude -15°
Summer sun

Angle set to latitude +15°
Winter sun

Fixed orientation. Orient panels due south (not magnetic south) and tilt to latitude plus 15° for winter optimisation. This is not the best angle for summer sun, but the extra sun in the summer will make up for the less-than-optimal angle.

Adjustable orientation. Orient panels due south (not magnetic south) and tilt to latitude plus 15° for winter optimisation. Adjust the tilt angle to latitude minus 15 for summer optimisation. It is generally not worth the effort to manually shift panel orientation more than twice a year (once in the spring and once in the autumn).

Tracker orientation. Two-axis and one-axis trackers are available. Two-axis trackers will automatically track the sun east to west and adjust the vertical tilt angle to optimise efficiency. Single-axis trackers track the sun east to west.

Shading. Even partial shading can make a huge difference in the output from solar modules. Shaded cells become loads instead of power sources, and rapidly reduce module output. Make sure that modules have the critical middle hours of the day clear of all shading, both for summer sun and winter sun. Detemine potential shading during different seasons at possible panel locations.

Orientation rules of thumb for photovoltaic installation

B16 Design to optimise productive-mode options in the designed system: designing for improved comfort conditions by the independent production of energy and as low-energy design in relation to the climate of the locality

In principle, ecodesign should not be dependent on external non-renewable sources of energy, such as fossil fuels, but should rely on solar energy, as do ecosystems in nature (in A4). Ecodesign should use productive modes in the designed system so that it generates its own energy as the design heads towards an objective of zero and/or partial use of non-renewable sources of energy. Productive-mode systems include: photovoltaics, solar collectors, and wind and water generators. The built environment should seek to become a net producer of energy rather than a consumer of non-renewable sources of energy.

It is important to keep in mind that the source of energy in ecosystems in the biosphere is the sun as a renewable source of energy. In responding to this by design (by ecomimicry), our sources of energy for our built environment should be similarly renewable and be solar as a productive mode. It is vital that this approach is eventually fully adopted in our built environment because in the long term our non-renewable sources of energy (eg fossil fuels) will be depleted and humankind will need to find other sources of energy.

However, the designer also needs to be aware that current technologies in productive energy modes, while advancing rapidly, are still very much in their early developmental stages. For example, many solar photovoltaic systems are still of low efficiency and costly, although developments are increasing energy-conversion efficiencies and addressing the cost of production and storage. The average residential unit uses about 1 to 5 kilowatts.

Photovoltaics

Photovoltaics (PV) is a locally generated productive-mode energy source that provides a clean, quiet and pollution-free energy source. As a general guide 1 square metre of PV panels will be able to generate approximately an average of 100 watts of electrical energy (in UK skies, assuming 300 watts in high summer). In the PV cell, when light falls on it, the extra energy imparted by a stream of photons of light absorbed by the cell permits a flow of electrons to take place and hence provides the electrical potential output. Currently the cost of producing electricity from PV cells is four to five times the costs of producing electricity from conventional sources. The three main types of PV being produced today are single-crystal (monocrystalline), polycrystalline (gallium-arsenide cells), and amorphous silicon cells. Different types of photovoltaic cells have different efficiency coefficients. These have been calculated and are listed below:

- monocrystalline silicon cells:

  efficiency coefficient: 14 per cent

  direct voltage: approx. 0.48 volts

  direct current: approx. 2.9 amps

- polycrystalline silicon cells:

  efficiency coefficient: 12 per cent

  direct voltage: approx. 0.46 volts

  direct current: approx. 2.7 amps

- amorphous solar cells – silicon plated on to a support substance (opaque module):

  efficiency coefficient: 5 per cent

  direct voltage: approx. 63 volts

  direct current: approx. 0.43 amps

- amorphous solar cells – semi-transparent:

  efficiency coefficient: 4 per cent

  direct voltage: approx. 63 volts

  direct current: approx. 0.37 amps

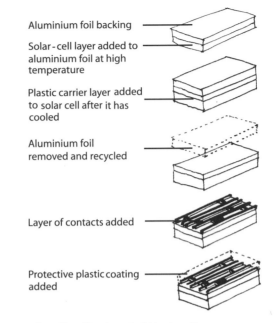

Aluminium foil backing

Solar-cell layer added to aluminium foil at high temperature

Plastic carrier layer added to solar cell after it has cooled

Aluminium foil removed and recycled

Layer of contacts added

Protective plastic coating added

Deposition of the micrometre-thick solar-cell layer demands a high temperature that would melt a plastic substrate, so the layer is intially laid down on aluminium foil.

● Solar cells laid in a plastic substrate

While single-crystal (monocrystalline) solar cells use expensive and energy-consuming semiconductor-grade silicon, polycrystalline and amorphous cells do not. Polycrystalline cells use a metallurgical-grade silicon, which is much cheaper. However, both single-crystal and polycrystalline cells use blocks of silicon, which must be sliced into thin wafers to create the cells. This slicing creates much waste in the form of dust and is a slow, energy-intensive process.

The manufacturing processes for amorphous PV cells use far less material than others and the product can be applied as a thin film to a variety of materials. Amorphous PVs using gallium arsenide have traditionally had an efficiency of 5–8 per cent as opposed to crystalline panels with 10–15 per cent efficiency. However, encouraging results of 20 per cent efficiency have recently been achieved for thin-film panels. Advanced systems have indicated achieving 30 per cent efficiency. The development of amorphous panels has led to architecturally integrated solar cells. The solar panel can now be combined with part of a traditional building material, reducing one of the costs of inputs into the construction process and replacing it with a pollution-free, electricity-producing material. The overall consequence is that PV becomes more affordable.

Being connected to the main power grid gives a PV user the advantage of not having to own and maintain a bank of costly batteries for electricity storage. Another advantage is the reduction in the need for new transmission lines, as distributed electricity generation would enable power to be used at its source. PV cells are usually connected in the form of modules, which are wired so that the electrical power can be extracted at a suitable voltage potential. The main component of the solar PV cell array is the power inverter. The inverter is a key component of PV power production; it transforms the direct current (DC) produced by the solar cells to alternating current (AC) at grid voltage.

Source	Cost/installed	Cost per kW	Typical capacity	Efficiency %
Microturbine	700–1000	0.07–0.10	30–300 kW	27–33
Fuel cell	2000–3500	0.07–0.10	Up to 200 kW	40–55
Solar	6000–10000	0.14–0.28	Up to 100 kW	15
Wind turbine	1500–3000	0.04–0.07	10 kW–2 MW	40
Diesel generator	350–400	0.04 + oil	Up to 4 MW	20–25

Energy-generation technologies •------

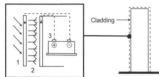

In the future nano solar cells could turn sunlight into electrical power. These supercheap solar cells – made of nanocrystal structures in an electrically conducting plastic, sandwiched between flexible electrodes – could be laminated in a thin coating on to the building cladding.

1. Sunlight penetrates the top electrode of the building's cladding and is absorbed by the nanostructures.
2. The solar energy excites electrons in the nanostructures, giving rise to an electric current that flows between the electrodes through the nanostructures and the polymer.
3. The electric current is collected by wires and used to charge a battery on the underside of the cladding, which provides power for appliances, and heating systems.

Nano solar cells •------

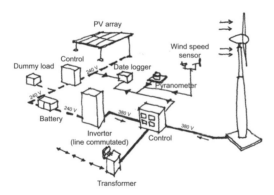

Hybrid wind and grid-connection
power generation system

The development of solar-cell materials that are ragged, long-lasting, cost-effective, easy to produce and efficient at energy conversion is the key issue confronting their designers. The future may lie in organic solar cells using nanotechnology to replace the heart of the existing solar cells, called a P–N–P (or positive–negative–positive) junction, with a simpler P–N junction. Theoretically, designers can design a synthetic molecule that traps incident solar energy, splits it into positive and negative charges and transports these charges to storage areas along a series of electron-collector rods. This solar battery would use two poles, anode and cathode; its development is dependent on finding materials with the right nanostructure.

Recent developments have been in nano-based devices optimised to conduct electricity using organic nanocrystals made from silicon and other materials. Solar cells can be made from bar-shaped semiconductor rods which are 2 to 5 nanometres wide and 60 to 100 nanometres long. By mixing these 'nanorods' with an electrically conducting polymer, the material behaves much like the traditional solar cell.

Each nanorod absorbs sunlight and turns it into a highly efficient flow of electrons along its length. If the material is sandwiched between two electrodes then any rods oriented vertically contribute to a usable electrical current. The material is potentially five to ten times cheaper than the conventional solar cell.

A recent development is the Graetzel cell, which is a dye molecule used to capture the energy from sunlight. The molecule absorbs the light, going into a higher state. In this higher energy state, the molecule separates the charge by passing an electron from the dye molecule to a nanoparticle of a white crystal of titanium dioxide (a pigment material used in white household paint.)

The separated charges (the positive charge remaining on the dye molecule and the negative charge shifted to the titanium dioxide nanoparticle) are then allowed to recombine using a set of electrochemical reactions. In this recombination some of the energy that was originally absorbed from the sun by the molecule is released as electrical current passing through an external circuit.

Graetzel cells currently have efficiencies exceeding 7 per cent and can be manufactured using silk-screening techniques. Other productive modes include the use of solar collectors, wind and water generators, etc. We should note that as these all involve mechanical systems, they require intensive and regular maintenance and replacement as a result of wear and tear.

Hydroelectric power

Hydroelectric power is another potential source of renewable energy. Nearly 20 per cent of solar energy is used to evaporate water on the surface of the earth. When the water vapour condenses and falls as precipitation it makes hydropower possible. Hydropower currently accounts for 10 per cent of the electrical power generated in the USA and 19 per cent of the world's electricity generation.

Geothermal energy

Geothermal energy, although not yet widely exploited – it currently makes up only 0.1 per cent of total world energy – also has potential as a renewable energy resource. Hot water and steam, which lie deep beneath the earth's surface in volcanic rock, geysers and hot springs, can be converted to electricity.

Biomass energy

Biomass, in the form of agricultural and industrial waste, can also be used to generate electricity to electrolyse water and produce hydrogen. The UK, for example, produces 30 million tons of solid waste a year. If this waste were incinerated for power generation, it could produce enough electricity to provide 5 per cent of the country's total requirement.

Hydrogen

The most important aspect of using renewable resources to produce hydrogen is that sun, wind, hydro and geothermal energies can all be converted into 'stored' energy that can be applied in a concentrated form whenever and wherever needed, and with zero CO_2 emissions. So, if the sun isn't shining, or the wind isn't blowing, or the water isn't flowing, or fossil fuels are not available to burn, electricity can't be generated and economic activity grinds to a halt. Hydrogen, therefore, is one very attractive way to store energy to ensure an ongoing and continuous supply of power for society.

Wind generators

Of solar energy, 2 per cent is converted into wind energy through atmospheric circulation. A typical wind generator is comprised of two- or three- bladed propellers approximately 50 metres in diameter. Wind generators have been built with blades up to 140 metres in diameter (in Hamburg, Germany). In an area where the average wind speed is 7.5 m/s, the propellers will generate about 250 kilowatts of electricity. As a general guide, a rotor-blade diameter of 2 metres can yield about 500 kWh of electricity per year.

Ecodesign must also take into account the high environmental consequences of, and high embodied energy entailed in, the production of these systems and their technologies, which may not justify their operational energy savings. The justification for these systems may lie in their capacity to imitate the way that ecosystems use solar energy, albeit that the processes at work in ecosystems are chemical (ie photosynthesis) whereas the processes

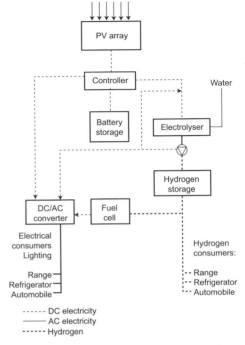

● Proposal for a solar hydrogen energy system

● Wind generators

Average wind speed	Rotor diameter in metres (capacity in kW)		
	1.0 m (0.25 kW)	3.0 m (1.5 kW)	7.0 m (10 kW)
4.0 m/s (9 mph)	150 (600)	1300 (867)	7000 (700)
4.5 m/s (10 mph)	200 (800)	1800 (1200)	10000 (1000)
4.9 m/s (11 mph)	240 (960)	2200 (1467)	13000 (1300)

● Estimated energy output of wind turbines in kWh/y and (kWh/y/kW)

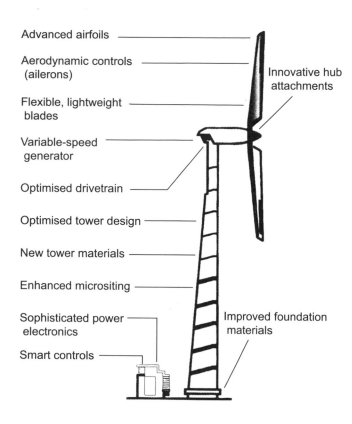

Advanced airfoils

Aerodynamic controls (ailerons)

Innovative hub attachments

Flexible, lightweight blades

Variable-speed generator

Optimised drivetrain

Optimised tower design

New tower materials

Enhanced micrositing

Sophisticated power electronics

Improved foundation materials

Smart controls

A new generation of wind turbines

- Check out local average wind speeds to help size wind systems. Local weather stations should be able to give a good idea of local wind velocities, but the best way to evaluate the site is with an anemometer-based wind-speed totaliser.

- Available wind power increases with the cube of the wind speed. This means that if the wind speed doubles, it has the potential for eight times the wind power.

- In areas with inconsistent wind, a low-cost microwind turbine to supplement the PV system is easier to justify than a larger turbine.

- Check manufacturer specifications and power curves carefully. Some models maintain power outputs in high wind while others drop off radically. Low turbine power output in high winds is fine for most areas because they are subject to high winds (above 11.645 m/s) for only short periods of time, but will not work well in areas with consistently high winds. If the area is characterised by low average winds, the low-speed section of the turbine power curve will be the most important.

- Most turbines are rated at around 12.516 m/s wind speed, which is a very windy condition. At 6.7 m/s, which is moderately windy, available wind power is only about 15 per cent of what is available at 11.175 m/s. At 2.5 to 3 m/s (light winds), wind turbines have little or no output. For realistic expectation, it is important to know the available wind speed or rely on the experience of others in the area that uses wind energy.

- Wind generators should be installed at least 6 metres higher than any obstructions nearer than 150 metres, and mounts should be well grounded. Towers can have tilt features that allow lowering of the turbine to the ground in the event of approaching severe weather, such as a tornado or hurricane.

in human-made productive systems are often electrical (ie photovoltaic cells) or mechanical (ie wind generators, etc).

The future may lie in the use of renewable forms of energy that are carbon-free, such as photovoltaics, wind, hydro and geothermal systems that split water into hydrogen and oxygen.

If enough buildings were in productive mode and could generate sufficient electricity collectively to ease the load on the national grid when connected, what we would have would be a system of 'distributed generation'. Here, the central power plants share distributed power with a connected number of smaller plants (eg in entire residential communities, large office buildings, major factories, etc) to ease the load on the grid by sharing surplus generated power.

The contention is that using clean technologies to generate power at the site where it is consumed can be far more efficient than generating it centrally. This is because sending electricity through transmission wires wastes energy, while producing electricity on site allows waste heat from the process to be captured and used (eg to heat the building) in a process called co-generation.

Again, the designer must be aware that at present most productive-mode systems are equipment and (human-mode) technology intensive, and that the more equipment intensive the designed system becomes, the more will be its embodied-energy content and the more items will eventually need to be reused or recycled or reintegrated at the end of the designed system's useful life.

Recent research has produced flexible fabric with solar panels that can be draped over just about any shape of built form, greatly expanding the opportunities for complex curvy building aesthetics and the number of places where solar energy can be generated. Unlike conventional solar cells, the new material has no rigid silicon base. Instead it is made up of thousands of inexpensive silicon beads sandwiched between two thin layers of aluminium foil and sealed on both sides with plastic. The aluminium sheets give the material physical strength and act as electrical contacts. The indicated overall efficiency of solar energy conversion is 11 per cent.

Other advances in solar cells include printable lighting panels using nanomaterials, solar cells made of semiconductor panels, self-orientating nanoparticles in conductive plastics, blending buckyballs with carbon-based molecules containing copper atoms, etc.

The collectors focus sunlight on pipes filled with mineral-oil heat-transfer fluids. The oil is heated to between 120 and 290°C, and then passes through a heat exchanger where a secondary fluid is vaporised. This high-pressure gas spins a turbine, generating electricity. The gas is then condensed back into a liquid and cycles back through the vaporiser to repeat the process.

Parabolic trough collectors

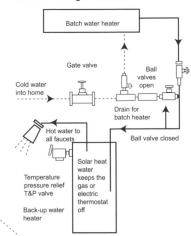

• Solar water heater installation

Solar panels attached to the back of the jacket store energy in a battery in the pocket. Changing of small devices can be through a USB connection.

• Mobile photovoltaic power plant

Summary

As we can learn from ecomimicry, ecosystems in nature use renewable sources of energy (solar energy) whereas human-made ecosystems in our built environment are still largely dependent on the use of non-renewable energy resources (eg fossil fuels to generate electricity). Without tapping renewable energy resources, our built environment will come to a halt. When planning the operational systems of a designed system, the ultimate goal in ecodesign should be to design net energy-production systems that produce and distribute more energy than they consume. This reduces the combined dependency of the human-made built environment on its consumption of non-renewable energy resources. Our ecodesign objective is biointegration, ie to emulate the ecosystems in nature (in A3 and A4) so that, analogous to the ecosystems in the biosphere, ultimately our built environment will rely exclusively on solar energy. At present productive-mode systems are technology and equipment intensive, and the designer is reminded of the need to design for the eventual replacement, reuse, recycling and reintegration of all these systems and their associated equipment back into the natural environment as well as the intensive embodied-energy content in their technological systems.

B17 Design to optimise composite-mode options in the designed system: designing for improved internal comfort conditions by composite means with low use of renewable sources of energy and as low-energy design in relation to the climate of the locality

Strategically, it is likely that ecodesign will result in a designed system that is a hybrid (see B15 and B16) employing a combination of passive, mixed, full and productive modes all acting together variably depending on the daily and seasonal external conditions of the locality.

Composite mode is essentially a composite of passive mode, mixed mode, full mode and productive mode, all designed to act in tandem as a low-energy design.

Composite mode may also use systems such as fuel cells, which were invented in the 19th century. Fuel cells in modules allow the end-users to customise the unit to their current power-generating needs by adding modules of more power as needed. Fuel cells are like batteries – but with one big difference. Batteries store chemical energy and convert it to electricity; when the chemical energy runs out, the battery is discarded. Fuel cells, by contrast, do not store chemical energy. Instead, they convert the chemical energy of a fuel that is fed into them to generate electricity. They do not require recharging and will continue to generate electricity as long as external fuel and an oxidant are supplied.

Fuel cells require hydrogen fuel. The hydrocarbon fuels are too 'dirty' to be used as primary fuels for the cell. A fuel cell is made up of a negatively charged anode on one side, a positively charged cathode on the other, and an electrolyte in the middle that is composed of an alkaline or watery acidic solution or a plastic membrane, allowing the electrically charged hydrogen atoms to travel from the anode to the cathode. Commercial fuel cells are composed of many individual cells stacked one on top of another. Hydrogen is fed into the anode side of the cell, where a chemical reaction splits the hydrogen atom into a proton and an electron. Freed electrons exit through the external electrical circuit in the form of direct-current electricity. The hydrogen ions (the protons) travel through the electrolyte layer to the positively charged cathode. The flow of electrons returns to the cathode, where they react with hydrogen ions and oxygen in the air to form water. Fuel cells work by using a process that is the reverse of electricity.

Like a battery, fuel cells convert chemical energy into electricity. In the case of a battery, when the battery has discharged its available power and the electrochemical reaction is exhausted, the battery is thrown away if it is not reusable. If it is reusable, it is 'recharged', which reverses the electrochemical reaction to separate the chemicals back into a state where they are ready to create more electricity. Unlike batteries, fuel cells use external fuel to convert chemical energy into electricity, so they don't need recharging, but they do

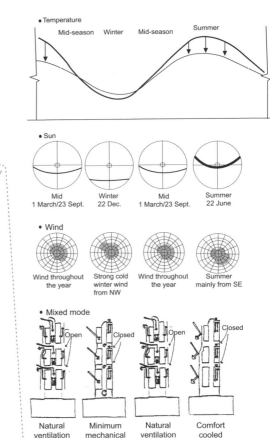

• Temperature

Mid-season Winter Mid-season Summer

• Sun

Mid
1 March/23 Sept.

Winter
22 Dec.

Mid
1 March/23 Sept.

Summer
22 June

• Wind

Wind throughout
the year

Strong cold
winter wind
from NW

Wind throughout
the year

Summer
mainly from SE

• Mixed mode

Open   Closed   Open   Closed

Natural
ventilation

Minimum
mechanical
air supply

Natural
ventilation

Comfort
cooled

• Composite mode
(Variable adjustments over the seasons of the year)

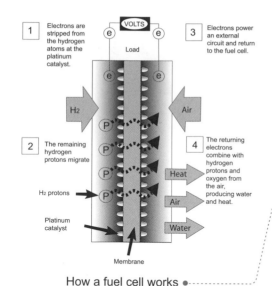

1. Electrons are stripped from the hydrogen atoms at the platinum catalyst.

VOLTS

Load

3. Electrons power an external circuit and return to the fuel cell.

H₂

Air

2. The remaining hydrogen protons migrate

H₂ protons

Platinum catalyst

Membrane

4. The returning electrons combine with hydrogen protons and oxygen from the air, producing water and heat.

Heat

Air

Water

How a fuel cell works

Electrolyte

Catalyst

Anode

Cathode

H_2

O

H_2O

e

e

e

Electricity produced

H2	Hydrogen
O	Oxygen
H2O	Water
e	H2 electron
P	H2 proton

The fuel cell's proton-exchange membrane

need a steady supply of fuel. Fuel cells generally work by separating an oxygen source from a hydrogen source using a non-conducting permeable barrier, called an electrolyte. Oxygen or hydrogen ions flow through the electrolyte to the other side of this barrier where they are encouraged by a catalyst to combine chemically to form water. To restore electrical balance, the resulting excess electrons left on one side (electrons cannot pass through the non-conducting electrolyte) are transported around the electrolyte through wires and a load, such as an electric motor.

There are five primary types of fuel cell, each distinguished by the type of electrolyte used to carry the charge between the fuel and the oxygen.

Fuel cells have no mechanical moving parts, are silent, and are up to 2.5 times more efficient than internal combustion engines. Their only outputs are electricity, heat and pure distilled water. Until recently they were not produced commercially (except for the US space programme), because they were bulky and uneconomical. They required large amounts of platinum as a catalyst, which made them far too expensive for mass production. However, the fuel cell is not necessarily ecologically preferable as to supply all existing uses of energy by fuel cells would entail the depletion of the earth's supply of platinum.

Fuel cells run on hydrogen, which exists in abundance but must be separated from water (H_2O) or natural gas (CH_4) before it can be used as a fuel. This is not technically difficult, but requires a special infrastructure that the existing fossil-fuel economy needs to modify. However, during the 1990s, technological breakthroughs drastically reduced the amount of platinum needed as a fuel-cell catalyst, and initiated the use of 'stacking' techniques that make it possible to create compact and highly efficient units.

At present, natural gas is the most common source of hydrogen, but separation of hydrogen from water with the help of renewable energy sources (especially solar electricity and wind power) will be the most economical and cleanest method, in the long run. When that happens, we will have created a truly sustainable system of energy generation. As in nature's ecosystems, all the energy we need will be supplied by the sun, either via small-scale solar devices or distributed as hydrogen, the ultimate clean fuel, and used in the efficient and reliable operation of fuel cells. Research studies indicate the potential use of micro fuel cells to power hand held and portable devices as replacements for conventional batteries.

In design terms, composite mode depends on operable components in the built structure or infrastructure to facilitate the different systems and modes to be adopted depending on the daily and seasonal climatic conditions. These components will have key influences on the shaping of the built form.

Summary

In most instances, the designer will combine a composite of modes (ie passive, mixed, full and productive mode options in B12 to B17) into the designed system to create internal conditions of comfort in an optimised low-energy built system with low use of renewable sources of energy, that is tailored to the varying climate conditions of the locality and its seasons, to the time of day (eg varying daytime use and night-time use), and to the facilities and their internal spaces).

Season	Spring	Summer	Autumn	Winter
	March · April · May	June · July · August	September · October · November	December · January · February
Wind rose				
Solar path				
Temperature and humudity	MAR · APR · MAY	JUNE · JULY · AUG	SEP · OCT · NOV	DEC · JAN · FEB
Orientation, built form configuration facade design				
Composite responses to optimise mid-season				

Summer

Passive mode: building massing and orientation

Passive mode: solar control and shading

Passive and mixed mode: natural ventilation strategy

Passive and mixed: evaporative cooling system

Passive mode: facade systems

Passive mode: building construction and control systems

Passive mode: facade systems and increased insulation

Passive mode: reduced building surface area

Passive mode: design for solar gain

Passive mode: wind protection

Winter

Diagram of a composite of passive modes

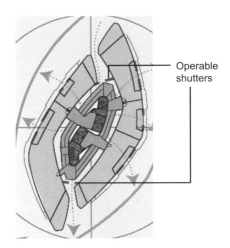

Operable shutters

Plan showing operable shutters
(Ecotower, Elephant & Castle, 2000)

Composite Mode showing adaptation of building operable shutters over different seasons of the year

Design to internally integrate biomass with the designed system's inorganic mass

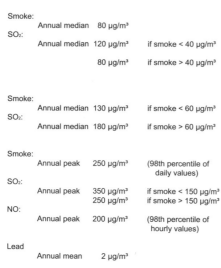

Smoke:
SO₂:

Annual median	80 µg/m³	
Annual median	120 µg/m³	if smoke < 40 µg/m³
	80 µg/m³	if smoke > 40 µg/m³

Smoke:
SO₂:

Annual median	130 µg/m³	if smoke < 60 µg/m³
Annual median	180 µg/m³	if smoke > 60 µg/m³

Smoke:
SO₂:
NO:

Annual peak	250 µg/m³	(98th percentile of daily values)
Annual peak	350 µg/m³	if smoke < 150 µg/m³
	250 µg/m³	if smoke > 150 µg/m³
Annual peak	200 µg/m³	(98th percentile of hourly values)

Lead

Annual mean	2 µg/m³

A draft directive on air pollution by ozone (CCM (92) 236 final) sets the following standard:

Ozone:

8 hour mean	110 µg/m³
1 hour mean	360 µg/m³ health protection warning
1 hour mean	200 µg/m³ vegetation protection threshold

Air quality standards and guidelines (EU)

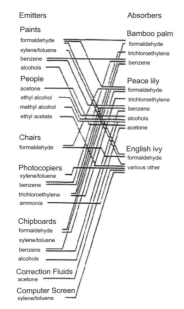

Emitters

Paints
formaldehyde
xylene/toluene
benzene
alcohols

People
acetone
ethyl alcohol
methyl alcohol
ethyl acetate

Chairs
formaldehyde

Photocopiers
xylene/toluene
benzene
trichloroethylene
ammonia

Chipboards
formaldehyde
xylene/toluene
benzene
alcohols

Correction Fluids
acetone

Computer Screen
xylene/toluene

Absorbers

Bamboo palm
formaldehyde
trichloroethylene
benzene

Peace lily
formaldehyde
trichloroethylene
benzene
alcohols
acetone

English ivy
formaldehyde
various other

Use of plants for improving IAQ

B18 Design to internally integrate biomass with the designed system's inorganic mass (eg by means of internal landscaping, improved indoor air quality (IAQ) considerations, etc)

The balancing of biotic and abiotic constituents in the composition of the designed system is not just an external endeavour, internally (in B7), ecodesign should also balance and integrate the designed system's internal built environment with adequate biomass to create ecologically complete integrated human-made ecosystems. It is necessary for ecodesign to integrate and to incorporate internal biomass (eg in the form of internal landscaping) to create balanced ecosystems. This should be integral with our other design endeavours to increase large-scale ecological continuities and linkages (eg by means of ecological corridors and land-bridges; see B8).

As mentioned earlier (in B7), it is crucial for ecodesign not only to reduce the existent artificiality and inorganic nature of our built environment but also to include certain planting types into the internal built environment in order to enhance the internal air quality (IAQ) by utilising their absorption of volatile organic compounds (VOCs) and other airborne contaminants that affect the health and well-being of the human users.

Indoor plants filter and purify the air by sedimentation and absorption. Leaf surfaces (especially hairy ones) trap dust and soot. Through photosynthesis, plants convert sunlight into chemical energy, absorb carbon dioxide from the air and replace it with oxygen. This not only gives fresher air, it also dilutes any airborne pollutants. By transpiration through their leaves and absorbing water via their roots, plants also regulate humidity, modify temperatures and balance ions in the air. Soil also cleans the air – its micro-organisms act as sponges and absorb gases and vapours, especially carbon monoxide.

Contaminants: addressing indoor air quality

Strategies to reduce the effects of VOCs, other than by increasing natural ventilation rates (achieved by increasing the air change per hour), include the use of charcoal filters and the selective use of certain houseplants. In the context of ecological building, it would be ideal to achieve and maintain comfortable room temperatures and humidities and to remove contaminants through internal foliage alone, without having to resort to any technical or mechanical means. The transpiration of the plants (and hence, evaporative cooling), as well as their production of oxygen and the elimination of contaminants play important roles in maintaining air quality.

Designers should be aware of studies carried out on the elimination of contaminants.

Formaldehyde, benzol and trichloroethylene were studied in relation to various plants. It is notable that the elimination is initially rapid but slows down after a period of two hours. It is as yet unclear whether the elimination process reaches a saturation point, or whether it decreases considerably or even ceases altogether after several days, since all studies to date have been carried out on a 24-hour basis. Long-term studies are necessary to determine the complete process.

Factors influencing indoor air quality (IAQ) include ventilation, humidity, lighting, contamination, furnishings and colour schemes, maintenance, cleaning, building use, building management and noise. The three primary sources of poor indoor air quality are hermetically sealed buildings and their synthetic furnishings, reduced ventilation and human bioeffluents.

However, more than 50 per cent of poor indoor air quality is due to inadequate ventilation and thus natural ventilation can contribute to greater internal comfort and user well-being. Typical air rates are about 0.5 to 3.0 ac/h depending upon density of occupation. Healthy humidity levels range between 35 and 65 per cent. Typical recommended values for air exchange per occupant range between 5 and 25 litres/second/person. However, the internal air quality can be enhanced by improved air changes (eg more than 4 ac/h); in some cases, designers have increased air changes by up to 6.8 ac/hr. However, at this air-change level and above, there may be disruptions to work surfaces (such as displacement of paper).

Current standards in the USA (ASHRAE Standard 62–1989) come with the proviso that ambient air quality requirements are site specific and not regional specific (ie they prefer ambient air quality at the proposed point of fresh-air intake). A built system's fresh-air intake should be located away from the built form's pollutive areas such as loading bays, building exhaust fans, cooling towers and other sources of contamination.

Indoor materials also introduce pollutants. Volatile organic components (VOCs) are carbon-based, chemical solvents distilled from petroleum or petroleum by-products. VOCs are often carcinogenic and, in quite small amounts, can cause or contribute to a wide range of serious human ailments. These range from birth defects and metabolic disorders to kidney and lung disease, memory loss and respiratory problems. VOCs and other deleterious chemicals are found in many of the most widely used construction and interior decoration materials, and are included to enhance the performance of the product. Current standards for VOCs specify outgassing levels at around 0.5 mg/m^3.

Examples of construction materials that contain VOCs are plywood made with isocyanurates, vinyl flooring made with polyvinyl chloride (PVC), many paints, glues and adhesives, and almost all maintenance and cleaning products that are petrochemical- or solvent-based.

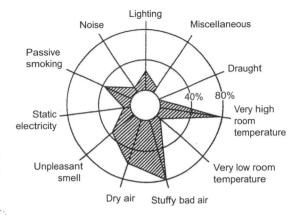

User most frequent internal environment complaints

Design to internally integrate biomass with the designed system's inorganic mass

	Sources	Health effects
Asbestos	Deteriorating, damaged or disturbed insulation, fireproofing, acoustical materials and floor tiles	Long-term risk of cancer and lung diseases
Biological contaminants (moulds, mildews, bacteria, viruses, animal dander, cat saliva, house dust, mites, cockroaches, pollen)	Plants, pets, animal urine, soil and plant debris; transmission via infected people and animals and contaminated central air-conditioning systems	Allergic reaction; infectious diseases; irritation to eyes, nose and throat; dizziness; fever; digestive problems
Carbon monoxide	Stoves, furnaces, fireplaces, space heaters, tobacco smoke, automobile exhaust from attached garages	Fatigue; chest pain; headaches, dizziness, impaired vision; nausea; fatal at very high concentrations
Formaldehyde	Pressed-wood products, urea-formaldehyde foam insulation, tobacco smoke, combustion sources, durable-press drapes, glues	Irritation to eyes, nose and throat; nausea; breathing difficulty; fatigue; skin rash, allergic reactions; may cause cancer
Lead	Lead-based paint, drinking water, contaminated soil, dust	Low levels can harm the nervous system, kidneys, and blood cells; high levels can cause convulsions, coma and death
Nitrogen dioxide	Stoves, heaters, tobacco smoke	Irritation to eyes, nose and throat; respiratory infections; lung damage
Pesticides	Insecticides, termiticides, disinfectants	Irritation to eyes, nose and throat; damage to nervous system and kidneys; increased risk of cancer
Radon	Contaminated soil and water; can accumulate in buildings	Increased risk of cancer
Respirable particles	Fireplaces, wood stoves, kerosene heaters	Irritation to eyes, nose and throat; respiratory infection; lung cancer
Volatile organic compounds (VOCs)	Paint and other solvents, wood preservatives, cleaners and disinfectants, aerosol sprays, air fresheners, moth repellents, hobby supplies, dry-cleaned clothing	Irritation to eyes, nose and throat; headaches; nausea; damage to liver, kidneys and nervous system

Indoor air pollutants

These materials (and others) contribute to the 'sick building syndrome'. The designer should seek to avoid introducing these contaminants and other toxic materials as far as possible, since human inhabitants are biotic components in the ecosystem. Every major material proposed for use should be researched, its chemical make-up analysed, and then it should be chosen or rejected on its environmental and IAQ impact, as well as the ecological impact of its production and distribution. For example, interiors should use 100 per cent wool carpet woven to avoid the use of adhesives in the backing (ie use jute underlays instead), low-toxic-emission particle boards, low-VOC paints and other finishes, and factory finishing of those products that have offgassing.

Ecological design needs to take into account IAQ and its impact on building users, since humans are also a species in the ecosystem. Good IAQ requires the following design provisions:

- An IAQ management plan for the construction process (eg for the protection of the ventilation system equipment and pathways from contamination) and, after completion of construction and prior to occupancy, the provision of cleaning for those ventilation-system components and pathways exposed to contamination during construction.

- Reduce construction contaminants in the building prior to occupancy (eg dust, particulates, contaminants related to water infiltration, and VOCs).

- Provide a filtration of the return-air side of the HVAC system components (eg minimum 65 per cent) during construction and replacement of air filtration media prior to occupancy.

- A permanent air-monitoring system capable of monitoring the supply and return of air, and ambient air at the fresh-air intake, for carbon monoxide, carbon dioxide, total volatile organic compounds (TVOCs) and particulates.

- A building material emissions testing programme, particularly for: adhesives; sealants; caulks; wood preservatives and finishes; carpets and carpet padding; paint; gypsumboard; ceiling tiles and panels; insulation–thermal, fire and acoustic; composite wood products; gaskets; glazing compounds; control joint filter; wall coverings; floor coverings; work surfaces; M&E sealants and linings; and flexible fabrics.

- Precautions to discourage microbial growth by meeting the recommended standards, including antimicrobial agents. Components that must meet current standards include: air filters and humidifier pads; M&E insulation; carpets; adhesives; fabrics; polymeric surfaces (vinyl, epoxy, rubber flooring, laminates); ceiling-tile coatings; and paints and other elements of the building's interior.

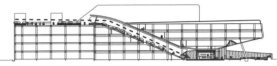

Example of an internal diagonal ecocell that extends from ground level to roof garden
(Mewah Oils, Klang, 2005)

Design to internally integrate biomass with the designed system's inorganic mass

● Chapter C ● Chapter B ● Chapter A ●

Plant	Form-aldehyde	Benzol	Trichloro ethylene
Banana	89	-	-
Bowstring	-	53	13
Chrysanthemum	61	54	41
Dracaena deremensis (Janet Craig)	50	78	18
Dracaena deremensis (Warneckii)	-	70	20
Dracaena deremensis (Yellow Variegated)	90	79	13
True aloe	-	-	-
Ivy	67	90	11
Devil's ivy	-	73	9
Spathe flower	67	80	23
Creeping hairy spurge	-	-	11
Ficus benjamina	50	-	35
Gerbera	86	68	-
Green lily	-	81	-
Chinese evergreen (*Aglaonema*)	86	48	-
Philodendron domesticum	71	-	-
Philodendron oxycardium	76	-	-
Philodendron selloum	-	-	-

IAQ enhancement using plants as filters: Percentage absorption of contaminants after 24 hours

Internal integration of biomass

In integrating biomass internally within built structures (see also B7, B8 and B23) the following need to be considered:

Plants as humidifiers

• Certain plants are especially well suited to the elimination of contaminants. For instance, during a single day in an office, an ivy plant is able to eliminate 90 per cent of the benzol contained in and released through tobacco smoke, artificial fibres, dyes and plastics. Aloes, bananas, spider plants and *Philodendron* are effective agents against formaldehyde, which may seep from insulating foam and particle board. Trichloroethylene from lacquers and glues is best eliminated with the help of Chrysanthemum and Gerbera species. It is certain that the microbes symbiotic with root systems, and not the plants themselves, are largely responsible for eliminating contaminants.

Indoor vegetation can enhance IAQ by helping eliminate formaldehyde, benzene and airborne microbes and by absorbing carbon dioxide and releasing oxygen, and by using the appropriate vegetation designers can also contribute to the regulating of the humidity of the internal environment. However, although proven experimentally, the processing rate of plants as biological filtering systems is slow. It works out to be approximately 1 per cent of the processing rate of bacteria. Therefore, to have any effect, rooms must have a large number of plants indicatively, 1 plant per square metre. The filtering works in two ways. First of all, the pores on the leaf surfaces (called stomata) take in the air together with the toxic substances, which are then collected, processed and filtered. This has been proven for formaldehyde. The other way works with the soil – harmful substances enter the soil and are absorbed by plant roots or processed by soil bacteria. Some of the best plants for biofiltering are the areca palm, the golden pothos, the rubber plant (*Ficus*), English ivy (*Hedera*) and the spider plant (*Chlorophytum*). Living walls of plants and moving water have been designed into office buildings as central air purifiers.

Plants can also serve as important internal ecological life-support systems. In the USA, NASA was among the foremost agencies researching the role of plants in an enclosed area. Studies during NASA Skylab missions revealed the problems facing the inhabitants of a closed facility. The monitoring of inside air during manned spacecraft flights detected the presence of more than 300 volatile organic chemicals (because the interior was constructed of plastic and other synthetic human-made materials).

Research has shown that houseplants can remove volatile organic compounds (VOCs) from sealed test chambers (NASA) and findings (c 1984) led to further evaluations of 12 common houseplants (jointly with the Associated Landscape Contractors of America) to remove formaldehyde, benzene, trichloroethyhene and other VOCs.

To date, 50 houseplants have been tested for their ability to remove various toxic gases from sealed test chambers. As formaldehyde is the most common toxin found in indoor air, a plant's ability to remove this substance from air was used as the standard for rating the plants. Formaldehyde is found in various resins, and it is used to treat many consumer products, including refuse bags, paper towels, facial wipes, permanent-press clothing, carpet backing, floor coverings and adhesives. It is also used in building materials like plywood, particle board and panelling. The health risks associated with formaldehyde include eye, nose and throat irritation and, more controversially, there are claims that it triggers asthma and chronic respiratory diseases.

Plants as humidifiers

- With regard to humidification, plants are better agents than electrically powered air humidifiers and even humidifiers combined with air-conditioning systems, because they do not provide a favourable breeding ground for bacteria. Studies show that internal design using houseplants can help provide an environment that mimics the way that nature cleans the earth's atmosphere. When their stomata open to absorb and release air and water, the internal air is stimulated. This allows the plants to capture toxins, which are transported to the root systems where microbes break them down. Saturation and rerelease of toxins is not a problem; the removal rate actually improves with exposure. Plants also emit phytochemicals that suppress spores and bacteria (eg the Boston fern). Another effective indoor plant is the gerbera daisy, which is held to be best at the removal of formaldehyde (found, for example, in facial wipes, carpets, gas stoves and plywood). The lady palm is best for removal of ammonia, and the peace lily is found to digest human bioeffluents. Research has indicated that the areca palm is most effective for indoor absorption. Four criteria can be used to rate the plants: their capacity to remove chemical vapours; their ease of growth and maintenance; their resistance to pests; and their transpiration rate.

Plants and temperature reduction

- Plants can only create a definite decrease in temperature in summer when all surrounding surfaces, with the exception of windows, are densely covered in foliage. Individual plants do not cause a noticeable change. Nevertheless, the use of plants in buildings should be given more attention in the future, since the overall effects are unquestionably positive, especially the psychological effect that verdant foliage has on the occupants. However, it must be acknowledged that plants need an environment that provides more than the minimum level for survival (ie the compensation point between photosynthesis and respiration). This can only be achieved by choosing the best plants, locating them correctly and combining plants that have long life expectancies. Bearing in mind that light drives

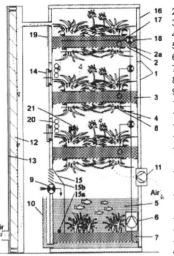

1. Glass cells
2. Mesh shelf
3. Fabric filter
4. Epiphytic plants
5. Aquatic cell
6. Rain pump
7. Biofilter
8. Rain spray bar
9. Water inlet valve
10. Water outlet
11. Blower
12. Optional lamp
13. Reflector
14. Sealing access hatch
15. Dechlorination chamber
16. Dehumidification cell
17. Moisture sensor
18. Valve
19. Shade
20. Sensors
21. Biota

Eco-aspirator for enhancing indoor air quality (IAQ)
(© John Paul Frazer)

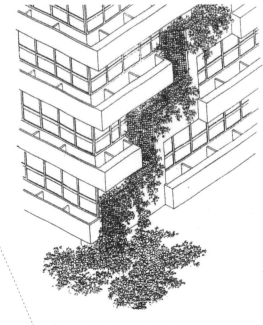

Stepped vertical landscaping concept

Design to internally integrate biomass with the designed system's inorganic mass

Contaminants	%	Building system problem	
Fungi	32	Ventilation inadequate	50.4
Dust	22	Filtration inadequate	55.6
Low relative humidity	16	Hygiene inadequate	41.7
Bacteria	13		
Formaldehyde	8		
Fibrous glass	6		
Exhaust fumes	5		
VOCs	4		
ETS	3		
High relative humidity	2		
Ozone	1		

Indoor air quality by problem type

Problem type	Average
Poor ventilation	56.6
Interior contamination	6
Microbes	16.9
Tobacco smoke	1.3

Indoor air quality factors

photosynthesis, plants should especially be used in very bright, naturally lit areas such as winter gardens, atria and large, open glassed-in office areas. When lighting conditions are poor, the photosynthesis and pollutant breakdown of plants are equal. If forced to grow in an environment below the compensation point, they receive too little light, begin to fade and eventually die.

- Ecological design is not just about the addition of increased biomass on the external and near-external surfaces of the built form but also involves the internal areas of the built form itself as places for indoor planting and landscaping. As mentioned earlier, plants are climate regulators. They are important components for buildings, whether outside, inside or incorporated into the built structure itself.

Indoor trees

- Integrating biomass internally into built forms entails the inclusion of indoor trees or trees in semi-enclosed conditions. Trees may be considered nature's air conditioners. During photosynthesis, trees suck up large amounts of water through their roots which is released into the atmosphere through their leaves when they transpire. As this water evaporates it cools the surrounding air; a similar effect is achieved when we sweat. In temperate climates during summer, an average-sized maple can release more than 50 gallons of water in one hour. One maple tree has the cooling output of a single large window air-conditioner.

In addition, an average tree absorbs up to 50 pounds of CO_2 through its leaves annually as a result of photosynthesis – storing up to 1 ton of carbon dioxide in its lifetime. During photosynthesis, the absorbed CO_2 and the energy from sunlight are broken down into carbon and oxygen. The latter is released into the atmosphere while the carbon is incorporated into the tree's growth. Because of transpiration and shading, the air surrounding a tree is, on average, 5°C cooler than its ambient view temperature. Tree-shaded neighbourhoods are up to 3°C cooler than neighbourhoods without trees.

Of course, aesthetically plants also enrich the indoor environment by adding rich colours and textures and generally making the indoor habitat more amenable for human occupation and well-being. For example, it is well known that in offices with plants there are fewer complaints about headaches, stress or the incidence of colds.

- Ecological design must therefore involve the addition of appropriate indoor planting to the internal areas of our new and existent built environments since plants can play a major role in ameliorating indoor air quality.

- At the same time, we should be aware that increasing biomass in the urban ecosystem through ecological design will bring attendant increases in other organic life that may affect human life. Modern urban structures and human-made ecosystems are not biologically 'dead'. In fact, there are a number of species that make up urban biodiversity without any design help at all. It's just that these species are generally an annoyance to humans: cockroaches, rodents and rats, spiders, fruit flies, ants, dust mites, moulds and fungi. These pests thrive in those urban environments that are usually hidden from the view of the building's human occupants – dark and damp places, cellars and basements, spaces between floors, walls, HVAC systems, underneath furniture and appliances, etc (see B7).

The incorporation and integration of more biomass into the internal environment will soften the 'hard-looking' built form and modify the appearance of the conventional internal environment of built structures and facilities. Studies have shown that the presence of plants in hospitals can contribute to accelerating the healing process in humans. Further studies indicate that mental disturbances can, in some cases, be traced directly to people's loss of contact with the earth and the natural environment. Currently, research is taking place on biophilia as a partly genetic tendency by humans to respond positively to nature. Gardening or simply observing a lush landscape is contended to have an emotionally restorative effect in promoting measurable improvements in mental and even physical health. People who were exposed to nature recovered from stress more quickly than others who were not. Hospitalised patients whose windows overlooked landscaped scenery recovered from surgery more quickly than those deprived of such a view. Research also shows that simply viewing a garden or a natural scene can quickly reduce blood pressure and pulse rate, and can even increase the brain activity that controls mood-lifting feelings.

In ecodesign, the balancing and biointegrating of the inorganic mass and properties of our design systems with more organic and biotic constituents has to be part of the overall endeavour in order to achieve greater ecological integration and linkage with the ecosystems of the locality (see B7). This has to extend to the internal environment of our designed systems. This design goal is pervasive in the ecodesign approach.

Summary

Ecodesign must not only deal with the external balance of the biotic and abiotic constituents of the built form but also with the internal balance of the organic constituents and content of the designed system so that it performs as a human-made ecosystem in order to achieve greater ecological integration and linkage with the ecosystems of the locality. The incorporation of internal landscaping and vegetation also contributes to improving indoor air quality (IAQ). This design goal is fundamental to the ecodesign approach.

Space	Standard maintained illuminance (lux)
Atria	
- general movement	50–200
- plant growth	500–3000
Assembly shops	
- medium work	500
Lecture theatres	300
Newsagents' shops	500
Offices	
- filing rooms	300
Paint works	
- colour matching	1000
Public rooms, village halls, church halls	300
Teaching spaces	300

● Designing lighting levels in built forms for plant growth

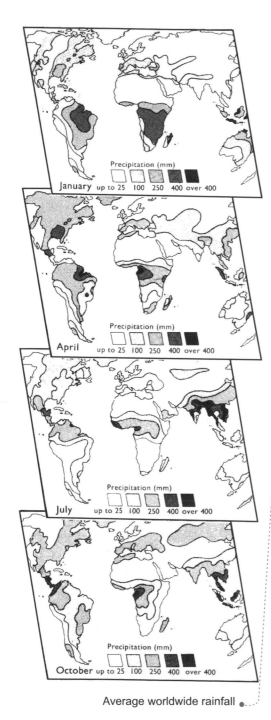

Average worldwide rainfall

B19 Design for water conservation, recycling, harvesting, etc: conserving water resources

A prime objective of ecodesign is the conservation of quality water resources through water recycling and rainwater harvesting where practicable for a given locality.

Water conservation is an important ecodesign goal because of the scarcity of good-quality water. Good-quality water has become a diminishing resource. Most humans could survive for several weeks without food, but not for more than a few days without water. In extremely hot climates just a few hours without drinking water causes death. There are those who contend that the water crisis threatens to dwarf the energy crisis in significance and severity. Of the global water supply, 97 per cent is in the form of saltwater. Only 3 per cent is fresh, only a fraction of that is accessible, and two-thirds of that is ice. Only 1 per cent is available for human consumption and use, agriculture and industry. The renewable freshwater on earth (rainfall) is only 0.008 per cent of all global water. Although about 4 trillion gallons of water (rainwater) falls globally daily in the form of precipitation, two-thirds of this is lost in evaporation, transpiration and runoff. Urbanisation, which leads to an increase in the impervious surfaces in our built environment, has long been recognised as a process that alters the water quality of urban and suburban aquatic systems. It increases sedimentation and thus the transport of nutrients into downstream (receiving) aquatic habitats. Site planning and layout planning in ecodesign must start by designing for surface-water management and natural drainage patterns.

This runoff is currently not available for use. Asia has 36 per cent of surface runoff but 60 per cent of the world's people. South America has 26 per cent of the runoff but only 6 per cent of the population. Globally, people already use 35 per cent of accessible supplies. An extra 19 per cent are used to dilute pollutants, sustain fisheries and transport goods. Humans currently use around half the total world supply provided by rainwater. At present, 1.1 billion people lack access to clean drinking water and more than 2.4 billion lack adequate sanitation.

The amount of water required by humans varies enormously depending on physical exertion and environmental and climatic conditions such as temperature and humidity. For moderate physical activity, used as the benchmark in calculations for energy balance, a person requires approximately 4 litres of water and/or its equivalent provided by water content of foods per day (with little or no activity in cool conditions), or 1460 litres per year. In terms of usage, a typical urban resident uses 7–15 cubic metres per annum, and a rural resident 2–4 cubic metres per annum. Water-deficient countries should strive to assure 100 litres per person per day. Average water use in office buildings is around 3000 litres per person per annum. An average city requires approximately 660 litres per person per day.

Water is an essential substance on earth. Wherever there is liquid water, organic molecules and an energy source, there is life. The biosphere is a thin membrane of organisms wrapped around the earth, yet it is so internally complex that most of the species composing it remain undiscovered. Water is the basis of this life. Water has no substitutes, and it flows naturally across political boundaries. It has been estimated that by 2015, 3 billion people, or about 40 per cent of the estimated world population, will be living in water-stressed countries that will have difficulty in meeting freshwater needs. Most of our planet's water is located in the oceans and is thus unsuitable in quality for residential, commercial or industrial use. The building industry uses 16 per cent of global freshwater annually. This percentage refers to the amount required to manufacture building materials and to construct and operate buildings. It does not reflect the impact of the building industry on water quality.

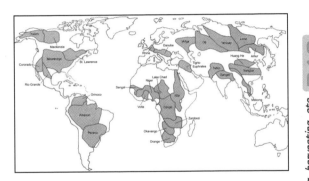

● Some of the world's major river basins

Our water resources also go through cyclical transformations like everything else in nature. Water circulates regularly through rivers, lakes, oceans and the atmosphere, making systemic detours through plants and animals. Plants grow and, through transpiration, they transfer water from the soil to vapour in the air. The rising water vapour condenses to form clouds, from which rain falls, enabling more trees to grow. Water vapour also condenses over the ocean. Algae in sea water produce dimethyl sulphide, which provides cloud-condensing nuclei, the particles around which water condenses to form clouds. The cloud vapour lowers the temperature, causing a differential in temperature and air movement. When the clouds condense over a landmass the result is rain.

The time that a water molecule spends at any one point in the cycle is as follows:

Location	Time
Atmosphere	9 days
Rivers	2 weeks
Soil moisture	2 weeks to 1 year
Large lakes	10 years
Underground water at slight depth	10s to 1000s of years
Ocean mixed layer to a depth of 55 yards	120 years
Seas and oceans	3000 years
Underground water at depth	up to 10,000 years
Antarctic icecap	10,000 years

Ground water

Population increases in urban centres, notably in developing countries, are exerting tremendous and increasing pressure on the use of ground water resources. Untreated human waste (see B20) remains the biggest pollution threat to water resources. Ground water is the main source of base flows for rivers, lakes and wetlands. It is also an effective buffer against drought. As global warming is expected to alter recharge patterns, the buffering action will become increasingly important. When rainfall is insufficient and rivers run dry, ground water remains a dependable source of water for drinking and irrigation. But worldwide ground water supplies are being depleted at an alarming rate. More than 50 per cent of the global water for drinking, washing and irrigation of crops comes from underground. As the demand for ground water increases, many of its sources are polluted by the dumping of toxic wastes and by the slow seepage of agrochemicals through the soil. Over-mining of ground water in many crop-producing areas is lowering the water tables, and changes in the flow paths of ground water bring pollutants into non-contaminated areas.

As the basis for establishing the priorities in water conservation, the world water use by sector is as follows:

Agriculture	70% (82% in low/middle-income countries, 30% in high-income countries)
Industrial and commercial	22% (10% in low/middle-income countries, 59% in high-income countries)
Domestic	8% (8% in low/middle-income countries, 11% in high-income countries)

Based on the above, the priority for water conservation as the focus of ecodesign of our built environment must be agriculture, followed by industrial and commercial use. Domestic use is the lowest priority and, therefore, while ecodesign strives and plans for a reduction of domestic consumption and elimination of waste, its impact will be secondary to conservation endeavours directed at agriculture and industrial use. Of the world's food, 40 per cent comes from irrigated cropland, and this irrigation accounts for two-thirds of the global usage (see above). The spreading water shortage threatens to reduce global food production by 10 per cent at a time when the population could double in 50 years.

For example, 60 per cent of the world's people are living in Asia and only have access to 36 per cent of the world's renewable freshwaters and global tensions over water scarcity are increasing. The most vulnerable and greatest water use is in irrigated agriculture, where ground water is being over-pumped, soils are being sanitised and there is already a shortage of freshwater. Approximately 180 billion cubic metres of water are being over-pumped on an annual basis. Countries that are in the water-stressed category account for about 26 per cent of global grain imports. Water stress will have immense effects in terms of food security.

Design considerations for water conservation in ecodesign

Generally, design to encourage the conservation of water and the reduction of waste. For example, the USA uses three times as much water per day (578 litres/person) as the average European country, and considerably more than most developing countries (eg around 160 litres/person/day).

Strategies to combat depletion of water resources through waste and inappropriate use include the following:

Capture storm runoffs

The practice of channelling storm runoff from roofs and impervious surfaces into sewerage systems and external drains should be replaced by capturing it (eg by porous paving systems, in storm-water storage cisterns (in urban areas), in bioswales and in retention ponds and lakes) in order to slow the flow of water and allow it to drain (eg within a few days to prevent the hatching of mosquito larvae) back into the ground rather than draining away. (See B6)

Increase water productivity

Ecodesign needs to increase water productivity, getting more out of each drop. In agriculture, drip irrigation is the most efficient way of getting water to crops, however, only 1 per cent of the world's irrigation areas is under drip irrigation. Other methods include shifting cropping patterns, reusing municipal wastewater for irrigation, and using natural varieties of crop, which are more drought tolerant. Building systems should include the use of low-flow plumbing fixtures and water-efficient appliances (eg urinals and WCs) and M&E equipment.

Residential use

Of all water use (eg in the USA), 47 per cent is accounted for by residential households, of which half is used for outdoor activities such as watering and landscaping. Until the water that we use for drinking and landscaping is transported and purified using renewable energy sources, every drop consumed is contributing to global warming. It takes energy to collect, purify and transport the water to the end-users. Energy is also needed to recollect, repurify and retransport the resulting wastewater that goes down the drain.

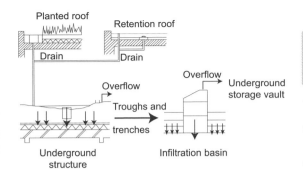

• Water-harvesting system from roof

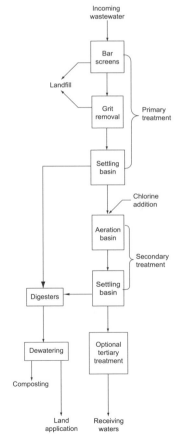

• Primary, secondary and tertiary treatment of wastewater

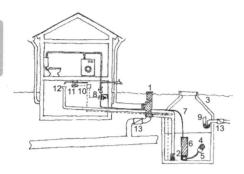

1. Self-cleaning filter
2. Filter
3. Cistern
4. Floating inlet filter
5. Inlet pipe
6. Multigo pump
7. Pressurised tube
8. Automatic valve
9. Overflow
10. Control panel
11. Magnetic valve
12. Drinking-water feed
13. Non-return valve

Example of a rainwater recovery system

Water-conserving planting

Planting water-conserving native plants and grasses instead of non-native ones can reduce watering (and irrigation) and maintenance costs (eg on fertilisers and pesticides) in landscaping by up to 85 per cent (eg using local drought-resistant species in drier environments, etc). Mulching can also reduce watering needs by up to 40 per cent. Landscaping, especially in arid regions, should be water efficient.

Reuse 'grey' water/wastewater

A typical large apartment or office building can use more than 454,600 litres of water in a single day. Once used, the water is more often than not released as wastewater. One way to reduce water consumption is to reuse such runoff water as undrinkable 'grey' water in non-potable washbasins and toilets. Most of these projects rely on plants to clean chemically saturated runoff water. In some cases, plants and other living organisms are used to transform wastewater into drinking water. In theory it is possible to recycle all of a building's wastewater.

The way to reduce wastewater is not to create it at all, for example, by using waterless urinals (a single flushing unit can use up to 65,000 litres of water a year). There are now two types of waterless urinal: a retrofittable design to fit existing units, and new waterless urinal bowls that incorporate a specially designed 'airlock' cartridge and barrier oil or other sealant liquid that allows urine to pass through to the waste pipe but prevents malodorous gases from returning to the room.

New environmentally friendly techniques for the purification of drinking water are the use of ultramembranes and ultraviolet light to kill off bacteria. Ultramembranes have pores that are so fine that they can physically screen individual cells. Ultraviolet technology is used in the 'after-disinfection' stage of water treatment as a second level of defence. Another method is to use UV light during the entire disinfection process where a photochemical process is used to create powerful oxidisers, that break down the organic compounds so that they can be consumed by aerobic bacteria that reside in active carbon filters.

Collect rainwater

A rainwater collector or a grey-water system can reduce or eliminate irrigation costs for homes and buildings. A grey-water system sends wastewater from the shower, dishwasher and washing machine through a filter so that it can be reused on the landscape. In the case of a household, this can save up to 100 gallons of water a day that would otherwise have gone down the drain.

Ozone as conservator

Ozone is an effective biocide. It is a short-lived, unstable gas that is created on site with an electrical generator, and immediately converts back to oxygen. In the process it oxidises fatty oil and breaks the bond between dirt and clothing. Used in laundry systems, especially in facilities that handle large amounts of textiles, such as hospitals and nursing homes, these systems save hot water (energy), reduce water and sewerage costs, reduce chemical use and improve sewerage quality.

Design for precipitation recharge, eg use of swales

Design and plan to ensure that precipitation falling on the site eventually returns to the environment to recharge aquifers and natural waterways without deteriorating their quality or quantity. Where contamination occurs, the designed system should provide for removal and/or recovery of contaminants. Water re-entering should not diminish its source, and should be returned to the natural environment in a state that enhances the aquatic habitat. The site-planning layout can use swales to return the runoff back into the land. Unlike drains, swales are contiguous with the surrounding landscape. The vegetation in the swales traps suspended solids in the runoffs, which then become embedded in the soil of the swales.

Specify low-use water fixtures

Encourage water conservation by specifying low-use water fixtures and appliances and by incorporating water-recycling systems that limit demand and reduce sewage. To be able to meet the water demands of the future, immediate improvements are needed in techniques for conservation, collection, storage, treatment and reuse. Water conservation includes using water that is of lower quality than drinking water, such as reclaimed wastewater effluent, grey water or runoff from ground surfaces, for such purposes as toilet flushing and the irrigation of vegetation. Rainwater runoffs can be directed to plants with high water demands, although drought-tolerant and xerophytic plants should be used where appropriate in landscaping. Water-conservation measures should also be implemented during construction.

As the basis for water conservation, we can summarise water use in typical fixtures as follows:

Fixture	Delivery rate in litres per minute
Kitchen taps	9.5 or less
Bathroom taps	9.5 or less
Showerheads	9.5 or less
Toilets and flush valves	6 or less per flush
Urinals and flush valves	6 or less per flush

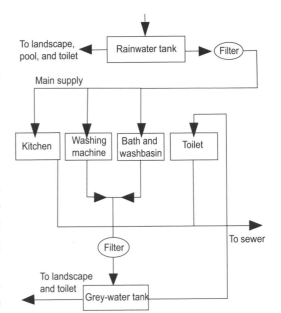

Integrated grey-water reuse system

The present standard toilet of 3.5 to 5 litres per flush (lpf) is the largest consumer of water in residences and offices. In ecological terms, the maximum preferred water use per flush is 5.3 litres per flush (in new water-conserving toilets) stipulated in many municipal building codes. Every toilet manufacturer now provides a number of models that meet this criterion. Before specifying the precise model, the designer should evaluate noise, solids evacuation, bowl cleaning and water surface area. Double-flush units save water by providing a partial flush for liquid wastes and a complete 6.05 litres per flush for solid waste. It is estimated that an average residence toilet uses around 28 flushes per day. A waterless or composting toilet may also be used where appropriate.

Urinals

Use urinals that have a maximum flow rate of 4 gallons per minute (gpm) and are spring-loaded or use waterless urinals. Lavatory fixtures should also be spring-loaded and have a maximum flow rate of 8.3 gallons per minute (gpm) at a test pressure of 0.042 kg/mm^2, but a higher test pressure ensures that a conservation device functions over a wide range of pressures. Electronic control devices can be used in commercial installations, but only where maintenance staff are competent to service them.

Shower fixtures and household appliances

Use shower fixtures rated for a maximum flow rate of 9.5 litres per minute at 0.056 kg/mm^2. In public facilities where water use is more difficult to monitor, shower fixtures can have a timed cycle linked to activation. They can also be spring-loaded with a chain operator, in which a hand chain-pull is released by use of a spring, automatically shutting off the fixture.

In kitchen and laundry areas install commercial appliances that are specified to be water saving. Refuse disposal exerts a huge load on wastewater treatment facilities and should be avoided. Composting provides a more useful alternative for food waste (see B20).

Reduce potable water usage

Reduce the rate of potable water usage through the use of:

• water-saving features and fittings;

• flow restrictors on most outlets;

• low-flush toilets;

• landscape plant species with minimal long-term irrigation needs;

- Connection to non-potable recycled water reticulation systems (eg connected toilets and external garden taps)

Plan to protect the wider environment

Where relevant, plan to protect forests and watersheds because these relate to runoff patterns, flooding patterns and control of the water cycle.

In the wider context, it is encumbent on the ecological designer to encourage water utility companies and central government to institute strong water policies to regulate ground water use as well as to price urban water to better reflect its value and future scarcity.

Ecosanitation

It is important to manage natural waste resources in a safe way for use in the urban setting. In fact, potentially the most viable and promising source of water for urban agriculture is recycled grey water, and the most promising source of fertiliser is sanitised human excreta together with animal manure. This is the evolving concept known as ecological sanitation, or ecosanitation. It may be defined as a system that makes use of human excreta and turns it into a valuable resource, which can be introduced into agriculture without polluting the environment and in a way that poses no threat to human health.

The collection and processing of these products and their use as resources through an ecosystem approach could result in a cleaner urban environment, potentially large-scale employment generation from expanded recycling activities, revitalisation of soils for rural agriculture and expansion of urban agriculture. That human faeces can be processed into humus that is pleasant smelling and as easy to handle as soil is not commonly realised. Black water, or toilet wastewater, contains 90 per cent of the nitrogen and 80 per cent of the phosphorus in wastewater. In carefully managed ecosanitation facilities, which include urine separation and composting, nutrients can be collected and recycled. Concentrated toilet and organic household waste can also be treated to produce energy via aerobic or anaerobic processes.

Guidelines for ecosanitation

- Adopt biological methods for the treatment of residential, commercial and infrastructure storm water.

- Use a wastewater treatment plant where sewage sludge is turned into biogas, for example to fuel gas cookers and cars, and biosoil used as agricultural fertiliser. Such a system can reduce water consumption by 50 per cent, remove 95 per cent of phosphorus in grey water, reprocess urine and faecal matter for agricultural use, and reduce the heavy metals

Form of pollution	Indicators
Water	Algal blooms
	Dissolved oxygen
	Evaporation
	Oliforms
	Nutrients
	Pesticides, herbicides, defoliants
	pH
	Physical water characteristics
	Sediment load
	Stream flow
	Temperature
	Total dissolved solids
	Toxic dissolved solids
	Turbidity
Air	Carbon monoxide
	Hydrocarbons
	Particulate matter
	Photochemical oxidants
	Sulphur oxide
Land	Land use and misuse
	Soil erosion
	Soil pollution

Pollutant indicators

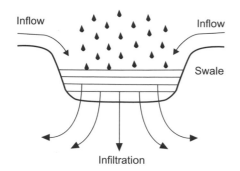

Use of bioswales for site-water management

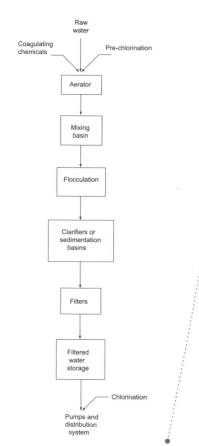

Typical drinking-water treatment steps

and other nutrient contents by 50 per cent. Storm water drains into the ground locally and road storm water is treated separately. Reduced-flow equipment is used throughout to keep water consumption as low as possible.

- Where the level of rainfall permits, use ecosanitation options that are low- or no-water technologies. The design can use rainwater for flushing toilets and watering green areas. Rainwater is collected in underground tanks and can also be deployed to feed landscaped water features. This will prevent lowering the ground water during the building phase and allow for an intermediate collection of all the rainwater that falls on to the buildings. Underground tanks can be used to meet the requirements with an additional storage buffer.

- Use natural ecological water balance as a slow-filtration method through a roadside swale system (eg approximately 11 kilometres in length), into bioretention systems where the water soaks into gravel-filled trenches and into landscaped green spaces. The water can be stored in the trenches where some permeates into the ground with the surplus flowing, say, to several recreational areas where further retention is facilitated.

- Reuse grey and black water. Note that a person produces 500 litres of urine and 50 litres of faeces a year (black water). If tap water is accessible, a person produces 20,000 to 100,000 litres of wastewater (grey water, if not mixed with black water).

If black water is collected separately with low dilution, it can be converted to safe natural fertiliser, replacing synthetic products and preventing the spread of pathogens and water pollution. If waste is mixed with a large volume of water, the large volume turns to a potentially dangerous flow of waste that has to be treated at high cost (as is done commonly in cities). This mixing makes simple treatment and higher quality reuse impossible because of faecal contamination and excess of nutrients. The reason for this wasteful handling of important resources is the long-standing failure to develop technologies for efficient flushing toilets. New concepts in sanitation can produce fertiliser from black water and facilitate reuse of treated grey water. Yellow water (urine) contains nearly all the valuable soluble nutrients.

A system can be adopted that is based on urine-sorting flush toilets (or no-mix toilets). Yellow water is collected with low or, better, no dilution and can be used directly on brown land – the nutrient composition suits many types of soil. Black water is converted to small volume by a two-chamber composting tank with a filtration system. Each chamber is used for a year and left without further change for another year. The resulting compost can be used as fertiliser. For countries with warm climates, the appropriate no-water sanitation option could include dessication-on-site toilets with two solar-heated chambers.

For example, more than 280,000 litres of wastewater are generated per household per year not from toilets, but from sinks, showers, baths, dishwashers and washing machines. Also called grey water, this 'waste' can be safely and easily reused to flush toilets and provide water for landscaping. Before using it for irrigation, grey water should be passed through filter systems. Even black water (sewage from toilets) can be treated and used to water landscape vegetation. Many plumbing codes have hitherto proscribed the use of grey-water because of concerns over health. Typically, separate lines and septic systems must be installed to keep grey and black water apart. In new construction this is not difficult, but when working with existing systems it can be costly.

Cisterns and catchment basins are ancient methods of meeting a building's water supply needs. Typically, a system of gutters from the roof collects runoff and channels it into a cistern. Ecologically conscious buildings employ these methods of collecting rainwater to reduce the need for treated water. Catchment areas are often designed to look like ponds or marshes. The rainwater collected by these methods is used for landscape maintenance. Often comparable in cost to drilling a well, rainwater-collection systems can be employed within a group of buildings or an entire community. In some municipalities, rainwater may be used as a back-up supply connected to the area's regular water system.

Designing for conservation of water can influence the shape and extent of the horizontal surfaces of the built form (eg its roof) as potential water collectors. Inventive solutions can include scalloped sunshades that also serve as rainwater collectors.

Summary

The designer needs to be aware that quality water is a crucial resource in the biosphere. Without water no living organism can exist. Ecodesign of the built environment and all its processes must conserve good-quality water that must be regarded as a valuable natural resource in the designed system through incorporating and planning for water-conserving systems and appliances, rainwater harvesting, water reuse and recycling (eg black water and grey water for downgraded use), and the recovery and return of rainwater and surface water back into the ground and retention ponds as against its loss by discharge into the drains. The design should also prevent legionnaires disease in domestic water systems. Potable water should be at an acceptable level of quality for human use (eg WHO standards). Composite systems could be used that combine solar collection and rainwater collection systems.

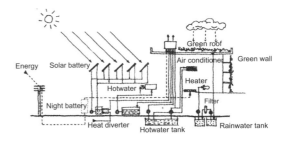

Combined solar-collection and rainwater-collection system

Source	Percentage (%)
Toilet	40
Bathing	15
Laundry	30
Kitchen	10
Others	15

Household wastewater

Process	Purpose
Preliminary treatment processes*	
Screening	Removes large debris (leaves, sticks, fish) that can foul or damage plant equipment
Chemical pre-treatment	Conditions the water for removal of algae and other aquatic nuisances
Pre-sedimentation	Removes gravel, sand, silt and other gritty materials
Micro-straining	Removes algae, aquatic plants and small debris
Main treatment process	
Chemical feed and rapid mix	Adds chemicals (coagulants, pH adjusters, etc) to water
Coagulation/flocculation	Converts non-settleable or settleable particles
Sedimentation	Removes settleable particles
Softening	Removes hardness-causing chemicals from water
Filtration	Removes particles of solid matters, which can include biological contamination and turbidity
Disinfection	Kills disease-causing organisms
Adsorption using granular activated carbon (GAC)	Removes radon and many organic chemicals such as pesticides, solvents and trihalomethanes
Aeration	Removes volatile organic chemicals (VOCs), radon, H₂S and other dissolved gases; oxidises iron and manganese
Corrosion control	Prevents scaling and corrosion
Reverse osmosis, electrodialysis	Removes nearly all inorganic contaminants
Ion exchange	Removes some inorganic contaminants, including hardness-causing chemicals
Activated alumina	Removes some inorganic contaminants
Oxidation filtration	Removes some inorganic contaminants (eg iron, manganese, radium)
*Generally used for treating surface-water supplies	

Basic water-treatment process ●

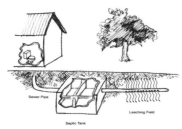

Septic system

B20 Design for wastewater and sewage treatment and recycling systems: controlling and integrating human waste and other emissions

A significant volume of the outputs from the built environment, aside from solid wastes, are wastewater and sewage emissions. As mentioned earlier, untreated human waste (not just sewage) remains the biggest pollution threat to water resources. In a day a human being produces an estimated 1150 grams of urine and 200 grams of faeces. The global urban and rural population is about 3 billion. Therefore, nearly 3500 million kilograms of human urine and 600 million kilograms of human faeces are generated in urban areas every day. Globally, the total is about 7 million tons of urine and over 1 millon tons of faeces each day. Further wastage of quality water is used in their discharge in sanitary systems. Ecodesign must address the consequences on the natural environment of this immense output of human waste.

Ecodesign must ensure that these biological emissions from the human users of built structures and facilities do not pollute the aquatic ecosystems and environments into which much of the waste is currently discharged. Untreated or partly treated sewage is one significant cause of water pollution globally and most of that pollution comes from cities in both developed and developing countries. Open defecation and water pollution with human faeces are major causes of diarrhoeal diseases and worm infestations, causing much of the world's morbidity and mortality. It is estimated that between 6 and 7 million people die each year from water stresses. The ecodesigner should ensure that appropriate waste-management systems are available even before the ground is broken.

Conventional wastewater-treatment technologies do not provide adequate treatment for full biointegration. They are technologically inadequate for several reasons. They produce sludge as a by-product. This sludge is often contaminated and toxic, and is disposed of by ocean dumping, landfilling, spreading on agricultural land, incineration or composting. Environmentally damaging chemicals are employed in waste-treatment processes. For example, aluminium salts are used to precipitate-out solids and phosphorus. Chlorine is widely used in ammonia control.

Also, conventionally, the wastewater from our built environment is discharged into pipes and carried to a wastewater-treatment plant. Here, the wastewater receives some treatment to remove the pollutants after which they are discharged into the environment. The usual three types of treatment are:

• Primary treatment: this first stage of treatment is largely a mechanical process. The wastewater passes through a series of screens that remove branches and other large objects. Then it enters settling tanks where most of the suspended solids settle out as sludge. Upon completion, about 30 per cent of the pollutants have been removed. The disposal of the sludge is dealt with below.

- Secondary treatment: the second stage of treatment is mostly a biological process. The sewage is mixed with bacteria that digest organic matter in the wastes. Upon completion, 85 to 90 per cent of the pollutants have been removed.

- Tertiary treatment: also called advanced wastewater treatment, this stage consists mostly of chemical processes. It removes dissolved substances not adequately removed by the primary and secondary treatments, particularly nitrogen and phosphorus. Upon completion, about 95 per cent of the pollutants in the original wastewater have been removed.

An ideal of green design requires that wastewater leaving a designed system be as pure as that entering. This can be achieved by the use of natural biological sewage treatment plants or 'living machines' and 'constructed wetlands' (ie a botanic purifying system) that use plants, fish, bacteria and snails to purify water on site to potable standards. In the 'living machine', waste water and anaerobically treated sewage flows into greenhouse tanks, where it is purified through the actions of plants such as seeds and floating weeds, and the processed water is used for raising fish. This is an alternative to conventional sewage treatment (see above), and as a biological sewage treatment and wastewater system it can have many environmental and economic advantages. Though it does not actually save water, it greatly contributes to the conservation of freshwater.

Another experimental system is the 'Bio-Geofilter' which can treat both waste water and sewage. After primary processing in a conventional domestic septic tank design, the output water still contains much nitrogen and phosphorus that could pollute waterways. The Bio-Geofilter intercepts the discharge from the septic tank and through hydroponics, uses it to grow vegetables and plants. These plants absorb the decomposed nitrogen and phosphorus as food for their growth, resulting in water that is clean enough for fish to inhabit.

Biological wastewater-treatment systems

Biological wastewater systems are a version of natural processes and an example of ecomimicry. Natural systems in ecosystems link wetlands, and marshes purify water. In the artificial marsh-type system, the sewage water passes through a series of artificial wetlands where it is purified by water-loving plants and micro-organisms, emerging cleaner than high-quality drinking water. The plant is essentially a large greenhouse containing six interconnected cascading tanks. The first one receives raw sewage. The second digests it anaerobically (ie in the absence of air). In the third tank oxygen is added to the, by now,

Principles for designing a 'living machine'

- Microbial communities. The primary ecological foundations of living machines are predicated upon diverse microbial communities obtained from a wide range of aquatic (marine and freshwater) and terrestrial environments. In addition, organisms from chemically and thermally highly stressed environments are critical. Genetic engineering cannot do what constellations of natural organisms can accomplish when they work in concert.

- Photosynthetic communities. Sunlight-powered photosynthesis is the primary driving force of these systems. Anaerobic phototropic microbes, cyanobacteria, algae and higher plants must be linked in a dynamic balance with the heterotrophic microbial communities.

- Linked ecosystems and the law of the minimum. At least three types of ecological systems need to be linked together to produce living machines that carry out self-design and self-repair through time. Such systems have a theoretical ability to span centuries and possibly millennia.

- Pulsed exchanges. Nature works in short-term/long-term pulses which are both regular and irregular. This pulsing is a critical design force and helps maintain diversity and robustness. Pulses need to be intrinsic to design.

- Nutrient and micronutrient reservoirs. Carbon/nitrogen/phosphorus ratio needs to be regulated and maintained. A full complement of macro and trace elements need to be in the system so that complex food matrices can be established and allowed to explore a variety of successional strategies over time. This will support biological diversity.

- Geological diversity and mineral complexity. Living machines can simulate a rapid ecological history by having within them minerals from a diversity of strata and ages. The geological materials can be incorporated into the subecosystems relatively quickly by being introduced as ultrafine powders, which can be solubilised over short time frames.

- Steep gradients. Steep gradients are required within and between the subelements of the system. These include redox, pH, humic materials and ligand or metal-based gradients. These gradients help develop the high efficiencies that have been predicted for living machines.

- Phylogenetic diversity. In a well-engineered ecosystem all phylogenetic levels from bacteria to vertebrates should be included. System regulators and internal designers are often unusual and unpredictable organisms. The development of various phyla has arisen to a large extent from the strategic exploration of the total global system over a vast period of time. This time can be compressed with the consequences of this evolution.

- The microcosm as a tiny mirror image of the macrocosm. This ancient hermetic law applies to ecological design and engineering. As much as possible, global design should be miniaturised in terms of gas, mineral and biological cycles. This big system relationship needs to be maintained in the living machine.

● **Principles for designing a 'living machine'**

Design for wastewater and sewage treatment and recycling systems

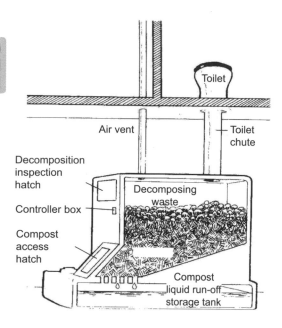

Toilet

Air vent

Toilet chute

Decomposition inspection hatch

Decomposing waste

Controller box

Compost access hatch

Compost liquid run-off storage tank

Example of low-treatment sewage system ●

clearer liquid to aid the treatment process. The fourth tank contains phytoplankton and bacteria while the fifth holds zooplankton, snails, shrimp and other organisms. The sixth tank looks like a tropical pond full of tilapia fish and waterplants. Some of the treated, but still nutrient-rich, water can be used to grow vegetables (eg tomatoes, cucumbers and melons) in a hydroponic system. Smaller tanks can be used for growing crayfish and a range of selected fish (eg tropical fish), which may thrive on the treated water. Inside the greenhouse that holds the sewerage works there could be a stream of clear water that runs to a garden or landscaped area below. This water is the end product of the entire treatment process.

The greenhouse or solar aquatics system approach requires little land. Each component has three simple and practical design criteria: high-quality effluent with potential for reuse, stable operation and aesthetic appeal. These systems can be designed for decentralised wastewater treatment for medium and small flows to service variably sized built systems ranging from towns and suburban developments to households. In these markets, a wastewater-treatment system can enhance the neighbourhood where it is located.

Biological toilets

In the 1960s, toilets were manufactured to use 25 to 34 litres (5.5 to 7.5 gallons) of water per flush. Today's new toilets use only 7.3 litres (1.6 gallons) per flush. An ecologically preferred toilet to use, however, is the compost toilet. Depending on the model, the toilet basically flushes waste into an odour-sealed chamber where it composts into an odourless fertiliser.

Biological treatment systems use much less energy, capital and far fewer chemicals than regular waste-treatment plants. They are less expensive to operate, can be an attractive educational feature in a building, and can provide natural habitats, fertilisers and food. Biological systems can be highly environmentally and economically effective.

Biological systems have the following features:

• natural, biologically diverse and resistant to discharges to the natural environment;

• reduce financial costs related to wastewater surcharges, water purchases, sludge disposal and chemical treatment and storage;

• capable of achieving tertiary treatment to meet stringent discharge by-law requirements;

• cheaper to operate than conventional systems when used to achieve a tertiary level of treatment;

• can be designed to be modular and expand to meet growing needs;

• custom designed;

• easy to operate and maintain;

• minimise or eliminate impacts of discharges into the environment;

- constructed on natural 'ecological engineering' principles;

- typically do not require chemicals that are harmful to the environment, and use a natural not a chemical process;

- can be designed to conserve and recycle wastewater. By using effluent from the biosystem for irrigation, toilet flushing and other non-potable uses the system saves potable water and resources;

- natural models based on ecomimicry (in A4);

- aesthetically resembling a botanical garden, can become a central garden that enhances the surroundings;

- incorporate abundant plant life that can be brought from the wastewater-treatment system and can be used to grow plants and, in some cases, vegetables hydroponically.

The greatest value in such systems is the inherent potential for reuse of the high-quality treated effluent. Potential reuse options include:

- agriculture and landscape;

- industrial activities such as cooling and processing needs;

- ground-water recharge;

- recreational and environmental uses such as for golf courses, parks and habitat restoration;

- non-potable urban uses, such as toilet flushing, fire protection and construction.

The system uses sunlight, a controlled environment and nature's bounty, including bacteria, zooplankton, plants, snails and fish to break down organic pollutants in wastewater. The treated water is used for irrigation, recycled back into toilets or discharged harmlessly back into municipal waste systems.

Basic design strategies include:

Gravity water storage

Employ gravity water storage where possible, as each segment of elevation of a storage tank provides about 300,000 kg/m² of static pressure

Dry toilets

Use possible alternative systems to the conventional water closet so that sanitary waste is processed in dry toilets where human urine and faeces are collected in a specially designed chamber that diverts urine to one receptacle and faeces into another, dries and sanitises the faeces further and makes them safely available to agriculture. Faeces are dropped below the

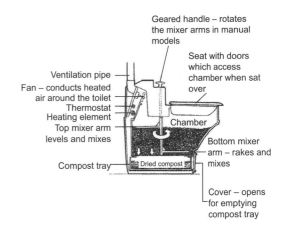

Geared handle – rotates the mixer arms in manual models

Seat with doors which access chamber when sat over

Ventilation pipe
Fan – conducts heated air around the toilet
Thermostat
Heating element
Top mixer arm levels and mixes

Chamber

Bottom mixer arm – rakes and mixes

Compost tray

Dried compost

Cover – opens for emptying compost tray

● Waterless sewage system

Design for wastewater and sewage treatment and recycling systems

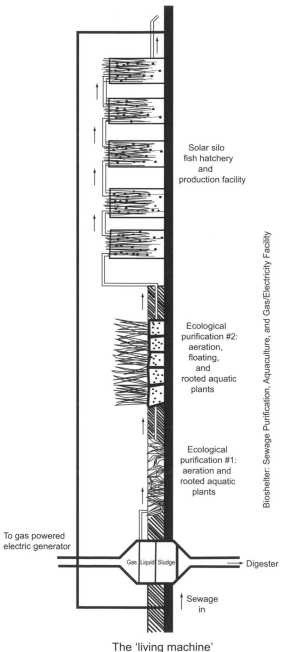

Solar silo
fish hatchery
and
production facility

Ecological
purification #2:
aeration,
floating,
and
rooted aquatic
plants

Ecological
purification #1:
aeration and
rooted aquatic
plants

To gas powered
electric generator

Gas | Liquid | Sludge

Digester

Sewage
in

The 'living machine'

Bioshelter: Sewage Purification, Aquaculture, and Gas/Electricity Facility

toilet opening into an enclosed compartment and treated with ash, lime or sawdust to increase dryness and raise the pH, which is necessary for pathogen destruction. Dried faeces are mainly composed of carbon and can be used as soil conditioners after a resting period of about six months. Urine, which is collected in a separate container, can be taken directly to fields to be further diluted with water and used as a fertiliser. Experiments indicate that farmers get higher yields with fertiliser derived from human excreta. Ecological toilets, properly handled, are suitable for new urban areas where planning for their inclusion can begin at the project's inception. It is also possible to install them in existing buildings. To incorporate ecosanitation for use in urban agriculture it will be easier to apply the concept to new cities from the start. Ecosanitation is any system that collects and safely reuses human excreta for agriculture with a view to saving water and preventing water pollution. It can also be used on golf courses, parks, rooftop gardens and to reclaim vacant lots. Such ecotoilets have multiple benefits in terms of sanitation, bioenergy and manure. There are many more indirect benefits; it is a system that gets rid of the health hazards of human excreta, does away with the need for large centralised, high capital input waste-processing plants and saves water.

Biogas digester

Use the biogas generation of anaerobic digestion as an alternative system. The anaerobic conditions inside the digester render the excreta harmless, making them suitable for use as manure or soil conditioners. In an example of a biogas public toilet in India, the digester is located underground and excreta from toilets flow into it under gravity. Biogas is produced inside the digester by anaerobic fermentation with the help of methanogenic bacteria. The biogas is collected over water in a separate gas holder or inside the digester itself, depending on design. One cubic foot of biogas is produced from the excreta of a person per day. Human-excreta-based biogas contains 65 to 66 per cent methane and 32 to 34 per cent CO_2, together with hydrogen sulphide and other trace gases.

The biogas purifying tank's main function is to process the daily sewage output of a particular building. It is usually made up of a precipitating tank, an anaerobic tank and a filtering tank. Sometimes a secondary or tertiary anaerobic tank and filter tank are used. For more complicated polluted sources a pre-process tank is substituted for the precipitating tank. It treats the fermented liquid and discharges it to the next two tanks, Biogas is the by-product of the process. The biogas purifying tank differs from other types of tank: the biogas tank is an anaerobic fermenting tank that produces large amounts of gas from a high concentration of the fermenting elements, the main task of which is the production of gas not the breakdown of sewage. A biogas septic tank is a combination biogas and septic tank. It ferments sewage anaerobically and discharges the water after a certain time period.

Biogas has multiple uses too, the most popular being cooking, lighting (through mantle lamps) and electricity generation using a genset.

Ecotoilets or ecosanitation facilities enable all organic wastes to be recycled, perhaps in an underground biogas purifying tank but not in an ordinary biogas tank or the usual septic tank.

The by-product of biogas production, manure, can be used as a fertiliser. The technology is based on filtration of effluent through activated charcoal followed by UV rays to make it colourless, odourless and pathogen-free.

Traditional mode ecosanitation and food production

Use traditional solutions for safe ecosanitation implementation in lower density urban areas. A traditional method of recycling human waste is to plant trees on old abandoned latrine pits, a method which is established in many parts of the world (eg in Africa). Where this technique is used, the growth of trees (usually fruit trees like papaya and banana, or species that are used for making shelter or poles, even dyes) is known to be spectacular. The concept of closing the loop is established.

Often it is in urban allotments and gardens that a rich diversity of old-fashioned, non-commercial varieties of fruit and vegetables are found, in contrast to the unnatural uniform characteristics of modern large-scale monoculture plots. Urban agriculture can help boost local shops and markets, regenerate the local economy and provide a much needed alternative to the major supermarket chains (see B21).

On city farms, compost soils are a natural solution to the provision of carbon sinks. However, there is a limit to which soils can act as carbon sinks after being amended by the continuous addition of compost – the compost can only have a certain level of humus (organic matter) content. Therefore, the only way to increase the capacity of soils to provide carbon sinks is to expand the area under humus-rich soil. It has been calculated that in a garden of 0.4 acres with an 20cm layer of organically rich topsoil amended by the addition of compost (up to 7.7 per cent organic matter from just 1 per cent at the beginning) 19 tons of carbon were sequestered over a ten-year period of soil improvement. That equates to three years of an average person's emissions in the USA.

Composting

Waste-food biomass is the power source behind urban food production. Composting not only increases the soil's ability to become a better carbon sink, it performs other crucial ecosystem services too. Studies show that regular application of compost reduces irrigation, fertiliser and pesticide requirements by 30 per cent. The recovery of urban nutrient resources could have major impacts on the replacement of nitrogen-fertiliser sources. A lack of organic fertiliser is a barrier to efficient urban agriculture. Many cities market their excess compost and mulch production. However, some cities, eg Portland (USA), have made recycling and resource efficiency a top priority, with installations of sophisticated recycling plants for resource recovery.

Compost in city farms also has the ability to soak up rainwater and prevent it from becoming storm water that ends up in a sewer. Estimates are that gardens and naturalised landscapes absorb between 15 and 20 per cent more rainwater than even standard grass lawns because without the tilth that organic matter like compost provides, even grass lawns shed rainwater too quickly.

Composting also stops the release of methane into the atmosphere. Instead of producing methane in landfills, it could be captured safely as biogas to provide electricity, steam, heat and CO_2 for horticulture.

Materials used during building operations can be managed as a resource: paper collected for recycling; food waste composted whether on site or at a nearby facility (if on site, then the compost can be used on the ground for landscaping to act as a carbon sink; access can be sold or given to building occupants; also, a greenhouse or a fruit and vegetable garden could be provided on site).

Waste energy from power plants could be used to provide heat for food-producing greenhouse operations in cities. Process heat is available from composting alone, along with soil nutrients and CO_2 itself in designed composting greenhouse systems. Waste energy can be scrubbed from landfill gas and used on a seasonal adjustment basis, whereby in winter it may be used for heat and in summer scrubbed to become CO_2 for horticulture.

The incorporation of all/any of the above systems will obviously influence the size and the shape of the built structure or facility and the provision of its infrastructure.

Summary

Ecodesign includes the design of systems to handle and dispose of the high volume of wastewater and sewage outputs from humans in our built environment. This should be done by means of biological treatment and recycling systems that reduce or eliminate the continued use of non-renewable sources of energy and of chemicals in waste treatment, curb or eliminate effluent discharge into aquatic ecosystems and reduce the continued dependency on the resilience of the natural environment to absorb these wastes. Site planning must start with a water-management plan and consider surface-water retention and natural drainage patterns of the land.

Material	Disposal environment			
	Terrestrial		Aquatic	
	Arid-land soil	Tropical and temperate soil	Ocean	Freshwater
Water	Highly beneficial	May be beneficial	No consequence	Little consequence
Organic compounds	Beneficial food for soil micro-organisms Fast biodegradation times desirable		Must be removed by oxidation in pre-treatment to prevent depletion of oxygen dissolved in water Fast biodegradation	
Nitrogen (N)	Extremely beneficial Limiting nutrient in plant growth	Beneficial May leach into ground water if added in excess	Probably OK Harm-limiting nutrient but dilution makes measurable effect unlikely	Highly undesirable Algal growth's second most limiting nutrient
Phosphorus (P)	Beneficial Leaching into ground or surface waters unlikely due to low mobility in soil	Beneficial Limiting nutrient in plant growth	Probably OK Harm-limiting nutrient but dilution makes measurable effect unlikely	Highly undesirable Algal growth's second most limiting nutrient
Potassium (K)	Beneficial at washwater concentrations		Effect unlikely	
Sulphur (S)	Beneficial		No consequence	
Sodium (Na)	Highly undesirable Toxic build-up likely	Undesirable but partly flushed from all but clay soils by rain	No consequence	No consequence
	Directly toxic to plants, destructive to soil structure			
pH (acidity/alkalinity)	pH lowering desirable	pH lowering desirable	No consequence	Little consequence
Chlorine (Cl)	Undesirable		No consequence	Little consequence
Boron (B)	Highly toxic to plants at washwater concentration		No consequence	Undesirable
Pathogenic micro-organisms	Harmlessly biodegraded under proper conditions		Diluted but could spread disease	Likely to spread disease
Industrial toxins	Disastrous		Highly undesirable Diluted but may bioconcentrate	Disastrous

Integration of emissions in the biosphere

Industrial and
commercial region
Important mining
Arable stock
Open range land
Subsistence farming
Nomandic farming
Forest for hunting
Forest for lumber
Fishing
Little or no
economic activity

Areas of productive and non-productive land ●

B21 Design for food production and independence: designing to promote urban agriculture and permaculture

Ecodesign should, where possible, provide for local self-sufficient food production in every designed system. This is vital because food production is one of the key sources of environmental degradation. While rural societies retain a dynamic balance of nutrients in their local ecosystems, urban districts take their food produce from distant localities. There is also a need to reduce our dependence on external sources of food supply as well as limiting the industrial consequences of food production, such as its transportation (especially over long distances), and the manufacture and distribution of related products. One approach is to introduce urban agriculture and permaculture into the potentially food-productive surfaces of the designed system (eg on the terraces, roofs, sky courts, etc, of the built form).

A fundamental pattern for understanding a city's impact is the relationship between its land area and the total amount of land required to provide it with its biological, material and energy resources – or its 'ecological footprint'. An ecological footprint is the productive land necessary to support humans in their lifestyle. For instance, humans in the developed world (ie the USA and Europe) source their food, minerals and petroleum from all over the world and all these processes use some of the world's limited productive land. Their 'footprints' are larger than those from developing countries. The world has only 1.5 hectares available for each person. But to support its present patterns of consumption the world needs 2.3 hectares of productive land per person. This excessive footprint is literally trampling on the world's available resources, eg 7.5 per cent of all arable land is abandoned every decade; the earth's forest, freshwater and marine environments have reduced by 30 per cent in 30 years; and a third of all fish species and a quarter of all mammal species are in danger of extinction. Just to maintain an urban existence, an average city of 1 million people requires more than 4 million pounds of food, 625,000 tons of freshwater and 9500 tons of fuel energy every 24 hours, most of which have to be transported over long distances.

The long-term future of our food supply is increasingly in question. The destruction of native plant cover by monocropping and sod-busting practices of tilling soil can all exacerbate the effects of an extended drought (eg the Californian dust bowl catastrophe of the USA in the 1930s) and result in the destruction of farmland. We need to question the ecological implications of the food that we eat, eg whether butter is produced from intensively milked cows fed on genetically modified maize, whether there are traces of antibiotics in battery-farmed eggs, are greenhouse gases emitted as a result of air-freighting orange juice from a plantation abroad, is there a loss of biodiversity caused by growing wheat on an industrial scale to produce bread, and the extent of the pressure put on landfills by excessive food packaging. Modern arrgriculture is unsustainably dependent almost exclusively on petrol and continues to deplete farmlands of topsoil and nutrients. Currently, for example, 4 per cent of all the energy consumed in the USA goes on growing food. Another 10 to 13 per cent is used to transport, process, package and deliver that food to supermarkets. In total, more than 17 per cent of the energy used in the USA goes on providing food to its people. In the USA a third of the original topsoil has gone and most of the rest is significantly depleted of nutrients and degraded by pesticides and chemical fertilisers.

The increased energy flow-through in agriculture has also resulted in more entropy in the surrounding environment. As the native soil base has been depleted and eroded because of intensified farming practices, so more synthetic fertilisers have had to be applied to sustain the yields. Nitrate pollution from fertiliser runoff is now a consequence of half of our agricultural practices; growing a single crop over extended acreage has created economies of scale and increased productivity and profits, but has required the use of greater amounts of pesticides. More traditional farming relied on the planting of diversified crops that attracted a range of insects, some of which are natural enemies of insect pests. Eliminating crop diversity in favour of monoculture crops left the fields without the beneficial insects, and crops became more vulnerable to insect pests, requiring a steady rise in the use of pesticides. Much of the sprayed pesticide runs off into the ground water and becomes a major source of water pollution in every agricultural region of the world. At present about 6 calories of fossil-fuel energy are needed to produce 1 calorie of food. If the food is imported or brought from a considerable distance, then more than ten times as much energy can be required.

The pesticides also destroy the remaining soil. The soil contains millions of microscropic bacteria, fungi, algae and protozoa, as well as worms and arthropods. These organisms maintain the fertility and structure of the soil. Pesticides destroy these organisms and their complex habitats, hastening the process of soil depletion and erosion. To meet the demands of a growing population, scientists created new superstrains of wheat and rice that greatly increased yield per acre. These high-yielding varieties doubled production in less than a decade in places like India and Pakistan, but they required vast inputs of petrochemical fertilisers and chemical pesticides.

Humans have built a worldwide agricultural infrastructure run by fossil fuels, and the short-term increase in yield has made it possible greatly to expand both the total human population and the number of people living in urban areas.

The new genetically engineered food crops have been touted as a solution. But these crops, too, require large inputs of energy, especially in the form of petrochemical fertilisers.

Research has thus far been unsuccessful at creating biotech crops that get their own nitrogen from the air rather than from the soil. Studies show contradictory results in terms of yield performance. The prospects for agriculture look even bleaker when we consider the fact that 11 per cent of the land surface of the planet is already used to produce food, which leaves little remaining arable land for agriculture. In desperation, human beings have begun to cut down large swathes of tropical rainforest in the Amazon basin (South America) and elsewhere to make room for agricultural production. The destruction of the rainforest eliminates precious habitats for many of the earth's remaining species of plants and animals. The soil base itself is too thin to support food production for more than a few years. The result is spreading erosion, and barren land no longer fit for human, animal or plant habitation.

To make matters worse, one-third of the world's agricultural land has been converted from growing food grains for human consumption to growing feed grain for cattle and other livestock. For instance, cattle production is now the most energy-consuming agricultural activity in the world. It takes the equivalent of a gallon of petrol to produce a pound of grain-fed beef in the USA. To sustain the yearly beef requirements of an average family of four people requires the consumption of more than 1182 litres of fossil fuel (petroleum). When that fuel is burned, it releases 2.54 kilograms of additional CO_2 into the atmosphere – as much CO_2 as the average car emits in six months of normal operation.

If well-off consumers in the West and elsewhere were willing to forego a diet heavy in meat and eat items from further down the food chain, ie a largely vegetarian diet, precious farmland could be freed up to grow food for millions of people.

Ecodesign should encourage the local production of food especially on any flat surfaces of the built form that are potentially suitable for food production, particularly in residential communities. Studies have shown that the contribution of non-local food production to global warming is between six and 12 times higher than that of local production, due to increased CO_2 emissions. Many of the older cities have productive small gardens and allotments. Some actually export food outside their local communities. For instance, an intensively planted garden patch of only 1 square metre (about 10.5 square feet) can provide a whole family with vegetables for a season. Fifteen to 20 per cent of the solid waste in cities is organic and could be a potential resource. Its nutrients, properly composted, could fertilise urban agricultural systems (eg rooftop crops) and provide a sizeable proportion of urban food requirements. Local food production also saves the energy costs of transportation (eg on average, in the USA, 28.35 kilograms of food travel 2400 kilometres from field to table before being eaten, which is more than ten times the calorific content of the food itself).

To support an average metabolic rate of 11,500 kJ (2750 kCal) per day, a person would have to consume approximately 1100 grams (dry weight) of carbohydrates or 650 grams of fat each day. On an annual basis, the energy requirement per person would therefore be roughly 400 kilograms of carbohydrates or 240 kilograms of fat. Carbohydrates are mainly obtained from plants but fat can be derived from either plant seeds or animals. In addition to energy, humans require nutrients. These are usually combined with energy in the food that humans consume, although the relative proportions can vary. Standard US agricultural practice today requires at least 4500 square metres, of land to feed a person on a high-meat diet or about 1000 square metres for a vegetarian. The Biosphere 2 experiment in Arizona showed that by applying intensive hand-growing methods using soil-based agriculture, only 307 square metres of land were required per adult, to provide all food, including grain and fodder for livestock (chicken, goats and pigs) in order to keep the Biospherians healthy. Therefore a hectare will support at least 33 people. This figure is for a year-round growing climate. For temperate climates based on this figure, we can multiply the figure by three to get about 1000 square metres per person.

Farm	fertiliser	11.6%
	tractor fuel	7.3%
	other	0.4%
Mill	transport	1.4%
	other	2.0%
	milling fuel	7.4%
	packaging	2.2%
Bakery	transport	5.0%
	other ingredients	9.4%
	baking fuel	23.6%
	packaging	8.3%
Retail	transport	12.2%
	shop heat and light	8.6%

● Indicative energy breakdown of a standard loaf of white bread

Organic farming

Organically reared animals and organically grown fruit and vegetables ideally harbour no artificial fertilisers, and none of the various legally permitted insecticides, pesticides, fungicides, herbicides, waxes, hormones, antibiotics or other additives present in non-organic food. Organic farming is an ecological approach to farming in which technologies are based on ecological knowledge rather than chemistry or genetic engineering. Organic food production is defined as a holistic food-production management system that provides and enhances agro-ecosystem health, including biodiversity, biological cycles and biological activity in the soil. The primary goal of organic agriculture is to optimise the health and productivity of interdependent communities of soil life, flora and fauna. It increases yields, improves pest control and builds soil fertility. In this approach, a variety of crops is planted (multiculture); these are rotated so that insects attracted to one crop will disappear with the next. Total eradication of pests is not preferred, because this would reduce the biodiversity necessary for a healthy ecosystem, such as the need for natural predators that keep pests in balance. Instead of chemical fertilisers, the organic approach enriches the fields with manure and tilled-in crop residue, thus returning organic matter to the soil to re-enter the organic cycle. Organic and biointensive farming can provide for a vegetarian's entire diet, plus the compost crops needed to sustain the system, on only 200–400 square metres, even starting with low-quality land.

Organic farming is sustainable because it embodies ecological principles that have been tested by evolution over time. There are soil benefits. Monocropping (eg growing only one type

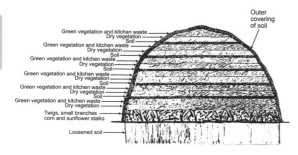

Outer covering of soil

Green vegetation and kitchen waste
Dry vegetation
Soil
Green vegetation and kitchen waste
Dry vegetation
Soil
Green vegetation and kitchen waste
Dry vegetation
Soil
Green vegetation and kitchen waste
Dry vegetation
Soil
Green vegetation and kitchen waste
Dry vegetation
Soil
Green vegetation and kitchen waste
Dry vegetation
Twigs, small branches
corn and sunflower stalks

Loosened soil

Biointensive compost pile ●

of crop such as wheat, rye, etc) and increasing applications of synthetic fertilisers destroys the soil. The principle adopted in organic farming is that a fertile soil is a living soil containing billions of living organisms in every cubic centimetre. It is a complex ecosystem in which the substances that are essential to life move in cycles from plants to animals, to manure, to soil bacteria and back to plants. Solar energy is the natural fuel that drives these ecological cycles, and living organisms of all sizes are necessary to sustain the whole system and keep it in balance. Soil bacteria carry out various chemical transformations, such as the process of nitrogen fixation that makes atmospheric nitrogen accessible to plants. Deep-rooted weeds bring minerals to the soil surface where crops can make use of them. Earthworms break up the soil and loosen its texture; and all these activities are interdependent, combining to provide the nourishment that sustains life on earth.

Organic food production preserves and sustains the global ecological cycles and nature's biodiversity, integrating their biological processes into the processes of food production. When soil is cultivated organically, its carbon content increases, and thus organic farming contributes to reducing global warming. Naturally reared plants also have a stronger resistance to infections and are better able to withstand climatic stresses. Organic farming protects water quality by not using agrochemicals and fertilisers that leach into the underground water table and into streams, rivers and reservoirs.

Enormous quantities of fossil fuels are used in the production of agrochemicals. Energy is needed for the manufacture of their basic ingredients, for the collection and delivery of these, and their conversion into finished products; for their distribution and for multiple applications.

Compost piles

Compost piles based on the decomposition of organic material into humus are the basic material in biointensive agriculture. Well-made compost has been shown to have plant-growing benefits far in excess of its simple 'nutrient analysis' and to be an active factor in enhancing plant resistance to pests. Chemical fertilisers, which are derived from increasingly expensive non-renewable petroleum products, have been shown to deplete the soil over time. As soil quality deteriorates, increasing quantities of chemical fertilisers are needed to sustain yields, causing harm to the structure of, and microbiotic life in, the soil. Biointensive food-raising methods avoid these problems through recycling organic waste products in the form of compost.

Animals raised on organic farms support the ecosystems above the ground and in the soil, and the whole enterprise is labour intensive and community oriented.

Ecodesigners might suggest that humans change their diet to eat less meat, or become vegetarian. Animal husbandry causes heavy ecological impacts and animals are often raised and killed under appalling conditions. Moreover, consumption of animal fat contributes to arterial and heart disease in humans.

Permaculture

Where appropriate, ecological design should also include the introduction of permaculture into the built environment in preference to urban agriculture. The term permaculture (or permanent agriculture) was first used to describe the whole-systems approach to agriculture. It is defined as the conscious design and maintenance of agriculturally productive ecosystems that have the diversity, stability and the resilience of natural ecosystems. Permaculture is the harmonious integration of landscape with people, providing their food, energy, shelter and other material and non-material needs in a sustainable way. Permaculture design is a system of assembling conceptual, material and strategic components in a biological pattern that functions to benefit life in all its forms.

Permaculture uses ecological principles to plan self-renewing and sustainable systems for food, water and energy. Every available space is used with close, multi-layer planting: ground plants under trees; vines trellised on walls; and trees and plants with multiple uses, in order to create a holistic balance of shelter, food and environment.

It proposes the following design principles:

- Connected layout: a network structure in which related elements are placed adjacently, and the output of one element is the input to the next

- Multifunctionality: each element performs more than three functions

- Circulation: matter and energy circulate within small areas of a geographical region or a built system

- Using natural systems: a creation of eminent that uses transition processes so as to provide an ecosystem for many species

- Social diversity: formation of richer lifestyles and social groupings through the symbiosis of diverse elements

- Maximisation of edges: the boundaries between areas with different characteristics are suited to forming rich and diverse ecosystems

There is a significant difference between the terms permaculture and urban agriculture. The philosophy behind permaculture is one of working with, rather than against, nature; of protracted and thoughtful observation rather than protracted and thoughtless action; of looking at systems with respect to all their functions, rather than expecting only one yield from them; and allowing systems to demonstrate their own evolution. A permaculture system can be designed into any rural or urban setting. It is an integrated system of design encompassing not only agriculture, horticulture, architecture and ecology but also money management, land-access strategies and legal systems for businesses and communities.

At the core the aims are essentially ecomimicry: to create systems that provide for their own needs, do not pollute and are sustainable. Central to permaculture are concepts such as conservation of soil, water, energy, and system stability and diversity.

Urban agriculture, on the other hand, is an all-encompassing term, which could include agriculture that adheres to permaculture or sustainable agriculture concepts, as well as agricultural practices that are more like conventional food-crop growing practices and involve high usage of fossil-fuel based chemicals. Permaculture takes human-controlled, energy-demanding, artificially designed landscapes and arranges them so that they work to conserve energy or even generate more energy than they consume.

Permaculture systems involve a number of guiding principles in their operation. Among the most important is the notion that one component of a design serves best when it serves several purposes at once, such as a solar greenhouse that warms a house, provides a nursery for starting plants early in the season, creates a quiet environment, etc. Another important principle is that edges between zones are potentially especially rich in productivity and services to people, agriculture and natural species. Mixing architecture and town planning three-dimensionally with complex permaculture systems shaped by regional climate becomes a context for appropriate technology and a flourishing human community. All of this has been technologically and conceptually available since the early 1980s.

The concept today encompasses anticipatory planning and design with the aim of creating stable self-supporting food-production systems as a sustainable culture based on ecological principles, which supply not only wholesome food for people but also energy and aesthetic aspects such as warmth, beauty and meaningful pursuits.

Permaculture design includes the mixing of appropriate technologies and agriculture according to design principles that accomplish high orders of integrity in complex whole systems. Urban permaculture amounts to the application of the same design principles to urban habitats, to produce an even higher order of integrity. Ideas on permaculture are also found in bioclimatic design such as the use of trees planted to shelter buildings and gardens from wind or to avoid shading areas that should get warmth and light.

Permaculture in densely built-up areas such as cities also helps to increase ecological diversity. Ecologically benign agriculture models, like permaculture, mimic the energy pathways and cycles of nature. The integration of food and urban systems can be achieved in a sustainable manner through system redesign. Urban agriculture is a vital element and process in an ecosystem's service systems, providing fresh, clean food and health as by-products of a redesigned urban eco-infrastructure, in an integrated resource-management strategy.

Throughout history, cultures have used their dwellings, workplaces and other communal areas to produce food. The FAO estimates that 800 million people worldwide engage in urban agriculture, with 200 million of these doing so for commercial reasons. Farming is done in city core areas, wedge areas and corridors out of the city and on the periphery. It is also done on rooftops, in vacant lots, in small greenhouses, on windowsills, and in pots or planter boxes. Productivity can be as much as 15 times the output per hectare of rural agriculture, but yields often suffer from inferior or insufficient inputs of water and fertiliser. Moreover, fear is prevalent that the food grown in urban conditions contains contaminants. However, various tests have shown that produce grown on rooftops actually contains less contamination than produce bought at local markets or grown on suburban plots.

Food production in urban environments has not yet received the attention from governments that it rightly deserves. There are many reasons why it should. The global food economy is heavily reliant in non-renewable resources. For example, fossil fuels are expended not only in transportation (food transportation comprises about 25 per cent of road and air traffic) but also in petroleum-based fertilisers, pesticides, herbicides and other chemicals. Local food production in urban environments minimises the need for long-distance transportation and wasteful, often non-biodegradable, packaging. Organic waste generated in urban areas can be composted and returned to the urban nutrient cycle to grow more food.

One way of maximising food growth in urban areas would be to have balconies for planting, which project above, but do not block the sunlight falling on, the plants below, and rooftop growing zones.

The provision of food production within our built forms will influence the shape and configuration of our built structure, facilities and infrastructure layouts to provide surface areas for food production and their irrigation.

Food item	Source country	Distance travelled (km)
Apples	USA	16,303
Sugar snap peas	Guatemala	8780
Asparagus	Peru	10,156
Pears	Argentina	11,079
Grapes	Chile	11,660
Lettuce	Spain	1541
Strawberries	Spain	1541
Broccoli	Spain	1541
Spinach	Spain	1541
Red peppers	Holland	100
Potatoes	Israel	3518
Tomatoes	Saudi Arabia	4965
Chicken	Thailand	10,688
Prawns	Indonesia	11,710
Brussels sprouts	Australia	16,994
Wine	New Zealand	22,988
Marlin	Indian Ocean	7261
Carrots	South Africa	9620
Peas	South Africa	9620
Total kilometres travelled		161,606

Transportation distances between source countries and UK, for the various food types

Agricultural biotechnology

Biotechnology is also crucial in preserving biodiversity through more productive agriculture. Biotechnology holds the promise of greater food production yields on the same land by developing insect-resistant crops, thereby eliminating the need to convert petroleum resources into pesticides and saving energy otherwise used in the latter's packaging, transport and application. It has been estimated that agriculture is heavily dependent on fossil fuels and non-renewable energy to the tune of 9.8 kCal of fossil energy per kCal of food energy. Through biotechnology and bioprospecting many 'wild' or 'natural' ecosystems may be converted to species and processes suitable for large-scale, highly controlled aquacultural or silvicultural production. Disease-resistant crops are also expected to help increase productivity and minimise the environmental impacts of farming, enabling producers to get the most out of their land and livestock in the safest, most efficient manner possible. This can help the best existent agricultural lands to be more productive, thereby reducing pressure on marginal lands, which may contribute to conserving biodiversity.

Summary

Ecodesign must take into account and integrate the food production requirements of the users of the designed system and achieve this as locally as possible, and so incorporate independent, community and local food production within the designed system. This will reduce the ecological footprint of the built environment as well as reduce other attendant ecological consequences (eg energy use in the transportation of food). The provision of planted terraces, edges, roof surfaces, ground surfaces, etc, will facilitate the subsequent incorporation or conversion of these into food-production areas.

B22 Design the built system's use of materials to minimise waste based on the analogy with the recycling properties of the ecosystem: designing for continuous reuse, recycling and eventual biointegration

To create our built environment, large volumes of material from the biosphere are extracted, processed and consumed in processes that include the production of our buildings, built structures and facilities, urban infrastructures (eg roads, drains, sewerage, bridges, ports, etc), and all those other things and artefacts that we manufacture (eg refrigerators, toys, furniture, etc) and produce (eg food). In ecodesign, we need to design our built environment as a human-made ecosystem possessing the recycling characteristics that mimic the way the ecosystem handles materials through continuous reuse and recycling.

This is necessary because the more our built environment imitates the recycling properties, structure, functions and processes in natural ecosystems, the easier will be its environmental integration. As part of our ecodesign strategies in approaching humankind's use of materials, we need to apply and adopt the principles of ecomimicry (A4). As mentioned earlier (in B2), the four key strategies in materials use are: reduce (in B2), reuse, recycle and reintegrate. Consuming fewer goods and improving process efficiencies (ie 'reduce') have the most impact (in B2). Reusing goods has a medium impact. Recycling has the least positive impact since it is at the tail end of the consumption cycle and is itself a process that requires additional energy and resources.

In endeavouring to use the ecosystem as a model for our approach to the use of materials in our built environment it is worth looking at its processes in some detail. Ecologists suggest that there is a parallel between the dependence of living things on energy flows and an ecosystem's dependence on the cycling of materials and energy. These principles can be validly applied universally to organisms and ecosystems and they are fundamental to the ecosystem model. A simple model would be one that used boxes to indicate the various components of the ecosystem on a scale, from the level of decomposers, and the materials that they break down, upwards. Energy flows into the ecosystem through photosynthesis and flows out by respiration. In reality, any element or individual within the system can occupy more than one box, which is to say that the roles within an ecosystem are complex and changing. The consumers at the top of the food chain die and become the material for the decomposers at the bottom to work on; such is the cycle.

The ecosystem model

The principles and premises of the ecosystem model are as follows (see also A4):

• The 'systems' of nature are inherently cyclical processes. Nature recycles resources in familiar ways such as in food chains. Another example would be the breakdown of decaying plant matter by organisms, which enriches the soil and promotes the growth of new plants, replacing those that have decomposed. The reuse of materials and energy allows the biosphere to maintain its stability and continue to exist over time. There is, thus, an analogy between the flow of resources in a natural system (an ecosystem) and in a built environment (a synthetic system). The use of materials is not a one-way street. This cycling of materials in a natural environment is one of the most salient features that define what an ecosystem is.

- The cyclical flow of materials is basic to ecosystems, and yet in most environments the cycle remains incomplete. The further up the hierarchy of ecosystems one goes, the greater is the efficiency – mature ecosystems are better able to retain material for recycling through the ecosystem (approaching a closed loop) than developing ecosystems. The biosphere as a whole is, of course, a closed system, but its component ecosystems are not. Producers bring energy into an ecosystem and it is eventually dissipated (partly) from the system. The degree to which the circle can be closed indicates how far the ecosystem has gone in its development towards maturity.

- In the ambient ecosystem of our built systems, which exists in an urban context, one finds a small producer base that is hardly important to the consumers, who are primarily humans. This is an ecological way of saying that plant life found in our existent urban developments is negligible as a food source and has a relatively minor role in the flow of energy through the ecosystem. A city is a dependent system; it draws its energy from other ecosystems external to it, for example agricultural producers in rural areas and, of course, from the dead ecosystems that power our cities through their decomposition into fossil fuels.

- Human-made ecosystems are less stable and predictable than mature natural ones, from which they are poles apart. The existent city, instead of being cyclical in its use of energy and materials, filtering them down to decomposers who can modify them for reuse, operates in a linear, one-way fashion. An enormous flow of imported energy takes the place of a natural cycle. A few natural ecosystems, such as rivers, provide an analogy to the city because of their linearity and sensitivity as one-way flows which are cyclic. The more broken and linear a cycle becomes, the more dependent is the ecosystem on imported energy and materials, because the internal flow no longer provides its needs. The importation of matter and energy may seem 'free' from within the ecosystem (like the flow of petroleum that once seemed endless), but, of course, because of the interrelationships of all the ecosystems in the biosphere, there is no such 'free lunch'. The linear, one-way consumption of resources in the human-made environment has damaged and fractured many ecosystems, causing effects such as the exhaustion of soils, drawing down of fossil-fuel resources and extermination of species.

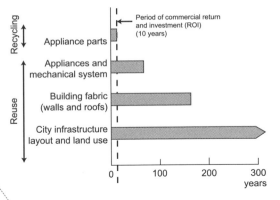

- Designing for continuous reuse and recycling 'to close the loop' as ecomimicry

Design the built system's use of materials to minimise waste based on analogy with the recycling properties of the ecosystem

Design the built system's use of materials to minimise waste based on analogy with the recycling properties of the ecosystem

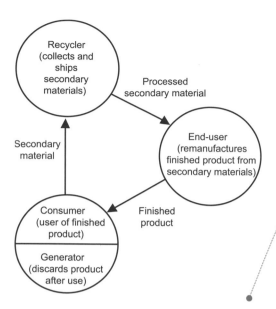

Definition of key recycling entities

Recycler (collects and ships secondary materials)

Processed secondary material

End-user (remanufactures finished product from secondary materials)

Secondary material

Consumer (user of finished product)

Finished product

Generator (discards product after use)

- The role of the decomposer strata in the existent urban ecosystem has also been drastically curtailed. This role is not integrated with the ecosystem and is wholly inadequate. Thus, one ecosystem component can be overwhelmed by the hypertrophy of another or by disruption. In the natural ecosystem, decomposition is carried out by a complex variety of organisms (including fungi and bacteria), all of which act as decomposers. But these decomposers actually occupy various trophic levels, and each breaks down dead matter on all the levels at and below it. Without decomposers, the outflow from the system (loss of material that should have been recycled through decomposition) becomes greater, leading to the production of 'wasted' resources trapped in dead animals and plants, and with no decomposers to break them down and return the much needed and sometimes rare materials to the system. In existing cities, materials that should have been cycled within the ecosystem or between systems are simply dumped.

- The rapidity of human consumption and the speed of natural regeneration are vastly divergent (imagine, for example, human beings waiting for more fossil fuels to be produced). A key element in ecodesign is not to make the built environment totally dependent on the natural one for the recycling of its outputs, for it is not capable of doing so. It is possible, however, to accelerate natural regeneration rates by human action, and this clearly needs to be done – if it can be accomplished without further environmental harm. One action that the ecological designer can take is to supply an adequate decomposer layer to his or her built environment. This amounts to imitating in a more faithful way the cyclical pattern of the ecosystem in nature, divergence from which has caused many environmental and human problems. Decomposition, production and consumption have to be commensurate. The human-made environment must shoulder some of the responsibility for recovery and not just depend on nature to assimilate and recycle its outputs, for that capacity has obviously been exceeded.

- Stage by stage the life cycle of our built systems should be examined using the interactions-framework (in A5) to check the impacts on the ecosystems of each activity taken at that stage. In the design of the relationship between the built structures and their environments, we can identify three basic strategies: the designer can attempt to control the ecosystem processes of the environment in relation to the building; or succumb to them; or seek to cooperate with them. In the last case, the constraints, restraints and inherent opportunities of the ecosystems of the locality and the hinterland to the urban complex have to be examined closely by the designer in the initial stages, following which all design efforts have to be based on an understanding of the ecosystem and directed towards finding compatible combinations and interactions between the natural and built environments.

- In most urban and city-centre sites, the ecosystem will already have been significantly devastated and nothing of the site's original ecosystem (its abiotic and biotic components) will remain, except perhaps the topsoil (and then only if there was no basement on the site), its ground-water conditions, its bedrock and the surrounding air, for example, a zeroculture site. In such cases, the environmental context for building becomes the city block, as well as the entire city and its hinterland. A major exception is in the developing world, where large cities are often laid out on greenfield sites with intact ecosystems.

- The environmental factors for ecological design are influenced by the built form and in turn influence the operation of the built form. In the ecological approach, the designer must see the environment in which the designed system is to be located as more than just a spatial zone with physical, climatic and aesthetic features. It exists as part of an ecosystem whose abiotic and biotic components and processes must be taken into account in the design. The layout and location of the built system also depend upon these environmental factors. In addition to these considerations, attitudes to the environment as an infinite source of resources and sink for waste have to be changed; we must acknowledge nature's limitations, particularly in terms of its regenerative capacities.

- The external dependencies of our designed system (ie its environmental dependencies, or L22 in A5) consist of the totality of the ecosystems in the biosphere and the earth's resources. All built structures and infrastructures spatially displace natural ecosystems by their presence and deplete the earth's energy and material resources by their creation, operation and final disposal. The use of terrestrial resources for the building further involves extensive modifications to the ecosystems at the points where those resources are extracted from the earth or made available. Thus, the designer is responsible for thinking about where the materials for the building are to come from.

- The interactions framework reminds the designer to account for the activities and processes inside and outside of the built structures and the interactions between the two. Here we need to stress the importance for the designer of mastering these impacts; the green approach to design takes into account the effects that all our built and manufactured projects and products have on the earth. Beyond the brute fact of spatial displacement – something is there that was not there before – there are more subtle and far-reaching effects. The resources and energy that go into most urban buildings and structures change the ecosystem's inventory of resources, energy and materials; during the structure's use, its existence and operation may facilitate or cause other human actions (most prominently further development). Hence, a design once executed can in a sense generate other structures, greater population, more resource use and other unintended or unforeseen developments.

- Nowhere has humankind altered the environment more than in cities, but their impact reaches far beyond their boundaries. The growth of cities was a crucial source of environmental

Design the built system's use of materials to minimise waste based on analogy with the recycling properties of the ecosystem

Design the built system's use of materials to minimise waste based on analogy with the recycling properties of the ecosystem

292

change. Their impacts extended to hinterlands, to downwind and downstream communities and, in some respects, to the whole globe. They absorbed ever larger quantities of water, energy and materials from near and far. In exchange, cities pumped out goods and services – as well as pollutants, refuse and solid wastes. Urban metabolism generated pollution effects and land-use effects. Only a few societies managed to accumulate capital for investment in pollution abatement at rates faster than pollution itself intensified (eg post Second World War Japan had enough money and ingenuity to find good uses for refuse, converting some into construction materials). And even in those that did, ruling elites usually found it easier to insulate themselves from pollution rather than to reduce it. So cities remained concentrated nodes of pollution far larger yet far less lethal than before, thanks to vaccination, antibiotics and other public-health measures.

Cities cover an estimated 1 to 2 per cent of the earth's land surfaces, their spatial growth reflecting only a small fraction of their environmental impact. The space needed to support a city, and to absorb its wastes, is its ecological footprint. Cities take in water, food, oxygen and other resources and discard sewage, refuse, carbon dioxide and other unwanted matter. Fast-growing cities (rather like growing and developing organisms) have higher metabolisms than those that have stopped growing. For example, seven-eighths of Hong Kong's food comes from outside the mainland. A quarter of its freshwater is piped in from China, which in exchange takes 40 tons of human excreta per day (for fertiliser). Assuring other cities an adequate water supply requires stronger measures, because of the physical character of modern cities. Roofs and roads prevent water from percolating down into the earth and increase surface runoff. Chicago in 1990 had only 45 per cent of its surface pervious to water. It was already subsiding in 1900, as its aquifer drained, and between 1940 and 1985 the city dropped up to 7 centimetres in elevation, causing damage to building foundations and its sewerage system.

- A definition of the ecological footprint is the amount of productive land and shallow sea appropriated nationally by each person around the world for food, water, housing, energy, transportation, commerce and waste absorption. The average amount is about 1 hectare (2.5 acres) per person in developing nations, but about 9.6 hectares (24 acres) in the USA. The average footprint for the total human population is 2.1 hectares (5.2 acres). However, for every person in the world to reach the present US levels of consumption with existing technology would require four more planet earths.

The ecological footprint of each modern city dweller's consumption has been estimated at 12 acres per person.

- Growing cities also need building materials such as timber, cement, brick, food and fuel. Prior to the advent of the railway, all these materials for building were transported by ship or road.

Railways and lorry transport meant that such materials could be sourced from much further afield, dispersing the environmental effects across broader hinterlands, thus enlarging the ecological footprint of cities.

- The higher the density and diversity of a city, the less dependent it is on motorised transport, the less resources it requires, and the less is the impact that it has on nature. As the city is designed to conserve energy and material, while turning wastes into resources (such as when it is building more soils than it is consuming, helping species to survive and actually giving back acreage to nature and creating new resources for its healthy evolution), the negative ecological footprint is turned on its head and the situation changes fundamentally.

- As with cities, so with buildings. In ecodesign, it is imperative to keep a building's ecological footprint within manageable levels. One way of doing this is to increase the ecological productivity of the site, for example through permaculture or by enhancing ecological biodiversity, thus increasing the building's ability to absorb and recycle the waste products from within its site and reducing the energy expended to reach the site (ie fuel used in transportation).

- In the future, to aid the purchaser in their selection, more and more products will be labelled 'climate neutral; meaning that the product has no net greenhouse gas emissions. For example, if a commercial company wants to label its product as climate neutral, it first has to do everything that it can to reduce the carbon dioxide emissions that occur during the manufacturing, transportation and retailing of the product.

Summary

Ecomimicry informs us that materials in ecosystems in the biosphere are recycled and if our built environment is to reverse its current state as a system of throughput, then, in a similar way, at the outset the designer must regard all designed systems as potential wastes, the eventual destinations of which (at the end of their useful lives or their after-lives) must be considered in terms of their continuous reuse, recycling and remanufacture, and their eventual benign reintegration back into the natural environment. The strategy is to design to facilitate continuous reuse and recycling of materials at each level within the built environment. Achieving this will diminish the eventual extent of the problem of the environmental sink for the designed system and its constituents in the biointegration (see A4) of all the outputs from our built environment with the natural environment. Of course, the designer will need simultaneously to ensure that the processes of reuse and recycling do not in themselves involve high consumption of non-renewable sources of energy, or require the intensive use of technology and equipment and so create further environmental problems or disruption.

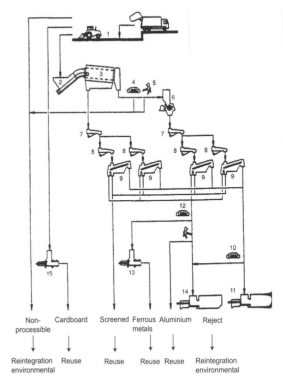

Non-processible — Cardboard — Screened — Ferrous metals — Aluminium — Reject

Reintegration environmental — Reuse — Reuse — Reuse — Reuse — Reintegration environmental

1. Tipping floor
2. Feeder
3. Rotary screen
4. Magnet
5. Visual control
6. Shredder
7. Flow divider
8. Flow spreader
9. Ballistic classifier
10. Magnet
11. Static packer
12. Magnet
13. Bailer
14. Static compacter
15. Bailer

Diagram of a mechanical recovery system (usually energy intensive)

B22

Chapter C • Chapter B • Chapter A •

Design the built system's use of materials to minimise waste based on analogy with the recycling properties of the ecosystem

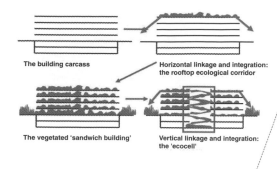

The building carcass

Horizontal linkage and integration:
the rooftop ecological corridor

The vegetated 'sandwich building'

Vertical linkage and integration:
the 'ecocell'

Designing for horizontal and vertical integration ●

B23 Design for vertical integration: designing for multilateral integration of the designed system with the ecosystems

In addition to the efforts in ecodesign to integrate our built environment with the natural environment horizontally (in B8), the designer must ensure that the designed system also integrates vertically with the ecosystems, both physically and systemically.

While it is often easier to physically integrate the designed system horizontally with the ecosystem of the locality, we will find that some built systems are so intensive in mass and have such an extensive footprint in their built configuration that attention needs to be paid to increasing their level of vertical integration. One approach to achieving this is by the creation of large vertical slots and incisions in the built form that bring biomass, vegetation, daylight, rainwater and natural ventilation into its inner depths.

These slots and incisions become ecocells – essentially a cellular void that is inserted at regular intervals into the built form and cuts across all its floors. These cellular voids have a spiralling ramp and bring daylight into the inner parts of the built form, provide opportunities for rainwater harvesting (for reuse and recycling), enable linked vegetation to enter the inner parts of the built form, provide opportunities for natural ventilation and recesses for the provision of recycling systems within the built form. A series of ecocells can be located within the built form so that it cuts through all the floors from the uppermost roof terrace, which can be landscaped, down to the car park.

As with the analogy of our built environment to a prosthetic limb (in C3), a higher level of integration can be achieved where our artificial system integrates not just physically but systemically with its host organism. In this regard, our built environment as the artificial system must similarly integrate physically and systemically with the processes of its own host organism, the ecosystems in the biosphere.

Systemic integration occurs when the artificial system integrates with its host organism to function holistically as part of the host system's systemic processes. For example the design marries the integration of operational functions with the ecosystem functions to enable them to act as a whole in recycling of nutrients, accessing energy pathways and flows, etc. Systemic integration works with living processes that respect the needs of all species while meeting those of humankind and engaging in processes that regenerate rather than deplete. It should create positive feedback loops and states of symbiosis between different functional elements.

Natural daylight

Rainwater collection and recycling

Continuous vegetation linkages

Natural ventilation

Sewage recycling tanks

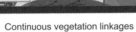

The ecocell as an armature for vertical integration

Material	By mass	By weight	By volume	By density
Steel and iron	1.57	2.73	0.05	1090
Copper	0.05	0.02	neg.	na
Lead	0.06	0.06	neg.	na
Aluminium	0.01	neg.	na	na
Concrete	63.33	53.75	0.09	1190
Brick and clay	15.01			
Brick	na	21.21	0.35	1210
Wood	19.64	22.01	1.10	400
Glass	0.33	0.22	neg.	na
Plastic	< 0.01	neg.	na	na
Total	100.00	100.00	2.4	830

Typical waste from building construction

These interactions begin with the choice of materials for the structure and the energy source to power the built system. The functioning of the building depends on a set of internal processes, the building's 'metabolism', which interact with the environment (into which, of course, their wastes and exhausts are discharged). The architect has to be aware of these processes and their effects, as well as the ecosystem's response to them. The designer might regard the creation of a built structure (eg a building) as a form of energy and materials management or as prudent resource management. Generally, sustainable development involves a partnership between ourselves and the physical conditions of the planet that sustains us; we are in an inclusive relationship with the biological and physiological landscape. This relationship has been weakened by industrialisation and urbanisation to the point where it has become necessary to design benign qualities into the environment positively. By analogy, the built environment's enclosures (buildings, etc) and its infrastructures (roads, drains, sewerage, water supply routes, etc) must physically and ecomechanically integrate with the ecosystems of the locality.

Summary

The designer must ensure that the designed system's systemic integration with the ecosystem is not just horizontal across the built form or across the project site (ie creating new ecological corridors or enhancing existent ones) but also vertical within the built form itself. In previous sections discussion of most of the design interfaces between the designed system and the natural environment has focused primarily on horizontal integration whereas in this section the design emphasis is on ensuring that there is adequate vertical integration within the built form by inserting vertical integration devices and systems to achieve a higher level of integration of the designed system with the natural environment.

Vertical integration from basement to roof
(AOC, Kuwait, 2005)

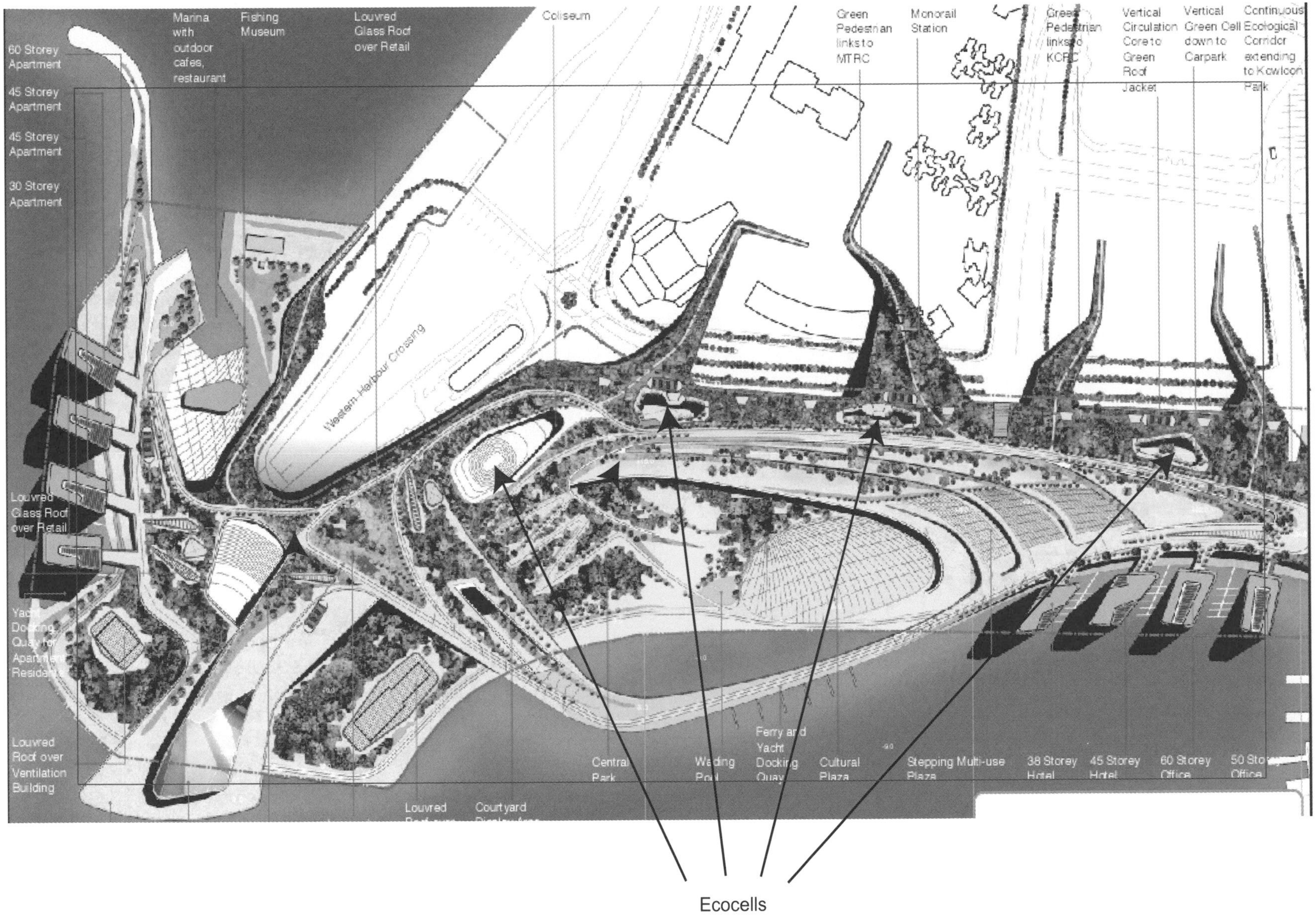

60 Storey
Apartment

45 Storey
Apartment

45 Storey
Apartment

30 Storey
Apartment

Louvred
Glass Roof
over Retail

Yacht
Docking
Quay for
Apartment
Residents

Louvred
Roof over
Ventilation
Building

Marina
with
outdoor
cafes,
restaurant

Fishing
Museum

Louvred
Glass Roof
over Retail

Coliseum

Green
Pedestrian
links to
MTRC

Monorail
Station

Green
Pedestrian
links to
KCRC

Vertical
Circulation
Core to
Green
Roof
Jacket

Vertical
Green Cell
down to
Carpark

Continuous
Ecological
Corridor
extending
to Kowloon
Park

Western Harbour Crossing

Louvred
Roof over
Display Area

Courtyard
Display Area

Central
Park

Wading
Pool

Ferry and
Yacht
Docking
Quay

Cultural
Plaza

Stepping Multi-use
Plaza

38 Storey
Hotel

45 Storey
Hotel

60 Storey
Office

50 Storey
Office

Ecocells

Horizontal and vertical integration using sandwich landscape layers and ecocells
(Kowloon Waterfront, Hong Kong, 2000)

B24 Design to reduce light and noise pollution of the ecosystems

Ecodesign must reduce and eliminate the light and noise pollution from the built environment into the surrounding natural environment as such pollution can affect the health of ecosystems, their fauna, flora and habitats.

Light pollution

Light pollution is caused by the upward and outward distribution of light either directly from artificial lighting fixtures or from reflection off the ground or other surfaces of the built environment. The effects are light glare, light trespass, sky glow and wasted energy.

Glare is direct light shining from an artificial lighting fixture (luminaire) that makes it difficult to see or causes discomfort. Light trespass is intrusive light that reaches into neighbouring properties and becomes objectionable. Sky glow refers to the composite illumination coming from an intensive urban environment (such as towns, cities and other developed areas) as a yellowish glow in the sky when viewed from a relatively dark area beyond that built environment.

In ecodesign consideration of light pollution is important because light pollution can affect natural systems, and is itself a symptom of waste from the human-made built environment. It is a drain on resources and is associated with the negative effects of climate change from the burning of fossil fuels.

The problem was first brought to general attention by astronomers who were increasingly unable to view the night sky from their research observatories. In fact, many of the observatories built during the 20th century are becoming severely compromised. Research indicates that in an unpolluted sky about 2500 individual stars should be visible to the human eye, but in a typical suburb with moderate illumination only 200 to 300 stars are visible. In cities, only a few dozen are visible.

Light pollution sources can affect the ecology of ecosystems more than 100 miles away. The major sources of light pollution are increasing urban development and growing populations in communities near parkland and national parks. Under ideal conditions, it might be possible to view a night sky with more than 15,000 visible stars plus the Milky Way. In the USA, only about 10 per cent of the population experiences these conditions regularly.

Light pollution is increasingly becoming a problem. Almost 50 per cent of artificial light is wasted (misses its intended target). Tall buildings in particular contribute significantly to light pollution. Other sources of light pollution include streetlights that fail to deliver all of their light downward, outdoor security lights around buildings, commercial signages and billboard illumination directed upward, landscape illumination directed upward or outward and light escaping from buildings at night. It is estimated that a third of outdoor artificial lighting escapes into the night sky. There is also the issue of wasted energy from inefficient lighting systems. Excessive lighting also means that utility companies are consuming more energy and emitting more pollution. In the USA, an estimated 25 KWh of wasted electricity produces nearly 19 million metric tons of CO_2 per year.

Light-pollution impacts on urban ecology include the disruption of the biological cycles of plants and animals. It poses a particular threat to migratory wildlife, especially birds, which are confused by lights. Some migratory birds may mistake building lights for the constellations that they normally use as aids to navigation. Among migrating songbirds, warblers are thought to be most affected, probably due to their pattern of migrating at night at low altitude. In addition there are fatal bird collisions leading to species being killed or injured by flying into buildings at night. Such birds were attracted to floodlights; once these were replaced by strobe lights, the numbers of birds killed fell to a few a year. That light pollution affects birds is evidenced by the fact that birds have been observed to follow the rotation of lighthouse beams. For example, blackbirds in London (UK) have been heard to sing at night because the artificial light and heat of the night mimics natural daylight.

The most extensive research on the impacts of light pollution on wildlife has been carried out on nesting sea turtle species. Light affects turtles who come up to the beach to nest. When bright artificial light is present, females may avoid coming ashore altogether or they may become disoriented, wandering on to roads, etc. Sea turtle hatchlings are also affected by light. They invariably hatch at night and instinctively head towards light, which they take to be the direction of the sea because the sea's surface is brighter (from the moon's reflection, or from bioluminescence) than the land. Thus, light pollution can cause the hatchling to head in the wrong direction.

Insect species are also affected by light pollution, especially species of moths, some populations of which seem more affected than others, signalling perhaps that some species have already evolved to adapt to bright lights.

As for plants, incandescent lamps for lighting the landscape have the potential to actively regulate the growth of most plant species and can prolong growth through the later summer months and autumn, thereby maximising the chance of plant injury from autumn frosts. However, certain frequencies and intensities of light are known to regulate the development and flowering of plants (photoperiod response), and it is thought that extending the day length will prevent or delay their response to shortening days where plants should become dormant and shed their leaves. Ecological studies have shown that sycamore species do not shed their leaves properly when they are too close to streetlights.

Humans are also affected by light pollution, they have evolved to need a certain amount of exposure to darkness, a light–dark rhythm. When enveloped in darkness human bodies produce melatonin, an important hormone that regulates the nightly cycle of rest and repair. Studies show that even at low light levels, night-time melatonin secretions are inhibited.

Studies have shown that about 3 foot-candles (fc) of light for outdoor lighting is a reasonable amount for security purposes. However, it is common to see light levels that are three to ten times higher, at 100 fc or more. Researchers have shown that just as important as illuminance level is the uniformity of light, the colour of light and coverage. Coverage influences whether there will be shadows, which is a security issue. In some cases, it has been shown that more light does not mean greater security. Glaring bright security light from dusk to dawn creates a blinding illusion of safety, but human threats may still exist.

Guidelines for reducing light pollution

For the designer, reducing light pollution is easy, and effects and impacts can be reversed. Some considerations to bear in mind in order to minimise light pollution when designing outdoor artificial lighting are:

• Design roadway lighting to minimise misdirected and upward light. Glare is particularly dangerous for drivers. It is usually present within a driver's field of vision when non-cutoff fixtures are used. Utilising full cutoff light fixtures significantly reduces glare and the 'veiling luminance' effect, improving visibility.

• Use materials and devices, such as reflectors, to be elevated and considered in lieu of additional lighting.

• Design so that architectural signages and commercial billboard lighting minimise light that does not illuminate the target area to keep spill light to a minimum. Certain types of advertising lights, such as searchlights and laser lights, need to be banned.

• Minimise or eliminate lighting of building exteriors during those hours when it is not needed. Automated time-switch lighting controls should be used.

• Limit the height of luminaires relative to the property boundary, thus preventing light trespass on to adjoining properties.

• Ensure floodlight-type light fixtures do not contribute heavily to light pollution (as they do if they are misaligned or used without visors). Wall-pack floodlights cannot be adjusted for directional control and are almost never a preferred choice for any outdoor lighting use. When improperly installed on buildings or poles, floodlights may even send more light upwards and sideways than within the intended target areas.

Within an office fit-out, the following strategies for ensuring energy efficiency of lighting can be followed:

- Replace base building fluorescent lights with energy-conserving lights (eg T8 fluorescent lights with 28 watt T5 lamps).

- Use light sensors on perimeter lights that automatically switch off when lighting levels are sufficient from natural daylight sources.

- Use manual switching for meeting and store rooms.

- Use controlled lighting in bathrooms.

- Programme after-hours switching mechanisms.

- Use dimming controls on accent lighting.

Large buildings contribute to light pollution, which affects the surrounding ecology and environment. A better understanding of these problems enables us to work towards ensuring ecological and environmental protection.

- Light pollution is an important issue to manage for skyscrapers in particular as it impacts on many animals.

- The death toll of birds caused by confusion from light pollution in skyscrapers is a major issue.

- Animals may change their behaviour and plants their growth patterns due to light pollution.

Sky glow

It is the excessively bright and poorly directed outdoor night lighting that causes light pollution, especially in intensive environments (such as large cities like New York). These are often termed 24-hour cities, because there is just as much activity at night as during the day. Often cities are as brightly lit during the evening as they are during the day, illuminated by streetlights, buildings and advertisements. Light pollution occurs when too much artificial illumination and unmanaged glare, emitted from improperly aimed and unshielded light fixtures, enters the night sky and reflects off airborne water droplets and dust particles causing a condition known as sky glow. Excessive lighting means that we are also forcing our utility companies to consume more energy and therefore emit more toxins into the environment.

As stated above, light pollution is a threat to wildlife, especially species that migrate. Migratory birds are confused by lights on skyscrapers and some migratory birds mistake building lights for the constellations that they normally use to navigate by. They spiral around the buildings and either collide with them or succumb to exhaustion and plummet to the ground suffering injuries or death. Half the number of 'migratory' birds that migrated in 1860 actually migrate now. This is partially a result of the unnatural thermodynamics in cities. Each year about 100 million birds across the USA are killed in crashes into windows or die from exhaustion after becoming mesmerised by lighted buildings.

Most bird collisions happen at relatively low altitudes in the early morning. The birds become disoriented by the building lights at night, particularly when it is overcast and there is a strong 'sky glow' effect, and then head for whatever foliage they can find in which to spend the rest of the night.

Other flying species are also killed in collisions with buildings, including bats (some five or six species), praying mantises and cicadas.

However, some animals have adapted to take advantage of light pollution; for instance, some bats use it to hunt the insects that are attracted to the light.

Light pollution also affects marine and aquatic species. For example, research indicates that cities near the coast are a threat to sea turtle hatchlings. Beaches along the USA's Atlantic coast are breeding grounds for Western Atlantic loggerhead, leatherback and green turtles. Artificial lights interfere with the turtles' natural instinct to move towards the brightest light source on the horizon. Hatchlings mistake urban lights for the reflection of moonlight, starlight and bioluminescence on the ocean. Confused by the light source, instead of heading for the sea after hatching, the turtles proceed inland where they are often killed by automobiles or predators.

Photoperiod response

Plants can also be affected by light pollution, though little research has been done on this issue. It is well known that certain frequencies and intensities of light regulate the development and flowering of plants – a process referred to as photoperiod response. Many trees and shrubs go dormant and lose their leaves in response to shortening days. Incandescent lamps for lighting the landscape have the potential actively to regulate the growth of most plant species and can prolong growth through the later summer and autumn, thereby increasing the chance of damage to plants from autumn frosts.

While not all plants respond to photoperiod, those that do can be affected by very low light intensities, well within the range of outdoor lighting. An experiment intended to grow wheat and potatoes together as potential food sources for a space station found that the long day length required for optimal wheat production blocked tuber formation in potatoes. Indeed, subsequent experiments found that irradiance levels as low as 3 foot-candles (fc) block tuber formation. Whether extended 'day length' from light pollution in urban and suburban areas might be killing off trees, shrubs and certain flowering plants by delaying dormancy is not known, but it is certainly a real possibility that warrants further investigation.

Although the effects of light pollution on plants have not yet been fully identified, it is still important to protect and maintain the trees that still grow in cities. Trees moderate climate, conserve energy and water, improve air quality, control rainfall runoff and flooding, lower noise levels, harbour wildlife, enhance the visual appeal of a city and reduce summertime temperatures by reducing the heat-island effect. Trees aid storm-water management, air quality improvement and energy conservation.

There is growing awareness of the problem of light pollution. In several cities, building owners and/or managers are asking their commercial tenants to switch off building lighting at night in an effort to help birds steer clear of the buildings. In several major cities, many skyscrapers have been dimming, or are turning off, their lights at night in order to mitigate the danger to birds. In some urban areas, public programmes have encouraged buildings to turn off outdoor lights and close window shades and curtains to reduce light pollution. In some cases municipalities have enacted legislation to control lighting.

Alternatives should be considered to reduce effects of existing light sources. One way would be to use improved shielded luminaries to direct light on to the pedestrians and the vehicular traffic and away from plants.

Solving light-pollution problems does not have to happen at the regional level; home users can replace old light bulbs with newer, more efficient, better designed ones. Offices and companies can retrofit inefficient mercury lighting in their buildings with low-sodium lighting that is designed to keep light from 'trespassing' into unwanted areas. Good lighting design reduces energy waste, curbs the impact on wildlife and improves night views of the sky.

Finally, tall structures such as skyscrapers also affect the migration of butterflies and moths, primarily due to their effects on air currents.

Noise pollution

Buildings contribute to air, noise and light pollution, which affect human health as well as impacting on the species in the ecosystems. A better understanding of these problems enables designers to work towards reducing their impact and improving the quality of life and effects on ecosystems.

Decibels (dB)*	Source of sound
0	Threshold of human hearing
10	Normal breathing
20	Rustling leaves, quiet room
30	Soft whisper, quiet library
40	Humming refrigerator
50	Average home or office
60	Normal conversation
70	Vacuum cleaner, busy street
80	Hair dryer
90	Threshold of hearing damage; Lawn mower, shop tools, city traffic
100	Tractor, farm equipment, power saw, Leaf blower, garbage truck, subway Train, newspaper press
110	Automobile horn, chain saw, Jet takeoff at distance of 2000 feet (610 m)
120	Threshold of pain; live rock concert, snowmobile siren
130	Motorcycle, firecrackers
140	Gunshot, siren at 100 feet (30 m)
160	Jet engine close up

* Data approximate. For example, different behaviours and equipment models have different dB levels. Typical conversation ranges from 50 to 70 dB, food blenders generally range from 85 to 90 dB, leaf blowers generally range from 95 to 155 dB, and so on.

Intensity of common sound sources

Examples of noise pollution generators are: busy airports, heavily travelled highways and city streets, rock concerts, chain saws, jackhammers, snowmobiles, leaf blowers and vacuum cleaners. The sounds emanating from these and thousands of other human products and pastimes are a form of pollution that is both a nuisance and a health hazard.

In many cases, hearing loss can be at least partially attributed to the noisy environment in which we live. In the USA, more than 20 million people are regularly exposed to industrial or recreational noise that could result in hearing loss. For instance, tests of 70 discotheque disc jockeys in their twenties found that one-third had significant hearing loss. Tests of 40 New York City firemen who had been exposed to siren noise for ten years or more found that 75 per cent had significant hearing loss.

Noise has also been linked to a variety of physical and psychological problems. Levels of 45 dB or more prevent an average person from falling asleep at night. Studies also show that noise affects humans and causes high blood pressure, irritability, indigestion and peptic ulcers, and may contribute to heart disease and mental illness.

Fauna have also been shown to suffer from exposure to loud noise. Researchers have raised the blood pressure of rhesus monkeys by exposing them to elevated noise levels. Noise from supertankers and military sonar equipment interferes with the communications systems of sea life, forcing changes in migration routes. Research shows that elk and wolves exposed to snowmobiles produce higher levels of glucocorticoids, hormones released when the animals are tested.

Sound intensity is measured in units called decibels (dB). The decibel scale is logarithmic: every increase of 10 decibels means a tenfold increase in sound intensity. Thus, 50 dB is ten times as intense as 40 dB and sounds twice as loud; 60 dB is 100 times as intense as 40 dB and sounds four times as loud.

Distance is a factor in determining effective decibel levels: the closer you are to a sound, the higher the decibel level reaching your ears. Close up, the sound of a jet aeroplane during takeoff is about 160 dB, but at a distance of 2000 feet (610 metres), it is about 110 dB – about the same as an automobile horn close up.

A factor in hearing loss is the length of exposure to loud sounds. Human hearing can be damaged by listening to 85 to 90 dB for more than eight hours a day, 100 dB for more than two hours, or 110 dB for more than 30 minutes. Any exposure to sounds of 130 dB or more results in permanent hearing loss.

Marine noise pollution

Research shows that the artificial noise created by ships and other human sources could be interfering with the reproduction and population recovery of certain marine life (eg whales). The very-low-frequency courtship songs of fin whales and blue whales often travel many hundreds, if not thousands, of miles under water. But so can very-low-frequency, human-made noises that have increased dramatically in the last 100 years of motorised shipping.

The song findings for fin whales (*Balaenoptera physalus*) also apply to the closely related blue whales (*Sibbaldus musculus*) and could hold true for some other species of baleen whales. The researchers concluded their report by noting: 'to the extent that growth of *Balaenoptera* populations is limited by the encounter rate of receptive females with singing males, the recovery of fin and blue whale populations from past exploitation could well be impeded by confusion resulting from misattribution of low-frequency sounds generated by human activity'.

Noise can be a source of stress for humans and cities can be noisy. Aggravation may increase with the level of noise but the level of annoyance is influenced by beliefs and judgements. Studies on traffic noise show that higher levels of aggravation are associated with judging the road as dangerous, having problems with neighbours and where land is used both for commercial and residential purposes. One interesting aspect of research on the effect of traffic noise is that younger humans are more affected by a given level of noise. This appears to be due to the fact that they hear better than people who are older. Not all noise is annoying and this depends on the context. Techniques have been developed for dealing with the noise of the city, such as habituation to noise.

In urban environments the main source of sound pollution is traffic noise, generated from the horns and exhaust systems of cars, smaller lorries, buses, rickshaws and motorcycles. This type of noise is augmented by faulty engines and defective silencers, narrow streets and tall buildings, which produce a 'canyon' in which traffic noise reverberates. With people staying up later, more demands are made on the city's transportation infrastructure at the expense of noise quality.

Road parameters also influence the level of traffic noise. For example, the propagation of traffic noise is significantly reduced in tunnels as opposed to open roads. Other factors in this category include road surface (eg stone is particularly noisy), gradient (steeper hills cause vehicles to work harder and thus emit more noise) and width (narrow streets lined closely with buildings trap noise and increase its effects).

The noise on city streets can reach dangerous decibel levels and can be significant enough to cause hearing loss. Some sounds found on a city street are sufficient to cause permanent damage. Experts agree that continued exposure to noise above 90 dB over time will cause hearing loss. To ascertain whether a sound is loud enough to damage your ears, it is important to know both the level of loudness (measured in decibels, dB) and the length of exposure to the sound. In general, the louder the noise, the less time required before hearing loss will occur. Research indicates that the maximum exposure time at 85 dB is eight hours. At 110 dB, the maximum safe exposure time is 1 minute and 29 seconds.

As a guide to the ecological designer, below are listed the sound levels for specific city sounds in our built environment in dB:

- 60   normal conversation

- 70   main road traffic

- 85   heavy traffic, noisy restaurant

- 90   truck, shouted conversation

- 90–115   subway/underground

- 95–110   motorcycle

- 110   baby crying

- 110   car horn

- 120   pneumatic drills, heavy machine

- 120   ambulance siren

- 130   jackhammer, power drill

- 143   bicycle horn

Summary

In designing the built form structures, facilities and infrastructure, the designer must consider the reduction and elimination by design of light and sound pollution. While light pollution is often regarded as a lesser form of pollution, light and sound pollution from the built environment affect not just humans, but also the fauna, flora and ecology of the locality.

B25 Designing the built environment as the transient management of materials and energy input flows: assessing inputs and outputs through the designed system and their consequences

Just as ecologists analyse the flows of energy and materials in ecosystems, so it is useful for the ecological designer to regard ecodesign as a form of management of energy and materials flow in a transient built form during its period of human use, which at the end of its useful life eventually flows back into the natural environment. This flow in the designed system can in principle be tracked from its source in the biosphere through its extraction, processing and manufacture to its position in the life cycle of the built structure and its eventual biointegration back into the natural environment. Generally, flows are generated not only between points of departure and arrival (or of entry and exit), but also between intermediate points.

The construction of a designed system requires significantly large inputs of energy and materials from the environment. Theoretically, these constitute the external-to-internal interdependencies of the built environment (ie L21 in the Partitioned Matrix) and include the inputs needed for its maintenance and for the disposal of its outputs. These include not only the energy and materials used to synthesise its physical substance and form but also those that are used to maintain it in all the phases of its entire life cycle. During its operation, outputs are also emitted and other impacts are inflicted upon the ecosystems. If we build with salvaged materials, we conserve more than half of the energy investment. In the ecological approach, the designer must map and quantify all external-to-internal exchanges and any resulting environmental impacts. From a holistic point of view, the use of inputs into the built environment is related to the discharge of outputs, the set of operations in the built environment, and the limitations of the earth's ecosystems and resources.

Current techniques include materials flow analysis (MFA) which calculates the transfer of natural and manufactured materials (resources and capital) out of a built system (eg building, region, city) in relation to those flowing in, as in inputs/outputs. It also examines the stocks, flows and transformation of energy and materials within the systems.

The interdependencies between the built and natural environment include the obvious spatial displacement of portions of the ecosystems caused by building; the amount of energy and output of matter; and the consequences of human activity within the built environment. In the broadest sense, the ecological consequences of the built environment must be considered to be not only those immediately related to the construction of buildings and other artefacts, but must also be understood to include all of the environmental interactions that derive from the use of built artefacts, their later disposal when no longer useful and their eventual recovery.

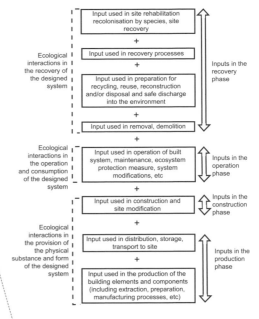

● The total inputs in the life cycle of a designed system

	Residential (%)	Commercial (%)
Paper	20–40	25–50
Corrugated cardboard	8–12	20–30
Plastics	6–8	10–15
Metals	4–8	2–5
Other wastes	40–50	18–24

● Outputs: Residential versus commercial waste

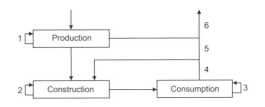

1. Recovery within production processes of the building material
2. Recovery of construction residuals from construction processes
3. Recovery from operations of the built system
4. Recovery of material from operation into construction processes
5. Recovery of material from operation into production processes
6. Redirected use of material elsewhere

● Strategy for the reuse and recycling of building materials

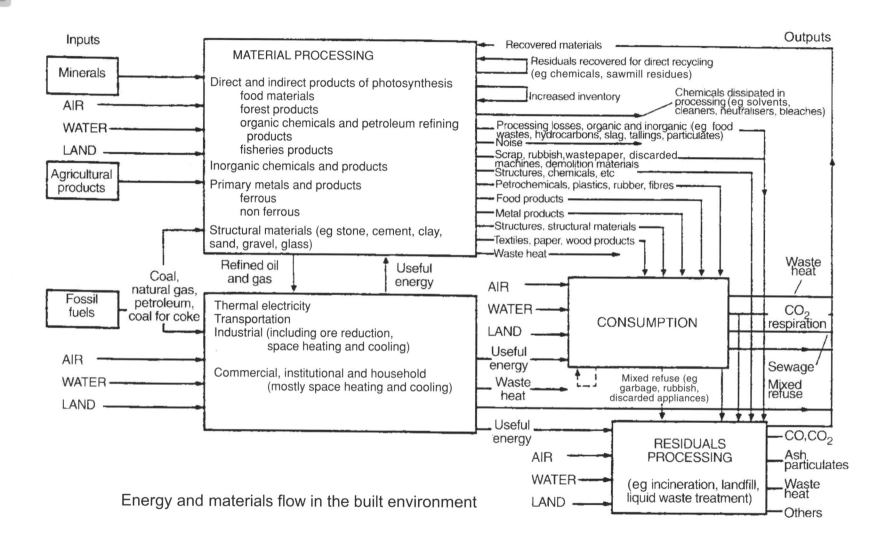

Energy and materials flow in the built environment

In order to conceptualise the consequences of 'energy and materials management', the process can be considered in terms of specific 'patterns' of energy use and the flow of materials from their origin in the environment, through their incorporation into buildings and lastly to their eventual end in environmental sinks. By considering the process thus, we are able to analyse all constructed objects in terms of the patterns of use that they represent. We can anticipate in design the extent of the demands and impacts that each individual pattern will exert on the earth's ecosystems and we can predict its likely future use of resources. The actions and activities that take place within a designed system over the course of its life cycle will determine the flow of inputs into the built environment and the expulsion of outputs into the environment beyond, and will have a specific impact on the earth's ecosystems as well as on its supply of resources. For example, about 50 per cent of all the energy consumption (ie inputs of L21 in A5) in a country (eg in the UK) and a similar proportion of carbon dioxide emissions (ie outputs) are associated with buildings. The majority (about 60 per cent) is used in residential stock, the remaining 40 per cent being divided between offices (7 per cent), warehouses (5 per cent), hospitals (4 per cent), retail (5 per cent), educational buildings (7 per cent), sports facilities (4 per cent), and hotels and other structures (8 per cent). These figures indicate that the major building type at which our energy conservation efforts should primarily be directed is the residential building followed by the office building. The strategies for the selection of materials for our green skyscraper or large building design are discussed below.

Once the schematic design for our building has been finalised, its physical components should be quantified and assessed for their anticipated impacts on the environment and to ascertain whether the design meets current standards for green design. In most conventional building situations, a set of 'Bills of Quantities' is usually prepared for the entire building (usually for bidding purposes). This quantification can easily be converted into weight equivalents (eg tonnage) of material, or into other volumetric quantifications, which can then be subsequently converted into energy-embodied equivalents and ecological-impact-embodied equivalents for comparative analytical purposes. Similarly, this process can be undertaken for the operational systems (M&E equipment) in the building.

The ecological approach considers synoptically the use of materials and energy by the built environment and its users, and the route that every material and component in the designed system takes must be managed and monitored not only in its economic context but in ecological terms throughout its physical life (from source until assimilation back into the ecosystems).

As described earlier, the design and creation of a building becomes a form of energy and materials management extended over the built system's entire life cycle. This is because

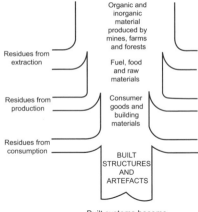

Residues: solids, particulates, gases, heat, liquids, etc

● The built environment as part of the
flow of enegy and materials

Inputs (tonnes per year)	kg per annum
Energy (fuel, oil, equivalent)	20,321,000,000
Oxygen	40,642,000,000
Water	1,018,082,000,000
Food	2,428,520
Timber	12,190,000
Paper	22,330,000
Plastics	21,330,000
Glass	365,770,000
Cement	1,970,000,000
Bricks	36,577,000,000
Metals	1,219,200,000
Outputs	
CO₂	60,960,000,000
SO₂	4,064,200,000
NOX	284,500,000
Sewage (sludge)	6,720,300,000
Industrial demolition waste	11,582,900,000
Household, civic and commercial wastes	3,962,500,000

Input-output flow of a city
(eg for London, 7 million population)

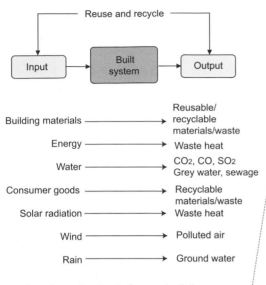

Inputs and outputs from a building as an artificial ecosystem

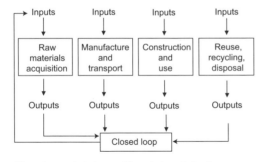

Life-cycles analysis to quantify and characterise the inputs and outputs of every stage in a product's life, to assess its overall environmental performance.

Typical material life cycle ●

all building activities involve the utilisation, redistribution and concentration of some component of the earth's energy and material resources, which are usually transported from distant locations into specific areas, a process that changes the ecology of that part of the biosphere as well as adding to the composition of the ecosystem. Therefore green design of skyscrapers and other intensive buildings involves the identification of the ways in which energy and materials are used in such buildings (structure, cladding systems, internal partitioning systems, fittings, equipment, etc). Furthermore, green design ideally anticipates their flows thoughout the life of the building up to the point of their recycling, reuse or reintegration into the natural environment (not forgetting the attendant impacts on the environment from their production in the period prior to construction).

Take, for example, the production of a bag of cement. First, land is lost for the extraction of clay and chalk; then large amounts of energy are used in the burning of materials to make that bag of cement (comparable to enough fossil-fuel energy to drive a domestic car for 30 kilometres). Further energy and pollution are created in transportation to the wholesaler then to the retailer, and later to the construction site. Yet more energy is expended (and carbon dioxide emitted) in concrete-making equipment on the building site and in the crane that hoists the cement up the building's frame. The complexities hidden within this deceptively simple example show the deeper level of consideration required of the designer who operates with ecological principles in mind. Similar chains of resource and energy use could be uncovered for every screw, nail and piece of wood or metal that goes into a built environment.

In effect, we can regard our built environment and cities as complex systems characterised by flows as continuous processes of change and development. There are two essential patterns of resource use: the linear and the cyclical. The linear pattern is favoured in the industrial world, where non-renewable resources flow once through the built environment where they are used then discarded. This is a transformative process by which resources are converted to wastes.

Ecological flow management
The key factors to carry out include:

• Ideally, in a cyclical pattern of resource use, a particular material or energy source would be extracted from the environment, used in a building, then transformed in an energy-efficient manner into a new resource. The process would then become a closed loop. A process that had formerly culminated in the production of a discarded material (waste output) would now end in the production of another resource (productive input). Make a more cyclical process out of one that already possesses cyclical characteristics to some degree.

A familiar cautionary note should be sounded: it will probably never be possible to achieve a hermetic cyclical pattern of resource use in the built environment. The recovery cycle is one stage where there will probably always be a quantity of resources lost. For instance, in the process of recycling scrap steel, approximately 10 per cent of the material is lost. Some materials cannot be put back into the system after initial use at all: inherent in the use of products like paints, solvents and cleaners is their dispersal in the environment. Other factors also contribute to the loss of material in the system, including friction and oxidation. Furthermore, thermal emission would represent a loss of energy even in an ideal system in which every element in the built environment was reused or recycled.

- Regard the built system as a mass of materials contained temporarily in the form of a 'building' for a brief period of use, after which its components will return to the continuous flow of use instead of regarding it, as is traditional, as a fixed and immutable quantity. Thereafter the components will return to the continuous flow and exchanges of energy and materials within the biosphere. This 'ashes to ashes' way of considering the built environment is analogous to the method used by ecologists to view the exchanges of energy and materials within an ecosystem.

- Focus on the flows of available energy or matter, particularly from primary producers – including green plants and other photosynthesisers – to sequential levels of consumer organisms in ecosystems (humans and their economies) and on the return flows of degraded energy and material (wastes) back to the ecosystem. The circulation of energy and materials in ecological systems is a dominant theme in ecosystem analyses. This ecosystem energetics is manifested in food chains, food webs and the cycling of elements, and involves the measuring of fluxes of material out (to other parts of the ecosystem or out of the system completely) and in (from other parts of the ecosystem or from outside the system completely), which can be very difficult to measure. The processing of material and forms of energy through terrestrial systems and the residence time of materials in different ecosystems link terrestrial ecosystems directly to other ecosystems (atmospheric and marine). In ecology, ecosystem energy and nutrient fluxes are modelled involving subtle, underlying assumptions about the constancy of ecosystems and the extrapolation of observations to larger spatial scales. We currently appropriate 40 per cent of the net product of terrestrial photosynthesis and 25 to 35 per cent of coastal-shelf primary production.

So, in ecodesign, the understanding of transfers of energy in and out of the building site and everything within it in the present, and projections of future energy flows, will be necessary.

- Regard the building over of sites as physical 'displacement' of the organisms that were originally found in the ecosystem. By building over this ecosystem, ecodesigners have

Inputs

40% of raw materials (by weight) are used in building construction globally each year
36% of a nation's energy inputs are used in buildings

Outputs

20 – 26% of landfill trash is construction trash
100% of energy used in buildings is lost to the environment

- Inputs and outputs from buildings

Designing the built environment as the transient management of materials and energy input flows

Waste composition (%)					
Generator segment	Paper	Cardboard	Plastic	Metals	Others
Office	65	15	6	2	12
Industrial	35	20	25	6	14
Retail	35	40	8	1	16
TCU	20	15	15	5	45
WWD	25	32	25	7	11
Public	45	10	5	6	34

TCU = transportation, communications and utilities
WWD = wholesale, warehouse and distribution

Quantities of commercial waste ●

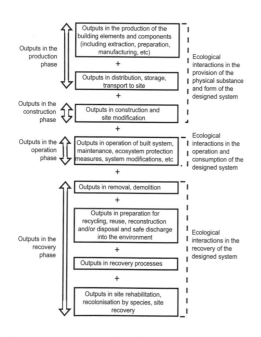

The total outputs in the life cycle of ●
a designed system

to take over the performance of the roles of the previous constituents displaced in the ecosystem, to maintain the flow of energy and nutrients. The human-made built environment's displacement of natural ecosystems is analogous to the behaviour of the strangler fig plant. The roots of the fig, which started as an epiphyte in the top of the canopy, wrap around the host tree. Eventually, the host tree is exterminated and replaced by the strangler fig plant, the prominent strangling roots of which now reach the ground and become the tree trunk and perform the functions of energy fluxes within the ecosystem.

• Have regard to the set of operations in the built environment and the limitations of the earth's ecosystems and resources. From a holistic point of view, the use of inputs into the built environment is related to the discharge of outputs. The interdependencies between the built and natural environments must be understood and addressed (see above). The relationship that commonly exists between the built and natural environments is open-ended and linear. This existing pattern might be described as a 'once-through' system in which resources are used at one end, and waste expelled at the other.

• Close the loop within the built environment by adopting the measures for output flow management conceived in the following ways (see also B27):

  • reduce the flow of outputs at the source of generation;

  • manage outputs after their generation;

  • implement final protective measures (ie reintegration); and

  • close the loop by the principle of designing for continuous reuse and recycling within our built environment.

The interactions framework (see A5) shows that the discharge and management of outputs are related systemically to the flow of inputs, the operations within the built environment and the assimilative capacity of the earth's ecosystems. In the design process, it is necessary for the designer to anticipate the net outputs associated with the proposed designed system (over its complete life cycle), the related impacts and interactions with ecosystems, the extent and type of inputs used in managing these outputs and the ways that they can be managed cyclically within the built environment.

• Reduce the outputs generated by the built system throughout its life cycle. The difference between human-made systems and natural systems is that the latter do not produce waste. 'Wastes' in natural systems are reintegrated or assimilated into the natural cycles in the biosphere. Human-made systems, because they have not been designed for recovery at the outset, are waste generating. For example, in many production processes in the built environment, the material outputs comprise up to 25 to 50 per cent by weight of the outputs. Outputs from construction processes include the rubble of the structure, concrete, bricks, timber cutoffs and metalwork. Solid outputs from the residential buildings during their period of use consist mainly of paper and fermentable organic matter but also frequently dust, cinders, textiles, glass, porcelain, wood, metals and plastics. Outputs from commercial buildings during their period of use are largely paper-based, but also include food wastes. Outputs from industrial buildings include building wastes, plastic, wood textiles, ash, gaseous emissions, liquid effluents from production processes and other toxic discharges. As the activities of the human-made environment increase in volume and diversity, so will the forms of output or waste.

The management of materials expelled by the built environment into the ecosystems is not ordinarily in the domain of the designer. Rather, related disciplines have dealt with such environmental protection issues as the disposal of solid wastes and pollution control, including air-and water-pollution engineering and the disposal of liquid effluents. This specialisation makes it difficult to consider the emissions of the built environment in a holistic way. Despite this structural impediment to solving environmental problems, it has nevertheless been recognised that exchanges of materials and energy need to be monitored. Evaluating such emissions is the first step towards improving those situations in which the ecosystem is threatened with contamination.

- Predict the kinds of wastes that will be produced by a building in the planning stage. To do this, it is useful first to look at and classify all outputs (and products) as potential pollutants. There are several possible classificatory schemes, for instance by state (solid, liquid, gaseous, particulate) or by degree of toxicity. If the second approach is chosen, for instance, it would entail looking systematically at all hydrocarbons, compounds of mercury etc, through the ranks of toxicity.

- Understand the wastes produced by the built environment by analysing their sources. For instance, outputs might include the by-products of the built environment's construction. Among these types of material would be waste lumber, main tailings and rejected building elements. Such materials can be collected, and if reuse is technically possible they can be distributed to new sites. If the materials cannot be reused, then they will have to be disposed of, but this must be done carefully in order to minimise environmental harm. Some forms of energy and materials generated by the built environment are by their natures impossible to recover. It will be impossible to entirely prevent energy loss from friction, heat loss and other forms of output. For these kinds of energy exchanges, the best that we can do is to try and minimise them through good design.

Buildings themselves, when they reach the ends of their useful lives, can be recycled, as can building materials, materials associated with demolition, product packaging and other potential wastes. Building, maintaining and demolishing parts of the designed structure will also generate materials, like dust, that can be collected and recycled. Given the vast array of materials and

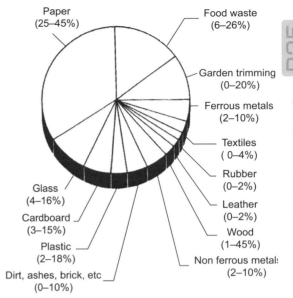

Paper (25–45%)
Food waste (6–26%)
Garden trimming (0–20%)
Ferrous metals (2–10%)
Textiles (0–4%)
Rubber (0–2%)
Leather (0–2%)
Wood (1–45%)
Non ferrous metal (2–10%)
Glass (4–16%)
Cardboard (3–15%)
Plastic (2–18%)
Dirt, ashes, brick, etc (0–10%)

Outputs: Typical physical composition of municipal solid waste

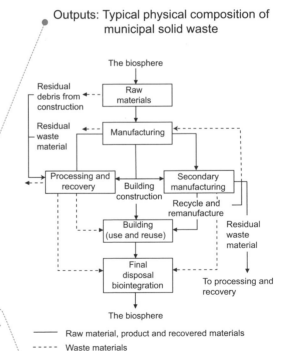

Model of use, reuse and recovery

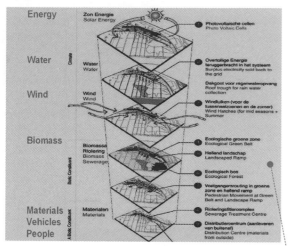

Designing the built form as a system of flows
(University of Amsterdam, Netherlands, 2000)

energy generated by every building activity, it is no wonder that pollution has been dealt with in such a piecemeal fashion.

The sheer number of potential pollutants has also frustrated conservation attempts.

• Limiting the quantity of materials and energy expelled by our large buildings into the environment will become a central objective of ecodesign. Some distinctions can be made among the non-recyclable materials and quantities of energy that a particular built form is inevitably going to produce. At the most basic level, some of these wastes will cause an increase in the volume of a particular material or energy source that already exists in the environment. In other (and worse) cases, potentially poisonous foreign materials will be spewed into the environment. The second category of wastes is obviously to be avoided by all possible means.

Material flows analysis (MFA)

Use material flows analysis (MFA) as a planning tool for guiding the design and the assessment of urban development to promote sustainability and economic revitalisation. MFA calculates the transfers of natural and manufactured materials (resources and capital) out of a city in relation to those flowing in as an input/output analysis. It also examines the stocks, flows and transformations of energy and materials within the city. This 'metabolic' framework of analysis provides a basis for 'sustainability auditing' and enables identification of leverage points for change such as: (1) where wastes in resources can be put to new uses by industry; (2) where public interventions, policies, improved regulations or infrastructure development will bring the greatest investment returns; and (3) where eco-innovations that provide import replacement products or resource-efficient services can revitalise urban areas.

Through MFA, it was found that eco-efficiency improvements to the building stock to achieve resource, energy and greenhouse gas reductions could be made with relatively little public financial investment (in some cases a profit) and more rapidly than major new 'green' developments or changes in land use and urban form (eg providing a strong case for redevelopment and adaptive reuse and retrofit rather than new development). Ecological reconstruction of urban residential development can achieve 'resource autonomy' and provide ecosystem services while reducing net resource consumption.

Advantages are:

* Forward looking and orients urban planning towards sustainability (or system design solutions) rather than monitoring and mitigating effects.

* Design-oriented and proactive, rather than formulistic approaches to design or regulatory constraints upon design.

* Enables the calculation of simplified cumulative and/or regional impact assessments – in lieu of measuring the total energy consumption of isolated projects and products in life-cycle assessments (LCA).

- The three basic criteria or indicators are: resource autonomy (where the built environment is designed to be self-sufficient in terms of temperature control, air quality, ventilation, rainwater reuse, lighting and energy requirements and operational performance); material renewability and reusability (where all the materials are either renewable or reusable; recyclable materials are avoided as they typically entail high levels of embodied energy); and ecosystem services (where the designed system maintains or increases the pre-development-level use of ecosystem services).

In assessing the flow through a built system, we need to recognise the amount of energy required to produce the built system itself. A complete energy audit of the energy flow of a built system will include the energy used to create the building materials (see B29) and components and to construct the built system, this being its embodied energy. Embodied energy is the 'direct' and 'indirect' energy used to manufacture, transport and install building products:

- Direct energy is the energy actually consumed in the construction of the built forms and is a relatively small portion of embodied energy.

- Indirect energy represents the energy consumed in the production of building materials and their associated transportation (see B10). Indirect energy represents the largest portion of embodied energy.

When full life-cycle analysis (LCA) is undertaken, embodied energy should be extended to include the energy associated with maintaining and repairing materials and components.

Summary

In the design of products, built structures, facilities or infrastructures, the designer should regard the designed system as the transient management of the flows of materials and energy through the built environment over its life cycle from its source to its eventual reuse, recycling or eventual reintegration. In assessing their consequences the designer should seek to quantify these flows. This is a radical re-envisioning of what architecture is, being here the transient assembly of materials and equipment for a period of human use, following which these are dismantled or demolished. This provides the designer with a methodical framework to assess the consequences arising from the creation of these

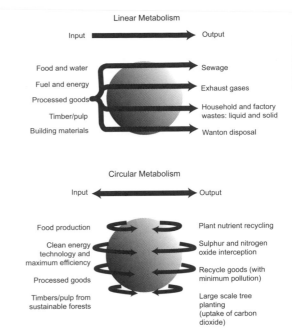

- Consumption models

flows, which arise from the use of global materials resources, the use of renewable and non-renewable energy resources and the use of the natural environment itself. More importantly, the assessment of flows provides the basis for designing their subsequent environmental integration, particularly in terms of the outputs from the built structure and how these can be systematically assimilated back into the ecosystems or into the biospheric processes.

B26 Designing to conserve the use of non-renewable energy and material resources

Ecodesign must seek to conserve the use of non-renewable energy and material resources (as a sustainable strategy) through efficiency of use, through prudent management of their flows and through continuous reuse and recycling. The predicted peaking in the production of oil is reflected in an increase in the cost of oil and in the shortage of supply. These will significantly affect the future design of our built environment whereupon low-energy design will become an even more critical aspect of ecodesign.

Ecodesign must be based on the wise and efficient consumption of materials and non-renewable energy sources. The energy that our built environment uses today is mainly from fossil fuels such as oil, gas and coal. They are non-renewable and will in time will be completely depleted. World oil resources are predicted to peak in production within the next ten to 20 years. Production of oil is considered to peak once half the volume of oil in any field has been extracted. Industry accounts for about 22 per cent of a country's energy use (in the UK) of which the largest is the chemical sector at 22 per cent followed by iron, steel and other metal industries at 14 per cent, other metal products, machinery and equipment at 13 per cent and food, drinks and tobacco at 12 per cent. Designers can play a crucial role in the reduction of material and energy use from the very start of the design process. However, it must be recognised that materials entail territorial changes in places other than the design's own site, on a scale beyond the designer's control. The idea of sustainability in ecodesign is to avoid using up natural resources and to avoid their depletion to a point of no return. This conservation approach, designing for temporal integration in ecodesign, has three main objectives:

- to maintain essential ecological processes and life-support systems;

- to preserve genetic diversity in ecosystems; and

- to ensure the sustainable utilisation of species, ecosystems and natural resources.

The integrative role of ecodesign is essentially one of temporal integration. Ecodesign seeks to use non-renewable resources in ways and at rates that will assure their renewal and prevent their irreversible exhaustion. In designing for temporal integration of our built environment it is crucial to note that currently humans are using fossil fuels at 250,000 times their rate of formulation (see A2). Humankind's ecological footprint has exceeded its global biocapacity by 21 per cent which means that humans are using natural resources faster than these can be replenished. The basic premise is that there are limitations to the availability of natural resources and a final limit, which depends on the earth's capacity to continue to provide the human-built environment with raw materials and fossil fuels.

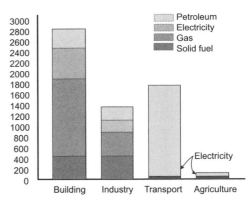

● Delivered energy consumption by sector and by delivered fuel type (UK, 1987)

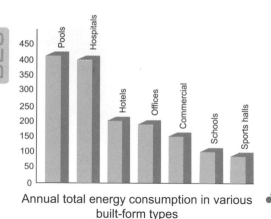

450
400
350
300
250
200
150
100
50
0

Pools
Hospitals
Hotels
Offices
Commercial
Schools
Sports halls

Annual total energy consumption in various built-form types

The general principles of 'resource management' can provide a means of resource conservation, as can more conventional approaches. The 'natural resources' that occur in the biosphere can be classified under a variety of rubrics. For example, resources can be grouped according to their sources of origin: forest products; non-metallic minerals and those products made from them and compound products. It must be understood that each building element found in the built environment possesses its own history of energy and materials consumption. Every part of a building or structure can produce pollution and ecosystem degradation. Producing a particular building element and making it available for use in a building project necessarily entails environmental consequences.

Natural resources are considered to include energy sources as well as materials extracted from the earth and exploited by humans. These are further categorised according to their availability and potential for regeneration. The distinction between renewable and non-renewable resources is the 'appreciation of their relative importance in relation to the variables which constitute environment'. Some hold that this distinction is basic to the ecological approach to resource conservation. The external dependencies of the built environment, and the resources on which it depends, are categorised as follows:

• Inexhaustible resources

Examples of these sorts of resources include air, water and solar energy. Although the total available quantity of each of these resources is virtually unlimited, the form in which they occur is subject to change. Such variation has particular consequences for the ability of these resources to sustain life. Any permanent degradation of their quality (for instance, as a result of pollution) therefore raises concern.

• Replaceable and maintainable resources

Examples of these resources include water, as well as flora and fauna. Simply put, replaceable and maintainable resources are those resources the production of which is primarily a function of the environment. In normal environmental conditions such resources will be produced indefinitely. However, any impairment of the environment will have an adverse effect on the production of the resources. This depends upon many factors, but especially on the deliberate and inadvertent interference of human beings in the production of these resources.

• Irreplaceable resources.

Examples of such resources include minerals, soil, fossil fuels, land and the landscape itself in its original state. These resources are known to be irreplaceable and their availability is related to the rate and type of exploitation by humans. Non-renewable energy resources are essentially the results of solar energy in the past, therefore they exist in a finite amount. Present consumption of these resources by humans is at a rate that makes natural regeneration rates negligible. This situation raises an acute multigenerational allocation problem: the more of these non-renewable resources that we use now, the less will exist in the future.

The categorisation of resources clearly indicates which of them demand our conservation efforts. The categories are flexible as new substitutes are found for traditional resources or as extraction and recovery methods evolve. Both developments – resource replacement and discovery of extraction techniques – have ramifications for supplies. Because building materials made from naturally occurring resources are used worldwide, the use of material as well as of energy resources in our building will have ramifications for the future availability of them all.

Common mineral and energy resources that are irreplaceable can be classified further, based on use:

• Non-renewable (metallic mineral) resources

These include abundant metals such as iron, aluminium, chromium, manganese, titanium and magnesium. Scarce metals are also among these non-renewable resources. They include copper, lead, zinc, tin, tungsten, gold, silver, platinum, uranium, mercury and molybdenum.

• Non-renewable (non-metallic mineral) resources

These also include minerals used in chemical fertilisers and for special uses: sodium, chlorides, phosphates, nitrates, sulphur. Some of these are mainly building materials: cement, sand, gravel, gypsum, asbestos and so on. Water is also a non-renewable resource and exists in lakes, rivers and ground water.

• Limited and non-renewable (energy) resources

These resources include fossil fuels, eg coal, oil, natural gas and oil shale, as well as materials suitable for nuclear fission or fusion.

• Continuous-flow (energy) resources

These include direct and indirect forms of use. Examples of direct use include: the flow of precipitated water, tidal effects of water, geothermal phenomena, wind power and climate energy. Examples of indirect use (eg through combustion) include: photosynthesised energy (eg wood), biomass and waste products used as fuel.

The categories above can be useful to the designer since they serve as a reminder of which are the renewable and which the non-renewable resources. The status of a resource should be taken into consideration both in design and in the management of inputs and outputs. The earth contains finite quantities of the non-renewable materials and energy resources.

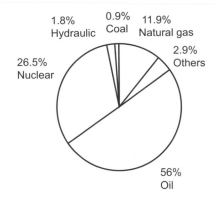

Primary energy consumption (by type) of a nation

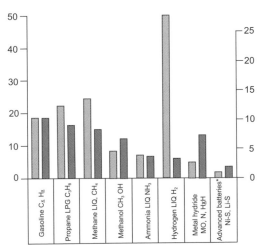

*Includes adjustment for different energy-conversion efficiency

Energy-density characteristic of fuels use in the built environment

Energy source
1. Coal
2. Oil
3. Gas
4. Fission
5. Falling water
6. Geothermal
7. Refuse
8. Algae
9. Wood
10. Wind
11. Tides
12. Waves
13. Ocean currents
14. Temperature differential
15. Solar
16. Fusion
17. Electrostatic
18. Gravity
19. Hydrogen
20. Water desalination
21. Ocean pressure
22. Phase transformation
23. Animate

Energy conversion techniques and engines
1. Heat engines/ converters
   (a) Steam engines
   (b) Gas turbines
   (c) Heat pumps
   (d) Internal combustion engines
   (e) Nuclear reactors
   (f) Rockets
   (g) Jets
   (h) Heating systems
   (i) Blast furnaces
   (j) Domestic appliances

3. Electric conversion
   (a) Generators
   (b) Electric motors
   (c) Lights
   (d) Heating

4. Mechanical conversion
   (a) Water wheels
   (b) Water turbines
   (c) Contraction engines
   (d) Helium/hydrogen balloons
   (e) Sails/wind

Energy storage
1. Bulk
2. Underground
3. Mines/caverns
4. Electrochemical battery
5. Pumped water reservoir
6. Compressed air
7. Hydrogen generation
8. Flywheel
9. Heat in water
10. Sodium, etc

Energy transport
1. Ship
2. Rail
3. Truck
4. Pipe
5. AC transmission
6. DC transmission
7. Cryogenic cable/ pipeline

Energy utilisation
1. Industry
2. Transportation
3. Residential/ commercial

Energy sources and systems

The ecological truth cannot be disputed. However, what does spark disagreement between resource conservationists are the quantitative questions: in what quantities do resources exist? Where are they located? How much of them can be extracted. Over what period of time the earth and the biosphere are closed materials systems, and consequently the present pace of continuous and accelerating human consumption cannot be sustained indefinitely. Available mineral deposits, including fuels and metals, were formed over the course of geological time, but they are being consumed far more rapidly than they could possibly be regenerated. As the increasing demands for minerals and fuel lead to the use of lower-grade resources, the problem of resource depletion can be temporarily resolved, but this resolution only comes at the expense of increasing pollution and ecosystem destruction.

Design guidelines for conserving non-renewable energy and materials resources

In designing for conservation of non-renewable energy and material resources, the designer needs to:

• Consider the human and technological parameters of non-renewable resources rather than those determined by geology. Some resources, such as precious metals, are depleted less for their utility and more for their economic value. The high market value of such substances provides a motivation in itself for their extraction – though also for their reuse.

• Minimise input (resources and energy) and harmful output (waste and emissions) throughout the life cycle of the product. How resources are used plays an important role in ecological reform. If input is minimised, the environmental costs drop because ultimately the polluter pays principle (PPP) will come to play an important role in all our industries.

• Acknowledge that a consequence of the use of any element in a built system is its history of direct and indirect interactions with ecosystems. The designer must recognise that each choice of building material has an impact on the earth's resources. The designer can analyse this impact by using the interactions framework. Every activity that is part of producing an element for incorporation in a built system will, first of all, exert spatial pressure in its immediate surroundings and will have an impact on local ecosystems. For instance, every building project also affects other interventions in the built environment. A building also relies on consumed energy and materials for its operation. Moreover, every part of the built environment produces outputs and waste energy, which may be expelled into the ecosystem and contaminate the environment. These comprise the sum of the ecological consequences of the exchanges of energy and materials between the natural and built environments (ie L21 in A5).

- Consider the following related factors to assess the total ecological impact. First, the designer must take into account the entirety of the processes and activities required to make each material or energy resource available for use in a designed system. Second, the displacement of natural areas by these activities and processes and their impact on natural systems in their immediate contexts are also considerations. Third, the total amount of energy and materials required by these processes and activities, and the respective impacts of such energy and materials on the ecosystems, must be analysed. Fourth, the total output of energy and materials from each of these processes and activities, and their environmental costs to ecosystems, has to be considered.

- Carry out a complete analysis of the ecological consequences of the built environment's components; this will undoubtedly become a time-consuming and complex task. It will entail an analysis of the ecological impact of using each material and energy resource employed in the built structure. This analysis becomes even more burdensome when it is remembered that each resource has to be viewed from its place of origin in the environment to its ultimate reabsorption (following demolition of the building or complex) into the biosphere. However, indicators can be used to facilitate the analysis. The varieties of environmental consequences are, of course, interrelated as demonstrated in the Partitioned Matrix (in A5). Their net impact constitutes the total ecological cost of using given energy and material resources to construct a building or group of buildings-related structures. Quantify the amount of energy used in built systems. Current accepted patterns of exploitation of material resources depend largely on non-renewable fossil fuels as energy sources. These non-renewable resources are becoming ever more scarce; in many cases, they can be recovered only by additional expenditures of energy, which in turn must be procured somewhere in the environment and thus cause additional environmental impact.

At present rates of use of non-renewable energy resources, within the next 50 years the world will probably run out of non-renewable fossil fuels (unless new sources of these fuels are discovered). It is thus imperative to use renewable energy sources as much as possible (eg solar, wind, geothermal). Wind energy is proving to be a viable option where local climatic conditions permit (ie average wind speeds of about 6 metres per second or more). Currently wind generators have efficiencies of 40 to 50 per cent, with an upper theoretical limit of efficiency at 59.3 per cent. Other alternatives include biomass, photovoltaics and other sources, all of which merit further development.

In general, major existing building developments depend upon fossil fuels and have been designed to be extravagant in their use of these non-renewable resources. This situation has resulted from the fact that, until recently, the built environment has seldom been

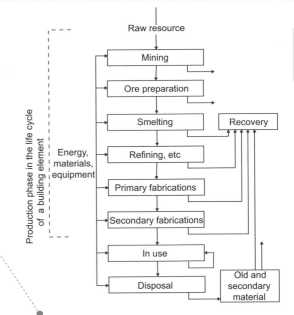

Production phase in the life cycle of a single building element

Designing to conserve the use of non-renewable energy and material resources considered in its totality from the perspective of energy consumption. Considerable amounts of energy are used to produce a building and to maintain it thereafter. Energy is consumed to operate a building, to move people and goods to and from it, and to demolish it when it is no longer needed. Buildings also exert a major impact on the flow of energy in their local area. Moreover, even the process of coping with environmental problems brought about by buildings requires expenditures of energy (for instance, recycling solid wastes and reducing air pollution are not 'neutral' activities, but require energy). Buildings and other associated structures consume about 30 to 40 per cent of the energy required by the human-made environment in a given year, and transportation takes up another 25 per cent. Increasing the supply of energy will be environmentally counterproductive, in view of the fact that greater quantities will result in increased use and in the concentration of materials, thus only encouraging resource consumption. Such an increase would only exacerbate current energy problems by facilitating existing patterns.

The availability of non-renewable energy resources has an impact on the availability of other material resources, and ultimately on the ability of the built environment to function. By using fossil fuels, we increase the earth's environmental difficulties. Clearly, as designers we must work to reduce overall energy consumption, which will lead to positive environmental consequences.

In order to assess the value of a designed system or the cost of a service, we add up the quantities of non-renewable energy resources that are required to produce the system or service. The net result of this accounting is the embodied energy value of the material. Certain products consume more energy per unit than others. If we consider the fact that any resource use has an unavoidable impact on the environment, and that most energy resources used in the existing human-made environment have been produced from non-renewable sources, then the ecological/environmental impact of the components of the built system can be accounted for during the design process by using a form of 'energy equivalents'.

The energy cost of a designed system must be considered in the broadest sense, that is over the course of its entire life cycle. The energy that goes into the operation of a built system during its life is considerable (around 65 per cent) in comparison with the energy used in its initial construction. For example, more dramatic is the finding that for every kilowatt hour of energy consumed in the construction of a commercial skyscraper (including energy used in the manufacture of materials, their transportation, and so on), an equal amount of energy will be used to operate the building each year over the course of its useful life.

Energetics

Within the field of ecology, energetics is the study of the ecosystem with respect to energy exchanges and metabolism (or efficiencies). Energetics converts the biomass of an ecosystem into energy and units. Energy passes through a built system, and this energy can be quantified using indices, which allow us to see the built environment in terms of the energy cost of producing building materials. The energy cost of a product provides an indication of its impact on the environment through the use of energy resources, and also lets us compare its cost to that of other products. This method can be used to assess the efficiency of current technology by considering together all the energy used in a product's creation, operation in the built environment and later disposal or recovery. Hence, the total energy costs of different construction processes and materials can be compared and their relative degrees of dependence on the earth's resources assessed.

There are a number of factors to take into account when selecting materials (see B27). If we are approaching design with a concern for environmental consequences, we must thoroughly analyse and quantify the energy and material resource requirements of a building over the course of its useful life, and we must inventory the ways in which the materials and resources impair the ecosystem (that is, we must determine their 'embodied ecological impacts'). Designers must also go beyond functionalism in selecting materials and energy forms for use in their projects. One design criterion should be the environmental impact of a particular energy source or material over the entire life of the building. When thinking about materials, it will be important for designers to consider whether a material is a renewable or a non-renewable resource. This assessment is actually complex, because each process in the built environment requires resources and exerts a particular impact on the external environment.

The purposes of incorporating these energy and materials considerations into design are several. First, the designer works to reduce the depletion of the fund of resources in the biosphere. Second, he or she attempts to minimise, through good design, the outputs expelled by the built environment into the ecosystem. Third, the designer works to reduce the built environment's use of resources from the natural world.

- Analyse the exchanges between the built environment and its ecosystems to amass information for evaluating a proposed building project. Such information supports a comparison of the total consequences of alternative design schemes with respect to the use of materials and energy. This comparison will in turn inform the choice of subsystems in the chosen design. The designer can also configure the designed system in such a way as to conserve non-renewable energy and materials. The designer can determine which aspects of the designed system require excessive quantities of resources and then target those profligate energy consumers that can be modified to achieve a more reasonable level

Building inputs	
Material embodied energy	MJ/kg
Kiln-dried sawn softwood	3.4
Kiln-dried sawn hardwood	2.0
Air-dried sawn hardwood	0.5
Hardboard	24.1
Particle board	8.0
Medium density fibreboard (MDF)	11.3
Plywood	10.4
Glued-laminated timber	11.0
Laminated veneer lumber	11.0
Plastics general	90.0
PVC	80.0
Synthetic rubber	110.0
Acrylic paint	61.5
Stabilised earth	0.7
Imported dimension granite	13.9
Local dimension granite	5.9
Clay bricks	2.5
Cement	5.6
Gypsum plaster	2.9
Plasterboard	4.4
Fibre cement	7.6
In-situ concrete	1.7
Pre-cast steam-cured concrete	2.0
Pre-cast tilt-up concrete	1.9
Concrete blocks	1.4
Autoclaved aerated concrete (AAC)	3.6
Glass	12.7
Mild steel	34.0
Galvanised mild steel	38.0
Aluminium	170.0
Copper	100.0
Zinc	51.0

- Process-energy requirements for common building materials

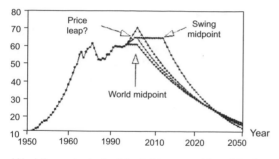

World's projected midpoint in use of fossil fuels.

of energy consumption. The objective of minimising environmental impact can be met by planning for efficient energy use and minimising resource consumption. Reducing energy use will in turn lead to a reduction in ecosystem effects – always keeping in mind that the building's impact profile takes in the whole of its useful life. Thus, designers can plan for resources to be recycled or recovered rather than simply wasted at the end of the production and operational phases of the designed system. Such strategies as lowering supply and flow rates, increasing the efficiency and performance of systems and designing new systems all contribute to resource conservation.

• Reduce the overall demand as a long-term solution through the modification of human patterns of needs (ie reduction in standard of living) and through the general practice of conservation in the use of material and energy resources (see B19, B20, B22, B25, B26, B28). It must be observed, however, that a decrease in the use of high-ecological-impact materials and forms of energy as a result of the efficient use of alternative materials would only reduce to some extent the overall impact on the biosphere. As has been mentioned, this optimal strategy also has larger social, economic and political ramifications that lie outside the scope of this work.

• Intervene on behalf of the environment during the design stage; it is then that many decisions are made that have a profound impact on the amount of energy and materials used over the course of the building's life. The original designer is the individual who initially specifies the types and qualities of materials that will go into the building, albeit with the input of others. The processing or fabrication methods that the designer chooses or advocates for the manufacture and recovery of a product will have enormous consequences for the amount of waste that will eventually be generated in the building process and beyond. Hence, the decisions that we make early in the design process are of great importance. For example, if a designer makes a poor choice of a certain material, its failure will require replacement. In this scenario, the amount of material used is doubled, as is the quantity of resources consumed. Even more direct environmental consequences result in the case of a failed product that is an inseparable part of a larger assembly that is in turn rendered useless and thus expelled into the environment as waste.

• In the area of materials processing, it is important to select fabrication methods that do not require excessive machinery or result in excessive waste (or both). Such processes will increase the total amount of materials and energy resources consumed per unit of building product. The use of materials, forms of construction, production technology, transport, assembly and dismantling of building components must all be planned in relation to energy content and ecological impact and the life cycle of the materials.

- The designer should think in terms of efficiency and reduce the total amount of resources required. With the consumption of energy and materials thus decreased, the overall flow of energy and materials through the built environment lessens. The designer should help ensure that processes built into the design of the building require the smallest quantity of materials and energy, choosing among the alternatives capable of performing a given service. In meeting this objective, the designer has to do more with less. Beyond working towards a rational use of energy and materials in the initial construction of a part of the built environment, based on resource conservation principles, the designer also takes into consideration the projected reuse and recycling of the selected elements.

- Humans are currently dependent on the use of the limited supply of fossil fuels for their energy needs. This source of energy is the result of hundreds of millions of years of gradual storage of solar energy by ancient living things. This source of energy is used to plant and grow crops, to process and cook food, to warm buildings in winter and to cool them in the summer, to run machinery, to make plastics, etc. Once this energy is used it cannot be recaptured. These fossil fuels should not be wasted and we need to conserve them and not deplete them.

Ecodesign is therefore low-energy design that conserves the use of such fossil fuels. We need to change our consumption habits and change our technology so that we use energy and materials at a much slower rate and thus achieve sustainability.

Of critical concern is the amount of energy used in built systems. Current accepted patterns of exploitation of material resources depend largely on non-renewable fossil fuels as energy sources. These are constantly becoming scarcer; in many cases, they can be recovered only by additional expenditures of energy, which in turn must be procured somewhere in the environment and thus cause additional environmental impact.

For example, global demand for power has tripled since 1950. The human-made built environment uses the energy equivalent of 10,000 million tonnes of oil every year and, according to the World Energy Council, energy consumption is likely to rise by 50 per cent by 2020. Most of this power comes from fossil fuels – coal and gas, and especially oil which has become the single most critical resource on the planet. The oil deposits on which our economies depend are tens of millions of years old. As for how much is left, it is hard to know. The technology for finding and extracting oil and gas deposits is constantly improving, bringing into production resources that were once considered beyond reach. It is also difficult to predict the rate at which fossil fuels will be consumed in future, as their use is complicated by a complex interrelationship between economic and political conditions. The best available current figures ('guesstimates') for known reserves are: coal about 250 years; oil about 40 years; and gas about 70 years.

Energy use	(%)
Running industry	37.3
Powering transportation	24.8
Driving cars	13.2
Driving trucks and buses	5.5
Flying planes	3.2
Driving farm and other off-road vehicles	1.2
Fuelling ships and boats	1.2
Fuelling trains	0.7
Heating homes and offices	17.9
Providing raw materials for chemicals, plastics	5.5
Heating water for homes and offices	4.0
Air-conditioning homes and offices	2.2
Refrigerating food	2.3
Lighting homes and offices	1.5
Cooking food	1.3
Other uses	3.0

● Percentage of energy consumed in the built environment (for a region)

As for the costs, finding oil reserves has now become a costly activity that is undertaken in the most extreme environments – remote deserts, the Arctic and deep under water – as the most easily accessible reserves have been exhausted. The average oil well is now more than 3 kilometres deep, and only about one-third of new wells actually hit oil. Bringing these far-flung resources into production is expensive. Transporting these fuels over thousands of miles from well to refinery adds considerably to that expense. For example, the largest oil field in the USA on the coast of Alaska 400 kilometres north of the Arctic Circle, is linked to the port of Valdez by a 1000-kilometre-long pipeline that crosses three mountain ranges and three major earthquake zones. After it reaches the petrol pump, most of the chemical energy that is released when petrol is burned in a car engine is converted not into the movement of the pistons but into waste heat. An electric car is hugely more energy efficient but only 1 per cent of cars on the road today are electric.

As for energy use, deciding on the internal environment and the operational consumption levels of certain intensive building types is probably the most important decision. In the conventional building, these elements consume up to 65 per cent of the energy used in a building over its life cycle.

• We need to be aware that while standards of comfort are used as the basis for design the impact and/or damage to the environment caused by human beings will be directly proportional to their living conditions and standard of living (see B3). Traditional and pre-industrial societies existing at subsistence levels obviously make far fewer demands on their environment. The further that people depart from a simple or rural way of life, the more demanding and complex are their interactions with the environment from which they drain ever increasing quantities of support and resources. Ecological footprint analyses support the argument that to be sustainable economic growth must be much less material and energy intensive than it is at present. Reduction of human environmental influence is possible, but only at the expense of a reduction in the quality and quantity of humankind's shelter and comfort. The less people demand from ecosystems, the less will be the human impact on them. In an already industrialised world, and in a society with high material and comfort expectations, the designer has a difficult task in reducing the environmental impact. The level of resource intake will depend on what the built environment's occupants will accept. The higher the perceived level of need, the more extensive will be the size of the built environment, and the greater the environmental impact. It all boils down to lifestyle and cultural issues. The ecodesigner has to deal with such issues in advance of preparing the design brief in terms of professional liability and user education (see B3).

• We need to seek wider controls (eg at the governmental level) for ecological tax reform in aid of resource conservation. If taxes were imposed on depletion and marketable quotas imposed on natural capital inputs to the economy, several outcomes might be expected:

the stimulation of the search for more material- and energy-efficient technologies; the pre-emption of any resultant cost savings, thereby preventing the economic benefits of efficiency gains from being redirected to additional or alternative forms of consumption; and the generation of an investment fund that could be used to rehabilitate important forms of self-producing natural capital.

There is a duality between engineering and nature that is based on the minimum use of energy. This is because animals and plants, in order to survive in competition with each other, have evolved ways of living and reproducing using the least amount of resource. This involves efficiency both in metabolism and optimal apportionment of energy between the various functions of life.

• Right from the start, the designer needs to place greater priority on the evaluation of the project's users and their needs rather than on responding to the demands for provision of hardware. Instead of taking the design assignment's demands for granted, the designer needs to look into ways in which the design might inadvertently contribute to creating what may prove to be unsustainable expectations regarding the nature and form of the built environment.

It is during the preliminary design stage that the designer is in a position to have the greatest influence on the extent of impact of the built structure. Therefore before the finalising of the design brief (which determines the extent of construction and enclosure) (in B3), a questioning of the project programme and the users' need of that locality is beneficial. We might find, for instance, that these needs might be met by other means without the provision of any enclosure at all, or by simply seeking a consensus among the users to reduce their level of natural resources consumption.

• The designer can optimise energy performance to above the prerequisite standard to reduce the environmental impacts associated with excessive energy use. For example, the designer can design the built form to comply with ASHRAE/IESNA Standard 90.1–1999 (without amendments) or the local energy code, whichever is the more stringent.

• Ecodesign should also encourage the use of on-site, self-supply renewable energy using non-polluting and renewable energy resources including solar, wind, geothermal, low-impact hydro, biomass and biogas strategies in order to reduce the environmental impacts associated with fossil-fuel energy use.

Seek to reduce ozone depletion. Strategies include the installation of base building level M&E and refrigeration equipment and fire-suppression systems that do not contain HCFCs or halons.

• Adopt practical measures such as installing metering equipment in the designed system to monitor:

* lighting systems and controls;

* constant and variable motor loads;

* variable frequency drive (VFD) operation;

* chiller efficiency at variable loads (kW/ton);

* cooling load;

* air and water economiser and heat-recovery cycles;

* air distribution static pressures and ventilation air volumes;

* boiler efficiencies;

* building-related process energy systems and equipment; and

* indoor water risers and outdoor irrigation systems.

• When using concrete for construction, the following guidelines should be adopted:

* reduce waste by carefully estimating quantities of concrete required on the jobsite;

* consider alternative foundation systems, for example pier foundations use far less concrete than poured full-height foundation walls or slab-on-grade foundations;

* consider a pre-cast concrete system;

* specify minimal admixture use – chemical additivies for controlling concrete properties and workability can offgas formaldehydes and other chemicals into indoor air, depending on what was added;

* specify fly ash added to concrete mixtures, this can improve workability and strength – proportions up to 15 per cent or more are possible;

* control washwater runoff, and avoid locations where runoff will enter topsoil or flow into surface water; and

* use concrete waste as fill whenever possible.

• Design to integrate temporally in addition to designing to integrate the built environment physically and systemically with the processes in the biosphere and the ecosystems.

For instance, as stated, the rate of production of fossil fuels takes hundred of years and if our rate of consumption of these is not in tandem with the rate of production, then it has been predicted that within the next 50 years or so we will run out of fossil fuels.

Key questions about the use of non-renewable energy and material resources are: first, how far into the future should the ecological designer plan for the designed system? Second, when designing for reuse, etc, beyond the designer's lifetime, should the responsibility for use devolve upon the user/owner rather than the designer?

By consuming the earth's resources beyond its capacity for renewal, humans are witnessing the instigation of current crises in energy, economics, depletion of biodiversity and human existence, such as social deprivation. Whereupon designing with a view to the future is essential because sustainability is not a static state of affairs, but a wide and diverse range of issues held together by a symbiotic relationship, like the billions of cells working together to maintain optimal body temperature, and having constantly to adapt to changes in internal and external conditions.

Interactions between ecosystems are dynamic processes and change over time. Ideally, the designer should anticipate the impact and the performance of the designed system in the local ecosystem throughout the entire span of the designed system's life – during which the states of the ecosystems will not remain static but will themselve be changing. The current restricted range of the designer's responsibilities would need to be expanded to include responsibility for the environmental impact of the designed system over its whole useful life. Simultaneously, some form of environmental monitoring would be needed to check the impact of the designed system on its environment during this period, including the changing state and response of the environment.

The designer has therefore to look at the impacts of the designed system over time. The creation of the built environment can appear more or less invasive or damaging depending on how far into the future we project its effects. The accumulation or intensification of activities and the ecosystem's regeneration time and capacity are important factors in whether the built system's effect is negligible and/or temporary or permanently destructive. Negative effects could be broken down into several stages or levels. Some disturbances, such as upstream dumping of damaging waste on a single occasion, will cause a temporary ecosystem change. Drastic intervention such as complete removal of biotic components down to the bedrock in preparation for building would have permanent effects.

As contemporary law and other determining professional institutions have conceived of the design process, designers are not currently responsible for the later disposal of the components of their works. This is a practice issue that needs to be addressed by the professional institutions.

• Design to reduce the inputs into the built environment, including not only construction materials but also the energy derived from non-renewable resources to effect their transportation, assembly and construction on the site as well as the energy required to sustain the internal environmental conditions through the operational systems to their eventual recycling or reuse or ecological reintegration.

From the point of view of the ecologist, a building is simply a transient place in the flow of materials and energy in the biosphere, managed and assembled by people for a brief period of use (a period usually economically defined).

• Design to account for the long-term ecological impact of the efforts of designers, which is not traditionally the responsibility of designers. One possible solution to environmental problems would be to make manufacturers or suppliers of building materials and components responsible for these long-term consequences. Under such a system, the designer would assemble the materials and components in a building with the understanding that these would eventually be 'remanufactured' or returned to the supplier or manufacturer.

Customarily, when a building reaches the end of its useful life it is demolished and the constituent materials discarded or salvaged for reuse elsewhere. In the present economic system materials flow one way – from their points of origin as natural resources, through their transformation and assembly into goods, to their sale to the customer. The consumer uses the building but it is not 'consumed'; strictly speaking, he or she discards it after use. Many products that are ordinarily considered to be 'consumed' actually only render temporary service in the built environment. Even when a building is demolished, its fabric remains as output to the environment in the form of discarded materials.

If this one-way flow of materials persists as accepted practice, the rampant discarding of waste building fabric will result in its accumulation in the ecosystem and this mass will subsequently strain the environment's carrying capacity. The eventual reuse of materials needs to concern designers from the outset. In the ecological approach, the designer must assess the potential for the building's components to be recycled.

Ideally, although this is not practicable in absolute terms, the design should primarily use local and nearby resources. This reduces the energy costs of transportation of the materials.

Greenhouse gases

The heating up of the earth is the result of a growing accumulation of gases in the atmosphere that are preventing heat from escaping from the planet. The 'greenhouse' phenomenon begins when solar radiation enters the earth's atmosphere, hits the surface of the earth, and is transformed into infrared energy and heat. The heat rises and bombards the earth's atmosphere with carbon dioxide and other gases, forcing the gaseous molecules to vibrate. The gas molecules act as reflectors, sending some of the heat back to the surface, creating a warming effect. Carbon dioxide, methane and other greenhouse gases provide an atmospheric blanket that allows enough of the heat generated by the sun's radiation to stay on earth to provide the right conditions for the flourishing of life. For the 10,000 years leading up to the industrial age, the balance of greenhouse gases was relatively stable, so that the temperature on the planet remained within a narrow range. However, the burning of massive amounts of coal, then oil and natural gas in the 19th and 20th centuries, changed the equation.

Nearly 75 per cent of the increase in CO_2 concentrations over the past 20 years is attributable to the burning of fossil fuels. The remainder is the result of deforestation and land-use changes, both of which release CO_2 into the atmosphere. While the land and ocean absorb half of the increase in CO_2 emissions, the rest migrates to the atmosphere.

There is potential for hydrogen to become the next source of energy for the built environment. Hydrogen is the lightest and most ubiquitous element in the universe. When harnessed as a form of energy it becomes 'the for ever fuel'. One proposal is to have hydrogen-driven micro power-plants on site with the end-user as 'distributed generation' connected to a vast, worldwide hydrogen energy web where users can share and sell energy to one another.

Today, nearly half the hydrogen produced in the world is derived from natural gas via a steam-reforming process. The natural gas reacts with steam in a catalytic converter. The process strips away the hydrogen atoms, leaving carbon dioxide as the by-product. Coal can also be reformed through gasification to produce hydrogen, but this is a more complex (and therefore more expensive) process than using natural gas. Hydrogen can also be produced from oil or gasified biomass.

Summary

The designer can adopt one of several means to design to conserve the use of non-renewable energy and material resources:

- Consider what materials and energy sources flow into the built system or building and ensure that these inputs suit the built environment's anticipated patterns of use as well as its projected lifespan. This fit will be easier to achieve when design assignments are still unbuilt and in the early design phase. However, even for existing built systems, the designer can take measures to ensure that the materials and energy used are efficient and produce relatively little in the way of waste products.

- Modify the design brief and programme to reduce the production of outputs.

- Reduce the levels of consumption of non-renewable sources of energy by the designed system's users, which will in turn lead to an overall decrease in by-products from the designed system.

- Change the processes taking place within the built system that are responsible for outputs. For instance, the construction, production and recovery processes within the human-made built environment could be modified to increase efficiency and thereby reduce waste. By using fewer non-renewable sources of energy and materials in the built environment as a result of increased efficiency, the designer can limit the destruction of the ecological environment.

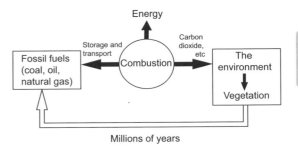

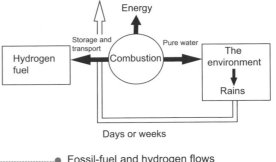

● Fossil-fuel and hydrogen flows

- Adjust the durability (period of useful life) of the designed system to suit its anticipated use as a designed lifespan.

- Integrate the internal processes of the designed system and its emissions to be within the resilience and carrying capacity of the surrounding ecosystem to assimilate the projected levels of emissions. Not only will the level of outputs need to be considered, but the timing and regularity of emissions will have to be taken into consideration as well. This will obviously depend upon the ecological carrying capacity of the locality's ecosystems and biospheric processes (in B4 and B5) with regard to those particular emissions (ie of waste energy and materials).

Energy efficiency is the ratio of energy services out to energy input. It means getting the most out of energy used.

Note:

Energy conservation is reduced energy consumption through lower quality of energy services (eg lower heating or air-conditioning levels through turning down thermostat levels, slower speed limits for cars, consumption limits for appliances, etc). It means doing without to save energy and is influenced by regulation, consumer behaviour and lifestyle changes.

The future may lie in the development of fusion energy. The largest effort to develop fusion energy is the JET (Joint European Torus) project (started in 1978). However, many of the scientific and engineering challenges in the development of fusion energy have yet to be resolved.

B27 Design for the management of outputs from the built environment and their integration with the natural environment: designing to eliminate pollution and for benign biointegration

Ecodesign requires the designer to be aware of all the outputs emitted from the designed system over its entire life cycle from its production through to its reuse and recycling, to ensure that these do not contaminate or negatively affect the natural environment, that they are either reused or recycled continuously within the built environment, and that they are benignly and seamlessly reintegrated into the natural environment at the end of the built system's life.

If we adopt the strategies of ecomimicry, namely put into practice what we have learned of how an ecosystem handles materials and wastes from each of its levels, then the principle simply stated is, 'waste equals food' in the ecosystems. Nature's ecosystems are cyclical whereas our present industrial systems are linear. In nature, matter is cycled continuously, and thus ecosystems generate no waste. Pollution begins the moment that a living organism violates the law that limits consumption to within the boundaries of existing resources and consumes more than it produces or reproduces.

Human systems generally take natural resources, transform them into products (and generate wastes along the way), and sell the products to consumers, who produce more wastes by discarding the products after use.

When transposed to our built environment, the principle in ecosystems of 'waste equals food' means that all products and materials manufactured, as well as the wastes generated in the manufacturing process, must eventually provide nourishment for something new. Generally stated, a sustainable business organisation would be one that is embedded in an integrated 'ecology of organisations', in which the waste (as outputs) of any one organisation would function as a resource for another. In such a sustainable industrial system, the total outflow of each organisation – its products and wastes – would be perceived and treated as resources cycling through the system.

In terms of the building industry, designing for long-term durability would include adaptable buildings – designs that not only work in the present but also adapt well for future users – pleasant, livable and humane. Buildings should also be flexible so that unexpected uses can be accommodated – 'long life, loose fit, low energy' – and have design elements that wear well. Designing for the future means design that works and lasts.

Adaptive use is the destiny of most buildings. It invites longevity and uses fewer resources in the long run. Remodelling and rehabilitation are essential. If architects have anything to

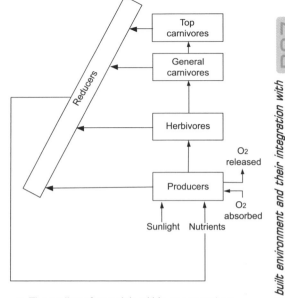

The cycling of materials within an ecosystem

Design for the management of outputs from the built environment and their integration with the natural environment

Material	Generated	Recovered	Recovery as per cent of generation
Total MSW	231.9	69.9	30.1
Paper, cardboard	86.7	39.4	45.4
Glass	12.8	2.9	23.0
Metals	18.0	6.4	35.4
Plastics	24.7	1.3	5.4
Rubber, leather	6.4	0.8	12.2
Textiles	9.4	1.3	13.5
Wood	12.7	0.5	3.8
Other materials in products	4.0	0.9	21.3
Food, other	25.9	0.7	2.6
Yard trimmings	27.7	15.8	56.9
Misc. inorganic wastes	3.5		

Generation and recovery of materials (USA, 2000)

learn from preservationists, it is how to design new buildings that will endear themselves to future preservationists 60 years from now. Take all that a century of sophisticated building preservation has learned about materials, space planning, scale, mutability, adaptability, functional tradition, functional originality and sheer flash, and apply it to new construction. Old buildings, like old forests, are appraised as intergenerational equity.

• Large developments are based on the idea of replacement. Piecemeal growth is based on the idea of repair. Since replacement means consumption of resources, while repair means conservation of resources, it is easy to see that piecemeal growth is the sounder of the two from an ecological point of view. But there are even more practical differences. Large development is based on the fallacy that it is possible to build perfect buildings. Piecemeal growth is based on the healthier and more realisitic view that mistakes are inevitable. Unless monetary resources are available to repair it every building, once built, is condemned to be, to some extent, unworkable. Piecemeal growth is based on the assumption that adaptation between buildings and their users is necessarily a slow and continuous business that cannot, under any circumstances, be achieved in a single leap.

• With growing environmentalism, another long-term issue is conserving the embodied energy of buildings and cutting down on the enormous solid-waste burden of demolished buildings. Recyclable materials are the obvious solution. Some industries, led by German car manufacturers, are adopting 'design for reuse' and 'design for disassembly' engineering. Design for disassembly in building construction is doubly appealing because it invites later reshaping of a building. The present design for demolition practice is facing a revolution that will change behaviour from the materials manufacturer through the architect to the carpenter. Nailing is archaic and it is easier to power-drive (and undrive) self-tapping screws. Timber-frame construction was the original design-for-disassembly building material. For instance, throughout medieval northern Europe, timbers were handed down from building to building for centuries. Galvanised steel studs are cheaper, lighter, straighter, easier to cut, don't rot and over 60 per cent are recycled. Assembled with wallboard screws, steel stud walls can be quickly taken apart and reused.

• Much current ecological design endeavour has focused on energy efficiency or conservation; greater importance needs to be placed on outputs management, which is to say the 'internal-to-external exchanges' from the built environment into the natural environment (L12 in the interactions framework). As we have mentioned earlier, to design our building as a completely closed system, without any exchanges of energy and material with its external environment, is not possible in practice, since external environment interactions are necessary attributes of living systems.

Having exhausted all the options of designing for recovery (see above), we may have to accept that a certain amount of environmental interaction and exchange cannot be avoided, and we will need to ensure that our design process is geared towards the reduction of initial energy outputs. This focus is crucial since, once an output is produced, it can only be managed at the cost of additional energy, materials and impact on the environment. In the case of the skyscraper and similarly large buildings, it is important to work at the outset to bring about a reduction in the amount of materials and energy that will be expelled by the building. Once the building is completed, certain limitations (discussed above) will impinge upon the recovery process.

The designer is in fact the 'outputs manager' for any given building project (in B27), working to minimise its negative environmental impact. First, the designer has to determine just what part of the built environment under his or her control is going to be expelled into the surrounding ecosystem. Using the interactions framework (see A5), the designer considers the whole range of emissions from the building. The designer has to know not only what materials and energies are going to be produced by the building(s), but also what forms they are going to take, with what parts of the natural environment they are likely to interact, what their effects on existing life forms are likely to be and, finally, where they will ultimately end up. The decisions that a designer makes concerning these potential pollutants are fundamental and must be integrated into the design process from the outset. As an outputs manager, the designer works throughout the process to control the amount of materials and energy expelled, modifying the design in order to reduce pollution. In those unfortunately unavoidable cases in which pollution from the new project cannot be helped, the designer must take steps to ensure the ecologically benign treatment of outputs.

- Decisions that affect pollution by the built environment are not presently considered to be the designer's prerogative in most instances. Instead, the problems of emissions are ordinarily shifted to others, such as pollution engineers, who sometimes rely too much on simplistic technological solutions that do not take account of the ecological complexities of our ecosystems.

- An ecologically simplistic approach limits the broad consideration of environmental consequences of the kind described above. If, for instance, any activity threatens to produce water pollution, a typical response would be to apply technical solutions to the problem. These might take the form of diluting the anticipated water pollution or treating the wastes prior to their emission. The ecological approach, on the other hand, would alter the activity at the source in order to reduce or eliminate the amount of pollution produced in the first place. Unfortunately, this second approach is rarely taken.

Type of material	Debris (%)
Wood	27.4
Asphalt/concrete/brick/dirt	23.3
Drywall	13.4
Roofing	12.0
Miscellaneous mixed	11.9
Metal	88
Paper	2.7
Plastics	0.5
Total	100.0

Metals have the highest recycling rates among materials recovered from construction and demolition (C&D) sites. Good markets for ferrous metals as well as copper and brass have existed for years. Steel as estimated has a C&D recycling rate of 85%.

Demolition debris from built forms •

First, the designer must know what is going to be discharged. He or she must determine the sources of outputs as well as their qualities and quantities. Second, the designer will want to know where the emissions will have an impact. Third, the designer must ask what type of damage will be caused and how regularly. Fourth, when the designer has determined the extent and character of the impact, he or she will have to assess whether it is significant. Having ascertained that the impact is significant, the designer will then analyse the range of solutions to the problem and propose various design responses aimed at limiting the pollution. Finally, once the building is in operation, the designer will want to confirm that the measures proposed for limiting emissions have been adopted and will also monitor their effectiveness.

Dealing with pollution

Waste product discharges

Design response to the reuse or recycling of potential waste products should be determined by balancing three objectives (see Partitioned Matrix in A5). These are: minimising the amounts of energy and materials imported by the building; decreasing the potential for wastes to be generated by the building; and minimising adverse effects on the ecological environment. In balancing these objectives, we should attempt to minimise the generation of wastes rather than focus on the ways in which they can be contained or treated. These latter processes are less effective ways of reducing strain on the earth, since they will necessarily require additional energy expenditures. It is best if the designer instead makes choices that lead to pollutants being minimised or entirely eliminated so that methods do not have to be invented or systems put in place to take care of them.

Protective measures

Where the design for recovery (eg reuse, recycling, remanufacture) cannot be adopted, the final options consist of protective measures. These will include the pre-treatment of pollutants – those by-products that are impossible to reuse in any way. By considering such measures, the designer will be minimising adverse impact on the environment.

Pre-treatment

In those cases where it is impossible to recycle potential outputs, the designer can also consider their pre-treatment. Through pre-treatment, the harmful qualities of emissions are neutralised. The material or energy is modified so that it causes less strain on the capacity of the ecological environment as it is absorbed. Pre-treatment methods can comprise either physical, chemical or biological transformations. Physical processes improve the materiality of the expelled material; for example, the size(s) of the particles that are discharged, the specific gravity of the materials, their viscosity, etc. Discharged by-products can also be made less harmful by altering them chemically. Such transformations can be brought about by reagents, which also must be chosen carefully since they can create additional environmental harm. Finally, biological processes work to isolate colloidal organic impurities and other materials in solution in a material that is expelled from the built environment. Biological reactions can also be staged in order to make the material more susceptible to absorption into the environment. The processes of filtration and sludge activation are both biological in nature.

Regardless of whether the process used is a physical, chemical or biological one, pre-treatment nearly always requires additional energy and materials. Pre-treatment also runs the risk of further environmental consequences. Our objective, therefore, in designing a pre-treatment system is to ensure that it can function with minimal harm to the environment. The process should also not completely exhaust the assimilative capacity of the environmental sink into which the products are going to be discharged. Pre-treatment is not a panacea: it does not reduce the total output of the built system. Rather, pre-treatment results in materials that are better suited – by virtue of their forms and the temporal and spatial patterns of their discharge – to assimilation by the environment. Ideally, pre-treatment should turn pollution into benign discharges, but it should only be contemplated after all possible steps have been taken to reduce the amounts of resources used and expelled by the building, and after a thorough analysis of the surrounding environment has been made.

Retention systems/storage

Some potential emissions (for instance, hazardous materials) cannot be treated, and therefore cannot be readily disposed of. For systems that are going to produce such materials, it is perhaps best to design a retention system. The offending outputs can then be stored temporarily until methods and opportunities for disposal are more favourable. This kind of design can also be employed to attune discharges to the assimilative capacities of the environment: materials can be stored until the receiving environmental sink is able to handle them. Hoppers, tanks and other storage systems can also be used to separate pollutants while awaiting further processing. In other cases, by storing wastes we can reduce their volume while we await better solutions for their removal, treatment, recovery or discharge. Obviously, storage will require space and equipment. It is better not to design processes that produce these outputs in the first instance.

	Common pollutant categories							
	BOD	Bacteria	Nutrients	Ammonia	Turbidity	TDS	Acids	Toxics
Point sources: municipal sewage-treatment plants	X	X	X	X				X
Industrial facilities	X							
Combined sewer overflows	X	X	X	X	X	X		X
Non-point sources: Agricultural runoff	X	X	X		X	X		X
Urban runoff	X	X	X		X	X		X
Construction runoff			X		X			X
Mining runoff					X	X	X	X
Septic system	X	X	X					X
Landfill/spills	X							X
Silviculture runoff	X		X		X			X

Pollutants and their sources ●

Storing emitted materials is only a partial solution, since it does not fundamentally alter them. Unfortunately, the most environmentally problematic materials – toxic wastes, hazardous and radioactive materials – have been dealt with in this manner. In addition to being stored in a variety of containers, these materials are sometimes subjected to compaction or refrigeration. Storage and treatment can take place at transfer stations or processing centres, or on site.

Dispersal

A nearly opposite approach to the storage of pollutants is their dispersal over a wide area. In certain circumstances, the designer may opt for casting the discharges over a large expanse of land, water or air. The concentration of the pollutant is thus lowered to the extent that it has a negligible adverse impact on any one area. For instance, to disperse gaseous discharges from an industrial plant over the widest possible area, a designer might recommend the construction of a high chimney. Or the industry might be spread over a larger area rather than concentrated in one place, in order to disperse the pollutants to a greater degree. The siting of industrial plants can also be determined with particularly sensitive areas in mind. Ideally, dispersion alone will not be counted on to solve pollution problems, since it does not essentially reduce the amount of harmful discharges released into the environment. As we are dispersing a pollutant, we should also be looking into ways of reducing its volume or eliminating it by redesigning the built environment.

Dilution

Environmentally harmful emissions can also be diluted in order to minimise their impact. Increasing the volume of some substances through dilution in a benign medium can sometimes make it easier for the environmental sink to accept them. Furthermore, the many sections of the environment differ in the degree to which they are capable of accepting pollutants. It may therefore be helpful in some cases to divert outputs from their places of generation. Thus the materials can be transported from an area that is unsuitable for discharge to one that is capable of assimilating the discharge, possibly as a result of its lower degree of previous contamination. This alternative should not be used excessively, since the environment is a finite area the unpolluted portions of which will eventually become exhausted. Furthermore, the transportation of pollutants consumes even more energy and causes additional environmental harm.

• When all preventive measures have been rejected as impracticable, the designer has no alternative to 'final protective measures'. With the knowledge that potentially harmful substances are going to be generated by the built environment, the designer takes steps to protect humans, animals, plants and other inhabitants of the natural environment from harm. Designing these protective measures can take two forms: designing for environmental treatment and designing for environmental desensitisation.

Environmental treatment

Designing for environmental treatment consists of making changes to the receiving sink so that the impact of discharges will be minimised. This is done in place of treating the outputs at their points of generation, and it is particularly useful as a means of counteracting the cumulative effects of a variety of emissions that will all end up in the same sink. The designer should seek as much as possible to anticipate the consequences of disposing of pollutants in the environment through a careful analysis of their impact on the local ecosystem. There are obvious drawbacks to this approach: it will require additional energy and materials, and it will offer only a limited short-term solution to environmental pollution problems. These drawbacks are of relatively less concern when responding to single disasters than to long-term environmental issues. For instance, this approach could usefully be employed in the case of an oil spill, when the environment in the area of this one-off accidental discharge could be modified to help it assimilate a greater amount of oil (Spofford, 1971).

Environmental desensitisation

Designing for environmental desensitisation entails making a receiving sink less sensitive to the impact of contaminants. This sort of design attempts to protect those elements of the environment that are susceptible to harm – including human beings, flora and fauna – from their degraded surroundings. In some cases, these potential receivers of the negative impact can be separated from the source by a buffer zone in the environment. Another example of desensitisation would be spraying a scented vapour on to a contaminated beach to lessen odours from pollutants. As is clear from this example, this approach is a last resort for environments that are not susceptible to any other methods, and it will certainly require additional energy and material expenditures.

Transportation, transformation, storage

Where it is unavoidable and discharged outputs enter the environment, they can be treated in one of three ways: by being transported within the ecosystem, by transformation from one form to another or by storage. Each of these approaches will have an impact on the environment. Transportation will require the use of an environmental medium, transformation will demand energy to accomplish the modification of the material's physical, chemical or biological makeup, and storage will take place in some other part of the environment, which may suffer an adverse effect as a result.

When a building discharges a given substance, that material (or amount of energy) can take one of a number of routes through the natural environment. These potential pathways must be analysed before the discharges are made, because even the most minute and seemingly inconsequential outputs can have serious environmental implications. For example, a 1.25°C increase in the surface temperature of an aquatic system, brought about as a consequence of thermal emissions, could have a serious impact on biotic communities living in the water. When the impairment of the ecosystems by a discharged material becomes significant, an ecological imbalance has occurred. Thus pollution is constituted by the entry into the ecosystems of materials or quantities of energy, produced by human beings, which harm or destroy those ecosystems. Pollutants can be substances that are not native to the ecosystem, or they can be materials or forms of energy that are familiar in a given ecosystem, but not in the large concentrations that result from human habitation and which are unhealthy for the environment.

Obviously, the degree of environmental impairment from a given pollutant is related to the ability of an ecosystem to assimilate that discharged material or energy. The assimilative capacity of the ecosystem with respect to any given pollutant will be variable over time and place. It will depend on local conditions as well as on the stochastic qualities of certain elements of the ecosystem. For instance, stream flow, temperature, amount of light and other factors will influence assimilative abilities; the character of the discharged materials or energies will also play an important role in determining the ability of the ecosystem to absorb such outputs.

Assessing discharge consequences

Whenever the amount of harmful energy and noxious materials discharged into the environment exceeds its ability to absorb them, this increased pollution sets off a chain of adverse environmental consequences.

• As we have already observed, a great amount of damage to one part of the environment may have a ripple effect on another. A pollutant can move throughout the environment, leading to changes in the qualities and quantities of resources in various areas. When a pollutant arrives in an ecosystem, it may upset the existing equilibrium, which then must be re-established. In cases of minor pollution, the disequilibrium may only be temporary: the pollution may cease and the system's equilibrium will be reinstated. But if a serious amount of pollution appears in an ecosystem and continues until the output exceeds the assimilative capacities of the system, then severe environmental damage can occur. This may even result in the destruction of the ecological environment, but in any event it will be damaged. In the latter case, the ecosystem will only contain those organisms that are able to survive in these degraded circumstances.

• In order to assess the assimilative capacity of the environment in the location where the discharge is to take place, the designer must determine the biological and physical capacities of the local ecosystem. He or she must also understand the characteristics of the materials to be expelled, as well as the patterns of their discharge. Thus the designer has to be able to specify the times and places of discharges in order to map concentrations of potential pollutants in the environment. Making such assessments is difficult, since emissions do not come from a single source but from a variety of them.

• In assessing an overall pattern of discharges a number of factors will have to be played off against one another. An extreme example would be an area in which heat was provided overwhelmingly by electricity, in which transportation was largely by electric-powered vehicles, in which gases from industry and steam plants were wet-scrubbed, but in which refuse was ground up and then dumped into the sewerage system and disgorged in raw form into waterways. In such a place, the air would be protected to a large extent. However, this area would be taxing its aquatic environment to the extreme. To take a contrasting example, a region in which municipal and industrial wastewater was treated effectively, and in which sludge and solids were incinerated, would be protecting its aquatic environments; however, it would be straining the assimilative capacities of the land and air. A third example would be a region that encouraged a great deal of recovery and recycling of waste materials while also achieving a low level in the production of residuals. If this degree of efficiency characterised the entire area and all production processes, there would be very little in the way of discharged pollutants entering the environment. Yet this region would require large quantities of materials and energy to fuel this level of recovery and recycling. The interactions framework in A5 helps us to make the difficult trade-offs that are required to achieve a balance in the area of environmental impact.

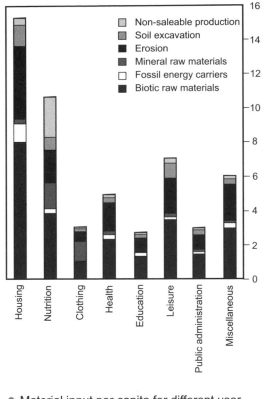

● Material input per capita for different user needs (Germany, 1990)

Counteracting the biosphere as 'sink'

However, at the end of the intended or designed economic life, the ecological physical life of our building's components, material or equipment persists; therefore some form of reuse or recycling must be identified for this final 'waste' to be managed. In order to avoid excessive discharges of wastes into the ecosystems at the end of the building's economic life, the extended use of the building element within the built environment is crucial.

• Ecosystems are the end point of waste, discharges and all other outputs of human-built systems. This is the idea of the biosphere as 'sink'. But, because ecosystems are finite and their ability to absorb these outputs is likewise finite, limits have to be placed on the discharge of waste products from the building lest the surrounding ecosystem's assimilative systems be overwhelmed. Taking a larger view, we see that the 'life' of the entire built

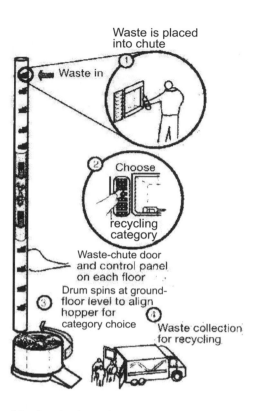

Waste is placed into chute

Waste in

① Waste in

② Choose recycling category

Waste-chute door and control panel on each floor

③ Drum spins at ground-floor level to align hopper for category choice

④ Waste collection for recycling

Mechanical waste separator ●┄┄┄┄┄

system is finite as well, and hence the designer has to consider what will be the final fate of the components of his or her building. When its usefulness is at an end, the building itself becomes waste, and its materials have either to be recycled or disposed of. Thus we can distinguish two aspects of the waste equation confronted by the designer: that relating to the amount of waste that will have to be processed during the building's life, and that which will have to be dealt with when, at the end of that life, the structure itself has to be disposed of. It is the ethical and professional responsibility of the ecological designer to consider both of these elements, for the responsibility for a building does not end upon hand over to the owners at the completion of construction; the designer's responsibility has to be from source to sink, covering the whole flow of the built system's components during its life cycle.

- Ecodesign acknowledges that all design has a global impact because of ecosystem connectivity. A building site, at least in the current understanding of the architectural and legal professions, is usually described by its low boundaries in a legally recognised way, much as a country is defined by internationally agreed borders. An ecosystem, by contrast, has evolved within natural boundaries, which may be criss-crossed by human lines and divisions, which, of course, the ecosystem does not respect. Just because the environment of the designer's site also has several or many other building lots contained within it does not mean that the designer can think of his or her particular site as discrete, an isolated entity that exists only within the legally specified, human-made lot lines. A site is not just a square on a map, but a place in the world; actions taken on that site have effects on local ecology that will extend to the other human-made parcels (ie building lots) in the same environment and beyond. As we have seen, the scale of such impacts of a design can be local, regional, continental and biospherical all at the same time.

- In the case of urban buildings such as skyscrapers, most sites, being urban, would usually have already been extensively degraded and rendered devoid of any biotic components. In such instances, the remaining environmental effects that the designer of the built system would have to take into account would be its impacts on the local micro-climate level (eg air pollution, thermal emissions, etc), its impacts on surrounding buildings, and all emissions and discharges of waste from the built system into the city's infrastructural system, which are then discharged elsewhere into the environment, both locally and globally (because of the connectivity of all natural systems in the biosphere).

- The designer must be aware that all designed systems, as open systems, emit outputs. These outputs, as waste, enter the surrounding ecosystem, whether they are in solid, liquid or gaseous form. In some cases, the outputs are brought back into the built system and recycled and reused, while other wastes may be unavoidably discharged into the ecosystem and have to be absorbed by the environment.

- The designer cannot simply take the view that once the wastes exit the built system they no longer have to be thought about, as if they had somehow disappeared by crossing the boundary of the built environment. Outputs from buildings, as from any built system, have to be absorbed into the ambient world; this may or may not require some degree of treatment to facilitate their assimilation by the ecosystem. Determining whether and at what level pre-treatment is necessary must, of course, be the responsibility of the designer, who will have to take into consideration various limiting factors. Meteorological features of the local environment determine the rate of waste dispersion by air; rainfall and the rate of ground-water runoff set limits on how much waste can be tolerated by riverine and other water systems; soil conditions not only affect land-based waste disposal but, because the environment's systems are linked, they will also determine wastewater reclamation and other factors. Similarly, topography, like soil conditions, affects the possibility of waste disposal through landfills and also plays a part in flooding and erosion – environmental dangers that the designer must also take into account.

- To help reduce atmospheric levels of greenhouse gas, carbon dioxide emissions from power-generating plants can now be captured and stored (carbon sequestration). The gas from fuel emissions, for example, can be extracted by using solvents, liquefaction, membrane separation or absorption to be stored in inert form over centuries. Saline reservoirs and unminable coal beds are also alternative carbon dioxide storage options.

- We should therefore regard the management of outputs from our designed system as a problem to be addressed ideally within the built environment itself, or at least in its immediate context. In the case of urban built forms, that will mean dealing with pollutants within the city itself. The transfer of emissions from the urban environment to outlying areas should only be contemplated in cases where pollutants cannot be reused locally or where they cannot be absorbed by the local ecological environment except at the cost of contamination and excessive expenditures of more energy.

- In those cases in which the designer cannot entirely preclude waste outputs from his or her building project, specialists in recycling as well as pollution-control engineers can use indicators to assess pollution levels. They can then determine the capacity of a given ecosystem to assimilate permissible forms of pollution. For example, for water pollution, algal blooms can indicate the presence of dissolved oxygen, evaporation, nutrients and faecal coliforms, as well as pesticides, herbicides and defoliants. The pH of water can also be analysed, as can the physical characteristics of a given body of water – such as sediment load, stream flow, temperature and turbidity – to reveal the presence of toxic and non-toxic dissolved solids.

- For those outputs (eg industrial emissions) that may potentially lead to pollution, certain indicators of the levels of permissible pollutants may be used to determine the assimilative capacity of the ecosystem (in B5). Such indicators, for instance, include:

Source	Carbon monoxide (CO)	Particulates	Sulphur oxides (SOx)	Unburned hydrocarbons (HC)	Nitrogen oxides (NOx)
Transportation	111.0	0.7	1.0	19.5	11.7
Fuel combustion in static sources, power generation	0.8	6.8	26.5	0.6	10.0
Industrial processes	11.4	13.1	6.0	5.5	2
Solid-waste disposal	7.2	1.4	0.1	2.0	0.4
Miscellaneous	16.8	3.4	0.3	7.1	0.4
Totals (1970)	147.2	25.4	33.9	34.7	22.7
Totals (1940)	85	27	22	19	7
Change over 30 years (%)	+73	-6	+54	+83	+224

● Pollutants released into the air in millions tons/annum (UK, 1970)

Design for the management of outputs from the built environment and their integration with the natural environment

Form of pollution	Indicators
Water	algal blooms;
	dissolved oxygen; evaporation; faecal coliforms; nutrients; pesticides; herbicides; defoliants
	pH
	physical water characteristics
	sediment load
	stream flow
	temperature
	total dissolved solids
	toxic dissolved solids
	turbidity
Air	carbon monoxide
	hydrocarbons
	particulate matter
	photochemical oxidants
	sulphur oxides
Land	land use and misuse
	soil erosion
	soil pollution

Earth and air analysis

In addition to water, pollution engineers can also analyse the air and earth to determine contaminant levels. Indicators in the atmosphere can reveal the presence of various forms of air pollution, including carbon monoxide, hydrocarbons, particulate matter, photochemical oxidants and sulphur oxides. The use and misuse of the land itself, which we might term 'land pollution', is indicated by obvious forms of soil erosion and soil pollution.

• Although it is convenient to think of indicators in terms of the parts of the ecosystem that are open to damage – earth, air and water – the impacts of the pollutants on the entire system and on the biosphere and its processes are also significant. The effect that various discharges from the built environment have on plant and animal species, populations, natural habitats and communities, as well as on the larger functioning of the ecosystem, should also be considered.

- The pollutants that we find in the environment are in fact a consequence of the decisions made in the earliest stages of the design process. From the moment that the designer makes a first schematic response to the requirements of a particular programme, he or she is determining what environmental impact the building will have. From the beginning, a built system should be designed in ways that minimise the production of those materials and quantities of energy that will contribute to the destruction of the environment. If this is done, then the building will not further tax the capacity of the ecosystem to absorb outputs. Since the environments that surround most of our intensive building types, such as skyscrapers, are densely developed, and their absorptive capacities are strained already in many instances, it is essential that new high rises and other urban buildings do not produce further large quantities of energy and materials that have to be assimilated.

- Many of the common building materials are associated with industrial processes that have the most serious potential for environmental pollution. One argument for their continued use is that many of these materials are potentially very durable and, if they are reused, the disadvantages of their manufacture may be balanced by their longer useful lives.

Output management

The appropriate measures for output management can be conceived as follows:

- reduction of outputs at the source of generation (eg by efficiency of production or systems adopted in the built environment);

- management of outputs after generation (eg through continuous reuse and recycling within the built environment); and

- application of final protective measures (eg by their benign and seamless reintegration into the ecosystems).

These measures may be related to the pathways taken by the outputs. For instance, to reduce the amount of waste materials produced by the built environment at the point of their potential generation, the designer can either modify the design or alter the methods used to manage those materials expelled from the building. The first step is to reduce the amount of materials and energy produced by the building and to ensure that those that are expelled exist in forms that are susceptible to effective management. Achieving these

Pollutant	Averaging time	California standards		National standards		
		Concentration	Method	Primary	Secondary	Primary
Ozone	1 hour	0.09 ppm (180 µg/m³)	Ultraviolet photometry	0.12 ppm (235 µg/m³)	Same as primary standard	Ethylene chemiluminescence
	1 hour	9.0 ppm (10 µg/m³)	Non-dispersive infrared spectroscopy (NDIR)	9 ppm (10 µg/m³)		Non-dispersive infrared spectroscopy (ND IR)
	8 hours	20 ppm (23 µg/m³)		0.053 ppm (100 µg/m³)		
Nitrogen dioxide	Annual average		Gas phase chemiluminescence		Same as primary standard	Gas phase chemiluminescence
	1 hour	0.25 ppm (470 µg/m³)				
Sulphur dioxide	Annual average		Ultraviolet fluorescence	80 ppm (0.03 µg/m³)		Pararosaniline
	24 hours	0.05 ppm (131 µg/m³)		365 ppm (0.14 µg/m³)		
	3 hours				1300 ppm (0.5 µg/m³)	
	1 hour	0.25 ppm (655 µg/m³)				
Suspended particulate matter (PM10)	Annual geometric mean		Size selective inlet high volume sampler and gravimetric a analysis			Inertial separation and gravimetric analysis
	24 hours			150 µg/m³	Same as primary standard	
	Annual arithmetic mean			50 µg/m³		
Sulphates	24 hours	25 µg/m³	Turbidimetric barium sulfate			
Lead	30-day average	1.5 µg/m³	Atomic absorption			Atomic absorption
	Calendar quarter			1.5 µg/m³	Same as primary standard	
Hydrogen Sulphide	1 hour	0.03 ppm (42 µg/m³)	Cadmium hydroxide STRactan			
Vinyl chloride (chloroethylene)	24 hours	0.010 ppm (26 µg/m³)	Tedlar bag collection, gas chromatography			
Visibility reducing particles	8 hours (10 am to 6 pm, PST)	In sufficient amount to produce an extinction coefficient of 0.23 per kilometre due to particles when the relative humidity is less than 70 per cent. Measure in accordance with ARB Method V.				
Applicable only in the Lake Tahoe air basin						
Carbon monoxide	8 hours	6 ppm (7 µg/m³)				
Visibility reducing particles	8 hours (10 am to 6 pm, PST)	In sufficient amount to produce an extinction coefficient of 0.07 per kilometre due to particles when the relative humidity is less than 70 per cent. Measure in accordance with ARB Method V.				

Ambient air quality standards

goals will mean modifying the project's design, and carefully selecting building materials and methods. At this early stage the designer takes steps to ensure that everything generated by the building can be managed effectively.

- There are several means of reducing the amount of waste products from a building. First, the designer considers what materials and energy sources are flowing into the building. These inputs should suit the anticipated patterns of use of the built environment as well as its projected life span (ie L21 in the Partitioned Matrix). This fit will be easier to achieve with projects that are in the design phase, but even for existing buildings the designer can take measures to ensure that the materials and energy used produce relatively little in the way of waste products. Second, the designer can modify the building programme in order to reduce the production of outputs. Third, it may be possible to reduce levels of energy consumption by the building's users, which will in turn lead to an overall decrease in by-products being turned out by the building. Fourth, the processes taking place within the building (L11) that are responsible for outputs can be changed. For instance, the construction, production and recovery processes could be modified to increase efficiency and thereby reduce waste. By using less energy and fewer materials in the built environment as a result of increased efficiency, we limit the destruction of the ecological environment. Fifth, the designer can adjust the durability of the building to suit its anticipated use and lifespan. Finally, the internal processes of the built environment (L11) should be coordinated with the ability of the surrounding ecosystem to assimilate the projected levels of emissions. Not only will the level of outputs need to be considered, but the timing and regularity of emissions will have to be taken into consideration as well.

- The management of waste products in the built environment usually requires additional expenditures of energy and materials with some added environmental costs. In the design and planning of the built environment, the designer should therefore ensure that difficult outputs are either minimised or not generated in the first place, as their disposal inevitably has to be considered.

- For a building that expels materials or wasted energy, the designer has the option of dealing with this pollution either before or after it is actually discharged into the surroundings. Some methods for managing outputs after their generation have already been discussed. In some cases, it may be possible to devise a use for materials or quantities of energy that might otherwise be expelled into the environment. In such cases, these potential outputs will be reused, recycled (or remanufactured). Where the design for recovery (eg reuse, recycling, remanufacture, etc) cannot be adopted, the final option consists of protective measures. These will include the pre-treatment of pollutants – those by-products that are impossible to reuse in any way (see under pre-treatment). By considering such measures, the designer will be minimising adverse impact on the environment.

Outputs from built environment	Flow in	Location	Flow out	Time scale for integration
CO_2	Fossil fuel burning, deforestation	Mass in atmosphere	Ocean absorption, uptake by afforestation	100 years
SO_2	Fossil fuel burning, ore smelting	Mass in atmosphere	Acid rain	1 week
Garbage	Production	Landfills, ocean dumping	Biological and physical degradation, burning, compost, recycle	10 years
Radioactive waste	Power plants	Waste repositories, now almost wholly in interim storage in power reactors	Radioactive decay	24,000 years for Pu
Nutrients (nitrates, phosphates)	Agricultural runoff	Water bodies in rivers, lakes, aquifers	Flushing, plant uptake, burial in sediment, evaporation	(Depends on, water body) 1 year; 100 years; 3 months
Beverage cans	Discarding	Stock everywhere	Recycle, degrade	5 years
Sewage	Production	Waterways	Biodegradation	1–3 years
Cars	Production, import	Car population	Junking, export,	10 years
Housing	Construction	Housing stock	Reuse, recycle Demolition, burning, land – fill	50–75 years

Outputs from the built environment and environmental integration

- One method of reducing waste in products is to design them based on containers. Those parts of the designed system as a product can be designed with containers for refilling. Refilling eliminates the need for making (and disposing of) replacement products or packaging. There are three basic refill systems: (1) the container that can be returned to the manufacturer for refilling; (2) the container that the user can take to the refilling point; or (3) the container that uses refill packs, which contain less packaging, to refill the originals. Many of the supplies that go to a building (eg food and fuel) come in containers.

- The designer will also need to consider the issue of consistency in component replacement. Some parts of the built structure, facility or infrastructure may be made of durable materials but fail to endure simply because one part wears out before the rest and can't be replaced. The capacity to replace these crucial parts can be incorporated into the design. Many common products in the built environment could be made reusable through basic design changes. One way is by modular design and assembly, which can make repairs and replacement quicker and easier to accomplish. When one component fails or becomes obsolete, the particular module can be easily removed or replaced. With modular design and assembly with mechanical joints (as against chemically bonded joints), the users themselves may even be able to do more of their own repairs and replacements, and facilitate the principle of continuous reuse and recycling. In the case of professional servicing where labour is often the primary expense, modular assembly can mean lower repair bills. A related concept is design for disassembly (DFD, B28), which is aimed at making it easy to take apart complex products and components.

- The designer must be aware that to design for reuse, recycling and recovery, extra storage space and in-built redundancy must be provided in the designed system and that construction joints or points of connection should be mechanically connected as against chemically bonded. At the minimum, there must be adequate storage space for the building-wide collection of materials, eg separated glass, aluminium, office paper.

- To reduce the amount of waste material produced by the built environment at the point of its potential generation, the designer can either modify the design or alter the methods used to manage materials expelled from the building. To recap, the first step is to reduce the amount of materials and energy produced by the building and to ensure that those that are expelled exist in forms that are susceptible to effective management. Achieving these goals will mean modifying the project's design, and carefully selecting building materials systems and methods. At this early stage, the designer should take steps to ensure that everything generated by the building can be managed effectively.

Computer-age wasteland ●

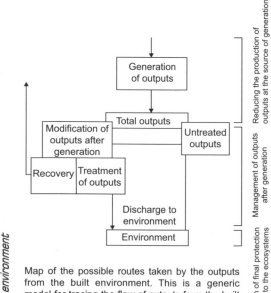

Reducing the production of outputs at the source of generation

Management of outputs after generation

Application of final protection measure to the ecosystems

Map of the possible routes taken by the outputs from the built environment. This is a generic model for tracing the flow of outputs from the built environment; it could be considered as a problem definition tool. The selection of the appropriate form of management for each individual output from a system will thus depend on the built system, the form of outputs discharged, the operating condition, the form of the inputs, the state of the environment and the interaction of all these factors.

Management of outputs

● In the case of solid-waste management, there are some basic choices: combustion, incineration, landfilling and composting. Each produces different outputs, and the choice depends on which output is desired. All these wastes are the outcome of the existent systems in the built environment and would be reduced or eliminated if the built environment were designed at the outset for continuous reuse, recycling and eventual biointegration back into the natural environment. If energy recovery from waste is sought, incineration and landfilling are choices. The total energy content of mixed solid waste is frequently only a little less than the energy content of a low-grade coal or lignite. If maximum energy recovery from waste is desired, then combustion is the solution. In combustion, virtually all the organic carbon is instantaneously converted to CO_2, high capital costs are involved, the process is impractical for wet organic wastes, and emission controls and ways of dealing with the consequences for biospheric processes must be implemented. Incineration of mixed waste is not the only combustion alternative, for example we can produce a refuse-derived fuel from paper or wood waste that can be co-fired in conventional power plants, but this adds cost as well as the question of emissions into the atmosphere. In controlled landfilling with methane recovery, something less than 50 per cent of the organic carbon is anaerobically converted to biogas (methane and CO_2) over a 20- to 30-year period; this biogas is available for local energy needs. Landfills, on the other hand, function like large, rather inefficient anaerobic digesters in the ground. However, research has shown that over 90 per cent of landfill biogas production can be recovered. There is no net energy benefit in the composting option, where the organic carbon component of waste is both converted to CO_2 and retained or sequestered in the end product of the composting process – humus/organic matter. Although energy is not recoverable (although heat is) composted wastes are useful as conditioners/amendments to boost the organic-matter content of soils.

Summary

The designer can adopt one of several means to reduce the amount of outputs emitted from the built environment. The ecological designer must design to conserve the use of non-renewable energy resources and non-renewable or scarce material resources as a sustainable design strategy. The key approach to the reduction of extraction and consumption of non-renewable energy and material resources is simply the reduction by design of user needs and use of these resources and to design for efficient material use and for continuous reuse and recycling of materials. Design will need to be modular and facilitate change and flexibility. Construction should optimise off-site prefabrication and pre-installation. To achieve these aims, all methods of construction and assembly technologies have to be universally applicable and adaptable to whatever scenario may evolve in the future.

B28 Design the built system over its life cycle from source to reintegration: designing to enable and facilitate disassembly for continuous reuse, recycling and reintegration

Whether the design assignment is for a product, a built structure, a facility or an infrastructure, the ecological designer must design for continuous reuse and recycling within the built environment before the end of its useful life eventually leading to its benign disassembly, and reintegration back into the ecosystems. To achieve this seamlessly, the design must influence the way that the various parts and components are assembled, put together, fixed and connected. The basic principle is to design for disassembly (DFD). To facilitate reuse, recovery and recycling, the product or material should not be made into composites as combinations of composite materials potentially result in one material becoming an impurity and so affecting the recycling of the other material.

There are three broad alternative strategies for a design approach based on the conservation of resources.

Strategies to reduce the supply and flow rate

• Reduce the existing consumption level by controlling the rate of resource use or lowering the standard of living.

• Reduce flow by reducing the total number of products or components turned out.

• Substitute other resources (eg renewable resources).

Strategies to improve the efficiency and performance of existing systems

• Encourage the recovery (reuse, recycling, regeneration) of existing components, provided that it does not increase environmental degradation and contamination.

• Increase the efficiency of recovery processes.

• Extend the useful life of a unit or a component.

• Control corrosion and wear to curb losses.

• Increase efficiency of production processes.

• Increase efficiency of the component or equipment use.

1. Use recycling and recyclable materials
2. Minimise the number of types of materials
3. Avoid toxic and hazardous material
4. Avoid composite materials
5. Avoid secondary finishes to materials
6. Provide standard and permanent identification of material types
7. Minimise the number of different types of components
8. Use mechanical rather than chemical connections
9. Use an open building system with interchangeable parts
10. Use modular design
11. Use assembly technologies compatible with standard building practice
12. Separate the structure from the cladding
13. Provide access to all building components
14. Design components sized to suit handling at all stages
15. Provide for handling components during assembly and disassembly
16. Provide adequate tolerance to allow for disassembly
17. Minimise number of fasteners and connectors
18. Minimise types of connectors
19. Design joints and connectors to withstand repeated assembly and disassembly
20. Allow for parallel disassembly
21. Provide permanent identification for each component
22. Use a standard structural grid
23. Use prefabricated subassemblies
24. Use lightweight materials and components
25. Identify point of disassembly permanently
26. Provide spare parts and storage for them
27. Retain information on the building and its assembly process

• Design for disassembly (DFD) principles

General design strategies for the redesign of existing systems/design of new systems

- Achieve materials and energy economy and low ecological impact by appropriate design and selection.

- Redesign existing systems for maximum performance.

- Design for ease of repair and recovery (eg by standardisation and simplification of materials and components).

- Design for optimum use of each unit of the component.

- Design for minimum use of materials per unit per component.

- Design for efficiency and low ecological impact in use.

- Design for efficiency and low ecological impact in processing and recovery.

The above examples are, of course, not exhaustive of all the possible strategies for designing for the conservation of resources. They are, however, indicative of the way in which our design effort should be directed. We should also be aware of the extensive outputs of waste during construction, and the designer must ensure that the builders have a waste-management programme that includes recycling and reuse of materials and responsible waste disposal.

In nature, building is a natural function. When building activities take place in nature, the organism (whether a bird, an ant or a bear) takes materials from a variety of sources and then concentrates them into one specific location (ie the equivalent of the 'project site'), and then assembles them into an enclosure for its activities and protection from the climatic elements or other hostile organisms. It is, therefore, an inescapable fact that all building activities involve the utilisation, redistribution and concentration of some component of the earth's energy and material resources (and in current construction practice) from usually distant locations into specific locations with the result of changing the ecology of that part of the biosphere as well as adding to the composition (usually inorganic) of the ecosystem of that locality. As we mentioned earlier, the further continued existence and maintenance of this newly added built environment is dependent on the earth's ecosystem and resources continuing to supply it with those inputs of materials and energy necessary for its operations.

In the case of humans, the distances over which materials are sourced and transported are intercontinental and the scale of enclosure is not only large but unprecedented. These 'inputs' into the built environment (see B3, L21) include not only constructional materials but also the energy derived from non-renewable resources to effect the transportation of the materials, their assembly and construction on the site as well as the energy required to sustain the internal environmental conditions through the operational systems (in L11) over the designed system's life to their eventual recycling or reuse or ecological reintegration back into the natural environment. However, the consequences of the above are not confined to the project site's ecosystem, but impact on the global environment as a whole. Both outputs and inevitable wastes are emitted (L12 in the Partitioned Matrix in A5).

For these reasons, the designer might regard the creation of a built form as a form of energy and materials management and, in effect, as essential prudent resource management. For example, the supply of electricity involves the conversion of fuel into energy, and these conversion processes deplete non-renewable resources; in addition, they can have a lasting negative effect on the environment through the related emissions caused over the entire life cycle of the building. As we have noted, green design takes account of the entire process and operation of the built system, including its final dismantling; in effect, the ecological designer designs the life and death of his creation. In ecological design, the designer is ethically responsible for the designed system, whether it is a building or a product, over its entire life cycle up to its after-life, ie what happens to the built system or product and its materials at the end of their useful lives. Therefore, the designer must not only understand the environmental implications of all the building's inputs and outputs, but must also seek to recycle all outputs as inputs to other processes (ie analogous to natural recycling in ecosystems). The designer must be concerned with how the designed system and all its component parts can be taken apart or disassembled in ways that will allow maximum levels of reuse and recycling.

Ecologically, the designer's design concerns extend even beyond the point at which the building is handed over to the client or users or in the case of a product when it is manufactured or sold. From an environmental perspective, the designer is ethically responsible for the disposition of the materials in the designed system from 'source back to source' and for the long-term fate of the designed system. Working within the parameters of a rigorous ecological approach, the designer determines not only how and at what environmental cost (in terms of demands for materials and impacts on the planet) a designed system can be built, but also analyses how and at what cost to the environment the built work will be used, managed and ultimately disposed of. In other design fields, this approach, embodying both initial design and subsequent use and disposal, is called design for disassembly (DFD) or design for reuse, recycling and remanufacture.

Entity	Process	Time scale
Plastic film container	Degrades	20–30 years
Aluminium can and tab	Degrades	80–100 years
Glass bottle	Degrades	1 million years
Plastic bag	Degrades	10–20 years
Plastic-coated paper	Degrades	5 years
Nylon fabric	Degrades	30–40 years
Rubber boot sole	Degrades	50–80 years
Leather	Degrades	Up to 50 years
Wool sock	Degrades	1–5 years
Cigarette butt	Degrades	1–5 years
Orange or banana peel	Degrades	2–5 years
CO_2 in atmosphere	Falls out to oceans	100 years
H_2O in atmosphere	Falls out	7 years
O_3 at ground level	Degrades to harmless products	Few hours
O_3 in stratosphere	Degrades to harmless products	Few hours
$CFCl_3$ in atmosphere	Degrades to products that do not increase stratospheric O_3	70 years
CF_2Cl_2 in atmosphere	Degrades to products that do not increase stratospheric O_3	120 years
$C_2F_2Cl_3$ in atmosphere	Degrades to products that do not increase stratospheric O_3	90 years
CH_4 in atmosphere	Degrades to products that are not as greenhouse active	10 years
CO in atmosphere	Degrades though main product is CO_2	0.4 years
Human excrement in woods	Biodegrades	6 weeks
Human	Reproduces	30 years
Building	Becomes unusable	50–75 years
Forest	Undergoes succession from clearcut to mature forest ecosystem	50–300 years
Fishery	Recovery from over-fishing	5–10 years
Whales	Recovery from over-whaling	50 years
Large appliance	Becomes unusable	15 years
Arable soil	Recovers from erosion	Centuries

Temporal integration: material degradation periods

The long-term ecological impact of such efforts is, of course, not conventionally the responsibility of designers. An alternative approach would be to make the manufacturers or suppliers of products or owners of built structures and components responsible for the long-term consequences of these items. Under such a regime, the designer would assemble the materials and components in a built structure or product on the understanding that these would eventually be 'remanufactured' or returned to the supplier or manufacturer for reprocessing or recovered for subsequent reuse or recycling.

Customarily, when a designed system reaches the end of its usefulness it is discarded or demolished (in the case of a structure or infrastructure) and the constituent materials discarded (eg in landfills) or salvaged for reuse or recycling elsewhere. In the present economic system, materials flow one way from their points of origin as natural resources, through their transformation and assembly into goods, to their sale to the consumer. At this point the environmental impact of materials and other components is forgotten as they are assembled into a larger work. The consumer uses the designed system but it is not 'consumed', strictly speaking: he or she simply discards it after use. Many products that are ordinarily considered to be 'consumed' actually only render temporary service in the built environment. For instance, even when a building is demolished its fabric remains as output to the environment in the form of discarded materials.

If this one-way flow of materials persists as accepted practice, the rampant discarding of waste materials will result in their accumulation in the ecosystem and this mass will subsequently strain the environment's carrying capacity. Even those elements that do not compound disposal problems during their period of use will still exacerbate environmental problems when discarded later. From the perspective of the life cycles of materials and that of the ecologist, built structures (even if they are architectural masterpieces) must be seen as potential waste. The eventual route and use of materials must concern ecological designers from the outset.

Designers obviously do not like to dwell on the prospect of their designs and built forms one day being demolished, but it happens anyway sooner or later. In the ecological approach, the designer must at the design stage assess the potential for the building components or the product to be recycled. While potential is not the same as actuality, such considerations assist designers in becoming aware of the need for their own participation in processes of recovery, reuse and recycling. These are then the end objectives of our role as designers in the management of materials and energy in our built environment. From the point of view of the ecologist, a building is simply a transient phase in the flow of materials and energy in the biosphere, managed and assembled by people for a brief period of use (a period usually economically defined).

As discussed earlier, nearly all existing design has been based on the mistaken assumption that the earth's natural resources (ie raw materials, fossil fuel, land and other materials) are infinite and the planet functions as a limitless sink for the disposal of any wastes that humans generate. The relationship that commonly exists between the built and natural environments is open-ended and linear. This existing pattern might be described as a 'once-through' system in which resources are used at one end, and wastes are expelled at the other. It might be suggested that just as the application of technologies may have inadvertently exploited the biosphere, so, if employed with a fuller understanding of the ecological systems, those same technologies could result in designs through which humanity could live in a better balance with nature.

In seeking to practise ecomimicry, we must work with the analogy that within ecosystems there is complete cycling of the basic elements of carbon, nitrogen, oxygen, phosphorus and sulphur. Within an ecosystem, the nutrients recycle from living organisms through organic wastes and other products back to new living organisms where energy flows in (in the form of sunlight) and out (as heat).

If everything that we produce is artificial and it all has to go somewhere eventually, then it serves us better before we design to regard everything in our design as potential waste or as something that eventually has to be reintegrated into the environment.

We extract materials from our environment, and through these extractive and productive efforts we engage in our most fundamental relationship with nature. The first question in design is to ask whether the extraction processes have undesirable impacts on the environment and whether these can be avoided.

Designing for disassembly (DFD)

- In designing for disassembly, many products are more advanced in their DFD development than are built systems in the building industry. With DFD the manufacturer must be able to take the products apart easily or dismantle them in order to redistribute the raw materials. A feature of designing for disassembly includes the use of simple clips, pins and screws as mostly non-chemical fixings (eg with very little glue bonding used). Where use of glue, for instance, is inevitable as when fabrics are adhered to partitions, the glue should be a water-based adhesive, applied strategically and as sparingly as possible not only to minimise the amount of adhesive used but also to allow refurbishment with other materials. The most successful products or built systems will be those that contain a small number of materials and components that can easily be disassembled, separated, rearranged and reused. These then are the bases for DFD.

The demand for labour (to carry out all the disassembling, sorting and recycling) increases, as waste decreases. Thus this approach might be described as the 'service-and-flow economy' and involves a shift from natural resources to human resources.

- Design the built environment products to be durable or for long life with lesser need for disposal or replacement. In the current economy based on the selling of goods, the obsolescence and frequent disposal and replacement of those goods is in the financial interests of the manufacturer, even though it is harmful to the environment and costly for the customers. By contrast, in the DFD service-and-flow economy it is in the interests of both manufacturer and customer to create long-life products using a minimum of energy and materials.

- Design for biointegration at the outset and use biodegradable products. Plastics and some other chemical-industry products can be designed to be decomposable or biodegradable by decomposers in the ecosystem, so that their components can return promptly to the earth's ecological cycles instead of lying in landfills for centuries.

At the moment most of our toxic synthetics remain on land and in the water indefinitely, with harmful ecological effects. We should not add to these.

- Design to defer environmental reintegration for as long as possible by retaining all human-made items within the urban ecosystem itself through recovery for constant reuse and recycling, and aim not to discharge, deposit or seek to reintegrate any of these items into the natural environment at all. These items become in effect constantly 'in-use'. To achieve this we need to design our built environment in such a way as to manipulate our use of the building materials essentially as continuous acts of reconstruction of what we take from nature remade into items for reuse or recycling.

- Design for environmental reintegration of those items that cannot be reused or recycled but which need to be deposited somewhere and reintegrated back into the biosphere's ecological processes and cycles in an environmentally benign way, rather than be deposited in landfills or just thrown away into the environment. Although designing for reuse and recycling means designing the materials from the designed item to be retained still 'in-use' within the built environment, eventually after they have exhausted their usefulness, many will become waste and will require reintegration.

- Every material thing that we create and, in effect, everything that we produce, reflects our relationship to the physical and biological world. Needless to say, at the present this relationship is one of estrangement and exploitation. We need by design to remake all our existent and new built environment so as to sustain humankind's place in nature in symbiosis with all other species and with the earth's ecological integrity.

- In principle, designing for reuse is to be preferred over designing for recycling. In the case of the recovery of any material for reuse, the only additional energy required is for transportation, whereas in the recovery process to recycle a material we need to break down the item (if a composite) and reconstitute the material altogether, which in some cases requires significant quantities of energy (eg the recycling of iron requires almost as much energy as was needed to produce it).

The designer must adopt a set of strategies towards the selection and use of energy and materials that will assist him or her in the design of the built environment. Essentially, these have to follow a cyclic pattern of use where possible, with minimal energy inputs and environmental degradation, from source to sink.

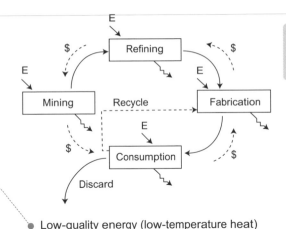

● Low-quality energy (low-temperature heat)

A summary of design strategies to promote designing for disassembly (DFD), reuse and recycling is as follows:

- Design for reuse as part of the strategy of DFD.

- Design for recycling as part of the strategy of DFD.

- Design for durability (prior to eventual reuse and recycling).

- Design to reduce the amount of material used (if scarce material or if non-recyclable).

- Design to minimise waste.

- Design for reintroduction into the natural environment.

- Design for remanufacture (as a lesser form of recycling).

- Design for repair and maintenance for reuse.

- Design for upgrading (and not for disposal).

- Design for refilling (instead of replacement).

- Design for replacement (as against wholesale disposal).

As a subset of the above, the principles of designing for disassembly (DFD) are as follows:

- Use recycled and recyclable materials where possible.

- Minimise the number of types of materials.

- Avoid toxic and hazardous materials.

- Avoid composite materials and make inseparable products from the same material.

- Avoid secondary finishes to materials.

- Provide standard and permanent identification of material types.

- Minimise the number of different types of components.

- Use mechanical rather than chemical connections.

- Use an open construction system with interchangeable parts.

- Use modular design and coordination.

- Use assembly technologies compatible with standard construction practice.

- Separate the structure from the cladding or external protective layer.

- Provide access to all built components.

- Design components sized to suit handling at all stages.

- Provide for handling the designed system's components during assembly and disassembly.

- Provide adequate tolerance to allow for disassembly.

- Minimise numbers of fasteners and connectors.

- Minimise types of connectors.

- Design construction joints and connectors to enable repeated assembly and disassembly and to withstand repeated disassembly.

- Allow for the possibility of parallel disassembly.

- Provide permanent identification for each component.

- Use a standard structural or coordinated-component grid.

- Use prefabricated subassemblies.

- Use lightweight materials and components.

- Identify point of disassembly permanently.

- Provide spare parts and allow for their storage.

- Retain information on the designed system and its assembly process.

In ecological terms, all our items and tools including built structures (the 'capital' of economists) are 'the exosomatic equivalent of organs' and, like bodily organs, require continuous flows of energy and material to and from the environment for their production and operation.

DFD also applies to products such as home appliances and electronics (durable goods such as refrigerators and washers), which must be designed in a manner that allows for easy disassembly when they are no longer needed. The individual components can be either readied for reuse and remanufacture, or their materials are easily separated for recycling.

Packaging must be minimal and devoid of advertising and must also be taken back by the manufacturer. Design for disassembly is particularly crucial in the automobile industry. Targets have been set that, by 2007, all European vehicles must be made so that they can be returned to the manufacturer at the end of their useful lives, and go through 'disposal processing' – where they will be taken apart and broken down into components that can be remanufactured, recycled or disposed of properly. The design of each product including automobiles must start from an understanding of what will happen to all of its components after the end of its useful life, and they must be identified so that they can be separated for reuse or recycling. The process of disassembly begins when the last owner returns the product back to the seller for free-of-charge recycling. The heavy machinery automobile is reconditioned for high-quality reuse. Recyclable items such as glass can be separated from other composites such as plastic and the plastic further separated into its various types for recovery. All metals can be shredded and then separated into ferrous and non-ferrous components for further processing.

These processes can be facilitated legislatively by 'take-back laws' with manufacturers already investing in disassembly plants. The concept must extend to the design of consumer durables and products.

In an ideal ecological industrial society, all products, materials and wastes become biological or technological nutrients that are easily biointegratable. Biological nutrients will be designed to re-enter the biosphere's ecological cycles to be consumed by micro-organisms and other creatures in the soil.

Management of outputs

The design measures for the management of outputs can be conceived in several ways. First, we can think about reducing the amount of outputs that are produced in the first place; this amounts to eliminating waste. Second, the designer can work to manage unavoidable emissions after they are generated. Methods of doing this will include remanufacturing and recycling. Third, we can act to protect those areas where materials and/or quantities of energy are going to be discharged.

In the management of materials and energy in the built environment, we can identify four possible design strategies of the pattern of use of energy and materials in the built form and its servicing systems. These are: once-through design; design of open circuits; design of closed circuits; and combined open-circuit design.

Once-through system

As the existing built environment has been configured, it constitutes a once-through system. That is to say, resources are consumed under the assumption that they are unlimited; hence outputs are discharged with little concern as to how they will affect the environment and with slight analysis of the routes that they will take to their ultimate sink.

Open-circuit system

An alternative approach is provided by the open-circuit system. Here, the designer capitalises on the ability of the environment to receive waste products from the built environment. The similarity between this system and the once-through system is that both use the environment as a receiving sink. However, in the open-circuit system the emissions do not exceed the ability of the ecosystem to absorb them. Thus, the level of discharge is held beneath the threshold at which environmental harm occurs. Presently, open-circuit design is achieved through careful geographic placement of discharges and through their pre-treatment. An example of an open-circuit system would concern the disposal of discharges from an industry located in a relatively pristine region with little pollution or contamination. The usual way of proceeding would be to dump the industrial discharge without regard for the land, which is considered to be an unlimited environmental sink. In an open-circuit approach, however, the environment would be evaluated and possibly modified before any system for the emission of industrial by-products was determined.

Closed-circuit system

The closed-circuit system is one in which most of the processes are undertaken within the built environment itself. The advantage of such a closed system is that impact on the surrounding ecosystems is minimal. Complete internalisation is possible only with respect to some outputs, since any system will rely on interaction with the environment for long-term survival, particularly for energy to keep the system operating. It also seems unlikely that discharges from the system could be entirely eliminated. Nonetheless, it may be useful to combine a closed-circuit system with open-circuit systems, especially when the assimilative capacities and other characteristics of the local ecosystems constrain a building's operation.

While ecological design should favour processes that are internal to the human-made environment as far as possible through continuous reuse and recycling, internalisation should not be pursued to the point where it creates new environmental problems for the surrounding ecosystem. A built environment that combines aspects of the open- and closed-circuit approaches has the advantage of reducing the level of environmental impact that would result from a once-through system, while simultaneously capitalising on the limited abilities of the ecological environment to assimilate discharges. As the designer embarks on a design assignment the thinking should be in terms of these three systems. The designer should work above all else towards eliminating the predominant once-through system and towards a closed-circuit system (ie designing for recovery; see below). As we have observed, a totally self-enclosed system will be unlikely or even impossible, but the designer can aim towards that objective, for instance by designing for reuse and recycling. Elements of the composite system combining open and closed aspects are also likely to be necessary.

Other considerations include:

- When a designer is attuned to the ecological consequences of the built environment, he or she is necessarily concerned with the lifespan of the building after it has been handed over to the owner or user. If the designer takes the environmental approach very seriously, he or she will be able not only to inform the owner of the environmental costs of the intended designed system, but also of the costs of its use and ultimate disposal once its useful life is over.

  Operating with this purpose, the designer will have a number of factors to consider. These will include the internal environmental interactions that result from the life of the built system. However, the impact of the built environment on the ecological one is not just a result of producing a building or complex, but also of using it. Moreover, the environmental consequences of the eventual disposal and recovery of the building must also be assessed, based on an understanding of the economics of real-estate investment and accepted patterns of use. As we have already observed, the actual physical life of a building can be much longer than its economic life. The environmentally sensitive designer will be concerned with both aspects.

- Patterns of resource use will also concern the designer, who must work to reduce the occurrences of linear patterns of use and will favour cyclical patterns instead. The goal of the green design process is a building or complex that minimises both its consumption of resources and production of wastes. Meeting this goal will probably mean recycling and recovery, and the designer must ensure that these processes do not require inordinate amounts of materials, energy and space in the environment.

- The stability of the natural environment is a major concern for the designer who introduces a building, which is a dynamic system, into it. Once a built system is dropped into the ecosystem, a whole chain of interactions is set in motion and this continues until the built structure is removed, the ecosystem recovered, and even beyond that point. The designer must think of all these interactions. From the moment that building materials are procured in the environment, through the moment at which scrap materials are dumped into environmental sinks, materials and energy are consumed by the built system at the same time that discharges are made. Therefore, for a designer to operate with a complete environmental consciousness, he or she must view energy and materials management in the most comprehensive sense. The designer must understand all of the ways in which the built system will interact with the natural environment over the course of its entire 'life'. Then, of course, the designer must work to minimise the negative interactions to every possible extent.

Even such an ambitious programme is unlikely to result in buildings in which no element is ever wasted; rather, systems should be made as efficient or benign as possible with respect to the consumption of energy and materials, and as minimally disruptive of the ecological environment as possible. This means minimising spatial impact on and pollution of the environment at the design and construction phases, as well as implementing recycling and recovery programmes. Designing with the recovery of materials as a goal may lead to a building's greater up-front cost, but in the long run proceeds from recycling and recovery may compensate for the higher expenses to some degree.

• To fully appreciate the environmental consequences of building, the designer must conceive of resource use as a cyclical pattern in which energy and materials flow through the environments (built and natural). The cycle can be viewed as it unfolds from the point of production, through the period of use to the moment of recovery of the materials again. The life-cycle model enables us to relate the activities that take place within and around the building to one another. All design should be informed by knowledge of this interconnectedness: thus, the ecological consequences of discrete activities can be assessed as part of a larger system.

• While it is generally agreed that our cities, buildings and other elements (such as transportation systems and infrastructure) must be interpreted as a complex system of material and energy flows, what is asserted here is that these flows must be managed to ensure that they are ecologically responsive. While the above discussion dealt with physical aspects of inputs that usually concern designers, we must acknowledge that in a truly comprehensive approach we would need to take into account the inputs of food to the occupants of the buildings. On the analogy of the framework presented for creating a skyscraper and other large intensive building types, we would look at the urban food system through all of its various stages as well: agriculture and horticulture, transportation, processing, packaging, refrigeration, storage, wholesaling, retailing, display, collection by the purchaser, further processing and disposal of all wastes from the food and its packaging. Collectively, these represent a major component of total environment impact and energy use. These aspects, though important, lie outside the scope of this work; however, they demonstrate that the ecological approach described here can be extended to all human activities and functions that take place in the built environment, and that no human activity exists in a vacuum or without an ecological context.

• It should be recognised at the outset that recycling efforts do not solve the underlying issues of the destruction of our resources.

The following are basic design strategies to close the loop:

Post-manufacture recycling (from beyond consumer use, ie in its after-life)

Products face either of two end results: they are absorbed into the domestic waste stream (landfilled or incinerated); or they can be recycled and reused. In an ecological sense, in close-loop heaven, products that are sent out would be brought back at the end of their life cycle. Until recently, this was unheard of, but that is starting to change. Laws are being drawn up in Europe that will require companies to take back their durable goods such as refrigerators, washing machines and cars at the end of their useful lives. In Germany, the laws start with the initial sale. Companies must take back all their packaging (or hire middlemen to recycle all the packaging for them). This shift of recycling responsibility from consumer to manufacturer means that it would be in the best interests of manufacturers to design a product that will either last a long time or can be disassembled easily for parts recycling and reuse (design for disassembly).

To address recycling within the built environment, it would be important to design a recycling system and recycling centre within it, whether on each floor, or centrally for a whole building.

Manufacturers also often use leftovers and production waste (post-manufacture waste) to make additional products. Shredded plastic bottles have found many uses, including the making of insulating clothing fibres. (The use of recycled plastic may harm the human body and has unknown consequences.)

Ecodesign from manufacturing, through use to after-life will give humankind the option of sustainability without destroying the biosphere, getting the services they want without the consequences of environmental devastation. Currently the disposable and energy-hungry products that litter our built environment loudly proclaim our disregard for other living things.

Reduce

Means buying and disposing less. As energy is needed to collect, to possess, to manufacture and to ship things, reducing means less burning of fossil fuels and fewer CO_2 emissions.

Reuse

Means to use a product more than once, whether for the same or a different purpose. It is better than recycling because the product doesn't need to be remanufactured before it can be used again. Thus large amounts of CO_2 emissions can be prevented when a product doesn't have to be disassembled, shredded, melted and reformed as when it is recycled, or when it doesn't need to be transported to a landfill. Reusing also means reducing, or purchasing less.

To close the loop, a system to complete biological and technological recycling is needed – imagine an industrial process that doesn't produce any waste; cars that have no emissions; packaging that becomes waste that eventually becomes food. The goal is to create products that are environmentally benign and do not disrupt nature's fabric (more than the products themselves, the materials as well as the process of creation have to be benign.

Although possibly the most outragous damage occurs in exploited developing countries, developed countries aren't spared either. The USEPA revealed the USA's metals mining industry to be the largest toxic polluter in the country, accounting for approximately 3.5 billion pounds of toxic pollution (of 7.3 million in total) in 1998. The next most polluting industry was electric utilities, at 1.1 billion pounds.

Recycling of construction waste

The reuse of building materials commonly saves about 95 per cent of embodied energy that would otherwise be wasted. Some materials such as bricks and tiles suffer damage losses of up to 30 per cent in use. The savings made by recycling of materials for reprocessing varies from up to 95 per cent for aluminium to only 20 per cent for glass. Some reprocessing may use more energy, especially if long-distance transportation is involved.

Using recycled concrete as aggregate has been calculated to save only 5 per cent of the embodied energy of concrete. Transport distance of crushed concrete is critical – limited to well below 50 kilometres. Using recycled fly ash or slag as a cement substitute for up to 40 per cent of the cement is useful, saving about 50 per cent of the concrete's embodied energy at that limit.

The construction of new buildings consumes 3 billion tons of raw materials every year. Construction waste can make up to 30 per cent of the municipal solid waste stream. Recycling construction waste has become an important industry especially in Europe. The Netherlands, for example, requires more than 75 per cent of construction and demolition waste (including concrete, asphalt, wood and gypsum) to be recycled. The rate in Germany and Belgium is more than 50 per cent. Today, it is estimated that North America recycles only 25 per cent. But due to possible landfill shortages and increased fees for dumping waste, this small industry is expected to grow by at least 10 per cent in the next decade.

Ecodesigners try to avoid materials manufactured by industrial processes that require toxic chemicals in the process or that contain chemicals in the end product, such as formaldehyde, VOCs, PVC, solvents, alkyds, CFCs and HCFCs.

The best way to reduce building construction is to reuse older buildings (ie the case for adaptive buildings) by retrofitting older structures. Older buildings are given a new life with new functions. Modular construction can also reduce the energy used to construct a building. Prefabricated construction using standardised units reduces the amount of energy used because it reduces the amount of construction work needed.

Design for recovery

It has been estimated that perhaps as much as a quarter of the volume of material resources consumed by buildings is recycled in the built environment.

Another way of recycling or reusing the built environment is to literally reuse it, by retrofitting older structures. Today's buildings are frequently 'reincarnated', becoming a new element of community life and gaining in commercial value. Flexibility-enhancing design includes walls, pipes and other interior elements that can easily be moved for future change of use or location, with 'flexibility' and 'demountable' being the key characteristics of these systems. Recycling within the built environment saves the energy and landfill space embodied in construction materials, which are responsible for 40 per cent of all materials flows and mainly end up as waste, the disposal of which typically costs 2–5 per cent of construction budgets.

The amount of energy required to dismantle the building is rarely, if ever, considered. In the minds of architects and developers, buildings are built to be permanent despite the fact that the economic lives of their components are becoming increasingly short.

Demolition and dismantling

Ecodesign includes designing for the deconstruction or the selective dismantling of a product or a built form, where it is disassembled into various parts and components for their reuse, remanufacture and recycling. This deconstruction involves the separation of different building materials and the reuse of recycled materials in superior utilisation options. While traditional demolition is highly mechanised, capital intensive and waste generating, deconstruction is labour intensive, low-tech and non-environmentally disruptive.

In the process of green design, we must consider the amounts of resources that will be used to dismantle the building and its components, and we should consider as well the amount of pollution and waste that will be generated in the process. As we have already observed, recycling building materials requires further energy expenditures. Thus, our choice of materials must be informed by a consideration of the relative environmental costs of recovering and reusing them in some form. When we consider the environmental costs of reuse, we must look not only at resource use but also at the impact that the process will exert on the ecosystem. Dismantling a portion of the built environment and recovering some or all of its components will necessarily have ecological consequences. For example, demolition may entail the use of heavy equipment that cannot be transported to a building site, set up and operated without creating some kind of impact on the immediate surroundings.

It may even become necessary to erect facilities to process the demolished materials on site, which will also create a stress on the local environment. Moreover, the recovery process may lead to emissions of various materials, possibly in the form of pollution. The designer must weigh his or her objective of cyclical resource use, as well as his or her choice of recovery process, against the qualities and quantities of emissions likely to be generated.

The availability of the raw materials will also inform our choices. The economic viability and ecological necessity of resource recovery are also a function of how rare or abundant a particular material is in the environment, and how easily it can be extracted for human use. Gold, for example, is regularly recovered because of its high economic value. Aluminium, on the other hand, is recovered not because of its rarity – it is in fact abundant – but because producing it from raw resources is costly in terms of energy while reprocessing it is relatively less expensive.

The possibility of recovery after initial use will be influenced by the form of construction that has been employed in the obsolete building or buildings. For instance, it is relatively easy and cost effective to collect steel and other metals from a building and melt down the scrap. Reinforced concrete, by way of contrast, is a building material produced by a chemical reaction and it cannot be separated into its component elements of sand, cement and steel. Its reuse is limited to employing the material in its downgraded form as landfill or hard core and, in certain instances, as reused concrete aggregate. Clearly, building systems produced by physical and chemical processes have a lower potential for recovery than those that are produced by mechanically joining elements that can later be disassembled.

It will probably prove difficult to favour structural systems capable of disassembly in larger, more complex buildings. Impermanent structural solutions will generally work on a small scale where the choices of materials, as well as of removal and recovery processes, are made by the architect and client. In larger projects like high-rise buildings and other intensive building types, a whole host of additional factors will have to be considered, including safety, stability and fire protection. The need for structural stability will also often dictate the use of those building systems that are the most difficult to disassemble. Furthermore, these large projects are designed within parameters established by various government bodies on the local, state and national levels, all of which have to be satisfied by the design. Certain means of achieving structural economies may make the production phase easier and more economical, but they will make dismantling and salvaging the building more difficult. Such processes include the use of continuous structural members, joints made in situ with physical and chemical processes and the use of complex components composed of multiple elements.

The designer must nevertheless consider the way in which the built structure will eventually be demolished or dismantled. The demolition methods will naturally have a significant impact on the qualities of the salvaged materials, as will the type or source of obsolescence. For example, a building or component made obsolete by weathering will also have been physically decayed by the elements. For components to be recycled, they must be in good condition or at least be capable of being repaired. They must also be compatible with new construction, particularly with regard to their dimensions, capability for performance and method of installation. With the eventual destination of the recovered elements in mind, the designer in effect predetermines how to demolish or dismantle the building. He or she will want to know whether the component parts of the building are to be reused or whether the materials are to be salvaged for regeneration. The decisions concerning dismantling are crucial, since it is at that point in the cycle of materials that wastes are transformed into new resources. Unfortunately, the vast majority of buildings now standing have not been designed with the ease of eventual dismantling and recycling in mind.

For a potentially wasted element of the built environment to become a resource, there must be a present-day need for it. Thus, a sort of design that imagines the ultimate recovery of building materials and components presupposes a continued need for those parts of the structure. If the elements of a building are not related to a material that has been used over a long period of time and that can be incorporated into a wide range of structural systems, for instance bricks, which have been used from Roman times to the present, then recovering them will be pointless. The recovery of materials of limited utility will only produce expensive waste. The geographical presence of the resource, and the existence of a local market for the salvaged elements, will also have an impact on the economics of recovery.

It could be stated that our entire human-made environment needs to be restructured so that it can become more efficient in its use of energy and material resources by recovering the bulk of the resources that are within that environment. It is generally held that a human life-support system based on a recovery pattern of use is the only structure that could operate for an indefinite period of time in a finite system. The feasibility of the recovery of any output depends on the technical means, the product output specification (or the design programme), and the availability of a potential use (or demand) for the recovered output.

Design for reuse (see earlier description of DFD)

The reuse of the material can be either primary (in its original form) or secondary (in modified form). Primary reuse means that the item is reused for the original intended purpose and does not require any additional reprocessing. Secondary reuse involves employing an item again but for a different purpose, and thus requires modifying it in a limited way. Secondary reuse involves creative reuse solutions for parts of the building that no longer serve their primary or intended function. Planning ways to reincarnate these components as part of the initial design phase would enhance both the probability and speed of their eventual reuse. The secondary use is predetermined and planned for. Reuse is preferred over recycling as it uses less energy and effort.

We should be aware of the danger of focusing on one aspect of use, which can give us a misleading picture of overall performance. The design must be seen within a life-cycle overview. Generally, the method of construction and assembly of materials affects reuse and recycling. The design of the connections and fixing of materials should:

- make the components easy to disassemble (eg mechanical methods of fixing) or DFD;

- reduce the number of different types of materials used;

- avoid using combinations of materials that are not mutually compatible;

- consider how materials can be identified (in the long term, some form of chemical tracing ingredients may be used); and

- ensure that it is possible to remove easily any components that would contaminate the recycling process (eg microprocessors).

Design for reuse could also be called designing with 'nuts and bolts'.

Design for recycling

Recycling is a resource recovery method that involves the use of an output after it has undergone some reprocessing, accompanied by a complete or partial change in form. This can also involve the collection and processing of waste products for use as raw materials in the manufacture of raw products. This is, however, more complex than simply designing for reuse, because the collection and distribution infrastructure for recycling may incur additional energy costs. To justify recycling of a material, the designer must ensure that the energy and resources saved (and the reduced impact on the ecosystem) are greater than those needed to make a fresh product. We should note that composite materials make recycling difficult.

The environmental benefit from using recycled materials comes from the fact that the impact on the environment is less than if a completely new material were used, because it has already been used once.

A useful distinction is now made between the ideal of recycling, in which a material is used in its pure form, and the usual norm of downcycling, in which the material is reused in a less pure and degraded form, still contaminated with other materials also used in the original product. In green building, the products used – whether building components, fittings or furniture – will also be designed so that they, or parts of them, or their constituent materials can easily be recovered and recycled rather than just being downcycled. These relatively new procedures result not only in benign products but also in far more efficient and less wasteful manufacturing processes. Recycling lessens the amount of wastes that the earth must absorb and also the resources to be extracted from it.

Design for durability

The current average life of buildings is 50 to 60 years in Europe, only 35 years in the USA, and 20 years in some parts of Japan. Even during their relatively short lives, many buildings undergo major reconstruction, to attract a different group of users, etc.

A long-life product, which is easy to reuse or to repair, means less overall waste. This is a simple approach to recycling by extending the life of resources and products with little or no change. Designing products so that they last longer than their predecessors is one way to reduce waste through reuse. Sometimes this can be done by employing a new technology, as in energy-efficient compact fluorescent lightbulbs, which last much longer than traditional incandescent bulbs. Another approach is to fabricate products using more durable materials.

In the USA, the average life of commercial building skins is only 20 years. Services are replaced every seven to 15 years, and interior space-defining elements every three to five years. Many commercial buildings have been virtually rebuilt during their brief lives. Pre-1940 buildings tend to be more durable than their modern counterparts. Institutional and

Categories of need for preservation	Building component examples
Unnecessary	Interior joinery, floorboarding, interior wall studs
Optional	Roof timber (pitched), ground-floor joists, tile battens
Desirable	External wall studs, timbers in flat roofs, cladding
Essential	Sole plates, load-bearing joinery, timber in contact with ground or concrete below damp-proof course

● Categories of preservation for different building components

Maintenance schedule				
	Activity 1		Activity 2	
Item	Action	Frequency pa	Action	Frequency pa
Outer surfaces				
Outer glass	Wash	12		
Other outer skin	-			
Windows				
Wooden frame	Wash	4		
Steel frame	Wash	4		
Aluminium frame	Wash	4		
Inner glass	Wash	12		
Floor finish				
Screed floor	Sweep	50		
Stone tile floor	Sweep	50		
Wood tile floor	Sweep	50	Buff	50
Plastic tile floor	Mop	100	Patch	5
Cork tile floor	Sweep	50	Buff	50
Vinyl floor finish	Mop	100		
Vinyl tile floor	Mop	100	Patch	5
Linoleum tile floor	Sweep	50	Mop	50
Linoleum floor finish	Sweep	50	Mop	50
Rubber tile floor	Sweep	50	Mop	50
Wool carpet	Vacuum	100		
Nylon carpet	Vacuum	100		
Block flooring	Sweep	50	Polish	10
Chipboard floor	Sweep	50		
Polished softwood floor	Sweep	50	Polish	10
Polished hardwood floor	Sweep	50	Polish	10
Internal wall surfaces				
Plasterboard				
Steel sheet				
Chipboard				
Inner glass	Wash	50		
Plaster + painted wall				
Plasterboard wall finish				
Wood wall finish				
Faced wall board finish				
Wooden board wall finish				
Plastered wall				
Painted wall				
Tiled wall	Wash	25		
Ceiling surface				
Painted ceiling				
Plastered ceiling				
Ceiling board				
Metal				
Tiled ceiling	Wash	12		

Maintenance schedule of some building elements

residential buildings also generally have a longer lifespan than commercial buildings, although this is also declining as the same materials and construction processes used in commercial buildings are now also being employed in residential buildings.

Such short-term vision for buildings has also become pervasive and institutionalised in places. Some countries suggest a 40 to 60 year lifespan for all normal built forms dependent upon the extent of maintenance required. Others see three categories of durability, the highest being 50 years for structure and elements that are difficult to replace or where failures would be difficult to detect, only 5 years for materials that are easily accessible and where failures are easy to detect, and 15 years for the rest.

Research has shown that the average age of residential buildings is 140 years in the UK, 103 years in the USA and 80 years in Germany. This contrasts rather significantly with the life cycle of similar buildings in Taiwan and Japan, which is about 30 years. The changing societal and population demographics, economic development, and changes to land and real-estate usage have all acted in tandem to affect the speed of residential remodelling. In Europe and the USA, the higher residential building life cycle is much closer to its 'physical endurance age' and thus closer to a sustainable development ideal.

Long-life or durable built forms are those whose lifespans can be measured in centuries rather than decades. If we build only once, the potential resource savings would be tremendous. Owners also gain by having an investment that will continue to generate income for a very long time. The incorporation of natural green systems would also minimise operating costs, reduce energy use, and create pleasant and healthy living environments.

Design for durability would also mean designing for adaptability, as a long-lived built system must be useful during the whole period of its existence. It may not be difficult to design a durable building, but the challenge is to design buildings that can be adapted to many uses over their long lives. Factors that significantly affect a building's lifespan fall roughly into four categories: planning, form/space, materials/construction and user satisfaction.

Design for efficient material usage (design for reduction)

This technique simply means an efficient use of materials by designing to reduce the amount of material used (if material is scarce or non-recyclable). It does not mean a minimalist design approach, though we should seek to conserve rare materials as much as possible or design for recycling and reuse.

Design to minimise waste (design for reduction)

This will require a good knowledge of the life cycle of the product and good information about the performance of different materials within the reuse and recycling chain. It also raises fundamental questions about the wisdom of designing products that have a life expectancy shorter than that of the materials of which they are made.

Design for reintroduction into the natural environment (reintegration)

This means designing to ensure that the materials are biodegradable and can be reintegrated back into natural systems after use.

Design for remanufacture

This involves the partial or total reconstitution of the output into its original form prior to use. This concept is sometimes referred to as 'products-in-service', where the supplier of the product or material will buy back the material after its use for remanufacture. The material is thus regarded as purchased in a form of 'lease' to the user. The supplier assumes responsibility for the eventual remanufacture, recycling or disposal of the material. Parts of the building can be designed at the outset to be disassembled, refurbished and reassembled when they eventually wear out, using new parts or parts retrieved from other products. Remanufacturing is commonplace in the automotive and defence-related industries. Remanufacture can save up to 70 per cent of the resources, labour and energy used to produce and distribute new products.

Designing for remanufacture involves:

- ensuring that parts are interchangeable between items;

- making components repairable or easily replaced;

- allowing for technological components to be replaced without affecting the overall frame of the product; and

- choosing a design aesthetic that allows for the easy update of that part of the building through the replacement of a few key components such as panels.

Design for repair and maintenance

Designing parts of the building (eg cladding) so that they can be conveniently maintained and repaired entails the availability of replacement parts, as well as the ability to take them apart and put them together again easily. Easy to follow manuals and accessible technical assistance from manufacturers can be instrumental here. But more than just designing

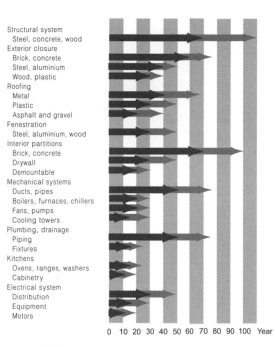

- Structural system
  - Steel, concrete, wood
- Exterior closure
  - Brick, concrete
  - Steel, aluminium
  - Wood, plastic
- Roofing
  - Metal
  - Plastic
  - Asphalt and gravel
- Fenestration
  - Steel, aluminium, wood
- Interior partitions
  - Brick, concrete
  - Drywall
  - Demountable
- Mechanical systems
  - Ducts, pipes
  - Boilers, furnaces, chillers
  - Fans, pumps
  - Cooling towers
- Plumbing, drainage
  - Piping
  - Fixtures
- Kitchens
  - Ovens, ranges, washers
  - Cabinetry
- Electrical system
  - Distribution
  - Equipment
  - Motors

0 10 20 30 40 50 60 70 80 90 100 Year

■ Expected lifespan
■ Extended lifespan

Temporal integration. Typical useful life
of various components and parts in this
built environment

to facilitate repair and maintenance, we should be aware that improper use, overuse and neglect all shorten a component's life, minimising reuse potential. It is therefore beneficial for all users to learn how to handle and operate the building and its components and systems correctly, utilise them reasonably to serve real needs, service them when called upon and store or protect them from the climate safely and intelligently.

Timely repair to the building can extend the life of its components. The opportunity to keep the building and its systems working is a vital component of reuse. Many building components are manufactured in a manner that makes them almost impossible to repair. For example, it is extremely difficult to service or to replace components that are welded together, chemically bonded or riveted (rather than fastened with screws that allow disassembly) or are permanently sealed in a housing. As a general guideline, when the cost of repair is no more than half of the cost of replacement, repair is always preferable.

Design for upgrading

A number of items in the building are amenable to upgrading as the owner's needs change or technological advances occur. For example, the building's building automation systems (BAS) computers can commonly be upgraded by adding a larger memory chip, a new drive or other similar parts. Several copying machines are also now being designed with the capacity to upgrade in mind.

Every year in the UK, 1.5 million computers are dumped in landfills and an equivalent number kept in storage unused. Upgrading aside, computer repair can be undertaken and the refurbished computers shipped to developing countries.

Design for replacement

The designer should also consider the issue of replacement. Some parts of the building may be made of durable materials but fail to endure simply because one part wears out before the rest and can't be replaced. The capacity to replace these crucial parts can be incorporated into the design. Many common building products could be made reusable through basic design changes. One way is by modular construction, which can make repairs quicker and easier to accomplish: when one component fails or becomes obsolete, the particular module can be easily removed or replaced. With modular construction, the users themselves may even be able to do more of their own repairs and replacements. In the case of professional servicing, where labour is often the primary expense, modular assembly can mean lower repair bills. A related concept is design for disassembly, which is aimed at making it easy to take apart complex products and components.

Designing from source back to source: life-cycle analysis

In ecological design, we must guarantee – as much as possible – the reuse or recovery of materials. In the selection of materials in our built environment, we must also consider the building and its components as having overall physical lifespans of perhaps 50 to 80 years, with subsystems (for example the cladding) having shorter lifespans (about 5–10 years), along with M&E equipment (eg 10–15 years). Different materials, components and equipment have their own lifespans, after which replacement and recovery need to be implemented.

The building's physical life is also different from its economic life. The economic life of a commercial building is considered to be that period during which it produces a financial return that justifies the investment made. In the case of an owner-occupied building, as opposed to a speculative project, its commercial life is that period during which it is used directly. The economic life of a building is thus distinct from its physical life, which is potentially much longer. There is, nonetheless, a correlation between the physical life and the period in which the owner of a building receives an adequate return on investment.

The ecological physical lifespans of components of a built system are potentially very long. The design professions today, however, are not constituted in such a way as to emphasise considerations of the physical lives of building components. Rather, the economic lives of buildings and their parts are the primary considerations in most projects. However, when we adopt the ecological approach, we necessarily concern ourselves primarily with the ecological lives of our built works.

Under the existing system, which emphasises economic considerations, real-estate financing, as well as the design process, is based on the expectation that commercial buildings will last around 30 years. This is the extent of the project's economic life, after which it is deemed worthless. Obviously most standing commercial buildings, by virtue of their construction out of durable materials, are capable of outlasting the relatively brief economic life imagined during the investment process. The 'throwaway' culture of much of contemporary building and design practice results in buildings that are uneconomical and unecological white elephants. Beyond the 30-year mark, these buildings are rendered nearly obsolete. Because their long physical lives were not taken into consideration during the design process they have become difficult to reuse or renew.

Obsolescence

There are a number of factors that may contribute to the obsolescence of an entire development project, building or building component. Here we can speak of varieties of obsolescence related to different causes, some internal and others external to the structure's design.

Factors that contribute to this process of loss of value include location obsolescence, which is to say that the building's original function may no longer be appropriate in its immediate vicinity, or the function may no longer be required as a consequence of social and economic forces (eg the rendering obsolete of the government buildings in Bonn after the removal of the German capital to Berlin). Developing technologies also pose challenges to existing buildings, since many may not be capable of adapting to such changes. The forces of nature themselves may also make a built system, or part of it, obsolete, since they cause wear in structures that may push them below established standards of comfort and safety. Finally, changing statutory regulations, such as building codes, may lead to the obsolescence of the buildings.

Very often, a value judgement needs to be made about the anticipated life cycle of the building. For instance, aluminium has a higher embodied energy than steel; however, at the end of its useful life in a building, it requires considerably less energy to recycle than does steel. Making aluminium from recycled aluminium uses 90 per cent less energy than making it from scratch, and cuts related air pollution by 95 per cent. Similarly, using recycled glass for glass manufacture saves up to 32 per cent of total energy required in the process, reduces air pollution by 20 per cent and water pollution by 50 per cent.

Thinking of the built environment in terms of cyclical phases, we can identify the ecological interdependencies between the components of the built environment as well as assess the environmental impact of each. This is the only legitimate way of determining actual environmental costs, and the most credible means by which the claims of entire buildings or individual products to 'green' status can be evaluated. Life-cycle inventory (LCI) provides a quantitative assessment of environmental inputs and outputs associated with a product. This method illustrates possible life cycles for energy and materials. At each phase in the cycles, we observe materials and energy being taken in, and other material and forms of energy being released as outputs. It is important to see whether these processes unfold on a particular location, which may sustain a negative environmental impact as a consequence of such activity. We can test our findings with the interactions framework.

By looking at the built environment from this perspective, we are led to consider energy and materials use well beyond the consumption phase, which is our usual focus as designers. It is easy to see the environmental consequences of building, but the processes by which the individual components were produced are often overlooked. Each component in a building project represents a certain amount of energy and material consumed, as well as an amount of pollutants emitted and a portion of ecosystems degraded.

It is possible to reverse entropy, but only by using up additional energy in the process and, of course, when used that additional energy increases the overall entropy. This is the case in

recycling (as against reuse where the only energy needed is in transportation and installation),
which requires the expenditure of additional energy in the collecting, transporting and
processing of used materials, which increases the overall entropy in the environment.

Summary

The ecological designer must make as comprehensive an assessment as possible of the
environmental consequences of each part and component of the designed system. Account
must be taken of every element of the designed system's life cycle and flow, from its source
as raw materials to its manufacture, use, reuse, recycling and eventual reintegration
including all the materials and energy resources used or consumed, as well as of the volume
of waste produced in the process. To facilitate this the design must start from the discipline
of pre-designed connections to enable disassembly.

In doing so, the designer evaluates the total impacts upon the natural environment made by
each element and constituent of the designed system throughout its entire life cycle. Taken
individually, the stages in the life cycle may only represent minor environmental harm, but
when the designer looks at them collectively inappropriate levels of environmental impact
may emerge, such as excessive waste of resources and degradation of the environment that
may be out of all proportion to the scale of the project.

Central to designing for disassembly is the understanding of assembly, which is dependent
upon: functional and dimensional coordination of components and subsystems, conventions
of jointing, and the processes of putting together and taking apart. The disassembly must
be largely achieved by means of non-destructive work.

Due to the way that the design profession and related disciplines are presently constituted,
and the way that the existent built environment's development process is structured, it is
evident that the life cycle of a built structure, facility or infrastructure is only viewed from
an economic perspective and this should change to include environmental factors.

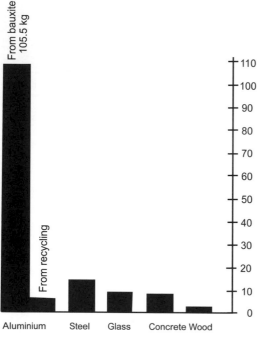

Comparison of energy costs of materials embodied

B29 Design using environmentally benign materials, furniture, fittings, equipment (FF&E) and products that can be continuously reused, recycled and reintegrated: assessing the environmental consequences of materials, etc, used in the designed system

Self-evidently, ecodesign must use materials and equipment (as well as all the items that are part of our built environment) that do not have negative environmental consequences. Besides the usual design criteria (eg aesthetics, costs, etc), the broad strategy is to select materials (ie as L21) with regard to:

• renewable sources and high recycled content;

• potential of the material for continuous reuse and recycling at the end of its useful life (eg as a consequence of replacement due to wear and tear);

• low embodied energy impact (including delivery to the site);

• low embodied ecological impact in production and manufacturing processes (ie low emissions, waste and pollutions);

• biodegradability (facilitating reintegration);

• local production (low transportation energy costs);

• low toxicity to humans and ecosystems; and

• method of installation and life cycle.

Even with the above general criteria, value judgements still need to be made in materials selection especially where the criteria for one conflict with those of another.

Product and material selection for the designed system can consist of the following steps:

• Identify the material categories.

• Identify building material options.

• Gather technical information.

• Review submitted information for completeness.

• Evaluate materials based on the above criteria.

• Select.

For example, in building projects, during the preliminary design phase or the schematic phase, materials can be classified into:

Site construction

- concrete

- masonry

- metals

- wood and plastics

- thermal and moisture protection

- doors and windows

- finishes

- specialities

- equipment

- furnishings

Special construction

- conveying systems

- mechanical

- electrical

Additional rules for material selection might be:

- Where two materials exist that will perform the same function for the same price, choose the less toxic of the two.

- Where practical, choose materials that are unrefined and as close as possible to their natural state as these required less energy to produce and less processing (ie less likely impairment as a consequence of processing).

- Use local materials wherever possible; the heaviest materials should be obtained from the closest source. By using local materials, we reduce transport energy, which can have a significant impact.

- Design for minimum energy consumption and maximum longevity. The embodied energy in the material tends to increase as the materials become more refined.

Design using environmentally benign materials, furniture, fittings, equipment (FF&E) and products that can be continuously reused, recycled and reintegrated

Chapter C • Chapter B • Chapter A

B29

Design using environmentally benign materials, furniture, fittings, equipment (FF&E) and products that can be continuously reused, recycled and reintegrated

	Ecological criteria to be evaluated (See Interactions Framework in A5)	Examples of design strategies to be considered	Examples of technological applications and inventions needed
Choice of building materials and construction systems	■ The depletion of global energy and material resources from construction ■ The impacts of that material and form of construction on the local ecosystems ■ The total inputs consumed in making available that material and in the construction ■ The total outputs emitted in making available that material in the construction and their impacts ■ The total global impact on the ecosystems as a result of the range of actions and activities involved in making available that material and form of construction ■ The energy and material costs of maintenance of that material and construction system ■ The ease and extent of reusability and recycling of that material ■ The ease and extent of environmental reintegration of that material	■ Use local source of materials ■ Design for ease of reuse in the same physical state within the built environment ■ Design for long life and multipurpose use to avoid short-term replacement ■ Design for reuse in a lower-grade from ■ Design for reuse elsewhere in the same state ■ Design for recycling ■ Design for environmental reintegration ■ Others	■ Demountable structures and system to permit further reuse (DFD or Design for Disassembly) ■ Materials derived from renewable resources ■ Recycled materials ■ Biodegradable materials that can be assimilated into the ecosystems ■ Development of the low-energy consumption and low-pollutive forms of materials ■ Others
Choice of servicing system	■ Depletion of energy and material resources during production, construction, operation and disposal ■ Discharges of outputs over their life cycle ■ Spatial impacts on the ecosystems of the project site ■ Ecosystem impacts caused by the actions and activities over the life cycle ■ Others	■ Use ambient sources of energy and materials ■ Reduce overall standard of user needs and comfort and reduce overall consumption levels ■ Optimise use of energy and material inputs ■ Assimilate outputs into ecosystems ■ Recycle within the built environment ■ Others	■ Ambient energy sources (eg, solar energy, wind power) ■ More efficient technical systems ■ Close the circuit in the systems by means of reuse and recycling systems ■ Design systems which have a symbiotic relationship with the ecosystems ■ Others

Strategies for selection of materials and forms of construction in ecodesign

Further rules for designing, specifying and building green are as follows:

- Maximise durability.

- Maximise energy efficiency.

- Maximise future reuse and recyclability (eg mechanical fastening is preferable to chemical or adhesive/solvent welding as this reduces the embodied energy after each reuse).

- Maximise ease of maintenance and long life of material.

- Maximise the reuse or recycled content: close the loop. Collecting and recycling is not the goal. We must incorporate the recycled products into the building and, when the product's current usefulness wanes, it should be recyclable into yet another useful product and not sent to the landfill.

- Maximise use of local and regional materials to reduce transportation energy costs.

- Minimise embodied energy: promote the highest and best use of a material to avoid wasting the embodied energy. The highest and best use of a 500-year-old redwood tree is not paper pulp.

- Minimise the use of hazardous natural chemicals (asbestos, lead, etc).

- Minimise use of synthetic chemicals: synthetic chemicals should be considered guilty until proven innocent.

As a general strategy, we need to be ecomimetic in our use of materials in the built environment based on the way that nature handles materials. In ecosystems, all living organisms feed on continual flows of matter and energy from their environment to stay alive. Although all living organisms continually produce waste, an ecosystem generates no waste – one species' waste is another species' food. Thus matter cycles continually through the web of life. It is this closing of the loop in ecosystems through reuse and recycling that must become the basis for the use of materials in our human-made environment.

Lessons could be learnt by imitating how ecosystems' processes are developed by natural selection over the course of time. Organisms in a complex, mature ecosystem adopt the following practices:

- Use waste as a resource material within the system (ie all wastes from one built environment can be resources for another).

- Diversify and cooperate to fully use the habitat (ie minimal waste).

- Gather and use energy efficiently (ie low energy in production, use, reuse, recycling and reintegration).

- Optimise rather than maximise (ie efficient use).

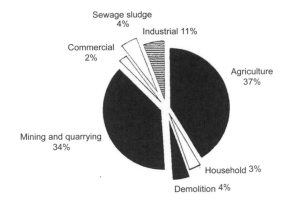

Estimated total annual waste (UK, 1980)

Design using environmentally benign materials, furniture, fittings, equipment (FF&E) and products that can be continuously reused, recycled and reintegrated

Design using environmentally benign materials, furniture, fittings, equipment (FF&E) and products that can be continuously reused, recycled and reintegrated

Appliance	Watts/hours
Coffee pot	200
Coffee-maker	800
Toaster	800-1500
Popcorn popper	250
Blender	300
Microwave	600-1500
Waffle iron	1200
Hotplate	1200
Frying pan	1200
Dishwasher	1200-1500
Sink waste disposal	450
Washing machine	
automatic	500
manual	300
Vacuum cleaner	
upright	200-700
hand	100
Sewing machine	100
Iron	1000
Clothes dryer	
electric	4000
gas heated	300-400
Heater	
engine block	150-1000
portable	1500
waterbed	400
stock tank	100
Furnace blower	300-1000
Air conditioner	
room	1000
central	2000-5000

Appliance	Watts/hours
Ceiling fan	10-50
Table fan	10-25
Electric blanket	200
Blow dryer	1000
Shaver	15
Computer	
laptop	20-50
pc	80-150
printer	100
Typewriter	80-200
TV	
25 inch colour	150
19 inch colour	70
12 inch colour	20
VCR	40
CD player	35
Stereo	10-30
Clock radio	1
AM/FM car tape	8
Satellite dish	30
CB radio	5
Electric clock	3
Radio telephone	
receive	5
transmit	40-150
Lights	
100 W incandescent	100
25 W compact fluorescent	28
50 W DC incandescent	50
20 W DC compact fluorescent	40

Appliance	Watts/hours
Compact fluorescent incandescent equivalents	
40 W equiv.	11
60 W equiv.	16
75 W equiv.	20
100 W equiv.	30
Electric mower	1500
Hedge trimmer	450
Weed eater	500
1/4 inch drill	250
1/2 inch drill	750
1 drill	1000
9 inch disc sander	1200
3 inch belt sander	1000
12 inch chain saw	1100
14 inch band saw	1100
7 1/4 inch circular saw	900
8 1/4 inch circular saw	1400
Refrigerator/freezer conventional	
20 cubic feet (pre-1993)	145-250
20 cubic feet (post-1993)	60-100
Sunfrost	
16 cubic feet DC	22.5
12 cubic feet DC	14
Vesfrost refrigerator/freeze	
12 cubic feet	30
Vesfrost, conventional	
15 cubic feet (pre-1993)	88
15 cubic feet (post-1993)	61
Sunfrost freezer	
19 cubic feet	50

Typical energy consumption levels of domestic appliances

- Use materials sparingly (ie reduce the use of materials).

- Do not pollute the system (ie favour reintegratable materials that do not end up in landfills).

- Do not deplete resources (ie ensure sustainable use from renewable sources).

- Remain in balance with the biosphere (ie ensure materials are biodegradable).

- Run on internal 'information' within the system (ie self-maintaining without external guidance).

- Use local resources (ie for low transportation energy costs).

We might start design by simply regarding everything produced by humans as eventual waste material or the human-made built environment (including our architecture, no matter how aesthetically satisfying) as eventual refuse or waste material. The question, then, is what do we do with this waste material? Some of it is readily biodegradable and can return into the environment through decomposition. Recent discoveries include the production of biodegradable plastic made from corn. Corn syrup is fermented to form molecules that when dehydrated string themselves into a polymer that is much like any other plastic, except that it is based on a renewable resource and is biodegradable (ie it will turn into compost when discarded).

The balance of the inert waste needs to be deposited somewhere, currently as landfill. Ecomimetically, we need to think about how a product or a building and its components can be reused and recycled at the outset, before their production and as built-in design right at the beginning. This determines the types of materials we can use and the way that these are connected to one another.

If the recovery of all human-made products were built into the design process by insisting upon all kinds of reuse, regeneration and recycling using minimal amounts of energy, the overall reliance of the built environment on non-renewable resources would be considerably reduced. The need for non-renewable resources would also decrease as a consequence. Given the fact that the quantities of non-renewable fossil fuels and other materials in the earth are finite, our ability to recover materials from the obsolete portions of the built environment must increase. We must also minimise the degree to which we waste resources and we must limit our use of resources that cannot be recovered after use. Some quantities of what we consider to be 'pollution' are in fact accumulations of resources in inappropriate locations, or derelict resources occupying non-functional spaces, which could be rehabilitated and put back into the human-made system. We would not think of such materials as pollution had they been recovered and put to new uses. Pollution can be regarded as 'a resource out of context'.

End use	kWh/year
Space heating	10,000
Electric (resistance)	500
Gas (fan only)	1000
Refrigerator	800
Freezer	4500
Water heater (electric)	100
Washing machine/stove	780
Clothes dryer	
Electric	1000
Gas	70
Air conditioner	
Room	1000
Central	2000
Lighting	1000
Other uses/devices	
Aquarium/terrarium	548
Audio system	50
Black-and-white TV	40
Blanket	120
Bottled-water cooler	300
Ceiling fan	50
Clock	25
Coffee-maker	50
Colour TV	250
Computer	130
Dehumidifier	400
Dishwasher	200
Exhaust fan	15
Engine heater	250
Furnace fan	500
Garbage disposer	10
Grow light and accessories	800
Hair dryer	40
Humidifier	100
Instant hot water	160
Iron	50
Microwave oven	120
Mower	10
Pool pump	1500
Spa/hot tub	2000
Sump/sewage pump	40
Toasters/toaster oven	50
Vacuum cleaner	30
VCR	40
Waterbed	900
Well pump	400
Whole house fan	80
Window fan	20

Summary of energy consumption of various items used in buildings

B29

Chapter C ● Chapter B ● Chapter A ●

Design using environmentally benign materials, furniture, fittings, equipment (FF&E) and products that can be continuously reused, recycled and reintegrated

Design using environmentally benign materials, furniture, fittings, equipment (FF&E) and products that can be continuously reused, recycled and reintegrated

Material	Embodied energy (GJ/tonne)
Concrete	1.0
Brick	3.1
Glass	33.1
Steel	47.5
Aluminium	97.1
Plastics	162.0

Embodied energy of key building materials

Rather than making certain human actions on the environment illegal, as some ecologists might prefer, we could argue that economic motivations will change industrial methods. This change hinges partly on the recognition that resources are finite and that basic ingredients such as water and energy will eventually be more profitable if they are considered renewable. If industrial processes in our built environment more closely resembled natural organisms they could eliminate most waste. If consumer goods were considered as services (like rental cars) they could be more efficiently managed. Nature needs compensation and the sources of water, arable land and air used by our built environment will need replenishing for our survival.

Though environmental policy-makers have focused on the growing glut of refuse and pollution, most of the environmental damage is done before materials ever reach the consumer. The four primary materials industries (paper, plastics, chemicals and metals) account for 71 per cent of the toxic emissions from manufacturing in the USA, and five materials (paper, steel, aluminium, plastics and container glass) account for 31 per cent of US manufacturing energy use. These are the industries at which we might most usefully target our ecodesign efforts.

The point here is that the selection of materials is not as straightforward as setting out a priority list of preferred items using a system of embodied energy 'weighting' for different material characteristics. Choice also depends on design (eg whether designed for recovery). The basis for the materials selection is explained below:

Materials selection

Renewable material sources are those with a high recycled content. Ideally, the selection of material should be from abundant or renewable sources to avoid depletion or unsustainable use. Design must reduce the use and depletion of finite raw materials and long-cycle renewable materials by replacing them with rapidly renewable materials. The preference is to use rapidly renewable building materials and products made from plants that are frequently harvested (eg within a ten-year cycle or less). At the outset, the designer can establish a project goal for rapidly renewable materials and identify materials and suppliers that can achieve this goal. Ecodesign must reuse building materials and products (including salvaged, refurbished or reused materials, products and furnishings) in order to reduce demand for virgin materials and to reduce waste, thereby reducing impacts associated with the extraction and processing of virgin resources.

Besides the usual architectural criteria of aesthetics and costs, the ecological criteria for selection are of utmost importance and include the potential of the material for reuse and for recycling (as a consequence of replacement due to wear and tear at the end of the building's useful life). Many of the common building materials are associated with those industrial processes that have the most serious potential for environmental pollution. One argument for their continued use is that many of these materials are potentially very durable, and if they are reused the disadvantages of their manufacture can be balanced by their longer useful lives.

Materials selection should address life-cycle performance issues including the impact of production processes on the environment, including:

• renewable resources;

• environmental impact of production processes;

• chemical emissions (offgassing) after installation;

• durability; and

• recyclability.

For example, some of the materials selected with these criteria include:

• recycled foam underlay with a non-toxic adhesive;

• linoleum;

• cork underlay;

• spotted gum timber flooring;

• sisal flooring with a natural rubber latex backing;

• low VOC-emitting paints; and

• pressed bamboo sheeting and cork for some wall finishes.

• potential of the material for continuous reuse and recycling at the end of its useful life (eg as a consequence of replacement due to wear and tear).

Materials must be selected based on their potential for reuse and recycling. A material may have a high embodied energy at the first use, but thereafter this is significantly reduced. For instance, recycling can save most of the energy on certain plastics and up to 75 per cent for aluminium. In regarding design as the management of the inputs and the outputs of the building, our concern has to begin with the objectives (being the end consequence of the management activity, hence 'management by objectives' or MBO). The objectives are simply to reduce the impact on and positively renew, restore and enhance the natural environment. This is best achieved by retaining the materials and components within the built environment by reuse. Materials with potential for reuse must be given priority over materials with potential for recycling, as reuse uses less energy inputs and effort, albeit both avoid discharge into the environment.

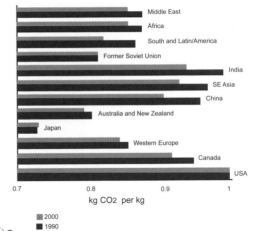

kg CO_2 per kg

■ 2000
■ 1990

CO^2 release per kilogram of cement produced

Design using environmentally benign materials, furniture, fittings, equipment (FF&E) and products that can be continuously reused, recycled and reintegrated

Design using environmentally benign materials, furniture, fittings, equipment (FF&E) and products that can be continuously reused, recycled and reintegrated

384

A material's potential for reuse and recycling might be given greater priority at the level of 'embodied energy' value. There is a mistaken belief that priority should be given to materials and components with low embodied energy values. On the contrary, the potential of a material for primary or secondary reuse is more important, for every time that a material is reused its original embodied energy is reduced (ie less about 50 per cent of its original embodied energy depending on the energy cost of reuse). Hence, the more times that a material or component is reused, the more its 'embodied energy costs' go down in value, thereby enhancing its suitability for first use.

As an initial strategy, materials from non-renewable resources should be made as reusable or as recyclable as possible to conserve the material. At the same time, in material selection, priority should be given to materials that have been used previously (ie 'waste' from an earlier structure) or that have been recycled. This immediately lowers the overall embodied energy figures in the building's mass.

To facilitate reuse, the connection between components in the built form needs to be mechanical for ease of demountability and reuse in an acceptable condition.

Low embodied ecological impact (including delivery to site)

'Embodied ecological impact' reflects the impact on the natural environment of the extraction and the production of the material or component (both globally and locally) at the source of manufacture, as well as the chain of activities leading up to its delivery on to the construction site. An indicator commonly used is the CO_2 emissions measured in kilograms. However, CO_2 emissions are not the only ecological impact in the production of a material; others include land devastation, pollution of waterways and energy costs of transportation.

For a more rigorous design approach, considerations should include:

- The records of suppliers of raw materials and components should be examined to ensure that their manufacturing processes are not unnecessarily polluting. As a minimum requirement, suppliers should be able to demonstrate that they have not contravened local legislation and acceptable ecosystem impacts concerning emissions.

- The processes by which specific ingredients are manufactured should be assessed for their impact on the environment (pollution in manufacture).

- Products (ranging from paints to toothpaste) can be produced in different ways with varying degrees of polluting effects. For example, paper produced by mills that use chlorine bleach should be avoided in favour of unbleached paper, or paper bleached using hydrogen peroxide.

- The impact of the materials on the environment after use should also be considered. Check whether they are fully biodegradable and whether there will be a contamination problem if the products end up in landfill sites.

- Saving water is as important in some regions as saving energy. Designers can aim to design products and parts that use far less water.

- Materials may be natural or synthetic, recycled or virgin, renewable or non-renewable. There are no clear-cut answers about which is least environmentally damaging. The belief that naturally occurring materials are to be preferred over human-made materials can be erroneous as these materials (eg tropical hardwoods) may be in very short supply or their production may result in environmental impairment or loss of biodiversity.

- Materials that occur near to their point of use have the advantage that they require less energy to transport. The use of locally occurring construction materials is argued by some to engender a more critical, regionalist design.

- The extraction process of some raw materials, such as aluminium and gold, can cause severe damage to local habitats. While the designer cannot take responsibility for what happens at the very start of the supply chain, this is one area where information should be requested wherever possible from raw materials suppliers or intermediaries. Material selection decisions should reflect the desire to support those materials whose mining and extraction activities cause the least damage.

Method of installation and life cycle

To facilitate reuse and recycling, consideration must also be given to the method by which the material is fixed to the building structure. Mechanical forms of fixing facilitate reuse, whereas chemical and altered forms of fixing inhibit it.

Low toxicity to humans and to ecosystems

Each material, product and component to be used in our building needs to be carefully studied for its physical contents, manufacturing history and performance record. The intention is to minimise the toxic content of the material and its effect on humans, who after all are one of the key species in the ecosystem of the building, and on the ecosystems. For example, office furnishings should be tested for the presence of formaldehyde, and paints with minimum volatile organic compounds (VOCs) should be applied to walls. All adhesives, architectural sealants (eg fillers), carpets, paints and coatings, wall coverings, floor finishes and furniture systems need to be carefully reviewed to reduce the presence of toxic elements such as formaldehyde, VOCs and other harmful chemicals commonly found in construction materials and all of which affect indoor air quality.

B29

Chapter C ● Chapter B ● Chapter A ●

Design using environmentally benign materials, furniture, fittings, equipment (FF&E) and products that can be continuously reused, recycled and reintegrated

Chapter C ● Chapter B ● Chapter A ●

Design using environmentally benign materials, furniture, fittings, equipment (FF&E) and products that can be continuously reused, recycled and reintegrated

The variety of chemicals found is usually complex and, as a result, difficult trade-offs need to be made. The criteria can be prioritised to help in decision-making. For instance, indoor air quality can be given first priority because it affects the building users more directly and because information on chemical composition is more readily available than data on manufacturing processes or disposal. Where particularly dangerous trade-offs in the upstream and downstream effects need to be made, there may be exceptions (Zeiher, 1996). For example, polyvinyl chloride (PVC) plastic emits highly toxic chemicals when incinerated, and thus its use is to be avoided wherever possible.

Establishing a material's toxic chemical content by knowing the quantity of chemicals it contains, the rate at which they emit gas, which can be transmitted to building occupants, and its other health hazard potentials is not an exact science. For example, a review of the United States Manufacturers' Material Safety Data Sheets (MSDS) is a first step in determining the presence of harmful chemicals in products. MSDS sheets, which are provided by the manufacturer upon request, list the names and amounts of major chemicals found in products. Next the information can be checked against the International Agency for Research on Cancer list of carcinogens and a number of handbooks on toxicology.

However, the lack of information from manufacturers makes general research by the designer on product types a pivotal requirement in the design decision-making process. Although MSDS sheets can be obtained, a certain expertise is required to interpret the scientific data.

Toxic solvents and alkyds such as benzene, xylene and toluene are found in many common building products (eg in oil-based paints) and can enter the bloodstream and cause respiratory problems, allergic reactions and liver damage. Chemicals used in the production of fabrics, carpets and pressed woods used in furniture systems include formaldehyde, diphenol ether and styrene, all of which are believed to cause numerous health problems, including suppression of the immune system.

The designer can circumvent some of these problems. For example, lead-free water-based latex paints might be employed, and wool/nylon blend, formaldehyde-free carpets can be used over 100 per cent natural jutepad with underlay. The furniture used in our building needs to be tested by an independent laboratory for the presence of formaldehyde.

Avoiding CFCs and HFCs

The designer should ensure that the selection of materials and systems avoids the use of ozone-destroying chlorofluorocarbons (CFCs) and hydrochlorofluorocarbons (HCFCs). About 50 per cent of all CFCs are currently used in buildings. The main measures to phase out CFC and HCFC uses are:

- designing buildings to avoid employing air conditioning that uses these;

- avoiding specifying insulation materials that involve these in their production;

- avoiding halon-based fire-control agents;

- designing buildings to maximise natural light and ventilation; and

- upgrading existing CFC air-conditioning systems with alternative systems, and avoiding the repeated use of CFC-related materials including HCFCs.

Asbestos

Another hazardous material is asbestos. The designer must ensure that the building is constructed without the use of asbestos or asbestos-containing material. Existing skyscrapers that are being adapted must have an asbestos operations and management plan.

Nature has four characteristics when it comes to manufacturing materials:

- life-friendly manufacturing processes (ie materials are manufactured in water, at room temperatures, without harsh chemicals or high pressures – as opposed to man's 'heat, beat and treat' way);

- an ordered hierarchy of structures;

- self-assembly; and

- templating of crystals with proteins.

Design for dematerialisation

Another approach is to design for dematerialisation as an ever more efficient use of materials. Commercially, this will continue as competition within markets and push industries to look for new ways to do more with less, that is, to use fewer materials and less energy to produce goods and services. New technologies also usher in dematerialisation, for example, the replacement of phone books with compact discs at phone companies that offer information services. For instance, a single disc carries 90 million phone numbers that would once have been displayed in 5 tons of phone books. So although total consumption may be rising, resource consumption per unit of output is declining, with less resource use and fewer wasteful by-products.

The dematerialisation phenomenon stands to benefit developing countries, as they are able to take advantage of such technologies from industrial countries and 'leapfrog over resource-intensive stages of development'.

Design using environmentally benign materials, furniture, fittings, equipment (FF&E) and products that can be continuously reused, recycled and reintegrated

Material	Canada	USA	NZ	Switzerland	Finland
Metals					
-Aluminium	236.3	192.0	145.0	261.7	468.0
-Nickel	168.3	58.0			
-Steel (general)	25.7	39.0	32.0	27.7	43.2
- Zinc	64.1		68.4	68.4	
Non-metallic minerals					
- Glass	10.2	19.8	16.7	21.6	16.5
- Gypsum	7.4	7.2		1.4	2.8
- Brick	4.9	5.8		3.1	
- Glass wool	22.3	14.0		18.0	23.4
Cement products					
- Cement	5.9	9.4	7.4	4.9	4.9
- Concrete	1.2	1.3	2.0	0.9	
- Mortar	2.2			1.4	
Plastic					
- Polyethylene	87.0			49.3	
- Polyolefin	97.0				
- Polystyrene	105.0			122.8	
- Paint (water based)	76.0	77.7			18.8
					76.7

Energy intensities of selected materials (MJ/kg)

Industrial ecology

The practice of 'industrial ecology' transforms production and consumption from a linear entropic process to a circular energy-efficient one. The term refers to the natural/social system in which humans are embedded with nature. One tenet of industrial ecology is 'dematerialisation', or the decline over time in the weight of materials used to meet a given economic function. The rates of dematerialisation would matter enormously for the environment, but are 'equivocal'. Stated another way, dematerialisation means using fewer raw materials and less energy per unit of output. The strategy for dematerialisation focuses on particular attributes of raw materials, rather than resources per se. For example, people need 'fuel', not necessarily oil. Materials that are malleable, conductive or strong, are not just silver, copper or steel. Seen this way, the development and production processes have near-endless opportunities for invention, exploration, substitution, and conserving technologies that expand the potential resource base.

As materials used for basic infrastructure and construction account for some 70 per cent of total materials consumed (excluding fuels), dematerialisation can make a considerable difference in resource consumption. The trend is telling. Today, it takes 35 per cent less steel to build a skyscraper than just a few decades ago. This has come about by the transformation that steel has undergone to become lighter in weight, but higher in strength. Other examples in resource reduction include automobiles and, in particular, the invention of fibre-optic cables. In this latter example, a single fibre-optic cable, just 65 kilograms of silica, can carry many times the number of messages carried by a cable made from 1 ton of copper. Wireless communication, if it replaces conventional wired communication, could further induce resource reduction and hence reduce environmental impact.

Everyday equipment, appliances and products must be designed to become significantly lighter. The average stove has become more compact, from 245.67 pounds per unit (in 1972) to 203.29 pounds (in 1987), a 17 per cent drop. The same trend is seen in water heaters, washers, dryers, air conditioners and freezers. Others, like refrigerators and dishwashers increased in size and weight within the same time period. Where packaging is concerned, not only have we seen a declining trend for grocery packaging, aluminium soft-drink cans have also witnessed dramatic decreases. When they were first introduced (in 1963), to produce 1000 cans required 54.8 pounds of metal. By the early 1990s, only 33 pounds were needed. An individual firm can save over 200 million pounds of aluminium annually. Besides, 50 per cent of recycled material in cans means even more resources conserved.

Dematerialisation strategies result from three kinds of design approach:

- Design for lightweighting (using less of the same material by design improvements).

- Design by substitution (replacing a dense and less efficient material with a less dense and more efficient one accomplishing the same task with a reduced weight, though not necessarily a smaller volume, of material.

- Design for reuse and recycling (from industry scrap as well as post-consumer sources). Recycling is a net 'dematerialiser' because it captures materials from a waste stream and reprocesses them. It depends on the ease with which the material can be isolated from the waste stream; whether large quantities of material are available in relatively uniform quantity; and how much embedded value remains within the discarded material.

Recycling can and often does reduce energy and material needs per product compared with a non-recycled product made of the same material. However, over time, resource conservation has often come about through substituting one very efficient material for another more traditional, energy- and resource-intensive material.

Other technological developments may widen recycling opportunities and prevent 'dissipative' transfer of material into the environment in ways that make recovery virtually impossible. The term 'dissipative' can be used to describe, for example, the brake pads on vehicles and tyres that 'leave finely distributed power on highways'. Their additives and laminates often result in such materials failing to achieve the same levels of resource conservation as can be achieved by using high-technology, complex materials.

Dematerialisation is an 'unsung environmental triumph' because it reduces environmental impacts associated with resource extraction and processing to make individual products, and may also reduce the 'transport intensity' of economic growth.

There is no waste at all in nature because all its 'manufacturing processes' are interrelated through all scales, from the local pond to the globe. What one organism no longer needs is used by another. The biosphere was constructed from these relationships, each further level of complexity emerging from a symbiotic relationship with the levels below. Industrial ecology imitates this interrelatedness. Waste becomes another sellable or exchangeable commodity. Instead of our producing, say, steel, and its waste being dumped as an unwanted product, that waste is used by another enterprise for another industrial process. For example, blast furnace slag from steel manufacture can be used as a cement replacement in concrete. The building industry in Japan uses up to 80 per cent blast-furnace cement to 20 per cent ordinary Portland cement However, making the waste of one production cycle the raw material of another has yet to become commonplace.

B29

Chapter C ● Chapter B ● Chapter A

Design using environmentally benign materials, furniture, fittings, equipment (FF&E) and products that can be continuously reused, recycled and reintegrated

Design using environmentally benign materials, furniture, fittings, equipment (FF&E) and products that can be continuously reused, recycled and reintegrated

390

The products we use	The potentially hazardous waste they generate
Plastic	Organic chlorine compounds, organic solvents
Pesticides	Organic chlorine compounds, organic phosphate compounds
Medicines	Organic solvents and residues, heavy metals (mercury and zinc, for example)
Paints	Heavy metals, pigments, solvents, organic residues
Oil, gasoline, and other petroleum products	Oil, phenols and other organic compounds, heavy metals, ammonia, salt acids, caustics
Metals	Heavy metals, fluorides, cyanides, acids and alkaline cleaners, solvents, pigments, abrasives, plating salts, oils, phenols
Leather	Heavy metals, organic solvents
Textiles	Heavy metals, dyes, organic chlorine compounds, solvents

Waste generated by manufacture of common products

Industries need not be located next to each other as long as they are connected by shared information and a mutual desire to use waste from each other's processes. Waste becomes designed where a process that creates a lot of waste, as long as it is useful, or wanted waste, may be better than one with a small amount of waste that has to be landfilled.

Considerations of use of materials during building occupancy

It is important not only to re-evaluate user requirements; the patterns of use in the building are important as well. For example, US businesses alone consume an estimated 21 million tons of office paper every year, the equivalent of more than 350 million trees. In fact, office paper is one of the top six contributors to waste outputs from offices and among the fastest growing by percentage. For instance, if the pattern of use in offices throughout the USA increased the rate of double-sided photocopying (eg through user education), it would save the equivalent of about 15 million trees.

The designer must be aware that to design for recovery, extra storage space must be provided in the building. At the minimum, there must be adequate storage space for the building-wide collection of separated glass, aluminium and office paper.

Low embodied energy impact (including delivery to site)

Buildings consume energy in extracting, transporting, manufacturing and erecting their materials and components. Green design seeks to minimise this 'embodied energy' by making maximum use of local materials (minimising their transport) of inherently low-embodied energy (wood being the lowest and aluminium among the highest).

In aggregate, the embodied ecological impact of a material can be evaluated at three levels: global sustainability; natural resource management; and local environmental quality at source of production.

Embodied energy in a material or assembled component is the energy expended (from non-renewable energy sources) in the extraction and processing of raw materials, their manufacture, transport and construction. Some hold that the embodied energy of a product is calculable with a high error margin.

It has been found that a major cost of the embodied energy in a material is incurred in transportation to the construction site. The contention is that local products are to be preferred as these will travel the shortest distance; however, this has to be set against the reuse potential of the material or component. A local or regional product that has limited reuse potential may have a lower overall embodied energy value than material imported over long distances but which can be reused many times. Furthermore, the local material may be in limited supply as a resource.

Much of the literature on energy 'contained' within the building materials relates to mass rather than to use, which can be misleading. For example, it may be incorrect to contend that glass is a preferable material to brick by virtue of its lower mass, and that therefore an external wall of glass is preferred to brick. Brick, while having a higher mass, also has better insulation properties than glass, thereby providing energy savings in the operational life of the building. On the other hand, glass may be easier to demount and reuse than brick.

Pre-assembly of materials has also to be factored in. For example, timber-frame construction can be up to 20 per cent less energy intensive than traditional timber construction. In a two-bedroom dwelling, the embodied energy is equivalent to between two and five years of energy consumed in its operational phase (by heating, light and power). Thus, while embodied energy is one factor in ecological design, affecting its initial costs, the operational energy costs by far exceed these in terms of energy use, but may actually be less when comparing embodied ecological impacts. Some studies in Europe indicate that the production energy (primary energy at approx. 2.0 MWh/m^2) contained in a building is approximately 20 per cent of the operating energy required over its entire lifetime.

Studies have shown that the level of embodied energy in a building is related to its mass. Generally, the lower the building's mass, the lower would be the total value of the overall embodied energy in its materials and equipment. A low energy embodied office building should not be more than 10 GJ/m^2 of primary delivered embodied energy.

Reinforced-concrete-frame construction has almost the same amount of embodied energy as steel, but it is less recyclable at the end of its useful life than steel. Structural steel can generally be recycled and reused in virtually the same way as before, whereas concrete can be reused only in a downgraded form (eg as rubble) and, with limitations, can be recycled again for structural purposes.

As embodied energy constitutes only about 35 per cent of the energy used in the lifespan of a building (ie L21 in the Partitioned Matrix in A5), the greater amount is used during its operational mode (up to 65 per cent, ie L11 in the Partitioned Matrix in A5). Hence, we should place greater importance on passive design so that during its operational stage the building will make the most of ambient energy, eg natural daylight, natural ventilation, etc, to minimise the remaining energy demands over its lifetime (considering a 60-year building lifespan).

The embodied energy/carbon dioxide calculations are a key indicator of environmentally conscious building design. However, when comparing embodied energy values of alternative construction types, it is not the embodied energy value per unit mass or unit volume of the material that is important. Rather it is the building that has to be compared, as alternative materials used for similar functions will have different properties. This comparative component

Building type	Embodied energy delivered GJ/m^2	Embodied energy primary GJ/m^2	Embodied CO$_2$ kg GJ/m^2
Office	5 – 10	10 – 18	500 – 1000
House	45 – 8	9 – 13	800 – 1200
Flat	5 – 10	10 – 18	500 – 1000
Industrial	4 – 7	7 – 12	400 – 700
Road	1 – 5	2 – 10	130 – 650

Overall embodied energy and embodied CO^2 for various building types

Design using environmentally benign materials, furniture, fittings, equipment (FF&E) and products that can be continuously reused, recycled and reintegrated

is termed the 'functional unit'. For example, although steel has a higher embodied energy per unit mass than reinforced concrete, it is considerably stiffer. The result is that much less steel is required to perform the same structural function as reinforced concrete.

Therefore, when making such calculations, what should be compared is the embodied energy of the 'functional unit'. In the example above, this might be effected by comparing a steel beam with a reinforced concrete beam, which performs the same function. But when comparing frame alternatives in office buildings, the functional unit should be the gross square metre area of the completed building, as many substantive factors result from adopting either a steel or concrete frame, such as the type of foundations and the structure's fire resistance.

Research comparing steel and reinforced-concrete-frame construction for office buildings has shown that there are no significant embodied energy/carbon dioxide differences between the alternative construction methods. Thus, there are no embodied energy/carbon dioxide penalties for designers selecting either material. However, a designer who selects high energy embodied materials must pay particular attention to their recycling or reuse after the end of the useful life of their building.

Because it takes so much energy to make a building, it is important to consider what will happen to its constituent materials once the building is no longer functional (see design for reuse and design for disassembly in B28).

Using recycled materials, deploying all materials to facilitate their eventual recycling, and designing buildings to be robust and adaptable to foster their longevity further conserves embodied energy. The difficulty of systematising such reductions is such that embodied energy is rarely, if ever, taken into account when judging the energy efficiency of a building.

However, by contrast, energy inputs for running buildings now tend to be much greater than embodied energy. In the UK, approximately 5–6 per cent of the total energy consumption is embodied compared with about 50 per cent used in buildings for space heating and cooling, water heating, lighting and power.

Biodegradable materials (see B28)

When we consider the use and selection of materials, the natural world is a vast store of design inspiration. Everything that humans want to do, the natural world has generally achieved, and without consuming fossil fuels, polluting the environment or putting the biosphere's future at risk. Materials used in a biomimetic world would be manufactured in the same way that the natural world makes its materials – using the sun's energy and basic compounds – to create fibres, plastics and chemicals that are fully biodegradable.

One of the major design issues that needs resolution is the systemic integration of our built forms and their operational systems with the ecosystems in nature. This integration is crucial to the entire proposition of ecodesign, for if our built systems and built forms do not integrate with the natural systems in nature then they will remain disparate as artificial objects in nature and their eventual integration after their manufacture through biodegradation and natural processes of decomposition is unlikely. While recycling and reuse within the human-made environment will contribute towards the problem of deposition of waste, we should ideally seek to integrate not just the inorganic waste into the ecosystems but also organic waste (eg sewage, rainwater runoff, wastewater, food wastes, etc).

Plant/wood-based materials

Wood is regarded as the greenest building material because it has the lowest embodied energy. However, because of the social and environmental impacts of large-scale deforestation, only wood from sustainably managed forests can be considered green. For example, the Forestry Stewardship Council (FSC) is an international non-profit organisation founded in 1993 in Bonn, Germany, to support environmentally appropriate, socially beneficial and economically viable management of the world's forests. The FSC is introducing an international labelling scheme for forest products, which provides a credible guarantee that the product comes from a well-managed forest. All forest products carrying the FSC logo have been independently certified as coming from forests that meet the internationally recognised FSC principles and criteria of forest stewardship. In this way FSC provides an incentive in the marketplace for good forest stewardship.

Plants can also be used as green building materials, bamboo and thatch from reeds being traditional examples of building materials. Today, the focus is on hemp and kenaf (ambary) because of their varied manufacturing applications and low-input production. Fibres of both plants can be used as reinforcement in composite materials.

New materials must be created that will reduce any harmful impact on the environment. Flax fibres can be combined with recycled polypropylene to produce a biodegradable laminated material with high tensile strength. Research into this process had two aims: to replace glass with a natural fibre, and to use a recycled material in place of plastic. It is hoped eventually to replace thermoplastic composite compounds with this environmentally friendly material.

Composite materials may not recycle well, as the technologies that produce composites introduce complexity to the material profile and make isolation of the materials from the waste stream more difficult.

- Compliance with laws and FSC principles
  Forest management operations shall respect all applicable laws of the country in which they occur, and international treaties and agreements to which the country is a signatory, and comply with FSC principles and criteria.

- Tenure and use rights and responsibilities
  Long-term tenure and use rights to the land and forest resources shall be clearly defined, documented, and legally established.

- Indigenous peoples' rights
  The legal and customary rights of indigenous peoples to own, use and manage their lands, territories and resources shall be recognised and respected.

- Community relations and workers' rights
  Forest-management operations shall maintain or enhance the long-term social and economic well being of forest workers and local communities.

- Benefits from the forest
  Forest-management operations shall encourage the efficient use of the forests' multiple products and services to ensure economic viability and a wide range of environmental and social benefits.

- Environmental impact
  Forest management shall conserve biological diversity and its associated values, water resources, soils, and unique and fragile ecosystems and landscapes, and by so doing maintain the ecological functions and integrity of the forest.

- Management plan
  A management plan – appropriate to the scale and intensity of forest management – shall be drawn up to assess the condition of the forest, yields of forest products, chain of custody, management activities and their social and environmental impacts.

- Monitoring and assessment
  Monitoring shall be conducted-appropriate to the scale and intensity of forest management – to assess the condition of the forest, yields of forest products, chain of custody, management activities and their social and environmental impacts.

- Maintenance of natural forest
  Primary forest, well – developed secondary forest and sites of major environmental, social or cultural significance shall be conserved. Tree plantations shall not replace such areas or other land uses.

- Plantations (draft principle not yet ratified)
  Plantations shall complement, not replace, natural forests. Plantations should reduce pressure on natural forests.

● Forest stewardship principles (FSP)

Design using environmentally benign materials, furniture, fittings, equipment (FF&E) and products that can be continuously reused, recycled and reintegrated

What must be kept in mind, however, is that the more we know about new materials and the environment the easier it becomes to draw appropriate conclusions about their environmental advantages.

Biopolymers

Investigations into new materials and processes have uncovered sustainable sources that can replace conventional ones that have proved environmentally harmful. Biopolymers, such as those made from potato starch and corn starch, have the same characteristics as certain plastics and can be moulded and formed in the same ways, but they are fully biodegradable. For example, such plastics are derived from corn and other plants. They are made into a variety of fibres, packaging and other forms but will break down naturally when they are discarded. The premise in operation here is that packaging is not just waste; it is a valuable raw material.

Soybean

Other crops have strong market potential due to their chemical composition. One of the most versatile being researched is the soybean. Soy-based products for construction include water sealants for concrete, and soybean oil paints and solvents for use as adhesives that can fingerjoint green or dry wood. Soy adhesives reduce formaldehyde requirements.

Foam insulation is another product that has been made from soybean. One example, called Bio-Based 500, is a semi-rigid, open cell, half-pound foam insulation.

Agriproducts

New uses of agriproducts are crossing into construction, eg research in California has identified potential benefits from using rice-hull ash as an additive to fly-ash cement; researchers are creating rigid urethane foam from soybean oil, which can be used for building insulation; and milk that is unfit for consumption can be recovered for use in paint.

Compressed strawboard uses an agricultural by-product. 'The strawboard used for partitions is manufactured from rice or wheat straw, by-products of farming. The straw is compressed into a board without the need for a binder. It is manufactured using a simple reciprocating ram, ie the straw is pressed between two heated plates at 210°C, using approximately 1.25 kWh per square metre of product.' Its advantages include the use of a waste by-product that would otherwise be burnt producing air emissions; it is based on a natural, renewable material; and it does not use formaldehyde binder, which eliminates the environmental impacts associated with manufacturing the resin as well as potential VOC emissions from the final product. VOC emissions are normally associated with MDF, plywood and particleboard. Better still, the biodegradable strawboard can also be recycled back into new strawboard, or can be used as mulch or compost. Where glues are employed to attach fabric to the strawboard, they are specifically chosen to be water-based to eliminate the VOC emissions usually associated with conventional adhesives.

Another example of an ecologically sound material has been developed that combines organic animal (wool) and plant (ramie) fibres to create a fabric that is cool in summer and warm in winter. It is also fully biodegradable, and is made without harmful dyes or production processes. It can be used for everything from clothing to packaging, all organically produced and meant to be biodegradable. After use, such items are meant to be thrown on a compost heap and broken down and returned to the soil as nutrients. This is the complete opposite of technological 'products of service', such as automobiles and television sets, which follow their own closed cycle of use and reuse (design for disassembly). When it is time for their disposal, many of their elements are meant to be remanufactured into similar products rather than being 'downcycled' into a material of lesser quality and material value.

See also further construction applications of agriproducts under soybean.

Plastics

Plastics are often not recycled in large quantities (with a few exceptions, such as plastic soda bottles). Plastics are often difficult to isolate from the waste stream because they occur in many different, often difficult to distinguish, resin forms. They often occur in composite form with other materials or in conjunction with other plastics. Moreover, plastics are an extremely efficient material – for many products, a little material goes a long way, so that only small amounts of any given resin are used per product. Thus, recovering that product does not yield much material for the effort undertaken. Plastics are the result of a kind of recycling. They are often made from what were once considered as waste gases and burned off in petroleum-refining processes. Plastic results from the very efficient transformation of gases into usable matter, with little residual matter remaining. This contrasts starkly with the mining of metals, which often requires the extraction of large amounts of material and the application of large amounts of usable materials. Recyling is a means of avoiding this waste-generating, energy-consuming process. Because plastics often derive from a very efficient residual-gas-using process, there are fewer 'avoidable costs' achieved through recycling than is the case with many metals, glass and paper.

Biodegradable plastics

Techniques for making biodegradable plastics that are biologically produced have been around for some time (having been invented at the Pasteur Institute in Paris as far back as the

Design using environmentally benign materials, furniture, fittings, equipment (FFSE) and products that can be continuously reused, recycled and reintegrated

Chapter C ● Chapter B ● Chapter A ●

Design using environmentally benign materials, furniture, fittings, equipment (FF&E) and products that can be continuously reused, recycled and reintegrated

1920s). However, it was only recently (in the 1980s) that industry sought to implement such techniques. A biologically biodegradable plastic was produced by fermenting strains of bacteria. These bacteria use a mixture of hydrogen, carbon dioxide and oxygen gases to produce a slow-release encapsulation material for pharmaceuticals and other things.

Bioplastics

Green 'bioplastics' are now also made from sugar cane, soybeans, corn starch and sweet potatoes – although hyped as 'new', that is far from the case, for the first plastics were made from cellulose, or pure vegetable fibre. Before this, so-called 'biodegradable' plastic bags were introduced in the 1980s by chemical companies, in response to calls for a more socially acceptable material. However, they were made mainly out of conventional oil-based plastic, but with corn starch added as a filler, which would supposedly be broken down by bacteria in a landfill. In fact, once the corn starch had been broken down, 95 per cent of the bulk of the bag still remained, in the form of 'plastic dust' that would never fully degrade, adding the risk of leaching into nearby ground water. In 1990, there was a real advance when a compostable, biodegradable plastic made entirely with corn starch was developed. It cost almost four times as much as conventional plastics, and it faced a lack of composting sites prepared to accept it after its use. Another biodegradable plastic was made from polylactic acid, a by-product of fermented sugars found in milk, beets, corn, potatoes and grains. Invented in 1833, it was later used in surgical sutures and screws because it actually breaks down harmlessly in the body. It can be safely recycled or incinerated and, if disposed of in a compost or landfill, it decomposes in six weeks.

Universities around the USA are also at the forefront of developing safe non-petroleum-based plastics. Researchers are developing a 'green' plastic from supercritical carbon dioxide (part liquid, part gas and much touted as a possible replacement for petroleum-based solvents). Supercritical carbon dioxide is also being used to generate new kinds of chemical reactions with the aim of eventually producing a range of environmentally benign and solvent-free plastics. A non-toxic methyl methacrylate monomer (primary ingredient of Plexiglas) has been developed without using petroleum by-products.

Other biodegradable bioproducts derived from organic sources include foam laminates and food-wrapping products from potato starches; recent research has also confirmed that wheat and corn starches can be similarly used.

Non-biodegradable plastics

These have no place in a future based on sustainable materials. Synthetic materials and, specifically, chlorinated organic compounds, are responsible for the appearance in the environment of dioxins, which have been described as 'vicious carcinogens linked to a marked increase in the use by industry of chlorinated chemicals – specifically PVC [polyvinyl chloride]'. After its carcinogenic properties, plastic's next fatal characteristic is being impervious to organic biodegradation. It will last forever. This trait, once regarded as its strong point, has now become its greatest disadvantage. Every piece of non-biodegradable plastic made will continue to haunt the natural environment – from marine life killed by ingesting what looked like jellyfish but was actually plastic to seals dying after becoming entangled in discarded nylon-mesh fishing nets that float ghost-like across the ocean – for centuries to come.

Even incineration will not make plastic disappear. Incineration at extremely high temperatures as a method of disposal only converts them into more toxic gases and particulate matter that disperses these airborne toxins more widely than would otherwise be possible through simple landfilling.

Plastics burn too easily. Burning plastic, as in an incinerator, releases noxious gases that are equal in their damaging effect on humans and other organisms to any biochemical weapon ever devised. Polypropylene wastebaskets, polyurethane foam mattresses, nylon carpets, the styrene-butadiene foam underlayer to carpets, polyethylene-insulated cable and polyurethane foam-padded furniture are all easily combustible and the fumes that they emit are fatally toxic to humans.

Warning logo for poisonous plastics

Design using environmentally benign materials, furniture, fittings, equipment (FF&E) and products that can be continuously reused, recycled and reintegrated

397

Chapter C • Chapter B • Chapter A •

B29

Design using environmentally benign materials, furniture, fittings, equipment (FF&E) and products that can be continuously reused, recycled and reintegrated

Type	Properties
Permanent	For products for which there will be no secondary use. Applications in medicine and related fields for products in direct contact with organic parts, eg parts of an implanted hip joint, shell of heart pacemaker, artificial veins, or blood-storage bags. Material, characteristics and lasting quality performance of primary importance, eg nylon 66. Quantity used negligible.
Reusable	Product can be used over and over again unchanged, eg plastic bucket. Complex tools or appliances can be repaired, upgraded in whole or in part, for resale. Enormous numbers of items involved. Wood, tin, enamel, glass and ceramics are ecologically and aesthetically preferable.
Recyclable	Thermoplastics and elastomers melt at a specific high temperature like glass and are easy to recycle. Thermosetting polymers do not liquefy and are very difficult to recycle; research is continuing into better methods.
Co-recyclable	Compatible materials can be recycled together to form a useful new material.
Biodisintegratable	Attempts have been made to embed a biodegradable trait into synthetic polymers so that they turn into mulch. These compounds perform badly in landfills through lack of moisture, but slightly better when composted. Radical improvements have produced plastics, now commercially available, that degrade 100 per cent less than two months after being discarded. Research continues into further control of the start of degradation.
Biodegradable	100 per cent biodegradable rather than biodisintegratable. PHA (polyhydroxyalkanoate), a member of the polyester family, is 'manufactured' directly by micro-organisms. Scores of bacteria have been found that produce this organic polymer, including PHBs (polyhydroxybutyrates), one of the first forms to become commercially available. PHA plastics can be moulded, melted and shaped like petroleum-based plastics, and have the same flexibility and strength. The same production methods can be used, eg melt-casting, injection-moulding, blow-moulding, spinning and extrusion.
Bioregenerative	Polycaprolactone film completely biodegrades within three months, leaving no residues. Research into paper products laminated with layers of corn-based cellulose materials proves they can resist water for six to eight hours and could serve as containers for drinks and fast-food items.
Bioenhancing	Carry additives to stimulate plant growth, prevent erosion in arid climates (artificial burrs), or carry plant seeds and seedlings embedded in growth stimulants.

Categories of plastics and their potential for recovery and degradation

Plastic	Properties	Uses
Acrylonitrile-butadiene-styrene	Tough, lightweight, impact resistant, long wearing, resistant to stains and chemicals, adheres to metals	Car components, appliance housings, shells for cellphones and laptop computers, ski boots, inline skates, bicycle helmets
Epoxies	Strong, electrical insulators, bond easily to metals	Protective coatings, adhesives, sealants
High-density polyethylene (HDPE)	Strong, stiff, resistant to chemicals and moisture	Containers (milk cartons, trash bags, yogurt containers, cereals box liners), piping
Low-density polyethylene	Tough, flexible, transparent, tear and moisture resistant, can be heat-sealed	Thin sheeting (bags, films, wrapping on tamper-proof boxes), coated paper (milk cartons), bottles (household cleaning products, food, motor oil)
Linear low-density polyethylene (LLPE)	Strong, resistant to punctures and tears	Packaging (shrink film, stretch film), trash bags, disposable nappies
Nylon	Easy to mould, resistant to chemicals and abrasion, non-flammable	Fibres (carpets, tyre cord, apparel, backpacks, tents), zips, non-lubricated gears and other machine parts
Phenol, formaldehyde resins	Tough, heat and fire resistant	Pressed wood products, thermal insulation, adhesives, varnishes and printing inks
Polycarbonates	Strong, tough, stiff, impact resistant, resistant to heat and moisture, maintain shape	Casings for cellphones, laptop computers, batteries, power tools, microwave cookware, helmets, windows, eyeglass and headlight lenses, medical equipment
Polyethylene terephthalate (PEE or PETE)	Tough, clear, resistant to moisture and gases	Containers (soft-drink bottles, other food and non-food containers), car tyres, carpet yarns, fibrefill, and the 'polyester' of knit fabrics
Polyesters	Tough, durable, resistant to heat, sunlight and many chemicals.	Food containers and wraps, microwave cookware, bathroom counters, clothing buttons
Polypropylene (PP)	Versatile, strong, tough, resistant to heat, moisture and chemicals	Packaging (hot liquids, medicine bottles, yogurt containers), fibres, moulded parts for cars
Polystyrene (PS)	Versatile, tough, easily moulded, maintains shape, clean temperature insulator	Packaging (CD/jewel cases, foam trays for foods as well as the clear film around the package), shells for cellphones and laptop computers, dishes, cups, toilet seats, toys (vehicles, action figures, play sets), insulation for refrigerators and freezers
Polyvinyl chloride (PVC), or vinyl	Tough, flexible, resistant to chemicals and moisture, non-flammable, impact resistant	Pipes and pipe fittings, floor tiles, house sidings and gutters, credit cards, packaging (shampoo bottles), wire insulation, medical tubing, plastic-coated cloth
Polyurethane	Versatile, tough, impact and abrasion resistant	Coatings for wires, hoses and tubing; waterproofing for coats, umbrellas and outdoor furniture, shoe soles, ski boots, inline skates, covers and door panels

Uses of various types of plastic

B29

Chapter C ● Chapter B ● Chapter A

Design using environmentally benign materials, furniture, fittings, equipment (FF&E) and products that can be continuously reused, recycled and reintegrated

Chapter C ● Chapter B ● Chapter A ●

B29

Design using environmentally benign materials, furniture, fittings, equipment (FF&E) and products that can be continuously reused, recycled and reintegrated

400

PVC

Polyvinyl chloride (PVC) was first introduced into the USA in 1929 (by BF Goodrich). It was hailed as a miracle material – after all, it was cheap, water-resistant, chemically stable, pliable and found multiple uses. However, it also had an untold danger, which was discovered too late to prevent a disaster. It had been known before that PVC gas had narcotic properties but, in a shameful disregard for the well-being of vinyl workers, this was never considered much of a problem where they were concerned. First, vinyl workers were found to be suffering from gastritis, skin lesions and dermatitis, then a rare hepatitis-like condition. Finally, vinyl was linked to cancer, specifically angiosarcoma of the liver (caused by exposure to vinyl chloride monomer gas).

Globally, over 50 per cent of PVC manufactured is used in construction, in products such as pipelines, wiring, siding, flooring and wallpaper. As a building material PVC is cheap, easy to install and easy to replace. PVC is replacing 'traditional' building materials such as wood, concrete and clay in many areas. Although it appears to be the ideal building material, PVC has high environmental and human health costs that its manufacturers fail to inform consumers about.

From its manufacture to its disposal, PVC emits toxic compounds. During the manufacture of the building block ingredients of PVC (such as vinyl chloride monomer) dioxin and other persistent pollutants are emitted into the air, water and land, thus presenting both acute and chronic health hazards. During use, PVC products can leach toxic additives, for example, flooring can release softeners called phthalates. When PVC reaches the end of its useful life, it can be either landfilled, where it leaches toxic additives, or incinerated, again emitting dioxin and heavy metals. When PVC burns in accidental fires, hydrogen chloride gas and dioxin are formed.

For virtually all PVC applications, safer alternatives exist, using more sustainable, traditional materials – such as paper, wood or local materials. PVC can also be replaced by a variety of other, less environmentally damaging, plastics – although most plastics pose some risk to the environment and contribute to the global waste crisis.

Polyvinyl chloride (PVC) is unique in its high chlorine and additives content, which makes it an environmental poison throughout its life cycle. Vinyl chloride is a known human carcinogen. PVC releases dioxin and other persistent organic pollutants during its manufacture and disposal and cannot be readily recycled due to its chlorine and additive content. Furthermore, the additives are not bound to the plastic and leach out.

PET

After the vinyl cancer scare, the search for the safest plastic for the bottling industry continued and, eventually, the PET (polyethylene terephthalate) bottle was invented. PET is now ubiquitous, thanks to manufacturers who quickly saw benefits in its lightweight, strong and unbreakable properties, but it threatens to swamp already brimming landfills. PET is, however, far from the worst product that the plastics industry has produced (it has the redeeming quality of a high recycling rate: 30 per cent in 1993 in the USA, see below). Styrofoam cups and platters take the longest to biodegrade even when compared to the worst plastic types. They also pose a dual assault on the environment, because the chemicals used to blow styrene plastic into foam are the same chlorofluorocarbons that deplete the ozone layer. The worst thing about polystyrene materials is that, for the most part, they are used only for a few seconds or minutes (to keep food warm) before being discarded – into landfills where they stay intact, leaching out toxins for an extended period.

PET bottles acquired a new lease of after-use life as the basic component for synthetic fleece material that mimics sheepskin. PET soda bottles are collected, shredded and crushed into tiny pieces called 'flake'. They are first washed in a purifying bath, then either bleached white (if clear) or left alone (if tinted green). Then the flake is melted and forced through a nozzle to extrude fine filaments the thickness of a human hair. These are teased and spun. These are a fully synthetic, petroleum-based product that is fully recycled and reused.

Polyurethane (PU)

Polyurethane (PU) is mainly used in insulation and soft/foamed products like carpet underlay. It uses several hazardous intermediates and creates numerous dangerous by-products. These include phosgene, isocyanates, toluene, diamines, and the ozone-depleting gases methylene chloride and CFCs, as well as halogenated flame retardants and pigments. The burning of PU releases numerous hazardous chemicals such as isocyanates, carbon dioxide, hydrogen cyanide, PAHs and dioxins.

Polystyrene (PS)

Polystyrene (PS) is widely used for foam insulation and also for hard applications like cups and toys. Its production involves the use of known (benzene) and suspected (styrene and 1,3-butadiene) human carcinogenic substances. Styrene is also known to be toxic to the reproductive system. PS can be technically recycled, but recycling rates are low, although higher than for PVC.

Acrylonitrile-butadiene-styrene (ABS)

Acrylonitrile-butadiene-styrene (ABS) is used as hard plastic in many applications such as pipes, car bumpers and toys (hard building blocks). ABS uses a number of hazardous chemicals. These include butadiene and styrene (see above) and acrylonitrite. Acrylonitrile is highly toxic and readily absorbed by humans by inhalation and directly through the skin. Both the liquid and its vapour are highly toxic. Acrylonitrile is classified as a probable human carcinogen, as are styrene and butadiene.

Polycarbonate (PC)

Polycarbonate (PC) is used in the manufacture of products such as CDs and refillable milk bottles and is usually made with the highly toxic phosgene – derived from chlorine gas. PC does not need additives but does need solvents for its production, such as methylene chloride, a carcinogen. Other solvents used may include chloroform, 1-2-dichloroethylene, tetrachloroethane and chlorobenzene. A number of processes have been developed to reclaim polycarbonate from compact discs and PC milk and water bottles, for downcycling into lower quality products such as crates or building applications, or for mixing in small quantities with virgin material for higher grade products such as bottles.

Polyolefins

Polyolefins such as polyethylene (PE) and polypropylene (PP) are simpler polymer structures that do not need plasticisers, although they do use additives such as UV and heat stabilisers, antioxidants and in some applications flame retardants. The polyolefins pose fewer risks than other plastics and have the highest potential for mechanical recycling. Both PE and PP are versatile and cheap, and can be designed to replace almost all PVC applications. PE can be made either hard or very flexible, without the use of plasticisers. PP is easy to mould and can also be used in a wide range of applications.

In comparison with PVC, PE and PP use fewer problematic additives, have reduced leaching potential in landfills, reduced potential for dioxin formation during burning (provided that brominated/chlorinated flame retardants are not used) and reduced technical problems and costs during recycling.

Biobased polymers, ie biodegradable plastics from renewable sources are seen as a promising alternative for plastic products which have a short life cycle or are impractical to recycle, such as food packaging, agricultural plastics and other disposables.

Biobased plastics can be made out of products obtained from raw materials produced by a natural living or growing system, such as starch and cellulose. The advantage of biopolymers is that they readily degrade and can be composted. Natural polymers include cellulose (from wood, cotton), horn (hardened protein) and raw rubber. Converted natural polymers include vulcanised rubber, vulcanised fibre, celluloid and casein protein.

Estimated decomposition rates of various types of material:

Styrofoam container:	> 1 million years
Plastic jug:	1 million years
Glass bottle:	1 million years
Disposable nappies:	550 years
Aluminium can:	500 years
Tin can:	90 years
Leather shoe:	45 years
Plastic bag:	20 years
Cigarette butt:	5 years
Wool sock:	1 year
Paper bag:	1 month
Banana peel:	3 weeks

It is contended that plastics head the list of outgassers (emitters of noxious vapours and fumes). Those who suffer from exposure to the outgassing are chemically sensitive; the name for their disease is EI/MCS, environmental illness/multiple chemical sensitivity. The only treatment for it is to avoid exposure to plastics whenever possible.

It is a myth that plastics and other non-biodegradable materials form the main bulk of landfill. Only 100 pounds out of 14 tons of refuse (figures from a study of nine municipal landfills made over a five-year period) constituted fast-food packaging (when all the concerns were for non-biodegradable styrofoam packaging). In fact, fast-food packaging, foam and disposable nappies together made up just a half of 1 per cent of landfilled refuse bulk weight. Research also found that the volume of all plastics, including foam, film and rigid toys, utensils and packages, amounted to around 20 to 24 per cent of all refuse. One of the biggest contents in landfills is paper.

Besides plastics, environmentally friendly building materials are now available that are made from recycled materials, from shingles to drywall to insulation. Wall insulation has been made of recycled newspapers.

Design using environmentally benign materials, furniture, fittings, equipment (FF&E) and products that can be continuously reused, recycled and reintegrated

Chapter C ● Chapter B ● Chapter A

B29

Design using environmentally benign materials, furniture, fittings, equipment (FF&E) and products that can be continuously reused, recycled and reintegrated

404

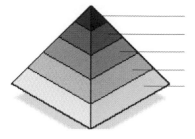

· Polyvinyl chloride (PVC) and other
  halogenated plastics
· Polyurethane (PU), polystyrene
  (PS), acrylonitrile-butadiene-styrene
  (ABS), polycarbonate (PC)
· Polyethylene-terephthalate (PET),
  polyolefins (PE, PP, etc)
· Biobased plastics

The plastics pyramid ●- - - - - - - - - - - - -

Pyramid of plastics

A pyramid of plastics can be used to assist those making material selections to avoid PVC use. The guidance focuses on the toxic characteristics of the potential alternative materials. It provides a qualitative ranking based on the environmental and health problems of PVC, addressing the production, additives and product emissions during use, disposal and recycling.

It does not include raw materials and energy inputs and therefore does not address all the criteria of a life-cycle analysis. It provides guidance for interim steps on the route to clean production. Ultimately, we should ask why we are using these materials and whether they are really necessary.

The pyramid of plastics is a ranking of plastics according to their hazardous characteristics. PVC, the most problematic plastic, is at the top of the pyramid, and biobased plastics, the least polluting of the plastics, are at the pyramid's base. It represents an ongoing process to qualify the main plastics in the economy. More plastics can be added as necessary and qualifications may change depending on new information on the material, such as on production processes or the use of toxic additives.

The addition of toxic additives can significantly change the environmental impacts of a plastic. For example, chloroparaffins or brominated flame retardants in polyolefins or biobased plastic products with heavy metal stablisers would significantly increase the hazard level of the plastic and therefore change its position on the pyramid of plastics. Furthermore, many additives are persistent organic pollutants (POPs) and can cause serious environmental damage.

It is essential that the production of biobased plastics does not involve the use of genetically modified organisms (GMOs) or allow the patenting of life forms.

Storage and collection of recyclables

Design can facilitate the reduction of waste generated by building occupants that is hauled to, and disposed of in, landfills and provide an easily accessible area that serves the entire building and is dedicated to the separation, collection and storage of materials for recycling including (at a minimum) paper, corrugated cardboard, glass, plastics and metals.

Building reuse: maintain existing walls, floors and roof

Extend the life cycle of existing building stock, conserve resources, retain cultural resources, reduce waste and reduce environmental impacts of new buildings as they relate to materials manufacturing and transport.

Maintain as much as possible of the existing building structure and shell (exterior skin and framing, excluding window assemblies and non-structural roofing material).

Consider reuse of existing buildings, including structure, shell and non-shell elements. Remove elements that pose a contamination risk to building occupants and upgrade outdated components such as windows, mechanical systems and plumbing fixtures. Quantify the extent of building reuse.

• We can also divert construction, demolition and land-clearing debris from landfill disposal. This requires the designer to redirect recyclable recovered resources back to the manufacturing process. Redirect reusable materials to appropriate sites.

• The designer must also develop and implement a waste-management plan, quantifying material diversion goals. Recycle and/or salvage a significant percentage (eg at least 50 per cent) of construction, demolition and land-clearing waste.

Local production (low transportation energy costs)

One of the major energy costs of built forms is the transportation of materials to the project site. For instance, timber has a very low embodied energy, but if it is shipped 200 kilometres to the site, this saving becomes negligible. The ecological designer must seek to increase demand for building materials and products that are extracted, harvested or recovered and manufactured within the region (eg within a radius of 800 kilometres), thereby supporting the regional economy and reducing the environmental impacts resulting from transportation.

Design efforts should include establishing a project goal for locally sourced materials and identifying materials and material suppliers that can achieve this goal. During construction, the designer needs to ensure that the specified local materials are indeed installed and quantify their total percentage.

Materials selected should encourage environmentally responsible forest management and use of wood-based materials and products certified for wood building components including, but not limited to, structural framing and general dimensional framing, flooring, finishes, furnishings and non-rented temporary construction applications such as bracing, concrete form work and pedestrian barriers.

The lack of green certifications and standards and difficulty in obtaining green-building-product information through mainstream building industry information resources may place an extra burden on the specifier.

Industry is beginning to use ecolabelling as a communications tool for manufacturers to convey the favourable environmental impact of their products and services as the basis for their selection for use in the built environment.

B29

Chapter C • Chapter B • Chapter A

Design using environmentally benign materials, furniture, fittings, equipment (FF&E) and products that can be continuously reused, recycled and reintegrated

Design using environmentally benign materials, furniture, fittings, equipment (FF&E) and products that can be continuously reused, recycled and reintegrated

Alerce	(Fitzroya cupressoides)
(Chilean) false larch, lahuan	(Pilgerodendron uviferum)
Brazilian rosewood	(Dalbergia nigra)
Chilean pine	(Araucaria araucania)
Guatemalan fir	(Abies guatemalensis)
Parlatore's podocarp	(Podocarpus parlatorei)
Afrormosia	(Pericopsis elata)
Ajillo	(Caryocar costaricense)
Central American/Honduran mahogany	(Swietenia humilis)
Cuban mahogany	(Swietenia mahogoni)
Gavilan blanco	(Oreomunnea pterocarpa)
Quira macawood	(Platymiscium pleiost achyum)

Endangered timber species

There are a number of differing approaches to materials selection and there are no absolute rules. One set of criteria used to select products may be by nature subjective, and a particular product may perform environmentally well under one criterion, but poorly under another. Trade-offs in the design and selection process between different criteria are inevitable. An eco-rating system could, of course, be developed as a guide. However, this would be based on partial analyses and weighted factors for the evaluation and comparison of one material to another and in totality could never be comprehensive. Such systems can provide only a general basis for materials, assembly of materials and equipment selection.

An example is the energy intensity index for materials. Energy intensity is the energy used in the production of a building material or component. It is either expressed as energy/mass or volume such as MJ/kg or MJ/cm^3 or energy/standard unit such as MJ/m, or MJ/m^2.

Summary

In ecodesign, the designer must select and use environmentally benign materials for the fabrication, construction and production of products, built structures and infrastructures. It is acknowledged that in practical terms it is not possible to design with zero consequences for the ecosystems as the use of any material and the production of any item in the built environment will have an impact (whether to a greater or less extent) on the external environment. Nevertheless, the design strategy is to use materials that have the least negative consequences for the natural environment and the maximum potential for continuous reuse, reycling and eventual benign reintegration into the natural environment (for recycling within natural processes and not statically as landfill). There are also a number of differing approaches to materials selection; there are no absolute determinate rules. One set of criteria used to select products may be regarded as subjective, and a particular product may perform well under one criterion, but poorly under another. Trade-offs between different criteria are inevitable. An eco-rating system becomes a comparative guide. However many of these guides are based on partial analyses and selective weighted factors for evaluation and comparison of one material to another and in totality may not be comprehensive. Nevertheless, these can provide a comparative basis for selection of materials and their assembly, or for equipment, on the simple basis that the selection is based on the item that has the least impact compared to others of the same type.

B30 Design to reduce the use of ecosystem and biospheric services and impacts on the shared global environment (systemic integration)

Ecodesign should consider and reduce the consequences of our built environment on the ecosystem services that affect the biosphere globally.

Indirectly humans and our built environment utilise the ecosystem services provided by nature, such as the provision of oxygen and the natural cleansing properties of the environment. Emissions from industrial processes are discharged into the air or to the waterways or simply to the land. Global impacts by the built environment include CO_2 emissions resulting from energy use, acid rain, ozone depletion due to CFCs (chlorofluorocarbons), HCFCs (hydro-chlorofluorocarbons), air and water pollution. It has been estimated that a kilowatt hour (kWh) of electricity causes the release of about 1 kilogram of CO_2 into the atmosphere.

What is discharged by our built environment at one location is transferred to other locations because of the interconnectivity in the biosphere. All the oceans are connected and constitute a single ecosystem. What is discarded at one place may poison waters almost anywhere else on the globe. Already numerous fisheries have been destroyed, or much reduced, and many beaches made unusable by humans.

The air is also a single ecosystem and may be even more fragile than the oceans. What humans do not throw into the sea is often burnt in the air. Burning does not destroy anything but converts it to something else, affecting human health as well as organisms, trees and plants. Acid rain created by the burning of fossil fuels in one part of the world descends a few days later on another part, killing its trees, poisoning its lakes and affecting ecosystem productivity. This air pollution includes the use of CFCs in air conditioners and refrigerators, which when released eat away at the ozone layer that protects the biosphere and humans from the sun's rays.

The result of our steady and increasing burning of fossil fuels is the continuous emission into the atmosphere of carbon dioxide, an odourless gas that is respired by green plants. There are not enough plants on the earth to convert all this carbon dioxide into the waste product of their transpiration, namely oxygen. Therefore the carbon dioxide in the atmosphere continually increases, leading to global warming. During the 20th century, global surface temperatures increased by nearly 0.6°C, mostly over the past 25 years. It is to counteract this that ecodesign must seek to revegetate our built environment as much as possible (see B7).

Global ecosystem services include ecosystem biodiversity. The reasons for concern over the loss of biodiversity pertains to the array of essential services provided by natural ecosystems. Such services include protecting watersheds, regulating local climates,

Climatic type	Example	Basic profile	Major design issues	Planning and urban design responses	Preferred built form
Hot-humid	Equatorial zone	• Hot diurnally and seasonally with minor temperature changes • Heavy rain • More comfort at high elevations	• Excessive heat • High humidity	• Ventilation: open ends and dispersed form • Widely open street to support wind movement • Extensive shadow • Dispersion of high-rise building to support ventilation • Combined variation of building heights • Wide, yet shadowed open spaces • Shadowing, planned tree zones	• Dispersed floor-plate configuration and loose built form with open ends to support cross-ventilation
Cold-humid (temperate)	Northern United States Canada	• Snowy • Windy, blizzard conditions • Very cold nights	• Low temperature • Winter and summer high precipitation • Windy	• Heating (passive and active) • Mixture of open and enclosed forms • Protected edges at winter windward side (with structure or trees) • Uniform building heights • Medium dispersed open space • Circumferential and interesting tree strips	• Mixture of dispersed floor-plate configurations and loose built forms (to suit summer conditions) and controlled enclosure to built form (to combat winter blizzard impact) • Variation of the two strategies during the mid-season
Hot-dry	Middle East North Africa Most of Australia Southwest United States	• Intense solar radiation • Large temperature amplitude between day and night • Dusty storms; torrential rain • Low cloudy days • Intense dehydration • High salinisation; evaporation exceeding precipitation	• Excessive dryness combined with high day temperatures • Dusty and stormy	• Compact forms • Shadowing • Evaporative cooling • Protective cooling • Protect urban edges from hot winds • Windward location near a body of water • Narrow winding neighbouring roads and alleys • Uniform city height • Small, dispersed and protected public open spaces • Circumferential and interesting tree zones • Use of geospace city concept	• Compact floor plate and 'tight' built form
Cold-dry	Inland plateau Central Asia Central Siberia	• Stressful and uncomfortable • Strong, dry cold wind	• Excessive low temperatures associated with dryness • Stressful wind	• Compact and aggregate forms, clustered forms • Protected urban edges • Narrow winding neighbourhood roads and alleys • Uniform city height • Small, dispersed and protected public open spaces • Circumferential and interesting tree zones • Use of geospace city concept	• Compact and combined floor plate and built form • Clustered built form
Seashore strips	Especially along the desert coasts of Peru, Northern Chile Kalahari – Southwest Africa Atlantic Coast – Moroccan Sahara Northwest coast of Mexico Somalia in East Africa	• Windy and stormy • Breeze system • High humidity • Erosion	• Humid regions • High humidity • Windy	• Moderately dispersed form, open urban edges • Wide streets perpendicular to the shore to receive ventilation • Variety of building heights • Wide public open spaces • Shadowing, planned tree zones	• Moderately dispersed floor plate and 'loose' built form, especially near stormy seashore
			• Dry regions • High humidity • Windy	• Open towards the sea, compact and protected towards the land • High-rise building mixed with low height • Small protected dispersed public open spaces • Shadowing, planned tree zones	• Compact floor-plate configuration and built form and protective considerations toward the land, yet open towards the seaside
Mountain slopes	Lower slopes Middle slopes High slopes	• Windy and increasing air circulation • Higher relative humidity than the lowland as elevation increases • Provides healthy and moderate climate • Enhance attractive views	• Windy	• Semi-compact form: mix of compact and dispersed • Horizontal streets and alleys to enhance the view • Low-height building • Small protected dispersed public open spaces • Use of geospace city concept	• Semi-compact floor plate and built form: mixture of compact and clustered configurations

Climatic types and bioclimatic urban design responses

maintaining atmospheric quality, absorbing pollutants, and generating and maintaining soils. Ecosystems, functioning properly, are responsible for the earth's ability to capture energy from the sun and transform it into chemical bonds, a form in which it is used to provide the energy necessary for the life processes of the fewer than 300,000 species of photosynthetic organisms and all the other 10 million or so species, including humans, that depend on them.

It could be argued that the existence or health of a forest or a population of fish depends on a system of ecological processes, relationships and species; and that many, if not most of these have no instrumental, aesthetic or inherent value, at least as perceived by society at large. Perhaps one of the most important things that ecological economists can do is to identify how these ecosystem functions are, in fact, valuable to people. The term 'contributory value' expresses the indirect benefits that species involved in predator–prey relationships, which are essential to the population stability of harvested species and species diversity in general, confer on ecosystems. All species have a contributory value, and the loss of any species represents an incremental decrease in the overall utility value of ecosystems.

Ecosystems are also responsible for regulating the recycling of nutrients, derived from the weathering of minerals in the soil and from the atmosphere, and making them constantly available for the maintenance of life. The populations of organisms that control pests on adjacent crops are often maintained in natural or semi-natural ecosystems nearby, as are many of the insects and other animals that pollinate these crops, ensuring the production of fruits and seeds. People are not very aware of these ecosystem services, nor of the role of biodiversity in their lives.

In designing for systemic integration, the approaches are as follows:

Assimilation
The emissions must be of the appropriate form and size for disposal into the biospheric media (air, water and land), within the capacity of that media to assimilate the emissions without contamination and within the media's ability to self-cleanse and self-renew.

Biodegradation
The emissions, by being exposed to the atmosphere, are decomposed over short periods of time by bacterial action and weathering. What is crucial is the degradation time and the ability of the locality to absorb the degradation material, eg as inorganic material or organic material. The latter can become nutrients (food) for the ecosystems.

Design to reduce the use of ecosystem and biosphere services and impacts on the shared global environment (system integration)

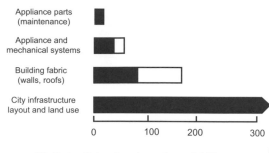

Appliance parts
(maintenance)

Appliance and
mechanical systems

Building fabric
(walls, roofs)

City infrastructure
layout and land use

0   100   200   300

☐ Potential extension of useful life

Replacement rate of different
elements of the built environment

Summary

Designing for systemic integration must start at the source, which means reducing the inputs and outputs of the designed system to reduce and eliminate at the outset its dependence on ecosystem and biospheric processes and natural environmental media to absorb and assimilate its emissions and outputs at the end of the built environments' useful life. This will reduce the negative consequences and load on the biospheric processes since all the environment's natural systems are interconnected, and impacts on one part of the biosphere may have consequences on another. The designer must be vigilant in monitoring the consequences of the outputs of the designed system on the ecosystems and biosphere through air, water and land. Our built environment should be in the service of the planet and not the other way round.

Design to reduce the use of ecosystem and biosphere services and impacts on the shared global environment (system integration)

410

B31 Reassess the overall design (ie product, structure or infrastructure) in its totality for the level of environmental integration over its life cycle

This is to remind the designer to avoid piecemeal compliance to all the key factors in ecological design and to refer them to the theoretical Interactions Matrix for comprehensive coverage (in A5 and B3).

Reassess the overall design (ie product, structure or infrastructure) in its totality for the level of environmental integration over its life cycle

Chapter C ● Chapter B ● Chapter A ●

411

Other
Considerations

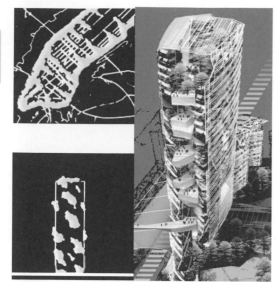

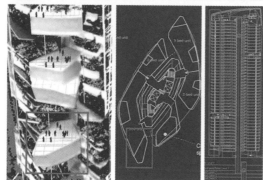

Sky courts detail (in Elephant and Castle Eco Tower, London)

C1 What is the green aesthetic?

One of the key concerns of the designer must be to establish precisely what the green aesthetic is. What should the green building or the green product look like?

This is a perplexing question as there is no ready answer. One contention is that ecological design or green design is more a philosophy or ethical choice than a building style or an aesthetic approach. While this is the case, the question of an appropriate aesthetic remains. The question of what is the green aesthetic or an appropriate green aesthetic still needs to be addressed by every ecological designer. This manual has to extend beyond a checklist of eco-ethical responsibilities and technical or remedial items for action. The formal and the environmental in design have to be juggled together to develop a new ecology-based aesthetic for architecture and the built environment. The work of ecodesigners might be valued as much for its aesthetics as for its environmental performance.

In addition to meeting the systemic aspects of ecological design, the ecologically responsive structure facility, infrastructure or product must therefore also be aesthetically pleasing, economically competitive and excel in user performance. If it does not meet these criteria, it is likely that it will not be accepted by the public. The economics of ecological design (or ecological economics) need to be rationalised if industry and the business world are to accept the benefits of green design beyond the ethical justification. The aesthetics of ecodesign must also permit a multiplicity of interpretations and visions by individual designers. This, then, is a further challenge confronting ecological designers today: what is the green aesthetic?

What is clear is that a designed system, whether a building or an enclosure, should have a balance of both the biotic and abiotic components in its content and that this will significantly affect its appearance and aesthetics. At present, there is a tendency to over-emphasise technological components, and current resultant purported green design appears remote from the image of nature. The presence of organic matter (in B7) on its external areas, most likely on those aspects of the built form that will receive the most sun, will give the design a fuzzy or 'hairy' or densely vegetated organic aesthetic. Some ecologists contend that ecological quality tends to look aesthetically 'messy'. What is good for the landscape may not look good and what looks good may not be good. The distinction between function and appearance may distress idealists who regard presentation as dissembling, but it is intrinsic to the concept of design, in which each design is recognised as one of any number of possible designs for a particular place.

Passive mode design options (in B13) also significantly affect the shaping and orientation of the built form to relate to the climatic conditions of the locality and may be complex in locations where there are great seasonal fluctuations.

Buildings that are ecotechnology driven or those stuffed with ecological gadgetry systems (such as solar collectors, double-skin walls and flue systems, etc) may tend to be mechanical in appearance. Others may seem much more organic in appearance. Ultimately, in terms of effective biointegration, it is the benign environmental systemic integration between our built systems and the natural systems in nature that is ecologically the more important aspect of the design, over its aesthetic aspirations.

It is the large and intensive building types that particularly need the attention of the world's ecological designers to make them as ecologically responsive and as aesthetically fulfilling as possible, for the sake of our sustainable future.

One aspect of ecodesign that influences built form is the way the designer relates that form to the landscape by regarding the landscape as an intrinsic part of the built form or infrastructure. For instance, the provision of continuity between landscape and the built form tends to favour earth-berms, mounded edges and mounded connections to the latter. We might contend that for the built form to function integrally it should appear fused within its environmental context using the elements of earth and vegetation (see B7) in such a way that they seem part of the natural environment – integration of the built form and infrastructure with its context (ie building as landscape, and landscape as building). The design's aesthetics should capture a true sense of connectedness and biointegration in nature.

The location of the ecocells (in B7) within the landscape also influences orientation and built form. These are vertical integrating devices. Finally, there are the systems that return water to the ground and the biosystems for treating human sewage, which may occupy part of the land. Where these produce emissions into the ecological systems, the precise location of the biosensors monitoring pollution and the carrying capacities of the ecosystems needs to be considered.

● Edge-planting (in Boustead Tower, 1985)

Summary

The efforts to harness solar energy during the 1970s failed because the built forms then were not beautiful; and ultimately such endeavours did not function well and often many were not even cost-effective. If ever we needed great designers, it is now as an environmentally based architecture needs to be widely aesthetically acceptable. While it appears that low-energy and ecological design strategies and solutions are applicable regardless of an individual designer's architectural style, as ecodesign advances there may be strong ecological determinants that influence building configuration, the range of materials used and the inevitable curbing of decorative excess. Since the best opportunity for improving a building's environmental performance occurs early in the design process, it is clear that at the outset we must make our built environment not only ecologically responsive but also seek to develop an ecological aesthetic if green design is to be a durable proposition. The complete change in the value-systems inherent in an ecologically responsive and sustainable approach to design imposed by implementing ecodesign and planning principles will probably eventually generate a new ecological aesthetic by virtue of its own merits.

This mock-up stylises a rainforest – closely spaced trees with flat, spreading crowns that fit together with those of neighbouring trees like the pieces of a jigsaw puzzle. You can see mosaics within mosaics. Leaves on stems, and stems on trees, are all organised so that there is minimum overlap. Each leaf is positioned so that it can absorb all the light that it needs to photosynthesise efficiently.

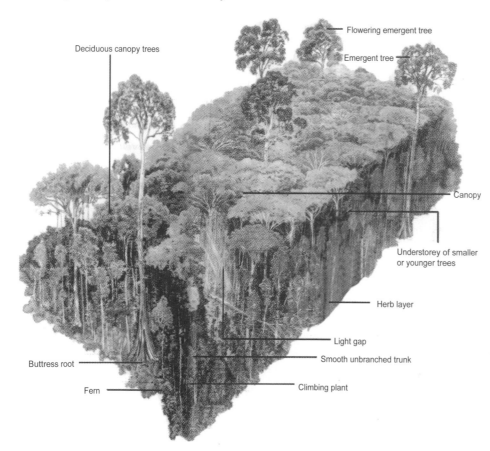

Deciduous canopy trees

Flowering emergent tree

Emergent tree

Canopy

Understorey of smaller or younger trees

Herb layer

Buttress root

Light gap

Smooth unbranched trunk

Fern

Climbing plant

C2 Issues of practice

If the best that ecodesign can achieve is a few ecostructures, conserved naturally vegetated zones, bike paths, recycling industries, wildlife habitat corridors or organic agricultural plots, then it will not lead to saving the world and ensuring our sustainable future. A much greater transformation is needed in global economic, political and social institutions. All of which require radical revisioning along ecological principles. Historically, every step in civilisation has been another notch in controlling and retarding nature. Buildings were enclosural and designed to keep nature's extreme temperatures out. Human-made parks and gardens were contrived to divert the power of botanical growth into the tame artefacts of domesticated crops, iron is mined to topple trees for timber, etc.

Other aspects that inhibit practical implementation of ecological design include:

- The working methods of environmental design professions inhibit change. Ecodesign must be a process of work that looks for the best solution at all stages of the designed system's planning and extended life, for human society and for all other species affected.

- The perception of higher costs as a consequence of green design. On the contrary, because of the elimination or reduction of mechanical components, green buildings generally should cost no more than conventional ones.

- The time taken for internal contradictions within existent practice to become ecologically intolerable. For example, trade-offs will probably always be made between fossil-fuel consumption, architectural effect and structural performance.

- Many of today's professionals do not have the necessary background in ecology and ecological design to comprehend fully the ecological approach. Students (postgraduates who spend an intensive year being trained in the principles of environmental design) often do not have time to integrate the new practice into their established ways of designing. One of the reasons why earlier 'ecological design' has been so haphazard and incomplete is that it is interdisciplinary. Most designers lack the knowledge of ecology, biology and the other fields that impinge on environmental issues. The theory presented in this book provides a basis for an integrated design framework so that the complex set of interdependencies can be factored into the design; otherwise, 'ecological design' will continue to be piecemeal or linear. Therefore, the interactions framework is the centrepiece of a holistic design theory.

With so many emerging fields of knowledge and study (eg resource conservation, pollution control and low-energy engineering), the criteria for more ecologically informed design will become increasingly complex. This will put further pressure on the practising designer who is already faced with more information available to solve a problem than he or she can possibly assimilate. In order to proceed, design must be selective and respond to the most significant issues within the context of the design problem.

- In practical terms, until it becomes a question of economic viability, ecological design will only appeal to the righteous, the frightened, or the enlightened.

- The need for ecodesign is in one discipline, but the necessary knowledge belongs to many others. The more complex the knowledge, the further removed it is from the architect. Design advisory tools (guidelines, precedents, standards) keep designers continually trapped within what is typically done.

- The environmental consequence of using a given resource goes back to the process by which it was made available for use; the early stage of the life of a material is not usually considered by the designer, who is trained to think only about the assembly of components into a structure located at a particular project site. Which designer, for example, is encouraged to think about the fact that mining and other extraction techniques associated with the metals used in architectural projects can lead to the destruction of natural habitats? Yet designers should know that when rocks containing minerals are removed from a mine, the waste rocks are customarily left somewhere nearby in the form of tailings or open dumps. Rising demand draws down stocks of the mineral and pushes production towards lower-grade ores, the land area on which the extraction process has an impact increases, while the quantity of waste rock rises. Not only are large amounts of energy and materials used to mine, transport and process materials for building, but equally large quantities of waste materials and energy are generated in the process.

- The solid-waste products and waste gases derived from the refining process have to be ejected into the environment. And when the mineral resources within the mine have been exhausted we are left with a degraded landscape which is full of holes, mountains of rock and scattered buildings and machinery now made obsolete. The open gouges in the earth's surface may make toxic or harmful substances available to ground water, producing dangerous runoff for decades after the mine has been abandoned. The cycle of waste, damage and energy-consuming processes continues to expand almost limitlessly. To reclaim a seriously damaged landscape requires yet more energy and material resources. Beyond the mine site, the transportation of its products, their use in the built environment and their eventual disposal eat up even more energy and materials, and produce yet further waste products. Let us not forget that no process takes place in a vacuum: each requires plants and machinery, building enclosures and a supply of energy and materials to operate.

- One reason why buildings are inefficient is because the compensation paid to architects and engineers is frequently based directly or indirectly on a percentage of the cost of the building itself or of the equipment that they specify for it. Designers who attempt to eliminate costly equipment therefore end up with lower fees, or at best with the same fees for a greater amount of work.

- The current perception of human beings' progress may need to be revised. We need to rethink the boundaries of 'civilisation'. We need to look at human civilisation, not as humans' progress in art and culture, nor science and technology, but 'as a relationship between humankind and nature'. This allows us to view civilisation as the degree to which societies modify their natural environments.

- We need to reassess human needs and set appropriate goals. Designing for sustainability is not complete (nor will it make much sense) without factoring in the habits and standard of living of the end-users of products: our human society itself. The root causes of society's excessive consumption and its effect on the environment have to be addressed. In an era of increasing globalisation, trade has enabled us to discount the value of local natural capital and has blinded us to the negative consequences of our over-consumption, which often accrues in distant export regions. Currently, society suffers from an addiction to quantity over quality – bigger rather than better for the natural system. That's the conventional Western attitude, anyway. The message that needs to be got across, especially to highly consumerised societies, such as North America, is that less does not necessarily mean worse, it just means different. Other cultures have much less at their disposal. Global-scale environmental problems are most often ascribed to increasing numbers of people demanding ever higher standards of living, coupled with the spread of technology and practices that pollute or fragment the landscape. If every person in the world were to strive for and achieve present US consumption rates with existing technology, four more planet earths would be needed to sustain them.

In an ecological world view, the conventional gross national product (GNP) should be replaced by the more comprehensive environmentally genuine progress indicator (EPI), which includes estimates of the environmental costs of economic activity.

Discussion on ecodesign

Does one species, bent on increasing its numbers and economic standards, have the right to proceed, at best unwittingly, at worst through ignorance and indifference, with this planetary-scale slaughter and devastation. Should not *Homo sapiens* rather use the species' evolved capacity to feel and reason to pause and take stock of the potential consequences of their behaviour, to make themselves collectively less destructive and, despite its lack of popular political support, rethink the global-scale value system that prioritises human numerical and economic growth above nearly all other competing values?

By far the most serious environmental problems of the 21st century will not simply be habitat loss or ozone depletion or chemical pollution or exotic species invasions or climate change alone, but rather the synergism of all these factors.

When an ecologist worries about the limited capacity of ecosystems or species to withstand all human disturbances and thus counsels humanity to lighten the load – even by economically costly adjustments – economists rightly remind us that there are limited human, technological and economic resources available for all laudable purposes, and we simply cannot afford to hedge against every potential ecological impact. We cannot afford (or even know how) to replace all natural ecosystem functions such as pest control, let alone replace species that we've driven to extinction. Once they're gone, they're gone, as ecologists remind us. It is not good stewardship or economics to mortgage our environmental future and leave the burden of finding solutions to posterity. But we are leaving them more wealth to cope with these burdens, the economists retort. Finding the balance of values across this cultural dichotomy is what the political process is supposed to do. And that process works only to the extent that we can get our values aired in the decision-making arena. That is especially hard to do when it is so easy to become confused by an exaggerated and baffling debate.

The basic nature, methods and goals of design should be rethought

- Architecture is a social art to which a large number of disciplines already contribute. In contrast, ecology is a natural science, and includes the question of human survival within the natural environment – an environment that humans are constantly using and changing, often in ways that undermine the sustainability of the species. The designer has to find ways to merge these two into one through ecodesign.

- Building is one of the primary ways in which people change the natural environment, not only by displacing it at the site, but also by using resources from far and near in constructing the building. It logically follows that designers and architects, who are responsible for the creation of built structures, should increase their knowledge of the interactions between architecture and the environment if they are to reduce the negative impacts of human constructions on the natural systems with which they share the biosphere. The teaching and practice of architecture and industrial design of products will therefore have to be modified to include an ecological analysis of the designed system, its use and eventual disposal.

• The need for ecological design is no longer seriously in dispute, but a comprehensive 'green' approach has yet to be embodied in the practice of design that includes architecture, planning, engineering and product design. For instance, in architecture theory tends to focus on two camps, which promote the spatial and climatic models respectively. A truly ecological approach would include both. Any built structure obviously causes a spatial displacement in its environment simply by existing, but it also alters the climate and natural environment through its operation.

Ecological design goes further, to include the interactions of architectural products and the built environment, which go beyond spatial displacement and effects at the project site. Thus, the types and quantities of energy and resources that go into the building's structure, their source and the environmental effects at the point of extraction all need to be considered. In terms of functioning, the internal processes of the built environment and its outputs also have to be examined and, in turn, so do the responses or 'feedback' of the ecosystem as a result of its efforts to absorb the outputs. The four components in the Interactions Matrix correspond to the sets of demands that any built environment makes on the earth's ecosystems. Each is related to other disciplines, such as those concerned with pollution, environmental protection and conservation. Therefore, further development of the framework would be by advancing the fundamental basis from which research on ecological design and all the problems of environmental impairment could be approached.

• The ecologist is obviously more concerned with the systemic aspects of architecture and the built environment than with its aesthetic or social dimensions (even though these aspects may indirectly have ecological implications, in the sense that they affect the behaviour of people in the ecosystem). The consumption of energy and materials and the flow from sources to environmental sinks is of more interest to the ecologist. For the ecologist, a building or a built structure or facility is a machine that consumes resources in the transient form of a human-made built form located at a particular project site, but which has a connection to large-scale effects in the biosphere. Ecologically speaking, the building is also a potential waste product, which has to be recycled just like a soft-drink can or a plastic bottle. Designers may resist viewing their artworks in this manner, and cling to the traditional view of the building as an outgrowth of the architect's aesthetic and its functional use. However, a building is both of these things. It is a structure with a particular social and economic function, which embodies the aesthetic theories of an individual or group of individuals, that also requires certain resources to be realised and creates certain environmental effects as a result of its creation and operation.

- The traditional conception of the architect's professional responsibilities will also be expanded. For instance, if the designer is aware of the implications of using certain forms of energy and materials that may be toxic, he or she is responsible for the resulting ecological effects. The designer is, from a green perspective, responsible for the choice of materials and systems and for the way that the structure and its components are used, recycled or discarded at the end of the building's life. Again, architects may resist the idea that their buildings will one day be torn down and replaced, preferring to think of them in a timeless aesthetic way; but such a view is not in keeping with an awareness of the need for sustainable building practices and the conservation of the environment and natural resources. Obviously, the amount of resource consumed in the creation of an urban building can be huge; whether this material eventually becomes waste will largely be determined by design choices before the building is even raised, and is therefore the designer's responsibility. More research needs to be done on the ecological impact of energy and materials use. But if the responsibility that is here being loaded on the architect's shoulders seems enormous, it has to be remembered that it is also an enormous opportunity to direct and determine how human beings interact with the natural environment and whether they behave in a way that makes their mode of existence sustainable.

- The built form will also need to be monitored throughout its life cycle for ecological effects, and a system will have to be put in place for doing so. Thus, the architect's and designer's job is not over once the building has risen over the project site, but continues from 'source to sink'. Much literature has accumulated on design methods, and a variety of approaches has been suggested. In approaching a design problem, the designer has to strike a balance that assigns a relative importance to the various elements, and may use this approach in one case, that approach in another. This case-by-case method, using various approaches as the environmental demands dictate, is an effective method of designing responsibly and ecologically. Different approaches have different strengths and weaknesses; as technology and systems advance and are further developed, the costs and benefits will change over time. Therefore, it is impossible to pre-select a set of standard solutions for design problems; all we can do is give the designer a philosophy and a method of working that are in themselves renewable and sustainable, and respond to each situation with the best knowledge currently available in order to create an effective design synthesis.

- As we are still in the early days of ecological design and its technology, we can only make predictions about the design options that a designer will have to consider. The interactions specified in the Partitioned Matrix will always be relevant, but the technical solutions to the ecological problems will evolve and need to be developed. Initial design decisions are vitally important and require further research. As has been mentioned, these will determine the degree of environmental dislocation and destruction, and the extent and feasibility of preventive or ameliorative actions.

- The fact that human beings change the environment by their behaviour does not have to be inherently destructive. The quantification of the impacts defined by the Partitioned Matrix gives no more than a statement of the extent of impacts on ecosystems and the corresponding resources needed to mitigate them. The designer's task is to integrate the designed system with its ambient ecosystem to minimise negative effects and, by means of design interventions, to achieve a 'steady-state' relationship with the environment. Further research needs to be done to develop quantitative data to support ecological design, covering the areas of interaction specified in the Partitioned Matrix and extending over the building's entire useful life. Some of the elements that need quantitative development are the quantities of energy and materials used in the building; global availability of these resources and their rates of depletion; ecological consequences of each input; permissible levels of outputs by the building and the routes taken by these discharges through the ecosystem; the energy and materials cost of outputs management; the appropriateness and efficiency of the building's operational systems; the extent of internalisation of system processes; the ecological consequences of the operational system processes; biodiversity and resilience of the building's ambient ecosystem; the global impacts on natural systems of the building; impacts on other human-made systems; and the global impact on renewable and non-renewable resources.

- Ecological design does not mean that the entire biosphere should be isolated from human intervention and turned into a nature reserve. Ecosystems change whether humans intervene in them or not; the goal of ecodesign is to manage the interaction of people and environments in the least harmful way possible, taking into account the limitations of ecosystems and biosphere resources and managing their use in a sustainable manner. In principle, buildings could actually have beneficial ecological impacts. Critical design choices will determine whether positive effects are achieved, and how. An organised and coherent use of ecological principles in design is still being developed; unfortunately, in many cases the information, theory and practical applications to achieve the desired effects are not yet available. Ecosystem modification by built systems has so far been largely ignored or misunderstood, and unforeseen effects are not uncommon. Ecological design will require us to transform our existing built environment and products and to create new ones to function, both individually and collectively, in tune with natural systems. The question, then, is whether we can understand the complexity of the natural world well enough (in B5) to integrate with it at all successfully (in A1 and B3) and to emulate it (in A4). For example, our current methods of understanding nature still rely on classical, reductive science. Ecological analyses are still unable to fully capture the synergies and intricate interrelations that distinguish the systems in the natural world. It is essential that more endeavours be made by researchers to achieve a deeper understanding of the environmental repercussions of our built environment, to anticipate them as a regular part of design and planning and to collect the data in a form appropriate to design analysis for the designer prior to design.

- Such gaps in our knowledge and practice should not dissuade the designer from incorporating ecological considerations into design. When data cannot be exactly quantified, indices can be used (such as the water-quality index). Better empirical data should follow. The provision of monitoring systems to facilitate environmental protection systems is essential. Here, again, more data are needed, since many potentially dangerous pollutants have not even been recognised or evaluated yet. The four components of the interactions framework also need to be further studied and reliable data developed on inputs and outputs of the built environment, the interactions of the systems of the ecosystem and the built environment and other factors.

- Of course, the larger social pattern of use and the pressure or desire for sustainable resource consumption and conservation are elements that go beyond the scope of the designer's power. But an ecologically minded designer can at least 'buy time' until society has developed more ecological consumption habits and more responsible value systems and styles of living – just as the designer has to wait for the development of new environmentally responsive technologies but can use the best that are available in the meantime (which can be made available through rapid prototyping) and make allowances for future developments. The pursuit of green design is itself an impetus for changing people's ideas about the relationship of their built environment to the natural world, and is also a spur towards the development of new, 'green' technologies. There is no reason why architects and designers cannot lead these developments rather than wait for them to happen, and every reason for them to start making our built environment as green as possible.

- What fundamental knowledge must designers possess? How can we work from principles when what we do is produce artefacts? How do we take knowledge from another discipline, but apply it within ours? In the past, our approach has been one of extension – designers have expanded the umbrella of their discipline to overlap with these other fields. For example, architectural education began to require more and more knowledge that was inherent to other disciplines, while many of these disciplines were also rapidly expanding their knowledge. The more that knowledge is extended, the more the designer has to be forced to trade knowledge for information. As a result, the designer often appropriates the knowledge from other disciplines as an ever growing database of strategies from which to pick something that seems appropriate for the design assignment or project at hand. The more complex the knowledge, the further removed it is from the designer. Design advisory tools are intended to guide the designer through a limited selection and optimisation process, whereas rating systems (eg LEED, BREEAM, etc) fully remove the designer from the decision-making process. Regardless of the name – advisories, guidelines, precedents or standards – this approach keeps us continually trapped within what is typically done. A pre-defined outcome subordinates that knowledge necessary to produce the desired solution: eg the sustainable product or built environment.

- Common subjects can bring diverse disciplines together. In ecodesign, whereas the designer wants to produce an artefact or a solution, others may want to understand a phenomenon.

- We need to establish our context as part of the larger problem of addressing environmental impacts. Having narrowed our context to the 'sustainable designed system', we have been doing precisely the opposite. We have presumed that built structures, facilities, infrastructures and products are autonomous entities and that by optimising each one with respect to its energy use we have done our part. This delimiting of the context ensures that the normative practice of architecture and design is unchanged, and it introduces new 'solutions' in the way we most easily understand them, through products and strategies or, in essence, artefacts that can be defined and specified.

- What if we expanded our context from the solution to the problem? Rather than designing, for instance, more efficient lighting systems for buildings, can we ask what humans need in order to see? Rather than focusing on the design of a sustainable building, could we not step back and ask ourselves how our disciplinary activities contribute to environmental degradation? Ultimately, we will come back to solutions for inherently, as designers, we make things. Let us, however, think in territories larger and broader than the things we make.

One way to ensure a more pervasive implementation of ecodesign might be legislatively through rewriting planning and building codes for ecodesign. For example, current codes ignore the environmental impacts of:

- the sourcing of resources;

- the acquisition or depletion of resoures;

- the transportation of resources;

- manufacturing processes;

- the efficiency of use of resources;

- whether resources can be reused or recycled at the end of the structure's useful life;

- disposal and reintegration of resources after use;

- the embodied energy of materials; and

- the contribution of each of the activities in the built environment to global warming.

Summary

In the 21st century, architecture and design, both of the built environment and products, are in an exciting experimental period, but they may be repeating the mistakes of our 20th-century predecessors by over-simplifying the difficult architecture–technology-environmental relationship.

To achieve an ecologically sustainable future, ecodesign has to be more than a number of designers and others in related design disciplines revising their approach to design. Ecodesign as an activity is not, and should not be, the exclusive domain of designers. In any case, design is used by other disciplines as a construct because it is interdisciplinary and integrative in a way that is tolerant of local differences and expertise.

Ecodesign and the instructions here should be adopted not just by designers but also by the key decision-makers from other disciplines, those in business and in government with the power to force through fundamental changes in industry and in society's socio-economic philosophical and aesthetic values. This reorientation should be accompanied by a merciless critique of our current built environment's technology, politics and economics to achieve globally the simple collective objective of the benign and seamless biointegration of everything that we humans do or build with the natural environment.

C3 The future of ecodesign: prosthetics design as the parallel basis for designing biointegration of artificial-to-natural systems

Ecodesign can learn from the problems of integration encountered in prosthetics design, which is the design by doctors and surgeons of artificial human body parts. Prosthetics seek effective biointegration of the artificial organ or part of the human body with its host human. The design of our built environment similarly seeks effective biointegration of our artificial human-made designed system with its host organism, ie the ecosystems in the biosphere.

We can compare ecodesign to prosthetics design as both endeavours share the common problems of the biointegration of the human-made artificial system with its host organic system. This analogy is relevant for designers seeking solutions to the problems of the integration of our built environment with the natural environment.

Prosthetics is the branch of surgery (including dentistry) dealing with artificial devices or prostheses. These are the mechanical, electrical or hybrid devices attached to or inserted into the human body to replace, supplement or improve the functions of the missing or defective or diseased human organs and parts. These are the artificial arms, limbs, breasts, knee caps, etc, that are human-made as against the natural parts of the human body. Designing these might be regarded as the ultimate challenge of artificial-organ manufacture as it represents the accurate biomimicry of human body tissues, organs and parts.

In ecodesign, our designed system is therefore analogous to the prosthetic system (or the artificial system), which must effectively integrate with its host organism. In the case of the prosthetic device, its host organism is the human body to which it is appended, and its success is dependent upon the effectiveness of this integration in the symbiotic relationship between the artificial prosthetic system and the natural host organism as well as the efficiency of the performance of the artificial system. In the case of our built environment, its equivalent host organisms are the ecosystems, and the success of its design is dependent upon the effectiveness of this integration as well as the performance of the designed systems themselves, and the symbiotic relationship between the artificial built environment and the ecosystems in the biosphere.

We might therefore regard ecodesign as a form of prosthesis design, being the design of the built environment analogous to designing the relationship between the prosthetic devices and the host human body. In applying this analogy, we must be aware that unlike machines and mechanical systems organisms have a holistic property where the whole is greater than the sum of its parts. By analogy, our built environment must be designed not just for mechanical integration but to be holistically integral with the ecological systems,

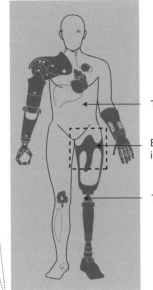

The host organism

Biomechanical integration

The prosthetic device

Ecological design as analogous to prosthetics design

The prosthetic leg •- - - - - - - - - -

their functions, processes and flows. Our built environment must not be designed as just mechanical additions to the biosphere.

The issue of effective system-to-host integration is therefore as crucial in ecodesign as in prosthetics. For instance, to be effective the prosthetic leg must be well integrated with its host organic system. We should note that the extent of integration for a simple prosthetic leg is at the biomechanical level. A more sophisticated level of integration would be its attachment to the host organism's nervous system, which in the case of prosthetics might involve internal open-wound insertions, which bring with them potential problems of septic infection.

However in prosthetics, system-to-host integration can also be effected externally without open-wound insertions. For instance, the host organism's instructions to the prosthetics can be transmitted externally by physical contact using phantom-limb responses and external receptive devices.

By analogy, a building (or our built environment) might be regarded as a combination of a life-support system and an enclosural system, both of which are physically embedded in the ecosystem of a particular place. Its physical presence (ie its built form's footprint, its entire mass and all of its related infrastructures) as well as its internal flows and processes are those aspects that must be integrated with the systems of the locality and its ecologic flows, processes of energy, materials and organic life (see B3, B7, B23).

How to achieve this integration effectively and in a seamless and benign way is therefore the key issue in ecological design. We might regard any design that does not integrate with the natural environment as an artefact that is divorced from the ecologic environment and thus cannot be regarded as ecological. The artefact becomes nothing more than an object in the ecosystem and, worse, should it continue to pile up or accumulate, it then becomes another human-generated waste product that has not become part of the natural cycles.

Generally, where this environmental integration is found to be missing or faulty, then it is at these locations or points that artefacts become the cause of environmental problems and impairment. All of our human-made systems and structures, indeed everything made by humans, that have become divorced from the ecologic processes of the natural environment are deemed wastes and unintegrated artefacts. From the ecological point of view they are artificial alien objects, and thus the antithesis of things natural. Artificiality and physical disparities then give rise to the problem of how to effect reintegration into the natural environment. By comparison, we find that in ecosystems this problem does not exist. There are no wastes as everything in an ecosystem that is produced by its organisms is recycled back into and often within the ecosystem.

The term artificial can be used here to refer to the artefacts, items, components and built forms that are human-made and not reintegratable. Mostly these are inorganic, non-biodegradable and not easily reintegrated into nature without the additional use of non-renewable sources of energy or combustion. It is this artificiality from our human-made built environment that must be eliminated.

Furthermore, integration and reintegration are not one-off actions. The process of integration must be carried out over the built form's entire life cycle, from its evolution and production, through its period of use and operation, to its demolition or removal from the ecosystems.

The relationship between today's technologically complex prosthetic devices and their host organisms (humans) is mirrored in our state of obligated dependence on the productivity and life-support services of the ecosphere (our host organism), this despite the increasing technological sophistication of our designs (the prostheses). This dependence simply reaffirms this manual's fundamental premise that ecological design is essentially about designing our built environment as artificial systems integral both mechanically and organically with the ecosystems in nature over their entire life cycles. Implicit in this is their eventual integration in a way that is benign to the natural environment and enables both the artificial prosthetic system and the natural host system to function successfully without collapse or failure.

Much can be learned by looking at the correlation in bionics, biotechnology and biomechanics. By analogy, if we look at an artificial limb such as a prosthetic arm or leg, the design issue of integration is essentially a physical or biomechanical one, as mentioned earlier. In the case of more complex prosthetic devices and systems such as artificial organs, however, the design issue can extend beyond mechanical integration into organic, systemic and temporal integration, as is the case with heart valves.

In the case of prosthetic device integration into the human body in human physiology, further distinctions might be made. There are several methods of such integration, which we can similarly apply to ecodesign: the *mechanical*, the *additive* and the *organic*. By analogy these are possible ways in which our built environment can integrate with its host organism, the natural environment.

For instance, in the case of the human ear, an example of an additive mechanical device is the normal hearing aid. A higher level of human-made machine or organism–prosthesis integration in the ear would be, for example, the use of cochlea implants that would enable the deaf to hear again through direct electronic-to-neural connections. The implants bypass the cochlear damage by receiving and converting sound into signals sent along electrodes to cells adjacent to the auditory nerve.

The improved prosthetic hand

This implant can be a simple electronic device that separates the multiple sound frequencies received by a microphone placed within the ear and outputs the strength of six or so frequencies through electrodes, which are implanted next to the nerve cells in the ear that would normally receive signals from sensor cells that transduce the motion of the small cochlear hairs. Depending on the implant, there may be anything from eight to 22 electrode points placed at different positions to maximise the range and frequency of stimuli sent to the brain. A microphone is worn behind the ear itself to pick up sound, which is sent to a processor where it is digitised into a coded signal sent to a transmitter coil. The coil then sends the signal via radio waves through the skin back to the implanted receiver. Although there is direct electronic-to-neural connection, this system is not entirely internal, as a microphone and transmitting coil are needed.

These implants enable people who would otherwise be deaf, to hear well enough to understand speech better than they would if using a regular hearing aid, which only amplifies sound. The electrodes of these artificial cochleae are permanently implanted, so there is a direct electrical connection between the electronics of the silicon device and the nervous system of the patient. For instance, analogously in ecodesign, we can install the equivalents to the implants in the form of a network of linked environmental biosensors and activators into our natural environment to monitor the systemic interactions between our built environment and the processes in the ecosystems.

Another example is prosthetic eyesight enhancement, which has recently undergone human trials. Here retina chips are inserted in a blind person's eye (in certain classes of blindness, eg muscular degeneration) to enable simple perceptions. The retinal implant is a silicon retina. The silicon microchip, just 2 millimetres wide, contains 5000 solar cells that convert light into electric impulses that travel through the optic nerve to the brain. In another system, a camera on the patient's glasses captures and transmits images to an implant. A battery pack is required to transmit power magnetically to a receptor worn behind the ear, which sends electricity to the implant to stimulate nerve cells. Current implants have 16 electrodes, but it is likely that the next generation implants could include up to 100 electrodes. Eye implants are much more complex than the artificial cochlea for the ear as they need to interface with the host organism's nervous system at tens of thousands of different nerves or neurons, due to the inherent complexity of the human eye. By analogy ecological design can be directed towards the insertion of implants in the ecosystems to enhance, for instance, ecosystem decomposer recycling processes to extend the ecosystem's carrying capacity or even to enhance photosynthetic processes.

These prosthetic examples are far more subtle than the more visually obvious examples of mechanical attachments for human amputees, for instance, which consist of metal shafts, joints full of magneto-restrictive fluids, single-board computers, batteries, connectors and loose wire harnesses without a hint of antiseptic packaging and everything visibly hanging out.

We need to note that in the design of prostheses, a high level of complexity of integration is not always needed. Following from the examples above, we might for instance suggest that we make similar neural connections between the nerves in the stump to a prosthetic arm or leg. However, this has not met with as much enthusiasm because in the case of leg prostheses, the possible payoff from having direct neural connection is not seen to be great enough to compensate for the other attendant problems it poses.

Another problem in organic integration is that of rejection of the artificial or alien matter inserted into the host organism (ie the human body), an area that needs a great deal more research and development. Again by analogy, there are a multitude of biological and microbial processes in the ecosystems that are difficult for ecological design to integrate or to imitate and which, like the problem of septic infections in prostheses with open wounds, are challenges that need to be resolved. In the case of our built environment nature does not find all human-made materials to be biodegradable, and many of our products have very long periods of degradation and reintegration. Devastated ecosystems are examples analogous to the rejection of, or negative reaction to, our artificial built environment by the natural ecosystems.

Beyond the prosthetic limb, the possible benefits from having a neural connection to the prosthetic device are greater. The latest research technique is to implant a silicon chip with holes through it right in the heart of a severed cluster of nerve cells. The human nerves are then permitted to regrow through the holes and circuits to measure electrical activities in the nerves and inject their own signals into the nerves. The chip communicates wirelessly to an external monitor strapped to the skin. In a similar way, the inorganic components of our built environment can be designed with holes, voids and perforations to enable key organic components of the ecosystem to grow and thread through them. A new development in prosthetic limb design is an artificial limb with built-in microprocessors that can be programmed to help the limb move more naturally, together with built-in sensors that measure movement and force.

Even in the case of the artificial heart, the level of integration is mainly mechanical but with an increasing level of organic integration. The first successful example of 'biocompatibility' is the artificial heart. In terms of development, this pioneering biomechanic integration was the first surgically supplied artificial internal body part. Unfortunately, the early patients

● The Prosthetic Heart
  (External Energy Source)

● Survival rate

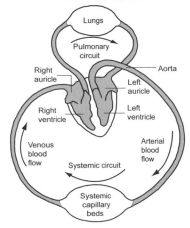

Human circulatory system
● The artificial heart (requiring) both
  mechanical and organic integration

431

were subject to infections and many ultimately suffered and died through complications. Since then, however, a smaller version of the artificial heart has been used successfully on hundreds of humans waiting to receive heart transplants. A recent development is the cardiac or heart-assist pump to aid a failing heart, again a mechanical component.

Even in the case of the most advanced artificial heart, the artificial organ has still to be powered by external sources of energy (eg batteries that are recharged externally). We are still unable to design an artificial heart that uses the energy of the human body to power itself. Similarly, our human-made built environment is still unable fully to exploit ambient sources of solar or other energy to fully power itself and is still greatly dependent on non-renewable energy, such as fossil fuels, to do so. To extend the analogy further, the successful achievement of biointegration (and in the case of the built environment, ecointegration) might result from the creation of hybrids; items which are neither human-made nor organic, but a successful composite of both.

In the case of prosthetic hybrids in the medical world, there are today thousands of human 'hybrids'. In terms of function, these people are part human, part machine; some may have electronic implants in their bodies that directly connect to their neural and nervous systems, which function much better as a result. By extension, the future of ecodesign may well lie in the design of hybrid built environments and artefacts as part ecosystem, part human-made.

Advances indicate that in the future, as in the case of artificial limbs and organs, it is likely the organic will truly integrate with the artificial as hybrids. This will occur, for instance, when artificial limbs are permanently attached to patients' bones and their skin merges with the covering of the prosthesis, and when it becomes technically possible to route the wires from human brains down into arms and even legs. In the future, too, it is likely that in ecodesign our built environment will also integrate with the natural environment at a similar level of complexity.

More recently, as against the use of totally artificial robotic prosthetic limbs in humans as described above, researchers have been working on using organic material such as organically cultured muscles (taken from other mammals) to eventually build the prosthetic limb with biological muscle in place of mechanical electric motors. The antithesis of mechanical addition and integration is organic or holistic prosthetic integration, which includes cellular-level manipulation of our bodies through genetic therapies. The analogy in ecological design is the use of biotechnology in ecosystem conservation. It may well be that the future of successful ecological design lies in an engineered biotechnological built environment (eg for bio recycling and regeneration of materials and production of energy). Here, as with prostheses, the designed solution becomes an effective prosthetic marriage of artificial materials (eg silicon and steel) with biological matter. The ideal is where the distinction between that which is organic and that which is prosthetic becomes seamless or disappears as in an authentic hybrid.

We need also to be aware that with current technology, simple organ transplantation requires a huge, highly skilled and specialised team approach and support. It requires people to remove the organs, people to tissue-type them, and people to preserve them. This may similarly apply to the early endeavours in the biointegration of our built environment.

In the case of genetic research, the inserting and deleting of genetic material is not essentially new. It is just capitalising on the ways in which the researchers have enabled all the components to communicate with each other. The real challenge would be to completely redesign by analogy with the case of the computer and its central processing unit. Applying this to the case of genetic engineering, some work has already started on the middle ground although complete redesign is still beyond current capabilities. It may be that, say, 30 years hence, it will be possible to programme cells within living organisms. Engineered biology and biotechnology will eclipse the importance of mechanical technology. Prosthetics technology will by then have merged with biotechnology and further into ecotechnology.

Currently many ecological designers are already designing buildings, structures and products that are analogous in part to artificial prosthetic devices. However, the next stage is to extend this into analysis of systems and networks as means of benignly integrating all of our built environment with its host organic system, the ecosystems in the biosphere, physically, systemically and temporally. Prosthetic systems might imitate organisms' responses to environmental change with the following types of plasticity:

- morphological plasticity (the organism having more than one body form);

- physiological adaptability (an organism's tissues can modify themselves to accommodate stress);

- behavioural flexibility (an organism can do something new or more than it could before);

- intelligent choice (an organism can choose, or not, based on past experience); and

- guidance from tradition (an organism can be influenced or taught by others' experience).

Ultimately, ecodesign is not just about designing our built environment and all its artefacts to biointegrate benignly with the natural environment. It is also about humans and their way of life and attitude towards the environment. It is pointless to have effective ecodesigned systems only for their benefits to be entirely negated by a profligately consumerist population.

Ten-degree servers would cover an area of approximately 1 million square kilometres

One-degree servers would cover an area of approximately 10,000 square kilometres, and would focus on regional information such as national park websites or cropland maps

One-minute servers would cover an area of approximately 1 square kilometre, and would allow users to locate websites for local restaurants, cinemas or train stations

A proposal for a global ecomonitoring system (GES) where the globe would be carved by latitude and longitude into ecological cellular zones of three different sizes. Dedicated servers assigned to each cell would hold the ecological data registered to local monitoring websites, maps and other information about that ecological area or ecosystem. Search engines could direct ecological status queries to one type of server, depending on the type of ecological data that is required.

Proposed Global Ecomonitoring System (GES)

Ecodesign needs to be matched with a radical change to an ecologically acceptable life style. For example, it is simply energy inefficient to design energy-efficient heating systems for a building to create high levels of comfort for its occupants when the same energy saving can be achieved by its occupants wearing warmer clothing in the cold season (or the reverse scenario, eg going without ties and jackets so mitigating the need for air conditioning in the hot season).

Ultimately a green and sustainable future demands an immediate revision of our way of life and global socio-economic industrial change. It should not need a global disaster to effect this change.

Crucially needed is a real-time [global early warning and monitoring system] for the biosphere, its processes and the ecosystems together with the human activities that have ecological consequences, so that immediate remedial action can be taken to prevent ecological disasters and events in any part of the globe. The satellite technology already exists for this. This system could be a combination of global information systems [GIS] and a global network of biosensors and physical sensors in the air, land and water that can detect and monitor biospheric and ecosystem changes and which respond in recognisable ways to environmental pollution and ecological indicators. The sensor technology and environmental sensing will also enable us to control and monitor the ecology of our human-built environments and any human activities that will have negative consequences on the built environment.

Summary

The future of ecodesign may lie in applying some of the principles of prosthesis design and identifying how effective biointegration can benefit the design of our built environment. The answer to future ecodesign may lie in the design of hybrid systems at three levels of integration with the host organism (the ecosystems in the biosphere): mechanical, additive and organic integration.

Appendix 1: timeline of key international developments relating to the global environment

1962   *Silent Spring* (Houghton Mifflin, Boston, MA) by the marine biologist Rachel
            Carson is published

1967–69   Environmental Defense Fund, Natural Resources Defense Council, and Friends of
            the Earth founded

1968   *Spaceship Earth* by Buckminister Fuller is published

1969   Oil spill in Santa Barbara, California
            National Environmental Policy Act passes Congress, US Environmental Protection
            Agency and Council on Environmental Quality established

1970   First Earth Day

1972   UN Conference on the Human Environment, 'Only One Earth', held in Stockholm
            UN Environment Programme launched
            RIBA Conference, 'Design for Survival'
            'Blueprint for Survival' in *The Ecologist* (UK) is published

1973   Dangered Species Act Oil Embargo
            The Club of Rome, *The Limits to Growth* (Meadows, D. et al.) (Universe, NY) is
            published

1974   F. Sherwood Rowland and Mario Molina release research that demonstrates that
            chlorofluorocarbons (CFCs) (introduced in the 1930s), the compounds contained
            in freon, tend to break down some components of the atmosphere, especially the
            ozone layer

1975   Worldwatch Institute established
            Convention on International Trade in Endangered Species of Flora and Fauna
            comes into force

1977   UN Conference on Desertification

1979   Convention on Long-Range Transboundary Air Pollution adopted
            National Academy of Sciences releases report on climate change ('Charney Report')

1980   World Conservation Union releases its World Conservation Strategy
            Global 2000 Report to (WCN) President released

1981   First meeting of the PLEA ('Passive and Low Energy Architecture') initiated by
            Professor Arthur Bohan of Miami University, USA

1982	World Resources Institute launched

1982   World Resources Institute launched
          UN Convention on the Law of the Sea adopted
          UN World Charter for Nature published

1985   Austrian meeting of World Meteorological Society, United Nations Environment
          Programme and International Council of Scientific Unions reports on the build-up
          of CO_2 and other greenhouse gases in the atmosphere
          Antarctic ozone hole discovered

1987   World Commission on Environment and Development (WCED), *Our Common
          Future*, (The Bruntland Report, Oxford University Press, Oxford)
          Montreal Protocol addresses the threat to the ozone layer by setting a time
          scale for the phase-out of CFCs and ACFCs

1989   Basel Convention on the Control of Transboundary Movement of Hazardous
          Wastes signed

1990   Building Research Establishment Environmental Assessment Method (BREEAM),
          UK, Building Research Establishment (BRE)

1992   Earth Summit, United Nations Conference on the Environment and Development
          held in Rio de Janeiro. The objective was the 'stabilisation of greenhouse gas
          concentration in the atmosphere at a level that would prevent anthropogenic
          interference with the global climate system'
          Agenda 21 (as the benchmark for international action to combat climatic change)
          adopted
          The United Nations Framework Convention on Climate Change (UNFCCC) was
          signed by world leaders (including US President)
          Convention on Biological Diversity signed
          Article (4), paragraph (2), subparagraph (b) of the convention instructs
          industrialised nations to aim to reduce their greenhouse gas emissions to 1990
          levels

1994   Global Environment Facility created
          UN Conference on Population and Development held in Cairo
          UN Convention to Combat Desertification signed

1995   World Trade Organisation established.
          The European Union bans the production of CFCs from the start of 1995 and will
          phase out use of ACFCs by 2015

1996	*Our Ecological Footprint: Reducing Human Impact on the Earth*, by Wackernagel, M. and Rees, W., New Society, Gabriola Island, is published
1997	Kyoto Protocol to the United Nations Framework Convention on Climate Change signed. The protocol requires industrialised countries to cut their emissions of greenhouse gases to reduce CO_2, Methane (CH4), Nitrous oxide (N_2O), Hydrofluorocarbons (HFCs), Perfluorocarbons (PFCs) and Sulphur hexafluoride (SF6) emissions by 5.2 per cent by 2010. Over 140 countries ratified the convention
1997	The USA Byrd-Hagel Resolution stating that the USA should subject any agreement that committed it to reducing emissions unless commitment obligations was imposed on developing countries as well
	ISO 14040 (the principle and framework of Life Cycle Assessment (LCA) becomes an international standard as part of ISO 14000 (Environmental Management) series of standards
1998	These commitments apply to industrialised or Annex 1 nations that include the USA, Canada, Japan, Europe, Australia, New Zealand and several countries in the Eastern bloc. Rotterdam Convention for the Application of Prior Informed Consent for Trade in Hazardous Chemicals and Pesticides signed
2000	Stockholm Convention on Persistent Organic Pollutants (POPs) signed
2001	USGBC (US Green Building Council, Washington, DC), Leadership in Energy and Environmental Design (LEED), Environmental Building Ratings System – Version 2.0
	LEED certification was created to give a definition to green building by establishing a common standard to promote whole-building practices, stimulate green competition, raise consumer awareness, transform the building market and products, and recognise the environmental consequences of the built environment
2002	World Summit on Sustainable Development held in Johannesburg
	UN Framework Convention on Climate Change Ministerial meeting (New Delhi)
2003	Kyoto Protocol comes into force (without US endorsement)
2004	Russia endorses the Kyoto Protocol
2012	Kyoto Protocal expires

Appendix 2: sustainable development

Sustainable development is the concept in international developmental affairs that seeks to balance the needs of the present with the future viability of natural resources and planetary ecology. The term sustainable development first came to prominence in the World Conservation Strategy (WCS) published by the World Conservation Union (WCU) in 1980. The idea was given prominence in the environmental debate by the 1987 World Commission on Environment and Development, led by Norwegian prime minister, Gro Harlem Brundtland. The commission's report, *Our Common Future* (The Brundtland Report of the World Commission on Environment and Development, 1987), articulated a growing concern about environmental degradation and the depletion of natural resources, an emerging crisis caused by industrial, technological and economic activity, fed by over-consumption in the industrialised world and exacerbated by rapid economic growth in developing countries. The commission called for a global commitment to 'sustainable development', defined as economic and social activity that meets the present needs of the world's population 'without compromising the ability of future generations to meet their own needs'.

Seeking to avoid what they see as looming social and environmental disaster, advocates of sustainable development urge measures including conservation and recycling, population control, and the development of alternative, renewable energy sources. The idea has triggered debate among ecologists, economists and politicians over the planet's 'carrying capacity', its adaptive and restorative potential, and the very definitions of the terms 'development' and 'sustainability'.

A sustainable built environment is defined as one which conserves non-renewable energy, material and ecological resources, reuses and recycles materials and outputs within the built environment, minimises the emissions of toxic substances and benignly reintegrates these throughout the lifecycle of the built systems with the environment, is seamlessly reintegrated at the end of its useful life, while sustaining an acceptable quality of human life and maintaining the capacity of the ecosystems at the local and global level.

Appendix 3: the Rio Principles

The Rio Principles include the following ideas:

- People are entitled to a healthy and productive life in harmony with nature.

- Development today must not undermine the development and environment needs of present and future generations.

- Nations have the sovereign right to exploit their own resources, but without causing environmental damage beyond their borders.

- Nations shall develop international laws to provide compensation for damage that activities under their control cause to areas beyond their borders.

- Nations shall use the precautionary approach to protect the environment. Where there are threats of serious or irreversible damage, scientific uncertainty shall not be used to postpone cost-effective measures to prevent environmental degradation.

- In order to achieve sustainable development, environmental protection shall constitute an integral part of the development process, and cannot be considered in isolation from it.

- Eradicating poverty and reducing disparities in living standards in different parts of the world are essential to achieve sustainable development and meet the needs of the majority of people.

- Nations shall cooperate to conserve, protect and restore the health and integrity of the Earth's ecosystem. The developed countries acknowledge the responsibility that they bear in the international pursuit of sustainable development in view of the pressures their societies place on the global environment and of the technologies and financial resources they command.

- Nations should reduce and eliminate unsustainable patterns of production and consumption, and promote appropriate demographic policies.

- Environmental issues are best handled with the participation of all concerned citizens. Nations shall facilitate and encourage public awareness and participation by making environmental information widely available.

- Nations shall enact effective environmental laws, and develop national law regarding liability for the victims of pollution and other environmental damage. Where they have authority, nations shall assess the environmental impact of proposed activities that are likely to have a significant adverse impact.

- Nations should cooperate to promote an open international economic system that will lead to economic growth and sustainable development in all countries. Environmental policies should not be used as an unjustifiable means of restricting international trade.

- The polluter should, in principle, bear the cost of pollution.

- Nations shall warn one another of natural disasters or activities that may have harmful transboundary impacts.

- Sustainable development requires better scientific understanding of the problems. Nations should share knowledge and innovative technologies to achieve the goal of sustainability.

- The full participation of women is essential to achieve sustainable development. The creativity, ideals and courage of youth and the knowledge of indigenous people are needed too. Nations should recognise and support the identity, culture and interests of indigenous people.

- Warfare is inherently destructive of sustainable development; nations shall respect international laws protecting the environment in times of armed conflict, and shall cooperate in their further establishment.

- Peace, development and environmental protection are interdependent and indivisible.

GLOSSARY

acid rain
Precipitation that has a pH below 5.6. Main contributors are sulphur dioxide from industrial burning of fossil fuels, and nitrogen oxide from automobile emissions, which is transformed into nitrogen dioxide.

aerobic digestion
Treatment of sludge or other thickened slurries that is typically used to decrease the solids content of a sludge or to remove pathogenic organisms. In concentrated slurries, aerobic digestion can generate considerable quantities of heat. Examples include extended aeration and auto thermal aerobic digestion (ATAD). Composting can be thought of as an aerobic digestion process using a relatively small water content.

Organic waste is utilised as a substrate for the growth of bacteria, which functions in the presence of oxygen to stabilise the waste and reduce its volume. The products of this decomposition are carbon dioxide, water and a remainder consisting of inorganic compounds, undigested organic material and water.

aerobic treatment
Removal of organic pollutants in wastewater by bacteria, requiring oxygen with water and carbon dioxide as the end results of the treatment process. Processes include trickling, filtration, activated sludge and rotating biological contactors.

agricultural wastes
Solid wastes of plant and animal origin, which result from the production and processing of farm or agricultural products, including manures, orchard and vineyard prunings, and crop residues, which are removed from the site of generation for solid-waste management.

air change
A measure of the air exchange in a building. One air change is an exchange of a volume of air equal to the interior volume of a building

air emissions
Solid particulates (such as unburned carbon) and gaseous pollutants (such as oxides of nitrogen or sulphur) or odours. These can result from a broad variety of activities including exhaust from vehicles, combustion devices, landfills, compost piles, street sweeping, excavation, demolition, etc.

air pollution
The presence of unwanted material in the air in excess of standards. The term 'unwanted material' here refers to material in sufficient concentrations, present for a sufficient time and under circumstances to interfere significantly with health, comfort or welfare of persons or with the full use and enjoyment of property.

aluminium can or container
Any food or beverage container that is composed of at least 94 per cent aluminium.

ambient air
Surrounding atmosphere.

ambient lighting
Lighting throughout an area that produces general illumination.

ambient temperature
Dry bulb temperature of the medium (air, water or earth) surrounding people, objects or equipment.

American Society of Heating, Refrigerating and Air-conditioning Engineers (ASHRAE)
Professional society in the USA for heating, refrigerating, mechanical ventilation and air-conditioning engineers.

amorphous silicon
A type of silicon in which the atoms have no order, as in glass, so it is not crystalline; also called thin-film silicon.

aquifer
A geologic formation, group of formations or part of a formation capable of yielding a significant amount of ground water to wells, springs, or surface water.

azimuth
The angle between true south and the point on the horizon directly below the sun.

azimuth angle
The angular distance between true south and the point on the horizon directly below the sun (negative before noon, positive after noon).

backyard composting
The controlled biodegradation of leaves, grass clippings and/or other yard wastes on the site where they were generated.

berm
A human-made mound or small hill of earth, either abutting a house wall to help stabilise the internal temperature or positioned to deflect wind from the house.

bioclimatology
The study of the relations of climate and life, particularly the effects of climate on the health and activity of living things. Bioclimatic design is design based on bioclimatological principles. The general approach is applicable to all climatic zones but varies depending on the local conditions and latitude of the site.

biodegradable
A substance or material that can be broken down into simpler compounds by micro-organisms and other decomposers into elements found in nature within a reasonably short period of time after customary disposal.

biodegradable material
Waste material that is capable of being broken down by micro-organisms into simple, stable compounds such as carbon dioxide and water. Most organic wastes, such as food wastes and paper, are biodegradable.

biodegradable plastic
Material subject to decomposition by micro-organisms, includes copolymers of natural and synthetic polymers that are produced by polymerisation of starch or cellulose with polystyrene.

biodegradation
Decomposition of material due to action of living organisms.

biological diversity
The variety and variability among living organisms and the ecological complexes in which they occur.

biological oxygen demand
Amount of dissolved oxygen used by micro-organisms in the biochemical oxidation process to break down organic matter.

biomass
Any organic (wood, agricultural or vegetative) matter; key components are carbon and oxygen.

biome
The largest terrestrial ecosystem. Biomes are distinct regional ecosystems of the world identifiable by their similar types of soil, climate, plants and animals no matter where they are located.

black body

A perfect absorber and emitter of radiation. A cavity is a perfect black body. Lampblack is close to a black body, while aluminium (polished) is a poor absorber and emitter of radiation.

black water

Wastewater generated within a household, including toilet wastes.

brownfield

Property that is no longer used for its original purpose and may be contaminated. Examples would be old petrol stations or abandoned factories.

buffer zone

Neutral area that acts as a protective barrier separating two conflicting forces. An area that acts to minimise the impact of pollutants on the environment or public welfare. For example, a buffer zone is established between a composting facility and neighbouring residents to minimise odour problems.

building envelope

The elements of a building that enclose conditioned spaces through which thermal energy may be transferred to or from the exterior, or to or from unconditioned spaces.

Building Research Establishment Environmental Assessment Method (BREEAM)

Green building rating system developed by the Building Research Establishment (BRE) in the UK (see Leadership in Energy and Environmental Design).

carbon cycle

The term used to describe how carbon circulates through the air, plants, animals and soil.

carcinogen

An agent that can cause cancer.

carrying capacity

The ability of a region to support the people who live there without degrading the resources that are available.

chimney effect

Tendency of air or gas in a vertical passage to rise when it is heated because it becomes lighter (less dense) than the surrounding air or gas. Useful in promoting cooling through enhanced natural ventilation.

chlorofluorocarbon (CFC)

Class of volatile, non-reactive, non-corrosive, non-flammable and easily liquefied gases. Group of substances derivative of methane or ethane with all or some hydrogen atoms replaced by chlorine and fluorine. Use discontinued because CFCs are believed to be responsible for destruction of stratospheric ozone. Formerly used as refrigerants, as propellants and in blown Styrofoam. Related compounds also containing bromine, eg, halons, are used as fire retardants

closed-loop recycling

The process in which an item is recycled back into the same product (as old aluminium cans are made into new cans). Reclaiming or reusing wastewater or process chemicals in an enclosed process in manufacturing.

co-generation

Production of two forms of energy from one source.

collector efficiency

Collector efficiency is a measure of the percentage of available solar energy that the collector will transmit to the heat transport fluid.

The calorimetric method uses a closed system consisting of a collector and small storage tank and provides a good method for determining the day-long efficiency of a collector. The instantaneous method uses an open system, an isolated collector, and is performed at solar noon under steady-state conditions.

collector, flat plate
An assembly containing a panel of metal or other suitable material, usually a flat black colour on its sun side, that absorbs sunlight and converts it into heat. This panel is usually in an insulated box, covered with glass or plastic on the sun side to take advantage of the greenhouse effect. In the collector, this heat transfers to a circulating fluid, such as air, water, oil or antifreeze.

collector, solar
A device for capturing solar energy, ranging from ordinary windows to complex mechanical devices.

Combined heat and power (CHP)
Local production of power and conservation of heat energy.

commercial waste
Waste materials originating in wholesale, retail, institutional or service establishments such as office buildings, stores, markets, theatres, hotels and warehouses.

compost
A humus-like relatively stable material resulting from the biological decomposition or breakdown of organic materials.

composting
The controlled degradation by aerobic micro-organisms of organic materials in solid waste to produce humus, a soil conditioner and fertiliser. Organic wastes such as food scraps and yard trimmings interact with micro-organisms (mainly bacteria and fungi) to produce a humus-like substance.

composting toilet
Toilets that compost human waste, require little or no water and do not create a health or odour problem when properly installed.

compost system
Controlled biological decomposition of organic refuse in which such materials are mechanically mixed, ground, or shredded, then decomposed to humus in windrow piles, or in aerated enclosures such as mechanical digesters or drums.

conservation
The planned management of a natural resource to prevent exploitation, destruction or neglect.

consumer
Also known as a heterotroph, it is any organism that is unable to manufacture or produce its own food, and therefore must rely on producers for food energy.

contaminant
Any physical, chemical, biological or radiological substance or matter that has an adverse effect on air, water, habitat.

Convention on International Trade in Endangered Species of Wild Fauna and Flora (USA) (CITES)
Provides lists of endangered species of timber and other natural products.

conversion
A form of recycling in which a waste material is turned into a useful material of substantially lower quality. An example is the use of crushed concrete and bricks as a granular base for roads and pavements. Also known as downcycling.

'cradle-to-cradle'
A term used in life-cycle analysis to describe a material or product that is recycled into a new product at the end of its defined life.

'cradle-to-grave'
A term used to describe the life cycle of materials, eg. the management of hazardous waste, from their point of generation to their final treatment and/or disposal.

crystalline silicon
A type of silicon in which the atoms have a regular diamond-like structure; also called single crystal or polycrystalline.

deciduous
Trees that lose their leaves seasonally, differing from coniferous.

decompose
To separate into constituent parts or elements or into simpler compounds; to undergo chemical breakdown; to decay or rot as a result of microbial and fungal action.

decomposer
An organism that nourishes itself by breaking down dead organic matter for energy and nutrients.

degradable plastics
Plastics specifically developed for special products that are formulated to break down after exposure to sunlight or microbes.

dioxin
The generic name for a group of organic chemical compounds formally known as polychlorinated dibenzo-p-dioxins. Heterocyclic hydrocarbons that occur as toxic impurities, especially in herbicides.

direct cooling
Direct cooling has four major components: keeping heat out; providing ventilation; underground construction, and evaporative cooling. Most of the strategies for keeping the heat out of a building involve avoiding direct solar gain. They include orienting the building away from intense solar exposure; using indirect daylighting instead of artificial lighting; shading roofs, walls and windows with overhangs, wing walls, and vegetation; adjusting surface-area-to-volume ratios.

direct irrigation
Above ground low-pressure watering system with flexible tubing that releases small, steady amounts of water through emitters placed near individual plants.

direct solar gains
Direct solar radiation passing through glass areas (mainly south facing) that contributes to space heating (kWh).

direct solar radiation
Direct solar radiation from the solid angle of the sun's disc. Solar radiation reaching a surface in a straight line from the sun.

disposable
Something that is designed to be used once and then thrown away.

drinking water standards
Water-quality standards measured in terms of suspended solids, unpleasant taste and microbes harmful to human health. Drinking water standards are included in state water-quality rules.

earth-sheltered design
Design of buildings that are partially or totally below ground, either as a result of digging into existing topography or filling over parts of the structure. Earth-sheltered design uses the constant temperature of the deep earth in a location to improve energy efficiency, and can be beneficial for use of contoured sites by decreasing maintenance and environmental impact.

ecological integrity
A natural system exhibits integrity if, when subject to a disturbance, it has a self-correcting ability to recover to an end state that is normal for that system, not necessarily one that is pristine or naturally whole.

ecology
The study of the relationship between living things and their environment. The word is derived from Greek words meaning the study of the home.

ecosystem
The interaction of organisms from the natural community to one another and their physical environment, acting together to form a whole.

ecotone
A habitat created by the juxtaposition of distinctly different habitats. An ecological zone or boundary between two or more ecosystems; also known as edge habitat.

effluent
The wastewater that is discharged as the result of a process.

embodied energy
Embodied energy accounts for all energy expended for production and transportation plus inherent energy at a specific point in the life cycle of a product.

It includes:
• energy involved in the manufacture of building materials
• energy consumed in the delivery of materials
• energy expended during construction
• energy required to demolish and dispose of construction

emission
Pollutant gas, particle or liquid released into the environment.

emission control
Any measure that reduces emissions into air, water or soil. The most effective emissions control involves redesign of the process so less waste is produced at the source. Common emission controls are dust collectors, wastewater-treatment plants, and in-plant solid and toxic waste reduction programmes.

emissivity
The ratio of the radiant energy emitted from a surface at a given temperature to the energy emitted by a black body at the same temperature.

energy
Ability to do work by moving matter or by causing a transfer of heat between two objects at different temperatures. Energy exists in several forms, which may be transformed from one to another, such as thermal, mechanical, electrical or chemical.

energy cost
The cost of energy by unit and type of energy as proposed to be supplied to the building, including variations such as time of day, season and rate of usage.

energy management system
A control system capable of monitoring environmental and system loads to adjust M&E output in order to conserve energy while maintaining comfort.

environment
The external conditions of an organism or population; the term 'the environment' generally refers to the sum total of conditions – physical and biological – in which organisms live.

environmental cost
A quantitative assessment of impacts such as resource depletion, air, water and solid-waste pollution, and disturbance of habitats.

environmental impact statement (EIS)
A document that details the potential environmental impact of a proposed action.

environmental medium or compartment
The part of the environment, typically air, water, soil and biota that contaminants are carried by or transmitted through.

environmental rehabilitation restoration
The act of repairing damage to a site caused by human activity, industry or natural disaster, and its rehabilitation into a viable ecosystem. The ideal is to leave a site in a state that is as close as possible to its natural condition before it was disturbed. Examples are replanting forests, stabilising soils, and filling in and replanting mine pits.

environmental sustainability
Cross-generational maintenance of ecosystem components and functions.

environmentally preferable
Products or services that have a lesser or reduced effect on human health and the environment when compared with competing products or services that serve the same purpose. The comparison may consider raw materials acquisition, production, manufacturing, packaging, distribution, reuse, operation, maintenance and/or disposal of the product or service.

episode (pollution)
An air pollution incident in a given area caused by concentration of atmospheric pollution reacting with meteorological conditions that may result in a significant increase in illnesses and deaths. Although most commonly used for air pollution, the term is also used for other kinds of environmental events such as a massive water-pollution situation.

evaporative cooling
The phase change of water from liquid to gas is a heat-absorbing process. The result is effective cooling of the air as water evaporates. This technique can be used to significantly reduce reliance on mechanical refrigeration, particularly in hot, dry climates.

flat plate collector
An assembly containing a panel of metal or other suitable material (usually with a flat black colour on its sun side) that absorbs sunlight and converts it into heat. This panel is usually in an insulated box, covered with glass or plastic on the sun side to retard heat loss. In the collector, the heat transfers to a circulating liquid or gas, such as air, water, oil or antifreeze; the heat is either utilised immediately or stored for later use.

fluorocarbon
Non-flammable, heat-stable hydrocarbon liquid or gas, in which some or all hydrogen atoms have been replaced by fluorine atoms. Formerly used in refrigerants, aerosol propellants, solvents, blowing agents, coatings, monomers. As with CFCs, fluorocarbons are classified as ozone-depleting substances (ODS) and have been banned from use as aerosol propellants.

focusing collector

A collector that has a parabolic or other reflector that focuses sunlight on to a small area for collection. A reflector of this type greatly intensifies the heat at the point of collection, allowing the heat collection fluid to achieve higher temperatures. This type of collector will work only with direct-beam sunlight.

food chain

The organisms in a line, where each is the food for the next in line.

food web

A food web is an intricate network of food chains. Because few organisms eat only one kind of food, a food web is a more accurate depiction of the complex nutritional cycles that exist in nature.

formaldehyde

Poisonous, reactive, flammable gas with pungent suffocating odour. Combines readily with many substances and polymerises easily. May cause irritation of eyes, nose, throat and respiratory system, tearing of the eyes, burns of the nose, coughing or bronchial spasm, allergic reactions. Contact may result in sensitisation. Carcinogen. Used in wood products, plastics, fertiliser, and foam insulation. Incorporated in synthetic resins by reaction with urea, phenols and melamine. Urea-formaldehyde (UF) resin is used in particleboard (eg, for subflooring and shelving and in cabinetry and furniture), hardwood plywood panelling (eg, decorative wall coverings, cabinetry, furniture) and medium-density fibreboard (MDF) (drawer fronts, cabinets, furniture tops). MDF contains a higher resin-to-wood ratio than other UF pressed wood products and is generally the highest formaldehyde-emitting pressed wood product, particularly when the surfaces and edges of these products are unlaminated or uncoated. Softwood plywood and oriented strandboard (OSB) produced for exterior construction contain dark phenol-formaldehyde (PF) resin. Pressed wood products containing PF resin generally emit less formaldehyde than those containing UF resin.

fossil fuel

Hydrocarbon deposits from plant remnants, including coal, peat, tar sands, shale oil, petroleum, natural gas. See Non-renewable resource.

green roof

Vegetation cover on roof surfaces. There are two types: extensive and intensive. Extensive green roofs (also referred to as ecoroofs or living roofs): thin soil layer with horizontally spreading, low-growing vegetation cover over entire roof surface that adds minimal loads to structure; serves as ecological storm-water management control by eliminating or delaying runoff. Also effectively reduces temperatures of the roof surface by absorbing heat from the sun, which may reduce the urban heat-island effect. Intensive green roofs (also referred to as traditional roof garden): thick soil layer or planters with vegetation, such as trees and shrubs that requires intensive care and maintenance; add substantial loads to building structure.

grey water

Domestic wastewater, composed of washwater from kitchen, bathroom and laundry sinks, tubs and washers. Does not include human waste.

ground cover

Material used to cover the soil surface to control erosion and leaching, shade the ground, and offer protection from excessive heating and freezing. Some ground covers are produced from garden waste compost.

ground water

Water beneath the earth's surface that fills underground pockets (known as aquifers) and moves between soil particles and rock, supplying wells and springs.   Ground water is a major source of drinking water and there is a growing concern over areas where leaching agricultural or industrial pollutants, or substances from leaking underground storage tanks, are contaminating ground water.

habitat

Place or type of place where an organism or community of organisms lives and thrives or a specific plant and animal species is naturally found; contains food, water, shelter and space.

hardwood
Deciduous trees with broader leaves and usually slower growth rates than the conifers, or softwoods. Common temperate-region hardwoods include dense, close-grained wood from oak, maple, cherry, walnut, beech, birch, cypress, elm and hickory. Hundreds of hardwoods are available from both temperate and tropical regions. Used in furniture and flooring, for appearance, excellent durability and resistance to wear.

harvested rainwater
The rain that falls on a roof or garden and is channelled to a storage tank (cistern). The first wash of water on a roof is usually discarded and the subsequent rainfall is captured for use if the system is being used for potable water. Good-quality water is available by this method in most areas.

hazardous material
Chemical or product that poses a significant threat to human health and/or the environment while being transported.

heat load
The total energy required for space heating.

heat loss
Heat flow through building-envelope components (walls, windows, roof, etc).

heat pump
A thermodynamic device that transfers heat from one medium to another. The first medium (the source) cools while the second (the heat sink) warms up.

heat recovery
Heat utilised that would otherwise be wasted. Sources of heat include machines, lights, process energy and people.

heating season
The period of the year during which heating the building is required to maintain comfort conditions.

Heating, ventilation and air-conditioning systems (HVAC)
The heating, ventilation and air-conditioning systems in buildings

hydrocarbon
Chemical composed only of carbon and hydrogen; petroleum crude oil is the largest source of hydrocarbons.

hydrochlorofluorocarbon (HCFC)
Hydrochlorofluorocarbons are generally less detrimental to depletion of the stratospheric ozone than related chlorofluorocarbons; generally used to replace chlorofluorocarbons. However, a total ban on all CFCs and HCFCs is scheduled to be effective 2030. See also Chlorofluorocarbon.

hydrofluorocarbon (HFC)
Hydrofluorocarbons have no ozone depletion potential, but are greenhouse gases and contribute to global warming. See also Chlorofluorocarbon.

hydrologic cycle
The term literally means the water-earth cycle. It refers to the movement of water, in all three of its physical forms, through the various environmental compartments.

impact
An effect on the environment or on living things.

---

impermeable

Restricts the movement of products through the surface.

impervious surface area

Area that has been sealed and does not allow water to infiltrate, such as roofs, plazas, streets and other hard surfaces.

incident angle

The angle between the sun's rays and a line perpendicular (normal) to the irradiated surface.

incineration

Treatment technology involving destruction of waste by controlled burning at high temperatures.

indigenous

Native to a region.

indirect gain

The indirect transfer of solar heat into the space to be heated from a collector that is coupled to the space by an uninsulated, conductive or convective medium (such as a thermal storage wall or roof pond).

indoor air quality (IAQ)

Acceptable indoor air quality is defined as air in which there are no known contaminants at harmful concentrations as determined by cognisant authorities, and with which a substantial majority (80 per cent or more) of the people exposed do not express dissatisfaction.

industrial waste

Materials (including liquid, sludge, and solid, or hazardous waste) discarded from industrial operations or derived from industrial operations or manufacturing processes; all non-hazardous solid wastes other than residential, commercial, and institutional. May also include small quantities of waste generated from cafeterias, offices or retail sales departments on same premises. Industrial waste includes all wastes generated by activities such as demolition and construction, manufacturing, agricultural operations, wholesale trade and mining.

inert solids or inert waste

A non-liquid solid waste including, but not limited to, soil and concrete, that does not contain hazardous waste or soluble pollutants at concentrations in excess of water-quality objectives, and does not contain significant quantities of decomposable solid waste.

infiltration

The uncontrolled movement of outdoor air into the interior of a building through cracks around windows and doors or in walls, roofs and floors. This may work by cold air leaking in during the winter or hot air entering in the summer.

infrastructure

A substructure or underlying foundation: those facilities upon which a system or society depends; for example, roads, schools, power plants, communication networks and transportation systems.

inorganic

Not composed of once-living material (eg minerals); generally, composed of chemical compounds not principally based on the element carbon.

inorganic compound

Compounds that do not contain carbon (with some exceptions, eg, carbon dioxide, carbonates and cyanides). Minerals, metals, ceramics and water are examples of inorganic compounds. Most tend to be very stable because they oxidise slowly or not at all. See also Organic compound.

insecticide

A chemical agent that destroys insects. These toxins act on the reproductive or nervous system of larval or adult insects.

insolation

A contraction of 'incoming solar radiation' meaning the amount of solar energy incident on a given area over a certain period of time. The total amount of solar radiation (direct, diffuse and reflected) striking a surface exposed to the sky. This incident solar radiation is generally measured in BTU per square foot per hour.

insulation

Material having resistance to transfer of energy, eg acoustic, electric, thermal, vibrational or chemical.

integrated waste management

Using a variety of practices, including source reduction, recycling, incineration and landfilling to minimise the amount of municipal solid waste.

internal gains

The energy dissipated inside the heated space by people (body heat) and appliances (lighting, cooker, etc). A proportion of this energy contributes to the space-heating requirements (kWh).

kilowatt hour

Energy unit equivalent to 1000 W used for 1 hour; also referred as a 'unit' of electricity: $1kWh = 3.6 MJ$.

labelling

A generic term that includes labels, markings or placarding.

landfills

Sanitary landfills are land disposal sites for non-hazardous solid wastes where waste is spread in layers, compacted to the smallest practical volume and cover material is applied at the end of each operating day. Secure hazardous waste landfills are disposal sites permitted for hazardous waste. Both types of landfill are selected and designed to minimise the chance of hazardous substance releases into the environment.

latitude

The angular distance north (+) or south (-) of the equator, measured in degrees of arc.

Leadership in Energy and Environmental Design (LEED)

LEED is an assessment system that is a sustainable/green checklist and rating system developed by the US Green Building Council. It differs from others because it follows the underlying notion that all buildings can be rated quantitatively according to verifiable documentation. The system requires regular documentations for certification which can be complicated and time consuming. Subsequent versions reduce the extent of paperwork. The system provides a quantitative statistical record of building performance.
Life cycle assessment assesses the whole environment aspect and potential environmental impacts all through the life cycle (ie. from cradle to the grave) of a designed system starting from the material extraction from the earth, followed by manufacturing, transport and air, and ending with the waste management including sense, recycling and eventual build disposal and reintegration.

life cycle

All stages of development, from extraction to production, marketing, transportation, use and disposal.

life-cycle assessment (LCA)

A process or framework to evaluate the environmental burdens associated with a product, process or activity by identifying, quantifying and assessing its energy and material usage and environmental releases, to identify opportunities for environmental improvements. Extraction and processing of raw materials, manufacturing, transportation and distribution, use/reuse/maintenance, recycling and final disposal are all considered.

life-cycle cost

All internal and external costs associated with a product, process or activity throughout its entire life cycle, being the amortised annual cost of a product, including capital costs, installation costs, operating costs, maintenance costs and disposal costs discounted over the life of the product. This definition has traditionally excluded environmental costs.

light shelf
Light shelves are horizontal projections at the building interior that reflect direct sun rays on to ceilings deep in a space. Light shelves work best on facades that are generally southfacing, since they work for long periods of time each day and can also provide shading of glazing below.

liquid
One of the three states of matter. Liquids are characterised as having a definite volume, but an indefinite shape.

longitude
The arc of the equator between the meridian of a place and the Greenwich meridian measured in degrees east or west.

Mechanical and Electrical (M&E) systems
The mechanical and electrical systems in buildings generally to provide improved internal conditions over external conditions and to service the building users (eg power supply, water supply, telecommunications, removal of sewage, etc). Referred to as HVAC systems in the USA.

metal
A mineral source that is a good conductor of electricity and heat, and yields basic oxides and hydroxides. One of the hidden treasures in garbage.

microbial
Pertaining to micro-organisms, such as bacteria, protozoans, yeasts, mould, viruses and algae.

mitigation
Measures taken to reduce adverse impacts on the environment.

monitoring
Periodic or continuous surveillance or testing to determine the level of compliance with statutory requirements and/or pollutant levels in various media or in humans, animals or other living things.

natural
Determined by nature, occurring in conformity with the ordinary course of nature; a state of nature untouched by civilisation.

natural resource
Material or energy obtained from the environment that is used to meet human needs; material or energy resources not made by humans.

niche
The effects an organism has on its surroundings and how the surroundings affect the organism.

nitrogen cycle
The circulation of nitrogen through plants and animals and back to the atmosphere.

nitrogen oxide (NOx)
One of the products of combustion of hydrocarbon fuels, along with the volatile organic compounds, that undergo photochemical reactions and produce ozone.

non-biodegradable
A substance that will not decompose under normal atmospheric conditions.

non-recyclable
Not capable of being recycled or used again.

non-renewable energy
Sources of energy such as oil, coal or natural gas that are not replaceable after they have been used.

non-renewable (resources)
Not capable of being naturally restored or replenished; resources available in a fixed amount (stock) in the earth's crust; they can be exhausted either because they are not replaced by natural processes (copper) or because they are replaced more slowly than they are used (oil and coal). Fossil fuels (coal, petroleum, natural gas) are examples of non-renewable energy sources.

nylon
Synthetic thermoplastic melt-spun fibre in the polyamide resin family. Crystalline solid characterised by high strength, elasticity, durability, high flexibility, low water absorption, resistance to abrasion, rot, and mildew. Used in manufacture of synthetic fibres, rope, carpet and moulded plastics. Some nylons are recyclable, though very little recycling is currently done.

nylon 6
Polymer derived from caprolactam. It is a very durable fibre among synthetics, second only to nylon 6,6. Used for textiles. It is made from a single polymer and thus can be 100 per cent recycled back into carpet fibre. Also called Zeftron (trademark for product manufactured by BASF). See also Nylon.

offgassing
The releasing of gases or vapours into the air.

operational costs
Those direct costs incurred in maintaining the ongoing operation of a programme or facility. Operational costs do not include capital costs.

organic
Composed of living or once-living matter; more broadly, composed of chemical compounds principally based on the element carbon, excluding carbon dioxide.

organic compound
Chemical compound based on carbon chains or rings, and containing hydrogen with or without oxygen, nitrogen or other elements. Organic compounds are the basis of all living things; they are also the foundation of modern polymer chemistry. There are several million known organic compounds, and their characteristics vary widely. See also Inorganic compound and Volatile organic compound (VOC).

organic waste
Natural materials, such as food and garden waste, that decompose naturally.

organically grown
Agricultural products that are grown with minimal use of synthetic fertilisers or pesticides. Various state and industry definitions are used to determine which products can be sold as organically grown.

organism
Living things ranging from a bacteria in the soil, to a plant, to an animal.

orientation
The orientation of a surface is in degrees of variation away from solar south, towards either the east or west. Solar or true south should not be confused with magnetic south, which can vary owing to magnetic declination.

oxidation
When a substance either gains oxygen or loses hydrogen or electrons in a chemical reaction. One of the chemical treatment methods.

oxygen cycle
The circulation of oxygen through the various environmental compartments. It is closely tied to the carbon cycle.

packaging
Any of a variety of plastics, papers, cardboard, metals, ceramics, glass, wood and paperboard used to make containers for foods, household and industrial products.

paper
Made from the pulp of trees. Paper is digested in a sulphurous solution, bleached and rolled into long sheets. Acid rain and dioxin are standard by-products of this manufacturing process.

particulates
Suspended small particles of ash, charred paper, dust, soot or other partially incinerated matter carried in the flue gas.

passive solar cooling
Building design that avoids unneeded solar heat, utilises natural ventilation and employs thermal mass (especially in hot, dry climates) to retain coolness.

passive solar heating
Building design that uses natural processes to collect, store, and distribute heat in a building. Most passively solar-heated buildings require an auxiliary heating system for periods when solar heat is unavailable or insufficient.

peak power
The maximum amount of power a PV module can generate under standard test conditions of irradiance and cell temperature; units of Wp (compare a 'wagon puller' who has both the strength to pull the load and can do so at speed).

pesticide
Lethal chemical that destroys pests, eg insects, rodents, nematodes, fungi, seeds, viruses, or bacteria. Term includes insecticides, herbicides, rodenticides, and fungicides. Any substance or mixture of substances intended for preventing, destroying, repelling, or mitigating any pest or any substance or mixture of substances intended for use in a plant regulator, defoliant or desiccant. Chemical pesticides include organochlorine, organophosphorus, carbamates, chlorophenoxy compounds, dinitrophenols and paraquat. The active ingredients are semi-volatile and some, particularly the organochlorine insecticides, are persistent in the environment. The carrier solvents and inert ingredients may exhibit similar or greater toxicity than the active ingredients, and can include volatile ingredients that offgas into indoor air. May cause central nervous system effects (dizziness, nausea). Direct indoor applications can subject building occupants to VOCs and pesticide residue. Alternative, safe forms of controlling pests include use of sticky or mechanical traps. Also known as biocide.

petrochemical
Chemical made from petroleum or natural gas feedstock, such as ethylene, butadiene, most major plastics, and resins. Also known as petroleum chemicals. See Hydrocarbon.

petroleum
A mineral resource that is a complex mixture of hydrocarbons, an oily, flammable bituminous liquid occurring in many places in the upper strata of the earth.

photovoltaic (PV)
Capable of generating a voltage as a result of exposure to visible or other radiation. Solid-state cells (typically made from silicon) directly convert sunlight to electricity. The electricity can be used immediately, stored in batteries or sold to a utility.

planned obsolescence
The practice of producing goods that have a very short life so that more goods will have to be produced.

plastics
Synthetic materials consisting of large molecules called polymers derived from petrochemicals (compared to natural polymers such as cellulose, starch and natural rubbers).

Material that contains one or more organic polymeric substances of large molecular weight, is solid in its finished state, and at some stage in its manufacture or processing into a finished article can be shaped by flow. Includes polymers, plasticisers, stabilisers, fillers and other additives. Many toxic chemicals are used in plastics manufacturing (eg benzene, cadmium compounds, carbon tetrachloride, lead compounds, styrene, vinyl chloride).

permeable
Having pores or openings that permit liquids or gases to pass through.

pollutants
Any solid, liquid or gaseous matter that is in excess of natural levels or established standards.

pollution
Harmful substances deposited in the environment by the discharge of waste, leading to the contamination of soil, water or the atmosphere.

polyethylene
Thermoplastic material composed of polymers of ethylene. Used for films, coatings, flexible containers. There are high-density (HDPE) and low-density (LDPE) forms. These are relatively low-toxicity materials.

polyethyleneterephthalate (PET)
Thermoplastic polyester resin made from ethylene glycol and terephthalic acid. Used to make films or fibres. High tensile and impact strength, high stiffness, high flex life and toughness. Used in blow moulding of soft-drink bottles, photographic film, electrical insulation. Common recycled polyester plastic resin used to produce polyester fibre and sheet plastics.

polypropylene
Thermoplastic resin made by polymerisation of propylene. Product is hard and tough, resists moisture, oils, and solvents, and is heat resistant. Used in moulded articles, fibres, film, toys. Melt-extruded polypropylene is used in indoor–outdoor carpets, outdoor furniture, non-woven materials, 'hard elastic' materials, carpet yarn, rope, artificial turf, packaging and primary carpet backing.

polystyrene
Tough thermoplastic polymer, made by polymerisation of styrene. Soluble in aromatic and chlorinated hydrocarbon solvents. Extruded polystyrene (XPS) rigid insulation has high insulation value and a void-free structure, making it largely impervious to water. XPS is manufactured using HCFCs as the blowing agent; HCFCs are strong greenhouse gases. Expanded polystyrene (EPS) board is sometimes used as an alternative to XPS to avoid use of HCFCs; however, EPS has a slightly lower insulating value and gaps between beads of EPS may allow moisture intrusion, which may require additional flashing or moisture-barrier films. Used in injection moulding, extrusion or casting for electrical insulation, fabric lamination, rigid foam and moulding of plastic objects.

polyurethane
Thermoplastic and thermosetting polymers. Used in rubbers with high abrasion resistance, foams, binders for paints to provide flexibility.

polyvinyl chloride (PVC)
Thermoplastic polymer of vinyl chloride. Rigid material with good electrical properties and flame and chemical resistance. Stabilisers are needed to prevent discoloration from light or heat, and plasticisers are needed for flexibility. Vinyl chloride monomer is a known human carcinogen. Due to environmental releases during manufacturing, PVC production is banned in many parts of Europe. The environmental organisation Greenpeace has developed an on-line resource guide to PVC alternatives. Hazardous when burned. Used in soft flexible films, including flooring, and in moulded rigid products, eg pipes, fibres, upholstery, sidings and bristles. Identified by a '3' inside a recycling triangle found on packaging.

population
Members of the same species sharing a habitat.

porosity
The percentage of the total volume of the material that is occupied by pores or other openings.

Portland cement
A kind of cement made by burning limestone and clay in a kiln. When water is added to the cement, the calcium oxide is hydrated to form alkaline calcium hydroxide. Although brief skin contact may be tolerated, some people develop extensive skin burns. Cement dermatitis may include skin dryness, rashes, etc. Unhydrated Portland cement is a respirable dust but is not a silica hazard. Used as the base for most grouts for ceramic mosaics and quarry and paver tiles. Also known as hydraulic cement or cement.

post-commercial recycled content
Material that has been recovered or otherwise diverted from the solid-waste stream during the manufacturing process. Does not include used, reconditioned or remanufactured components. Also known as preconsumer recycled content.

post-consumer recycled content
Material or finished product that has served its intended consumer use and has been discarded for recovery. This material is part of the broader category of recovered material. Examples include newspapers, magazines, beverage containers, building materials, etc.

potable water
Water suitable for drinking.

primary treatment
In wastewater treatment, the removal of coarse and fine floating and suspended solids from raw sewage. See also Secondary treatment and Tertiary treatment.

producer
An organism, like a plant, that can make its own food through a process like photosynthesis.

product
An outcome or an object; the amount, quantity or total produced.

recover
To reclaim a resource embedded in waste.

recovered materials
Waste materials and by-products that have been recovered or diverted from solid waste. Excludes those materials and by-products generated from, and commonly reused within an original manufacturing process.
Those materials that have known recycling potential, can be feasibly recycled, and have been diverted or removed from the solid-waste stream for sale.

recovery rate
All discarded materials that have been recovered through various recovery strategies including garden waste, composting and reuse. Designated materials recovered plus returned via deposit divided by the total designated materials available.

recyclables
Materials that still have useful physical or chemical properties after serving their original purpose and that can, therefore, be reused or remanufactured into additional products. Waste materials that are collected, separated and used as raw material.

recycle

To separate a given material from waste and process it so that it can be used again in a form similar to its original use; for example, newspapers recycled into newspapers or cardboard.

recycled content

That portion of a product that is made from recycled materials. This may include both pre- and post-consumer materials. Buying products with recycled content helps support recycling.

recycling

The act of extracting materials from the waste stream and reusing them. The extraction and recovery of valuable materials from scrap or other discarded materials. Metals are separated electrostatically. Recycled mixed plastics are used for products that do not depend on colour, clarity or strength, eg, carpet backing. Higher-value recycled products require sorting of plastics, based on differences such as density, physical properties, solubility or light sensitivity. True recycling is the conversion of a waste material back into its original form. An alternative is conversion into another material. See also Conversion.

recycling loop

A process through which materials that might otherwise be wasted are collected and processed for conversion into new products that otherwise would have been discarded.

reflectance

The ratio or percentage of the amount of light reflected by a surface to the amount incident. Good light reflectors are not necessarily good heat reflectors.

regeneration

Restoration of logged forestlands and mined sites. Drainage, soil replacement, replanting and fertilisation are usually involved.

region

The combined geographic area of two or more incorporated areas; two or more unincorporated areas; or any combination of incorporated and unincorporated areas.

relative humidity

The ratio of the amount of water vapour in the atmosphere to the maximum amount of water vapour that could be held at a given temperature.

renewable resources

A resource that is capable of being naturally restored or replenished at a rate equal to, or greater than, its rate of depletion. A resource capable of being replaced by natural ecological cycles or sound management practices. Examples of renewable energy resources include solar, wind, hydro, geothermal and biomass resources. Renewable resources are sometimes referred to as regenerative, non-depletable or current-income energy.

A naturally occurring raw material or form of energy, such as the sun, wind, falling water, biofuels, fish and trees, derived from an endless or cyclical source, where, through management of natural means, replacement roughly equals consumption ('sustained yield').

repairability

The ability of a product or package to be restored to a working or usable state at a cost that is less than the replacement cost of the product or package.

residue

Materials remaining after processing, incineration, composting or recycling have been completed. Residues are usually disposed of in landfills.

retention basin
An area designed to retain runoff and prevent erosion and pollution.

reusability
The ability of a product or package to be used more than once in its same form.

reuse
The recovery of a material for additional use without reprocessing (eg glass bottles reused by a dairy).

The process of minimising the generation of waste by recovering usable products that might otherwise become waste.

The use of a product more than once in its same form for the same purpose; eg a soft-drink bottle is reused when it is returned to the bottling company for refilling; finding new functions for objects and materials that have outgrown their original use; to use again.

rock bed
A container filled with rocks, pebbles or crushed stone, to store energy by raising the temperature of the rocks, etc.

roof pond
A body of water on the roof of a structure that is exposed to solar gain, which it absorbs and stores. The thermal energy is radiated into the building uniformly and at a moderated temperature, in both sunny and cloudy conditions.

runoff
Water (originating as precipitation) that flows across the surface of the ground – rather than soaking into it – eventually entering bodies of water, may pick up and carry with it a variety of suspended or dissolved substances. In many cases, the runoff is a leachate composed of toxic compounds.

salvage
Recovery and reclamation of damaged, discarded or abandoned material, eg during demolition or renovation.

secondary treatment
In wastewater treatment, biological treatment for removing floating and settleable solids, oxygen-demanding substances and suspended solids. Includes trickling filters or activated sludge processes. Disinfection is the final stage of secondary treatment. See also Primary treatment and Tertiary treatment.

sedimentary rocks
One of the three types of rock that comprise the crust of the earth. They are the result of the weathering of pre-existing solids.

sewage
The waste and wastewater produced by residential and commercial establishments and discharged into sewers.

shading coefficient
The ratio of solar energy transmitted through a window to incident solar energy that is normal to it. Used to express the effectiveness of glazing or a shading device.

sick building syndrome (SBS)
A pattern of health complaints related to poor indoor air quality. Unlike building-related illness, sick building syndrome does not have known causation or definite symptoms, nor can it be diagnosed medically. It may be a multi-factorial problem (eg, inadequate ventilation, deficiencies in M&E operation, exposure to indoor air pollutants such as tobacco smoke, VOCs, mould). Symptoms include nasal stuffiness, dry and irritated eyes, throat and skin; headaches; generalised lethargy and tiredness leading to poor concentration. Symptoms typically disappear upon leaving the building.

silica gel
Highly absorbent silica used as a dehumidifying and dehydrating agent, as a catalyst or catalyst carrier.

sludge
The semi-solid to solid residue left from wastewater treatment as solid matter that settles at the bottom of septic tanks or wastewater-treatment plant sedimentation tanks; must be processed by bacterial digestion or other methods, or pumped out for land disposal, incineration, or composting.

softwood
Wood from a coniferous tree, such as pine, fir, hemlock, spruce or cedar. Softwoods are fast-growing and primarily used for construction. See also Hardwood.

soil
The thin layer of the earth's crust that we live on and that has been affected by weathering and decomposition of organisms. The loose top layer of the earth's surface in which plant life can grow.

solar collector
A device designed to gather and store energy from solar radiation, ranging from ordinary windows to complex mechanical devices. The three major types of active solar collectors used in building applications are flat plates, evacuated tubes, and a variety of linear concentrators. Flat plates are the most common type used for heating and hot water. Evacuated and concentrating collectors are often used for applications requiring higher temperatures. See also Photovoltaic.

solar energy, useful
The amount of solar energy contributing to the total heat load. It is expressed in absolute figures (kWh) or per unit collector area (kWh/m^2).

solar radiation
The energy-carrying electromagnetic radiation emitted by the sun. This radiation comprises many frequencies, each relating to a particular class of radiation:

• high-frequency/short-wavelength ultraviolet;
• medium-frequency/medium-wavelength visible light;
• low-frequency/high-wavelength infrared.

This radiation is relatively unimpeded until it reaches the earth's atmosphere. Here some of it will be reflected back out of the atmosphere, some will be absorbed. That which reaches the earth's surface unimpeded is referred to as 'direct' solar radiation. That which is scattered by the atmosphere is referred to as 'diffuse' solar radiation. The combination of direct and diffuse is called 'global'.

solid waste
Solid product or material disposed of in landfills, incinerators or compost. Can be expressed in terms of weight or volume.

solar water heater
A water-heating system in which heat from the sun is absorbed by collectors and transferred by pumps to a storage unit. The heated fluid in the storage unit conveys its heat to the domestic hot water of the building through a heat exchanger. Controls regulating the operation are needed.

stack effect
Pressure-driven airflow produced by convection, by the difference between confined hot gas in a chimney or stack and cool air surrounding the outlet. The stack effect can overpower a building's mechanical system and disrupt ventilation and circulation.

The tendency of air or gas in a duct or other vertical passage to rise when heated owing to its lower density in comparison with that of the surrounding air or gas. In buildings, the tendency towards displacement (caused by the difference in temperature) of internal heated air by unheated outside air owing to the difference in density between outside and inside air.

succession

The progressive changes in an ecosystem that eventually result in the establishment of a stable community.

sun space

A well-glazed space, generally southfacing, that collects heat and supplies some of it to another space (typically adjoining). Temperatures within sun spaces are normally not controlled and change daily and seasonally.

surface-area-to-volume ratios

One potential and often misleading indicator of building energy performance. The smallest ratios apply to buildings that are spherical or, more practically, squarish in shape. Disregarded is the fact that surface area can also be very useful if it increases the potential for passive solar heating, natural ventilation and/or daylighting of buildings.

surface water management systems

Systems designed, constructed, operated and maintained to prevent surface water flowing on to waste-filled areas.

sustainable

The ability to support, endure, or keep up. Meeting present needs without compromising future resources. In order for recycling to be sustainable, it is essential for the public to buy products made with recycled materials.

sustainable development

The management of resources in a way that enables people living today to meet their needs without jeopardising the ability of the earth's future inhabitants to meet theirs.

task lighting

Any form of light that is focused on a specific surface or object. It is intended to provide high-quality lighting (often flexible) for a predetermined activity.

tertiary treatment

Final stage in wastewater treatment to remove nitrates and phosphates and fine particles. The process is also known as advanced sewage treatment and follows removal of raw sludge and biological treatment. See also Primary treatment and Secondary treatment.

The third step, sometimes employed, at a municipal wastewater-treatment plant. It consists of advanced cleaning, which removes nutrients and most BOD (Biochemical Oxygen Demand).

thermal chimney

A section of a building where solar heat or thermal currents are controlled in a manner that stimulates an updraught and the exhaust of heated air. This draws fresh air into occupied areas of the building through open windows or vents, providing a passive cooling system.

thermal conductance

The thermal conductance through 1 square metre of material of a given thickness for each 1 K temperature difference between its surfaces (W per sq.m. K).

thermal mass

Material that absorbs heat or coolness and releases it slowly over a long period of time. Earth, water, and masonry materials can provide excellent thermal mass in passive heating or cooling-system design.

The mass of the building within the insulation, expressed per volume of heated space (kg/m^3). 'Primary thermal mass' receives direct sunlight; 'secondary thermal mass' is in sight of the primary thermal masses and so receives radiative and convective energy from the primary thermal mass; 'remote thermal mass' is hidden from view of both the primary and secondary thermal mass and so receives energy by convection only.

thermal pollution
Discharge of heated effluent into natural waters that may upset the ecological balance of the waterway due to change in temperature, threatening the survival of some types of life or favouring the survival of others.

thermal storage
Thermal storage enables a solar-gain system to collect more heat than is immediately required and store it for later use.

thermal-storage wall
A masonry or water wall used to store heat from the sun. Typically, the generally south-facing side is painted a dark colour to improve absorption.

time lag
The period of time between the absorption of solar radiation by a material and its release into a space. Time lag is an important consideration in sizing a thermal storage wall or Trombe wall.

toxic
Defined for regulatory purposes as a substance containing poison and posing a substantial threat to human health and/or the environment.

toxic substance
In very general terms, any material considered to be hazardous to human health or the environment, eg benzene, carbon tetrachloride, chloroform, dioxane, ethylene dibromide, methylene chloride, tetrachloroethylene, 1, 1, 1-trichloroethane, trichloroethylene.

tracking
The process of altering the tilt of a module throughout the day in order to face the sun and thus maximise the power output.

trophic level
The term used to describe each level of energy consumption within a food web. Energy within a food web always flows in only one direction, starting with the producers.

ultraviolet radiation
Electromagnetic radiation with wavelengths shorter than visible light. This invisible form of radiation is found in solar radiation and plays a part in the deterioration of plastic glazings, paint and furnishing fabrics.

U-value
See Thermal conductance.

volatile organic compound (VOC)
An organic compound that readily evaporates under normal conditions or temperature and pressure. Examples of VOCs include: benzene, trichloroethylene and vinyl chloride. Also included are the precursors, along with the oxides of nitrogen, that undergo photochemical reactions and produce ozone.

waste
Anything that is discarded, useless or unwanted; opposite of conserve, as in 'to waste'.

wastewater
The spent or used water from individual homes, a community, a farm or an industry that contains dissolved or suspended matter.

watershed
The land area that drains into a river, river system or other body of water or to a common outlet such as the outflow of a lake, the mouth of a river or any point along a stream channel.

wetlands

Environment characterised by shallow or fluctuating water levels and abundant aquatic and marsh plants. Includes marshes, swamps, bayous, bogs, fens, sloughs and ponds.
An area that is regularly saturated by surface or ground water and subsequently is characterised by a prevalence of vegetation that is adapted for life in saturated soil conditions.

white goods

A term used to describe large appliances such as refrigerators, washers and dryers. The terminology was derived from the standard white colour of these appliances that existed until recent years.

window-to-wall ratio

The ratio of glazing area to the gross exterior wall area.

wind turbine

A machine that generates electricity from the wind by turning a generator-connected wind propeller.

wing wall

Vertical projection on one side of a window or wall used to increase or decrease the wind pressure or solar incidence on the wall or window. Small outside walls on a building set perpendicular to an exterior wall next to a window. A negative pressure zone is created by the wing wall stimulating air movement (breeze) through the window.

xeriscape

Landscaping for water and energy efficiency and lower maintenance. The seven xeriscape principles are: good planning and design; practical lawn areas; efficient irrigation; soil improvement; use of mulches; low-water-demand plants; good maintenance.

Allaby, M. (1986), <u>Ecology Facts</u>, Hamlyn, London, UK

Allaby, M.(1998), <u>Oxford Dictionary of Ecology</u>, Oxford University Press, Oxford, UK

Allen, W.L. (Ed.), (June 2004), 'The End of Cheap Oil', in <u>National Geographical</u>, Publ. National Geographical Society, Washington, USA

Amato, A. and A. Eaton, (1998), 'Life Cycle Assessment', Paper presented at the Steel Construction Institute's 'Sustainable Steel' conference, Orlando, USA

Ardalan, N. and Bakhtiar, L. (1993), <u>The Sense of Unity: The Sufi Tradition in Persian Architecture,</u> Publ. for the Centre for Middle Eastern Studies No. 9, The University of Chicago Press, Chicago, USA

Arvill, R. (1970), <u>Man and Environment</u>, Penguin Books, London, UK

Ashby, R. (1971), <u>Royal Commission on Environmental Pollution, Second Report: Three Issues in Industrial Pollution</u>, H.M.S.O., London, UK

Ashby, R. (1973), <u>Royal Commission on Environmental Pollution, Third Report: Pollution in some British Estuaries and Coastal Waters</u>, H.M.S.O., London, UK

Ashby, R. (1956), <u>Introduction to Cybernetics</u>, Chapman & Hall, London, UK

Atkinson, W.I. (2003), <u>Nanocosm: Nanotechnology and the Big Changes Coming from the Inconceivably Small</u>, Amacom American Management Association, New York, USA

Audubon Society Hq. In L.C. Zeiher (1996), <u>The Ecology of Architecture: A Complete Guide to Creating the Environmentally Conscious Building</u>, Whitney Library of Design, New York, USA

Axelrod, A. (2003), '<u>Science A.S.A.P</u>', Prentice Hall Press, USA

Aynsley, R. May (1998), <u>Natural Ventilation in Passive Design</u>, RAIA Environmental Design Guide, TEC2, RAIA Publishing, Australia

Baker, N.V. (1992), <u>Energy and Environment in Non-Domestic Buildings: A Technical Guide</u>. Cambridge: Cambridge University Press with Cambridge Architectural Research Ltd. and The Martin Centre for Architectural and Urban Studies, UK

Barabasi, A.L. (2003), Linked: how everything is connected to everything else and what it means for business, science, and everyday life, Penguin Group, USA

Beatley, T. (2001), 'Going Green', in <u>Urban Land Europe</u>,Urban Land (March 2001)

Behling, S. and S.(1996): <u>Sol Power: The Evolution of Solar Architecture</u>, Prestel Publishing, Munich,Germany

Bird, M.(2001), 'Direct Out', in <u>TIME</u> (14 May 2001), Publ. NY, USA

Dr. Birkeland, J.(2002), <u>Design for Sustainability: A Sourcebook of Integrated Ecological Solutions</u>, Earthscan Publications Ltd, London, UK

Boyce, A. (1997), <u>Preserving the Legacy: Introduction to Environmental Technology</u>, John Wiley & Sons, Inc. New York, USA

Brown, G.Z. (1985), <u>Sun, Wind, and Light: Architectural Design Strategies</u>, John Wiley & Sons, New York, USA

Buchanan, M. (2002), <u>Small Worlds and the Groundbreaking Theory of Networks</u>, W.W. Norton & Company, USA
Bunch, B., Tesar, J. (2003), <u>Discover Science Almanac: The Definitive Science Resource</u>, A Stonesong Press Book, Hyperion, New York, USA

Burall, P.(1991), Green Design, The Design Council, London, UK

BRECSU (Building Research Energy Conservation Support Unit), (1995), Energy Consumption Guide No. 19, Hong Kong

Brown, Lester, Christopher Flavin, and Sandra Postel, (1991), Saving the Planet, W.W. Norton & Company New York /, USA

Brundtland, G.H. (1987), in World Commission on the Environment and Development (WCED). Energy 2000: A Global Strategy for Sustainable Development, Zed Books, London, UK

Cain, S.A. (1970), 'The Importance of Ecological Studies as a Basis for Land-Use Planning', Biological Conservation, Vol. 1, Elsevier Publishing Co., UK

Callenbach, E.(1998), Ecology: A Pocket Guide, University of California Press, Berkeley, USA

Capra, F. (2003), The Hidden Connections: A Science of Sustainable Living, Flamingo, UK

Cohen, J.E. (1995), How Many People Can the Earth Support?, W.W. Norton New York /, USA

Cole, R., (2004), 'Changing context for environmental knowledge', in Building Research & Information
 (2004) 32(2), March-April, 91-109, Spon Press, UK

Carolin, P., and T. Dannat, UK (1996), Architecture, Education and Research: The Work of Leslie Martin: Papers and Selected Articles, Academy Editions, London, UK

Carr, Marilyn, (Ed), (1985), The AT Reader: Theory and Practice in Appropriate Technology, Intermediate Technology Publications, London, UK

Chapman, P.(1973), 'The Energy Cost of Producing Copper and Aluminium from Primary Sources', Open University Report ERG 001, Rev. Doc.

Chapman, P. (Feb 1974), 'The Energy Cost of Producing Copper and Aluminium from Primary Sources', Metals and Materials, pp. 107-111

Chappel, C.L. (1973), 'Disposal Technology for Hazardous Wastes', Surveyor, Nov. 2, 1973, pp. 501-502

Clarke, R.(May 1972),'Soft Technology: Blueprint for a Research Community', Undercurrents 2

Clinic for Occupational Medicine, Örebro, Sweden, (November 1994), 'The Healthy Environment', Southeast Asia Building, p. 54.

Cole, Ray, et al. (1995), 'Linking and Prioritising Environmental Criteria', Proceedings. Task Group 8, International Research Workshop, Toronto, Canada, November 15-16, 1995, School of Architecture, University of B.C.,Canada

Colinvaux, Paul, R.(1973), 'The Ecosystem as a Practical Model', in Introduction to Ecology, John Wiley & Sons, New York, USA, pp. 229-245

Commoner, Barry (1972), The Closing Circle, Confronting the Environmental Crisis, Jonathan Cape, London, UK

Cook, E. (Sept 1971), 'The Flow of Energy in an Industrial Society', Scientific American, Vol. 225, No. 3, pp.134-147

Cooke, G.D., R.J. Beyers, and E.P. Odum (1968),'The Case for the Multispecies Ecological System with Special Reference to Succession and Stability', Biogenerative Systems, NADA Spec. 165, pp. 129-139

Cranbrook, Earl of, and D.S.Edwards (1994), <u>A Tropical Rainforest: Biodiversity in Borneo at Belalong, Brunei</u>, The Royal Geographical Society, London

Crosbie, M.J. (1994), <u>Green Architecture: A Guide to Sustainable Design</u>, Rockport, Mass: Rockport Publishers

Crosby, T.(1973), <u>The Environmental Game</u>, Penguin Books, London

Cuito, A. (2000), <u>Ecological Architecture: Bioclimatic Trends and Landscape Architecture in the Year 2001</u>, Loft Publications, Barcelona, Spain

Daly, Herman. (1991), <u>Steady-State Economics</u>, Island Press, Washington D.C.

Darling, Fraser F. (1969), 'Wilderness and Plenty', Reith Lectures, BBC

Darling, Fraser F., and R.F. Dasmann, (June 1972), 'The Ecosystem View of Human Society', Realities

Dasmann, R.F., J.P. Milton, and P.H. Freeman (1973), <u>Ecological Principles for Economic Development,</u> John Wiley & Sons, London

DeBlieu, J. (1999), <u>Wind: How the flow of air has shaped life, myth, and the land</u>, Houghton Mifflin Company, Boston, USA

Demkin, J.A. (Ed), (1996), <u>Environmental Resource Guide (ERG)</u>, The American Aluminum Institute of Architects, John Wiley & Sons, Inc., New York

Desmecht, J., A. Dupagne, J. Hauglustaine, and J. Teller, (1998), <u>Low-Energy Social Housing, Marchin (Belgium): A Case-Study Revisited</u>, Environmentally Friendly Cities, Proceedings of PLEA '98. (Lisbon, Portugal, June 1998). James & James Science Publishing Ltd., London, pp. 237-240

Dickinson, G., and Murphy, K. (1998), <u>Ecosystems: A functional approach</u>, Routledge, London and New York

Dixon, P. (1998), <u>Futurewise: Six faces of global change</u>, Profile Books, London, UK

Durrell, Lee (1986), <u>Gaia State of the Ark Atlas</u>, Doubleday, New York

Drinkell, P. (2002), 'The Bionic Connection', in <u>Discover</u> November 2002, pp.49-51, Publ. USA

Edwards, Brian (1996), <u>Towards Sustainable Architecture, European Directives and Building Design</u>, Butterworth Architecture, Oxford

Edwards, Brian (1998), <u>Green Buildings Pay</u>, E&FN Spon, London

Emery, F.E. (Ed) (1981), <u>Systems Thinking: Selected Reading</u>, Part 4, Penguin Books, Harmondsworth, pp. 12, 241-260

Emery, F.E. and E.L. Trist (1965), 'The Casual Texture of Organizational Environments', <u>Human Relations,</u> Publ. UK. 18, pp. 21-32

Eisenberg, E. (1998), <u>The Ecology of Eden</u>, Picador, USA

E. Trianti-Stourna, K. Spyropoulou, C. Theofylaktos, K. Droutsa, C.A. Balaras, M. Santamouris, D.N. Asimakopoulos, G. Lazaropoulou, N. Papanikolaou (1998), 'Energy conservation strategies for sports centers: Part A. Sports halls', in <u>Energy and Buildings 27</u> (1998), 109-122, Elsevier, Amsterdam, NL

Fathy, Hassan (1986), <u>Natural Energy and Vernacular Architecture</u>, Chicago: Published for United Nations University by University of Chicago Press

Bibliography

Fazal, A. (1995), 'The Future of Cities: Sustainable Settlements in Asia Pacific', in A. Awang et al., <u>Towards a Sustainable Urban Environment in Southeast Asia: Urban Habitat and High-Rise Monographs</u>, Kuala Lumpur: Institute Sultan Iskandar of Urban Habitat and High-Rise (ISI), p.3, Malaysia

Fisher, S. (2004), 'Ecological Corridors', Research Essay (Private Communication)

Flavin, C. (1986), <u>Energy and Architecture: The Solar and Conservation Potentia</u>l. Worldwatch Institute, Washington D.C., USA

Flavin, C. and N. Lenssen (1994), <u>Power Surge: Guide to the Coming Energy Revolution</u>, W.W. Norton & Company, New York, USA

Fordham, M. (August 1997), 'Thinking Big', <u>Architectural Review</u>, pp. 87-89, London, UK

Fox, A. and R. Murrell (1989), <u>Green Design</u>, Architecture Design and Technology Press, London, UK

Frey, H. (1999), <u>Designing the City: Towards a more sustainable urban form</u>, E&FN Spon, UK

Fuller, R.B. et al (1963), <u>World Design Science Decade 1965-1975.</u>, Southern Illinois University Press Carbondale, Ill:, USA

Gabel, M. (1975), <u>Energy, Earth and Everyone</u>, Simon & Schuster, New York, USA

Gabel, M. (1975), <u>Energy, Earth and Everyone: A Global Energy Strategy for Spaceship Earth</u>, Straight Arrow Books, San Francisco, USA

Gallo, C. (Ed) (1998), <u>Bioclimatic Architecture</u>, Publ. Italian National Agency for New Technology, Energy and the Environment, IN/ARCH Italian National Institute of Architecture, Rome, Italy

Garber, S.D. (2002), <u>Biology: A Self-Teaching Guide</u>, Second Edition, John Wiley & Sons, Inc., USA

Gerardin, L. (1968), <u>Bionics</u>, Weidenfeld & Nicolson, London, UK

Ghazali, Z.M. and M.A. Kassim (1994), 'How to Reduce Wastes and Save Materials' in A. Curarg et al., (Eds), <u>Environmental and Urban Management in Southeast Asia</u>, Urban Habitat and High-Rise Monographs, Kuala Lumpur: Institute Sultan Iskandar of Urban Habitat and High-Rise (ISI), pp. 183-195

Ginsburg, J. (2001), 'Once is Not Enough', in <u>Business Week</u>, April 2001, New York, USA

Girardet, H. (1992), <u>Earth rise: How Can We Heal Our Injured Planet?</u>, Paladin, London, UK

Girardet, H. (1992), <u>Earthrise: Halting and Destruction, Healing the World</u>, Paladin, UK

Girardet, H. (1999), <u>Creating Sustainable Cities</u>, Schumacher Briefing No. 2, Green Books for The Schumacher Society, Dartington, UK

Givoni, B.A. (1994), <u>Passive and Low Energy Cooling of Buildings</u>, Van Nostrand Reinhold, New York, USA

Glancey, J. (2001), 'What does green mean?', in <u>Guardian</u>, 4 August 2001, UK

Glass, J. (2001), <u>Ecoconcrete</u>, British Cement Association, Berkshire, UK

Goldbeck, N. and D. Goldbeck (1997), <u>Choose to Reuse</u>. Woodstock, Ceres Press, New York, USA

Goldsmith, E. (1971), '<u>Limits of Growth in Natural Systems</u>', General Systems 16, London, UK

Goodstein, D. (2004), <u>Out of Gas: The End of the Age of Oil</u>, W.W.Norton & Company, NYC, USA

Gordon, A.(Sept. 1972),'The President Introduces his Long Life/Loose Fit/Low Energy Study', <u>RIBAJ</u>, pp. 374-375

Gore, A. (1992), <u>Earth in the Balance: Forging a new common purpose</u>, Earthscan Publications Ltd, London, UK

Graves, W. (Ed), (November 1998), 'Water: The Power, Promise and Turmoil of North America's Fresh Water', <u>National Geographic</u> Special Edition

Guangyu, Huang, and Yong, Chen (Eds), (2002), <u>Ecocity: Theory and Design Approach</u>, Science Publications, China (www.sciencep.com)

Guruswamy, L.D., and McNeely, J.A. (Eds), (1998), <u>Protection of Global Biodiversity: Converging Strategies</u>, Duke University Press, Durham and London, UK

Guzowski, M., R. Horst, and S. Sorensen (1994), <u>Daylight Impact Assessment, Phase One</u>: Literature Speech for Northern States Power Company. Report published by The Designer Group with the Weidt Group, The Regional Daylighting Center, pp. 2-7

Hagan, S. (2001), <u>Taking Shape: A new contract between architecture and nature</u>, Architectural Press, Oxford, UK

Hart, S. (1992), <u>Harvard Business Review on Corporate Strategy</u>, Harvard Business School Press, USA

Halliday, S. (2000), <u>Green Guide to the Architect's Job Book</u>, RIBA Publications, London, UK

Harris, S.(2001), 'The Solar Solution', in <u>The Industry Standard</u>, April 2, 2001, (www.thestandard.com), USA

Hawken, P., Lovins A.B., and Lovins L.H. (1996), <u>Natural Capitalism: The Next Industrial Revolution</u>, Earthscan Publications Ltd. London

Hayes, R., in T. Peters (1997), <u>The Circle of Innovation: You Can't Shrink your Way to Greatness</u>, Hodder & Stoughton, p. 429, UK

HBI (Healthy Building International Inc.), <u>Building Investigation Experiences</u>, HBI Inc.

Herendeen, R.A. (1998), <u>Ecological Numeracy: Quantitative Analysis of Environmental Issues</u>, John Wiley & Sons, Inc., New York, USA

Herring, H. (2000),'Is Energy Efficiency Environmentally Friendly', in <u>Energy & Environment</u>, Vol. 11, No. 3, 2000, UK

Herrick, T. (2001), 'Weighing the Evidence of Global Warming', in <u>The Asian Wall Street Journal</u>, Friday/Saturday/Sunday, March 23-25, 2001, UK

Hertel. H. (1966), <u>Structure, Form, Movement</u>, Reinhold, New York, USA

Herzog, T. (Ed), (1996), <u>Solar Energy in Architecture and Urban Planning</u>, Prestel, Munich, Germany

Hickman, L. (2005), <u>A Good Life: The Guide to Ethical Living</u>, Eden Project Books, USA

Hillier, B., (May 1977), 'Architectural Research: A State of Mind', <u>RIBAJ</u>, p. 202 London, UK

Hillman, M., with Fawcett, T. (2004), <u>How We Can Save the Planet</u>, Penguin Books Ltd, London, UK

Holling, C.S., and O. Gordon (June 1971), 'Towards an Urban Ecology', <u>Bulletin of the Ecological Society of America</u>, USA

Holling, C.S., and M.A. Goldberg (July 1971), 'Ecology and Planning', <u>AIPJ</u>, Vol. 37, No. 4, pp. 221-230

Holling, C.S., and M.A. Goldberg (May 1973), 'The Nature and Behaviour of Ecological Systems'. <u>An Anthology of Selected Readings for the National Conference on Managing the Environment</u>' International City Management Association, Washington, D.C. pp. 1-21, USA

Hough, M. (1984), <u>City Form and Natural Process: Towards a New Urban Vernacular</u>, Croomhelm, London, UK

Hough, M. (1995), <u>City Form and National Process</u>, Routledge, London, UK

Howard, N.J., and P. Roberts (Sept 1995), 'Environmental Comparisons', <u>The Architects' Journal</u>, Vol. 21, UK

Howard, N.J., and H. Sutcliffe (March 1997), 'Precious Joules', <u>Building</u>, Vol. 18, pp 48-50, UK

Hughes, M.K. (Aug. 1974), 'The Urban Ecosystem', <u>Biologist</u>, Vol. 21, No. 3, pp. 117-127

Ichinowatari, K., (Ed), (1981), 'Solar and Underground Houses' in <u>Process Architecture</u> Number 21, Process Architecture Publishing Co. Ltd., Tokyo, Japan

Kachadorian, J., (1997), <u>The Passive Solar House</u>, Chelsea Green Publishing Company, White River Junction, Vermont, USA

Karyono, T.H. (1996), 'Architectural Science, Informatics and Design', in J.W.T. Kan (Ed), <u>Proceedings of the 30th Conference of the Australia and New Zealand Architectural Science Association</u> (ANZAScA), Dept of Architecture, Chung Chi College, Chinese University of Hong Kong, July 17-19, 1996, pp. 207-221

Kelly, K. (1994), <u>Out of Control: The New Biology of Machines, Social Systems and the Economic World</u>, Perseus Books, Cambridge, Massachusetts, USA

King, G.K. (Ed), (2001), 'Green Architecture', in <u>Dialogue: Architecture + Design + Culture</u>, December 2001, Publ. Meei Jaw Publishing Co. Ltd, Taipei, Taiwan

Klaus, D. (1995), 'Klima and Gebaudeform' in <u>Technologie des Okologischen Bauens</u>, Birkhäuser, pp. 18-33, Berlin, Germany

Kluger, J. (2004), 'Just too loud', in <u>TIME</u>, 5 April 2004, NYC, USA

Kneese, A.V., S.E., Rolfe, and J.W. Harned (Eds) (1971), <u>Managing the Environment, International Economic Cooperation for Pollution Control</u>, Praeger Publishing, New York, USA

Knowles, R.L. (1974), <u>Energy and Form, An Ecological Approach to Urban Growth</u>, The MIT Press, Cambridge, Mass., USA

Kurn, D.M., S.E. Bretz, B. Huang, and H. Albari (1994), 'The Potential for Reducing Urban Air Temperature and Energy Consumption Through Vegetation Cooling', in Lawrence Berkeley Report No: LBL-35320, LBL, California, USA

Larson, D., Matthes, U., Kelly, P.E., Lundholm, J. Gerrath, J., (2004), <u>The Urban Cliff Revolution: New Findings on the Origins and Evolution of Human Habitats</u>, Fitzhenry & Whiteside, Ontario, Canada

Laszlo, E. (2002), <u>The Systems View of the World: A Holistic Vision for Our Time</u>, Hampton Press, USA

Lawson, B.(1996), <u>Building Materials, Energy and the Environment: Solarch</u>, School of Architecture, University of New South Wales, RAIA, Australia

Leadership in Energy & Environmental Design (LEED) , (2000), <u>Green Building Rating System for New Construction & Major Renovations</u> (LEED-NC), Version 2.1. (November 2002) (Revised 3/14/03), Publ. US Green Building Council, Washington, USA

Ledger, B., (1988), 'Collecting landfill gas has a double environmental benefit. It stops methane – a powerful greenhouse gas – from entering the atmosphere, and the gas can be used to generate power', Publ. <u>Canadian Consulting Engineer</u> (June/July 1998), Ontario, Canada

Leeb, Stephen & Donna (2004), <u>Oil Factor: Protect yourself and profit from the coming energy crisis</u>, Warner Business Books (USA)

Leontief, W.(August 1970), 'Environmental Repercussions and the Economic Structure: An Input-Output Approach', <u>Review of Economics and Statistics</u>.

Lewis, O., and Goulding, J.(Eds), (1995), <u>European Directory of Sustainable and Energy Efficient Building 1995</u>, James & James (Science Publishers) Ltd, UK

Lloyd, J. (1998), <u>Architecture and the Environment. Bioclimatic Building Design</u>, Laurence King Publishing, London, UK

Lopez Barnett, D., Browning William D. (1995), <u>A Primer on Sustainable Building</u>, Rocky Mountain Institute Green Development Services, USA

Lomborg, B.(2001), 'The truth about the environment', in <u>The Economist</u> August 4th 2001, UK

Lovins, A.B. (1977), <u>Soft Energy Paths</u>, Harmondsworth, Penguin Books, New York, USA

Lovins, A.B. et al. (1991), <u>Harvard Business Review on Business and the Environment</u>, A Harvard Business Review Paperback, Harvard Business School Press, USA

Lynas, M. (2004), <u>High Tide: How Climate Crisis Is Engulfing Our Planet</u>, Harper Perennial, UK

MacKenzie, D. (1997), <u>Green Design, Design for the Environment</u>, Laurence King Publishing, London, p.8, UK

Majumdar, M. (2002) (Ed), <u>Energy-efficient buildings in India</u>, Tata Energy Research Institute & Ministry of Non-conventional Energy Sources, Thompson Press (India) Ltd., India

Malin, N.(2002), 'Life-Cycle Assessment for Buildings: Seeking the Holy Grail', in <u>Environmental Building News</u>, Vol.II, Nov. 3, March 2002, Building Green, Inc., Brattleboro, Virginia, USA

Marras, A. (Ed), (1999), <u>ECO-TEC, Architecture of the In-Between</u>, Princeton Architectural Press, New York, USA

Martin, L. (May 1967), 'Architects' Approach to Architecture: Sir Leslie Martin', <u>RIBAJ</u>, Vol. 74, pp. 191-200, UK

Mason, J.(2002), 'Sustainable story of success', in <u>Financial Times</u>, Wednesday November 6, 2002, UK

Mascaro, L.G., Dutra, G.and F. Finger (1998), 'Environmental Aspects of the Urban Precincts in a Subtropical City', in <u>Environmentally Friendly Cities, Proceedings of PLEA '98</u>, Lisbon, Portugal, June 1998, James & James Science Publishing Ltd., pp. 99-102, London, UK

Maser, C.(1988), <u>The Redesigned Forest</u>. San Pedro, R&E Miles, California, USA

McDonough, W., & Braungart, M. (2002), <u>Cradle to Cradle</u>, North Point Press, New York, USA

McGarvey, R. (2004), 'Energy: Powering the Recovery', in <u>Harvard Business School</u>, May 2004, USA

McHale, J.(1967), 'World Dwelling', Perspecta, The Yale Architecture Journal, 12, pp. 120-129, USA

McHale, J. (1970), The Ecological Context, Braziller, New York, USA

McHarg, I. (1969), Design with Nature, Garden City, Natural History Press, New York, USA

McKibben, B. (1989), The End of Nature, Random House, New York, USA

McLaren, V.W. (1996), 'Urban Sustainability Reporting', Journal of the American Planning Association, Vol. 62, No. 2, p. 84, USA

McNeill, J.R. (2000), Something New Under the Sun: An Environmental History of the Twentieth-Century World, W.W. Norton & Company, New York, USA

Meadows, D.H., and D.L. Meadows (1972), The Limits to Growth, University Books, New York, USA

Mellanby, K. (1972), The Biology of Pollution, Edward Arnold, London, UK

Miller, J.G. (1965), 'Living Systems: Basic Concepts', Behavioural Science, Vol. 10, Oct. 1965, pp. 193-237, USA

Miller, R.E. (1966), 'Interregional Feedback Effects in Input-Output Models: Some Preliminary Results', Papers & Proceedings of the Regional Services Association, Vol. 17, pp. 105-125.

Moore, F. (1996), 'Concepts and Practice of Architectural Daylighting', in Fenestration R&D. Lawrence Berkeley National Laboratory Energy & Environmental Division Publishing, p.9, USA

Moriyama Masakazu, Takebayashi Hideki (1999), 'Making method of "Klimatope" map based on normalized vegetation index and one-dimensional heat budget model', in Journal of Wind Engineering Industrial Aerodynamics, Elsevier, Amsterdam, the Nertherlands

Morrison, W.I. (1972), 'The Development of an Urban Interindustry Model: 1. Building Input-Output Accounts', Environment and Planning, Vol. 5, pp. 369-385.

National Academy of Sciences: One Earth, One Future, National Academy Press, Washington D.C.,USA

Nihon Sekkei (1984), Energy Conservation Measures for High-Rise Building. Tokyo: JETRO (Japan External Trade Organization) Publishing, Japan

Odum, E.P. (1963), Ecology, Holt, Reinhart, Winston, New York, USA

Odum, E.P. (1969),'The Strategy of Ecosystem Development', Science, Vol.164, April 1969, pp.262-270, USA

Odum, E. P. (1971), Fundamentals of Ecology (Third Edition), W.B. Saunders Company, Philadelphia, USA

Odum, E.P. (1972), 'Ecosystems', in W.White and F.J. Little, (Eds), North American Reference Essays of Ecology and Pollution, North American Publishing Co., pp.66-69, Philadelphia, USA,

Odum, H.T. (1971), Environment, Power and Society, Wiley-Interscience, New York, USA

Odum H.T., and L.L. Peterson (Oct. 1972), 'Relationship of Energy and Complexity in Planning', Architectural Design, October 1972, pp. 624-628, USA

Olgyay, V. (1993), Design with Climate, Princeton University Press, Princeton, N.J. , USA

O'Reilly, W. (1996), Sustainable Landscape Design in Arid Climates, The Aga Khan Trust for Culture, Geneva, Switzerland

O'Riordan, T. (1971), Perspectives on Resource Management, Pion Ltd., London, UK

Orr, D.W. (2002) The Nature of Design: Ecology, Culture, and Human Intention, Oxford University Press, NYC, USA

Orr, D.W. (2003) 'The Case for the Earth', in Resurgence No. 219 July/August 2003, Resurgence, Bideford, UK

Paehlke, R. (1989), Environmentalism and the Future of Progressive Politics, Yale University Press, New Haven, USA

Papanek, V. (1985), Design for the Real World: Human Ecology and Social Change, Academy Chicago Publishers, Chicago, USA

Papanek, V. (1995), The Green Imperative: Ecology and Ethics in Design and Architecture, Thames and Hudson, London, UK

Patterson, W.C. (1990), The Energy Alternative: Changing the Way the World Works, Optima, MacDonald & Co. Ltd., London, UK

Pearson, D. (1989), The Natural House Book, Simon & Schuster Inc., New York, USA

Penporties, B., and P.D. Pedregal (1998), 'Application of Life-Cycle Simulation to Energy and Environment Conscious Design' in Environmentally Friendly Cities, Proceedings of PLEA '98, Lisbon, Portugal, June 1998, James & James Science Publishing Ltd., pp. 517-520, London, UK

Peranio, A. (1973), The Environmental Crisis – A Cybernetic Challenge, Haifa, Israel: Technion, pp. 122

Phillips, C. (2003), Sustainable Place: A Place of Sustainable Development, Wiley-Academy, UK

Pijawka, K.D., and Shetter, K. (1995), The Environment Comes Home: Arizona Public Service's Environmental Showcase Home, Herberger Center for Design Excellence, College of Architecture and Environmental Design, Arizona State University, USA

Platt, R., Rowntree, R.A., and Muick, P.C. (Eds), (1994), The Ecological City: Preserving and Restoring Urban Biodiversity, The University of Massachusetts Press, Amherst, USA

Ponting, C. (1991), A Green History of the World: The Environment and the Collapse of Great Civilizations, Penguin Books, UK

Raeburn, P., and Ginsburg, J. (2001), 'Green Power', in Business Week, 9 April 2001, USA

Raju, M.K. (1996), 'Success Stories in Energy Conservation as Relevant to Thailand', in Proceedings of the Conference on Energy Conservation: Thailand Means Business, NRG-CON, August 22-23, 1996, Thailand

Ramphal, S. (1992), Our Country, the Planet, Island Press, Washington, D.C., USA

Ratner, Daniel & Mark (2003), Nanotechnology: A Gentle Introduction to the Next Big Idea, Prentice Hall, New Jersey, USA

Ray, C. (1970), 'Ecology, Law and the Marine Revolution', Biological Conservation, Vo'. 3, no. 1, USA

Register, R. (1987), Ecocity Berkeley: Building Cities for a Healthy Future, North Atlantic Books, Berkeley, California, USA

Register, R. (2002), 'Ecoscape Eco-Industry Eco-Culture', Proceedings of the Fifth International Ecocity Conference, The Fifth International Ecocity Conference, Shenzhen, China, August 19-23, 2002, Ecocity, USA

Reynolds, M.E. (1990), Earthship: How to build your own, Solar Survival Press, New Mexico, USA

Reid, D. (1995), Sustainable Development: An Introductory Guide, Earthscan Publications Ltd. London, UK

Rifkin, J. (2003), The Hydrogen Economy: The Creation of the Worldwide Energy Web and the Redistribution of Power on Earth, Jeremy P. Tarcher/Penguin, New York, USA

Roaf, S., and M. Hancock (Eds) (1992), Energy Efficient Building: A Design Guide, John Wiley & Sons, New York, USA

Robertson, J. (1990), 'Healthy Buildings International Pty Ltd., Increasing Human Performance by Improving Indoor Air Quality', Paper (unpubl.), New South Wales, Australia

Rohmann, C. (1999), World of Ideas: A Dictionary of Important Theories, Concepts, Beliefs, and Thinkers, Ballantine Books, New York, USA

Rosenfield, A.H., J.J. Rowan, H. Akbari, and A.C. Lloyd (1997), 'Painting the Town White and Green', Technology Review, Feb/March 1997, pp. 52-59

Rydin, Y., and Myerson G. (1996), The Language of Environment: A New Rhetoric, UCL Press, London, UK

Saini, B.S. (1970), Architecture in Tropical Australia, Lund Humphries for the Architectural Association, London, UK

Salem, O.S. (1990), 'Towards Sustainable Architecture and Urban Design: Categories, Methodologies and Models', Rensselaer Polytechnic Institute, Troy, New York, unpublished manuscript, USA

Salmon, C. (1999), Architectural Design for Tropical Regions, John Wiley & Sons, Inc., New York, USA

Sastri, V.M.K. (1991), 'Building Energy Audit Techniques', Workshop on Building Energy Management, Bangkok, Thailand, 22-26 April 1991

Shahi, G.S. (2004), BioBusiness in Asia: How Asia can Capitalize on the Life Science Revolution, Pearson Prentice Hall, Singapore

Shugart, H.H. (1998), Terrestrial Ecosystems in Changing Environments, Cambridge University Press, UK

Sitarz, D. (Ed), (1994), Agenda 21: The Earth Summit Strategy to Save our Planet, The Earth Press, Boulder, Colo, USA

Sjors, H. (1955), 'Remarks on Ecosystems', Svensk Botanisk Tidskrift, Vol. 49, H1-2, Sweden

Skinner, B. (1969), Earth Resources, Prentice Hall, Inc., Englewood Cliffs, N.J. , USA

Slessor, C. (1997), Eco-Tech: Sustainable Architecture and High Technology, Thames & Hudson, London, UK

Slobodkin, L.B. (2003), A Citizen's Guide to Ecology, Oxford University Press, UK

Smith, P.F., and Pitts, A.C. (1997), Concepts in Practice Energy: Building for the Third Millennium, B.T. Batsford Ltd., UK

Sorenson, J.C. (1972), 'Some Procedures and Programs for Environmental Impact Assessment' in R.B. Ditton and T.L. Goodale, (Eds), Environmental Impact Analysis: Philosophy and Methods. Environmental Impact Analysis, Proceedings of the Conference in Green Bay, Sea Grant Publishing, WIS-SG-72-111, pp. 97-106, Wisc. , USA

Sorenson, J.C., and J.E. Pepper (1973), Procedures for Regional Clearinghouse Review of Environmental Impact Statements – Phase Two, draft., Association of Bay Area Governments, Berkeley, California, USA

Sorenson, J.C., and M.L. Mass (1973), Procedures and Programs to Assist in the Environmental Impact Statement Process, University of California, University of Southern California, SG-PUB-No. 27, USC-SG-AS2-73, Los Angeles, USA

Spellerberg, I.F. (1996), <u>Conservation Biology</u>, Longman Group Ltd., Harlow, UK

Spellman, C. (Ed) (2003), <u>Re-envisioning Landscape/Architecture</u>, Actar, Barcelona, Spain

Speth J.G. (2004), <u>Red Sky at Morning: America and the Crisis of the Global Environment</u>, Yale University Press, New Haven, USA and London, UK

Spofford, W.O. (1971), 'Residuals Management', in W.H. Matthews, F.E. Smith, and E.D. Golberg, (Eds), <u>Man's Impact on Terrestrial and Oceanic Ecosystems</u>, MIT Press, pp. 477-88 cambridge, Mass., USA

Spofford, W.O. (1973), 'Total Environmental Management Models' in R.A. Deininger, (Eds), <u>Models for Environmental Pollution Control</u>, Ann Arbor Scientific Publishing, Inc., Ann Arbor, Mich. , USA

Steele, J. (1997), <u>Sustainable Architecture: Principles, Paradigms and Case Studies</u>, McGraw-Hill, New York, USA

Stein, M. (2000), <u>When Technology Fails: A Manual for Self-Reliance & Planetary Survival</u>, Clear Light Publishers, New Mexico, USA

Stewart, G.H., Ignatieva M.E. (Eds) (2000), <u>Urban biodiversity and ecology as a basis for holistic planning and design</u>, Lincoln University International Centre for Nature Conservation Publication Number 1, Canterbury, New Zealand

St. John, A. (Ed) (1992), <u>The Sourcebook for Sustainable Design</u>, Architects for Social Responsibility, Boston, Mass, USA

Strong, S.J., with Scheller, W.G. (1987), <u>The Solar Electric House: Energy for the environmentally-responsive energy-independent home</u>, Sustainability Press, Massachusetts, USA

Suzuki, Yumiko (2001), 'Environmental management offers low risk for quick thinkers', in <u>The Nikkei Weekly</u>, April 2, 2001, Publ. Tokyo, Japan

Suzuki, Yumiko (2001),'New law to put Japan in recycling lead', in <u>The Nikkei Weekly</u>, April 2, 2001, Japan

Swaffield, S. (Ed), (2002), <u>Theory in Landscape Architecture: A Reader</u>, University of Pennsylvania Press, Philadelphia, USA

Szokolay, S.V. (1996), <u>Solar Geometry</u>, PLEA: Passive and Low Energy Architecture International in association with Department of Architecture, The University of Queensland, Brisbane, Australia

Takeuchi, Kazuhiko (Ed) (1995), <u>Ecological Landscape Planning</u>, PROCESS: Architecture 127, Process Architecture Co. Ltd., Tokyo, Japan

Taylor, A. (2001), 'Winds of change blow slowly for energy sector', in <u>Financial Times</u>, 14 March 200`, London, UK

Taylor, P. (1986), <u>Respect for Nature</u>, Princeton University Press, Princeton, USA

Teitel, M., and Wilson K.A. (1999), <u>Genetically Engineered Food: Changing the Nature of Nature</u>, Park Street Press, Rochester, USA

Treloar, G. (2000), 'Streamlined Life Cycle Assessment of Domestic Structural Wall Members', in <u>Journal of Construction Research</u> (2000) 1, 69-76, UK

The Presidential Commission for the New Millennium in Korea, (2000), Proceedings of the World Congress on Green Design (9-21 November 2000), COEX, Seoul, World Congress on Environmental Design for the New Millennium, Seoul (Seoul2000@millenniumed.org) Korea

Thomas, R. (Ed) (1996), <u>Environmental Design: An introduction for architects and engineers</u>, Publ. E&FN Spon, London, UK

Todd, N.J., Todd, J. (1993), From Eco-Cities to Living Machines: Principles of Ecological Design, North Atlantic Books, Berkeley, California, USA

Tolman, E.C., and E. Brunswick, (1968) 'The Organism and the Causal Texture of the Environment', Psychological Review, Vol. XLII, pp. 43-77

Tubbs, C.R., and J.W. Blackwood (1971), 'Ecological Evaluation of Land for Planning Purposes', Biological Conservation, Vol. 3, No. 3, April 1971, pp. 169-72, USA

Tuluca, A. (Ed), (1997), Energy Efficient Design and Construction for Commercial Buildings, McGraw-Hill, New York, USA

Turner, T. (1998), Landscape Planning and Environmental Impact Design, UCL Press, p. 95 London, UK

Vale, R., and R. Vale (1991), Green Architecture: Design for a Sustainable Future, Thames & Hudson, London, UK

Van Der Ryn, S., and P. Calthorpe (1991), Sustainable Communities: A New Design Synthesis for Cities, Suburbs and Towns, Sierra Club Books, San Francisco, USA

Van Doren, C. (1991), A History of Knowledge: Past, Present, and Future, Ballantine Books, New York, USA

Van Dyne, G.M. (1966), Ecosystems, Systems Ecology and Systems Ecologists, ORNL-3957, Oak Ridge National Laboratory, Oak Ridge, Tenn,, USA

Van Dyne, G.M. (Ed) (1969), The Ecosystem Concept in Natural Resource Management, Academic Press, New York, USA

Van Hinte, E. (1998), Smart Design, The Netherlands Design Institute, Amsterdam, the Nertherlands

Van Straten, M. (1999), Organic Super Foods, Octopus Publishing Group, UK

Victor, P.A. (1972), Pollution: Economy and Environment, Allen and Unwin, Ltd, London, UK

Viljoen. A (Ed), (2005), Continuous Productive Urban Landscapes: Designing Urban Agriculture for Sustainable Cities, Architectural Press, USA

Villecco, M. (Ed) (1978), Energy Conservation in Building Design, Washington, D.C., USA

Von Weizsacker, E., A.B. Lovins and L.H. Lovins (1997), Factor Four: Doubling Wealth, Halving Resource Use, Earthscan Publications Ltd., London , UK

Wagstaff.,J., (2004), 'Must Our Machines Die?', Far Eastern Economic Review (May 20, 2004), Hong Kong

Waldholz, M. (2003), 'Flower Power is Winning Respect', in The Asian Wall Street Journal, 27 August 2003, Hong Kong

Wann, D. (1996), Deep Design: Pathways to a livable future, Island Press, Washington, D.C. , USA

Warren, R. (1998), The Urban Oasis: Guideways and Greenways in the Human Environment, McGraw-Hill, New York, USA

Watkins, S., and King, D. (2001), 'A Geographical Guide to Eco-Shopping', in Geographical, March 2001, UK

WCED, Our Common Future, The World Commission on Environment and Development Oxford University Press, Oxford, UK

Wells, M.B. (1971), The Great Ecologic Colouring Book of Life and Death and Architecture, The Conservation Account, Cherry Hill, N.J. , USA

Wells, M.B. (July 1972), 'An Ecologically Sound Architecture is Possible', pp. 433, <u>Architectural Design</u>, UK

Wells, M. (1984), <u>Gentle Architecture</u>, McGraw-Hill, New York, USA

White, G.F. (Nov. 1972), 'Environmental Impact Statements', <u>The Professional Geographer</u>, Vol. XXIV, No. 4, pp. 302-9 , USA

Whitefield, P. (1993), <u>Permaculture in a Nutshell</u>, A Permanent Publications & Permaculture Association co-publication, UK

Whitehouse, D. (2004), '<u>The Sun: A Biography</u>', John Wiley & Sons, Ltd., UK

Wilen, J.E., (1973), 'A Model of Economic System – Ecosystem Interaction', <u>Environment and Planning</u>, Vol. 5, pp. 409-20, UK

Willard, B.E., and J.W. Marr (July 1970), 'Effects of Human Activities on the Alpine Tundra Ecosystem in Rocky Mountain National Park, Colorado', <u>Biological Conservation</u>, Vol. 2, No. 2

Williams, E.R., and P.W. House (Feb 1974), <u>The State of the System Model (SOS): Measuring Growth Limitations Using Ecological Concepts</u>, U.S. Environmental Protection Agency, Socio-Economic Environmental Studies Series, EPA-600/5-73-013, Office of Research and Development EPA, U.S. Government Printing Office, Washington, D.C. , USA

Wines, J., and Jodidio, P. (Eds), (2000), <u>Green Architecture</u>, Taschen, Cologne, Germany

Wilhide, E. (2002), Eco: <u>An essential sourcebook for environmentally friendly design and decoration</u>, Quadrille Publishing Ltd, UK

Willis, A.M., Tonkin, C. (1998), <u>Timber in Context: A guide to sustainable use</u>, Natspec 3 Guide, Construction Information Systems Australia, New South Wales, Australia

Wilson, A. (2004), 'Kohler's New High-Performance, Low-Flush Cimarron Toilet', in <u>Environmental Building News</u>, Vol. 13, No. 6, June 2004 (p.8), Publ. Building Green Inc., Brattleboro, Virginia, USA

Wolverton, B.C. (1996), <u>Eco-Friendly Houseplants</u>, Weidenfeld & Nicolson, London, UK

Woodwell, G.M. (1971), 'Effects of Pollution on the Structure and Physiology of Ecosystems' in S.W.H. Matthew, F.E. Smith, and E.D. Golberg, (Eds), <u>Man's Impact on Terrestrial and Oceanic Ecosystems</u>, MIT Press, pp. 47-58 Cambridge Mass, USA

Woolley, T., Kimmins, S. Harrison, P., Harrison, R. (1997), <u>Green Building Handbook: Volume 1: A guide to building products and their impact on the environment</u>, Green Building Digest, E&FN Spon, UK

Woolley, T., and Kimmins, S. (2000), <u>Green Building Handbook, Vol.2: A guide to building products and their impact on the environment</u>, E&FN Spon, UK

World Resources Institute (1994), <u>World Resources 1994-95</u>, Oxford University Press, New York, USA

Wright, G., and Slagle, T. (1998), 'Skyscraper Solar Spires', in <u>Solar Today</u> (September/October 1998), USA

Wright, G. (2002), 'Greenroof Los Angeles', in <u>Birdscapes</u>/Winter 2002, US Fish & Wildlife Service, USA

Yannas, S. (1994), <u>Solar Energy and Housing Design: Volume 2: Examples</u>, Architectural Association, London, UK

Yannas, S. (1994), <u>Solar Energy and Housing Design: Volume 1: Principles, Objectives, Guidelines</u>, Architectural Association, London, UK

Yeang, K. (July 1974), 'Bases for Ecosystem Design', <u>Architectural Design</u>, pp. 434-6, UK

Yeang, K. (July 1974), 'Energetics of the Built Environment', <u>Architectural Design</u>, July 1974, pp. 446-51, UK

Yeang, K. (1974), 'Bionics—The Use of Biological Analogies for Design', <u>Architectural Association Quarterly (AAQ)</u>, Vol. 6, No. 2, London , UK

Yeang, K. (1994), <u>Bioclimatic Skyscrapers</u>, Ellipsis London Ltd, London, UK

Yeang, K. (1995), <u>Designing with Nature: The Ecological Basis for Architectural Design</u>, McGraw-Hill, New York, USA

Yeang, K. (1996), <u>The Skyscraper Bioclimatically Considered: A Design Primer</u>, Academy-Editions, London, UK

Yeang, K. (1998), <u>T.R. Hamzah & Yeang Selected Works</u>, p.7, The Images Publishing Group Pty Ltd, Australia,

Yost, P. (June 2001),'Maximum Transport Distances for Reclaimed Materials', in <u>Environmental Building News</u>, Vol. 10, No. 6, Publ. Building Green Inc., Virginia, USA

Zeiher, L.C. (1996), <u>The Ecology of Architecture: A Complete Guide to Creating the Environmentally Conscious Building</u>, Whitney Library of Design, New York, USA

Zelov, C., and Cousineau, P. (1997), <u>Design Outlaws on the Ecological Frontier</u>, Knossus Publishing Easton, USA

Zold, A., and Szokolay Steven V. (1997), <u>Thermal Insulation: Passive and Low Energy Architectural International Design Tools and Techniques,</u> Plea Notes, Australia

G

H

R

S

U

water/wetland wall 139, 142

waterless toilets 275–6

watersheds 117, 118

whales, effect of marine noise pollution 305

wildlife effect of light pollution 299, 302

    effect of noise pollution 304

    see also animals; birds; insects; marine/aquatic species

Williams' alpha diversity index 121, 122

wind and built-form orientation 220

    indoor ventilation by 194, 211–18, 231

wind pockets 215

wind scoops 192, 211

wind speeds apparent temperature affected by 190

    Beaufort scale 213

wind tower ventilation 218

wind tunnel testing 215

wind turbines/generators 240, 246, 247–8, 321

    advanced design 248

    energy output rating 247

window fans 232

windows 220–1

    heat loss through 203

    opening 214, 215

wing walls 212, 214, 215, 216

wireless communication systems 388

wood embodied energy 376, 390

    recycling of 89, 334

    waste 89, 296, 313, 336

    see also timber-frame construction

wood-based materials 393, 405

wool/ramie fibres 395

World Commission on Environment and Development 436, 438

World Conservation Strategy 435, 438

world's largest cities 19

Y

'yellow' water 270

Z

zeroculture sites 99, 290–1

    design strategy for 100, 101